A Modern Guide to Foodservice Equipment

Revised Edition

A MODERN GUIDE TO FOODSERVICE EQUIPMENT

Arthur C. Avery

A CBI Book
Published by Van Nostrand Reinhold Company Inc.
New York

A CBI Book
(CBI is an imprint of Van Nostrand Reinhold Company Inc.)

Library of Congress Catalog Card Number 84-19554
ISBN 0-442-20837-5

Printed in the United States of America

Published by Van Nostrand Reinhold Company Inc.
135 West 50th Street
New York, New York 10020

Van Nostrand Reinhold Company Limited
Molly Millars Lane
Wokingham, Berkshire RG11 2PY, England

Van Nostrand Reinhold
480 La Trobe Street
Melbourne, Victoria 3000, Australia

Macmillan of Canada
Division of Canada Publishing Corporation
164 Commander Boulevard
Agincourt, Ontario M1S 3C7, Canada

16 15 14 13 12 11 10 9 8 7 6 5 4 3 2 1

Library of Congress Cataloging in Publication Data

Avery, Arthur C.
A modern guide to foodservice equipment.

"A CBI book."
Includes bibliographies and index.
1. Food service—Equipment and supplies. I. Title.
TX912.A93 1985 647'.95'0687 84-19554
ISBN 0-442-20837-5

To my wife, Nanette, whose encouragement, correction, and typing led to the completion of this book. Without her love and support, I never would have made it.

Contents

Preface

This book was written with three purposes in mind. The first of these was purely selfish. I needed a textbook for a class that has increased to over one hundred students. The second is that I wanted to encourage the formation of more classes in food-service equipment in other schools, as I find that most cooks, chefs, and managerial personnel know little about the potential benefits and requirements of their equipment. The third was that I wanted to provide a reference book in which the foodservice equipment buyer could find the specification details and capacity information needed to purchase the necessary equipment, and, when purchased, use it to the best advantage while keeping it clean and well maintained.

The material in the book is a digest of research generated during fifteen years as Director of the U.S. Navy Food Science and Engineering Division. Information was recorded by a number of fine scientists and engineers in approximately one thousand reports, of which a large percentage were on equipment. Some of the equipment developed as a result of this program included the high capacity fryer, oven, griddle with a fence around the outside, the forced convection oven, the submarine range and small group cooking center, high humidity refrigerator, improved mechanical cow, mixer-kettle, refrigerated kettle, tray prescraper, the oven meat-doneness control, and many other pieces of equipment. Much equipment evaluation that took place led to better equipment being made available by industry manufacturers.

However, some of the developed equipment was suppressed or never caught on with the food-service industry, including the electric oven that heated on all six sides and adjusted in oven height according to the product; the automated scullery where trays of dishes were washed and loaded into dispensers without human hands; an automated toaster that could be loaded with eight loaves of bread and provide toast for any serving line speed; 40-quart milk can mixer-dispenser; aluminum tray rack; inflight cooking center; tube storage systems for submarines; Dacron coffee leachers which could be used for three months; universal mixer kettle that pressure cooks and fries, deep fat fries, kettle cooks, refrigerates, mixes, and peels vegetables, in addition to many others.

So much applied technology is needed in the foodservice industry and most of this could be available tomorrow if the foodservice people would insist on it. There is no reason why large volumes of fat should be heated, griddled food should be cooked on one side at a time, cooked food needs a large heated oven compartment, ranges need to waste so much heat, broilers needlessly lose heat, and humans need to judge for doneness.

The foodservice equipment industry has been most cooperative in the writing of this book by providing specification sheets and photographs and, in some instances, articles on the equipment they manufacture. I appreciate all of this help. However, much of the material is subjective in nature. It is regrettable that more research on equipment is not being done, with the results made available to the foodservice industry through the offices of the Society for the Advancement of Food Service Research, where data could be evaluated and used to inspire further research and authoritative reports.

I would like to express thanks to the West Lafayette, Indiana High School and the Restaurant, Hotel and Institutional Management Department, Food Stores, Shreve Hall, and Graduate House West of Purdue University, all of whom were generous in allowing me to take pictures of their fine facilities for inclusion in this book.

ARTHUR C. AVERY
West Lafayette, Indiana

Introduction to Foodservice Equipment

Foodservice equipment is any equipment involved in quantity foodservice functions of: receiving, storage, preparation, service, and warewashing. In the past, the processes involved in researching, selecting, specifying, purchasing, integrating into the kitchen design and feeding system, installing, utilizing, cleaning, and maintaining foodservice equipment have been omitted, in part or wholly, from the training and educating of foodservice personnel.

Frequently the consequence of this omission has been the selection of equipment ill suited for the purposes for which it was purchased. The purchased equipment has been over or under proper capacity, thus slowing service or increasing cleaning problems. The workers have been unable to use the equipment to its fullest potential and have not known how to clean it properly and keep it in good running order.

The purchase of equipment occurs when a new foodservice operation is being built, a food operation expands in size or menu, menu emphasis changes, or a piece of equipment needs to be replaced. Reasons for this last could be high maintenance costs, obsolescence, need for more automatic controls, or over or under capacity. Sometimes a salesperson or advertisement or trade show sells the manager on the desirability of a particular piece of equipment either for itself or because a new or old piece of equipment will be enhanced by the new addition.

The selection of a particular model, make, or design of equipment takes place most often as a result of the buyer's experiences in the place he manages and in the places he has worked, the literature he has read, and the equipment he has seen in kitchens other than in his own, in purveyors' showrooms, or at trade shows. Next to this the buyer is influenced by recommendations from foodservice consultants, equipment purveyors, friends, and employees.

An example of this selection by past experience was clearly brought out to me when enlisted chiefs (chief petty officers) from the submarine fleet were given carte blanche on any foodservice equipment that they wanted to recommend for the first atomic submarine. All of the equipment recommended and purchased was what was used in World War II submarines. It wasn't until the Food Science and Engineering Division of the Navy researched new equipment most needed by submarines that equipment changed. Civilian buyers, too, are prone to repeat their experience in their equipment purchases.

Specifications to ensure that the buyer gets what he envisions in equipment are usually tied to a particular model. If detailed at all, the specifications parrot the information on the manufacturer's specification sheets. To open up bidding by a number of manufacturers, the military, United States government, most state governments, many universities, city school systems, large restaurant and health care chains, and other multi-unit organizations buy by general specification. For them, a specification is a detailed description of the features desired in the piece of equipment that they want to purchase. The details of specification writing will be discussed in Chapter 2.

Preliminaries to Writing a Specification

Before writing the specification, the buyer should ask himself such questions as:

1. Do I need and can I afford the equipment that I have in mind? Would a simpler, smaller, or less expensive piece of equipment do the job required?
2. What capacity of equipment is needed? Should I get exactly the capacity I need now and make adjustments later or plan on my future needs in the capacity I buy now?
3. Is the needed equipment available? Does the purveyor of this equipment provide local service or is other local service available for the selected equipment? (If not, reconsider the equipment purchase.)
4. Does the equipment fit into the remainder of the kitchen according to dimensions, capacity, appearance, and utility usage?
5. Can, and will, my workers use the equipment effectively? Do they have the skills and physical attributes to use it? Will the equipment last for a reasonable period of time under the use that will be given it?
6. Is the equipment safe for the workers to use? Is it easy to keep clean and maintain?
7. Do I know everything that I should know about the equipment? Will it produce a profit for my company or will it be a millstone around my neck?

Is the Equipment Purchase Worth It?

Probably the most difficult determination that an equipment buyer must make is whether or not a new piece of equipment will make money in excess of what it costs. Delineation of both savings by use of the equipment and costs of having and using the equipment must be estimated and calculated to determine whether the savings are greater than the costs. The following formula, amplified from Lendal Kotschevar, can be used for this:

$$\frac{A + B}{C + D + E + F - G} = > 1 \text{ to be a good buy}$$

where: A = savings in labor over the life of the equipment
B = savings in material over the life of the equipment
C = cost of purchase and installation
D = cost of utilities to operate the equipment over its life
E = cost of maintenance and repair of equipment over its life
F = interest on money in C if left in a savings bank over the life of equipment
G = turn-in value of the equipment

An example might be a potato peeler with a use life of nine years, a projected labor savings of \$500 and material savings of \$200 per year, purchase and installation cost of \$1,000, utilities cost of \$50 and maintenance of \$20 per year, 7 percent interest compounded annually on C, and turn-in value of \$200.

$$\frac{9\ (\$500 + \$200)}{\$1000 + 9\ (\$50 + \$20) + \$838 - \$200} = 2.8 \text{ (good buy)}$$

Some agencies will not accept a value of 1 as a good buy but insist that it be 2, 3, or more because most of the figures are estimates and some considerable leeway is in order. For computation purposes, one may use the projected years of use set for depreciation purposes by the U.S. Internal Revenue Service or a median of fourteen years for foodservice equipment, or one may consult the following list that I use:

Equipment	*Projected Years of Use*
broilers	9
dish and tray dispensers	9
dishwashers	10
food slicers	9
food warmers	10
freezers	9
deep fat fryers	10
ice-making machines	7
milk dispensers	8
ovens and ranges	10
patty-making machines	10
pressure cookers	12
range hoods	15
scales	9
scraping and prewash machines	9
serving carts	9
service stands	12
sinks	14
steam jacketed kettles	13
steam tables	12
storage refrigerators	10
vegetable peelers	9
work tables	13

With the increased use of stainless steel, these figures are on the low side by about five years, or close to the IRS figures. However, in some cases, equipment has lasted twice as long as the projected years. Use life of equipment is dependent on measurement tolerances and materials used in its manufacture, skill and care given by users, frequency of use, and loading and the utilities used.

Placing the Order

After the need and desirability of purchase have been established and the buyer has drawn up a good specification, he must place the order by use of a purchase order. This merely requires the seller to produce a piece of equipment in accordance with the specification for the buyer in exchange for a given amount of money. If the credit of the buyer is not good, the seller may insist on payment when the equipment is delivered either to the seller's or buyer's back platform according to the purchase document and mutual agreement. Installation may be done by the purveyor, the construction engineer, a separate firm, or the buyer. This, along with the crating, shipping, and payment details, is reflected in the purchase document or the specification.

The purchase can be made from the manufacturer, but this is seldom the case except with quantity buyers such as restaurant chains and the government. Usually the purchase is made from a local purveyor who will usually be expected to service the equipment as well as sell it. If it is written into the specification, he will train the kitchen personnel in its use as well as install it as a condition of purchase. In a few cases, the manufacturer or purveyor of a certain food material will market a piece of equipment that will be used with his product exclusively, or "one-stop" suppliers of food materials will contract to provide equipment as well as food and other supplies. A few buyers obtain equipment from government surplus sales, restaurants going out of business, and similar sources.

FIGURE 1.1. It is important that equipment be installed professionally and placed so as to be properly supported. Courtesy Vulcan-Hart Corporation.

Installation

In a new facility, the installation of the equipment is usually done by the general contractor, but in an established operation, the purveyor, a local foodservice repairperson, or an electrician or a plumber may be asked to do the job. As in most service purchases, one usually gets that for which he contracts, and in foodservice, this can be disastrous. Dishwashers may run in reverse to the flow of dishes, steam jacketed kettles may be connected to the wrong pressure steam, gas equipment may be vented improperly, and displays may be hard to see and controls hard to reach. Investment in factory-trained experts to do the installation is money well used (see figure 1.1).

Training

Many new pieces of foodservice equipment are improperly or insufficiently used because the workers have never been trained. I have seen Vertical Cutter/Mixers used only for bread crumbs or meats when vegetable cutting, mixing, or making salad dressing and similar products could be done if the workers had been trained to use the equipment fully. Training of the kitchen personnel to use new equipment should be part of each equipment specification or purchase description. This provision should not be considered lightly, as the benefits from the purchase of a new $3,000 or $4,000 piece of equipment may be negated to a large extent if the operator of this equipment does not receive proper training and supervision. Times, temperatures, methods, and adaptations are important and should be made specific in execution.

Applications

The regular applications of all available equipment should be well known and operating data presented in usable form adjacent to the equipment to which it applies. All too often, available standard kitchen equipment is used improperly, if at all, because the cook cannot remember the magic combination of application, time, and temperature. With some pieces of equipment, such as the microwave oven, the manufacturer strives to assist the cook by installing push buttons that time most frequently prepared items. The cook needs only to remember to use the standard amounts or portions on which these times were based and press the proper button.

It should be emphasized that attempts to use a manufacturer's standard time–temperature capacity data for all equipment, even for a particular model, may require some adjustments. This is due to difficulties in building all units with exactly the same use characteristics under various use conditions. Thus, one should use the manufacturer's data and that given in this book as an estimate from which to develop more exact data. This information may be developed by the same method used by many home cooks: Use the time–temperature–load data recommended by the manufacturer or an educated guess, and keep a record of this data together with the quality of the product. When next using the equipment, thoughtfully make adjustments up or down until the proper combination is obtained to get the optimum product. Record this on a card kept beside the equipment and also on the recipe card for the product.

There is other information specific and important to each piece of equipment. This should be developed to make fullest use of each one. Research should be done to determine what each piece of equipment can do in an emergency and what operations it does best. In many cases, the purchase of a piece of equipment to be used infrequently can be made completely unnecessary by use of another piece of equipment designed for another purpose. For example, a deep fat fryer may be used to water cook vegetables on a continuous basis as they are needed on the serving line, to cook pieces of ham if the serving line runs short of an entrée, or to roast pieces of beef in fat if the oven breaks down or an oven load is not needed.

Substitutions for Needed Equipment

Many pieces of equipment can be stretched by imagination and research to perform tasks for which they were not designed. Knowledge of these capabilities can, at times, be used to replace a piece of nonfunctioning equipment or to provide added capacity for available equipment. This may be done by changing the cooking media from that normally used, adding some simple modification to the equipment, or using another piece of equipment that will give the needed additional functions.

Cleaning and Maintenance

Properly cleaned and maintained equipment commonly has longer use life, seldom breaks down, uses less energy, and is used more thoughtfully than equipment that is allowed to deteriorate. If the workers are cognizant of the needs of the equipment, they are usually aware of the dangers of using it and thus are less prone to accidents.

Proper cleaning and maintenance must be planned step-by-step and the workers trained to carry out each step. All instructions should be mounted adjacent to the equipment in waterproof coverings so that they are available to guide the inexperienced worker and to remind the worker who cares for it customarily. The supervisors, too, should be well versed in the established programs and must ensure that they are carried out completely. The procedures outlined in this book may be used as a basis for setting up the desired programs. However, these should be modified to reflect the manufacturers' requirements and the owner's experience.

QUESTIONS

1. What is the purpose of specifications?
2. Before writing a specification, what questions does a buyer ask himself?
3. What is the formula for determining a good buy on equipment?
4. Why does a buyer usually make purchases from a local distributor?
5. Why is training of personnel a consideration in the purchase of equipment?
6. What is the benefit of research in the purchase of new equipment?
7. Beyond its accepted uses, what information does one strive to develop about new equipment?
8. What are the main benefits of properly cleaned and maintained equipment?

BIBLIOGRAPHY

KOTSCHEVAR, L.H., TERRELL, M.E. 1977. *Food Service Planning: Layout and Equipment.* John Wiley and Sons, New York.

LONGREE, K., BLAKER, G. 1977. *Sanitary Techniques in Food Service.* John Wiley and Sons, New York.

Writing an Equipment Specification

Even though a manager has in mind the design characteristics of a piece of equipment he wishes to purchase or the things that he wants it to do, he still must put them down on paper in such a way that the dealer or manufacturer knows, without a doubt, what he wants. This can be done in a few typed lines if the manager wants a particular piece of equipment from one manufacturer but it may take fifteen to twenty printed pages if design characteristics, performance, and other purchase factors must be made general enough so that a number of manufacturers or dealers may compete for the order.

The National Association of Food Equipment Manufacturers, the National Restaurant Association, and many other organizations have trade shows to acquaint dealers and foodservice managers with available equipment. Many dealers also have displays of representative equipment. It is only natural that managers will see something at these places that they want. Then it is an easy matter for them to ask the manufacturer what reputable dealer handles this equipment in their area. This is important because, although the manager may order equipment directly from the manufacturer, if something goes wrong with it, he wants to have someone near at hand to repair it. More often than not, the manufacturer's recognized dealer has the expertise to do the repairs.

In most cases, the manufacturer's representative at the shows or the dealer will have specification sheets that will include most of the information that the manager needs to write a purchase description of the equipment that he wants to buy. For a counter deep fat fryer, this information might be presented by the purchaser in the following way:

1. General. The unit shall be 51 cm wide by 76 cm deep (front to back) and 38 cm high including 5.1-cm (2-in.) legs (20- × 30- × 15-in.). The unit shall be thermostatically controlled in a range of 121–232°C (250–450°F). It will fry 28 kg (61 lbs) of 1.3-cm (0.5-in.) potatoes from raw to done in one hour and preheat to 177°C (350°F) in five minutes. The kettle will hold 13 kg (29 lbs) of fat.
2. Electrical. The unit will operate on three-phase, 60-cycle-rated 230 voltage with a wattage of 12 kw.
3. Make and model. The unit shall be similar, or equal, to the Model F 100 manufactured by the Jones Manufacturing Company.

This is a simplified version of a specification. It is an accurate description of the technical details and requirements that the purchaser has in mind for a particular piece of equipment he wants to buy. In an even simpler form it might be:

> Jones fryer like the one I saw in your store but for 230 volts instead of 208 volts. You said you would deliver it to me for $500.

If the purchaser considered anything to be in doubt, he would cover it in the purchase description:

> It will have a two-year parts and one-year labor warranty. It will come with two half-size and two full-size tinned steel wire baskets.

At this point it is more of a purchase description than a specification. The first example was more like a specification as it gave the dealer some latitude in what he would offer by saying, "similar or equal." Of course, he must conform to the specification details that are given, and he must prove that any substitution is "similar or equal."

Most independent foodservice operators have a specific piece of equipment in mind, and they do not want to have to consider "similar or equal" equipment. They write a simple purchase description indicating a specific model of a particular type of equipment from one manufacturer. Any other technical details would be added where necessary or if different from those in the equipment shown. Most often, voltage is the requirement specified. To that might be added details of delivery such as FOB dealer's warehouse or restaurant back platform, to be installed by dealer or someone else, any tests to be performed, any instructions to be given, warranties, and details of payment.

A specification must be drawn up and administered where the choice of equipment cannot be limited to one model of one manufacturer or where the purchasing system requires that a purchase be open to all purveyors known to be reputable and selling the required product or one similar to it. Those buyers often using specification buying are: the United States government, restaurants, hotels, nursing and retirement homes, catering chains, state and city school or institutional systems, private schools, college and university systems, foodservice cooperatives, large individual hospitals, and similar agencies.

To ensure that the purveyor has a fairly clear idea of what the buyer wants, a purchase description, either a simple specification or a much more explicit one, may be used. In the purchase description or simple specification, the purveyor would have no doubt as to what the buyer wanted because it would be equipment of his that he had demonstrated and discussed in some detail with the buyer. However, if he had never discussed what the buyer needed with him, then he would require some verbal or written description of requirements in order to decide what, if anything, he had that fitted the buyer's needs. The specification attempts to cover everything about which the purveyor may have questions so that he may make a bid with the assurance that he can provide what is needed. A formal written specification might include the following information:

1. Title. This is a commonly used name for this type of equipment: fryer, deep fat (electric).

2. Scope. (This is sometimes omitted from all but the most detailed military specifications.) This describes in general terms what is wanted: a heavy-duty device for cooking batch lots of foods in an open top vessel while they are immersed in fat.

3. Classification. This narrows the alternatives as to types, sizes, styles, models, grades, mountings, and other factors: counter model, with approximately 13.7-kg (30-lb) fat capacity that will deep fat fry 27 kg (60 lb) of 1.3-cm (0.5-in.) strips of potatoes from raw to done in one hour.

4. Specific requirements. This delineates in all necessary detail what the buyer has in mind:

General description. The fryer will consist of a corrosion-proof removable fry kettle set in an insulated stainless steel shell that is supported 5.1 cm (2 in.) off the countertop. It will be heated by thermostatically controlled lift-out electric tube elements arranged across the bottom of the kettle.

Materials. This gives a delineation of metals, compositions, gauges, finishes, insulation, soldering, welding, fasteners, and similar requirements: the fry kettle shall be of 16-gauge, Type-304 stainless steel with a No. 4 finish and the shell of 18-gauge, Type-304 stainless steel with a No. 4 finish. The insulation shall be of a heat resistant, nonpacking rock wool and will be at least 5.1-cm (2-in.) thick on all sides. The insulation will be covered with 20-gauge soft steel sealed tightly to the outer shell, etc.

Details on utilities. Included here would be voltage and phase requirements, amperage, insulation, dielectrics, resistance, and fusing insofar as it is important to the buyer: the fryer will operate on 230 volts, three-phase with 33 amperes per line wire or a total of 12 kw, etc.

Controls, regulators, displays, and their placement. The fryer will be provided with an adjustable, automatic thermostat that will provide a range of fat temperature control between 121–204°C (250–400°F) in increments of 5°. When set at 177°C (350°F) it will maintain that temperature ± 2.8°C (± 5°F) with only the fat in the kettle. The control will be mounted where it is readily visible and is not easily struck, will not get covered with fat, or heat above 52°C (125°F). The thermostat bulb will be placed in a position where it reflects the fat temperature accurately but is not subject to being struck by the fry basket, etc.

Performance. The buyer should give the purveyor a good idea of the various products for which he proposes to use the equipment. For instance, he might plan to use a fryer for potato strips, fish squares, croquettes, doughnuts, pies, and shrimp.

Special details. This could include details on heating elements, legs, accessories, design details not previously covered, motors, compressors, special features, and similar requirements: will utilize Calrod-type heating elements and be provided with 10-cm (4-in.) telescoping legs, a basket lift-out device on a one- to thirty-minute timer, etc.

Certification requirements. There are a number of professional testing groups that have set up certification of standards programs for foodservice equipment in those areas of greatest controversy. Many design requirements can be covered by requiring certification by these agencies. In the deep fat fryer example, seals of approval from the UL (Underwriters' Laboratories) would cover electric switches, displays, wiring and similar things, AGA (American Gas Association) would cover details related to gas equipment, and NSF (National Sanitation Foundation) would certify compliance with certain sanitary design requirements. If the device happened to be a steam vessel, then ASME (American Society of Mechanical Engineers) certification of the safety of the vessel's use up to a certain steam pressure might be required.

Warranties and maintenance requirements. Most

operators want to be sure that the supplier will stand behind his equipment for a certain period of time; it may be six months or it may be five years, depending on the equipment and the frequency of possible breakdown. For this reason they specify that part replacement and perhaps requisite labor will be the responsibility of the purveyor for an indicated period of time. This may be spelled out for selected parts of the equipment. For example, the fryer coil may be under warranty for five years while a timer may be under warranty for only one year. Many times the warranties and maintenance services are established policies of the purveyor or manufacturer, and the buyer includes them in his specification only to be sure that he has the purveyor's agreement that he is entitled to the service.

Manuals required. Many buyers do not know what instructional materials the purveyor has or is planning to give him. In most cases, the buyer should request at least three copies each of the design and installation manuals. These operating instructions give the worker an idea of average cooking times, temperatures, and loads, plus any special mechanics of use, as the list of parts numbers provided in the manuals can speed the replacement process if the equipment breaks down. Instructions on cleaning and maintenance, which are also provided, should be simplified and placed in waterproof covers next to the equipment, where they will be needed most.

5. Quality assurance. This should detail the following:

Inspection. The purveyor should know where, when, and in what detail the equipment he provides in response to the buyer's specification will be inspected. Inspection may take place in the manufacturer's factory, the purveyor's warehouse, the buyer's kitchen or a user's kitchen. It may be prior to the equipment's being constructed (this being done on a piece of display equipment, equipment manufactured for another buyer, or on a piece of equipment in use in another buyer's kitchen). As is most often the case, it may be tested in the buyer's kitchen before or after being installed permanently. The detail for which a piece of equipment will be inspected is limited as to what was covered in the specification.

Performance tests. If the buyer is fairly sure that there is equipment available with the fat load and heat input that he has specified, which will produce the amount critical to his operation, he should indicate this as a requirement in the specification. If no one can provide a piece of equipment that will perform as specified, then the purchaser must change some of his specifications. Usually this will be in power input or allowing a larger size of device so that it will perform as required. While often limited to one product, there is no reason why two or more products should not be used in the performance tests. It is important that the test product be described exactly, the method of utilization be delineated, if important, and the test time period be specified. Thus, for our specification example, the performance test might read: will prepare 27 kg (60 lbs) of 1.3-cm- (0.5-in.-) square strips of potatoes from raw to done in one hour. A griddle might be required to cook from raw to well done so many 10-cm- (4-in.-) diameter, 1.9-cm- (0.75-in.-) thick beef hamburgers in one hour. It is important that any performance testing be conducted as listed in the specification.

6. Delivery requirements. This would include packing, if important, details of shipping, including means, marking, delivery date, and details of installation if it is to be done by the seller. Manufacturers will seldom be responsible for installation, but dealers, if they have trained personnel, often will do it. It is to the buyer's advantage to have experts do the installation.

7. Administrative details. This can cover information as to bidding, opening and awarding of bids, how the contract will be handled, how discrepancies will be resolved, how payment will be made, etc.

8. Drawing and diagrams. Where custom-made equipment is involved, modifications are desired, special wiring or piping is required, or other equipment, such as a conveyor, must be integrated, then drawings or diagrams may be a part of a specification (figure 2.1). They should be checked carefully to ensure that they conform with the written requirements of the specification and are drawn to a designated scale.

9. Author of the specification. It is seldom that a specification is so clear that a purveyor or manufacturer does not have some questions about it. For this reason the specification should have the name, address, and telephone number of either the author of the specifications or the person who should be contacted to give details or explanations not covered in the specification. This person should have authority to give approval for exceptions to what is in the specification and see that if an exception is given to one bidder that it is given to the others also.

Checklist for Specification Writing

1. Is the specification, as written, free of any possibilities of misunderstanding? Is the language used familiar to the trade? Use of manufacturer's spec sheets for reference will usually take care of this. Gauges, finishes, types of materials, fasteners, controls, displays, heating elements, coatings, and similar terms should be in common usage.

2. Is everything important to the buyer included in the specification? If a griddle should be of a certain area, be a specific distance from the floor, and have a 15-cm (6-in.) fence around it, all of these requirements should be in the specification.

3. Is the specification free of all requirements of a frivolous nature that are unimportant to the buyer? Everything that is in a specification is a restriction that may eliminate some bidder who might otherwise have an outstanding piece of equipment and be able to give the buyer a good bargain. If the buyer cannot see the necessity for some detail in a manufacturer's specification sheet, he should not put it in the specification. One should give careful consideration before including anything which is not a usual feature on the equipment of a number of manufacturers. Specifying a feature used only by one manufacturer limits competition, and something that must be custom-made adds to costs greatly since it requires preparation of special drawings and manufacture by the most highly paid workers.

4. Are similar parts described in identical terms so that the manufacturer is not confused and led to believe that custom manufacture is necessary?

5. Is the design well balanced? Will the feet, frame, and floor be adequate to support the weight of the equipment? Are the hinges adequate for the size and weight of the door? Will the drawer slide work freely with a loaded drawer? Are materials of similar use life used?

6. Are better quality, more expensive material, heavier gauge, finer finish, added functions, or more or better controls than necessary being furnished in light of the expected functions to be performed and the use life of the equipment? While an oven front of stainless steel is desirable, the side, back, bottom and top panels could be made of cheaper steels that could be coated to provide adequate corrosion protection. While a table top supporting heavy mechanical equipment may warrant 12-gauge stainless steel, one to be used for salad preparation and salad making will do quite well with 14–16 gauge.

7. Does the equipment specification cover the details and accessories important to the use of that equipment in the buyer's place of business? Often one is confused as to what is provided when a standard piece of equipment is purchased. If a 57-

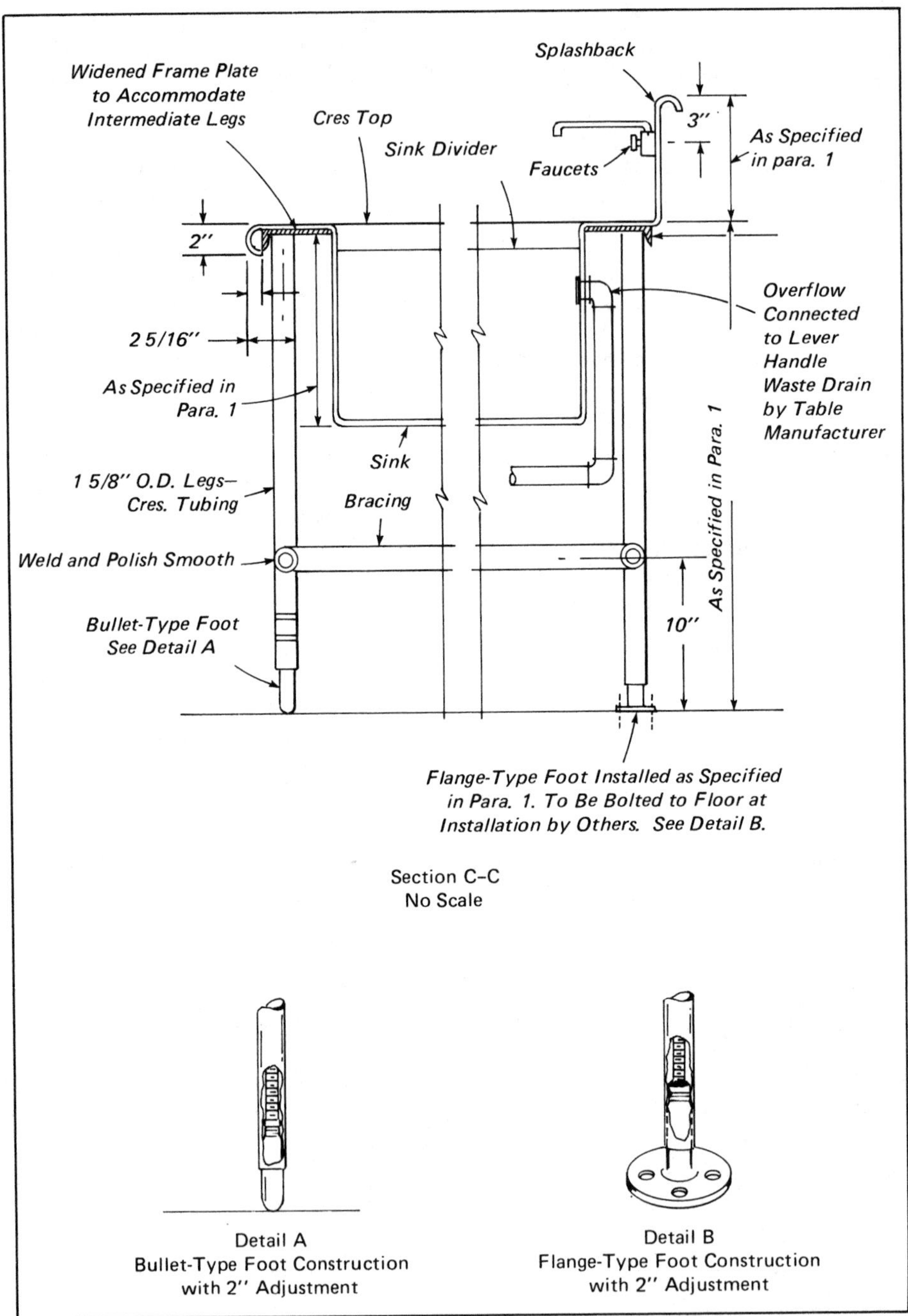

FIGURE 2.1. Drawings may be needed in specifications to express details of design.

liter (60-qt) mixer will be used for 38-liter (40-qt) quantities, does the mixer being purchased have the necessary adapters? Does the specification cover faucets, traps, valves, electric connections, and other expected accessories? If a food slicer is to be used to slice tomatoes, will it come with the necessary holder? Of a similar, but opposite, nature is being sure that accessories are needed. For years the U.S. Navy bought food mixers with a coffee-grinding attachment despite the fact that all coffee they purchased was ground.

8. Is the dealer going to install the equipment? If so, how much preparation of site, utility connections, and drains can he expect? In most manufacturers' specification sheets, these required items are delineated as to placement, number, and size, and usually the dealer who installs will expect these to be the minimum he will need.

9. Before specifying a piece of equipment, the buyer should learn if there are any state, county, or city regulations with which he might have to comply. A garbage grinder may be prohibited because the local sewage disposal plant or sewers cannot handle the garbage. A heavy, gas-using piece of equipment might be prohibited because of a local gas shortage. Local sanitation ordinances may have special requirements not anticipated by the National Sanitation Foundation.

10. Try to get the manufacturing done by workers with long experience in the work. Failing on this provision, be sure to specify that the work be "good commercial practice."

11. Include in the specification that all parts, pipes, and wiring that might need maintenance or repair be readily accessible. Before buying the equipment, check to be sure that the equipment complies.

12. If buying from a manufacturer or dealer, ascertain that capable local repair services are available with adequate spare parts to repair and maintain the selected piece of equipment. If one must get a repairperson from the factory to repair a dishwasher, or if a local repairworker must send to the factory for spare parts, sometimes the cost can be prohibitive and the delay can be disastrous. If local repairworkers are represented as being available, it is well to determine if they are factory trained and have a good reputation.

13. If a specification is written to attract a number of bidders, it should be written loosely enough so that the equipment from a number of manufacturers will comply with the specification details. Usually good competition in bidding will mean lower prices. If bidding is required by law but the buyer has a specific piece of equipment from one manufacturer that he is determined to buy, a very tight specification written around that manufacturer's specification sheet for that piece of equipment is the way to do it. However, the specifier needs to be prepared to justify everything that is in that specification as another manufacturer may protest the specification as being unnecessarily discriminating. A tight specification usually will mean fewer bids and higher prices.

Specification writers are urged to go to the trade shows, find all equipment that fits their needs and then get the various specification sheets. These, then, can be used to write a clear, concise specification that will record unequivocally exactly what is desired.

QUESTIONS

1. Where may a buyer view equipment that he might want to purchase?
2. What does a buyer use to tell purveyors what he needs?

3. What is the simplest way for the buyer to indicate that he wants a specific piece of equipment?
4. How does a buyer go about getting many bidders on a piece of equipment?
5. What are the major parts of an equipment specification?
6. What information is covered under materials?
7. What is a performance test?
8. What agencies are involved in certification, and what does each certify?
9. What local information does a buyer need before writing a specification?
10. What does one check relative to equipment repairs before buying?

BIBLIOGRAPHY

ANON. *Fry Kettles, Model F101.* Wells Manufacturing Corp., San Francisco.

AVERY, A.C. 1978. The art of writing specs. *Food Management* 13, No. 2, 40–42, 66–68.

BUREAU OF SHIPS, U.S. NAVY. 1956. *Military specification, range outfit, electric shipboard, MIL-R-1927 (ships).* Washington, D.C.

CANFIELD, J.H. 1970. The salesman's introduction to specification writing. *Food Service Equipment Dealer* 22, No. 11, 17.

LASCHOBER, J. 1959. Specifications for cooking equipment. *Institutions Magazine* 45, No. 3, 61.

MONTCALM, R. 1966. *Use of Specification for the Purchase of Equipment.* Walter Reed Army Medical Center, Washington, D.C.

Designing for Humans

In former years, foodservice labor was in plentiful supply and fairly well trained, but today a mushrooming foodservice industry and changing occupational goals have erased the lines of potential workers waiting outside the kitchen door. Skills have decreased as well, so most foodservice operators have turned to special equipment and convenience foods to provide the needed hands and skills. However, some workers are necessary to prepare, operate, clean, and maintain the equipment that is used. If the equipment is to be used efficiently and effectively, the design of the equipment, its arrangement, and the environment in which it is used must receive full consideration to achieve full productivity from the workers.

In order for the equipment and workers to combine productively, one must call on the science variously known as ergonomics, human factors, or human engineering. This may be defined as adapting tasks, equipment, and working environment to the sensory, perceptual, mental, and physical attributes of the worker. The employee works best if equipment is designed to do the job most effectively, if it is suited to his capabilities, and if it is placed in pleasing surroundings.

Other industries and fields have done well by using human engineering, for example, to enable the airplane pilot to read a multitude of visual displays and operate many controls to fly a sky monster successfully, to permit a power shovel operator to lift tons of material and drop it precisely into a truck, and to help the submariner to move many feet under the ocean's surface without disaster-causing errors. Thus, there is no reason why application of human engineering cannot allow the foodservice worker to be equally efficient and productive.

To accomplish this in foodservice, human engineering should adhere to the following principles:

1. Design and arrangement of equipment should be such that the equipment's use requires a minimum application of human physical effort.
2. Only essential information should be provided for the equipment, and this should be presented when and where it is required with maximum clarity. It should be arranged in a step-by-step order.
3. Control devices on equipment should be easily identified, minimum in number, logical in placement, and in consonance with displays in operation. They should relate precisely to the functions they control.
4. Equipment should be designed to provide maximum productivity while utilizing the worker's physical and mental attributes most effectively. It should take into account the dimensions of the worker and his strengths.
5. Equipment should be selected on the basis of need in utilizing specific ingredients to prepare a selected menu, grouped in most used combinations, and arranged in order of most frequent interuse proceeding from left to right. Those tasks demanding the greatest skill should be grouped around the worker having these skills, and his movements to provide for his needs should be minimal.
6. The environment in which the foodservice worker operates should be designed and controlled to allow him to be most productive, comfortable, and happy with his job. This control involves consideration of lighting, facility and equipment coloration, temperature, humidity, noise, smells, facility design, floor conditions, and safety, among others.

The aim of human engineering is to provide a working environment in which the worker is as alert, accurate, able to think, and free of debilitating and endangering fatigue during the last hour of his shift as he was during the first. Fatigue is the factor that can best be controlled by attention to human factors, and it does influence the others. Fatigue, most generally caused by tensions, can result in the following:

1. decreased attention to what is happening around the worker
2. slowed and impaired perception
3. fuzzy thinking and decreased patience
4. lower motivational level
5. reduced physical performance
6. increased number and length of pauses
7. sore and aching muscles
8. increased number of accidents
9. wastage and losses in food and cleaning materials and less care in using expensive equipment, thus causing costly equipment breakdown
10. decreased reference to, and use of, written instructions and recipes
11. less use of accurate measurements, processing times, and temperatures

This fatigue and resultant lowered productivity are often influenced by the following causes:

1. High temperatures and/or humidity. The worker can work just as hard as under more favorable conditions, but he pauses more frequently and for longer periods of time and looks for pseudoreasons to stop working (conversation, more personal time, trips for unneeded things, and similar time wasters). He works carelessly, refuses to follow recipes, and is more accident prone.
2. Available light level is too low or glaring, work area contrast with background is insufficient or too great, or food and skin show up in unnatural colors.
3. High noise level or sharp impact noises. These

cause the body to tense, sometimes without the worker knowing it. This tension causes fatigue. This happens most often in the dishroom and the potwashing area.

4. Long periods of mental or physical work where the body is held in a stooped or bent static position. The worker wastes much energy in maintaining such a body position and thus becomes tired more rapidly. This is caused most often by work surfaces which are too low and make the worker hunch or bend over his work. Sometimes it is the result of a work area too high causing the worker to lean back.
5. Standing too long. This happens in many kitchens but is most common with counterworkers. Most evidence shows that the majority of workers are more productive when seated, and few kitchens provide proper seating to allow this or, better yet, a combination of standing and seated work.
6. Repeated major body changes (loading and unloading a dishwasher from locations some distance from the dishwasher). Usually this is the result of poor kitchen layout.
7. Insufficient knowledge or unfamiliarity with the task or machine (repairing a dishwasher or making up a difficult recipe for the first time). Some managers counter insufficient knowledge by training two or more workers for each job.
8. Heavy physical exertion (scrubbing floors or hand-carrying products from Receiving to Storage).
9. Working at a disliked task (cleaning garbage cans, scrubbing walls, or deliming the dishwasher).
10. Work requiring careful attention to detail (checking payroll figures or keeping accounts).
11. Rushing to meet deadlines (getting ready for a banquet when understaffed).
12. Mental or emotional stress (cook fighting with a waitress, sickness at home, or problems with a spouse).

While the last four problems can be helped but not solved by human engineering, the others are open to solution.

Temperature, Humidity, and Air Movement

In a drug factory it has been found that a worker who can fill 47 bottles at 24°C (75°F) is reduced to 27 bottles at 32°C (90°F). It has always been believed that high temperature and high humidity control are not economically feasible in foodservice, particularly the kitchen. This is because the effects of these environmental conditions on the worker have not been realized and thought has not been given to their control and the benefits to be derived.

It is known that more work is done in good weather than bad and in excessive cold than in excessive heat. Other industries have found that the average person works best if his skin temperature is 33–34°C (91–93°F), which means a kitchen should be at 20–22°C (68–72°F) in winter and 23–26°C (74–78°F) in summer. Relative humidity of 40–45 percent is most comfortable. Below 30 percent, as often occurs in heated areas in the winter, there is excessive drying out of surfaces that must be constantly moist (eyes or nasal membranes). In summer in kitchen spaces where much moisture is generated (dishrooms and potcooking areas), the opposite is true. Humidity runs up to 90–95 percent; dishes do not dry, wiped table tops remain wet, and most important, perspiration does not provide its cooling action by evaporating. Thus the worker becomes more and more uncomfortable and unhappy.

By placing humidifiers in the forced air ducts of the air heaters, humidity can be increased to a comfortable 30–45 percent even when the outside air would provide only 5–10 percent humidity if brought in and heated to room temperature. Dehumidifiers are used by many stores that cannot afford air conditioners. Removing enough humidity to provide 40–45 percent relative humidity reduces the apparent temperature by as much as 10 degrees.

Fans are a common way of cooling kitchen workers, or at least making the workers feel that management is thinking about them. Some fans are mounted in hoods to remove radiated heat from cooking and holding equipment as well as dishwashers and cleaning equipment. They do little for the workers unless balanced by an intake fan in the wall opposite the equipment hood. Drawing stale air from the dining room is not the answer. While most ventilating engineers prefer to place the intake fan high on the wall to sweep away the hot, moist air as it travels across the room, I prefer to have the intake fan low in the wall so that the cool and often drier incoming air stays low where the workers are positioned. Some kitchens use an additional exhaust fan close to that in the hood so that the total exhausting capacity is greater than the incoming air, thus keeping the kitchen under a slight negative pressure. This prevents kitchen odors from being forced into the dining room. While a person may need about 30 cu m of air per hour, most foodservice consultants try to achieve twenty air changes per hour in a large kitchen and thirty in a small kitchen. I have found that about half this amount is often sufficient.

Hoods over the entrance and exit ends of dishwashers should be used to remove dishwasher humidity or the dishes will not dry properly and the dishroom workers will be uncomfortable.

At times it has been found that additional fans blowing directly on the worker are necessary to cool him by evaporation of perspiration. Regrettably, most of the fans are directed against the back of the worker instead of his front and top of his head where he has twice as many sweat glands. Fans should blow air from a low level where it is cooler. If the cooks are wearing long-sleeved uniforms, only 12 percent of the skin is exposed to the fan's evaporating air waves, and this is undesirable. T-shirts raise this exposure to 30 percent, and shorts allow 60 percent exposure, thus increasing cooling. Having fans blowing parallel to the walls increases air circulation around the room; window fans are most efficient if they blow the same way as the outside wind; and during the winter, fans should blow toward the ceiling to use that air for space heating.

Refrigerated water fountains have been frowned on in some kitchens because claims have been made that workers develop stomach cramps as well as waste time without balancing benefits. Research indicates that this is not the case unless workers drink to excess. Actually, cold water makes workers more productive and happy.

Air-conditioning in kitchens has long been considered economically unfeasible despite research from a major university that shows that kitchen workers are 10–25 percent more productive in the summer if kitchens are air conditioned. U.S. Navy research indicated that 15 percent more work was done at 24°C (75°F) than at 32°C (90°F). The resistance to air-conditioning has stemmed from the feeling that with many pieces of equipment pouring heat into the kitchen and the hoods and ventilation systems laboring to pump it out, any air-conditioning system sufficiently large to cope with these factors would be too expensive to buy and operate. If properly planned for, this is not true, and if considered along with energy conservation, it may pay in both dollars and employee comfort.

Some of the measures that may be used to make air-conditioning more financially suitable and, at the same time, reduce kitchen temperatures are as follows:

1. Heavily insulate all steam and hot water pipes, potsinks, dishwashing and silverware sinks, coffee urns, steam jacketed kettles, steamers, pressure cookers, and similar equipment. Increase insulation on ovens.
2. Place hot water heaters, refrigerator compressors, and condensers remotely from the kitchen.
3. Insulate the building.
4. Preheat equipment only for that amount of time necessary.
5. Use overhanging eaves, sun-reflecting windows, films and screens, and other means to reduce sun heating.

6. Cover all steam jacketed kettles, pots, griddles, fryers, and similar equipment during preheat and after use whenever feasible.
7. Use low temperature lights.
8. Whenever possible, use the preheat and residual heat of cooking equipment for starting and finishing cooking or keeping foods hot.
9. Adjust gas flames so that they do not come up around the sides of the pot but contact only the pot bottom.
10. Air out building at night during the summer. Take advantage of the outside air when cool.
11. Cook at 85°C (185°F) instead of a rolling boil in pots and kettles to reduce clouds of steam. A slow boil requires only one-quarter to one-third the energy that a fast boil does and performs the same job.

Lighting

Physiologists have estimated that 25 percent of the worker's energy is expended in seeing and thinking. Others have not found this to be so. However, it is commonly agreed that if the eyes feel tired, the body feels tired and responds only to the most urgent commands.

Eyestrain and the resultant fatigue is contributed to by the following factors:

1. glare, light rays that come directly from the source to the eye
2. distracting brightness on the periphery of vision
3. prolonged close work
4. constant adjustments from near to far or light to dark
5. lack of convenient and pleasing areas of visual relaxation
6. inadequate lighting
7. poor contrast between objects and background (separating silverware on a stainless steel table or peppercorns on a black table)

Eyestrain manifests itself by:

1. severe dilation of pupil of eye
2. high blinking rate
3. increased muscular tension together with nervousness and fatigue
4. nausea and psychological irritability in extreme cases

In foodservice operations, good light and color conditioning as contrasted with much of what has been available in the industry has the following beneficial effects:

1. improved production rates (87 percent of industrial motions are controlled by sight)
2. better quality products, fewer rejects and unusable items
3. reduced eyestrain and fatigue
4. reduced accidents and misuse of equipment
5. shortened worker training
6. improved worker morale, lowered absenteeism, and reduced labor turnover
7. better housekeeping and faster cleanup
8. better public relations
9. saving of money

In these days of energy shortage, there is reduced use of general illumination for foodservice spaces and more concentration of light on the specific kitchen tasks. In general, the amount of light provided is regulated by:

1. The size of the area involved in the task.
2. Contrast between the central product being made and the work background.
3. The reflectance of the background.
4. The time allowed for seeing. There is a range of light amount that is best for each task. Too much slows seeing and is expensive, while too little causes one to grope wastefully in his seeing function.

The visual acuity at the point of work is a function of:

1. the type and light intensity of the lamp

2. the type of fixture and how well it is maintained
3. location of the fixture or fixtures
4. freedom from dazzle or reflectance back to eyes from the work or background surfaces affected by (a) too great contrast in field of view (contrast should be about 1:3 in field of view and not more than 1:10 peripherally); (b) abrupt changes in light intensity; (c) light source too bright

Common Types of Fixtures

Direct light rays are beamed directly from the light source to work surface and often into the worker's eyes or reflected from a shiny surface where they cause sight-impairing glare. This is the most efficient type of lighting, but unless properly placed and shielded, it causes glare, obscuring shadows, and poor contrasts. Bright lights should not be located within 60 degrees of the center of the visual field. Shields should be used to keep the rays out of the eyes. Often less glare is apparent if several low-intensity light sources are used instead of one major source.

Indirect lighting shuts off direct rays from lamp to worker's eyes by bouncing the light off a reflective shield, wall, or ceiling. This provides glareless, even light with few shadows. However, this type of lighting is inefficient in the amount of energy required for a given level of lighting. Efficiency is impaired further by dirty reflectors or ceilings.

Diffuse lighting uses translucent shields to spread out the glaring rays from the lamp so that they are no longer objectionable to the eyes. While it is less efficient in the use of energy than direct lighting, it is more efficient than indirect. However, there is some minor shadowing, and its efficiency, too, can be reduced by dirty shields.

Combination lighting is commonly available depending on the particular lighting needs. One frequently used in offices, kitchens, and schoolrooms has a deep grid directly under the lamps to force the direct rays down onto the work surface without side glare, translucent side panels to provide diffused side lighting, and reflection off the ceiling or reflectors for general lighting. Where lighting on a work surface only is desired, often the gridded portion of the fixture is used alone.

Types of Lamps

What lamp to use is usually based on the amount of light required, the necessary color characteristics, and more recently, the relative energy efficiency of the lamp in producing light. The yellow-white incandescent lamps present both food and the human skin in the best light. This makes them a good choice in fine dining rooms, but they are relatively inefficient in the use of energy, produce considerable heat, and have a short use life. They use a very simple fixture. Fluorescents use a more complex and costly fixture, but they provide four to four and a half times the amount of light per watt of expended electricity. However, their color characteristics are not as desirable. They last about nine to ten times as long as incandescents. Fluorescents come in a wide range of color variations. One university research project rated a number of them in the following order of desirability for foodservice:

1. Incandescent lamps.
2. Soft white fluorescents.
3. White fluorescents.
4. Standard warm white fluorescents are preferred in service areas. Color improved warm white gives a tanned color and is good with prepared and baked foods.
5. Standard cool white fluorescents are preferred in maintenance areas. Color improved cool-white ones are not energy efficient but give a semblance of natural light and are used to accent green vegetables and lean meat.
6. Gold fluorescents.

7. Daylight fluorescents.
8. Pink fluorescents.
9. Blue fluorescents.
10. Green fluorescents.
11. Red fluorescents.

There are a number of new longer-life and better-quality fluorescents including a square one that were not evaluated in this study. The square lamps do not appear to provide as much glare as the round fluorescents.

Proper choice of lamp is important. As an example, a state institution was having trouble getting young females to work in the vegetable preparation room with an old woman. "She looks like an old witch," they said. And she did! Daylight fluorescents gave her skin a ghoulish appearance. The light fixture was placed almost directly over her head deepening her wrinkles so that she looked like what one thinks of as a witch. Replacing the daylight with soft white plus a pink lamp and moving her table back from the light gave her the rosy appearance and shallow wrinkles of the benevolent grandmother which she was. I often use two soft white plus one pink in kitchens to improve the appearance of the worker's skin and the food material with which he works. Green fluorescents are sometimes used to enhance a salad bar while pink or red are used frequently to make roast beef being sliced on the serving line more red. An installation suggestion is to place fluorescent fixtures parallel to the worker's line of sight as they produce less glare than when crossing his line of vision.

For outside use in parking lots and sidewalks, one may want to consider the use of multi-vapor or sodium lamps which have considerably more light output per watt of input. A new sodium (high-pressure sodium) lamp provides 86 percent of light output and lasts 20 times as long as incandescents. One should replace old fluorescents with newer ones that may be up to 14 percent more energy efficient. At its best, as a general rule, lighting only converts 24 percent of energy input into light. The remainder goes into heat.

There is considerable disagreement among authorities on the amount of light needed in food-service spaces. It has been found that good light increases production 4–35 percent over bad. I recommend the following FC (foot candle) levels. A foot candle approximates the amount of light from one candle flame held one foot away.

Area	*Minimum Light Levels in Foot Candles*
corridors	10
storeroom where labels on cans must be read	20
storerooms where only case labels must be read	15
rough work areas where only large print is read	20–30
areas where recipes and penciled instructions must be read	30–50
clean end of dishwasher	70–100
office where accounting is done and fine figures must be read	100–150
cashier's stand	50
intimate restaurant	5–10
intimate restaurant cleaning	20
family restaurant	30
fast food restaurant	75–100
service areas	50–100

Beyond 30–50 light levels, they must be tripled or quadrupled to be an obvious improvement. Some states require 70 FC but I have found this to be too much with stainless steel. Note that the lighting in the dining areas of intimate restaurants, family restaurants, and fast food restaurants should be even and without glare, that is, there should be no direct rays from the light source to the customers' eyes.

Too high concentration of light in the work area or too much contrast between work and background can be corrected by dimming or removing lamps.

To increase customer's check average, light the food selection brightly in a cafeteria or smorgasbord, but light the tray rail or area where the customer stands dimly.

Color

Practically as important as lighting in the food-service establishment are the color considerations. They can increase the productivity of the workers, alter the apparent architecture and atmosphere of the dining facilities, and provide desired influences on the customers. Particularly in hospital kitchens, but in others as well, it was thought beneficial to either paint the kitchen interiors white or use white tile to emphasize the worker's dedication to sanitation. While it might have made dirt easier to see, it had a tiring effect and was depressing to worker morale. If one observes a man leaving an all-white kitchen, he walks out hunched over and depressed, but gradually straightens and brightens up as he moves away.

I have found soft yellows and peach to be the most productive for kitchens as they show both food and skin in natural colors. Tiring colors are the white, purple, brown, orange colors, and harsh shades of blue and yellow green. Kitchen wall colors should be no darker or lighter than soft yellows or peach, and should be 50 percent reflective (figure 3.1).

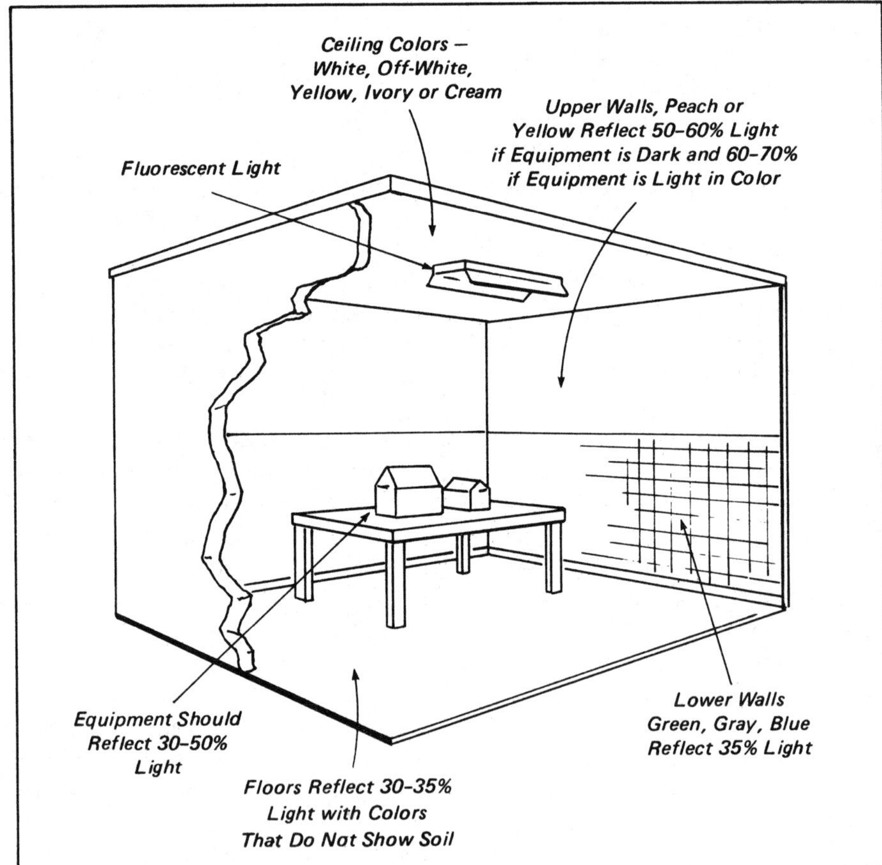

FIGURE 3.1. Color and light reflectance in the kitchen.

To improve foodservice, do some of the following:

1. Use warm reds, brown, yellows, gold, peach, and sometimes orange to enhance foods. Green plates and green lights sell more salads.
2. Use bright colors in fast food operations and restaurants which cater to low-income patrons and soft, warm colors in table service restaurants and those which cater to patrons in the higher-income brackets.
3. Avoid colors such as gray or green that do not flatter people.
4. Use light colors in small rooms to create the illusion of size and dark colors to seemingly decrease size.
5. Where there are no windows, use soft, warm colors.
6. High, lofty ceilings may appear lower if dark colors are used on them. Horizontal wall lines should be emphasized as well.
7. Low ceilings can be made to seem higher by using light colors on the ceiling and emphasizing vertical wall lines with dark colors.
8. End walls in long rooms may be painted warm, dark colors to square the room.
9. Mix warm and cool colors in a dining room to make it more interesting, but avoid too many colors, which may become tiring to the patrons.
10. Paint adjoining rooms harmonious colors.
11. To submerge undesirable features into the background, paint them the same color as the background. To make a dangerous object, such as a pillar, more obvious, paint it a bright color that contrasts with the background.
12. Light, cool blues and blue greens help to make a too sunny room appear cooler as well as more spacious.
13. Use bright lights, low room temperatures, loud and fast music, and purple violet, yellow green, and musty tones in a fast food restaurant where customers should eat quickly and leave. Use dim lights, temperatures of 24–26°C (76–78°F), soft, unobtrusive music, and warm hues of red, yellow, and peach in a fine restaurant where people should relax and linger over their drinks and food.
14. Peach and yellow colors and bright lights on the food cause people to load their trays.
15. The heat repelling qualities of white are well known. For example, white topped buses are 10–15 percent cooler than dark topped buses, and white helmets are 22 percent cooler than black ones. Since most food heating and service equipment radiates heat, it is desirable that foodservice workers wear light, loose-fitting white clothing in summer to reduce the amount of heat that is absorbed by the skin.
16. Before using a color in foodservice, consider how it will look under both natural and artificial light; many darker colors may look black.
17. Painting rest rooms white or purple tends to discourage workers from lingering. Some soft pastel shades tend to make workers spend too much time in rest rooms.
18. Kitchen ceilings should be painted off white and reflect 85–95 percent of the light that strikes them. Sidewalls should be peach or soft yellow and reflect 50–60 percent if equipment is dark and 50–70 percent if equipment is stainless steel or light colored. Floors should be fairly light colored and reflect 25 percent of the light.
19. Use color coding for danger or relief areas: (a) yellow or yellow and black checks to indicate obstacles; (b) orange to mark dangerous moving parts; (c) blue tags or tape to mark a switch or control which is being repaired and should not be operated; (d) red for fire equipment; and (e) green and white for first aid and safety equipment.

Noise

While designers go to great lengths to subdue

dining room noise to an expectant hush by use of draperies, deep carpets, alcoves, pads under the table cloths, and acoustic ceiling tiles, the kitchen and related spaces are often noisy. Noise is measured in decibels, and a kitchen employee can adjust to noise as a jack hammer operator does. Even though the employee says he is relaxed, his body continues to tire because noise builds up tension. Particularly noticeable are sharp impact noises. Managers who have gone to great lengths to reduce the noise that is responsible for typing and other machine operating errors and high employee turnover in offices have, in some cases, found that office noise levels are too low, and minor impact noises attract too much attention. Thus, sufficient noise must be added back in the form of music or machine hum to make these impact noises unnoticeable.

Almost everything in a kitchen and dishroom shouts at the worker. To make himself heard above the hubbub, he raises his voice and soon the kitchen noises rise to a crescendo. Noise levels of 40–50 decibels are pleasing, levels of 80–90 decibels become uncomfortable, 100 decibels are temporarily painful, and 120-decibel noise may be permanently deafening.

The clatter of pots, pans, and dishes in an atmosphere of stainless steel and ceramic tile cannot help but reverberate noise unless steps are taken to deaden the rattling noises and trap sound waves. Some of the measures that can be used include:

1. Workers must be admonished to talk rather than shout.
2. Carpeting (if approved by the Department of Health) can be used in any areas of the kitchen where the grease and water falling on the floor are not excessive. By reducing dish breakage, it quickly pays for itself.
3. Lift dishes from bussing boxes to dishroom tables rather than dump them. In addition to reducing noise, it reduces dish breakage. Use of heavy plastic dishes and rubberized, or otherwise coated, dish racks also helps.
4. Undercoat the tables holding dishes with asphalt or similar material, or use rubber or plastic mesh mats on the tables to lower the noise.
5. Locate noisy machines such as refrigerator motors and compressors remotely, or enclose them with noise absorbing batts of fiberglass or similar material.
6. Use coarse draperies or similar material to entrap sound.
7. Under maximum noise levels, honeycomb panels 46–61-cm (1.5–2-ft) deep of coarse cloth may be used overhead. Where gymnasiums have been converted to classrooms without ceilings, the honeycomb panels decrease the escape and interference of noise.
8. With the noise levels in the average kitchen, usually all that is needed are acoustic materials on upper walls and/or ceiling if health authorities will permit them. Most acoustic materials are compared on the basis of their noise reduction coefficients (NRC). The NRC uses total reduction of 500 cycles per second sound as 1.00. An acoustic panel with an NRC rating of 0.89 would be a much better sound reducer than wood panels with an NRC rating of 0.06. Some of the ratings of common kitchen and acoustic materials are:

Material	*Thickness*	*NRC*
plaster, smooth on masonry		0.02
wood panels		0.06
fiberglass tile	0.62 in.	0.53
fabrics (18 oz)		0.55
carpeting (40-oz hair-felt underlay)		0.60
acoustic tile, perforated	0.62 in.	0.67
acoustic veneer, perforated	0.62 in.	0.67
acoustic cane fiber	0.62 in.	0.69
sound-conditioning tile	0.62 in.	0.70
asbestos board, perforated	2.19 in.	0.85
acoustic panels	0.62 in.	0.89

While music may add to the noise level in a kitchen, it does reduce some of the tension effects of noise. One factory found that music played at the start and end of each shift and for a half hour in the middle of the shift increased worker productivity 7 percent during the day and 17 percent at night. The best music to work by was hit tunes, snappy waltzes, and semi-classical music. Religious music, or music which caused the worker to want to dance or clap hands was the worst.

Odor

Odor is not too much of a problem in most kitchens as customers, management, and workers associate bad odors with poor sanitation and the foodservice people take steps to eliminate them. Actually, under heavy odor conditions such as those in air raid shelters, people lose their appetite and thirst, lose sleep, and may have mind aberrations. High humidity and temperatures intensify these reactions.

In the kitchen, offending materials are removed and the odors vented to the outside. Other expedients used under special circumstances are cleaning with oxidizing compounds, odor absorption by activated charcoal (this solution is used in air raid shelters and submarines), counter-odorants or neutralizers, and pleasant fragrances. The last two must be used with care as some foods, particularly butter, pick up powerful odorants. One of the most commonly used neutralizers is Neutrox Gamma. Some are so powerful they have been used to neutralize odors of pig and mink farms.

Work Space and Equipment Design

Maximum efficiency in a man-machine system such as that in a foodservice kitchen must be designed as a whole with the worker complementary to the machine and the machine complementary to the abilities of the worker. Design of the work space and included equipment should allow the body muscles to be flexed moderately, provide a minimum of static positioning, and be biomechanically efficient.

At best, the body uses only 30 percent of its calories for work, and if this is wasted in static positions, it is not available for work. When stooped, only 5 percent of the body's energy is used for work, but if the body is vertical, 20–27 percent is available for heavy manual labor.

One should select equipment and plan work areas and tasks that will allow the torso to remain in a natural vertical position without frequent twisting or bending, low head ducking, and reaching out. Workers should be able to work with free, smooth, continuous motions rather than jerky ones. The work load should be adjusted so that the heart beats little more than 30 beats above resting. Heavy weights should be kept close to the center of gravity and be handled with a maximum number of muscles. The best muscular action is dynamic. Muscles contract and relax frequently, providing good blood circulation.

In foodservice, the body is most productive if the trunk is vertical, the upper arms are parallel to the trunk, the lower arms are at right angles to the upper arms, and hands are palms up. The elbow is most powerful at this point. In turning knobs, the arm is strongest if the hand is first turned outward; the knob is then grasped, and the hand turns inward. People can exert greatest strength and skills with their hands in front of the body. Best lifting is done with the back straight and vertical, arms extended down to grasp handles on the load a little above its center of gravity with the point of grip about 40 cm (16 in.) above ground level.

Seated, the most power can be exerted with a jerk rather than a steady pull with the arms straight out from the shoulders, or about 70 cm (28 in.). However, steady pull has a better control with a slight flex of the elbow and the feet braced and the load grasped about 20–25 cm (8–10 in.) above the seat top height.

Working Heights and Areas

While standing increases static energy consumption over lying down by 8–10 percent, kneeling increases it by 30–40 percent, and stooping 50–60 percent. Thus, it becomes apparent that work area heights that cause energy wasting in stooping are to be avoided. For the most part, tables at which people stand to work are best set at about 2.5–7.6 cm (1–3 in.) below worker elbow height for light work and highly manipulative tasks such as sandwich and salad making, cookie cutting, and portioning. Usually, this means heights of 94–99 cm (37–39 in.) for women and 99–104 cm (39–41 in.) for men (figure 3.2). It is well to have the table feet adjustable so that the table can be regulated to the height of the person who uses it most frequently. Heavy work tables, where the back must be used in the task, might be at 76–91 cm (30–36 in.) or the point where the worker's wrist bends when the arm hangs by the side. At least 11 cm (4 in.) of kick space should be left under the front of the table for toes. Where tall pieces of equipment are placed on tables, the tables should be of a height such that the most frequent task for which it is used can be done below elbow height. For tables where all the work done is by seated workers, the table top should be from 66 cm (26 in.) to a maximum of 78 cm (31 in.) with 58–61 cm (23–24 in.) clearance beneath for legs and possibly 5–21 cm (2–8 in.) for a footrest. If possible, the table top should be at elbow height but, at most, should allow comfortable resting of the elbows.

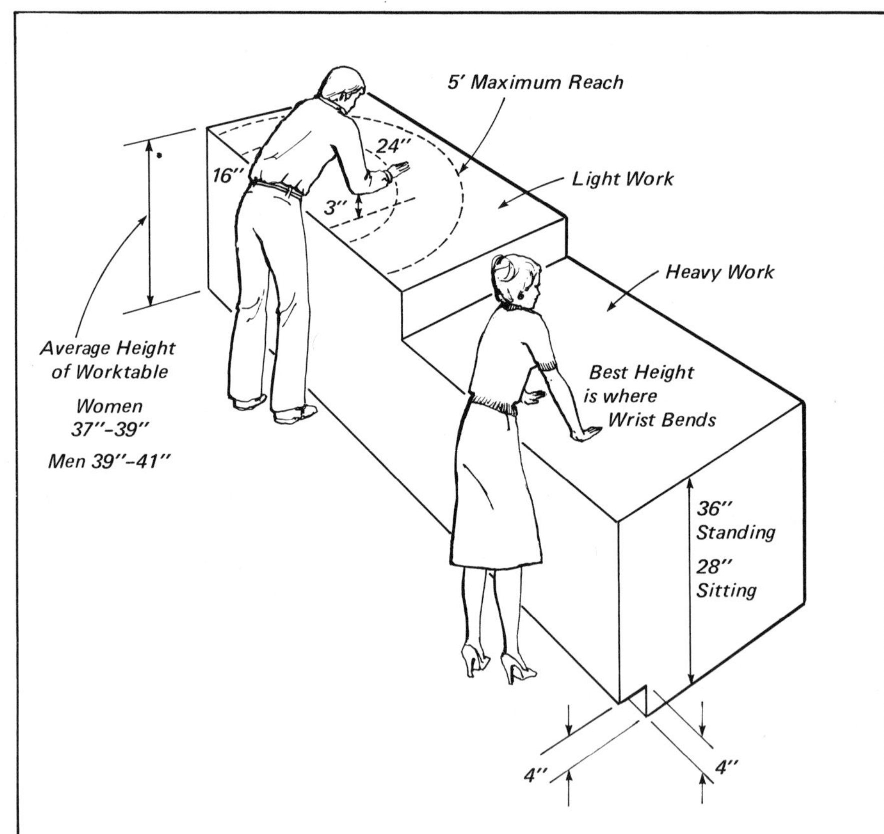

FIGURE 3.2. Optimum work table heights and working area.

The table top work area should be arranged so that the tasks are performed in an arc of 46 cm (18 in.) from the worker's belt buckle or two arcs of 41 cm (16 in.), one from each elbow. Supplies may be placed out to 61 cm (24 in.) from the belt buckle. Observations will show this arc concept is somewhat faulty as the worker, when looking straight ahead, sees reliably in an arc of 30 degrees and with usual head movement up to 70 degrees with a maximum of about 120 degrees. This means that much of the area outside of the easily seen area should be ignored for use in placing supplies or finished work.

Traditionally, the placement of hand tools has been in a drawer under the front of the work table. This is poor practice because it requires motions both to open and to close the drawer. It is also time-consuming to search for the needed utensil, which may have sharp edges and points to deal with, forcing the worker to move from in front of it to open the drawer. If a drawer is used, it should be self-closing so that it need not be closed by hand, and the utensils should be placed in a rack in the front of the drawer with each tool having a particular inset. A foot-pedal drawer opener is helpful. If health authorities will allow it, the best location for both tools and condiments is on one or two shelves placed above the work table at 61 cm (24 in.) from the table front. From here they may be selected quickly because they are in the space customarily covered by the eyes—23–37 degrees below horizontal when standing. Tools and condiments used by the left hand should be stored on the left of center, and those used by the right hand should be stored right of center. If over-the-table shelving is not permitted, the drawer space below the table top should be utilized by a shelf 15–20 cm (6–8 in.) below the table top to store tools and pans such as sheets pans. Extending the shelf 2.5–5.1 cm (1–2 in.) out from the table top improves visibility of its contents. A lower shelf 15–20 cm (6–8 in.) from the floor will serve as storage for tall pots and pans.

Chairs

Without using the body, a sitting person can apply more strength and be more productive than one who stands. Chairs used for standing-up work tables should be adjustable to allow the worker's elbow to be at the same height sitting as standing. Usually, this means adjustable seat levels 61–79 cm (24–31 in.) high with swivel adjustment. Chair foot braces should not be of the bar stool ring type but should be a broad support 45 degrees in front of the vertical. Chair backs or braces are usually adjustable and swiveled, and the top edge is about 36–41 cm (14–16 in.) above the chair seat but below the shoulder blades where they would interfere with shoulder blade action. The back should be narrow enough to avoid elbows bumping as they move back and forth. All work chair seats should angle back from front to rear about 4 to 5 degrees (leisure chairs about 18 degrees) and the surface should be nonslip, nonridged, and fairly hard in padding (no form fit).

Regular work chairs for use with the sitting-down work tables and dining room chairs should be of such a height that, as the person sits, the front edge of the chair does not press up into the thighs, thus shutting off circulation. A person should be able to place his hand between the chair seat and his thigh while his feet are set firmly on the floor. Seats for women should be 36–43 cm (14–17 in.) high; for men, 38–46 cm (15–18 in.). Fixed heights of 38 cm (15 in.) for women and 42 cm (16.5 in.) for men are commonly used. Strangely, most chairs are set at 43 cm (17 in.), although this is the proper height for few people. A height of 41 cm (16 in.) would be a better universal height as it would be usable by 75 percent of the men and 65 percent of the women.

In width, the chair seat should be about 43 cm (17 in.) and 39 cm (15.5 in.) in length for women, and 46–48 cm (18–19 in.) for men. Padded back rests 33 cm (13 in.) wide and 10–15 cm (4–6 in.) deep should be swiveled and adjustable just below shoulder blade height as they are in a typist's chair. Chair backs for dining room chairs generally tilt back instead of forward, and height does not matter except that they should be low enough so that they will not catch the waitress's elbow.

Heights of Other Equipment

Sinks have long been too high and too broad on the top front edge and too deep for hand pot or dish washing. The front edge should not be over 5.1 cm (2 in.) wide and 94–99 cm (37–39 in.) high for women and 99–102 cm (39–40 in.) high for men. Sink bottoms should be at the height of the worker's thumb tip with the arm at the side or an average of 69 cm (27 in.) from the floor for women and 74 cm (29 in.) for men. The pot soak sink may be 15 cm (6 in.) deeper as long as small utensils are not placed in it.

Steam jacketed kettles should have top edges no more than 97 cm (38 in.) high and have sufficient room under the drain for the pots that will be used.

Although space saving, three-deck roast or bake ovens or two-deck forced convection ovens are not desirable from the worker's standpoint. In the three-deck oven, the top deck is too high and the short worker cannot see into the back pans and may burn himself on the drop-down door. The bottom deck cannot be checked easily, and the worker may burn himself on the top of the door frame. Two decks only should be used, and these should be mounted on legs at least 51 cm (20 in.) high. One deck of forced convection oven on a high stand is preferable to two.

Ventilating hoods over cooking equipment and supporting tables should be at least 1.9 m (6.3 ft) above the floor.

Dishroom tables and conveyors should be 91–97 cm (36–38 in.) from the floor, and shelves above this equipment, if used for racks in stripping trays, should allow 25–36 cm (10–14 in.) clearance. Overhead conveyors used to return racks should be constructed so that the rack clears the floor by 1.9 m (6.3 ft) when it is suspended (figure 3.3).

Storage shelving should be in increments and on wheels so that it is possible to load the shelves at Receiving and handle them in and out of the storeroom as a unit. Batches may be loaded into two-basket supermarket carts at Receiving and transported in them as they progress around the kitchen. The baskets substitute for low shelving.

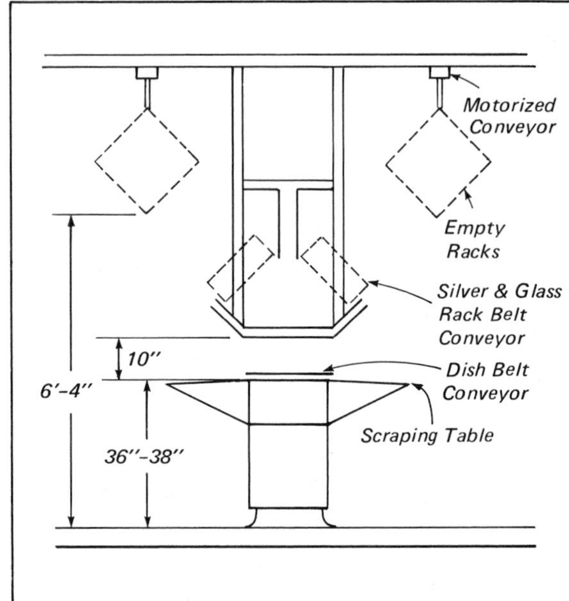

FIGURE 3.3. Dishroom heights.

Storerooms should be set up so that heavy goods may be handled on pallets and carts close to the floor. Most frequently used items should be stored between waist and shoulder height with most selected combinations placed close together and close to the door if the workers retrieve their own materials. Shelving that tilts forward with a bar across the lower end may be loaded from the rear, and the older stock slides to the front for first use.

Stairs and Ramps

Where a food facility is on two or more floors and stairs are used to travel between them, the stairs commonly become a source of accidents. The angle of the set of stairs may range been 20 and 50 degrees with the horizontal but the preferred range is between 30 and 35 degrees. A 25-degree angle uses the least energy. Stairs should be constant in height to avoid tripping. The risers commonly range from 13–20 cm (5–8 in.) with the steeper stairs using the greater height. From front to rear,

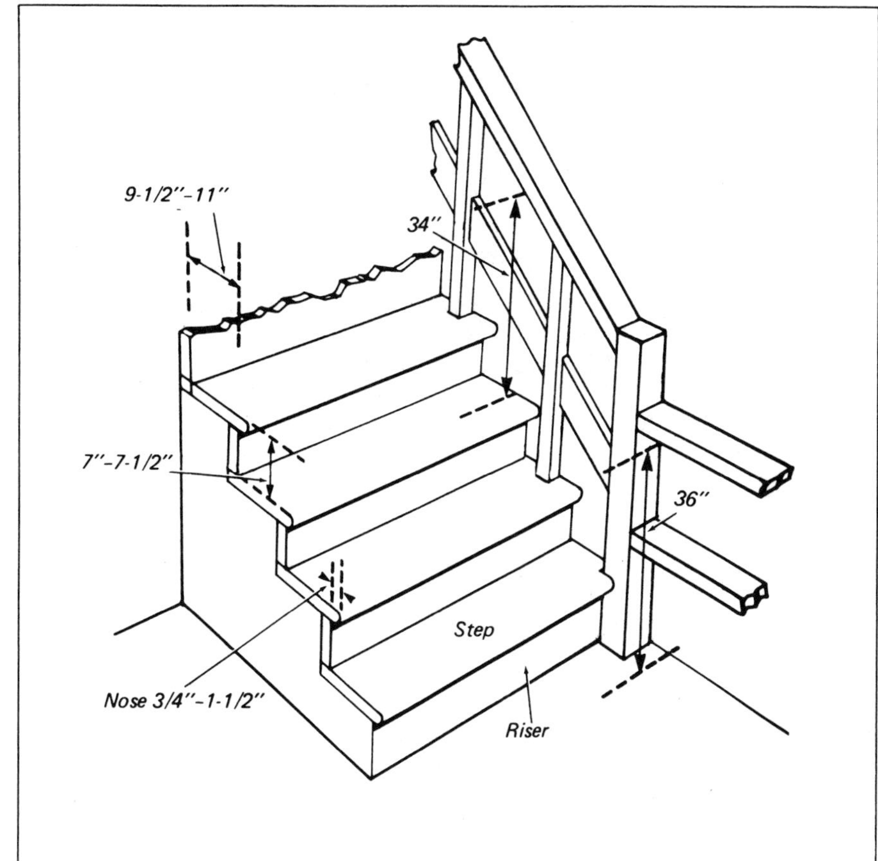

FIGURE 3.4. Stair dimensions.

the steps should be at least 24–41 cm (9.5–16 in.) deep with the deeper one being for the less steep staircase. Nosing out over the riser may be 2.5–3.8 cm (1–1.5 in.). There should be a landing for every 10–12 treads and a railing no wider than 6.4 cm (2.5 in.) should be placed so that it is 86 cm (34 in.) above the stair front edge and 91 cm (36 in.) above the landings (figure 3.4). In the interest of safety, it is well to paint the front edges of the stairs bright yellow and sprinkle some fine sand or silica in the paint of the step surface or use nonslip tread material to prevent skidding and slipping. This type of accident happens frequently when workers wear shoes with worn, rounded heels.

Where ramps are used, they should be no more than 20 degrees from the horizontal with 15 degrees preferred. They should be nonslip with a band of yellow at the start and end and along the edges if a person can fall over the edge. A 91-cm (36-in.) railing may be desirable on each side (figure 3.5).

Aisles

Aisles, in the past, have tended to be too wide when space and workers were readily available. I have seen military and institutional kitchens with aisles up to 4.27 m (14 ft) wide. Contrast these with some older submarine galleys with aisles 0.6 m (2 ft) wide and one can surmise that there are more efficient aisle widths. Recommended are the following aisle widths (the lower number is preferred):

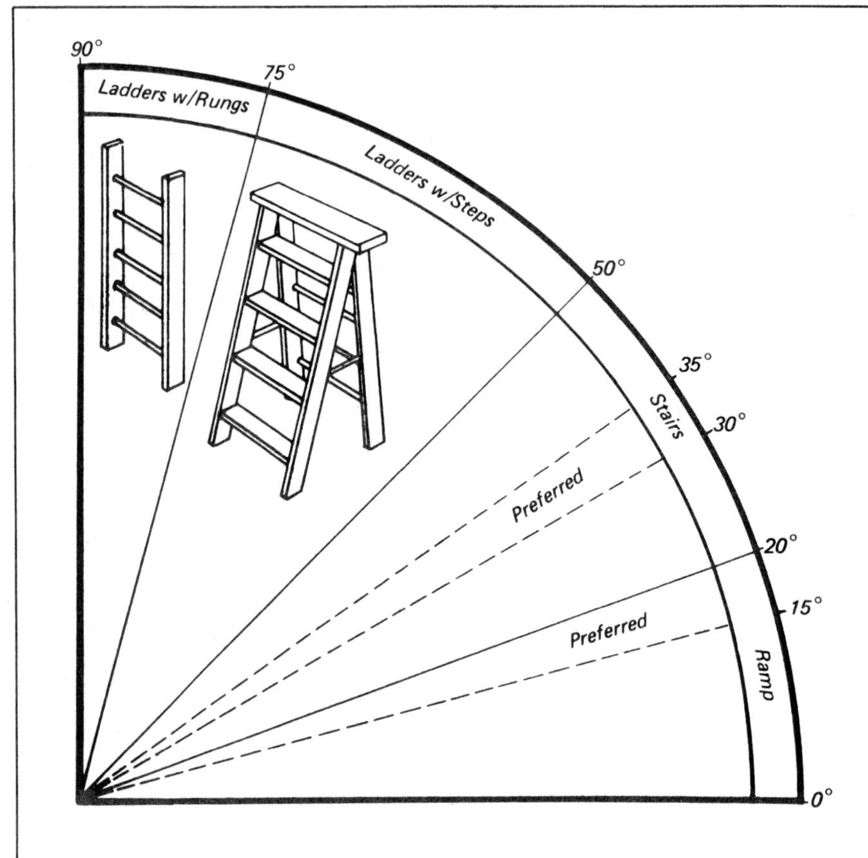

FIGURE 3.5. Angles of incline for ramps, stairs, and ladders.

Aisle Width	*Use*
76–91 cm (30–36 in.)	an employee uses one side of aisle
91–107 cm (36–42 in.)	employees work on both sides of aisle
107–122 cm (42–48 in.)	employee must pass behind workers on each side of aisle
51 cm (20 in.)	a cart must move down aisle (width of cart plus 20 inches)
132 cm (52 in.)	employees must walk past each other
91 cm (36 in.)	employees use oven, cabinet, or refrigerator
97 cm (38 in.)	employees use range oven
97 cm (38 in.)	employee must walk past one standing person
66 cm (26 in.)	employee must walk between two walls
91–97 cm (36–38 in.)	employee must bend over
114 cm (45 in.)	employee must get down on hands and knees

Some of the other human factors included in aisle design are:

1. Avoid glass doors that are not marked by lines, stars, or other means to prevent people from injury by shattering them as they walk through apparently open glass door.
2. Avoid one-way traffic aisles as foodservice workers tend to use them as two-way.
3. Avoid aisles against blank walls as they are wasteful of space and provide access from only one side.
4. If possible, avoid doors which open into corridors or aisles as people tend to run into them. Doors which open back into the rooms are often forbidden by law in public places as people in a panic may pile up against a door that opens in instead of out. Sliding or folding doors may be used, although a sliding door may be a panic obstacle.
5. Aisles should be inspected frequently to ensure that they are free of boxes, crates, dollies, or carts over which workers may fall. Similarly, aisles should not have projections from the equipment, posts, or building with which the worker may collide.
6. Make aisle crossings at right angles to minimize total aisle space.
7. Try to locate aisles for minimum travel but, at the same time, avoid locating heavy traffic aisles where considerable work is done. Locate traffic guides on walls or floors, particularly blind corners, to prevent accidents.
8. Locate equipment no closer than 1.8 m (six feet) to swinging doors.

Displays and Controls

In purchasing equipment or arranging work areas, it is important to keep people and their capabilities, habits, and weaknesses in mind. Displays or indicators must be placed where they will attract attention when it is needed. Their placement must allow information that must be read and interpreted in terms of some action by hands or feet on a control to be accurately reported. This process is not always simple as people tend to routinize repetitive tasks so that they need not think about them but can throw their minds into fantasy. In fact, people seem to be more productive if they do not need to think about their every move. However, if visual displays must be read to maintain the operation of a machine, then the dreaming worker's attention must be attracted by the display or some sound or light. The following factors must be considered relative to displays:

1. The display should be placed as close to the worker's line of sight as possible so that when he looks at the product cooking on range, griddle, or fryer he can read the display with a slight eye raise. This is commonly 15–45 degrees below the horizontal line of sight. The display should be tilted so that the eye views it at 90 degrees to the line of sight.

2. The display should not be too far away to read numbers or letters accurately when the worker stands or sits normally. If the worker must lean forward, either the display is poorly placed (too low or too high), too far away, or the figures and letters are not sufficiently large or clearly presented. Most will be on the front of equipment (ovens, steamers, ranges, or refrigerators) or above the work surface on the back of the equipment (deep fat fryer). However, some steam pressure gauges on upper and lower decks of three-deck ovens and dishwashers are too low, too high, too far away, or not placed properly for accurate reading.

3. Display, along with the control, should be placed or identified so that there is no doubt as to what it is sensing or controlling. The display should imply the form of the operator's response. If the display indicates on the dial that the temperature of the device is to the left of the desired point, the operator should be able to turn or move

the control to the right to achieve the desired temperature rise.

4. As many devices in the kitchen have a number of displays on the equipment, it is best to have each type of measurement use a different type of display to minimize mistaken readings. For example, a white light may indicate that current is on; a green light, that the heating elements are energized; a dial, steam pressure; a bar, temperature, and a buzzer, that the cooking cycle is finished. Usually, a red light should be used only to indicate an unsafe or dangerous condition.

5. The displays should be designed so they are easy to read. Most designers prefer circular scale displays to curved arcs. I prefer the straight vertical or horizonal scales for short scales. Pointers should be similar to the dial markings and extend to the numbers but not mask them. It is well to have the pointer close to the dial to avoid misreadings through parallax. The end of the pointer opposite the point should be omitted or shaped so that it will not be confused with the point indicator end. On the dials, capital letters are best with black letters on a white background and no more than ten graduations between numbers. The letter or number dimensions of width to height should be in a ratio of 3:5; the stroke of width to height, 1:6 or 1:8. At 91 cm (36 in.) the letters or numbers should be a minimum of 0.8 cm (0.33 in.) high, and at 183 cm (72 in.) they should be 1.9 cm (0.75 in.) high. I prefer to mark a green band along the periphery of the dial in the acceptable use range and a band of red on each side of this to indicate something that is too high or too low. Thus, on a deep fat fryer's temperature dial, the green band may extend from 149–177°C (300–350°F) and the red band from 93–149°C (200–300°F) and 149–204°C (350–400°F).

Factors that must be considered with controls are as follows:

1. Controls should be selected, located, and oriented so that their motion is compatible with the associated display.
2. The number of controls should be kept to a minimum.
3. Control movement should be as short as possible and consistent with the accuracy, speed, and strength needed. There should be enough resistance to movement so as to prevent inadvertent movement. In foodservice, with the large number of unskilled workers, the control should be able to stand abuse. Controls should be designed so that hand or foot slippage will not occur.
4. Some indication of when the control is malfunctioning is desirable, as is some indication of positive response to increased tension applied to the control when greater performance is required.
5. Foodservice controls are best placed on the right side of the equipment. Placement in front of a range requires stooping to use it and allows grease and food to drip on the control. This should be avoided. Placement on the back of the equipment should be checked to ensure that, when reaching over the equipment, splash and spatter will not injure the worker. The control should never get above 52°C (125°F), burn temperature. A control that is too hot will not be adjusted, and equipment performance will suffer.

Work Space Design for Older Workers

With the shortage of skilled workers in foodservice and changes of state and federal laws that raise the retirement ages of older workers, more attention must be given to the human engineering of work environment and jobs so that best use can be made of this valuable resource.

At about forty years of age, most individuals start to lose some of their hearing and sight. Ability to smell and taste starts to decrease and people become more forgetful as they start losing ability to make imprints on the memory. However, the older worker has not lost as much ability to produce as one might think. It has been found that the sixty to sixty-five year old is usually more experienced than his younger associates and gives greater attention to detail and seeing that a job is done properly. He has learned to seek the best way of doing each job, is rarely late or absent, is injured infrequently since he has learned to be careful and keep his hands in sight, and he has pride in his work and his ability to earn his own way. However, as is true with younger people, it must be recognized that not all older people suffer the same degree of aging in body and mind. A person who has kept his mind and body active at sixty years may be more youthful than a person of forty who has done little to keep his mind and body active.

It has been found that, as an average, the sixty- to sixty-five-year-old worker has lost little of his productivity; he knows more, works steadier, and does the job the best way. True, he has lost about 10 percent of his physical strength in back and legs, but his arms are strong. He does have a poorer immediate memory, thus instructions should be given in written form or posted in his work area in large writing or print. He prefers to work in a 24–27°C (75–80°F) room and is somewhat susceptible to glare and area noise. He does not respond to pressure well and finds it difficult to increase his operating speed. Do remember that he has lost some of his ability to taste and smell and tends to overseason foods. Broth should be checked occasionally, especially if feeding young people. Light should be about 10–20 FC greater than for the twenty year old.

At this point, one might be saying, "Is he worth fooling with?" He is a good blue chip investment! He produces far more than those under twenty-five years of age, is on par with the twenty-five to thirty-five year old, and takes his hat off only to the thirty-five to forty-five year old when it comes to productivity.

With skilled workers in short supply and high employee turnover, the older worker can be a good investment in foodservice.

QUESTIONS

1. By what other two names is human engineering known?
2. What is the definition of human engineering?
3. What are five of the results of fatigue?
4. What are five causes of fatigue in foodservice operations?
5. What is the most desirable temperature for a kitchen in summer? in winter?
6. Does too little humidity have a physical effect on the kitchen worker? If so, what?
7. How many kitchen air changes per hour do most architects seek for a large kitchen?
8. What effect on productivity in percent does research show results from air-conditioning kitchens in summer?
9. Name five measures that can be used to make kitchen air-conditioning more feasible.
10. What happens to the body if the eyes feel tired?
11. Name five factors that contribute to eyestrain.
12. Name and describe the four most commonly used light fixtures.
13. What type of lamp is best used in fine dining rooms? Why?
14. What lighting level is needed in kitchens where recipes must be read and doneness ascertained?
15. What colors are recommended for kitchen walls? Why?
16. Name five of the color codings for danger areas.
17. What is the most pleasing noise level in kitchens?
18. Name five measures that can be used to reduce noise levels in the kitchen.
19. Relative to the elbow, what is the desirable height of a light work table? Relative to the worker, what is the proper height of a sink bottom?
20. What is the best location to store hand tools?
21. What should the width of an aisle be through which a 76-cm (30-in.) wide cart must pass?

22. Where should a temperature dial be located relative to the worker?

23. What should one check relative to the relationship of display and control?

24. How does one alter the kitchen environment to make it better for the sixty-year-old worker?

25. How does the sixty-year-old worker rate in productivity as compared to the eighteen to twenty-five year old?

BIBLIOGRAPHY

ANON. 1959. Surfaces, materials affect acoustics. *Institutions* 45, No. 5, 120.

ANON. 1963. Do kitchens need color? *Fast Food* 62, No. 3, 42.

ANON. 1965. Color is great. *Fast Food* 64, No. 3, 124.

BENNETT, E., DEGAN, J., and SPRIGEL, J. 1963. *Human Factors in Technology*. McGraw-Hill, New York.

BERONEK, B. 1965. The elements of comfort: Sound. *Institutions* 57, No. 3, 63.

BIRREN, F. 1955. *New Horizons in Color*. Reinhold Publishing, New York.

BORSENIK, F.D. 1969. Human engineering: Environmental aspects. *Cooking for Profit* No. 228, 23.

CHESKIN, L. 1951. *Color for Profit*. Liveright, New York.

COCKLE, W.N. 1958. Ventilation. *Institutions* 42, No. 2, 39.

GRANDJEAN, E. 1973. *Ergonomics of the Home*. John Wiley and Sons, New York.

KETCHUM, H. 1959. Color in institutions. *Institutions* 44, No. 4, 76.

KOTSCHEVAR, L.H. 1967. Sound and noise. *Food Management* 2, No. 9, 10.

MCCORMICK, E.J. 1970. *Human Factors Engineering*, 3d ed. McGraw-Hill, New York.

MCFARLAND, R.A. 1946. *Human Factors in Air Transport Design*. McGraw-Hill, New York.

MILLER, R.K. 1973. You can reduce plant noise. *Food Engineering* 45, No. 3, 133.

MURRELL, K.F.H. 1965. *Ergonomics*. Chapman and Hall, London.

MURRELL, K.F.H. 1965. *Human Performance in Industry*. Reinhold Publishing, New York.

RICHARDSON, M., and MCCRACKEN, E. 1966. Work surface levels and human energy expenditure. *Journal of the American Dietetic Association* 48, No. 3, 192.

SOLIS, D.S. 1965. Creating environment with lighting. *Kitchen Planning* 2, No. 1, 15.

STEIDL, R.E. 1968. *Work in the Home*. John Wiley and Sons, New York.

VAN COTT, H.P. 1972. *Human Engineering Guide to Equipment Design*. U.S. Department of Defense, Washington, D.C.

WOODSON, W.E., and CONOVER, D.W. 1964. *Human Engineering*. University of California Press, Berkeley.

Sanitary Design of Equipment

Sanitarians and the National Sanitation Foundation (NSF) have been striving for years to encourage designs in foodservice equipment that make using it in conjunction with the storage, preparation, cooking, and service of food reasonably safe. Today, while it cannot completely compensate for some poor operational practices, most of the equipment in use is fairly well designed in terms of sanitary considerations.

The basis for improved equipment design has come from the standards formulated in 1944 by health authorities and equipment manufacturers which are administered by the National Sanitation Foundation. The standards serve the following functions:

1. Giving users of foodservice equipment that bears the NSF seal of approval the assurance that the equipment meets most health standards and has passed a critical inspection.
2. Giving manufacturers the advantage of being able to apply uniform construction methods to equipment that will be sold in the various states and yet meet most of their individual standards.
3. Providing an opportunity for health authorities to present a united front in securing the basic elements of safe equipment.

Before a manufacturer can use the NSF seal, his manufacturing methods and designs must be investigated, tested, and approved by the National Sanitation Foundation.

Materials

In general, materials used in the manufacture of food storage, preparation, cooking, service, and washing equipment should be capable of withstanding normal wear, infestation by vermin of various types, attack by foods, beverages, regular kitchen chemicals, and other elements of the kitchen environment. They should not impart toxic material, odor, or color to food as some pot and ceramic materials have done in the past.

Surfaces, where food is not likely to be in contact, should be smooth to ease cleaning, and noncorrosive or made that way by noncorrosive treatment or nonlead paint that won't crack, chip, or spall. Soft solders in the food areas should be at least 50 percent tin, have a minimum of lead, and be free of cadmium (previously a pot material), bismuth, and other toxic materials. Hard solders should be similarly free of toxic elements, and welding should use corrosion-resistant metal similar to the parent materials.

Stainless Steel

While iron and carbon in various combinations are known as steels, there are many special groups that have a certain group of characteristics that set them apart. One of these steel groupings is stainless steel, which is used where one wants resistance to oxidation (rust) or corrosion, and possibly high strength, resistance to high temperature, shiny appearance, and ease of maintenance. There are thirty or more stainless steels. Most of them have a low carbon content and fairly high chromium content. Those that interest us in foodservice have considerable nickel as well. Common stainless steels range from 11.5 to 27 percent chromium and have low carbon content in order to get a high degree of hardness. Thus cutlery steel may have 1.2 percent carbon, although most stainless steels have 0.2 percent or less. No. 302 stainless steel, one of the most commonly used stainless steels in foodservice, is composed of 18 percent chromium, 8 percent nickel, and 0.15 percent carbon; No. 304 is similar but has only 0.08 percent carbon. Weldability is improved by reducing the carbon content. Addition of a little sulphur improves machinability, and addition of copper and molybdenum increases resistance to corrosion. This type is little used in the food industry except where vinegars and brines are used often. Manganese can substitute in part for nickel.

Stainless steels are bright, attractive, and easy to keep sanitary. Thus they have ready application in both kitchen and serving-line equipment. They have a self-renewing coating that protects against oxidation and corrosion. However, they discolor in locations subject to high temperatures. The bright appearance readily shows dirt and thus promotes cleaning. It does not dull with judicious cleaning; that is, cleaning with the proper materials.

Due to its considerable cost per unit of weight, stainless steel users are closely attuned to the minimum thicknesses needed for various purposes. Gauges of 8, 10, and 12 may make good supports; gauges 12 and 14 go into table tops; gauges 14, 16, 18, and 20 make up side panels where some structural strength is needed; and gauges 20 and above are used to provide facing and other attractive exteriors. The inch and millimeter thicknesses for gauges 8 to 24 are as follows:

Gauge	*Inches*	*Millimeters*
8	0.1644(11/64)	4.1758
10	0.1345(9/64)	3.4163
12	0.1046(7/64)	2.6568
14	0.0747(5/64)	1.8974
16	0.0598(1/16)	1.5189
18	0.0478(3/64)	1.2141
20	0.0359(1/32)	0.9119
24	0.0239(1/40)	0.6071

Polishing requires much labor, energy, and material so if it is not needed, a lower degree of finish may be specified. Most finishes are designated by standard finish numbers, but these may be qualified by the grit as well.

Finish Number	*Description*
No. 1	hot rolled, annealed and pickled, dull rough
No. 2B	full finish, bright, smooth, cold rolled
No. 2D	full finish, dull and smooth, cold rolled
No. 4	Standard finish for foodservice equipment, primarily for that in the kitchen; may be made bright satin finish by abrasives
No. 6	high tampico, brush finish with soft velvety luster used for tableware; highly buffed it is 2B
No. 7	high glossy polish with mirror or highly reflective finish from fine grinding; much used for serving lines and paneling around serving lines

The No. 4 satin finish is considered to be best for kitchen use as it does not have as much glare hazard as the No. 7 finish under the 70-FC light level prescribed in many states; yet, it is easy to clean and maintain.

Plastics

The plastics available to foodservice are too numerous to discuss in their entirety in this book. Some 5,700 companies make several dozen major plastics into many products using about twelve methods. Some of the more important will be briefly mentioned.

The acrylics are used in a variety of clear products under the brand names Lucite, Plexiglass, and others. Lucite may be used for food covers and Plexiglass for refrigerator doors.

The melamines that are used in a variety of plastic dishes, Boontonware and Texas Ware, are also used in countertops such as Formica.

Fiberglass, utilizing glass fibers in a thermosetting resin that is usually a polyester, makes up many trays, bus boxes, and formed serving-counter fronts.

Nylon is used for cylinders in which flatware is washed, conveyor plates, tips of dishwasher plate holders, and many other places where friction is needed.

Phenolics, usually brown, make up many of the customer trays.

Polyethylene, a thermoplastic, is used for many flexible bowls and storage containers, bus boxes, and garbage cans.

Polypropylene, a high-impact plastic, is used frequently for dishwasher racks and similar applications.

Styrene has a high impact strength, but as it cannot withstand temperatures much above 71°C (160°F), its use is limited to covers, cold storage, packaging, and similar applications.

Other plastics are used for cart bumpers, radiator grills, shields, silverware holders, shelving, facings, laminates, etc.

Other Metals

Years ago, practically all foodservice equipment, except that in which flames were confined, was made of wood. Today it is recognized that, while it is cheap, light, strong, and beautiful, wood is not sanitary in contact with food. It wears rapidly and absorbs liquids and odors. As a result, most of the equipment is now metal or plastic. It may be a single metal such as aluminum, black and cast iron, or copper, an alloy such as stainless steel, brass (copper and zinc plus other metals), monel metal (two-thirds nickel and one-third copper), and soft steel (iron and a small amount of carbon).

Aluminum is used for utensils, equipment interiors and exteriors, carts, panels, steam jacketed kettles, and other equipment. Anodizing the aluminum minimizes the oxide that blackens everything. Iron is still used in pots and pans, some griddles, range tops, gas burners, and some similar equipment. Formerly copper was used in steam jacketed kettles (the U.S. Navy still calls these kettles coppers). Today it is used in electric wiring, some piping, and some utensils, particularly those used on alcohol heaters. To some extent, it is used in paneling, lighting fixtures, and ornaments. Its main use is as a coating to speed distribution of heat in utensils, coffee urns, and kettles.

Brass is used in bearings, some faucets, and shut-offs.

Formerly, monel was used in many of the applications where stainless steel is used today. Many of the early counter and table tops were made of monel metal until the cheaper and less stain-susceptible stainless steel became available in quantity.

Steel is used for oven and range interiors and exteriors, shelving, and frame and support elements in most of the equipment covered with stainless steel. It may be treated with acid (pickled) and coated with zinc (galvanized) to make sinks or keep equipment legs from rusting. Steel may be aluminized to protect it from corrosion and reflect heat in ovens or copperplated in pots and pans to give better heat distribution. It may be coated with tin to make food cans and utensils or coated with nickel or chrome to provide a shiny, easy-to-clean covering for various appliances and decorations, particularly around serving lines.

Coatings

Coatings are placed on various base metals, particularly iron and steel, to protect them from corrosion, make them easy to clean, allow them to have desirable colors or heat characteristics, or to give them good food-release qualities. They can be enameled, bonderized, glass coated, painted, or baked on.

Acrylic enamel is an organic coating made from synthetic resins on a metal, usually steel, surface. It resists heat, stains, and hot-water-detergent mixtures. It is susceptible to some kitchen chemicals and abrades rather easily.

Baked enamel is an alkyd paint on a base metal dried with heat 93–204°C (200–400°F). It does not nick or chip easily, but it does scratch and wears off where the hands rub against it. Acids, chlorine, bleach, and alcohol damage the finish.

Porcelain enamel is a glass fused to a metal base at 760–871°C (1400–1600°F) so that the finish is nonporous and does not scratch easily, rust, or stain, but it can chip on sharp metal-to-finish contact. It must have a base coat, and the enamel must be at least 0.13 mm (0.005 in.) thick for refrigerators and 0.09 mm (0.0035 in.) for freezers and should never be more than 0.38 mm (0.05 in.) thick.

Silicone is an intermediate substance between the organic and inorganic materials that has some of the qualities of glass on surfaces of grids, ice cube trays, and baking utensils to give good release. It scratches off rather easily but can be washed in soap and hot water.

Teflon is a fluorocarbon resin that is sprayed on oven or pan interiors and griddle and other utensil surfaces where good food release and cleanability are needed. It must be heat treated at 371–399°C (700–750°F). It is inert to most chemicals and solvents but must be washed with detergent and hot water to keep it from discoloring. Originally it was rather easy to scrape off with a sharp spatula, but with some of the new hard base finishes, it is scratch resistant.

Sanitary Qualities of Materials and Finishes*

Food Contact Surfaces

Surface materials in food zones should be smooth, corrosion resistant, nontoxic, stable, and nonabsorbent under use conditions and should not impart odor, color, or taste, or contribute to the adulteration of the food. Exposed surfaces in the food zone should be finished so as to be easily cleanable.

Surfaces in Heated Food Zone

Surfaces maintained at cooking temperature in the food zone should be of nontoxic materials and capable of withstanding repeated normal cleaning.

*This section has been adapted from *Materials and Finishes Guide with Selected Test Procedures*. National Sanitation Foundation, Ann Arbor, Michigan, by permission.

Griddles should have a finish at least as smooth as a 125-microinch finish. The surface of broilers, salamanders, and similar items should have a cleanability equal to good-quality cast iron surface.

Splash Contact Surfaces

Splash contact surfaces should be smooth and of an easily cleanable and corrosion-resistant material, or should be rendered corrosion resistant with a material which is noncracking, nonchipping, and nonspalling. Paint should not be used except as specifically provided in the applicable standard.

Nonfood Contact Surfaces

Nonfood contact surfaces should be smooth and of corrosion-resistant material or should be rendered corrosion resistant or painted. Parts of the equipment directly over and adjacent to the food zone and parts that have both food contact and nonfood contact surfaces should have nonfood contact surfaces rendered corrosion resistant, and if coated, the coating should be of a noncracking, nonchipping and nonspalling type.

Wherever specific materials are mentioned, it is understood that the use of materials proven to be equally satisfactory from the standpoint of sanitation and protection of product is acceptable.

Sanitary Design

In general, foodservice equipment should be designed so as to prevent presence of vermin, dust, dirt, splash, and spillage from the food zone as may be encountered under the expected use conditions. It should be easily cleaned, maintained, and serviced either in the assembled or disassembled state. The design should permit ingredients and foods to be added and the finished foods to be removed in a sanitary manner.

Corners or Angles

All internal angles of 110 degrees or less made by two or more planes of metal coming together should be rounded in a smooth radius of 3.2 mm (0.125 in.) for two planes and 6.4 mm (0.25 in.) for three metal planes. (I recommend radii of 12.7 mm (0.50 in.). The exposed external angles and corners should be sealed and smooth (figures 4.1 and 4.2).

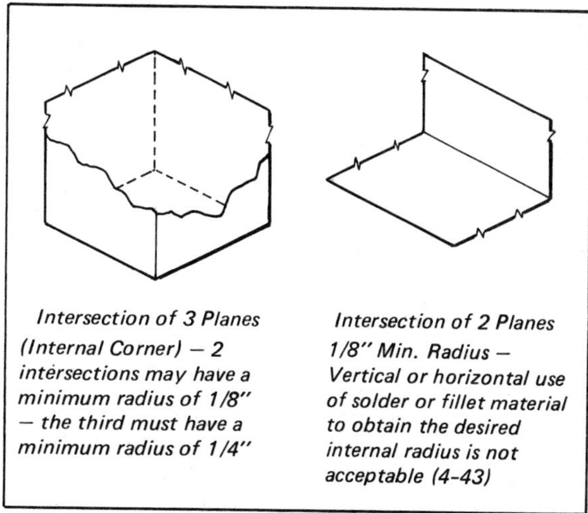

FIGURE 4.1. Internal angles or coving should be of a radii that will not accumulate residues. Courtesy National Sanitation Foundation.

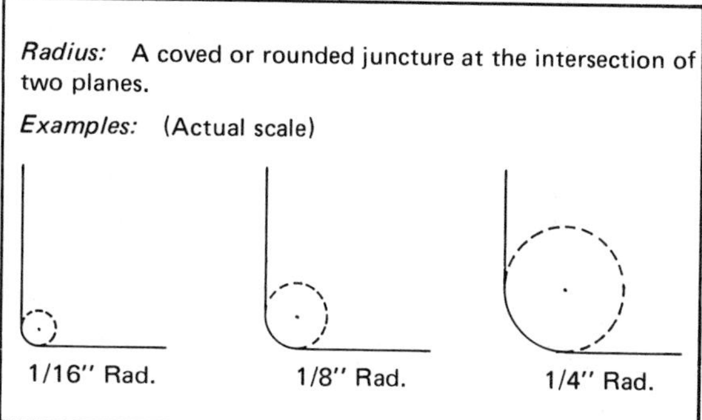

FIGURE 4.2. Various radii. Courtesy National Sanitation Foundation.

Wherever solder is used, it should be smooth with flux and catalytic material neutralized and removed. Soft solder should be limited to joining metal or sealing seams between adjoining metal surfaces. Hard solder can be used for filling strong joints and seams in the liners of refrigerated equipment. Welded areas in surfaces in contact with food or requiring cleaning should be ground smooth.

Exposed screw or rivet heads and projecting studs should be eliminated from food contact surfaces except in pots and pans where the low profile brazier head rivets are allowed.

For the most part, these same requirements apply to splash and nonfood contact surfaces except that paint is allowed on normally dry surfaces, but it is not allowed on food contact surfaces. Also, requirements for fasteners are not as rigid as long as food or similar collecting possibilities are held to a minimum.

Reinforcing and Framing Requirements

Reinforcing and framing members not totally enclosed or within walls should be constructed so as to be easy to keep clean. All framing and support elements should be placed and designed so that harborage for vermin is eliminated. This means that hollow sections must be sealed and horizontal reinforcing members and gussets must not be placed so as to allow food or other material to accumulate on them. Thus angle materials should have one leg pointed downward or formed integral with the sides as with drawer slides or removable shelves. Vertical channel sections should be either completely closed (my preference) or open to the floor (figure 4.3).

Panels and Doors

Panels applied to the outside or inside of equipment should be fastened by means that minimize projections and openings. Where removable panels are necessary, they should be of adequate size but small enough to be handled by one person and designed to fit the requirements of the zone in which they are to be used. Where drainage inside or out is necessary, the bottoms or gutters should be self-draining.

Doors should be fabricated according to use with single or double panel walls and with or without intermediate insulation. Without insulation they should be constructed without channel sections at the bottom to be easily cleanable, and if they have double walls they should be closed around the four sides and corners. Hinges in food or splash zones should be of simple take-apart

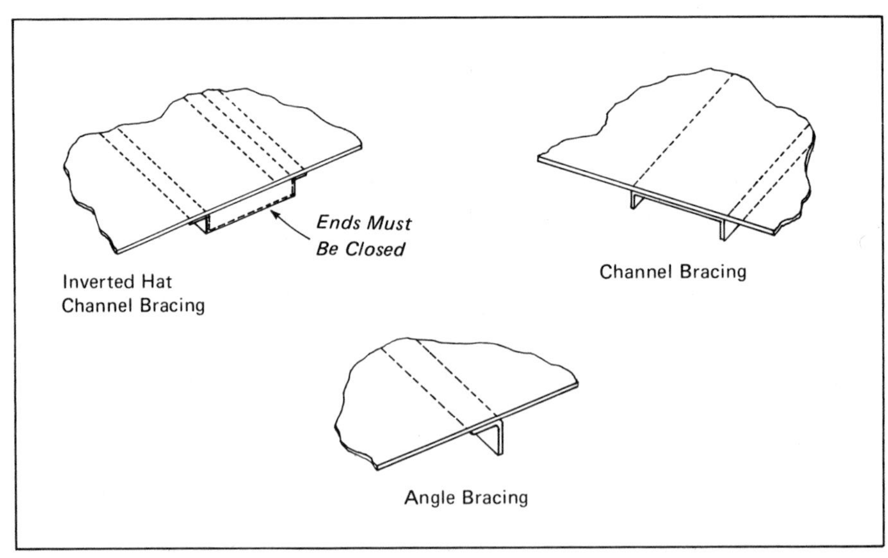

FIGURE 4.3. Design of reinforcing elements. Courtesy National Sanitation Foundation.

construction to facilitate cleaning in spillage situations. Piano or fixed pin hinges should not be permitted in food or splash zones. Sliding doors should be readily removable. Where insulated doors are used, the gaskets should be easily cleanable and replaceable and should not have grooves or projections. The edges of sliding doors should be protected against chipping by tight-fitting protective channels, suitable stripping, or nonfriable glass with smooth edges. The guides should be built to reduce collection of food and other material and should be easily cleanable. Deep channel tracks should not be used.

Tops

All exposed edges and nosings on horizontal surfaces that make up tops should be integral with the tops and made smooth. Nosings should be open 1.9 cm (0.75 in.) to permit ease of cleaning or be completely closed against the body of the unit on all sides to prevent harborage of insects. Where the edges of tops or shelves are flanged down or turned back, the return under-flange should be less than 12.7 mm (0.50 in.) and angled down with the space between the top and the flange not less than 19 mm (0.75 in.) and the space between the sheared edge and the frame angle not less than 19 mm (0.75 in.) to ease cleaning (figures 4.4 and 4.5).

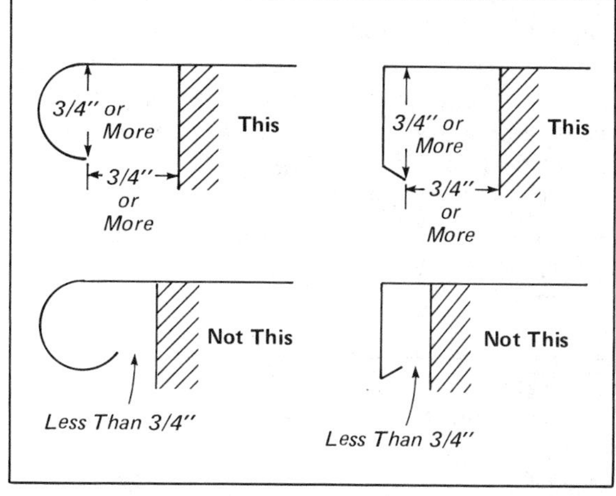

FIGURE 4.4. Nosings should either be sealed to the top or open to permit ease of cleaning. Courtesy National Sanitation Foundation.

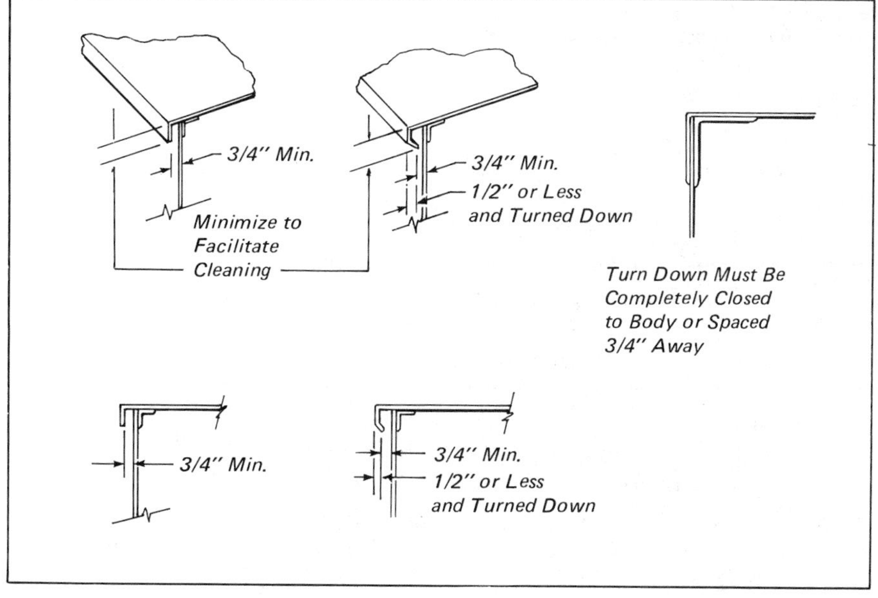

FIGURE 4.5. Adequate space should be left between turned down top and body. Courtesy National Sanitation Foundation.

Where tops or top plates come together, they should be welded, soldered, joined with adequate trim strips or draw fastenings or other sanitary means that ensure against breaking open under normal use (figure 4.6). Where openings in the top are necessary, they should be protected by a raised rim at least 4.6 mm (0.18 in.) above the top, but where it opens into a waste receptacle there should be a watertight turned-down edge extending at least 13.7 mm (0.5 in.) below the table top. A 9.7 mm (0.38 in.) raised edge may be used instead of this or both may be used. The food waste cones leading into the garbage grinder should be fastened into the table tops by continuous smooth welding or an equally effective gasketed or soldered structure.

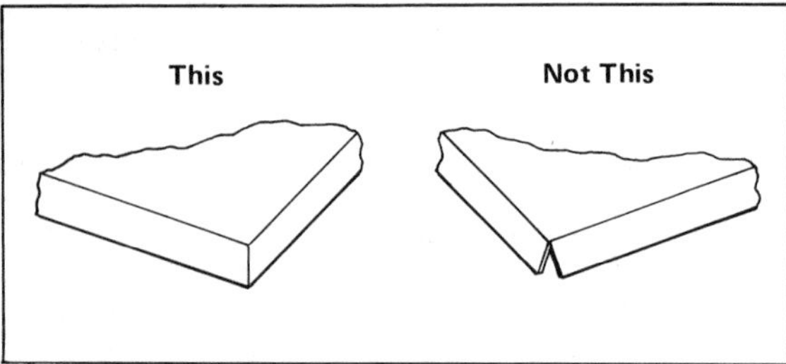

FIGURE 4.6. All external corners or angles are to be sealed and finished smooth. Courtesy National Sanitation Foundation.

All hardware should be smooth material fabricated with integral or plated finish that is easily cleanable. It should be secured so that it can be easily replaced if broken. The hardware should have no open seams, recesses, or unnecessary projections.

Breaker strips should be installed in such a manner that debris, food particles, water, or seepage do not enter between the breaker strips and the capping and/or the liner. Steam tables and cold pans should have the tops removable or have openings of a size and location that permit access for cleaning. There should be drains at least 2.5 cm (1 in.) IPS (iron pipe size).

Legs or Feet

Unless placed on a raised platform or sealed to the floor, legs or feet of a tubular nature should raise the equipment to a clearance of at least 15.2 cm (6 in.) from the floor. They should have sufficient rigidity so as to require a minimum of cross-bracing. They should be fastened to the equipment and in contact with the floor so as to prevent the accumulation of dirt and vermin. When the outside of the leg is greater than the outside dimension of the foot by 1.3 cm (0.5 in.) or more in the same plane, the foot shall at minimum adjustment extend 2.5 cm (1 in.) below the leg. All openings to hollow sections should be of drip-proof construction with no openings greater than 0.76 mm (0.03 in.). All other openings to hollow sections should be sealed. Legs and feet should be of simple design and free of embellishments and exposed threads (figure 4.7).

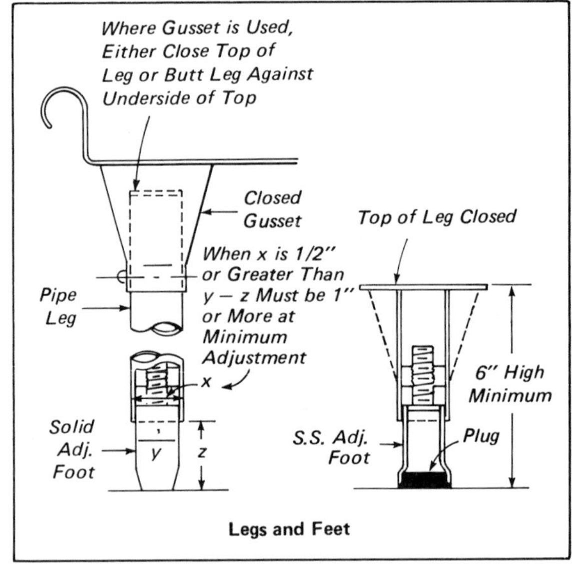

FIGURE 4.7. Legs and feet should be sealed against the entrance of vermin. Courtesy National Sanitation Foundation.

Exterior Attachments

Open display stands, with or without cross rails,

should be of solid or tubular construction. Tubes should be of welded or seamless construction. Assembly method should ensure easily cleanable joints. These include, but are not limited to, welding and sweating. The brackets should be of substantial, smooth, easily cleanable design, fabricated of materials having integral or plated finish. Counter trays should have similar requirements in their construction.

Display cases shall be fabricated so as to eliminate dust-collecting projections or moldings and minimize open joints and sharp corners. Sliding doors should be easily removable. Hinged doors need not be removable when designed for easy cleaning. Food shields should be used to effectively protect unwrapped foods and to intercept the direct line between the average customer's mouth and the food. The design should assume that the mouth of the average customer is 1.4 m (4.5 ft) to 1.5 m (5 ft) from the floor. Of course, the school child's mouth would be closer to the floor. Such shields should be fabricated of easy-to-clean sanitary materials.

Food and flatware containers, bins, and drawers should be of coved construction and should be smooth and welded or die stamped. Fillet material and solder should not be used to cover the angles or corners of food containers or drawers. All insets or receptacles for unpackaged moist foods and beverages should be removable, drainable, and easily cleanable. Such containers should be of open-mouth type, covered and conforming to the requirements of pots and pans. Rims should be easily cleanable. Rolled type beads should be closed and sealed. Handle and handle assembly parts should be attached to the utensil so as to eliminate inaccessible cleaning areas, recesses, and open seams.

The drawer carriages should be easily removable for cleaning. Bins should be in a totally enclosed space, or when not enclosed, they should be provided with a tight-fitting cover.

Flatware dispenser containers should be readily removable for cleaning and be easily cleanable. They should be constructed so that the flatware can be touched and picked up by the handles only.

Dishwashing Equipment

Dishwashing and prewashing machines should be designed and constructed to make the tanks, superstructure, and other parts easy to clean and to minimize places where dirt collects and where bacteria and vermin may find shelter. Tanks of the dishwashing machine should be of integral construction or integrally welded. All joints and seams should be sealed and made smooth. In the superstructure there may be overlapping sheets as long as there are no dirt-catching horizontal ledges. Integral piping in the dishwashing machine should be held to a minimum to reduce loss of pressure and temperature. It should not be placed so as to obstruct access openings or interfere with cleaning. Fresh water supply piping ahead of the backflow protective device should not pass through the tank or hood of the machine where outer surfaces of piping can be contacted by sprays or tank water. All water inlets should be protected against backflow by vacuum breaker or air gap (figure 4.8).

An automatic thermostatic control with a maximum differential of 8.3°C (15°F) should be provided in the wash and pumped rinse of all commercial spray type dishwashers relying on heat sanitation of dishes, in order to maintain these waters at the required minimum temperatures.

Thermometers with the sensing elements placed in the water entering the spray arm or manifold should be installed to show the water temperatures of all tanks. The thermometer dials should be placed so that they can be easily read but not readily broken. These thermometers must have an accuracy of ± 1.7°C (3°F). Appropriate markings should be provided on the thermometer to indicate the specified temperatures or range of temperatures of the water being measured. The graduated dial should be at least 4.7 cm (1.75 in.) in diameter.

Scrap trays should have openings smaller than those in the wash or pumped rinse spray arms, and these trays should be readily accessible and removable for cleaning. All recirculated waters should pass through these trays.

Conveyors should be constructed so that they

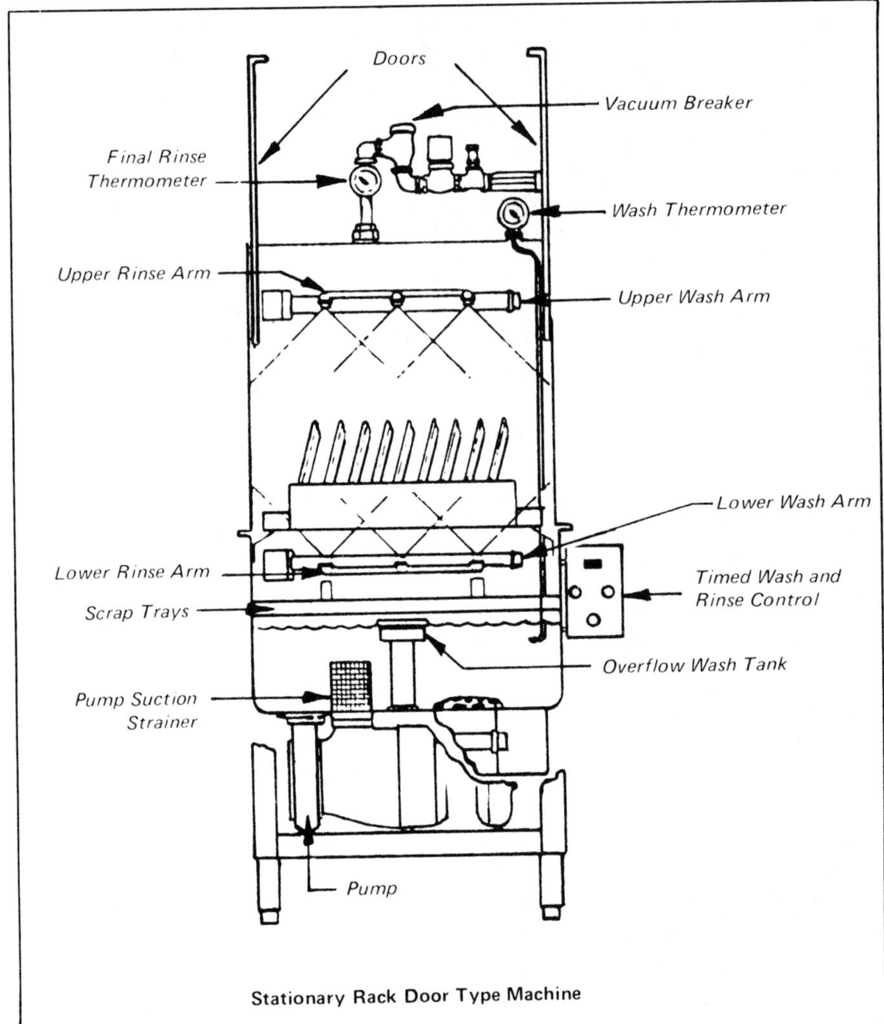

FIGURE 4.8. All parts of a dishwasher should be easy to reach and clean. Courtesy National Sanitation Foundation.

present a minimum of obstruction to the sprays. They should be accurately timed to subject every dish to the wash and rinse sprays for the times required for each type of machine.

Racks should be so constructed that dishes and trays are masked to a minimum extent from the sprays. Overcrowding should be discouraged, and it should be easy to place dishes in the proper position where they will be fully covered by the sprays. The racks should be made of materials that will withstand wear, action of detergents, and such other elements as may be found in the environment. Materials in the dish zone should be noncorroding, nontoxic, nonabsorbent, stable and should not impart taste or adulteration to the foods. Surfaces exposed to dishes should be easily cleanable.

Scraping blocks should be of synthetic rubber or other nonabsorbent material.

Sinks or sink bowls including partitions should be considered as food zones and should be drawn or welded and made smooth and otherwise fabricated in accordance with food zone design, with solder or fillet material not being acceptable in obtaining desired radii. The space between bowls or sinks should be completely filled or sealed or a minimum clear space of 5.1 cm (2 in.) should be provided between bowls or sink compartments which should be open at front, bottom, and back. Self-rimmed type warewashing and food preparation sinks are not desirable.

The use of sink drains which include a removable strainer without remote drainage control is satisfactory. Overflow gutters between two sink compartments should be approximately 15.2 cm (6 in.) wide and have a removable strainer plate or basket. Drains should be a minimum of 3.8 cm (1.5 in.) IPS except for fountain and underbar sinks which should be not less than 2.5 cm (1 in.) IPS (figure 4.9).

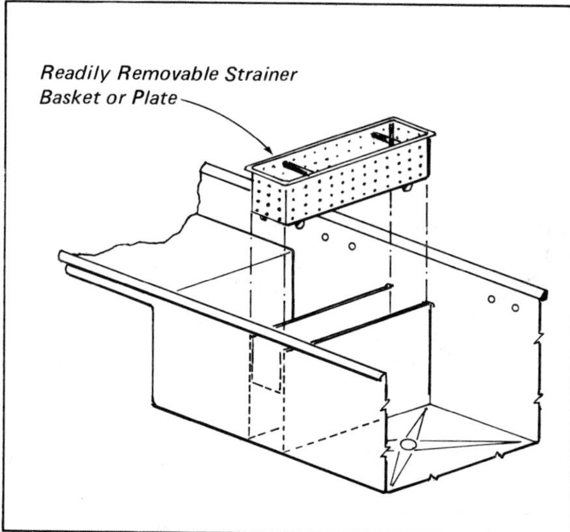

FIGURE 4.9. Sink with readily removable strainer basket is desirable. Courtesy National Sanitation Foundation.

Refrigeration

The food zones and those portions of the splash and nonfood zones requiring routine cleaning should be designed and constructed to accommodate this necessity. Design features should be according to those previously discussed in this chapter. Refrigerators should have maximum operating temperatures of 4.4°C (40°F); refrigerated short-term cabinets, 7.2°C (45°F); and freezers, −17.8°C (0°F). Temperature sensing and indicating devices should have an accuracy of ± 1.12°C (2°F) in the critical range and they should be of an easy-to-read type located where they are readily visible. The sensing element should be easily cleanable and located where it correctly reflects the representative temperature of the stored foods in the appropriate temperature zone.

Doors should be designed so that their opening and closing will not sweep dirt or other contaminants from the outside to the inside. Door sills should be flush with the interior floor of the walk-in refrigerator or freezer. Doors must be equipped with a mechanism to permit them to be opened from the inside even when locked on the outside.

Miscellaneous Sanitary Requirements

Rack slides should be constructed to minimize food collection, and must be readily removable for cleaning (figure 4.10).

Drawers and bins should be constructed to minimize food collection and to facilitate easy cleaning. There should be no recesses in drawer pan assembly hardware (figure 4.11).

All canopies and hoods should have smooth, easily cleanable surfaces. Where reinforcing must be used on the interiors, it should be located so that it will not act as a dam to grease or moisture running down the surface. There must be an easily cleanable gutter at the bottom to collect the drip material (figure 4.12).

Cutting boards should be made of hard maple, pecan, filled rubber, or other nonabsorbent, cut-resistant, nontoxic, easily cleaned material that does not dull the knives' edges used on it. The cutting boards should be of a size that is readily portable and easily removable for cleaning. Thickness should be no more than 4.7 cm (1.87 in.)

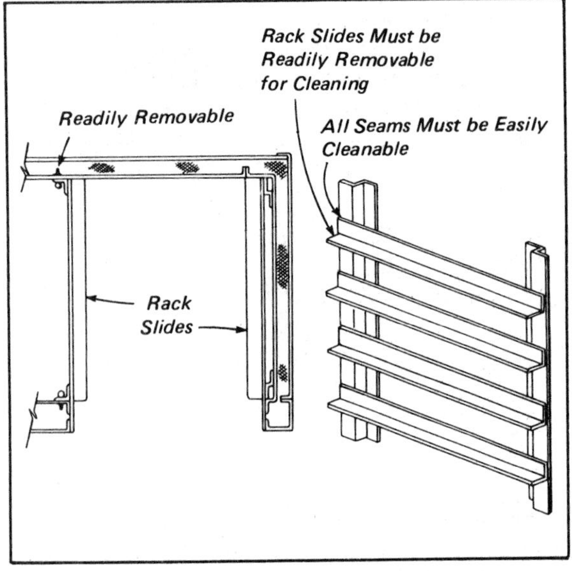

FIGURE 4.10. Rack slides should be constructed to minimize food collection. Courtesy National Sanitation Foundation.

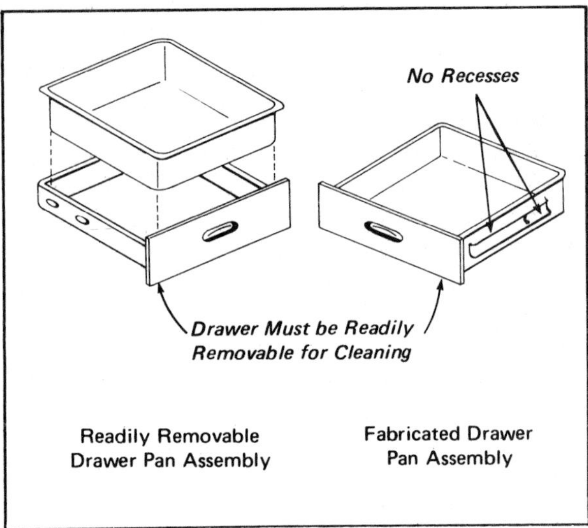

FIGURE 4.11. Drawer pan assemblies. Courtesy National Sanitation Foundation.

FIGURE 4.12. Grease drippings in hoods should be directed toward easily cleaned gutters. Courtesy National Sanitation Foundation.

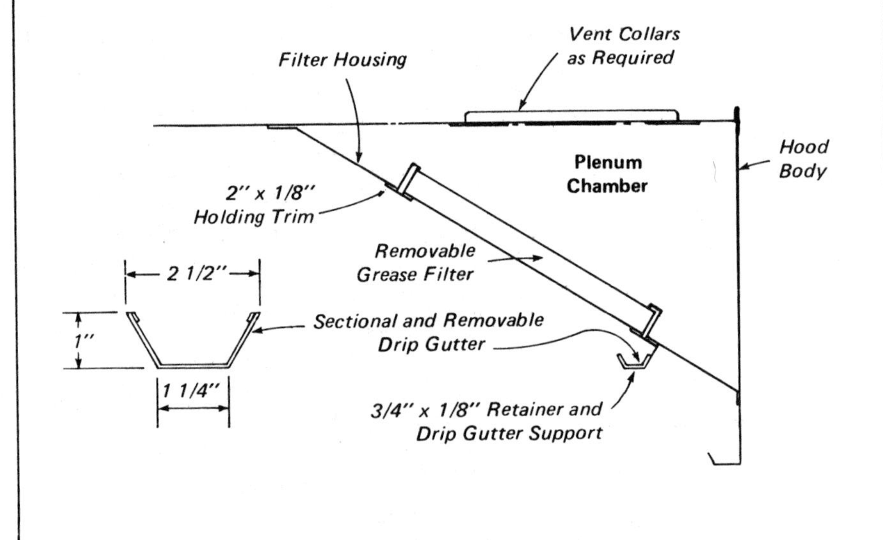

Boards made of multiple pieces bonded at right angles to the cutting surface should have the surfaces to be bonded machined to 0.025 mm (0.001 in.) and pressed together at pressures not less than 150 psi or more than 250 psi. Reinforcement should be with 0.1 cm (0.37 in.) bolts.

QUESTIONS

1. What is the authority behind sanitary design?
2. What are the functions of the NSF standards?
3. What should be the qualities of materials used in food service?
4. What is the composition of No. 302 stainless steel?
5. What gauges of stainless steel are used for table tops?
6. What finish is used for stainless steel in kitchens? for serving lines?
7. What plastic is most used for dishes?
8. For what is brass used in food service?
9. What coating is used for its release qualities?
10. Where should paint not be used in food service?
11. What are the requirements on coving when two and three planes of metal come together?
12. In using framing, what is the requirement regarding vermin?
13. What should be the composition of welding material for joining two plane surfaces?
14. What regulates the location of sneeze guards?
15. What is the requirement as to location of thermometers in dishwashers?
16. What materials should be used in cutting boards?

BIBLIOGRAPHY

ANON. 1958. *Relative Corrosion Resistance of Stainless Steels.* Peter A. Frasse & Co., New York.

ANON. 1976. *Food Service Equipment Standards.* National Sanitation Foundation, Ann Arbor, Mich.

ANON. 1977. *Standard No. 2 for Food Service Equipment.* National Sanitation Foundation, Ann Arbor, Mich.

KOTSCHEVAR, L.H., and TERRELL, M.E. 1977. *Food Service Planning: Layout and Equipment.* John Wiley and Sons, New York.

Ranges

The range is the basic item of multipurpose cooking equipment for quantity food preparation. While designed for surface heating of food in pots and pans, it can be procured with griddle surface or broiler, oven for baking, roasting, and holding and can be used for shallow or deep fat frying. Because this requires using pans of fat on the heating elements, it is dangerous.

As there are other pieces of equipment that individually perform the various range functions more effectively with less requirement for skill and consumption of energy, most institutions and large restaurants are using the range less and other equipment more. Some kitchens are built without ranges. The counter and floor mounted steam jacketed kettles, the steamers and pressure cookers, the fry pans, grills, griddles, broilers, deep fat fryer, and conventional or convection ovens do it all. Some may have several counter top hot plates for small quantity cooking.

Where ranges appear to be most used are in chef or older cook-dominated kitchens, restaurants with large menu selection, small restaurants, institutions, and churches or clubs where food preparation is done on an occasional basis.

Description and Specification

Most ranges are floor mounted, and the cooking is done in pots and pans on burners or heated plates at waist height. They may be heated by gas or electricity (figure 5.1).

FIGURE 5.1. Ranges with solid top, open top, and griddle top. Courtesy Vulcan Hart Corporation.

The framework of the range should be of heavy-duty, well-braced steel, welded so that it is rigid. The paneling may be of stainless steel but is usually 18–16 gauge steel with a baked-on acrylic, black Japan porcelain enamel or similar heat stable coating. While black is traditional, some manufacturers provide the range in gray. It is recommended that the front be of No. 302 or 304 stainless steel of the same gauge as the sides and a No. 4 satin finish. If baked-on coatings were used, resistant stains might cause workers to use abrasive materials that would remove the coating. The exposed steel would then be subject to rust. The range is generally insulated on all necessary areas with about 5.1 cm (2 in.) of fiberglass or spun rock wool insulation.

The supports may be of a die-formed two-sided bracket type with adjustable feet of 15-61 cm (6–24 in.) or more length tubular legs with sealed construction and adjustable feet. More and more operators are buying ranges with 13-cm (5-in.) casters. Some use a 5.1-cm (2-in.) base on the bottom of the range and mount this on a concrete platform that is integral with the floor. Some kitchens that use high stock pots set the range down into a well in the floor so that the tops of the pots are low enough for their contents to be observed and stirred easily. This means that the controls are too low for ease of use, but that is probably more desirable than pot tops that are too high. Ranges may be obtained in which the entire range top can be changed quickly for another type.

Gas Range

The tops of gas ranges are available in a great variety of forms. They may have open (grate) tops where a cast iron or steel framework supports the pot above the burner and the gas flame impinges directly onto the pot bottom. It is fast and does not require preheating. There is a minimum of metal to absorb heat that will not be used. Also, the bowing or bulging of the pot bottom has little effect on the rate of heat transfer. Open gas burners have a heat input of 15,000–20,000 Btu per burner. The latter is most common. The units are commonly 28–33 cm (11–13 in.) wide and may be 61 cm (24 in.) or more from front to rear. There is usually a sliding tray under the unit to catch drips and debris that fall through the grates. Aluminum reflectors may be used under the individual units as well (figure 5.2). Some of the new burner designs, which may be up to 25 percent more energy efficient than the old, should be investigated.

FIGURE 5.2. Double open top range. Courtesy Vulcan Hart Corporation.

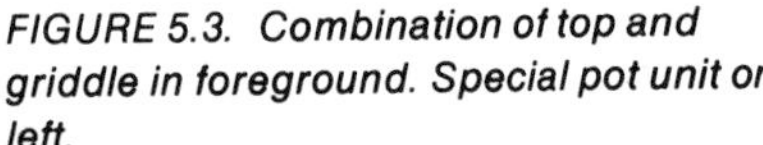

FIGURE 5.3. Combination of top and griddle in foreground. Special pot unit on left.

A second kind of top is the cast iron or steel plates 28–48 cm (11–18 in.) wide, although they are most commonly 30 cm (12 in.) wide so that three of them can make up the top of a standard 91 cm (36 in.) wide range. The front to rear dimension is usually 61 cm (24 in.), although it may vary. Thickness varies from 3.2–1.3 cm (1.25–0.5 in.). These units are called hot tops, boiling plates, closed tops, uniform heat tops, and hot plates, although this last is sometimes used for the round plate (figure 5.3). Heat input varies from 15,000–24,000 Btu for the 30-cm (12-in.) wide plate up to 35,000 Btu for the 46-cm (18-in.) wide one. One manufacturer applies 40,000 Btu to a plate 38 cm (15 in.) by 71 cm (28 in.). Some plates are dual purpose and do pot cooking and griddling. In most cases, the thermostats control the temperature between 121°C (250°F) and 454°C (850°F). The plates may have fins or ridges on their bottoms to conduct more heat to the plate top.

The range griddle is the same as the free-standing griddle, and this will be discussed in Chapter 13. It can be of widths from 30 cm (12 in.) up to the width of the range, usually 91 cm (36 in.). From front to rear (depth) it is usually 61 cm (24 in.) and the metal is between 1.25 and 2.5 cm (0.5–1 in.) in thickness. Often it has a stainless steel fence or raised edge around the two sides and the back. There are one or more grease troughs and at least one grease container. Heat input should be the same as the regular griddle (figure 5.4).

A few manufacturers make special high-heat units in solid-top ranges. They may have a re-

FIGURE 5.4. Open top range to right, griddle to left, and oven beneath. Courtesy Vulcan Hart Corporation.

movable ring and cover directly over the burner to get direct heat on the pot. The bottom side of the solid top may be lined with a ceramic brick, have raised concentric rings around the ring to concentrate heat at the center, or both. There are raised rays which go out to the edges of the hot top to carry heat outward. At least one model has two rings, covers, and burners side by side in the front of the range, and the raised rays on the under side carry heat to the rear. These units may range in heat input from 31,000 Btu per burner up to 80,000 Btu and can obtain temperatures up to 593°C (1100°F). Another similar piece of equipment is the stockpot range whose top dimensions are 46 × 56 cm (18 × 22 in.); it stands from 56–61 cm (22–24 in.) high. It is heated by 40,000 Btu (figure 5.5). Ranges may be purchased with part of the top as a 12–16-gauge stainless steel table top.

FIGURE 5.5. Stockpot range with multiple removable rings. Courtesy Vulcan Hart Corporation.

There is usually a raised back on the rear of the range to a height of 5–15 cm (2–5 in.). The vents may come up through this, and sometimes it is extended above pot height and a shelf is placed on it. In other cases where efficient use of space is necessary, a salamander or broiler may be placed over the back of the range in place of the shelf.

Under the range top there may be nothing but legs, a supporting storage cabinet, or a single deck oven. Most operators adopt this latter option because if they rarely use the oven for roasting or baking, they may use it as a hot-food storage cabinet.

The smaller ranges cannot provide enough space for an oven that will hold a 45-×-66-cm (18-×-26-in.) roast or sheet pan. In most food operations, the oven is of little value unless it can accommodate these pans. Most operators want range ovens that are 56–66 cm (22–26 in.) wide, 69–81 cm (27–32 in.) from front to rear, and 30–38 cm (12–15 in.) high, which means that they can handle the standard pans.

The oven interiors may be made of aluminized steel or enamel plates that may, or may not, be removable for cleaning. Continuous cleaning oven interiors may be made of steel coated with porcelain enamel. The oven should be insulated with a minimum of 5 cm (2 in.) of rock wool or spun glass around the body of the oven and 3.8 cm (1.5 in.) in the door. At least one oven has aluminum foil added as additional insulation. There should be from one to three slides up the side of the oven interior for racks. The racks are generally made of welded strip steel wires. Heat input should be at least 3–4 Btu per 15.6 cu cm (1 cu in.) of oven interior. The heat is thermostatically controlled from 79°C (175°F) to 288°C (550°F).

The oven door should have the interior metal of the oven on the inside and the exterior metal on the outside. The door hinges should be heavy duty and easy to keep clean (NSF approved). In the open position, the door should hold a minimum of 90 kg (220 lb). Some models will hold 113 kg (250 lb). The reason behind this is not only to support heavy pans of food but also the workers who will use the door as a platform when they clean the overhead hood. The door should be counterbalanced by dead weight, springs, or other means. The dead weight method has the fewest maintenance problems. There should be a handle on the oven door that is rigidly supported far enough away from the door surface so that the cook's hand does not come in contact with the door. It should never get hot enough from radiated heat to be a burn hazard. This temperature is 52°C (125°F). The handle material should be one that does not readily absorb or accumulate heat.

The burner units vary according to the manufacturer, and in many cases, a range may have a different type burner unit for each purpose.

Electric Range

Most electric ranges come with units that duplicate, in part, those available in gas ranges. In place of the open burner, the electric range has tubular metal elements in which the resistance wires are encased. They are arranged in circular fashion with some space between elements and cover most of the hot plate area. The lighter weight ranges have the elements in a round form as they contact the pot, while the heavier duty ranges have flattened elements. The range elements are somewhat fragile and sometimes break up when subjected to heavy pots that contain over 19 liters (5 gal.). The flattened elements are more sturdy, but they, too, have problems handling heavy stock pots. Only the solid tops are safe (figure 5.6).

FIGURE 5.6. Flattened electric range top units.

As further protection, the elements can be slightly recessed and covered by a cast iron hot top or French plate up to 1.25 cm (0.5 in.) thick. The tubular elements can press against or be clamped to the plate, or resistance coils can be recessed in a ceramic base and press against the plate bottom. The plates can vary in diameter from 15 cm (6 in.) to 27 cm (10.5 in.) and in electrical input from 1.25 kw for the small ones up to 2.5 kw for the large ones. Speed units may have up to 3.5 kw input. Most of the hot plates have four settings, high, medium, low, and off, although some have infinite control units. Some have enamel or stainless steel drip collectors under the units.

Electric ranges may be obtained with heavy cast iron or boiler plate steel hot tops. These are similar to the gas hot tops in that they are plates usually 30–46 cm (12–18 in.) wide by 61 cm (24 in.) from front to rear and 1.25–3.2 cm (0.5–1.25 in.) thick. They sometimes, but not always, come in a set of three per range top. These units may be utensil heating alone or some may be used for griddling. Ranges may have any combination of hot plates, hot tops, griddles, and table tops. The hot top is heated by tubular heating elements imbedded in the bottom or clamped to it. The 30-cm (12-in.) hot plate may have a heat input of 5–5.3 kw and the 46-cm (18-in.) unit may have 7.5 kw. The thermostat controls temperature on an average between 93°C (200°F) and 454°C (850°F). They may also have three heat switches to go with the thermostats (figure 5.7).

The electric range griddle is very similar to the conventional free-standing electric griddle in that it is usually 61 × 91 cm (24 × 36 in.) in size with a stainless steel fence around three sides and a grease trough on one or more sides that drains into a grease receptacle. There are other sizes (length and depth) available to be compatible with needs. They may be of cast iron or boiler-plate steel and range in thickness from 1.2 to 2.5 cm (0.5 to 1 in.). Most range griddles are underpowered for maximum production. It is desirable to have at least 22–24 watts input per 6.25 sq cm (1 sq in.). The thermostats control the temperature between 38°C (100°F) and 232°C (450°F). In some griddles, the thermostat controls 23 cm (9 in.) of griddle front and in others it controls 30 cm (12 in.).

FIGURE 5.7. Electric range with two French plates (right), two hot top units (left), and oven (bottom). Courtesy Toastmaster, McGraw-Edison.

Ovens in electric ranges are of similar size and construction to gas ovens, but they are generally sealed so cooking moisture will not be lost unless the vent or door is open. In gas ovens, the compartments are often open to the flue that vents gas waste products, causing meats to suffer high roasting losses. They are thermostatically controlled between 93°C (200°F) and 260°C (500°F) and use 0.7–0.9 w per 15.6 cu cm (1 cu in) of oven interior, which is desirable. The oven, too, can come with three heat switches to go with the thermostat control.

At least two manufacturers provide an electric range with a forced convection oven. Several others have self-cleaning ovens that heat the oven walls until the food spatter turns to ash that is easily wiped off. The rack in the oven should be used to determine whether the range is perfectly level.

Dimensions

Overall, both gas and electric ranges may extend in width from 30–299 cm (12–90 in.), from front to rear 77–107 cm (30.5–42 in.), and from floor to range top 81–91 cm (32–36 in.), although back extensions, shelves, or broilers may make the overall range height greater.

Other Purchase Considerations

1. Convenient access to all parts that may need maintenance, repair, or cleaning.
2. Conformance of design with pertinent standards of the National Sanitation Foundation, Underwriters' Laboratories, and American Gas Association.
3. Rust-resistant finishes on exteriors, oven interiors, burner assemblies, drip trays, burner box linings, and areas that may corrode.
4. Well-insulated, grease-resistant wiring.
5. Controls placed where they are easy to see and adjust by a standing adult. They should not be placed where they may get above 52°C (125°F) or where they may have food dropped on them.
6. Use of new electronic igniters on gas ranges to replace the ever-burning pilot lights that waste so much gas.
7. In gas units, use of burners that are fast and give proper heat distribution.

Determination of Needed Capacity

The capacity needs for the griddle and oven may be determined much the same as Chapter 13 on griddles and Chapter 6 on ovens indicate. Pot or pan cooking capacity calculations vary according to:

1. Pot material and design.
2. Bottom and side thickness, bottom diameter, and side height.
3. Whether or not a cover is to be used on pot or pan.

4. Food material composition, texture, and temperature.
5. Amount and initial temperature of liquid used.
6. Temperature at which cooking is carried out: warm, simmer, steam, boil, sauté, shallow fry, or deep fry.
7. Heat available for transfer from range to utensil.
8. Extent to which other equipment will be used for customary range-top functions: steam jacketed kettles, steamers and pressure cookers, fry pans, bainmaries, steam tables, fryers, and ovens.

Although these calculations may be made, they are complex and may be specific to the operations of a particular cook. Most manufacturers and dealers recommend a certain number of ranges to feed so many people in a cafeteria, hospital, school, or table service restaurant. This recommendation might be:

Meals per Day	*Number of Ranges*
300	2
500	3
1,000	4
under 300	1

This method is often wrong because of the many variables, differences in menu needs of the various establishments, and degree of using convenience foods.

The only way to calculate range-top needs is to determine the products that must be in pots and pans at the time of maximum use, generally a few minutes before service. Then one considers the amounts, pot sizes needed, and whether or not the products need quick high heat or slow steady heat. This should tell the operator how many of each type of heating units will be needed. This will be a rough estimate at best, but it is better than using standard figures since this aspect of foodservice is difficult to standardize. It is also one reason for considering other more predictable pieces of equipment for cooking, if possible.

Basic Use and Operation

Although the use of the griddle top and oven of the range can be standardized and usable time-temperature data can be given, the pot and pan heating facilities defy standardization for the various makes of equipment. Through trial and error and data keeping, an operator can get standard time-temperature for the utensil, the amounts of food prepared, and the procedures used in the operation. After finding a time-temperature relationship that results in a good quality product, the operator should insert on the recipe card the pot size, heating unit, setting, and process time used, along with the other pertinent recipe and processing instructions. The most popular range-top dishes are stews, beef a la Deutsch, chili, pot roast, soups, sauces, vegetables, Swiss steak, lobster Newburg, chicken a la king, and ragout.

Basic to all pot cooking is the use of pots 2.5 cm (1 in.) larger than the range units available. The gas flame should be adjusted to just contact the pot bottoms. The flame is hottest at this point, somewhere between 816°C (1500°F) and 1649°C (3000°F). Flames streaming up the sides of the pot waste heat and add little to the cooking speed because the hottest part of the flame is not under the pot. Electric and plate units should make full contact with the pot. The pot material should be a good heat conductor such as aluminum, copper bottom stainless steel, or aluminum-clad stainless steel. The bottom should be approximately 3 mm (0.12 in.) thick with the sides one-half of this. Except when reducing the volume of a sauce or cooking members of the cabbage family, the pot should be kept covered during heating and holding. This reduces energy consumption. Pots and pans bulging on the bottom should not be used with solid-top heating units since the heat transfer is not good.

Hot top ranges should use no more units than needed, and these should have pots tightly grouped together.

Ranges should have work tables on at least one side for preparation of food to be cooked, portioning cooked food, and storage of pots and pans beneath them. Hand tools and much used condiments should be on a shelf over the back of the table when health authorities will allow it; if not, a shelf placed 15–20 cm (6–8 in.) below the table top can be used. Storage of hand tools in drawers is awkward and dangerous. On the opposite side of the range should be a sink to which pots may be slid to drain. As part of the sink, there should be an overhead mixing faucet with a flexible hose that will permit filling of pots anywhere on the range top.

The possibility of having at least two individual pot cooking units with automatic temperature control units that sense and control a set temperature of the pot contents should be explored. This makes the nutrient value- , color- , flavor- , and texture-saving 85°C (185°F) simmer easier than by use of a hand-held thermometer.

Special Applications

When the range is the only cooking device in the kitchen, many adjustments are made to use it for purposes actually better served by individual pieces of equipment that are better engineered. For instance, commercial gas and electric fryers are better controlled and much safer than using a black pan on a range top, either solid top or open units. There are still many schools, hospitals, restaurants, and ships that do their deep fat frying in pans with sides 10–15 cm (4–6 in.) high. Needless to say, the quality of fried foods from these expedients is unpredictable, and the danger of fire is ever present.

Probably the most frequent auxiliary use of the range top is for frying pan and skillet preparation of eggs or omelets to short order or special order. Bacon, sausage, and cottage-fried potatoes are fried in similar manner. Small operators find that the frying pan uses less heat than a griddle. However, considerable skill is needed to gauge the proper heat input and time relationship for the hot tops, open burners, French plates, and hot plates. Thermostatically controlled griddle operations can be standardized.

Another use of the range top is steaming of vegetables or seafood (clams, lobsters, or crabs). A stock pot with a rack in the bottom to keep the food out of a small amount of boiling water and a tight cover to keep the steam from escaping is commonly used. In some cases, the cooks have developed baskets with folding handles to speed the loading and unloading of the steamer. A way of speeding the steam cooking process is the use of large pressure cookers that enable one to cook at temperatures up to 121°C (250°F).

Seldom is the range top used for baking. If it is used, old home-type portable ovens that fit over one or two heating elements may be used for baking or roasting. A flat pan on which a rack to keep the food off the pan's surface and over which a deep cover is put may be used for baking or roasting. Temperature control is very difficult in either.

Alternatives to the Range

Certainly, the foodservice industry has searched for alternatives to the range. It was looking for equipment that could be controlled accurately and would require a minimum of human observation and control, both of which were lacking in the average range. While not perfect, the present-day griddle, steam jacketed kettle, steamer, pressure cooker, fry pan, and the new ovens are an improvement over the conventional range. They could not be much worse as a university study showed that only 12 percent of the energy of an open burner and 9 percent of a solid-top range heated the contents of a 4-quart aluminum pan. The remainder was wasted.

Some efforts have been made to redesign the range. Probably the most effective and energy efficient of these was a range that used a small heat exchanger to heat air that was circulated about the range to heat pots or the oven and then brought it back to the heat exchanger for reheating and reuse.

Another unit had the heating element in the bottom of the aluminum pot or griddle, and the efficiency of heat transfer was very high. However, electrical connections were hazardous, and at times great sprays of sparks were created when water would get into the electrical interfacing between the pot and the range.

The U.S. Navy developed a submarine range that utilized the same floor area, 1987 sq cm (1176 sq in.), as the old range (figure 5.8). It increased griddle capacity by increasing wattage input and having a fence around three sides of the griddle. Pot capacity was increased by changing the pots to a square shape and bringing the sides of the aluminum pots down around the heating elements that had been increased in wattage.

FIGURE 5.8. Submarine range with griddle (left), three pot-heating units (right), and two 8-in. high ovens (bottom).

At the same time, the oven capacity was doubled by decreasing the oven height from 36 cm (14 in.) to 20 cm (8 in.) and making two decks instead of one. This oven would handle up to a 7-kg (16-lb) turkey. If turkeys larger than this were to be cooked, they could be split in half. The halves required one hour less cooking than the whole turkey. The low ovens provided less space that had to be saturated with moisture from cooking meat so roasting losses were greatly reduced. It is well to keep this in mind when purchasing ranges and try to purchase one with an oven height and capacity close to the size of the products which are to be cooked in it.

Another U.S. Navy range was designed as a complete cooking unit for twenty people in an area 76 x 76 cm (30 x 30 in.). To avoid sea rails (cross bars to hold pots on the range top in heavy seas), the solid-top heating elements were cast as indentations that would tightly surround the bottom of a 30-x-51-cm (12-x-20-in.) steam table pan. This brought the heating surface up the sides of the pans and increased the amount of heating area on the pan. The pots were 30 cm (12 in.) in one dimension and varied in the other dimension according to the size wanted—one-third, one-half, or the full length of the indentation. Height varied according to capacity needed.

The griddle on this range was similar to a steam table pan in size and was made of thick aluminum. The deep fat fryer was a half-size pot with an immersion type tubular heater in a unit which plugged into the back of the range and came down into the pot from the back. Heating took place from the heating unit plus the range hot top. The oven could be used as a heavy-duty broiler or conventional oven. It would take 30-x-51-cm (12-x-20-in.) pans. The fuses were on a slide-out rail so they could be checked easily and replaced. There are many ideas in this range which should be considered for ranges of the future.

Saving Energy

It has been shown that the range is inefficient in its use of energy. Because of this waste of energy, many food operations do not have ranges but use more efficient equipment, such as pressure cookers to cook vegetables and forced convection ovens to roast meat. However, many small foodservice operations or chef-dominated kitchens use the range because of its versatility. If one must use the range, the following energy-saving tips should be kept in mind:

1. If gas is used, the flame should be adjusted to a good blue color and should just meet the pot or pan bottom. Flames that touch the sides of the pot are wasteful. Electronic ignition can save as much as $80 per year, as compared to pilot ignition. For both gas and electricity, the pot should be about one inch greater in diameter than the flame or burner. Highly reflective foil placed beneath the burners directs the heat upward toward the pot.
2. The pot should have a dull finish and be made of black aluminum or some other heat-conductive material, to absorb heat and conduct it quickly to the interior. The bottom should not be more than .25–.32 cm (.1–.125 in.) thick. The pot sides may be half this thickness. For steaming, pot sides may be as thick as the bottom if it is desirable to heat the pot contents from the lower part of the sides as well as from the bottom. The pot cover should be composed of thin material, in two layers with a sandwich of air in between, and it should be tight fitting.
3. Solid-top ranges should be used as little as possible because too much gas is wasted in preheating the mass of metal in the top, leaving much unused heat residual in the metal after cooking. In addition, it is impossible to cover all the heat-radiating surface. Because bowed-bottom pots make incomplete contact with the solid top, they waste heat and should not be used on solid-top ranges.
4. As with steam jacketed kettles, range pots use half the heat if their contents are cooked at 85°–93°C (185°–200°F) rather than a slow boil. However, it uses about three times as much heat to maintain a heavy boil as it does a light one.
5. Some energy is saved if pots of food to be heated on the range are filled with hot tap water rather than cold. The hot water heater heats water more efficiently than the range. Time is saved, too.

Cleaning

Wipe up all spills as they occur. For open-top ranges:

1. Allow to cool, remove grids and trays beneath burners, and scrub them in the potwashing sink using both a fiber and wire brush.
2. Allow to soak if necessary.
3. Rinse in hot water and drain dry or wipe dry with a towel.
4. Brush burners with a wire brush. Ignite units to check for clogged holes. Clean these with a wire or some round, pointed object. Periodically, soak burners in grease solvent and hot water to remove burned-on grease. Rinse in hot water and dry.
5. Reassemble units.

For solid-top ranges or griddles:

1. Allow to cool.
2. Wet down and scrape baked-on material with dough cutter or similar sharp edge.
3. Scrub with a minimum of manufacturer-recommended detergent and hot water. Use a stiff brush.
4. Wash trough and drains and, if present, take grease receptacle to sink for washing and rinsing.
5. If material sticks on surfaces, soak them in cleaning solution until it dissolves.
6. Rinse all surfaces and wipe dry.
7. Coat heating surfaces with a cooking oil to prevent rust.

All other exposed surfaces should be washed with cleaning solution, rinsed in clean water, and wiped dry with a clean cloth. The oven should be cleaned the same way as a conventional stack oven.

Maintenance

1. All surfaces should be checked for baked-on soils and these should be scraped off with a sharp tool. Do not use steel wool or abrasives since they will scratch or remove finishes on stainless steel surfaces.

2. Check gas burner for proper combustion as indicated by the blue flame and for contact with the surfaces to be heated. Check burners for clogged burner holes. Check for broken grates. Be sure wire used for cleaning burner holes is of proper size.

3. Check electric heating elements for loose connections and good contact with pots heated on them.

4. Check griddle and hot tops for temperatures that conform to those indicated on the thermostats. Disk type thermocouples or high-temperature griddle thermometers may be used for this purpose. The temperature should be taken at the point when the power-on light goes out or the gas flame cuts back. The thermocouples should be placed near the center of the plate. The temperature should be within 8°C (15°F) of the thermostat setting. One should note the temperature drops on the plate before the power or gas returns. If they are beyond the cycling range indicated by the manufacturer, a maintenance person should be called.

5. Check for loose or faulty connections, leaking gas pipes, frayed wires, loose handles, or control knobs, and indicator lights that have failed.

6. If the gas flame lifts from the burner unit and does not make contact with it, there is incomplete combustion. To correct it, reduce the primary air input to the burner. If ignition occurs in the burner instead of on the ports, the same solution is recommended. Yellow tipping and yellow flame mean that the flame is getting insufficient air, and the air supply should be increased.

7. The range burners should be checked at least once a year by an expert (a factory-trained maintenance person).

QUESTIONS

1. What are the various types of gas and electric range tops?
2. Name five foods particularly suited for range top preparation.
3. Where are ranges most used?
4. If the gas flame lifts from the burner, how can it be corrected?
5. How does one correct a yellow gas flame?
6. What is the electric counterpart of the open gas burner?
7. What is the cleaning procedure for the open gas burner?
8. How are electric elements used with hot top plates?
9. What are pot dimensions in regard to burner or heating element size?
10. How does one calculate range top capacity needed?
11. Name five ways of saving energy in range use.

BIBLIOGRAPHY

ANON. 1974. *Ranges*. General Electric Company, Chicago Heights, Ill.

ANON. 1976. Range top rules modern command post. *Institutions Volume Feeding* 79, No. 7, 29.

KIEFER, W. *Vulcan Mini Service Manual*. Vulcan Hart Corp., Louisville, Ky.

LONGREE, K., and BLAKER, G. 1971. *Sanitary Techniques in Food Service*. John Wiley and Sons, New York.

SCHNEIDER, N., and JAHN, E. 1968. *Commercial Kitchens*. American Gas Assoc., New York.

WILKINSON, J. 1975. *The Complete Book of Cooking Equipment*, Revised Edition. CBI Publishing Company, Inc., Boston.

Conventional Ovens

An oven is a heated cavity in which food is cooked. The heat may be introduced by conduction through metal or other material, convection by natural or forced air movement, or radiation of electromagnetic waves, of which infrared and microwave are the most used. The food may be cooked by any or all of the noted heat sources.

Some of the more common types of ovens include:

- conventional roast
- conventional bake
- general purpose
- range
- conveyor and reel
- forced convection and pulse
- microwave
- pizza
- infrared and quartz
- barbecue
- combination
- portable and counter top

Only the most used ovens will be discussed in this book. The roast, bake, general purpose, and range ovens will be dealt with in this chapter and the forced convection, microwave, reel and conveyors, infrared, and pizza ovens in succeeding chapters.

Ovens are not new. Since there has been fire, there have been ovens. Cave dwellers and Indians had reflector ovens made of rocks and logs as well as pit ovens. Martha Washington had ovens in the sides of her kitchen fireplace. When the metal kitchen ranges were developed, it was only natural that they have ovens to complement the range top and make them what, at the time, was thought of as a complete cooking unit.

Description and Specification

In general, most conventional baking, roasting, general purpose, and range ovens are heated, insulated boxes. They may be single as in a range or stacked two, three, or four decks high for roast, bake, or general-purpose ovens (figure 6.1). They are front loaded through drop-down hinged doors. Food is placed in pans that may be set on a shelf or, most often, on the deck. Heat is applied. Doneness is ascertained by observation, reaction to an object inserted into the food, temperature sensing by use of a thermometer, time-temperature relationship, or some combination of these.

FIGURE 6.1. Three-deck bake oven (electric). Courtesy Toastmaster, McGraw-Edison.

The frame should be of angle irons, preferably 3.2 x 3.2 x 0.32 cm (1.25 x 1.25 x 0.12 in.) welded together to make it perfectly rigid. The outer sheathing should be 16–18-gauge carbon steel, although some manufacturers use 20–24 gauge on sides, top, and back. Fronts should be one piece and at least 16 gauge. Preferably they should be of No. 302 stainless steel (one manufacturer uses No. 430) with No. 4 finish. The interiors of the cooking cavities should be made of 16–18-gauge sheet steel treated to resist corrosion and reflect heat toward the interior. The cheapest of these is galvannealed, followed by aluminized steel, and the most expensive is stainless steel.

The doors should be 16-gauge steel like that of the oven front. The inside of the door should be of a thickness double that of the oven interior to protect the door against the sliding pans. The oven decks may be made of 1.9-cm (0.75-in.) transite or corplate (asbestos and cement mixture with high emissivity), 2.5-cm (1-in.) Rokite, 10–12-gauge reinforced sheet steel, nonabsorbent ceramic mounted in steel, or all-purpose pebble steel adequately reinforced.

The door should be equipped with heavy-duty hidden hinges, sturdy enough to hold 91 kg (200 lb). The door should be counterbalanced by springs or, better yet, dead weights. When dropped down, the door should be level so that a pan may be slid out of the oven onto it. It is well to have double-pane shock- and heat-treated windows in the door so that one may view the cooking food without opening the door. The door handle should be made of material that absorbs little heat. It should be offset far enough from the door so that the handle does not get above the burn temperature of 52°C (125°F). There may be a separate drop down door in gas ovens so that one may see the gas elements.

The exterior may be coated with dull heat-resistant black, silver gray enamel, permalucent gray, and similar heat-resistant finishes on soft steel along with the No. 4 finish of stainless steel.

The ovens should be insulated with 10 cm (4 in.) of fiberglass, vitreous fiber, or rock wool. At least one manufacturer places aluminum foil down through the middle of this. Range ovens use about 5 cm (2 in.) of insulation. The oven compartment should be tightly sealed to prevent moisture, which decreases its efficiency, from getting into the insulation. Care should be taken that the insulation is well fastened so that it does not settle and leave areas uninsulated. Doors commonly have insulation of roughly 5.1 cm (2 in.). Most ovens have a separate base 10–13 cm (4–5 in.) high and this may have 10 cm (4 in.) of insulation, rock wool, or fiberglass.

The base may be set on a concrete platform, on wall-supported or angular brackets, or tubular legs. It is desirable that the legs have adjustable feet so that the oven, as installed, has level decks and will turn out level cakes. If the oven is set on a counter, it should have at least 10-cm (4-in.) legs to facilitate cleaning beneath it. Some have 5-cm (2-in.) or 15-cm (6-in.) legs. While stacked roast or general-purpose ovens commonly come in three decks, it is not good human engineering to have them this way. The top oven is too high for one to see into the roast pan, and the cook can burn himself on the dropped-down door when he reaches into the oven. At the same time, the bottom oven is too low to see into and the cook may get burned on the door frame as he reaches into the oven. Unless forced to do otherwise, the cooks will use the center oven 75 percent of the time. Thus, unless restricted by space, it is best to limit stacking to two ovens and place them on 51–61-cm (20–24-in.) legs. The bottom oven deck should not be below 61 cm (2 ft) and the deck of the top oven should be below the armpit. Legs commonly come in lengths from 15–76 cm (6–30 in.) for floor mounting. Figure 6.2 shows an even simpler arrangement, the single-deck oven.

The heating elements in the gas oven are below the bottom deck plate, and the combustion products go through the cooking chamber. This speeds preheating, but causes the cooking moistures from the roasting meat to go up the flue instead of saturating the air as they would in a sealed compartment. Thus, roasting losses are high. Several manufacturers have sealed off the oven compartment, circulating the heated air around the outside of the compartment instead. Thus the oven air can become saturated with moisture and reduce the drawing of the water from the roasts. In both cases, they may use a steel plate below the bottom deck to even out the temperature.

FIGURE 6.2. Single-deck gas oven. Courtesy Vulcan Hart Corporation.

Gas Btu input may range from 20,000–40,000 in a two-pan bake oven and 22,000–56,000 in the two-pan roast and general-purpose oven. One pan is 46 x 66 cm (18 x 26 in.). A four-pan oven may range between 38,000 and 65,000 Btu, and a six-pan unit might run up to 67,000 Btu. It is desirable to be able to preheat the oven to 232°C (450°F) in 20 minutes, but many ovens take 30 minutes or more. It is well to get an oven that provides 3–4 Btu of heat per 16.4 cu cm (1 cu in.). The on-off cycling of the unit should not cover more than 17°C (30°F). The oven should have a thermostat that gives precise temperature control between 66°C and 288°C (150°F and 550°F), a light which will tell when the oven is not up to temperature, and an on-off control. It is desirable to have an automatic pilot and an automatic shut-off that will turn off the gas if the pilot flame fails. Also desirable is an external thermometer dial indicating the internal temperature of the oven cavity and a 1–120-minute timer.

The electric ovens generally use tubular electric elements with one set under the deck and the other at the top of the oven cavity. These provide 6–7 kw per two-pan oven compartment. This is divided so that the top element often has a bit less power than the bottom. At least one manufacturer has a roast or general-purpose oven with a shelf in it. The shelf has a plug-in heating element that converts the single oven, in effect, to a two-deck oven. The normally 6-kw oven is converted by the heating elements into a 9-kw oven. In an electric oven, one should have as a goal a power input approaching 1 watt per 15.6 cu cm (1 cu in.) of oven interior. It should not cycle more than 17°C (30°F). For controls, both the top and bottom elements have high, medium, low and off controls that may regulate the heating element to an electric input of 3.1, 2, 0.775, and 0 kw, respectively. Overall, a thermostat controls the oven between 79°C and 288°C (175°F and 550°F). There is a signal light that indicates when the power is on. It is also desirable to have a 0–120-minute timer and an indicating thermometer. In many bake ovens and a few general-purpose ovens, there is a steam inlet to allow injection of steam for hard-surfacing baked products (figure 6.3).

Both the sealed gas ovens and electric ovens have vents in the rear of the cooking compartment that may be regulated by a lever that is generally in the control panel. Some ovens have special high-temperature compartment lights that make it easier to tell product condition.

FIGURE 6.3. Electric roast ovens (left) and gas bake ovens (right).

Several ovens have linings or coatings that act together with high temperature to turn grease and splatter into an easily removable ash.

At least one manufacturer uses a high-density heating cable wrapped against the external walls of the oven compartment. Research indicated that this method of heating uses less energy than conventional top and bottom heating elements. The unit is supposed to maintain the cooked product for 24 hours at the internal temperature to which it was cooked. This is similar to the method advocated in the delayed service technique.

Many years ago both the U.S. Navy and a home range company had a control based on a meat probe of steel or aluminum that was placed into the cold point of a roast. This probe was connected to an external dial thermometer by a stainless steel flexible cable that plugged into the oven wall. A desired internal cooking temperature would be set on the thermostat dial and when the indicator reached that point, it would actuate an alarm and shut off the electricity. The home oven unit would reduce the oven temperature to that set on the dial and maintain it until the process was terminated. Several institutional ovens have used this control. A few use thermocouples with the leads coming out between the closed door and oven frame to register product temperature, which is read on a potentiometer. There is at least one other control that may be installed in a commercial oven that will allow one to read the temperatures of any one of six probes with an accuracy ±2° in a temperature range of 49–71°C (120–160°F). It comes with an alarm.

In many kitchens, the space occupied by the oven is critical, and dimensions of the oven must be considered in the purchase specification.

While roast, bake, range or general-purpose ovens may be as small as 55 cm (22 in.) wide, 41 cm (16.25 in.) deep (from front to rear), and 25 cm (10 in.) high for table top use, they may be 155 cm (61 in.) or more wide, 210 cm (83 in.) or more deep, and 262 cm (103 in.) plus high. The most common dimensions for a three-deck roast or general-purpose oven are 141 cm (55.5 in.) wide, 91 cm (36 in.) deep, and 198 cm (78 in.) high. However, as noted before, it is recommended that roast and general-purpose ovens be limited to two decks so that both will be close to waist height (figure 6.4).

The internal dimensions of the ovens, too, vary from 36–107 cm (14–42 in.) wide to 43–160 cm (17–63 in.) deep and from 10–66 cm (4–26 in.) high; the most common measurements are approximately 94 cm (37 in.) wide, 72 cm (28 in.) deep, and 32 cm (12.5 in.) high for roast ovens and 18–20 cm (7–8 in.) high for bake ovens. Ovens deeper than the length of one sheet pan are not recommended because one needs to use a peel to move pans to and from the back of the oven. In addition, space equal to the depth of the oven must be furnished in front of the oven in order to wield the peel.

FIGURE 6.4. Electric combination oven, with bake oven (top) and all-purpose ovens (bottom). Courtesy Toastmaster, McGraw-Edison.

In general, electric ovens are more energy efficient than gas ovens but may be more expensive to run, because of the much higher cost of electric Btu in some localities.

Determination of Needed Capacity

In calculating needed roast oven capacity, one needs to decide what products should be prepared in the oven and in what combinations. Of these, one must decide which ones put the greatest demand on the oven to the point that they regulate needed capacity, particularly at, and during, serving time. One needs to know how many portions of this food will be needed in what time frame, how many portions will fit on a pan, how many pans fill a deck, the number of batches wanted, and how long it takes to cook a batch. On the surface, this looks complex, but it is simple enough to lend itself to a formula.

For example, you are baking fish in three 20-minute batches for an institution of 300, of which 80 percent will take the fish. The oven holds two sheet pans, and each sheet pan holds 20 portions. How many decks will you need?

$$\frac{300 \text{ patrons} \times .80 \text{ (\% taking)}}{20 \text{ portions per pan} \times 3 \text{ batches} \times 2 \text{ pans per deck}} = 2 \text{ decks}$$

However, if these patrons are being fed in a cafeteria line at a rate of eight per minute, then the two decks are not enough.

$$2 \text{ decks} \times 2 \text{ pans per deck} \times 20 \text{ portions per pan} = 80 \text{ portions in 20 minutes}$$

at the same time the serving line demands

$$20 \text{ minutes} \times 8 \text{ patrons} \times .80 \text{ (\% taking)} = 128 \text{ portions.}$$

The first batch would last

$$\frac{80 \text{ portions in batch}}{8 \text{ patrons per minute} \times .80 \text{ (\% taking)}} = 12.5 \text{ minutes.}$$

Thus, if the first batch was done just in time to start serving, the second batch would have to start 20 minutes minus 12.5 minutes, or 7.5 minutes before the first batch came out of the oven. In this case, four decks would be needed. The third batch could be out of the oven in 20 minutes, and the first two batches would take 25 minutes to serve.

Basic Use and Operation

With a new oven, the decks should be cleaned off with a soft brush. Then the paint and preservative fumes inherent in the manufacture of an oven should be drawn off by opening the vent wide, setting the thermostat at 149°C (300°F) and the element controls at medium, and operating the oven for eight hours.

When the oven is to be used for most baked products, it must be preheated. This involves setting the thermostat at the desired temperature and turning the oven on. Where possible, foods requiring the lowest cooking temperature to be used for that meal should be done first. Gradually, you would work up to the hottest temperature immediately before service. This reduces energy requirements, but it is not always desirable. Some low temperature products should be served immediately after cooking, whereas some high temperature products need not be. In any case, during preheating, both the top and bottom element controls should be turned to high during preheat. In a high heat input oven, the preheat period should be no more than 20 minutes, but with most of the available ovens, preheat will take 30 minutes or more. To decrease electrical demand, it is well to stagger preheating of the decks so that all will not be on at the same time. After the power-on indicating light goes out, some manufacturers recommend waiting 10–20 minutes for the heat to stabilize before loading. In roast ovens the preheat may start when the product is placed in it because high initial temperature is not necessary.

In loading, if only one deck has a thermostat, that deck should be loaded first so that the drop in temperature characteristic in loading will activate the thermostat to start the elements heating again. The loading process should be carried out as fast as possible. Each deck should be loaded evenly with space between the pans and the sides of the oven. Material should never be added to a section after other material has started to bake. This results in unbalanced baking. If the bakery products need to have strong bottoms, heat the oven 14–28°C (25–50°F) above baking temperature before adding the product, and then reset the thermostat to the proper temperature after inserting the product. If more strength is needed in the product top, then 10–15 minutes before removal time, raise the thermostat 14–28°C (25–50°F). Except for products that should not be subjected to any steam, the vent should be closed to maintain a saturated atmosphere that will keep meat roasting yields high and reduce heat losses.

In general-purpose ovens where a shelf as well as the deck is used for baking, it is probable that the product on the deck will bake normally on the bottom but will be light on top; the product baked on the shelf will not be done on the bottom but will be properly browned or overbrowned on the top. To avoid this, half way through the baking period, interchange the products on the shelf with those on the deck.

The spatter of fat on the oven walls from roasting meats can be minimized by roasting the meat in special roasting bags that should be perforated to release the surplus steam. Pot roast, too, can be given adequate moist atmosphere in the roasting bags. The bags have the advantage of retaining most of the expressed meat liquids for use in gravy. Meats brown well and do not have a steamed appearance. Roasting losses are a bit high but most of that loss remains in the bag for other uses. It is possible to overcome the high roasting losses by greatly reducing the oven temperature.

At times aluminum foil is used to cover meats and roast potatoes. The foil is effective in shielding meats against excessive browning and in saving expressed liquids, and it does present drab potatoes in shiny armor to the customer. Other than this, it has the disadvantage of reflecting heat and adding to the cooking time. It gives the products a steamed atypical appearance.

Unevenness of color in baking is caused by the

choice of pans. Products that depend on absorption of heat by the pan and then conduction to the food are often uneven in cooking results since shiny pans reflect heat and dark pans absorb it. A thin pan conducts heat faster than a thick one of the same material. A warped pan conducts heat at uneven rates as the part in contact with the deck transmits heat faster than the part not in contact. Where pans are available in various materials, they probably conduct heat at different rates. As an example, stainless steel is more costly and less desirable than aluminum for sheet pans and roast pans.

Thought should be given to using the modern bake oven for roasting despite its 18–20 cm (7–8 in.) height. If its deck can be covered with roasting meat, it is probable that it will give lower roasting losses compared to the roasting or general-purpose oven because there is less space to be saturated with moisture from the meat. With the top element closer to the roast, it can be used with more finesse in providing product coloration. It will roast whole turkeys up to 16 pounds and half turkeys of any size. Halving turkeys saves one hour of roasting time.

Ovens should have tables or racks or both in front of them so that loading and unloading can be done with one motion each. Tables beside the oven necessitate a back and forth motion that may generate a messy and dangerous slosh of liquid.

Some of the common products prepared in ovens include baked vegetables, stuffed tomatoes, cabbage and peppers, bacon, sausage, oven fried or roasted duck, chicken or turkey, pork, beef, veal, lamb, baked and steamed fish, braised meats such as Swiss steaks and stews, escalloped dishes, casseroles, souffles, omelets, meringues, shirred eggs, melted cheese sandwiches, pies, cakes, cookies, breads, rolls, and puddings. For the type of pans, oven temperatures, and baking times of these foods, see table 6.1.

TABLE 6.1. Conventional Oven-baked Foods—Temperature and Times

Food	*Pan*	*Temperature*	*Time (min)*
Breads			
Biscuits	baking sheet	218°C (425°F)	12–15
Brown	bread pan	163°C (325°F)	90
Cornbread	baking sheet	218°C (425°F)	30
Crumb cake	baking sheet	191°C (375°F)	30
French	baking sheet	218°C (425°F)	30
Muffins	muffin tins	218°C (425°F)	18
Pizza	baking sheet	232°C (450°F)	20
Rolls	baking sheet	218°C (425°F)	12–15
Sweet dough	baking sheet	218°C (425°F)	10–15
White	bread pan	218°C (425°F)	35–40
Cakes			
Chocolate	baking sheet	191°C (375°F)	25
Devil's food	baking sheet	191°C (375°F)	25
Fruit	bread pan	121°C (250°F)	150
Plain	baking sheet	191°C (375°F)	25
Pound	bread pan	149°C (300°F)	140
Sponge	baking sheet	182°C (360°F)	25
White	baking sheet	191°C (375°F)	20–30
Cookies			
Brownies	baking sheet	177°C (350°F)	25
Chewy nut bars	baking sheet	163°C (325°F)	30
Fruit bars	baking sheet	177°C (350°F)	30

TABLE 6.1. (continued)

Food	Pan	Temperature	Time (min)
Cookies			
Ginger	baking sheet	191°C (375°F)	10
Hermits	baking sheet	191°C (375°F)	10–12
Molasses	baking sheet	191°C (375°F)	8–10
Sugar	baking sheet	204°C (400°F)	10
Vanilla wafers	baking sheet	191°C (375°F)	8–10
Desserts			
Apple brown betty	roast pan	191°C (375°F)	45
Apple crisp	baking sheet	191°C (375°F)	40–45
Baked apples	baking sheet	191°C (375°F)	60–90
Baked custard	roast pan	163°C (325°F)	45
Bread pudding	roast pan	163°C (325°F)	60
Cranberry apple crunch	baking sheet	191°C (375°F)	40
Gingerbread	baking sheet	177°C (350°F)	25
Baked entrées (nonmeat)			
Baked rice and cheese	roast pan	177°C (350°F)	30
Cheese souffle	roast pan	191°C (375°F)	30
Macaroni au gratin	roast pan	204°C (400°F) (top heat)	15
Plain omelet	hot roast pan	163°C (325°F) (low top and bottom)	30
Scrambled eggs	roast pan	177°C (350°F)	Stir every 4–5 minutes
Entrées (fish)			
Baked fish	baking sheet	191°C (375°F)	25
Baked tuna and noodles	roast pan	191°C (375°F)	30
Salmon casserole	roast pan	191°C (375°F)	30
Salmon loaf	roast pan	177°C (350°F)	45
Entrées (meat)			
Bacon slices	baking sheet	191°C (375°F)	10–15
Baked beef hash	roast pan	177°C (350°F)	45
Baked ham slices	roast pan	149°C (300°F)	120
Beef roast	roast pan	149°C (300°F) use thermometer rare 60°C (140°F) medium 71°C (160°F) well 77°C (170°F)	
Braised beef steak	roast pan (covered)	177°C (350°F)	120
Braised liver	roast pan	177°C (350°F)	30
Braised pork chops 1.3 cm (0.5 in.)	roast pan	163°C (325°F)	60
Braised spare ribs	roast pan add sauce	204°C (400°F) 163°C (325°F)	30 90–120
Ham loaf	roast pan	177°C (350°F)	90
Hamburger pie	baking sheet	218°C (425°F)	15
Ham souffle	roast pan	177°C (350°F)	90

TABLE 6.1. (continued)

Food	Pan	Temperature	Time (min)
Entrées (meat)			
Meat loaf 2.5 kg (5.5 lb)	roast pan	163°C (325°F)	90
Pork and noodle casserole	roast pan	177°C (350°F)	30
Roast lamb 1.8–2.7 kg (4–6 lb)	roast pan	149°C (300°F)	180
Roast pork loin 2.7–3.6 kg (6–8 lb)	roast pan	177°C (350°F)	240
Pies (22 cm [9 in.])			
Apple	pie plate	218°C (425°F)	30
Blueberry	pie plate	218°C (425°F)	30
Custard	pie plate	204°C (400°F)	30
Mince	pie plate	218°C (425°F)	45
Pumpkin	pie plate	218°C (425°F)	40
Poultry			
Baked chicken and noodles	roast pan	177°C (350°F)	40
Barbecued chicken	roast pan	177°C (350°F)	75
Chicken jambalaya	roast pan	204°C (400°F)	55
Chicken Tetrazinni	roast pan	218°C (425°F)	20
Maryland fried chicken	roast pan	177°C (350°F)	60
Oven fried chicken	roast pan	163°C (325°F)	90
Roast chicken (cut up)	roast pan	163°C (325°F)	60
Roast duck 1.8 kg (4 lb)	roast pan	163°C (325°F)	120
Roast turkey 4–5 kg (9–12 lbs)	roast pan	177°C (350°F)	210–270
Vegetables			
Baked beans, navy	roast pan	177°C (350°F)	60
Creole lima beans	roast pan	177°C (350°F)	60
Potatoes, baked	baking sheet	218°C (425°F)	60
Potatoes, browned	roast pan	218°C (425°F)	90
Potatoes, Lyonnaise	roast pan	232°C (450°F)	25
Potatoes, scalloped	roast pan	191°C (375°F)	35
Squash, baked acorn	baking sheet	204°C (400°F)	60

Source: Navy-Marine Corps Recipe Service

Special Applications

The oven may be used as a good substitute for tending certain foods on the range top or in a steam jacketed kettle. As an example, when reducing the volume of a sauce or cooking a product slowly, one can avoid stirring and constant gas or electrical adjustment by placing the food in a low, wide stock pot and cooking it in a roast or general-purpose oven at 107°C (225°F) or slightly above. The vent should be left open to permit steam to escape.

In another adaptation, one may add 3.8 liter (4 qt) of boiling water to 1.4 kg (3 lbs) of rice together with 14 g (0.5 oz) salt and 15 ml (0.5 oz) vegetable oil in a tall steam table pan and stir well. Place the pan in a preheated oven at 177°C (350°F) for 30 minutes without stirring. At the end of that time, place it in the steam table for service.

If boil over is threatened, wiping the inside of the top edge of the pan with fat will help. The uncommon uses of the oven are unlimited.

A special rack to hold food close to the upper heating elements may be used to convert it to a broiler. This works somewhat slower than a conventional broiler. The rack legs should be adjustable in length for accommodating various products.

Many range ovens, as well as roast, baking, and general-purpose ovens, are used as warming or holding ovens. The temperatures generally recommended for holding food are given in table 6.2.

TABLE 6.2. Temperatures Generally Recommended for Holding Food

Food	Temperature
Bacon	93–107°C (200–225°F)
Beef, rare	57– 63°C (135–145°F)
Beef, medium, well done	66– 71°C (150–160°F)
Biscuits, muffins, rolls	71– 77°C (160–170°F)
Casseroles	93– 99°C (200–210°F)
Fish and other seafood	71– 77°C (160–170°F)
Gravy	71– 77°C (160–170°F)
Pastry and pies	71– 77°C (160–170°F)
Pizza, lightly covered	93–107°C (200–225°F)
Potatoes, baked	93– 99°C (200–210°F)
Potatoes, mashed	66– 71°C (150–160°F)
Poultry, fried	82– 93°C (180–200°F)
Poultry, roasted	71– 77°C (160–170°F)
Vegetables	71– 77°C (160–170°F)

Ovens which have steam injection for hard rolls may have the oven atmosphere saturated with steam and then can be used for storage of meat roasts and poultry at, or slightly below, the internal temperature to which they had been cooked. The meat stays hot, and the holding loss is low. Beef may be held up to 24 hours but pork probably should be limited to 3 to 4 hours.

Alternatives to Ovens

A few hospitals use the Integral Heating System where the food is heated in a covered plate by a resistive coating on the bottom of the plate. It is insulated by a plastic shell. The plate, in effect, becomes a small oven.

Large gatherings frequently exhaust available cooking facilities, particularly for preparing meats. Cooks are forced to cook the food elsewhere or go back to our forefathers' methods and cook over open fires on spits that turn the roasts, or use metal grates over the coals.

The Indian cooker, a deep round hole in the ground, may be used. A fire is built over round stones and allowed to burn down to coals. Pots of food, roasts rolled in leaves, and unhusked ears of corn are placed on the coals, covered with canvas and other insulative material to hold the steam in the hole.

A similar cooking expedient is the New England clambake where a shallow pit is dug and lined with rocks. A raging fire is maintained until the rocks are very hot. Then the fire is scraped out, and the rocks are covered with wet seaweed. This, in turn, is covered with layers of washed clams, lobsters, fish, potatoes, sweet corn in the husk, and sometimes other items, all interspersed and covered with layers of wet seaweed. Heavy canvas is placed on top to hold in the resultant steam and heat. After several hours, the pit is opened, and the food is served with clam or fish chowder, corn fritters, and watermelon.

Saving Energy

1. As with other foodservice equipment, the more conventional ovens are filled, the closer they approach maximum energy efficiency. The larger the amount of unoccupied space, the lower the degree of energy efficiency. Thus, ovens should be purchased in sizes close to the size of the most usual loads. Oven heights, in particular, should be close to product heights, to save product and energy. Do not preheat ovens any longer than necessary: with meat roasts and similar foods, the oven need not be preheated at all. This saves about 10 percent on energy.

2. Ovens with heating elements wrapped around the oven compartment, or at least on four sides, are more energy efficient than those heated from top and bottom or bottom only. Self-cleaning ovens, if not used for self cleaning (burning off of spatter) are energy efficient, since they are built to heat on all sides.
3. Cooking at a low temperature, particularly roasting meats, is doubly efficient, because it saves both product and energy. Total energy can be saved with many baked products by cooking at a higher than normal temperature if it does not damage the product.
4. Being able to complete the cooking process without opening the oven door saves energy and reduces roasting losses. Doneness may be determined by using a food thermometer to sense the product's cold point and report it on an external thermometer dial.
5. As with stove top cooking, black or dull pans conduct heat better than shiny pans. Dull or black aluminum pans, therefore, are a better choice than stainless steel or iron. Shiny foils, too, should not be used to wrap potatoes or meats, since they increase cooking time. If the product must be browned, consider using low-sided pans to facilitate browning and reduce cooking time.
6. Ovens retain much heat after normal cooking operations. This heat should be used for cooking rice and pastas, reducing sauce volumes, and holding hot foods after the heating units have been shut off. Keep in mind that increasing oven insulation 50 percent improves energy utilization in ovens, and electronic ignition saves 20–30 percent over pilot light use.

Cleaning

1. Allow oven to cool.
2. Scrape each deck to remove baked-on material. If the decks are removable they should be washed periodically in detergent and water, rinsed, dried, coated with oil, and subjected to 177°C (350°F) oven heat for 30 minutes.
3. Brush material out of the oven interiors. Be sure to brush out all materials from the hinge areas and surfaces where the door makes contact with the frame. Check to make sure that the door makes good contact all the way around. Water should be well contained in a cloth or sponge and not allowed in any way to run over the surface of the oven interior as it is washed.
4. Brush out burner compartment and remove any spills.
5. Wash oven door thoroughly inside and out.
6. Wash outside of oven with detergent and water. Rinse and wipe dry.
7. Clean any bare metal with the cleaner recommended by the manufacturer. Do not use wire brush, steel wool, or caustic cleaners on aluminized finishes.

Maintenance

1. Check the oven for loose handles, control knobs, or other parts.
2. Check oven interior for baked-on deposits that have resisted normal cleaning procedures. Some of these may succumb to a coating of salt and high oven heat. Under any circumstances, the residue should be scraped free.
3. The gas flame should be blue. All ports should be operating. If not, they should be cleaned with a round, pointed object.
4. Check to see if the oven compartment light works. If not, replace the bulb with a high-temperature bulb of the proper wattage. If the power-on light does not operate when the oven is heating, it should be replaced.
5. Clean the vent orifice several times a year, and check the closing lever for free action periodically.
6. Check the thermostat against a thermocouple or oven thermometer set close to the location of the thermostat. The reading should be made against the thermostat setting at the time the energy shuts off or reduces.
7. Look for frayed wires, leaking gas lines, and improper door operation.

QUESTIONS

1. What is the definition of an oven?
2. What is the size of the framing elements in an oven?
3. What is transite?
4. What is the usual reflective interior of ovens?
5. What insulation thickness is common for the oven shell? doors?
6. Why should roasting losses be higher in gas ovens than electric ovens?
7. What is desirable gas and electricity input for ovens?
8. Should one have the vent open or closed when roasting meat?
9. What information is necessary to determine needed capacity accurately?
10. How does one load an oven?
11. How may one avoid spatter in roasting meats?
12. What are the advantages and disadvantages of using aluminum foil in meat roasting?
13. What is the advantage of black pans over shiny ones?
14. What are the advantages of using a bake oven for roasting meat?
15. How does one check the thermostat of an oven?
16. Describe five measures that can be taken to make conventional ovens more energy efficient.

BIBLIOGRAPHY

ANON. 1969. *A Brief Encyclopedia of Commercial Ovens.* Middleby-Marshall Oven Co., Morton Grove, Ill.

ANON. 1973. *Oven Menu Ideas.* Food Service Equipment Dealer, Chicago.

KOTSCHEVAR, L.H., and TERRELL, M.E. 1977. *Food Service Planning: Layout and Equipment.* 2d ed. John Wiley and Sons, New York.

LONGREE, K., and BLAKER, G.G. 1971. *Sanitary Techniques in Food Service.* John Wiley and Sons, New York.

SCHNEIDER, N.F., and JAHN, E.A. 1968. *Commercial Kitchens.* American Gas Assoc., New York.

WEST, B.B., WOOD, L., HARPER, V.F. 1967. *Food Service in Institutions.* 4th ed. John Wiley and Sons, New York.

WILKINSON, J. 1975. *The Complete Book of Cooking Equipment.* CBI Publishing Company, Inc., Boston.

Forced Convection Ovens

Most conventional gas and electric ovens are designed with heating elements under the bottom of the cavity, or both under the bottom and in the top. It is wasteful of heat and time to heat this cavity. At least one manufacturer has wrapped electric heating coils around the cavity, and a few ovens, particularly the home type, have elements in the sides to assist self-cleaning. For cooking alone, these elements are more energy efficient than top and bottom elements alone.

Another wasteful factor in the conventional oven is the use of only a small amount of the total cavity available for cooking most foods. Some cooks attempt to use a shelf in the oven to get two-level cooking, but halfway through the cooking time the food must be shifted from shelf to oven bottom and vice versa to get even cooking. The U.S. Naval Supply Research and Development Facility tried to overcome both the inefficient heating of the oven cavity and unused oven space by making a radiant heat oven that heated on all six sides and adjusted to the size of the food being cooked so that none but the needed space was heated and used. It worked well but was too complex for U.S. Navy use.

Then, the U.S. Navy adapted the existing conventional oven to take multiple shelves without having to move the food because of unevenness of heating. This was done by placing a fan in the oven compartment to move the heated air in a turbulence that made it possible to place food anywhere in the oven cavity and have it cook fairly evenly. After further research by the American Gas

Association, Michigan State University, Keating of Chicago, and others, the first commercial forced convection oven became available. Since then, most of the makers of conventional ovens have come out with their version of the forced convection oven.

Among others, the most prominent types of convection ovens are:

1. Forced air circulation. A fan drives heated air at high velocity and thereby evens out oven cavity temperature.
2. Thermionic. There is low velocity air movement but high air volume.
3. Muffle. A sealed oven compartment heats with, or without, the use of a fan.
4. Roll-in convection. This uses either a multiple rack assembly of shelves that roll into the oven from a cart, or a wheeled multiple rack that goes into the oven on the floor or onto an oven bottom close to the floor. The heating elements may be in, adjacent to, or separate from the oven cavity (figure 7.1).
5. Pulse type. This uses alternating gusts of very hot air and then cold air. The first provides the cooking heat; the second keeps the food surface from overcooking.

In all of these cases, the moving air strips away the cool layer of air next to the food and brings hot air in contact to speed cooking. The advantages and disadvantages of forced convection ovens are:

Advantages	*Disadvantages*
good speed of cooking	excessive cooking losses
good browning action	thick surface layer on food
high-density use of cooking cavity	uneven surface effect
lower cooking temperatures	some uneven cooking
more production in less floor space	cake batter blown to one end of the pan (older ovens)
less labor	air movement too strong for meringue (modern ovens)
overall cost reduction	
more energy efficient in well-insulated ovens	

FIGURE 7.1. Roll-in convection oven. Courtesy Despatch Industries, Inc.

Description and Specifications

Differences in the ovens furnished by the various manufacturers vary in the following design criteria:

1. Methods of air circulation. The two main ways of creating air movement in forced convection ovens are:

With turbulence or free flow, the fan moves the air in swirls and eddies. The air is heated through the oven walls or it is drawn in through the center of the baffle, passes over electric heating elements behind the baffle, and then is blown around the outer edges of the baffle into the oven cavity. The design and placement of pans and height of product affect the flow of air and heating efficiency. Some turbulence units have two-speed fans (figure 7.2).

With directed or controlled flow, the air is heated in the rear, top, or side heat exchanger and a top or rear mounted fan directs the air through ducts and hollow walls into the oven cavity through perforated or slotted panels and back into the center of the fan in a definite path. To even out the rate of heat flow, some models have small vents close to the heat source and fan, and larger holes as the distance from the heat source increases.

2. External dimensions. The most commonly used forced convection ovens have external dimensions which vary between 60–155 cm (23.6–61 in.) in width, 64–110 cm (25.1–43.4 in.) in depth, and 55–107 cm (21.75–42 in.) in height. With legs on cabinet, the oven may be 168 cm (66 in.) or more high. The most common dimensions are 96 x 96 x 81 cm (38 x 38 x 32 in.) to which one would add legs or cabinet to bring it up to approximately 152 cm (60 in.) in height. In selecting an oven size, one should be sure that it fits into the space available.

3. Cooking cavity dimensions. These vary from 33–84 cm (13–32.9 in.) in width, 37–72 cm (14.5–28.25 in.) in depth, and 36–79 cm (14.2–31

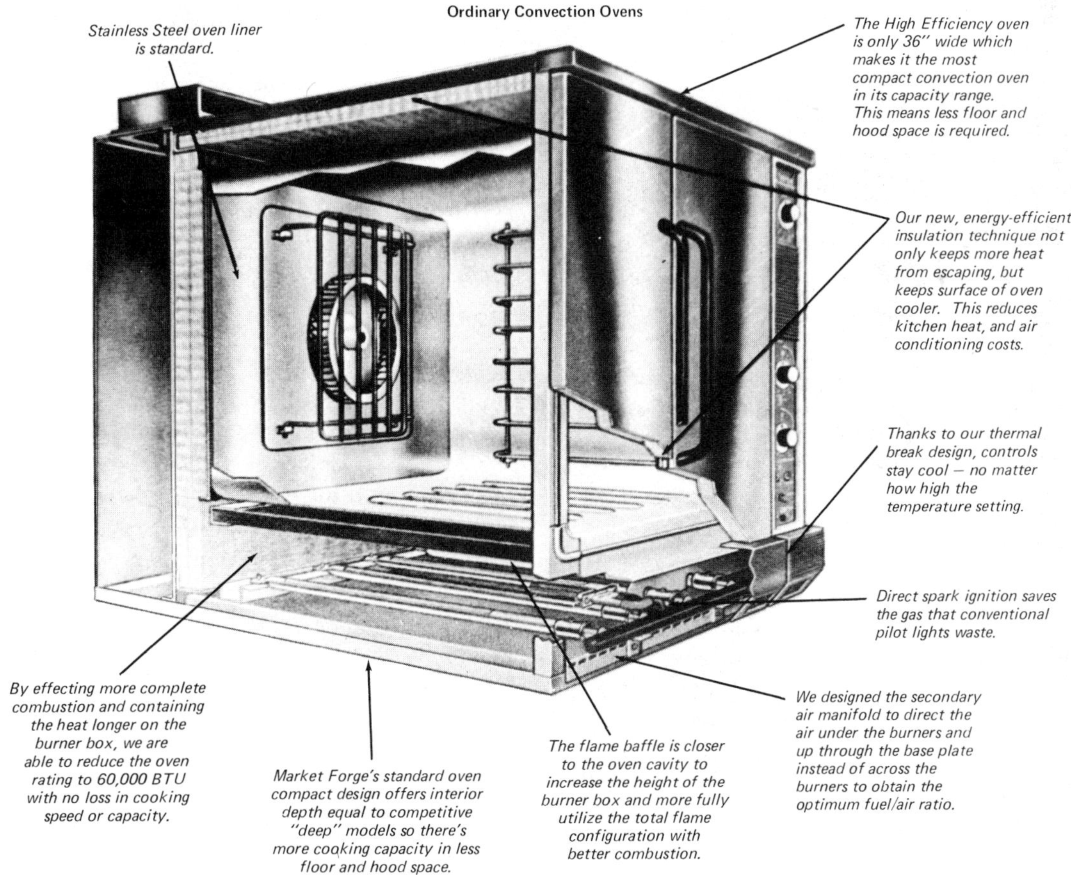

FIGURE 7.2. Gas convection oven design. Courtesy Market Forge.

in.) in height. However, the most common dimensions are 74 x 53 x 51 cm (29 x 21 x 20 in.). One should select an oven with a cavity size in area that will take the maximum pan size that will be used with at least 2.5 cm (1 in.) free for air circulation on all sides. If multiple pans are to be used, there should be 2.5 cm (1 in.) around the perimeter plus some space between the pans for air circulation. Height of oven selected will require balancing what is available against the amount of product to be cooked at one time considering the manufacturer's recommendations as to vertical shelf placement and pan arrangement for the particular product (figure 7.3).

FIGURE 7.3. Interior of forced convection oven.

4. Heat input. This varies between 5.3 and 37 kw for electricity and 40,000 and 120,000 Btu for gas in the average forced convection ovens. One should aim for 1–3 watts per 16 cu cm (1 cu in.) of oven space for electricity, and 4–8 Btu for gas. The oven should preheat to 204°C (400°F) in 15 minutes. The majority of the fans (0.5–2 HP) operate at 1,750 RPM.

5. Rack slides or guides. Usually, eight to eleven slides with a clearance of 3.2–5.1 cm (1.25–2 in.) between racks are found in most ovens. It is desirable to have racks that pull out half to two-thirds of their length without tilting. In some cases, particularly for reheating refrigerated or frozen school lunches, the ovens are set up to permit the roll-in or slide-in of a complete oven load of racks as one integral unit from a special cart. This permits the unit to be loaded at the central commissary or kitchen and wheeled into a specially designed refrigerator or freezer at the point of use until just before meal time. At this time it is transported to the forced convection oven for heating to service temperature. When heated, the rack is reloaded on the cart and wheeled to the point of service.

6. Exterior finishes. These may be secured in high-heat aluminum, 16–20-gauge stainless steel with no. 4 finish, 14–20-gauge mild steel with porcelain enamel, vitreous enamel, or other baked-on finishes.

The interiors may be obtained in stainless steel, aluminized steel, porcelain, vitreous enamel, easy-to-clean Teflon, catalytic chemically coated steel, or pyrolytic self-cleaning porous porcelain that starts oxidizing spatter at 144°C (300°F) and does a complete job at 232°C (450°F).

7. Insulation. Most forced convection ovens are underinsulated. The materials may be rock or mineral wool, marinite, pressed vitreous fiber, or other material. While the preferred thickness is 10 cm (4 in.) on all sides and at least 5.1 cm (2 in.) in doors, most ovens have far less than this. For instance, one oven has 10 cm (4 in.) in the sides, only 2.5 cm (1 in.) in the bottom, 4.4 cm (1.75 in.) in top, and 3.8 cm (1.5 in.) in the door. Another oven has 6.4 cm (2.5 in.) in the top, bottom, and sides and 3.8 cm (1.5 in.) in the door.

8. Doors. These may be French type, hinged on each side and interconnected so that as one opens, the other opens too. In another oven, the two doors are hinged so that one opens up and the other drops down. One manufacturer has the counterbalanced door drop down like a conventional oven. Several have the door hinged on one side or the other only. A majority of the ovens use the two doors that split to the sides. Most of the oven doors are stainless steel on the exterior surface, although a few use materials such as aluminum or enameled steel. The interiors may be stainless steel or the same material as the oven interior, which might be aluminized steel or porcelain. The doors may have single or double glass windows or solid metal and insulation. Some have gaskets and some use only metal-to-metal contact. Others are recessed into the oven when closed, and some fit flat against the front of the oven. The ovens may have no latches, positive lock latches, or magnetic latches, while door handles may be of bracket type or offset tubular type. They may unlatch the oven when pulled (figure 7.4).

FIGURE 7.4. French-type doors in forced convection oven. Courtesy U.S. Range Co.

9. Legs. These may be adjustable or fixed tubular or bracket type in lengths from 10 cm (4 in.) to 51 cm (20 in.). The oven may sit on another oven to double oven capacity in a kitchen that is short of space. This expedient is not recommended as the bottom oven is too low to use easily and the top oven is too high. Some kitchens have the oven placed on a set of shelves or a closed cabinet with doors or drawers. At least one kitchen has a refrigerator under the oven.

10. Indicators and controls. These depend on the individual manufacturer (figure 7.5). Found on a gas oven might be:

- thermostat: 79–260°C (175–500°F)
- main switch and a signal light
- switch for interior lights (an oven may have two to four lights, or no lights)
- fan switch (in most ovens the fan and heat go off when the door opens)
- a light telling when the fan is on
- gas control with safety pilot
- one or two timers (1 to 60 minutes and 5 minutes to 5 hours)

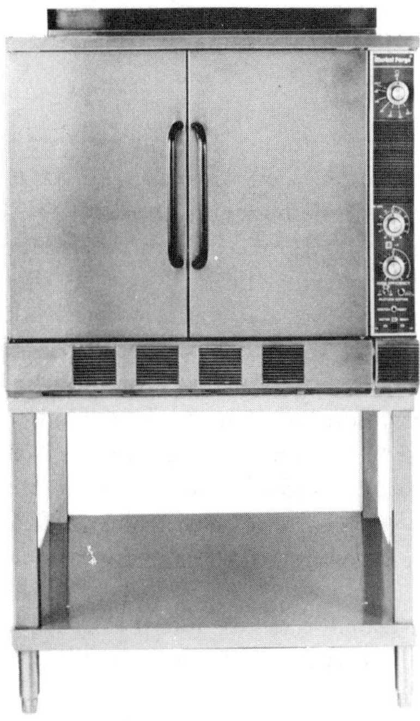

FIGURE 7.5. Controls on gas convection oven. Courtesy Market Forge.

An electric oven may have:

- electric interlock to shut off the heating elements and fan when the door is opened
- power switch to energize elements
- light to indicate power is on
- light to indicate that oven is up to temperature
- thermostat: 93–260°C (200–500°F)
- temperature dial
- one or two timers

At least one manufacturer has a load control that makes adjustments for the number of pans to be heated in the oven.

Special Forced Convection Ovens

There are some manufacturers who make special large forced convection ovens to handle the previously mentioned roll-in multiple-shelf racks from carts and self-contained multiple-shelf carts that hold up to forty pans on one loading. Among these are the following:

1. A combination refrigerator-forced convection oven can be filled with a rack load of school lunch meals or hamburgers and kept refrigerated or frozen until a timer actuates the heaters. Very hot air blows across the food and, as the intense heat starts to work its way into the product, the heat flow shuts off to be replaced by a cold blast that keeps the food surface from overbrowning. This alternation keeps up until the food is cooked or reheated to a set temperature, then the oven temperature is reduced to a set holding temperature. At least one user claims a 50 percent reduction in cooking time over conventional ovens.

2. An oven forces heat into the rack of food first from one side and then from the other.

3. One oven will take one to four racks of pans at a time and then turns them as the food in them cooks under forced convection heat.

Determination of Needed Capacity

It would seem that the calculation of needed capacity of forced convection ovens would be simple, and one would only need divide the number of pans of food required for a certain time period by the number of pans one can put into the oven and multiply by the number of batches that can be cooked in that time. Such is not the case. For most products, all shelves cannot be used at full capacity. For example, for one oven only three of nine shelves can be used for bread with only four loaves to a shelf; for frozen fruit pies, five shelves with two pies to a shelf can be used. When reheating TV dinners, nine shelves can be used with three dinners to a shelf.

For capacity determinations, it is best to run tests using recipe, pans, and raw material for an often prepared product that will place the greatest demand on the oven. Failing this, use the manufacturer's data. If you need approximately six hundred 170 g (6 oz) portions of macaroni and cheese in one hour and get approximately 25 portions per pan, this means about twenty-four 30 x 51 x 6.3 cm (12 x 20 x 2.5 in.) pans will be needed. The manufacturer's literature indicates that, if six shelves are used for macaroni and cheese with two pans per shelf, two batches can be baked each hour. Thus, six shelves multiplied by two pans per shelf multiplied by two batches equals twenty-four pans, or enough capacity for the need. It is well to remember that capacity data for one manufacturer cannot be used safely for calculations on the oven of another manufacturer. For instance, one oven will bake a 2.3 kg (5 lb) sheet cake in 16–18 minutes, another in 15 minutes, and yet another in 18 minutes.

Each manufacturer does have recommended combined capacity data to help people who cannot calculate their needs. For instance, one manufacturer recommends the following:

- the single small model for 112-person capacity
- the single large model for 140-person capacity
- the double small model for 224-person capacity
- the double large model for 280-person capacity

I have found that data such as these generally err on the side of overcapacity.

Basic Use and Operation

The forced convection oven is not much more difficult to use than is the conventional oven (figure 7.6). To use a gas oven, go through the following steps:

1. Insert the number of shelves that can be used for the particular product being cooked. Place them in the recommended positions.
2. Set the thermostat at the desired point and turn gas knob to burners on. To compensate for the temperature lost in loading, some cooks set the thermostat 28–42°C (50–75°F) above the cooking temperature and then, as they load the oven, they return the thermostat to the desired temperature.
3. When the indicator light goes off, the oven should be loaded quickly with the pans in the same vertical and horizontal planes. To speed loading, a rack or table should be located in front of the oven for one motion loading and unloading. If meat, fish, or poultry is being cooked, place one or more pans of hot water in the bottom of the oven to saturate the air and prevent excessive moisture losses from the product. Be sure that the fan is shut off during loading.
4. Shut the door and set the timer.
5. When the bell or buzzer rings denoting the cooking time is complete, remove the product and reload.
6. If a lower temperature is to be used for the next load, reset the thermostat to the new temperature and open the door not connected with the interlock (often the left one) until the oven is down to temperature and the indicator light goes on.
7. For daily shutdown, turn both the oven thermostat and the power switch to off. The gas valve may be left in burners-on position or may be turned to off. Door should be left ajar.

FIGURE 7.6. Forced convection oven in use. Courtesy Vulcan Hart Corporation.

The electric oven operation is similar:

1. Turn on main power switch with doors open.
2. Arrange shelves for the particular product as with the gas oven.
3. Close doors and fan should start operating clockwise.
4. Set thermostat for desired preheat temperature (it may be set above desired temperature as with the gas oven). After reaching the set temperature, allow the oven to cycle once to even out temperature (30–35 minutes), although this is not entirely necessary.
5. Open oven and load quickly. Place pan of hot water in the bottom of the oven to saturate the oven atmosphere for meat, fish, and poultry. Reset the thermostat, if necessary.
6. Set timer to desired number of minutes.
7. When bell or alarm rings, remove food from oven and reload. Temperature may be reduced as with the gas oven.
8. On completion of use, turn the thermostat and power switches to off and leave the oven doors ajar.

Time-Temperature Relationships in Oven Use

Some users of forced convection ovens use the same time-temperatures as they use for conventional bake and roast ovens. In addition to overcooking the food, this loses much of the benefit to be derived from the convection oven. Work done at Michigan State University by Borsenik and Newcomer (1959) showed that a convection oven would reduce cooking time of meat loaf 38 percent over a conventional oven at 177°C (350°F) and 47 percent at 121°C (250°F) using 23 percent less electricity and giving comparable shrinkage.

In research done by Schoman and Ball for the U.S. Navy (1961) on 9 kg (20 lb) roasts of beef, he found that he could roast them in the same time at 149°C (300°F) as he could at 204°C (400°F) merely using 0.57 cu m (20 cu ft) per minute of air circulation at the lower temperature. The yields were 57.9 percent at the high temperature and 65.7 percent at the lower. They continued their research with various combinations of air circulation, temperature, and steam pressure. Some of their findings were as follows:

1. As temperature was reduced, cooking time and meat yields increased. Power consumption decreased.
2. As volume of air movement increased, cooking time was reduced but so was the meat yield.
3. As steam pressure increased, cooking time decreased as did meat yields.
4. The optimum combination was 100–114°C (212–237°F) temperature, air movement of 0.21–0.28 cu m (7.5–10 cu ft) per minute, and a moisture saturated oven atmosphere at 0 kg (0 lbs) pressure.

In setting up cooking time-temperature relationships with today's forced convection ovens that evolved from the various research projects, one must use that combination of time, temperature, shelf placement, and location on the shelves that will give the finished product desired in the time frame desired. Also, the vagaries of the particular make of oven with which one is working must be considered because, in spite of the research, these ovens still suffer from some unevenness of heat distribution. The top of the oven is commonly hotter than the bottom, and there are hot and cold areas. In heating pans of frozen oatmeal, the U.S. Army found that in some forced convection ovens there were pans that were 38°C (100°F) colder when the first pans reach 71°C (160°F). In a test run several years ago, by the time the first pan of frozen oatmeal reached 71°C (160°F), the slowest was at 33°C (92°F), and when the slowest was at 71°C (160°F), the fastest was up to a too-hot 97°C (206°F). It took 120 minutes to heat the fastest to 71°C (160°F) and 160 minutes to heat the slowest to the same temperature. With four pans to a shelf, the fastest pan was on the right rear of the third of ten shelves and the slowest was on the left front of the eighth shelf.

One can do a fair duplication of the above tests by placing small aluminum dishes 2.5–5.1 cm (1–2 in.) deep with an equal amount of water such as 200 ml (6.8 oz) in each one in centers of the positions usually occupied by steam table pans in the oven. The evaporation of water should be timed for each pan with a stop watch to the point of dryness. This gives a good idea of the hot and less hot areas in the oven and the proportionate difference. Pans of food may be placed in positions of similar time requirement with proportionate time adjustments being made.

Also to be considered are the cycling variations. The conventional oven cycles through a range of 17°C (30°F) or more, and a forced convection oven cycles through range of 8–10°C (15–18°F). Every food varies in the way it cooks in a forced convection oven as contrasted with a conventional oven. The following are temperature reductions that may be used to make adjustments in conventional oven recipes:

cookies	14°C (25°F)
cakes and quick breads	28°C (50°F)
yeast products	42°C (75°F)
casseroles	14°C (25°F)
meat roasting	28°C (50°F) or more

A few operators try one-third to one-half of their conventional oven times and the same temperatures until they learn differently. Time reduction is usually less as the product increases in thickness.

Tips on Convection Oven Use

Cakes with very moist batter may be moist on top when finished, as they quickly saturate the oven atmosphere and moisture settles on the product. If the oven has a vent, it should be opened. If not, one should try to crack the oven open enough to let the steam out but not enough to operate the fan and heat interlock, which will shut off the oven.

Some ovens will overbrown the cake surface before the cake center is baked. One may be limited to 2.3 kg (5 lbs) of batter per 46-x-66-x-3.8-cm (18-x-26-x-1.5 in.) sheet pan. Overly thick cakes tend to "peak" and "crack." For cooking defects caused by the oven, see table 7.1.

The biggest problem with forced convection ovens is overloading. Manufacturers' instructions should be followed until they are found to be wrong. Then, usually by trial and error, one can reduce the load to the proper point. The more distance between the cake pans, the better the color will be. For manufacturer-recommended processing data, see table 7.2.

In roasting big pieces of meat, the University of Wisconsin Memorial Union uses pans of water in the oven bottoms. They roast the first hour at 93°C (200°F) and then increase the temperature to 107°C (225°F) until the meat is done. Yields and color are excellent, and the roasting time is only 30–60 minutes longer than when done at 163°C (325°F). One manufacturer recommends roasting meat for two hours at 93°C (200°F), one hour at 107°C (225°F), and the remainder at 121°C (250°F). Meat racks should be used in the pans.

One manufacturer recommends defrosting and reheating covered frozen meals at 260°C (500°F) for 20–30 minutes.

All pans should be centered vertically and horizontally on the various racks for best results. Partial loads should be placed on center shelves.

Pans where the level of the product is much below the top of the pan should not be used or the color will be poor.

Pans of water are of little value in the oven bottom when cooking hamburgers as they cook too fast.

Pies should be loaded on a 46-x-66-cm (18-x-26-in.) sheet pans to collect boil-over and speed loading. The usual load is four pies per pan. Pans which are 30 x 51 cm (12 x 20 in.) should be loaded sideways and 46-x-66-cm (18-x-26-in.) pans lengthwise. Both should be kept away from the walls for best air circulation.

The oven should not be loaded when the fan is running.

Yeast products should be fully proofed before being put in the oven. They tend to bake fast in a

TABLE 7.1. *Cooking Defects Caused by Oven*

	Overbaked	*Underbaked*	*Low baking temperature*	*High baking temperature*	*No bottom heat*	*Too much food*	*Uneven oven*	*Load too small*	*No water in oven*	*Excessive air*	*Load placed wrong*
Shrinkage of cakes	X										
Cake falls		X									
Solid pie crust			X								
Light color pie crust			X								
Pie crust soaked			X	X	X						
Pie watery			X								
Pie crust tough				X							
Unbaked bottom pie crust					X						
Pie crust sticks					X						
Low bread volume				X							
Dark bread crust				X						X	
Over volume bread			X								
Bread does not keep			X								
Poor bread texture			X								
Bread crust too thick			X							X	
Uneven baked colors				X		X					X
Uneven baked thickness							X			X	X
Undone cake center				X				X			
Excessive meat shrinkage				X		X			X	X	

Source: Adapted from Market Forge Operating Instructions S-112A.

TABLE 7.2. *Manufacturer-recommended Processing Data*

Product	*Shelves*	*Temperature*	*Time (min)*
Angel cake	3	121°C (250°F)	25–30
Apple turnover	5	177°C (350°F)	15
Beef pot pie	5	204°C (400°F)	30–35
Beef roast rolls			
5.4–6.8 kg (12–15 lbs)	3	135°C (275°F)	150
Biscuits	5	204°C (400°F)	6
Bread 0.45 kg (1 lb)			
24 loaves	3	171°C (340°F)	25–30
Bread, corn	5	168°C (335°F)	25
Brownies	5	149°C (300°F)	18–25
Buns, cinnamon	5	166°C (335°F)	20
Cake, sheet			
2.3 kg (5 lb)	5	163°C (325°F)	16–25
Cake, chocolate	5	163°C (325°F)	20

Forced Convection Ovens

TABLE 7.2. (continued)

Product	Shelves	Temperature	Time (min)
Chicken, quartered			
1.1 kg (2.5 lb)	5	177°C (350°F)	30
Cookies, sugar	5	149°C (300°F)	12–15
Crisp, cherry	5	149°C (300°F)	25
Halibut steaks, frozen			
142 g (5 oz)	5	177°C (350°F)	20–30
Hamburger patties			
5 per 0.45 kg (1 lb)	11	204°C (400°F)	8–10
Lamb chops (small)	5	204°C (400°F)	6
Lobster, stuffed			
0.68 kg (1.5 lb)	5	204°C (400°F)	10
Macaroni and cheese	5	177°C (350°F)	30
Meat loaf	3	163°C (325°F)	40–45
Pie, apple, fresh			
0.57 kg (20 oz)	5	177°C (350°F)	25–30
Pie, berry, frozen			
0.62 kg (22 oz)	5	177°C (350°F)	34
Pie, pumpkin	5	149°C (300°F)	30–35
Pork chops, stuffed	5	191°C (375°F)	25–30
Potatoes, Idaho			
120 count	5	204°C (400°F)	50
Pizza, frozen			
13 cm (5 in.)	6	232°C (450°F)	5–7
Rolls, dinner	5	177°C (350°F)	15–25
Sandwiches, melted cheese	5	204°C (400°F)	8–10
Steaks, shell			
0.28 kg (10 oz)	5	232°C (450°F)	7–8
Turkey rolls			
8.2 kg (18 lbs)	3	154°C (310°F)	210
Veal roast			
6.8 kg (15 lbs)	2	149°C (300°F)	190

Source: "Oven Menu Ideas," *Food Service Equipment Dealer*, Vol. 2, Section 2, Oct. 1973.

forced convection oven, and if not fully proofed, the product volume will be poor.

Special Applications

When cooking rice, for each 30-x-51-x-6-cm (12-x-20-x-2.5-in.) pan, mix 0.9 kg (2 lb) rice, 1.9 liters (2 qt) water, and 10 g (2 tsp) salt. Cover with foil and cook at 177°C (350°F) for 45–50 minutes.

When cooking spaghetti or macaroni, place a perforated insert in a 30-x-51-x-6.3-cm (12-x-20-x-2.5-in.) pan. Break 0.9 kg (2 lb) of spaghetti into 8–10-cm (3–4-in.) pieces and add to the pan in a mixture of 2.8 liters (3 qt) of water, 10 ml (2 tsp) of oil, and 10 g (2 tsp) salt. Stir until all of the spaghetti is wet, cover pan with foil, and cook for 30 minutes in a 177°C (350°F) oven. Remove perforated insert and drain.

Alternatives to the Forced Convection Oven

The nearest substitutes for the forced convection oven are the conveyor and reel types of ovens. These have a certain amount of hot air movement around the food which strips away the cool air layer as does the forced convection oven. They are large quantity cooking devices, but they occupy more space than the forced convection oven and are not as fast.

If one can do with less speed and cooking capacity per square foot of kitchen area, the conventional bake, roast, and general-purpose ovens will do. If less capacity, but more speed, is desirable then the quartz infrared and microwave ovens may be the answer. If high deck temperature can be used, the pizza oven or hearth broiler may be used, and if high top temperature is desirable, the overhead broiler is available. If crust and surface drying are not necessary, the various steamers and pressure cookers may be used for a large variety of products that might be oven cooked.

Saving Energy

1. Electronic ignition should be used in place of pilot ignition. This can save at least $20 per year.
2. Baking should be done at a temperature 10–24°C (50–75°F) lower than in conventional ovens. This increases yield and uses less energy per pound of food. When roasting meats, place several glass dishes filled with hot water at the bottom of the oven, to help saturate the air with moisture and reduce moisture losses in the meats.
3. In baking, as high a temperature as possible should be used, so long as the food can be cooked on the inside properly without overcooking the outside. If the product center is raw at the end of the cooking period and the outside is properly browned, the temperature should be decreased 15–25 degrees and the cooking time increased.
4. Oven lights should be turned off during the cooking process. This will increase the life of the bulbs and save energy.
5. Try experimenting with vertical aluminum skewers for baked potatoes. The pins should

FIGURE 7.7. Forced convection ovens can present special cleaning problems.

reduce cooking times 15–25 minutes, thus saving energy and reducing food shrinkage. Aluminum foil wrap should not be used, since it increases cooking time.

6. The lowest rack of the oven should be loaded first and the others loaded according to the manufacturer's recommendations.
7. Meringues and light batters should be cooked for 7–10 minutes before the fan is turned on. This saves a slight amount of energy and, more important, provides a more even surface and sets the meringue.
8. The oven should be filled to capacity whenever possible.

Cleaning

1. Shut off heat and fan and allow oven to cool with the doors ajar (figure 7.7).
2. Daily wipe off the outside of the oven with a cloth dampened in mild detergent. Clean with the metal grain (finish marks). Rinse with fresh water and wipe dry with a soft cloth. Do not use scouring powders or pads as they will scratch the surface. Once a week polish with a silicone-based polish.
3. Take the racks, rack supports, drip pan, and removable panels out of the oven for washing, rinsing, and drain drying in the pot sink area. Remove the fan baffle by removing thumbscrews. Wash baffle in pot sink, wipe off fan blades with a cloth wet with detergent and water, and replace.
4. Never use soaking wet cloths or sponges or pour water into the oven. Wipe fixed panels with a cloth dampened in detergent and water. Rinse with a cloth moist with clean fresh water.
5. Hardened spills may be sprinkled with salt and baked until charred. Then they can be removed with a spatula or dull knife. Do not use oven cleaning chemicals in pyrolytic-, catalytic-, or Teflon-coated oven surfaces or the special properties may be lost. The oven cleaner can generally be used on the oven door interior, but this treatment is seldom needed. Check around the door for hardened deposits, and if found, scrape them free.
6. The oven controls should be wiped off at the same time as the oven exterior and with the same damp cloths.
7. Reassemble the oven with the clean and dry oven interior parts. If oven odors remain, heat the oven to 260°C (500°F) for 30 minutes.

Maintenance

1. With gas ovens, check the flame to ensure that it is blue and contacting the burner. If not, adjust the airflow into the manifold.
2. Check door-oven interface for baked-on soil accretions, and scrape them off with a dull blade if they are present. This will prevent air and airborne moisture from leaking from the oven cavity.
3. Check door latch and hinges for looseness. Adjust, if necessary.
4. Observe oven-interior lights for burn-outs. Replace any with special high-temperature bulbs designed for oven use. Do not use regular household bulbs.
5. Check knobs on timers and thermostats for looseness and indicator lights for burn-outs. Tighten and replace, as necessary.
6. Check gas inlet pipes for leaks and electric connections for looseness.
7. Check timers before using and at least once a month with a good stop watch for periods of 10, 30, and 60 minutes and maximum time of control. Timers can vary as much as 20 percent from what they should be. If they vary more than 5 percent either way, make mental adjustments each time the timer is used or have it replaced.
8. Check thermostat before using, and at least once a month check with a wire thermocouple and a hand-held potentiometer or temperature indicator. Set thermostat successively for 93,

149, 204, and 260°C (200, 300, 400, and 500°F). As power-on light goes out indicating that each temperature is reached, check the temperature at the thermocouple, which should be suspended in the center of the oven and protected against direct airflow with a shield. A difference of over 5.6°C (10°F) should be adjusted by maintenance workers.

QUESTIONS

1. What are the five types of forced convection ovens?
2. What are the advantages and disadvantages of forced convection ovens?
3. What are the two types of air movement in the forced convection ovens?
4. What should be the gas input and electric input per cubic inch of oven interior?
5. What are the desirable thicknesses of insulation on sides and doors of the forced convection ovens?
6. What types of doors are available and which is most used?
7. What are the three special types of sides and doors of the forced convection ovens? How do they work?
8. What was the desirable combination of air movement, temperature, and steam pressure as advocated by Schoman and Ball?
9. What is the biggest problem with forced convection oven use?
10. How does one increase yields in meat roasting?
11. What are the alternatives to the forced convection oven?
12. How does one check the timers of an oven?
13. How can a cook measure evenness of heat distribution?
14. What caution should be observed when replacing oven lights?
15. Where are tables placed in conjunction with ovens?
16. Describe five measures that can be taken to make forced convection ovens more energy efficient.

BIBLIOGRAPHY

ANON. 1966. *Equipment Engineering Specifications*. Blodgett Ovens, Burlington, Vt.

ANON. 1969. *General Electric Convection Ovens*. General Electric Co., Chicago.

ANON. 1972. Is your oven capacity adequate? *Food Service Marketing* 34, No. 6, 16–20.

ANON. 1973. *Menu Ideas* (leaflet). Restaurant Equipment Dealer, Chicago.

BORSENIK, F., and NEWCOMER, J. 1959. Experimental oven ups speed, lowers fuel consumption. *Institutions Magazine* 45, No. 12, 12, 24, 72.

DAVENPORT, M., and MEYER, B. 1970. Forced convection roasting at 200 and 300°F. *Journal of the American Dietetic Association* 56, No. 1, 31–33.

FINK, K., ALDRICH, P. and IRMITER, T. 1966. Forced convection roasting of loin cuts of beef. *Journal of American Dietetic Association* 48, No. 5, 404–408.

OATS, G. 1969. The convection oven: a new twist on an old art. *School Lunch Journal* XXIII, No. 9, 26–33.

SCHOMAN, C., and BALL, C. 1961. The effect of oven temperatures, circulation, and pressure on the roasting of top rounds of beef (yield and roasting time). *Food Technology* 15, No. 3, 133–136.

WILKINSON, J. 1975. *The Complete Book of Cooking Equipment*. CBI Publishing Company, Inc., Boston.

Quartz Infrared Ovens And Pizza Ovens

Many counter operations, buffets, and small table-service restaurants have a need for a fast general-purpose cooking device which will occupy a minimum of space and have the following functions:

- heat half and full size steam table pans of frozen or unfrozen foods
- perform short-order cooking
- bake pizzas of various types
- bake hot breads

The quartz infrared oven will do most of these tasks well.

Most of the quartz infrared ovens are countertop units that use electric radiant heat top and bottom and may, or may not, have racks and swing down doors. In use, the oven is preheated to a set temperature between 121° and 399°C (250° and 750°F), the product is put on a rack or the deck, and a timer is set to indicate when the product will be ready for removal. Generally, the oven is maintained at a ready-to-use temperature because of the considerable time needed to bring it up to cooking temperature from ambient. Some advantages and disadvantages of the oven are:

Advantages	*Disadvantages*
speed	long preheat time
quality of product, good browning	human burn hazard
control of both top and bottom heat	hotter in back of oven
occupies little space	fire hazard
	needs rack at high temperatures

can use both glass and metal pans	some products must be covered
self-cleaning, top and bottom elements	need conventional oven, also
	low cavity height
	wide cycling range, 56°C (100°F) in some cases

Description and Specification

The quartz infrared oven is generally covered with 18–20-gauge stainless steel inside and out. The cabinet and door have 5.1 cm (2 in.) of insulation. At least one manufacturer has a fan that keeps the oven exterior below 38°C (100°F). The door is the drop-down type with sturdy hinges or brackets that support it in the drop-down position at the same level as the oven bottom. The rack and load may be pulled out without actually reaching into the cavity. The oven is supported on adjustable legs that should be at least 10 cm (4 in.) high (figure 8.1).

The top and bottom of the oven cavity are 0.6 cm (0.25 in.) thick ceramic glass or quartz, behind which are the heating elements. The 1800–5000 watts of the oven are equally divided between the top and bottom elements. The remainder of the oven interior and door is stainless steel. The thermostat bulb may be between the heating elements and the ceramic plate at the top element.

With the exception of breads and pastries that are baked at comparatively low temperatures, most foods are best cooked on a rack at heights of 1.9 cm (0.75 in.) or 3.8 cm (1.5 in.). One manufacturer has a wire rack that provides a height of 1.9 cm (0.75 in.) when placed in the oven one way and 3.8 cm (1.5 in.) when inverted. For controls, most of the ovens have on-off, cook-clean, and top-bottom switches, heater indicator light, temperature setting dial, and timer dial (1–60 minutes).

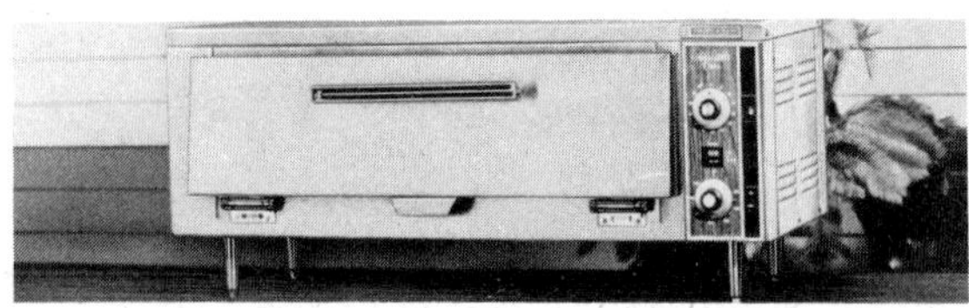

FIGURE 8.1. Infrared oven. Courtesy Lincoln Manufacturing Co., Inc.

The external width of the oven varies from 46 cm (18 in.) to 98 cm (39 in.), from 25.4 cm (10 in.) to 66.7 cm (26 in.) in depth, and from 30 cm (12 in.) to 56 cm (22 in.) in height. The oven cavity varies from 46 cm (18 in.) to 69 cm (27 in.) in width, from 30 cm (12 in.) to 61 cm (24 in.) in depth, and from 10 cm (4 in.) to 36 cm (14 in.) in height. Part of the wide range in exterior height is due to the variability in leg length.

Determination of Needed Capacity

As most quartz infrared ovens will hold only one or two 30-x-51-cm (12-x-20-in.) steam table pans, there is not much difficulty in determining capacity needs. One has only to decide what foods to heat, in what quantities, and in what time. If five pans of food must be heated in one hour and the calculated total cooking time for them is less than 60 minutes, then a single one-pan oven will suffice. If 8–10 pans are needed or the total heating time is over 60 minutes, the requirement would be a two-pan oven or two one-pan ovens.

Basic Use and Operation

Because ovens built by different companies vary in the operating steps to be followed, the procedure used for one oven will be given here to demonstrate what is involved.

1. Press power switch to on. Timer should be on hold.
2. Turn temperature dial to 343°C (650°F).
3. Press top-bottom heat switches to on until heat indicator light goes off. This should be on at each use as some ovens cycle through a range of up to 56°C (100°F).

4. Set cook-clean switch to cook. Set temperature dial to desired cooking time, insert food, and close door.
5. Set timer dial to proper cooking times.
6. When buzzer sounds, remove food and turn timer to hold.

In working with quartz infrared ovens, begin by using the manufacturer's instructions and process time until these are found to be erroneous. In most cases they will be less than required. A record should be kept of additional times and the original times corrected for the next use. Some cooks use 75 percent of conventional cooking times. However, while this may work with some products with a thickness of 5.1 cm (2 in.), it would not work with others of 2.5 cm (1 in.) thickness.

The variables that should be considered in setting processing times for the quartz infrared oven are:

1. Initial temperature of the product. As the temperature of the product becomes lower, the heating time becomes longer. Heating from the frozen state adds the heat needed to bring the product up to thawing through the thawing process plus the thawed heating or cooking heat needs.

2. Density of the product. The denser the product, the more time it takes to heat it, and generally, the lower the cavity temperature should be. Consideration should be given to the fact that the cold spot in the food will continue to receive heat for some time after it is removed from the oven.

3. Depth of product in the pan. In infrared heating, the depth should not be more than 5.1 cm (2 in.) as it will tend to overcook either on the top or bottom before heating through.

4. Temperature of cavity. The higher the cavity temperature, the faster the heating process will be. Care must be exercised in selecting foods for high-temperature cooking to ensure that the food can quickly conduct the heat to its interior before the exterior becomes overheated.

5. Use of top or bottom heat, or both. Broiled foods will need only top heat; those where conduction is most important will depend on only bottom heat. However, most foods can use both top and bottom heat, the former to brown the product and the latter to heat the pan and the cavity.

6. Placement in cavity. Initially, most quartz infrared ovens cooked products placed in the bottom of the oven cavity. This tended to cause burning-on of some foods on the pan bottoms and excessive drying out of the outer surfaces of the food while waiting for the top and the food mass interior to heat. Some users reduced bottom heat to allow the top heat to complete its functions but this increased total time. A better answer to the problem is to raise the food off the oven bottom by use of a 1.9 cm (0.75 in.) rack. This reduces bottom overcooking and, at the same time, moves the food closer to the top elements, which speeds top cooking. To assist broiling, additional height was needed in a rack to move the food closer to the top, or broiling element. As mentioned before, one manufacturer built this added height into the 1.9 cm (0.75 in.) rack which could be inverted and support the broiling food 3.8 cm (1.5 in.) off the oven bottom. This does add to the danger of burning in fat-rich foods.

The oven is hotter in the rear than in the front of the cavity. For some foods this does not matter, but for most foods it is best to turn the food halfway through the cooking period.

7. Type of pan. Shiny aluminum utensils reflect heat and add to the cooking time by 10–20 percent over black aluminum pans. Utensils made of aluminum have better heat conductivity than stainless steel and thus have shorter cooking times (see table 8.1).

8. Oven heights. When two ovens of different heights are compared as to cooking speed, the lower one should be faster and use less energy.

9. Wattage. This is by no means the least consideration. Most quartz infrared ovens have

TABLE 8.1. **Pans Used in Quartz Infrared Ovens**

Code Number	*Pan Size*	*Material*
1	30 x 51 x 6.3 cm (12 x 20 x 2.5 in.)	corrosion-resistant steel
2	30 x 25 x 6.3 cm (12 x 10 x 2.5 in.)	corrosion-resistant steel
3	30 x 19 x 6.3 cm (12 x 7.5 x 2.5 in.)	corrosion-resistant steel
4	30 x 51 x 6.3 cm (12 x 20 x 2.5 in.)	aluminum
5	30 x 25 x 6.3 cm (12 x 10 x 2.5 in.)	aluminum
6	10 x 23 x 3.8 cm (4 x 9 x 1.5 in.)	aluminum foil
7	25 cm (10 in.)	aluminum skillet
8	23 cm (9 in.)	aluminum pie pan
9	23 cm (9 in.)	aluminum cake pan
10	15 x 23 x 2.5 cm (6 x 9 x 1 in.)	aluminum bake pan
11	34 x 22 x 4.4 cm (13.5 x 8.75 x 1.75 in.)	glass
12	23 cm (9 in.)	glass cake pan
13	7.6 x 20 x 4.4 cm (3 x 8 x 1.75 in.)	aluminum loaf pan
14	120 ml (0.5 cup)	glass custard cup

fixed wattages with change possible only by turning off either the top or bottom element. At least one oven does have variable wattage. In general, with all other factors equal, the greater the wattage input, the shorter the cooking time.

Each manufacturer has set processing times and has developed details of preparation for a number of foods and conditions where they feel their equipment fills a foodservice need. Review of some of the results from testing these indicates that some of these times are less than half of the actual times required. Table 8.2 contains researched times and recommended use details for a 2500-watt quartz infrared oven as developed by Schwartz and Avery (1975).

TABLE 8.2. **Quartz Infrared Oven Cooking Details**
(Low rack 1.9 cm [0.75 in.] and high rack 3.8 cm [1.5 in.] from deck)

Food Product	*Pan Number*	*Product Depth*	*Temperature*	*Time (min)*	*Details*
Meat and Fish					
Barbecued spareribs (fresh)	1	5.1 cm (2 in.)	343°C (650°F)	30–35	baste every 10 min; low rack
Beef Burgundy (precooked)	5	3.2 cm (1.25 in.)	399°C (750°F)	30–35	cover at 20 min; low rack
Beef and cheese patties (fresh)	10	0.6 cm (0.25 in.)	343°C (650°F)	8	low rack
Chicken cacciatore (precooked)	5	3.8 cm (1.5 in.)	343°C (650°F)	25–30	break ice and cover after 15 min; low rack
Haddock (precooked, partially frozen)	1	3.2 cm (1.25 in.)	399°C (750°F)	23	low rack
Haddock steak (fresh)	2	2.2 cm (0.88 in.)	343°C (650°F)	16–20	low rack
Hamburger patties (fresh)	10	1.3 cm (0.5 in.)	343°C (650°F)	11–13	do not turn; high rack or none
Hot dogs	10	1.3 cm (0.5 in.)	343°C (650°F)	5–6	high rack
Lasagna (precooked)	2	7.6 cm (3 in.)	399°C (750°F)	42–45	cover after 20 min; low rack
Lobster tails (fresh)	wrap in foil	2.5 cm (1 in.)	343°C (650°F)	15–18	low rack

TABLE 8.2. ***(continued)***
(Low rack 1.9 cm [0.75 in.] and high rack 3.8 cm [1.5 in.] from deck)

Food Product	*Pan Number*	*Product Depth*	*Temperature*	*Time (min)*	*Details*
Meat and Fish					
Marzetti (precooked)	5	4.4 cm (1.75 in.)	343°C (650°F)	36–38	low rack
Rainbow trout (fresh); 227 g (8 oz)	2	2.5 cm (1 in.)	343°C (650°F)	12–15	cover after 8 min; low rack
Salisbury steak (precooked)	2	3.8 cm (1.5 in.)	343°C (650°F)	30–35	cover after 15 min; low rack
Stuffed peppers (precooked)	5	5.1 cm (2 in.)	399°C (750°F)	30–35	cover after 20 min; low rack
Submarine sandwich	foil bag	5.1 cm (2 in.)	343°C (650°F)	18	no rack
Sweet-sour pork (precooked)	6	2.2 cm (0.88 in.)	399°C (750°F)	18–20	cover; low rack
Turkey and dressing (precooked)	4	2.5 cm (1 in.)	399°C (750°F)	27–32	cover after 15 min; low rack
Veal parmigiana (precooked)	5	3.2 cm (1.25 in.)	343°C (650°F)	25	cover after 15 min; low rack
Yankee pot roast (fresh)	4	3.2 cm (1.25 in.)	399°C (750°F)	30–35	cover after 15 min; low rack
Vegetables					
Asparagus (frozen)	2	7.6 cm (3 in.)	399°C (750°F)	25	cover last 10 min; no rack
Cauliflower, casserole (frozen)	6	2.5 cm (1 in.)	343°C (650°F)	26	no cover; low rack
Corn on cob (fresh)	foil bag	5.1 cm (2 in.)	343°C (650°F)	10–15	low rack
Corn (frozen)	2	7.6 cm (3 in.)	399°C (750°F)	18	stir 3 times; no rack
Potatoes, baked	none	Medium	343°C (650°F)	25–30	no wrap; low rack
Potatoes, cottage fried (fresh)	7	2.5 cm (1 in.)	343°C (650°F)	10	stir every 3 min; no rack
Potatoes, escalloped (frozen)	2	3.2 cm (1.25 in.)	399°C (750°F)	18	low rack
Potatoes, French fried (frozen)	12	0.6 cm (0.25 in.)	343°C (650°F)	10	single layer; no rack
Spinach (frozen)	12	7.6 cm (3 in.)	399°C (750°F)	40	Stir 3 times; no rack
Heated Entrées					
Bacon	10	0.3 cm (0.13 in.)	343°C (650°F)	2.5–3	no rack
Beef and noodles (precooked)	2	5.1 cm (2 in.)	399°C (750°F)	9	low rack
Beef, T-bone steak	10	2.5 cm (1 in.)	343°C (650°F)	9–12	turn after 5 min; low rack
Chicken a la king (precooked)	3	3.2 cm (1.25 in.)	343°C (650°F)	15	low rack
Chicken, baked (fresh)	10	1.8 kg (4 lb)	288°C (550°F)	17–25	cover after 10 min; low rack
Fish fillets (fresh)	1	3.8 cm (1.5 in.)	343°C (650°F)	10–12	low rack
Hamburger patties (fresh)	10	1.9 cm (0.75 in.)	343°C (650°F)	9	do not turn; high rack
Pork chops, baked (fresh)	2	2.5 cm (1 in.)	343°C (650°F)	15–20	low rack
Seafood au gratin, (precooked)	9	5.1 cm (2 in.)	399°C (750°F)	20	low rack
Submarine sandwiches	wrap in foil	5.1 cm (2 in.)	343°C (650°F)	7	no rack

TABLE 8.2. (continued)
(Low rack 1.9 cm [0.75 in.] and high rack 3.8 cm [1.5 in.] from deck)

Food Product	Pan Number	Product Depth	Temperature	Time (min)	Details
Miscellaneous					
Bagels (fresh)	10	3.8 cm (1.5 in.)	343°C (650°F)	10–15	no rack
Biscuits (fresh)	10	1.2 cm (0.5 in.)	399°C (750°F)	10	cover after 5 min; low rack
Cake, chocolate (fresh)	9	3.2 cm (1.25 in.)	288°C (550°F)	15–18	no top heat; low rack
Coffee cake (fresh)	9	5.1 cm (2 in.)	260°C (500°F)	20–25	low rack
Cornbread (fresh)	10	3.8 cm (1.5 in.)	288°C (550°F)	15–20	low rack
Crepes (fresh)	7	0.3 cm (0.13 in.)	343°C (650°F)	1.5	do not turn; no rack
Eggs, fried (fresh)	7	1.2 cm (0.5 in.)	343°C (650°F)	0.5–0.75	preheat pan; high rack
Omelet, cheese (fresh)	7	0.6 cm (0.25 in.)	343°C (650°F)	2.5–3	do not turn; no rack
Pancakes (fresh)	7	0.6 cm (0.25 in.)	343°C (650°F)	1.5–2	no rack; turn over before serving
Pie, pecan (frozen precooked)	8	2.5 cm (1 in.)	288°C (550°F)	15–17	no top heat; low rack
Pizza (fresh); 33 cm (13 in.) diameter	pizza pan	1.2 cm (0.5 in.)	343°C (650°F)	9–10	rotate at 5 min; no rack
Rolls, Parker house (frozen)	10	1.3 cm (0.5 in.)	288°C (550°F)	7	no top heat; low rack

Safety Considerations

One should wear asbestos gloves when reaching into the oven because the door, oven top and bottom, product pan, and the rack are all very hot and conventional hot pads are not enough.

The cook should never leave the vicinity of the oven while it is turned on, particularly if food is cooking, because of the fire danger.

Cooking on the high shelf should be done in a 5.1-cm (2-in.) high sided pan as fats may ignite. If they do, one should not panic but reach in with asbestos gloves, remove the flaming pan, set it on a metal table, and cover the top with a sheet pan that should always be close by. This will smother the flame and no harm will result. One should not try to smother the flame in the oven because it will rekindle. Do not pour water on the flame as it may spatter and spread the flame or burn the operator. A fire extinguisher should not be directed into the oven cavity as the material may shatter the quartz plates and splash the fat. A carbon dioxide extinguisher should be near in case the fire spreads outside the oven.

Large quantities of fat should not be used to cook anything in the oven. If fats fry out of sausage or bacon in quantities, the cooking pan should be removed from the oven and the surplus fat poured off before putting the pan back into the oven.

Special Applications

Most of the special applications of the quartz infrared oven have to do with its broiling ability. Operators want a broiler without the great heat output of a conventional broiler. Large restaurants use it for baked Alaskas, and smaller ones use it to toast and heat sandwiches, melt the cheese on apple pie, and brown casseroles made of precooked ingredients. Some use it to take the rawness from roast beef, quickly toast bread, soften the peels on citrus fruits, brown and heat grapefruit and orange halves, heat soups, and melt cheese on certain soups. As it is a newcomer to the restaurant equipment lists, much research remains on finding more uses for the equipment.

Pizza Ovens

Pizza ovens have most of the descriptive factors of conventional bake ovens. They generally range in external width from 65 cm to 198 cm (25.5 in. to 78 in.), in depth from 67 cm to 109 cm (26.5 in. to 43 in.), and in height from 18.4 cm to 20 cm (7.25 in. to 8 in.). The common size is approximately 137 × 91 × 48 cm (54 × 36 × 19 in.). Interior measurements vary from 56 cm to 152 cm (22 in. to 60 in.) wide, 69 cm to 91 cm (27 in. to 36 in.) deep, and 18.4 cm to 20 cm (7.5 in. to 8.0 in.) high. Heat input is about 7.2 kw per deck and is evenly divided between the elements under the deck and in the top of the oven cavity. The average gas oven may use 85,000 Btu per deck. Preheating to 288°C (550°F) takes about forty-five minutes in the electric oven.

Most of the pizza ovens use a welded frame of angle iron similar to the conventional roast and bake ovens. To this are bonded external sheets of 16-gauge steel. This may be corrosion-resistant steel with No. 4 finish, but most of the coatings on the sheet steel are baked-on or vitreous enamels in black or some shade of gray. It is recommended that the front be of 16-gauge corrosion-resistant steel because fumes that come out around the door stain it, and it sometimes requires abrasive cleaners to remove the stain from the door frame. This action would remove the enamels. The walls should be insulated with at least 10 cm (4 in.) of mineral wool or some other heat-stable insulation material of equal insulating qualities. Ovens with less insulation add much heat to the kitchen. In place of insulation in the oven bottom, most ovens have a 13-cm (5-in.) base with 10 cm (4 in.) of insulation under the bottom oven deck.

The legs may be of tubular steel or 14-gauge angle iron frame. It is desirable to have adjustable feet so that the oven may be leveled easily. Length of legs may be from 15 cm to 76 cm (6 in. to 30 in.) or more. The more decks used, the shorter the legs will be. The bottom of the top deck should be no higher than the armpit, and the lower oven should be no lower than the waist. This limits the oven combination to two oven decks. Three-and four-deck combinations should not be used except in cases of critical space shortage.

The oven door is best coated on both sides with corrosion-resistant steel, although some have aluminized steel on the interior and baked-on enamel for the exterior. While some doors have 3.8 cm (1.5 in.) of insulation, it is preferable to have 5.1 cm (2 in.). The doors may be counterbalanced with springs, but weights are more desirable since they require less maintenance. There are usually double-pane heat-treated glass windows in the doors so that progress of the baking pizza may be followed without opening the door; however, some doors are solid. The hinges should be sturdy enough to hold 91 kg (200 lb) of weight, and the door should drop down to the level of the oven deck. A handle should be placed far enough away from the door so that its temperature does not get above 52°C (125°F). Corrosion-resistant steel, bakelite, and similar materials are used in handles. These materials plus the construction help to maintain the desired temperature of the handle.

The oven interiors are usually made of aluminized steel to reflect the interior heat that strikes the walls and top. The decks are commonly made of heavy material that will store and give off much bottom heat. Materials include 5.1-cm (2-in.) tile or 2-2.2-cm (0.75-0.88 in.) coreplate, or 2-cm (0.75-in.) pizza plate. Transite is used in some cases because of its high emissivity, and steel decks are used sometimes. Most of the ovens have the door wide enough for the deck to be removed. The ovens have vents where the generated steam may escape so that a crisp crust formation is possible. They may have one or more lights.

Like the conventional ovens, the pizza ovens have four stop switches for both the top and bottom heating elements. The stops are set at 3.5 kw, 2.14 kw, 0.875 kw, and off. A thermostat controls temperature from 121°C to 315°C (250°F to 600°F). It has an off position. Some have on-off switches. There is a power-on light and a manual timer which, in some ovens, runs from 0 to 60 or 120 minutes. Gas ovens have a gas shut-off valve. If the oven has lights, there is a light switch.

The most common size of pizza oven will hold six 30-cm (12-in.) pizzas. With pizza ovens, capacity needs are calculated similarly to those of the infrared oven. If a pizza oven will bake six of a specific size and twelve are needed, then two ovens will meet requirements.

Pizza Oven Utilization

In the making of pizzas, the pizza is prepared on an aluminum pizza pan and placed in the oven with a wooden or metal peel. In general, the larger the pizza, the longer the cooking time. While manufacturers advertise five-minute baking, it takes a small, thin pizza to be prepared in that time. Four pizza restaurants in Lafayette, Indiana, were surveyed on the baking of 25–30-cm (10–12-in.) pizzas, and the temperatures used varied from 204°C to 302°C (400°F to 575°F) and baking times from seven to fifteen minutes.

Pizza ovens may be used to cook most of the foods prepared in conventional ovens except those that have a height over 20 cm (8 in.). Most of these foods can be cut so that they will fit into the pizza oven. For instance, turkeys over 7.3 kg (16 lbs) will not fit, but if they are divided lengthwise, the two halves can be roasted very well in a 20-cm (8-in.) oven and in an hour less time.

Alternatives to Quartz Infrared Ovens and Pizza Ovens

The main replacements for the quartz infrared oven are the microwave oven, the pressure cooker for speed, and the hearth broiler for browning. The forced convection oven does have some of the infrared oven attributes, but actually there is nothing quite like it. It is unfortunate that more restaurant operators are not willing to take the time to learn how to use the infrared oven to its fullest advantage and train kitchen personnel to use it without fear. Conventional ovens, forced convection ovens, and the mechanical oven may be used for pizza baking. The pizzas are acceptable, if not as good as those baked in a pizza oven.

Cleaning

1. Wipe up spills as they occur.
2. Set oven for "clean" and thermostat for 454°C (850°F). Leave both top and bottom units on for one hour with the door closed. The oven will shut off automatically.
3. When oven has cooled, wipe out the interior of the cavity to remove the ash.
4. Coat the door interior, when cool, with a good oven cleaner.
5. Wash oven exterior with a soft cloth, hot water, and detergent.
6. After the oven cleaner has been allowed to act for the recommended time, rinse the oven interior with clean water in the same way as the exterior.

Maintenance

1. Check the quartz plates for fractures. If plates are broken, replace them.
2. Check the heating elements periodically for burn-outs. To test the top element, cover the high rack with slices of day-old bread placed in the oven at 343°C (650°F). Set timer for about three to five minutes. At the end of that time, remove the rack and examine the tops of the toast. While there should be some difference in color (darkening) from front to rear, across the width of the rack the coloring should be fairly uniform. If there are white segments, it is probable that the top heating elements have burned out, and the maintenance service should be called to replace them.

   A similar test should be run on the lower element using the low rack. In this case, examine the bottom of the pieces of toast for uneven heating and the possibility of burned-out elements.

3. To test the thermostat, suspend a thermocouple in the middle of the oven and check it on a potentiometer when the oven "heat indicator" light goes off, indicating that the oven has reached the set temperature. It should not vary more than 8°C (15°F). If it varies more, it should be brought to the attention of the maintenance service.
4. Check the various indicator lights for lighting. Replace any burned-out lights.
5. Check the control knobs for looseness. Tighten the knobs.

Some door warpage may occur at high temperatures, but one manufacturer claims that the door will recover when cool and that tightness of fit is not essential to proper use. At least one oven has no door.

QUESTIONS

1. What is a quartz infrared oven?
2. What are the advantages and disadvantages of the quartz infrared oven?
3. What are the variables that must be considered in developing process times for the infrared oven?
4. What are the two primary dangers in infrared ovens and how does one protect against them?
5. What are some of the special applications?
6. What special advantage does the infrared oven have in regard to cleaning?
7. How does one clean the inside of the door?
8. What is the test for burned-out heating elements?
9. How is accuracy of the thermostat tested?
10. What are the primary uses of the infrared oven?
11. How high is the interior of a pizza oven?
12. What is the main requirement of a pizza oven deck?

BIBLIOGRAPHY

ANON. Antiquated food preparation. Is it eating into your profits? (leaflet). Irex Corp., Riverdale, N.J.

ANON. Litton quartz infrared oven/Model HE 5000 (leaflet). Litton Industries, Minneapolis.

ANON. Food preparation and cooking times (leaflet). Groen Division, Dover Corp., Elk Grove Village, Ill.

ANON. 1975. Use and care instructions for your Wearever Astro 12/200 oven. Lincoln Manufacturing Co., Fort Wayne, Ind.

JOECHEL, S. 1960. And don't forget infrared for heating a product. Reprint. *Product Engineering,* Feb.

SCHWARTZ, M., and AVERY, A. 1975. Purdue University's report on infrared oven. Purdue University, West Lafayette, Ind.

Mechanical Ovens

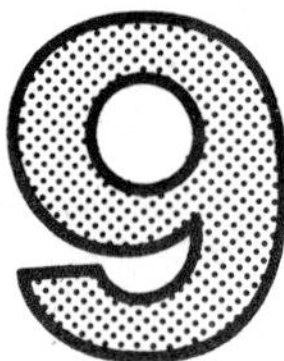

The mechanical oven with trays evolved from the conventional bake and roast ovens. Rather than having to travel from oven to oven to load and unload and to check on doneness, the cook or baker can do all of this in one location. A forced convection oven has advantages in heat distribution and speed; however, it must be small in order to control turbulence. The moving tray oven has many of the benefits of the forced convection oven but, at the same time, is a quantity production oven. Another advantage is the handling of the product at a comfortable height.

The revolving tray, reel, or ferris wheel oven became the major bakery oven of the 1930s. Like the ferris wheel, pans were suspended from double wheels that revolved in a gas or electrically heated chamber. The pans were pivoted so that they would remain level no matter what their position on the wheel. As these ovens turned out remarkably good products at low labor and energy cost, the next step was to increase the oven's capacity. Some reel ovens reached heights of two or three stories. They were expensive to install and operate and were unwieldy. Today the maximum number of trays for this type of oven is twelve (figure 9.1).

To get greater capacity in the moving tray oven, the trays are attached to chains that move from front to the rear horizontally. Then they circle around the wheel or transfer arm to a lower level. Here they return to the loading area at the front of

FIGURE 9.1. Reel type mechanical oven. Courtesy Despatch Industries, Inc.

the oven. In some cases, the food merely goes from one end to the other where it is unloaded. Then the tray or belt returns to the start for reloading. At the oven front, the tray is raised to the unload-load position. A food may take several trips through the oven before it is manually or mechanically unloaded (figure 9.2).

There are some ovens that move in a circular horizontal path at three to five levels. These are known as rotary ovens.

Although originally designed for baking, all of these ovens may be used for both roasting and baking. They are used in large institutional kitchens and commercial commissaries as well as large restaurants.

The ovens may be heated by: (1) direct burning of gas or heating by electric elements in the oven cavity; (2) indirect heating where the burning takes place in a separate chamber and the heat enters the oven through flues; or (3) recirculating heating that is similar to the indirect except that a portion of the gases, after circulating through the oven, is brought back to the combustion chamber for heating.

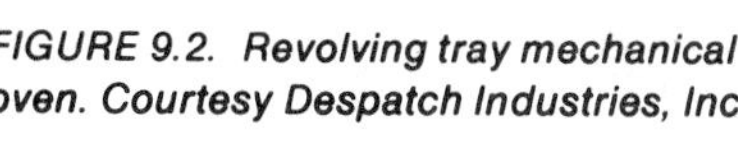

FIGURE 9.2. Revolving tray mechanical oven. Courtesy Despatch Industries, Inc.

Although unrelated to the mechanical ovens in operation or quantity food cooking, the pizza oven does have an important place in the family of ovens. Although specialized to provide high bottom heat for the baking of pizza crusts, the pizza oven does have overhead heat to brown the crust and melt the cheese. This makes it a general-purpose oven.

There is at least one manufacturer who combines the mechanical oven with the pizza oven in a multi-tier rotary oven. In from one to ten tiers, it will handle up to 43-cm (17-in.) pizzas at different temperatures from 38–482°C (100–900°F) with both top and bottom heat and at different times. Another manufacturer has a revolving tray oven which is advocated for baking pizzas (figure 9.3).

FIGURE 9.3. Revolving shelf pizza oven. Courtesy Despatch Industries, Inc.

Description and Specification

It would be difficult to give meaningful general specification details on mechanical ovens. Three of them, the reel, the traveling tray, and the rotary oven will be described briefly.

Reel Oven

A reel-type oven may have five trays that are 66 cm (26 in.) long and 142 cm, 188 cm, or 239 cm (56 in., 74 in., or 94 in.) wide. It would be 238 cm (7 ft, 10 in.) wide, 221 cm (7 ft, 3 in.) deep, and 208 cm (6 ft, 10 in.) high for the 142-cm (56-in.) wide tray oven. For the 188-cm and 239-cm (74-in. and 94-in.) trays, the oven widths would be 284 cm and 335 cm (9 ft, 4 in. and 11 ft), respectively. The indirectly heated oven is 13 cm (5 in.) wider. For the smaller tray oven, it would require 140,000 Btu of gas for direct heat and twice that amount for indirect heat and 39 kw if electrically heated. If the motor (0.33 HP) fails to work, there is a crank to move the reel so that the oven may be unloaded. The door is 30 cm (12 in.) high and varies in width according to the width of the tray. The tray has a clearance of 30 cm (12 in.). The door lifts vertically.

Exteriors may be white enamel, stainless steel, or forty-seven varieties of colors. The interior is aluminized steel. Provided with the oven are:

1. a temperature control with a range of 38–343°C (100–650°F)
2. on-off and igniter switches
3. a tray indicator to show what number tray is at the unloading door
4. a reversing switch to control tray position
5. interior light
6. a 1–60-minute timer

If the pans jam between the tray and the oven door frame, there is a control that shuts off the rotor motor.

The 142-cm (56-in.) tray oven will cook fifteen 46-x-66-cm (18-x-26-in.) sheet pans, twenty-five 31-x-51-cm (12-x-20-in.) steam table pans, one hundred 0.45-kg (1-lb) loaves of bread, or eighty-five 23-cm (9-in.) pies at one time. Twice these amounts of low height foods may be cooked if a wire rack is added to double-deck each tray. However, in most ovens, much unevenness of cooking and coloring often results.

Traveling Tray Oven

Most of the traveling tray ovens are rather sizable and probably have no place except in a large bakery or other food manufacturing plant. One of the smaller traveling ovens has ten trays 66 x 284 cm (26 x 112 in.). To take care of these requires an oven 4 m (13.5 ft) wide, 5.8 m (19.1 ft) long, and 2 m (6.66 ft) high. This gives about 18.8 sq m (202 sq ft) of hearth area, which will handle approximately 458 kg (1010 lbs) of dough. To bake this dough, about 500 Btu per 0.45 kg (1 lb) of dough or 2,500 Btu per 0.09 sq m (1 sq ft) of hearth is needed. The exterior is 18-gauge steel with a coating of white porcelain on the front, sides, and rear. The top is covered with 18-gauge steel sheets. Inside this exterior sheathing is a ventilated 15-cm (6-in.) space and inside this is 20 cm (8 in.) of granulated rock wool on the sides and 25 cm (10 in.) on the top. The 18-gauge steel base is covered with 8.8 cm (3.5 in.) of the granulated rock wool. Inside the insulation is a lining of aluminized 18-gauge steel.

The loading door covers the full length of the tray at the front of the oven. The conveyor consists of a chain with a 13-cm (5.25-in.) pitch and 6.3-cm (2.5-in.) rollers to really carry the weight of the tray on the tracks. The driving is done by a 3/4 HP motor operating through a variable speed changer, worm gear speed reducer, and driving sprockets operating on the conveyor chain. This oven has a hand wheel to drive the conveyor if the electric drive mechanism fails. The trays can be made to move forward or backward or stop by pressing buttons. A tray indicator shows the number of the tray at the loading door. A tray timing device times the stopping period from five to sixty seconds, as set. A timer may be set between one and sixty minutes and sound an alarm when the time is up.

Rotary Oven

This oven utilizes circular shelves that move horizontally around a central axis. The ovens vary in external width from 122 cm to 231 cm (48 in. to 91 in.), in depth from 132 cm to 234 cm (52 in. to 92 in.), and in height from 193 cm to 206 cm (76 in. to 81 in.). The exterior finish may be black enamel or stainless steel, or may be decorated to taste. They may have one to four 69-x-74-cm (27-x-29-in.) stainless steel doors and occupy floor space 1.6 sq m to 5.3 sq m (17.5 sq ft to 56.7 sq ft) in area. They are heated by 96,000 Btu of gas with electric ignition. They will maintain temperatures up to 316°C (600°F).

Most ovens have three to five shelves which vary in diameter from 91 cm to 193 cm (36 in. to 76 in.). The shelves may be 1.9-cm (0.75-in.) expanded steel, 0.6-cm (0.25-in.) aluminum alloy, or 1.9-cm (0.75-in.) transite. The distance between shelves is 16.5 cm or 22 cm (6.5 in. or 8.5 in.). There is an indicating thermostat, quartz light, a switch to operate the rotor at 4 revolutions per minute, and gas burner controls. The capacity ranges between one and twenty-five 46-x-66-cm (18-x-26-in.) sheet pans.

Determination of Needed Capacity

The determination of the capacity of a mechanical oven is no different than for a conventional oven. To buy a mechanical oven that would bake 2,000 loaves of bread each eight-hour day, take the baking time of bread in a mechanical oven (35 minutes), add the loading and unloading time, possibly 10 minutes, or a total of 45 minutes per batch. Divide this into 480 minutes of an eight-hour day, and this shows eleven batches will be needed. Eleven batches divided into the 2,000 loaves needed indicates that an oven which holds 182 loaves will be required. A five-tray oven where the trays are 66 x 239 cm (26 x 94 in.) will do the job, according to the manufacturer's literature.

If other products govern the size of the oven, then one similarly determines the number of a particular size of pan needed for each batch and finds an oven that will hold that number. If the manufacturer does not have this information available, then one calculates the number of pans that will fit on the various sizes of trays and finds an oven that has the tray size–tray number combination that makes up the desired capacity. Then one must determine whether he has enough space to install the oven.

At least one manufacturer provides information on the sizes of ovens to be purchased for preparing various numbers of meals. For instance, 1,000 meals a day would require an oven with five 66-x-96-cm (26-x-38-in.) trays; 2,000 meals would require an oven with four 66-x-239-cm (26-x-94-in.) trays.

Basic Use and Operation

The operation of the mechanical tray oven entails preheating the oven by setting the thermostat to the desired temperature and turning on the heat to bring the oven to the desired temperature. Then the oven is loaded as quickly as possible and the door is closed quickly to prevent loss of heat. At the end of the cooking cycle, the food is removed and the next load is added. Mixed loads of products may be cooked if they use the same temperature and the removal time for each tray is kept in mind.

Mechanical Oven Uses

University Hospitals, Iowa City, "fries" chicken by dipping the chicken in evaporated milk and cornflake crumbs and baking it on greased sheet pans for one hour. They find that casseroles of various fresh fillings and a great variety of toppings add variety to patients' meals. The mechanical ovens do a good job of cooking these. Souffles are cooked in rotary ovens at Greenbrier Hotel in White Sulphur Springs, West Virginia. At the University of Maryland, custards are baked at 163°C (325°F) in baking pans set in roasting pans of water. Plaza Hotels in San Antonio, Texas prepare suckling pigs in the mechanical ovens. Ohio University in Athens finds the chicken avocado casserole is a top favorite and that casseroles, in general, are the most often prepared items in the mechanical ovens. See tables 9.1 and 9.2 for manufacturer's time-temperature recommendations for products cooked in mechanical ovens.

Special Applications

Mechanical ovens seem to have no special applications, but they can be used for most of the foods prepared in conventional roast, bake, general-purpose, and forced convection ovens. Some mechanical ovens cannot handle very large roasts of beef or turkeys because of the clearance above the tray. A few institutions without deep fat fryers fry chicken in roast pans half full of fat, placed in mechanical ovens. While the quality of the product is good, frying chicken or other foods in this way is extremely dangerous from the standpoint of possible fires and employee burns from fat. Under no conditions should this be done.

Alternatives to the Mechanical Oven

Most of the conventional ovens and forced convection ovens may be, and are, used in place of the mechanical ovens.

Cleaning Large Conveyor Ovens

1. The oven front and door should be washed after each day of use. The exterior of the oven should be washed weekly with warm water and detergent.
2. Spills on the trays should be cleaned up as they occur.
3. Most large mechanical ovens have an opening where a worker may enter the oven when it is cool. He should first clean the floor of loose material with a vacuum cleaner. Then the oven may be washed with hot water and detergent. Some use a gong brush, others a

cloth. After washing, the surfaces should be rinsed with clean water. In moving the shelves with a person inside the oven, only the hand crank should be used.

4. The trays are most difficult to clean. Where easy-to-remove soil is present, cloths moistened in detergent and warm water are used. Where it will not be troublesome, some individuals use gong brushes. The surfaces are rinsed and wiped dry. In most ovens, the trays may be removed and washed in the pot sink. The brackets may often be removed for cleaning in the pot sink.
5. After cleaning, the oven should be heated and operated for thirty minutes to dry all interior surfaces.

TABLE 9.1. ***Manufacturer's Time-Temperature Recommendations for Mechanical Oven—Meats***

Product	Temperature	Time (min per lb)
Beef		
Standing rib, well done	163°C (325°F)	33–35
Rolled rib, well done	163°C (325°F)	add 5–10 min to above
Rump, boneless	163°C (325°F)	30
Lamb		
Leg, medium	163°C (325°F)	30–35
Shoulder, bone in	163°C (325°F)	35
Pork		
Ham, whole, 6.35–7.26 kg (12–14 lb)	163°C (325°F)	16–18
Ham, half, 5.44–7.26 kg (14–16 lb)	163°C (325°F)	18–20
Leg, fresh, whole	163°C (325°F)	35–40
Loin, fresh	163°C (325°F)	35–40
Veal		
Leg	163°C (325°F)	30–40
Loin	163°C (325°F)	30–35
Shoulder, bone in	163°C (325°F)	35–40

Source: Despatch Oven Company, Food in Revolution, Oct. 1963.

TABLE 9.2. ***Manufacturer's Time-Temperature Recommendations for Mechanical Oven—Baked Goods***

Product	Temperature		Baking Time
	Starting	Baking	(min)
Baked goods			
Apple pie, fresh	218°C (425°F)	199°C (399°F)	35–40
Bread, white	210°C (410°F)	194°C (380°F)	30–35
Corn muffins	204°C (400°F)	185°C (365°F)	17–19
Cup cakes	177°C (350°F)	177°C (350°F)	24–26
Danish pastries, ring	182°C (360°F)	182°C (360°F)	12–19
Sheet cakes	163°C (325°F)	163°C (325°F)	50–56
Sugar cookies	177°C (350°F)	177°C (350°F)	18–22

Source: Despatch Oven Company, Food in Revolution, Oct. 1963.

Maintenance

There is no specific regimen to be followed in maintaining all mechanical ovens. Each manufacturer has a list of those things which should be checked. Rather than use unskilled personnel to do the maintenance work, it is recommended that professional, or otherwise skilled, maintenance workers be called. They should follow the factory-prescribed program set up by the manufacturer. One manufacturer recommends that the oil level in the speed reducer be checked once a month and brought up to the filler plug. The electric motor is to be oiled once a month with light machine oil. The main shaft should be oiled with just enough No. 2 cup grease to prevent rusting. No lubricants should be used on the bearings inside the oven as they are supposed to run dry.

Versatile Small Conveyor Ovens

Research in foodservice equipment is being directed toward minimizing energy absorption by equipment, cooking media, and environment, and toward concentrating heat on the food. Under optimum circumstances, wasteful one-time passages of heat could be minimized, and heat remaining in the cooking media returned to the heat generator as reusable energy. Continuously timed cooking cycles are another design aspect in development. They would reduce human error and lower the level of skill needed in operating the oven.

Several small conveyor ovens fulfill most of the requirements for the oven of tomorrow. One is the Wearever Impinger Oven, which heats air on one side of the conveyor in much the way that air is heated in a forced convection oven. The hot air is forced into distribution ducts, which carry it above and below the conveyor, where the food is being moved. The hot air is directed down and up (impinged) upon the moving food from ports in the distribution ducts (figure 9.4). No air is directed toward heating the oven interior or walls. After food contact, the hot air is drawn back into the heater and reused. In fact, the oven does not have doors—it has an open space—since the drawing action of doors would interfere with the controlled circulation of hot air.

Directing the heat on the food, removing the cool condensed moisture layer from the food, and quickly replacing it with hot air all increase product cooking speed. Pizzas cook about four times faster than in the average pizza oven and pans of frozen entrees cook twice as fast as in regular ovens. Biscuits bake in seven minutes, lobster tails cook in eight, frozen cookies in eight, and frozen hamburgers in 5.5 minutes.

While they vary in size, the average Impinger oven is 199 cm (78.5 in.) wide and 142 cm (56 in.) deep. They can be used as either single or double decks (figure 9.5).

Both the oven and interior are made of stainless steel. The stainless-steel belt, made of flexible wire, is 81 cm (32 in.) wide and 183 cm (72 in.) long and can be adjusted to travel through the oven in 2.5–20 minutes. The baking chamber is 89 cm (35 in.) long. There are eight multi-holed distribution ducts, but some holes can be covered with column plates if the entire width of the belt is not needed. Both belt and ducts can be disassembled for cleaning. The belt clearance is 8.3 cm (3.25 in.). Operating tempera-

TABLE. 9.3. Typical Processing Times for Conveyor Ovens

Product	*Time*	*Temperature*
Hamburger patties	5 min 50 sec	260°C (500°F)
Meatloaf (frozen)	40 min	163°C (325°F)
Bacon (thin sliced)	3 min 40 sec	288°C (550°F)
Pizza (thin)	5 min	260°C (500°F)
Macaroni-and-tuna casserole	25 min	177°C (350°F)
Sliced meat and cheese sandwich	3 min	260°C (500°F)
Muffins	17 min	149°C (300°F)
Biscuits	7 min	204°C (400°F)

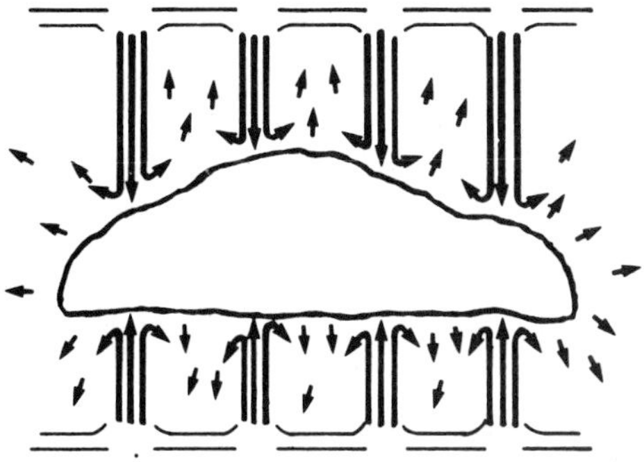

FIGURE 9.4. Heat is impinged on top and bottom of food in an Impinger oven. Courtesy Lincoln Manufacturing Company.

tures of 149°C (300°F) to 316°C (600°F) are provided by 120,000 Btu-capacity gas burners. There are electric units at 27 kw, smaller ovens for operators who want counter units, larger ovens, and two-deck units.

Oven Utilization

Cooking is timed from the moment the front edge of the pan enters the oven cavity until it starts to emerge at the exit. Belt speed can be varied according to needed time, or the product can be put through two or more times.

FIGURE 9.5. Wearever Impinger Oven. Courtesy Lincoln Manufacturing Company.

In conducting preliminary tests for using the oven with a new food, it is usual to lower the recipe temperature by 14°C (25°F) and decrease cooking time by one half. The temperature and time can then be adjusted, as in a conventional oven, until the proper degree of doneness and coloration is obtained. Thin products will cook in a short time at high temperature, since heat can reach the center quickly. Dense foods must be cooked at a lower temperature for a longer time, to prevent overcooking of the food surface before the heat reaches the product center.

Cleaning procedures are specific to each manufacturer's equipment. Follow their instruction sheets.

QUESTIONS

1. Describe the revolving tray, traveling tray, and rotary ovens.
2. What are the three ways of heating mechanical tray ovens?
3. What are the other names for the revolving tray oven?
4. If the drive motor fails, how is the oven unloaded?
5. How does one determine the capacity needed in a mechanical tray oven?
6. How may custards be baked in a mechanical oven?
7. Why are some mechanical ovens unable to handle large roasts?
8. What is the final step in cleaning a mechanical oven?
9. What is the feasibility of using the mechanical oven for frying?
10. What advantage does the impinger oven have over conventional ovens?
11. What is the effect on baking temperature and time when cooking thin foods?
12. What gives the impinger oven its special cooking effect?

BIBLIOGRAPHY

ANON. 1964. Cooking in quantity with a mechanical oven (leaflet). Middleby-Marshall Oven Co., Morton Grove, Ill.

ANON. 1966. Model L, built-for-life traveling tray oven (leaflet). Middleby-Marshall Oven Co., Morton Grove, Ill.

ANON, 1969. A brief encyclopedia of commercial ovens (leaflet). Middleby-Marshall Oven Co., Morton Grove, Ill.

ANON. Proposal and specifications, Despatch reversing airflow, rack type bakery oven, 52 bun pan capacity. Despatch Oven Co., Minneapolis.

ANON. Food in revolution (leaflet). Despatch Oven Co., Minneapolis.

ANON. Ovens: Revolving tray for baking, roasting (booklet). A.J. Fish Oven Co., Beloit, Wis.

ANON. 1973. Things you should know about ovens. *Quickservice Magazine* 3, No. 9, 20–25.

Microwave Ovens

Whereas conventional ovens may use convection, conduction, and radiation to heat a cavity and the food placed in it, the microwave oven depends on radiation alone to heat the food (figure 10.1). The cavity is not heated except as steam is formed from the product.

During World War II men aboard ships using radar noted that certain materials in front of the radar wave-projecting equipment got hot. At the same time, Dr. Percy Spencer, working on microwave applications for Raytheon Corporation, found that a candy bar melted in his pocket. Attributing this to the microwaves, he built a cavity and directed microwaves into it. This became the first microwave oven. After the war, several companies, including Raytheon, began to investigate the introduction of microwaves into an oven for the

FIGURE 10.1. Microwave oven. Courtesy Litton Microwave Cooking Products.

purpose of cooking food. Some of these ovens were very large. One built for the U.S. Navy would have held an ox. The magnetrons stood 0.9 m (3 ft) high. Because they were expected to do everything a conventional oven would do, but faster, they were not too successful.

Microwaves are very short electromagnetic waves that move with the speed of light and have a wave length between that of the ultra-high television band and the infrared bands which are important to much cooking and other heating equipment. They have wave lengths between 1 mm and 1 m (0.04 in. and 39 in.). The wave lengths from the industrial, scientific, and medical bands assigned to microwave ovens are 915 and 2450 Megahertz (MHz, a million cycles per second). Wave lengths of 915 MHz are 32.7 cm (12.9 in.) long and those of 2450 MHz are 12.23 cm (4.82 in.) long. In the magnetron, the heated cathode gives off negatively charged electrons that are attracted by the anode that surrounds it. An induced magnetic field around the anode bends the electrons into an orbital path past resonant cavities in the anode. This causes them to oscillate at high frequency. An antenna picks them up and directs them into the wave guide and down into the cavity.

A simplified version of how microwave heating occurs is to assume that food molecules are polar but are randomly oriented. Under the effect of microwave electric field reversal, they attempt to follow and this spin and generate heat. They are restricted by various factors such as the rigidity of ice or the viscosity of molasses. Some loss of heat effectiveness occurs when they cannot turn completely but, because of the reduced movement, penetration is greater in ice than in water.

Erroneously, microwave cooking is called "cooking from the inside out." This is not the case as the microwaves start to give up their capability to reverse molecules at the surface of the food if the molecules there are polar. However, the waves do penetrate to varying depths depending on the moisture content and density of the food. The 915 MHz wave loses about half of its strength in 7.6 cm (3 in.) of water and 0.8 cm (0.33 in.) of steak, while the 2450 MHz wave loses half its strength in 1.3 cm (0.5 in.) of water and 0.25 cm (0.1 in.) of steak. It will penetrate about 3.8 cm (1.5 in.) maximum in beef.

The most important factors that affect microwave penetration are the food's specific heat, chemical and physical state, temperature, and density, and the wave length used.

While its penetration is greater, the 915-MHz wave heats food somewhat slower than the 2450-MHz wave as its product molecules do not spin as fast and thus do not generate as much heat. In addition to reducing wave length to speed cooking of a food, one can increase power input. For each doubling of wattage input into the cooking cavity, cooking time is approximately halved. Chicken being roasted may take the following time reduction pattern:

Power input (watts)	*Cooking time per pound (min)*
200	24
800	6
1600	3
4000	1.2

In its operation, the microwave oven takes 110- or 220-volt current and converts it to the 4000- to 6000-volt current needed by the magnetron for conversion into microwaves. These waves are carried down to a resonant chamber where they bounce around (until absorbed by food) and generate heat. Cooking power is directly proportional to microwave intensity per square inch of surface. The microwave power is usually about 50 percent efficient in its conversion to heat. Microwaves may be conducted, reflected, absorbed, and transmitted.

Microwave ovens have the following advantages and disadvantages:

Advantages	*Disadvantages*
fast cooking	cooks some foods unevenly
does not present a cleaning problem if it has no browning unit	has hot and cold spots
	requires an expert to repair it

cool cooking	must be grounded
presents no burn or fire hazard	needs skilled operator for full use
has great variety of uses	easily overcooks food
designed for safety	does not brown most foods

Description and Specification

The microwave oven may be said to have ten major components:

1. The power supply converts line current to a voltage that the magnetron can handle to develop microwaves.
2. Most restaurants use one or two magnetron units; manufacturing plants using microwaves for drying use them in multiple units along a processing conveyor. The magnetron must be cooled by air, and this heat comes out into the kitchen.
3. The wave guide or transmitter is a device for moving the microwaves from the microwave generator to the oven cavity.
4. The coupling device transfers the energy from the wave guide to the cavity.
5. Disk or propeller type wave stirrers are needed because energy waves have a tendency to bounce around the cavity walls in regular patterns and strike the food in set places causing local overheating. They are located at the point where the waves enter the cavity. This problem of spot overheating is solved, in some cases, by placing the food on a turntable that moves the food in a circle as it cooks.
6. The rectangular cavity assists the wave stirrer in its prevention of standing waves, but the cavity may be of almost any shape.
7. A shelf is sometimes used to get the food off the oven bottom so that it may be subjected to microwaves from all sides.
8. One or more cutoff switches are integrated with the door to shut off microwaves to the cavity when the door is open. Much attention is given to leakage of microwaves from the cooking device. Thus the door plays a major part in containing the waves in the cavity and also serves as a means of introducing and removing food from it.
9. Switches, timers, and indicating lights assist the cook in making proper use of the oven.
10. Stainless steel or vinyl on steel sheathing or housing protects the wiring and other dangerous works of the microwave oven. They also make it attractive and easy to keep clean. The magnetron and other internal parts may be in the top, back, side, or base of the cabinet.

Power Aspects

While restaurant or institutional microwave ovens vary in wattage output from 200 to 3000 watts or more, most commercial ovens range between 600 and 2000 watts. To make available this output from 100 to 120 volts or 220 to 240 volts current, the device must start with more than twice the desired wattage. Examples of wattage from various manufacturers are:

Input	*Output*
2200	1000
3250	1350
1700	750
2800	1200
4800	2000
5450	2500

Power efficiency, the percentage of the power input that is made available as microwaves in the cooking cavity, is determined by the following formula:

$$\frac{\text{output in watts}}{\text{input in watts}} = \text{percentage efficiency}$$

An example would be:

$$\frac{\text{output 2500 watts}}{\text{input 5000 watts}} = \text{50 percent efficiency}$$

The ovens mentioned above would have the following percentage efficiencies: (1) 45, (2) 42, (3) 44,

(4) 42, (5) 42, (6) 46. By comparison, electric range top units have an efficiency of 60–65 percent, commercial electric ovens have 10–25 percent, and a U.S. Navy oven has 35 percent. As far as cooking is concerned, about 20–25 percent of the wattage going into the microwave oven raises food temperature.

Many microwave ovens do not have the wattage output indicated by the manufacturer. They may vary from 10–30 percent. Also, the power output of a microwave oven may change considerably over one day of use. A quick way to check the power output is to place one pint of water in a glass dish and take its temperature before and after a one-minute cook. The difference in degrees Fahrenheit multiplied by 17.5 gives the approximate wattage output.

A similar test can be run by heating one liter of water in a glass container for one minute and measuring the temperature change in degrees Centigrade after stirring. This, multiplied by 67, gives the power ouput of the oven.

Heat Distribution

Another consideration is the wave distribution within the cooking compartment. This compartment is generally made of deep-drawn stainless steel to reflect the microwaves. Aluminum is used sometimes. To permit the food to be accessible to waves from all sides, it may be placed on a wire, plastic, or glass shelf that can rest on the oven bottom or in several fixed positions up to 15 cm (6 in.) from the bottom of the cavity. Many ovens have no shelf. If a sheet cake is placed on the shelf or bottom and the power is turned on, the cake will rise in big brown bubbles in some places and remain uncooked in others. This is caused by the waves going in fixed paths. To compensate for this deficiency, a cook may move the food around the oven compartment or turn some foods over. The manufacturer has sought to minimize the deficiency by installing slotted disk or vane type stirrers that reflect the microwaves in many directions. Actually, the designers prefer to have most of the waves strike in a circle around the center of the oven where the food is commonly placed. Another expedient used is a turntable, usually plastic, that spins the food around under the area where the wave guide directs the microwaves into the oven.

However, some knowledge of the unevenness of a microwave oven is desirable before a purchase is made. Various techniques used to determine this are:

1. Cupcakes in glass cups may be distributed over the oven floor or shelf and evenness of baking observed after an adequate period of baking.
2. Glasses or cups of water distributed evenly over the oven bottom or shelf can be measured for temperature rise. In one test, Wilhelm and Satterlee (1971) found that nine water containers varied in temperature from 67°C (152°F) to 84°C (183°F) with the two extremes being adjacent to each other and the hottest in one corner. In another oven, the temperature variation was from 41°C (105°F) to 59°C (138°F), but in this oven the glass of water that was hottest in the previous test was the coldest in this test.
3. A glass plate, of a size that covers the oven bottom, can be covered with liquid egg white and subjected to a short cook. The hot spots will quickly turn white while the low heat areas will remain clear. Because it is difficult to get an even egg white coating, this test is little used.
4. I recommend use of heat-sensitive paper such as Thermofax. The oven bottom or shelf is covered with heavy black building paper on which the heat sensitive paper is placed to cover the top surface completely. The oven power is turned on until a definite pattern of dark spots or areas is apparent on the test paper. Dark areas indicate hot spots. This technique does not sense waves reflecting from the oven bottom.

Safety

One of the points of contention in the purchase and use of microwave ovens is the possible danger involved in their use. The radiation that might escape from the microwave oven is non-ionizing, which means that it does not normally cause irreversible chemical changes. Some scientists indicate a wide range of physical harms are possible from microwave radiation, but the literature is bare of any authenticated cases of human damage. However, it is claimed that burns, cataracts, pacemaker interference, and temporary sexual impotence are possible. None has been shown.

The U.S. Department of Health and Human Services' performance standards for microwave ovens provide for no more radiation than 1 mw/cm^2 or 1 mw per sq cm measured 5.1 cm (2 in.) from the oven. This stringent requirement is placed on the oven at the manufacturer's plant. In a restaurant, it should not be any higher than 5 mw per sq cm. The measurement requires a special meter. While fluorescent tubes or neon tubes may be used to indicate some leakage, they cannot be used to determine the level of loss. If there is any doubt about the safety of the oven, the maintenance service should be called.

While the entire oven is suspect for leakage and should be checked, in actuality the space between the door and the frame is the most frequent source of leakage. A few doors, especially those of the smaller ovens, are solid, but most microwave oven doors are made of aluminum or stainless steel and have small perforations in the door so that the product may be viewed without opening the door. The holes are too small for the waves to escape. Many ovens have a glass over the screen to prevent introduction of objects through the holes. The door and frame are designed to fit tightly so that microwaves do not escape. As a second safeguard there is a choke seal in the regular door seal. This sets up an electronic field to neutralize any microwaves that get as far as the seal.

To obviate the danger of opening the door with the power on, the ovens have an interlock switch that automatically shuts off the microwave input when the oven door is open. However, foolish workers in the past have depressed the switch by hand and opened the door, thus exposing themselves to danger. To counter this, most ovens now have two switches, at least one of which is not noticeable and cannot be circumvented easily. Some ovens have interlocks that shut off power when the outside sheathing or wrap is violated and another that shuts off the power if the shelf is not in place.

Ventilation

Many microwave ovens are underventilated. Although they may have a screen through which air is forced by a fan at some location in the cooking cavity, any large amount of moist food will cause a considerable number of water droplets to condense on the oven walls. Except when the oven is to be cleaned, excessive moisture wastes heat and is undesirable. A rough test of ventilation efficiency may be conducted by baking four 170-g (6 oz) potatoes or heating 907 g (2 qt) of water in a 34-×-25-cm (13.5-×-9.75-in.) glass dish for ten minutes. If the oven walls are heavily coated with water drops, the ventilation is suspect. The air going into the cavity is usually filtered.

Supplemental Heating

Browning foods has been a problem with microwave cooking since its inception. Various types of salt-heavy or dark coatings on the food have been tried as well as use of materials that absorb much of the microwave and pass it on to the food surface as heat. Manufacturers were reluctant to install infrared browning units as then they would lose the cool-cooking feature of microwave. However, in time, infrared elements were installed in some microwave ovens as broiler elements to brown the top of foods. Generally it takes at least fifteen minutes of cooking before any browning action is noted.

Another solution is the browning dish, which is made of a high-heat ceramic. This dish may be placed in the oven to absorb microwaves and generate heat within itself. When it is hot, steak or cottage-fried potatoes may be placed on it, and the dish returned to the oven for the normal cooking period. Halfway through this period, the steak is turned and the potatoes stirred to give a typical browning. Often the second browning (after the food is turned) is not very effective, since the dish has lost much of its initial heat. This expedient is probably not useful for more than one portion at a time.

At least one manufacturer makes a forced convection-microwave oven that can both cook fast and brown. Another oven has microwaves entering the cavity top and bottom. While this does not improve browning, it seems to turn out better baked items. Still another oven has a steam atmosphere that does not brown either, but it is said to reduce food moisture losses.

Controls and Protective Devices

Microwave ovens have been prone to suffer magnetron damage from operating the ovens with little or no load. This causes heat to back up to the magnetron. Today this is not so much of a problem. The newer ovens have a thermal cut-off in addition to the magnetron air-cooling system to protect the magnetron. One oven has a ferrite isolator that diverts the reflected energy away from the magnetron. Several systems cut off automatically when there is no load in the oven. Circuit breakers may also be used to protect against electrical overload.

There are a variety of timers available. Those frequently used for microwave ovens are: (1) electro-mechanical dial type, from seconds to twenty or thirty minutes (figure 10.2); (2) electro-mechanical push-button type; and (3) solid state push-button type.

When the cooking time is completed, usually an alarm sounds and power shuts off. At least one domestic microwave oven manufacturer has added a meat probe that constantly senses the temperature of a food being cooked. When it reaches a set temperature, it sounds an alarm and shuts off the oven. Allowance should be made for continuing rise in temperature after the power shuts off.

The combination of indicator lights and controls varies. Most ovens have power on-off switches and power-on indicator lights. There may be lights to indicate that the oven is ready to cook and others to indicate when the cooking is going on and when the process is complete. Some have hidden on-off switches to prevent the turning on of the oven during nonoperational times. There is a button to start the cooking process. Some have defrost controls that alternately turn the oven on and off for set periods of time from 15 to 120 seconds. A few ovens

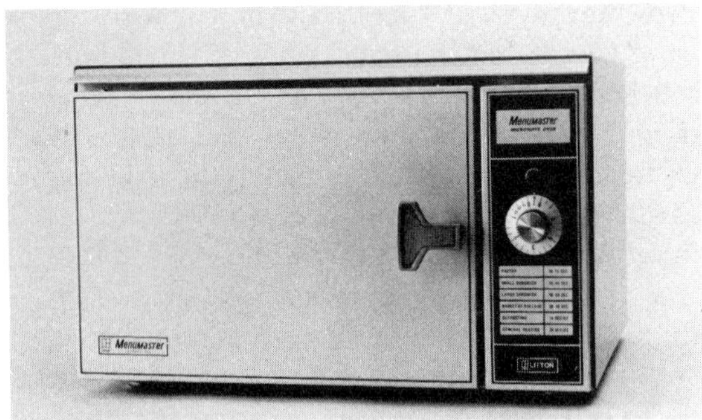

FIGURE 10.2. Microwave oven with six-minute timer and menu chart. Courtesy Litton Microwave Cooking Products.

have controls that regulate several levels of heat input.

Standby wattages range from 50 to 500 in the various ovens. Some ovens have the feature of reducing this further if the oven is not used. Preheat times run from mere seconds to several minutes, but this is not close to the thirty minutes required for some conventional ovens.

Dimensions

The microwave oven cavity ranges in width from 30–51 cm (12–20 in.), from 30–43 cm (12–17 in.) in depth, and from 13–31 cm (5–12 in.) in height. The external measurements of the oven range from 46–81 cm (13–32 in.) in width, from 36–74 cm (14–29 in.) in depth, and from 33–82 cm (13–32 in.) in height. This means that the oven capacity is only a small proportion of the space occupied by the cabinet, ranging from 8 to 32 percent in the various models. However, conventional electric bake and general-purpose ovens are not much better as the baking cavity is approximately 24 percent and the roasting cavity 32 percent of the cabinet without legs or base.

The microwave oven usually has short legs or a low metal base with rubber or plastic supports beneath it and is set on a counter.

Inspecting Agencies

There are a number of agencies that oversee various aspects of the microwave oven: (1) The Federal Communications Commission sets the two radio frequencies that microwave ovens may use, and they monitor them to prevent violation; (2) The Underwriters' Laboratories check the electrical aspects of the equipment against their standards; and (3) The National Sanitation Foundation ensures that manufacturers who use their NSF seal meet their sanitation standards.

Determination of Needed Capacity

Capacity to be purchased in a microwave oven probably defies accurate calculation if a number of diverse products are to be prepared in it. However, the calculation is simple if the oven is to be used for one or several products of consistent size, dimensions, density, and temperature. If a 227-g (8-oz) beef goulash casserole takes 80 seconds to heat to 71°C (160°F) from 4°C (40°F) in a 1000-watt oven and it takes 10 seconds to place the casserole in and take it out of the oven, then one casserole can be done every 90 seconds, or 40 per hour. If twice this capacity is needed, one would assume that a 2000-watt oven could provide the desired capacity, but such is not the case. Certainly the casserole will heat in 40 seconds, but adding the 10-second handling time for each casserole and dividing the total into one hour gives a production rate of 72 casseroles per hour.

Some would say, "Place two casseroles in the oven at the same time." In a conventional oven, this would mean almost no difference in cooking time, but in a microwave oven approximately 75 percent must be added to the cooking time for each casserole. Thus, 80 seconds plus 60 (80 x 0.75) plus 10 seconds for each casserole for handling would mean a total of 160 seconds, or 45 casseroles per hour, assuming that heating is even to give a good product in each casserole. Usually, this is not the case, and the casseroles must be moved about and turned for even cooking. Four baking potatoes might have to be switched from front to rear one-third of the way through the cooking and diagonally two-thirds through the process to get even heat treatment.

Actually, most capacity determinations are based on projected use of the equipment. If single items of a simple nature are to be reheated or short-order cooked, then the smaller cavity and lower wattage oven (under 1000 watts) will do. In fact, it is not good for a large oven to cook small amounts because it may overheat both food and the magnetron. Often the several items or jobs are put on a preset timer push button that puts a minimum of demand on operator skill. As complexity of use, need for increased capacity, or time of processing become important, the larger and higher powered units become necessary (1000–2000 or more watts).

One company makes the wattage-usage breakdown as follows:

1. Uses for a 700-watt output, 33-x-33-x 18.6-cm (13-x-13-x-7.3-in.) cavity are warming rolls and bread, heating pastries, pie, desserts, food portions, and small sandwiches at waitress station, snack bar, or coffee cart.
2. Uses for a 1000-watt output, 33-x-33-x 18.6-cm (13-x-13-7.3-in.) cavity are heating pies, pudding, baskets of rolls, plates of hors d'oeuvres, hot towels, hot plates, and temperature boost of plates, special diets, special orders, takeout orders, heating casseroles or beverages, and reheating steam table vegetables for kitchens, dining room serving stations, hospital serving pantries, drive-ins, and cafeterias.
   The average full-service restaurant would use the microwave oven 10 percent of the time for cooking, 20 percent for defrosting, and 70 percent for heating.
3. Uses for a 2000-watt output, 61-x-36-x-25-cm (24-x-14-x-10-in.) cavity are defrosting large and small items, primary cooking of fish and vegetables, finishing items browned elsewhere, bulk reheat of cooked meats and foods going into the steam table, heating complete plates, baking quantities of potatoes, sandwiches, or desserts for restaurant kitchens, hospitals, institutions, supermarkets, banquets, and cafeterias.

Basic Use and Operation

Many salespeople claim that time is the only control that one must consider on the microwave oven, whereas one must consider time, temperature, pan, and position in a conventional oven. This is not true. If anything, the microwave oven is the most complex piece of equipment with which the cook must deal. In addition to all the assistance the manufacturer may give the cook, he must do much experimentation on his own to take full advantage of the microwave oven's potential. Among others, the following factors control the cooking process:

1. Frequency of microwaves. While they penetrate deeper, the 915 MHz microwaves cook slower than the 2450 MHz waves of the same wattage. At present, only the latter is used in commercial cooking.

2. Claimed and actual output wattage. In the final analysis, the latter is the only one important to the cook. If he receives recommended recipes based on a 600-watt output and his oven can put out only 400 watts, then all the recipe times must be adjusted upward.

3. Initial temperature of the food. If a food must be reheated to 71°C (160°F) for service, it would take less time if the product started at 21°C (70°F) than if it started at 4°C (40°F) as fewer Btu would have to be introduced into the food.

4. The internal temperature to which a food must be cooked. The higher the temperature, the greater the cooking time is as the rate of Btu production remains constant. Heating with microwaves usually saves on Btus as the times are set to bring the food to no more then serving temperatures while other devices overheat food.

5. Specific and latent heats of the foods. Considering that one Btu of heat will raise 454 g

(1 lb) of water 0.6°C (1°F), it is used as the standard and given a specific heat of one. Other foods do not require this much heat to raise 454 g (1 lb) 0.6°C (1°F). Haddock requires only 0.8 Btu per 454 g (1 lb) to raise it 0.6°C (1°F) in a thawed state and 0.43 Btu per 454 g (1 lb) in the frozen state. However, to change water from 0°C (32°F) in the frozen state to 0°C (32°F) in the thawed state requires 144 Btu per 454 g (1 lb) of water or 112 Btu per 454 g (1 lb) of haddock. Thus, as specific and latent heats are different for most foods, they must be considered. Most fats have specific heats around 0.5 Btu per 454 g (1 lb); thus they heat more rapidly than the meats to which they are attached. An example is beef with a specific heat of 0.76 Btu. The fat would heat faster than the meat. This is desired because the cook usually wants the meat cooked to an internal temperature around 66°C (150°F) and wants the fat to melt as much as possible, so he tries to put the fat portions of the meat in one of the oven hot spots.

6. Taking temperatures of food to ascertain readiness for service or doneness. Determination of the spot at which the temperature should be taken is, in itself, a research project because the cold spot is not always in the middle. For instance, in a turkey log, the cold spot may be 2.5 cm (1 in.) from the bottom of the roast.

7. Temperature at which the cold point should be when the food is removed from the oven if the final temperature is to be at a certain point. Allied with this is the length of time that one should wait for this temperature adjustment to take place for each food. In some foods no wait is necessary but in others, a fifteen- to twenty-minute wait is needed.

8. Size of the load and how it should be distributed around the oven cavity. This is of considerable importance. Small pieces of food cook faster than large pieces. Good separation helps to get more even cooking. A mass of food such as mashed potatoes or a casserole heats better if depressed in the center and arranged around the perimeter of the dish.

9. Shape of the load. This is related to size. A 1-kg (2.2-lb) block of food in the form of an equal-sided cube will take much more time to cook than if it is cooked in a 1.3-cm (0.5-in.) thickness. For foods that one wants to cook quickly, one uses a thickness that the microwave will penetrate quickly and relies very little on conduction.

10. Shapes containing a mixture of thick and thin parts. In a roasting chicken, it is recognized that the thin wings and legs will be cooked before the thick breast and thighs. Shielding in the form of reflective foil is wrapped around the thin parts for at least a part of the cooking period.

11. The utensil. This can affect the cooking process. A glass dish passes 95 percent of the microwaves through to the cooking food while a shiny aluminum dish or foil would reflect most of the microwave directed toward the food and slow up the cooking process. A pan with a high lossiness would absorb many of the waves and pass some heat by conduction onto the food where it makes contact. However, this would shield the food from direct contact with the cooking waves, except perhaps from the top. This means that a large part of the cooking would have to take place by slow conduction except from the area which the microwaves could strike.

12. Adjustment for the added heat that comes from the browning element, browning dish, conventional oven heating elements, or forced convection heating elements in addition to the microwaves.

There are other factors that affect food heating or cooking, some of which are precooking in other equipment, vapor pressure in cavity, dielectric properties of foods, food density, size of oven, and coating on foods.

Desirable Features in Microwave Oven Containers

1. They should have low microwave absorption rates. Included in this category are most glasses, many plastic foams, plastic bags and dishes, paper, and some china (figure 10.3). The container should be tested by placing it in the oven with the power on for twenty seconds. If it gets quite warm, it should not be used.
2. Small amounts of mass will extract the heat from a cooked food by conduction.
3. They should be of a width and height that will fit into the oven. Shallow containers with thin layers of food usually are most desirable.
4. Round dishes or those with rounded corners are preferable. Foods tend to overheat in right-angle corners.
5. They should be able to withstand temperatures of 204°C (400°F), as well as low temperatures.
6. They should be capable of standing rough handling.
7. Nonporous utensils are preferred.
8. Aluminum foil can be used if the food is much greater in amount than the foil. Foil should not touch walls or bottom of the oven as it will arc.

FIGURE 10.3. Microwave oven and plastic steam table pan.

Cooking Hints

1. On casseroles and plates, arrange food around periphery and leave center depressed or empty (figure 10.4). Try to keep small or thin pieces from being exposed by themselves. Cover the casserole or plate with plastic film to keep in the steam and aid cooking. If film fits tightly, perforate it several times to release steam, if necessary. Foods with crusts such as pot pies should not be reheated with a cover as this will cause the crust to be soggy. Do not heat two different casseroles at the same time as they will not cook at the same rate.
2. In defrosting portions of chicken or meat, place them in the 1000-watt microwave oven for fifteen to thirty seconds, let stand thirty seconds to one minute, turn over and repeat defrost and stand cycles, if necessary. In most cases this should be enough. If not, repeat until food is thawed. After thawing, the product may be returned to the microwave oven for heating or cooking. Frozen casseroles are best if thawed for twenty-four hours in a refrigerator before heating.
3. Vegetables in small plastic bags may be cooked in those bags if they are slit several times on top to allow the steam to escape. Care must be taken not to overheat them as they lose their green color when overheated. Water must be present in the cooking of some vegetables such as asparagus to soften the pectin. Carrots tend to shrivel, and sweet potatoes become gummy in microwaves.
4. Bread, pastry, and breaded products should be reheated uncovered at low power. If low power is not available, a glass of water placed in the oven may accomplish this.
5. Sandwiches with precooked filling and pretoasted bread may be wrapped and heated in the wrapper if it is perforated.
6. Corn, cooked in the husks, makes a very good product. Chopped cabbage and Brussels sprouts cook very well in microwaves.
7. Products that may be cooked satisfactorily in

FIGURE 10.4. Microwave oven being used to cook entrées. Courtesy Litton Microwave Cooking Products.

the microwave oven are tender meat, poultry with or without stuffing, cut-up chicken, fish products, cured meats including bacon, baked potatoes, if punctured (they will shrivel less if they are wrapped in plastic), colored vegetables (these must not be overheated), casseroles, starch-thickened foods if stirred twice, hot salads, scrambled eggs, fresh fruits, hot breakfast cereals, high moisture cookies, cakes, pies, and crusts.

8. Products which do not lend themselves to microwave cooking include large pieces of meat, whole eggs, low-moisture cookies, tough meats, stewing chickens, yeast breads and biscuits, and high cellulose and starchy vegetables.
9. Cooking chicken from the frozen state reduces bone darkening.
10. Cooking vegetables with little or no water reduces the loss of water-soluble vitamins. Adding seasoned oil or butter speeds cooking.
11. Gel-forming capacity of egg proteins in a custard is destroyed by fast high-heat cooking as the protein is denatured, thus causing toughening. Some success may be attained by cooking custards and angel food cakes in a pan of water.
12. Tender cuts of meats appear to cook better in a low-powered oven or an oven in which power is reduced.
13. Deep fat frying may be carried out in a microwave oven if special high-temperature glassware is used along with high smoke point fats. The fat temperature must be monitored frequently to avoid overheating. If the fat begins to smoke heavily, the oven should be shut off.
14. If heating over 3.6 kg (8 lb) of food, a convection oven or pressure steamer will cook faster than a 2000-watt microwave oven.
15. In making microwave-heated sandwiches, bread which is rich in egg and shortening should be used, or toast and butter, if appropriate. The meat should be sliced thinly and placed loosely on the bread with a minimum in the center and it should be heated uncovered. Usually frozen sandwiches do not heat well as the bread is overheated before the filling is thawed and heated.
16. In reheating plated meals, put the potato and the fat side of the meat on the outside of the plate with the bone side of the meat and the easy-to-heat vegetables toward the center of

the plate (figure 10.5). Most foods will cook best in a microwave oven when they are not more than 5.1 cm (2 in.) thick.

17. Fish cooked in a microwave oven is similar to that conventionally steamed or poached. Fish should be cooked until it barely flakes when prodded with a fork or until the fins pull out easily. In cooking the fish, the tail should be pointed toward a corner of the oven or be shielded as it will cook faster than the rest of the fish. If browning under the broiler is desired, the fish should be precooked to 85 percent of doneness in the microwave oven and then broiled. To preserve moistness in the fish, brushing it with butter or fish stock will help. Wrapping it in wax paper is another method.
18. Use less liquid in casseroles, cakes, and similar dishes, since the microwave does not dry foods as conventional ovens do.

It is difficult to use the cooking times given for a particular manufacturer's oven in another oven, but the following processing times are those developed for one manufacturer's 1300-watt output oven (see table 10.1). With slight adjustment, they

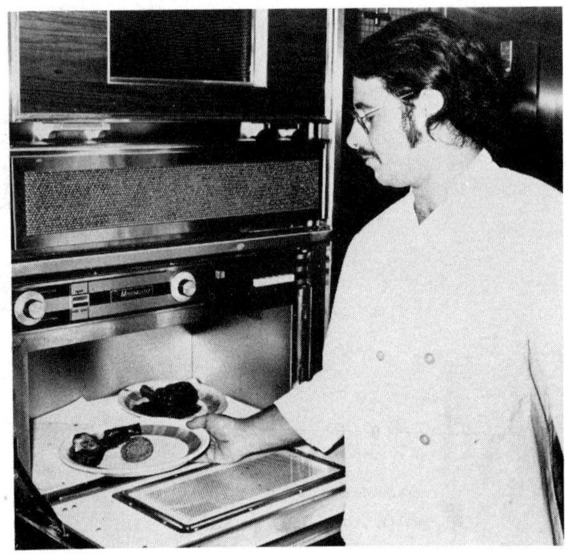

FIGURE 10.5. Plated meal being reheated in microwave oven. Courtesy Litton Microwave Cooking Products.

TABLE 10.1. Food Preparation in a 1300-Watt Microwave Oven

Food	Starting Amount	Starting Temperature	Time	Instructions
Cooking				
Apples, escalloped	113 g (4 oz)	4°C (40°F)	20–25 sec	place blanched product around perimeter of container, depress center, and butter product
Beans, green	113 g (4 oz)	4°C (40°F)	30–35 sec	same
Carrots, julienne	113 g (4 oz)	4°C (40°F)	25–30 sec	same
Cauliflower	113 g (4 oz)	4°C (40°F)	25–30 sec	same
Corn on cob	1 ear	21°C (70°F)	70–80 sec	butter ear, wrap in waxed paper, cook and then let stand 3 min
Corn niblets	113 g (4 oz)	4°C (40°F)	25–30 sec	place blanched product around perimeter of container, depress center, and butter product
Peas, green	113 g (4 oz)	4°C (40°F)	20–25 sec	same
Potato, au gratin, Delmonico, Lyonnaise	113 g (4 oz)	4°C (40°F)	30–35 sec	same

TABLE 10.1. (continued)

Food	Starting Amount	Starting Temperature	Time	Instructions
Potato, Idaho, baked	227 g (8 oz)	21°C (70°F)	3.25 min.	rub with oil, cook one side 2.5 min, turn and finish, wrap in foil 3 min
Bacon slices	2	4°C (40°F)	30–35 sec	heat between paper towels
Roast beef sandwich	113 g (4 oz)	4°C (40°F)	15–20 sec	place precooked meat lightly on pretoasted bun with most meat toward sides
Eggs, scrambled (2)	142 g (5 oz)	4°C (40°F)	35–40 sec	mix with small amount of milk and melted butter, heat covered 20 sec and stir, and finish
Frankfurter	85 g (3 oz)	4°C (40°F)	15 sec	pregrill after scoring, place in toasted bun with meat down, and heat
Hamburger	113 g (4 oz)	4°C (40°F)	20–25 sec	presear, add to pretoasted roll and heat
Lobster tail	170 g (6 oz)	4°C (40°F)	90–100 sec	split tail, cover with butter, heat covered, let stand 2 min
Trout	227 g (8 oz)	4°C (40°F)	1.5 min	coat with butter and cook each side 45 sec
Heat and Reheat				
Apple pie, slice	170 g (6 oz)	21°C (70°F)	15 sec	
Beef Burgundy casserole	198 g (7 oz)	4°C (40°F)	55–60 sec	place product around periphery, depress center
Beef goulash casserole	227 g (8 oz)	4°C (40°F)	60–65 sec	same
Beef stew	198 g (7 oz)	4°C (40°F)	55–65 sec	same
Bread, loaf	small	21°C (70°F)	8 sec	
Creamed chicken casserole	198 g (7 oz)	4°C (40°F)	55–60 sec	place product around periphery, depress center
Chili con carne casserole	170 g (6 oz)	4°C (40°F)	60–65 sec	same
Macaroni and cheese casserole	198 g (7 oz)	4°C (40°F)	55–65 sec	same
Roll, dinner		21°C (70°F)	4 sec	
Shrimp creole	198 g (7 oz)	4°C (40°F)	50–55 sec	place around periphery, depress center
Spaghetti and meat balls	198 g (7 oz)	4°C (40°F)	60–65 sec	same
Tart, fruit	113 g (4 oz)	21°C (70°F)	15 sec	
Turkey tetrazzini	198 g (7 oz)	4°C (40°F)	60–65	place around periphery, depress center
Defrost				
Cornish hen	485 g (17 oz)	−18°C (0°F)	65–75 sec	heat covered 30 sec, let stand 2 min, turn over, and finish
Halibut steak	227 g (8 oz)	−18°C (0°F)	25–30 sec	heat 15 sec, turn over
Steak, club	227 g (8 oz)	−18°C (0°F)	25–30 sec	heat 15 sec and turn over
Vegetables in carton	1.4 kg (48 oz)	−18°C (0°F)	3 min	heat 2 min, turn over, and finish

Source: Operative Manual, Litton Menumaster 70/50 Microwave Oven, Litton Microwave Cooking, Minneapolis, MN.

may be used as the starting point for setting times for other microwave ovens. For instance, if a 184-g (6.5-oz) hamburger took 30–35 seconds to cook at 1300 watts, then at 2000 watts it would take 32.5 seconds (the average of 30 and 35) x 1300/2000 watts (0.65), or 21 seconds. At 1000 watts it would take 32.5 seconds x 1300/1000 watts (1.3), or 42.25 seconds.

Adjustments must be made for differences from quantities noted in this guide, as well. For a liquid as the load is doubled, the process time is roughly doubled, but for some foods doubling the load means an increase of only 30 percent in cooking time. One manufacturer uses a blanket 75 percent for each added increment of food.

A rule of thumb method for determining a processing time is to try a period of time that one feels is slightly short. If the product is not up to temperature when tested with a thermometer, it should be given another short cook. If the product is then done, the combined times should be noted and used the next time the product is heated.

Special Applications

1. warming baby milk bottles or jars of baby food
2. decontaminating flour and cereals and destroying molds
3. heating syrup for griddle cakes and heating molasses to make it more fluid
4. liquefying dried glue
5. drying wet newspapers
6. drying bread crumbs and croutons
7. heating wet towels for customers and compresses for hospital patients
8. canning fruits such as tomatoes and pickles
9. heating liquids to boiling and adding to jars of food and bringing loosely sealed jars to a boil
10. drying plaster of Paris and papier-mâché articles
11. softening spreads for easier spreading
12. crisping soggy potato chips or pretzels
13. heating brandy for flaming desserts
14. reheating leftover griddle cakes or waffles (figure 10.6)

Alternatives to the Microwave Oven

For the most part, foodservice managers buy microwave ovens for fast thawing, heating and reheating small quantities of food, and cooking short-order items. While they cannot compete on the cooking speed for individual portions, there are fast pieces of equipment that can turn out far more portions per hour. For instance, a forced convection oven can turn out 264 hamburgers in ten minutes while a 2000-watt microwave might turn out 40 in that time. A 1300-watt microwave oven would turn out one portion of peas in twenty seconds of cooking time while a fast pressure cooker would do a 30-x-51-x-5.1-cm (12-x-20-x-2-in.) steam table pan of peas in only one minute. A 1300-watt microwave oven can provide a portion of scrambled eggs in thirty-five to forty seconds, while an infrared oven can fry two eggs in the same time, and a pressure cooker can poach a whole pan of them in thirty seconds. Broilers are equally fast. A deep fat fryer is very quick in cooking foods in single portions or in quantity.

FIGURE 10.6. Multiple microwave ovens provide quick reheat for items used in short-order cooking.

Time Saving in Microwave Ovens

1. The microwave oven is most energy efficient when used in cooking individual portions or small quantities. As the quantities get larger, microwave ovens save less time and energy efficiency is decreased.
2. Microwave ovens can melt chocolate in 1–2 minutes, warm muffins in 10 seconds, reheat baked apple pie in one minute, bake a potato in 4 minutes, fry bacon in one minute and soften hard sugar in 1.5–2 minutes.
3. Avoid cooking cheese, whole eggs, cream, pizzas, condensed milk, breaded foods, mayonnaise, chicken liver, kidney beans, and similar foods. Energy is wasted and many of these products do not turn out well.
4. High-sided pans should not be used, since they shield the food and waste energy.

Cleaning

1. Wipe up all spillage as it occurs. Do not allow any food accumulations to occur on oven interior surfaces, stirrer blades, or the door.
2. When interior soil indicates cleaning is desirable, place a large dish of water in the cavity and heat it until the interior of the oven is well coated with water drops.
3. Turn main on-off switch to off.
4. Wipe out oven interior, stirrer, shelf, and light cover with a soft sponge or cloth which has been dampened with a mild detergent and warm water. Rinse all surfaces. Do not use scouring pads, abrasive cleaners, or any other materials that may scratch the surface.
5. With warm water and detergent, wipe the inside door surfaces, particularly areas that make contact with the door frame. Wipe door frame contact surface. Make sure no crumbs or residues remain on either one. Rinse off surfaces with clean water.
6. Dry all washed surfaces with a soft, dry cloth.
7. Wipe off oven exterior with a soft cloth, warm water, and a mild detergent. Rinse. Wipe dry with a soft cloth.
8. Clean the air intake filter at least once a week by washing it in the pot sink or dishwasher. If grease remains, use a grease-removing compound. Rinse well and dry.

Maintenance

1. Turn on oven and when ready to cook, place a glass of water in the cavity and operate it for a minute on the timer. Do all of the indicator lights go on and off in proper order? If not, replace those that are burned out. Is the timer accurate and does it shut off the power at the end of the prescribed time?
2. Is the oven cavity light on? If not, replace it with a manufacturer-recommended bulb.
3. Check the door hinges for tightness and the door and frame contact surfaces for scratches. If a radiation meter is not available to check escaping radiation, use a small fluorescent tube or neon bulb to get a rough indication of escaping microwaves. If they light up in any way when passed around outside the door or other possible escape points, call maintenance to check the oven with a meter.
4. Check all control knobs for looseness, and tighten those that require it.
5. Periodically, use the technique indicated in the section on power aspects to determine whether the oven is maintaining proper output.
6. Only skilled personnel should do maintenance on the magnetron or power supply. Factory approved and trained maintenance personnel should check the oven periodically.

QUESTIONS

1. What is a microwave oven and what special attributes does it have?
2. What are the advantages and disadvantages of microwave ovens?

3. What is the effect on processing time of doubling the power output of the microwave oven?
4. How does one test a microwave oven for power output?
5. What are the major components of a microwave oven?
6. What is the formula for determining the power efficiency of an oven?
7. To test for heating evenness in the microwave oven, what is the procedure?
8. What two design features are used to improve wave distribution?
9. What utensils are good for microwave cooking? What ones are poor for the process?
10. What human physiological changes can occur from microwave radiation?
11. How does one get browning on foods cooked in a microwave oven?
12. What are the agencies that oversee microwave ovens?
13. What factors affect processing time of food in microwave ovens?
14. What foods are not well prepared in microwave ovens?
15. How does one determine the amount of process time increase to make for doubling the amount of food to be cooked?
16. What is the main energy-saving feature in proper microwave oven use?

BIBLIOGRAPHY

ANON. 1970. Consumer microwave oven systems conference, Cornell University. Association of Home Appliance Manufacturers, Chicago.

ANON. 1972. Regulations for the administration and enforcement of the radiation control for Health and Safety Act of 1972. Bureau of Radiological Health, Rockville, Md.

ANON. 1975. Microwave oven application and equipment guide. Litton Microwave Cooking, Minneapolis.

ANON. 1975. Menumaster microwave oven, system 70/50, operating manual. Litton Microwave Cooking, Minneapolis.

COPSON, D. 1962. *Microwave Heating in Freeze Drying Electronic Ovens and Other Applications.* AVI Publishing Co., Westport, Conn.

DAVIS, D., PRATT, D., REBER, E., and KLOCKOW, R. 1971. Microwave cooking in meal management. *Journal of Home Economics* 63, 97–100.

LUDVIGSON, V. 1971. An exciting new world of microwave cooking from Litton. Litton Systems, Minneapolis.

PETERSEN, A., and FOERSTNER, R. 1971. Evaluation of microwave oven cooking performance. *Microwave Energy Application Newsletter* 4, No. 1, 3–8.

POLEDOR, A., AVERY, A., and MCDONALD, M. 1974. Evaluation of microwave ovens. Purdue University, West Lafayette, Ind.

POLLAK, G., and FOIN, L. 1959. Study of microwave cooking device. U.S Naval Supply Research and Development Facility, Bayonne, N.J.

VAN ZANTE, H. 1973. *The Microwave Oven.* Houghton Mifflin, Boston.

WILHELM, M., and SATTERLEE, L. 1971. A 3-dimensional method for mapping microwave ovens. *Microwave Energy Application Newsletter* 4, No. 5, 3–5.

Deep Fat Fryers

Foodservice customers order deep fat fried food because they like its appetizing color and appearance, the distinctive flavor, and the crispness without apparent greasiness. The foodservice operator likes deep fat fried foods because they attract customers, require little advance preparation, cook rapidly, and can be cooked to order so that there are few leftovers. In fact, there are many fried foods that use up leftovers. Many of them are low food cost items, and the fryer uses little kitchen space for the number of food servings produced (figure 11.1).

By definition, the deep fat fryer is a device that cooks food by immersing it in heated fat. In form, the fryer may be a square, oblong, or round fry kettle that is mounted in, or on, a rectangular cabinet. To this, heat is applied by gas to the exterior of the container or in large tubes that pass through the fat. Electric heating elements, also, may be used. These are immersed in the fat along the sides or bottom of the kettle. Generally, the fat temperature is controlled thermostatically. The food is introduced into the fat by means of a welded rod, wire, or sheet metal basket. Cooking time is determined by observation of doneness in the product by the cook, use of electric or mechanical timers, or timed basket lift-out devices.

The present fryer is a far cry from the old black fry pan or kettle that cooked on top of the wood, coal, or oil ranges of the past. It was a constant fire hazard. In turn, the present fryers will give way to fryers that will cook by means of

FIGURE 11.1. Conventional deep fat fryer with two baskets. Courtesy Vulcan Hart Corporation.

centrally heated liquid media piped to the various cooking devices. They will be self-loading and unloading. The Amfare unit had this feature. Figure 11.2 shows a high-production, continuous-batch fryer of an advanced type.

Successful frying in present-day fryers requires the following:

1. well-designed, fast-recovery fry kettles
2. high-quality foods
3. high-quality fats designed for deep fat frying
4. proper food preparation, frying, and fried food holding procedures
5. proper care of fat and fryer

Description and Specification

When buying a deep fat fryer, it is not enough to choose one blindly from a dealer's showroom or trade show. The fryer should be checked to determine whether or not it fills certain specifications and requirements. In a fryer, the following should be investigated:

1. Is it constructed of noncorrosive metals?
2. Does it have a sturdy frame which brings the fryer top up to proper height?

FIGURE 11.2. Continuous type fryer. Courtesy Crown-X.

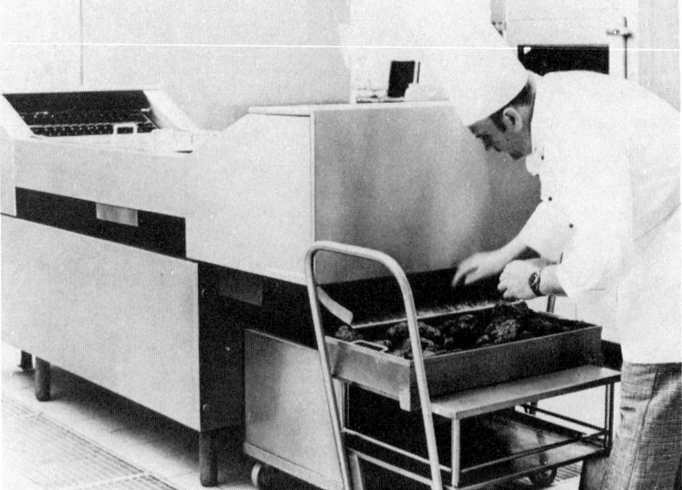

3. Will the dimensions fit your space and does it have flexibility of use?
4. Does it have desirable heat input and rapid recovery?
5. Does it have a satisfactory design for the job for which it will be used, and is it easy to clean?
6. Will it use fat economically and provide good flavor protection?
7. Is it easy and safe to use?
8. Does it have accurate thermostats and displays which give good, safe reliable control?
9. Does it have an easy and safe fat-draining system?
10. Does it have sturdy, easy-to-handle, free-fat-flow basket construction?
11. Does it have the desired accessories?
12. Does it conform to pertinent Underwriters' Laboratories, American Gas Association, and National Sanitation Foundation regulations?

Materials

In the past, fry kettles have been made of black iron, aluminum, and mild sheet steel; today most are made of 18-gauge 18–8–3 stainless steel and, to a lesser extent, mild steel. Aluminum in various forms can be used, but care must be exercised to use only cleaners approved for cleaning aluminum or deep pitting will occur. Nickel can be used, but it is expensive. Copper, bronze, or brass should not be used because they act in the breakdown of fat. Materials should be durable, nonabsorbent, smooth, and easily cleanable. Cabinets may be either free standing or built-in and can be of lighter gauges of stainless steel or 18-gauge mild sheet steels with baked-on enamels. Some operators use stainless steel on the surface where abrasive cleaners might remove the enamels, and enameled sheet steel on other surfaces where abrasives need not be used. Usually doors are 22-gauge mild steel with enamel coating but may be made of stainless steel.

The frame may be of soft steel angle iron and is placed in locations where it is not likely to corrode. The frame can be made of stainless steel, but it is expensive to use it for this purpose. The frame plus base or legs should be such that the fry kettle is at proper work height. This height varies according to the worker's height, and thus it is desirable, for electric fryers in particular, to have adjustable stainless steel feet. The top of the fry kettle plus the depth of the fryer basket should be slightly below the height of the worker's elbow.

Legs should allow the bottom of a floor-mounted fryer to clear the floor by at least 15 cm (6 in.) to permit easy cleaning beneath it. If the fryer is on casters and can be pulled out for cleaning, this clearance is not critical. It is not necessary to have the clearance if the fryer is mounted and sealed down to a raised concrete or other platform at least 5 cm (2 in.) high. Table or counter top fryers should have a clearance of at least 5 cm (2 in.) to permit cleaning beneath them.

Solders should not be more than 5 percent lead and should contain no toxic filler. Silver solder should not contain cadmium or toxic materials. Weld areas and welds should be equally resistant to corrosion.

Gas burners and immersed electric heating elements should be of materials that can stand constant cleaning. Immersed elements should not react with fat.

Dimensions and Flexibility of Use

In the past, deep fat fryers and griddles usually have been crammed under a postage-stamp-sized hood in the production area of the kitchen. Now some designers are placing the fryers and griddles on wheels and are wheeling them close to the serving area when they are in use. In the future, it is probable that most of the kitchen will be on wheels and rearranged each day to carry out best the demands of the day's menu.

While this may not happen tomorrow, designers are increasing the areas under ventilation hoods so that tables can be brought up beside equipment that must be tended closely. Because areas under hoods are expensive, equipment must fit tightly. This makes purchase dimensions important. They are even more important when a fryer is replacing another lifted out of a solid line of equipment. One must be sure to measure the space available carefully, as well as the fryer to be placed in the vacated space. Wherever possible, it should fit in tightly, providing a minimum of space and hard-to-clean crevices.

Fryers are available in a variety of widths from 28 cm (11 in.) on up and with various depths and heights. In addition to being of the correct width, it is desirable that fryers be of the same height as the adjacent tables to smooth the path of assembly line frying.

Heat Input

The amount of heat applied to the fat and the quantity of fat present, in part, determine the maximum fryer basket load and the quantity of food that can be fried per hour. While it did not increase the quantity of food that can be fried per hour substantially, fryer manufacturers tried to overcome the inherently slow frying time and low product capacity of low-heat input fryers by increasing the volume of fat to provide a heat reservoir. While it did increase frying speed and basket loads, the large fat capacity fryer was bulky, wasted heat, did not increase hourly production rate by any great degree, and was costly in fat usage. A more reasonable answer to the problem was to increase the heat input to the fryers so that fryers would need less fat, radiate less heat, produce more pounds of fried food per hour, and occupy less space. Gas fryers went from well under 2000 Btu input per pound of fat to 2400–3000 Btu per pound of fat, and today some are rated as high as 4000 Btu. They are also designed to get more heat into the fat by increasing the heated metal surface in contact with the fat. Electric fryers went from 1 kw of electrical input for 3.6–4.5 kg (8–10 lbs) of fat up to 1 kw for 1.1 kg (2.5 lbs) of fat. Today some are at 1 kw for 1 kg (2.2 lbs) of fat (figure 11.3). The minimum that a buyer should accept is 2400 Btu per 0.45 kg (1 lb) of fat if the unit is gas fired, and 1 kw per 1.1 kg (2.5 lbs) of fat if the fryer is electric. If the fryer is electric and uses 20 amperes or more, the circuit should be balanced 3-phase. It should be possible to fry one part of food to six parts of fat by weight in the new fryers and one part to eight in the older, slower fryers.

FIGURE 11.3. Electric deep fat fryers with lift-out elements.

Design for Use and Cleanability

A fryer should be designed for the use to which the operator plans to put it. A doughnut manufacturer wants a comparatively shallow fryer with plenty of surface area; a fryer of potatoes wants a rather deep fryer and a minimum of surface area. If much breading will fall from the food, it will char and hasten the breakdown of the fat. A cold zone is needed in the bottom of the fryer with, perhaps, a crumb tray that can be emptied frequently. On the other hand, if little residue drops down in the fat, they may not be necessary. Sometimes the residue of some foods, such as doughnuts, floats and can be easily skimmed off. One fryer has the fat resting on a tank of water that acts as a cold zone. The cold zone should be 41.7–56°C (75–100°F) below the cooking fat temperature. This could be dangerous, however, as the water could be stirred up into the hot fat, causing a steam explosion.

Where speed is desirable, the pressure fryer

has been developed. The top of the fryer fastens down to hold steam under pressure over the top of the fat. The steam may come from the cooking product or be injected into the space. Chicken that cooks in twelve to fourteen minutes in a conventional fryer may cook in eight to nine minutes in a pressure fryer. This difference in time may be cut in half by placing a cover on a conventional fryer to hold in the steam. Some operators feel that a pressure fryer shortens the use life of fat (figure 11.4).

FIGURE 11.4. Pressure fryer shortens cooking time. Courtesy The Broaster Co.

Where a cover is used with a conventional fryer, care must be taken to lift the rear of the cover first to release the steam before it can flow back into the cook's face.

Some research done by the military seems to indicate that the time saving in the use of the pressure fryer may be illusory. The manipulations required in the use of the pressure fryer make the total time to process a batch completely about the same in the rapid-recovery conventional fryer as in the pressure fryer.

Because air is deleterious to fat, the fryer should be designed to allow minimal air contact with the fat. This means that the small-surface deep fryer is least injurious to the fat. A kettle cover that floats on the fat surface when the fryer is not in use is desirable to reduce oxidative deterioration of the fat. It is probable that fryers which use pumps to move the fryer fat continually through built-in filters are allowing too much oxygen to come in contact with the fat. However, research on this is fragmentary.

Most fryer manufacturers now strive to get a large number of Btu into the fat by applying much heat against a small heating surface. This makes temperatures of the material rise, and the high temperature, in turn, is hard on the use life of the fat. Most desirable, but little considered at present, is application of heat to the fat at a lower temperature but over a large area. In some cases, this lower temperature of heating the fat is accomplished with high-pressure steam in tubes in the fat or by use of super-heated liquids.

Another problem in deep fat frying that must be considered is the foam that forms when moist foods are fried. Often this may be solved by allowing head space in the fry kettle above the surface of the fat. Some designs increase the head space so that the foam will not create a cleaning problem by boiling over the top. When a fat foams excessively, it means that too much water has been allowed to remain on the food, that the fat is breaking down, the fat is too hot, or the fat is inferior. Hot spots in the kettle, gum left on kettle surfaces, or too much fat may also cause foam.

Ease of cleaning must be designed into the fryer. The kettle shell must be smooth and easy to clean. All surfaces in contact with the fat must be accessible to abrasive cleaning. The various sections and heating elements should be joined with a minimum of hard-to-clean surfaces, connections, cracks, and crevices. The easier the fryer is to clean, the more frequently it will be cleaned.

Saving and Protecting the Fat

Fat can be saved by decreasing the temperature differential between the heat source and the fat. A reason for throwing fat away is fat turnover during the day of frying is insufficient to dilute the breakdown products of the fat properly. In selecting a fryer, care must be taken to select a fryer size that will require addition of 15 percent or more of the fat load each day of use. If some days require much more frying capacity, thought should be given to using two fryers—a small one for the short- and small-order frying and a large fryer for additional needed capacity.

Holding the fat at too high temperatures for too long periods of time is the main cause of fat deterioration. Control of this is a matter of production procedures—frying and holding fat at lower temperatures and shutting off the fryer entirely during slack business times. Covering fryers on a standby basis also helps.

Ease and Safety of Use

The buyer should determine whether or not the fryer will work well with adjacent equipment such as tables, shelves, drawers, and refrigerators. Also, he ought to determine its human engineering characteristics. Can the cook see when the product is properly browned? Can he read dials and accurately adjust the controls? Can he reach all parts of the equipment to use it and clean it without standing on something or having to assume awkward positions? Can he see surfaces to tell whether they are clean? If he must move the equipment, are the wheels or slides adequate?

Control and Display System

Accurate, easily used thermostats are a must. The thermostat should be accurate within plus or minus 5 degrees of the set temperature over a range of 93–204°C (200–400°F), otherwise it is difficult to time batches of food as one is not sure of the starting temperature. A fryer off by 8–14°C (15–25°F) may increase fat content of food by 10 percent. These thermostats fail from time to time, and if they do not shut off the heat automatically, the fat is liable to burst into flame within five to six minutes. A back-up or safety thermostat, fusible link, or circuit breaker is necessary to shut off the fryer (figure 11.5). The secondary independent safety switch has been on Underwriters' Laboratories requirements since 1973. It can be observed as a separate unit with a separate capillary from that of the regular thermostat.

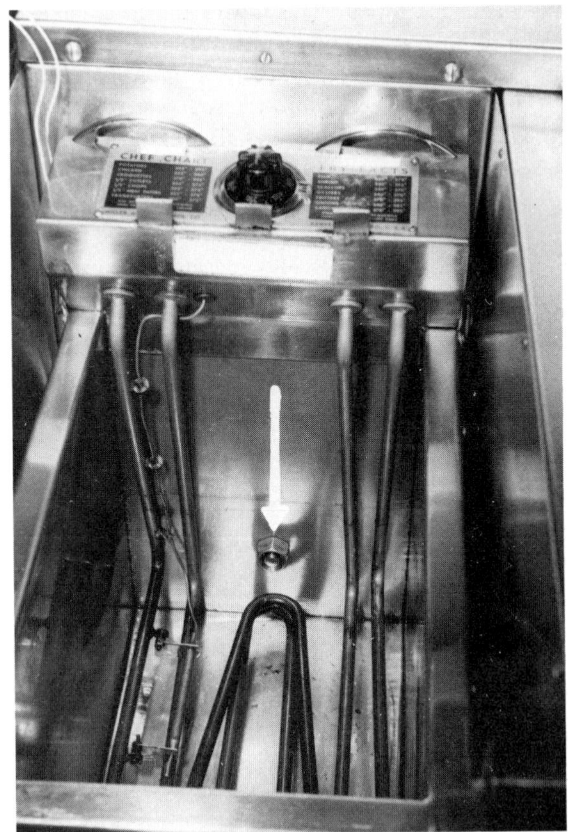

FIGURE 11.5. Backup thermostat with fusible link in deep fat fryer.

Other displays and controls necessary for good fryer operation are frying cycle time, a signal light to indicate when power is on, and an on-off toggle switch to shut off the power manually. Some have lights that indicate when the fat is at the

FIGURE 11.6. Thermostat for deep fat fryer in a location where it might get too hot to handle readily.

proper temperature. They should be located where they are easy to see, and hand controls should not get above 52°C (125°F), that is, burn temperature (figure 11.6).

A thermostat bulb should be placed where it reflects the fat temperature accurately but not where the fry baskets will strike and damage it.

Another fire-fighting idea to consider in installation of the fryer is to place a switch for the heat source going into the fryer in a position where it can be shut off without risk if the fryer bursts into flame. The best location for the switch is beside the kitchen exit door.

Easy and Safe Fat Drainage

Removal of the fat from the fry kettle for straining and for cleaning of the fry kettle is a use consideration that must be faced. If the quantity of the fat is not great, most fryer designs allow the frying elements to be lifted out of the fat. The fat is then poured from the kettle through a cloth or paper filter after which the kettle is taken to the sink or pot washer. Care must be taken to fasten the heating elements securely so that they will not drop on the worker.

Large fry kettles have drains to which a filter can be attached extending down from the bottom in the center or front edge of the kettle. It is usually 2.5 cm (1 in.) in diameter with a plug or gate valve. Counter fryers often have a 1.2-cm (0.5-in.) drain. Some large fryers use a siphon to remove the fat from the kettle to a container covered with a cloth or paper filter. There are also mechanical pump filtering devices that do the same job.

Baskets should be of sturdy construction to withstand hard service and allow good fat circulation. Materials should not react with fat to cause its breakdown. Most baskets are made of stainless steel or, less satisfactorily, tinned steel. Handles should be placed where they will not get slippery or too hot to handle. In size, the baskets can utilize a fraction of the fryer surface or all of it. The basket construction can be of open space to dump the food, be compartmented, or be of file construction to hold the product pieces apart. It should be considered that most fry baskets should not be filled more than half or two-thirds of capacity. Baskets should be of easily cleanable construction, usually welded wire, rods, or perforated sheet metal that will allow good fat circulation (figure 11.7).

Desired Accessories

According to the needs of the particular feeding operation or the affluence of the owner, various fryer accessories can be considered. Probably needed, but often ignored, is an indicating thermometer to check the fryer thermostat. In form, it can be a simple hand-held model to check fat temperature periodically and should be accurate to plus or minus 2 degrees through the thermostat range of perhaps 93–204°C

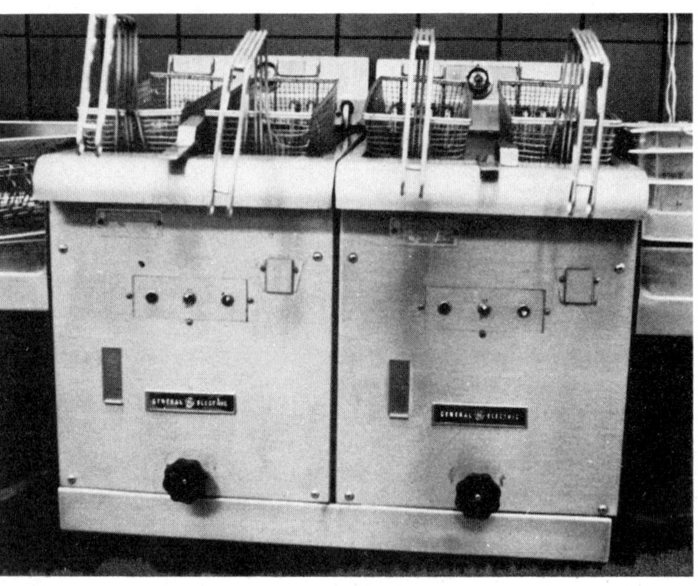

FIGURE 11.7. Baskets for deep fat fryer.

(200–400°F). More to the point is a continuous sensing model in the form of a bar, fan, or circle with the sensing bulb constantly set in the fat near the thermostat. The indicator is best placed at chest height on the wall directly behind the fryer. It speeds recognition of improper frying temperatures to have the thermometer dial marked in green through the proper frying range of 149–177°C (300–350°F) and the scale below and above this range marked in red to indicate improper or dangerous fat temperatures.

Another desirable accessory is the fryer basket lift-out device that may be purchased built-in or added to many common fryers. The experienced cook determines the proper basket load (one that does not take the fryer temperature below 149°C (300°F) and that will recover to initial temperature by the end of the frying period). He fries the load for the period of time that gives the best color, texture, and flavor and then sets the basket lift-out timer. Then he can turn the job over to a low-skilled worker who needs to know only how to weigh out the basket load and press the timer button. Lift-out devices produce items more consistent in quality than could a cook's judgment alone, and one inexperienced person can operate more fryers than a skilled cook.

Crumb trays, cold zone baskets, fat filters, infrared holding lamps, and similar accessories are available from most manufacturers on demand.

Conformance to Established Standards

Not all purchasing standards need to be spelled out in the form of purchasing specifications. Some of the professional societies have developed generally agreed on standards that can be requested as certification in a group as part of an equipment specification. In deep fat fryers, those most commonly requested are: AGA (American Gas Association), pertaining to gas contact details; UL (Underwriters' Laboratories), concerning electric current handling parts; and NSF (National Sanitation Foundation), for whose equipment sanitation qualities certification can be obtained. A buyer of fryers would be well advised to require the certification pertinent to the type of equipment in which he is interested. He can buy a great amount of professional competence this way.

Determination of Needed Capacity

In determining needed deep fat fryer capacity, many equipment salespeople must make decisions based on a minimum of information. They use what they call rules of thumb. One of these used for determining size of deep fat fryers is based on getting the buyer to estimate how many meals he will need to produce per hour. This number divided by 5 gives the fat capacity of the fryer. Thus, 150 meals per hour divided by 5 translates into a 13.6-kg (30-lb) fat capacity fryer. One hopes it is a fast-recovery fryer.

In another method, the salesperson multiplies the total estimated number of customers per hour by 1.5 to get the number of portions of fried food per hour. Then, knowing by experience how many portions of fried food his various fryers average per hour, the salesperson feels confident in prescribing a fryer size. I have found that this 1.5 factor commonly used applies only on Friday. The other days of the week a one-half portion of fried food per patron is more reliable. One expert indicates a fryer should have a fat capacity such that the fryer will cook 1.5 to 2 times its fat capacity per hour.

Much more accurate and usable is the calculation based on facts. Start with a load of product that is the maximum for a given make and size of fryer. It should not drop the fat from its initial temperature to below 149°C (300°F); at the same time, it should return to the original fat temperature by the time the product is done so that the next load can be inserted. Then determine the total time for each frying cycle: loading the basket, frying until cooked, and draining the product over the fryer for one minute before removing.

To get the number of portions per hour that can be prepared in a fryer, use the following procedure: divide total time of frying cycle in minutes into sixty minutes to get the number of batches per hour that can be fried. Multiply the number of patches per hour by the portions that can be fried per batch to get portions per hour. Divide this by 60 to get portions per minute per fryer. Divide this into serving line needs per minute to get the number of fryers needed. An example of the calculation is as follows:

How many fryers are needed to support a serving line rate of six customers per minute if seven pounds of cooked food per batch are fried in a seven-minute cooking and one-minute draining time if each cooked portion is six ounces?

Cooking 7 min + draining 1 min
= 8 min cycle per batch

$$\frac{\text{60 min per hour}}{\text{8 min cycle}} = \text{7.5 batches per hour}$$

18.7 portions per batch × 7.5 batches per hour
= 140 portions per hour

140 portions per hour ÷ 60 min
= 2.3 portions per min

$$\frac{\text{6 portions needed per min}}{\text{2.3 portions for one fryer}}$$
= need for three fryers to support serving line rate of six per min.

In another case, a school cafeteria has 500 students going through the serving line in one hour. Of these, 80 percent will take the 113-g (4-oz) portion of fried entrée that loses 10 percent of its weight in frying.

$$\frac{\text{113 g (4 oz) cooked serving}}{\text{90\% raw weight}}$$
= 125 g (4.4 oz) raw weight

500 × 80%

$$= \frac{\text{400 portions needed} \times \text{125 g weight entrée}}{\text{1000 g in 1 kg}}$$

or

500 × 80%

$$= \frac{400 \text{ portions needed} \times 4.4 \text{ oz weight entrée}}{16 \text{ oz in 1 lb}}$$

= need of a fryer that will cook 50 kg (110 lbs) raw entrée per hour.

If the frying cycle is nine minutes frying and one minute draining, then six batches are needed per hour. If one available fryer takes a load of 6.8 kg (15 lbs) of entrée without falling below 149°C (300°F) and the other fryer takes 9 kg (20 lbs), the latter is the one to buy because

$$\frac{50 \text{ kg (110 lbs) cooking capacity needed}}{6 \text{ batches}}$$

= need for fryer that will fry 8 kg (18 lbs) or more per batch.

Usually, the food used to determine fryer capacity is the one that is prepared frequently and requires the greatest fryer capacity per hour. If chicken is cooked from raw to done in the fryer, it is used as the basis for calculations. If precooked chicken is used, then perhaps potatoes, if done in one step, may be used to determine fryer capacity. The U.S. Navy uses fish fillets because their potatoes are precooked in the steamer and the two-step fry (blanch and finish fry) is used. Chicken is steam cooked, also, before finish frying.

Basic Use and Operation

Installation

The manufacturer's qualified distributor should install a fryer, whenever possible, since this person is usually an expert. The manufacturer's operating manual should be checked for detailed installation instructions, and the equipment name plate should be examined for proper voltage and current characteristics. Care should be taken to see that all supports and protective material used in shipping are removed and equipment inspected for shipping or manufacturer's damage or nonconformance with the specification.

All of the installation should conform to local fire, equipment, and sanitation codes. Most distributor's installation workers are aware of these. Be sure that new equipment is properly integrated with the old in terms of horizontal and vertical alignment. It should have legs adjusted so that it is level with no rocking. The fryer should be located near the serving line where there can be tables beside it, or wheeled carts or tables may be brought adjacent to it (figure 11.8).

Before use, the fryer should be cleaned thoroughly inside and out. The outside should be wiped with a clean cloth to remove the rust preventative. Sometimes detergent and water, plus a clean rinse and dry wipe, are needed. Then it should be filled with hot water and fryer cleaner to within 2.5 cm (1 in.) of the top. It should be heated

FIGURE 11.8. Fryer located with table area on left and right of fryer.

but not boiled. The top surfaces should be swabbed off, but the controls and displays should be wiped off carefully with a moist cloth. Then it should be drained and rinsed several times with fresh water to remove cleaner. After this it may be filled with fat and brought up to frying temperature. The thermostat should be checked with a thermometer.

Handling Fat for Fryer Use

The coloring of fried foods has little to do with the composition of the fat. It is a chemical reaction (Maillard) that depends on a certain time-temperature action on certain composition surfaces. The crust is a dehydration of the surface, usually formed when the fat gets above 156°C (312°F) and the surface gets below 3 percent moisture. Quality of the fat is particularly important as it makes up a large part of the finished product—40 percent of the potato chip, 35 percent of the potato stick, 20–25 percent of the doughnut, 12–15 percent of shrimp and scallops, 10 percent of fish sticks, and 7–10 percent of French fried potatoes. The fats provide flavor and tenderize and soften the crust.

Frying fats should be those constructed especially for frying. They should be top-grade commercial shortenings with a high smoking point and resistance to breakdown. The flavor should be bland, neutral, and resist carrying food flavors. The fat should be low in absorption and resist gumming or polymerization.

When adding fat to the fryer, it is best to use liquid fat or to melt it before adding it to the fryer. The cans may be placed in steam jacketed kettles, set on a solid top range, or placed unopened in the pressure cooker or steamer. Failing this, the fat may be packed around the heating elements and the fryer turned on with the thermostat set at about 107–121°C (225–250°F) until the fat is melted, taking care not to scorch the fat. The thermostat is then turned up to the desired frying temperature. Some fryers have a fat-melt feature or a switch that goes on and off intermittently.

Fat level should be at least 2.5 cm (1 in.) above the heating elements to start, and at no time should the heating elements come out of the fat. It is wasteful of heat and possibly dangerous in terms of fire.

During frying, free fatty acids in the fat rise from 0.05 percent at the start to as high as 7–8 percent. Rising up to 0.8 percent can cause the fat smoking point to drop from 218°C (425°F) to 163°C (325°F). This is one of the reasons that the operator should gauge his fryer size so that 15–25 percent of the fat is replaced each day. Thus, the deteriorative elements of the fat are constantly diluted. Some operators never remove and throw away the fat, and others must replace the fat every few days.

Preparation of Products

If it can be done safely, refrigerated foods should be brought to room temperature before frying as this lowers the load on the fryer and reduces energy consumption. However, most frozen foods are best cooked from the frozen state. Those frozen foods that can be thawed without deterioration should be because it is easier on the energy bill.

Products to be fried should be as dry as possible because, although steam going through the fat helps deodorize it, it also helps to break down the fat and causes spatter and foam. The conversion of water to steam also uses undue amounts of energy. Food may be air dried, blotted dry with absorbent materials, or whirled dry in special centrifugal dryers.

Foods that require long periods of frying time should be precooked since they absorb much fat in the cooking and shrink excessively under the batters, causing the batters to fall off. Another reason for precooking is to be able to finish-cook a greater amount than the fryer can handle from raw to done. Many operators blanch potatoes and chicken in the steamer or pressure cooker and then finish-fry it in the deep fat fryer for the desired color, crust, and flavor. In addition to saving time, some people find that they cut their fat consumption more than half and reduce potato loss 20 percent by steam blanching.

Croquettes should be formed several hours before frying as they hold their shape better when this is done.

Where possible, basket loads of chicken, and particularly potatoes, should be premeasured into loads that will not drop the fryer temperature below 149°C (300°F) and which will recover the fat temperature to its initial level by the time the product is done. The cook can weigh each basket load or tie a wire or string across the basket at the proper load level. Usually the basket load will be one-half to two-thirds of the fry basket's total capacity. Insofar as possible, try to separate basket loads into pieces of the same size as each size piece requires a different cooking time. In a high-energy conventional fryer, legs and wings of chicken may cook in ten minutes at 152°C (305°F), thighs in 13 minutes, and breasts in 12 minutes.

All loose crumbs should be removed from breaded foods prior to frying so that they will not fall off in the fryer. Some workers shake the basket several times over the crumb tray before placing it in the fryer. With double-breaded moist foods, letting them stand a few minutes between breadings to absorb the loose moisture is recommended. For products that fall apart during frying, binders of wheat flour, egg white, or cornstarch may be used.

An assembly line type of work center is set up for deep fat frying. For some products a table for raw materials on the left side of the fryer and one for the cooked material to the right of the fryer is all that is needed. An infrared lamp or heater over the cooked food helps to keep it hot and crisp. Frying chicken requires a larger assembly on the raw food side of the fryer. Laid out from left going toward the fryer might be the raw chicken pan, egg and milk dip, crumb pan, and the holding pan. Then comes the fryer and the cooked food pan. The operator would use his left hand to handle the chicken up to the crumb tray and his right hand to handle it thereafter. Each food to be fried should be set up in a somewhat similar assembly line.

Frying Process

The frying process should be such that after the product has been prepared satisfactorily for frying and the proper basket load has been established, the fat will add the desired crust, color, and flavor and, in some cases, cook and tenderize it. All other things being controlled, the cooking temperature and the time remain to be manipulated. This is the frying process.

Once it was thought that the frying fat temperature should never fall below 149°C (300°F) and for finishing the final product, it should not. However, it was found difficult to prepare crisp French fried potatoes that would not become limp as the water from the moist interior worked out and softened the exterior crust. Then it was decided that two-stage frying was the answer. The first, longer period, would cook the potato and drive off some of the moisture, and the second, shorter period, would evaporate the moisture that had worked out of the potato interior and give it the proper color and crispness. This worked, in part, but potatoes still became limp because the moisture content was too high.

The high initial frying temperature of 177–191°C (350–375°F) of the first stage hardened the surface of the potato and made further removal of moisture difficult as the water was still there to soften the crisp crust of the final product. Research showed that if the first stage was carried out below 149°C (300°F), the fat content became higher, the hard case did not form, and moisture was easily driven off. One research group found that initially the temperature of the fat would drop and then level out as moisture was lost. Then, when the temperature of the fat would rise a certain number of degrees from its lowest point, the French fries were at the desired moisture level. The white fries were removed until mealtime when they were fried at regular frying temperature of 177°C (350°F) to the desired color and a crispness that remained during the holding period.

Various foods have different time–temperature

relationships that are best for each product. A thick food, such as raw-to-done chicken, that must cook through and yet not have a thick tough crust, must cook at a temperature of 152–163°C (305–325°C) for a long period of time; one that is thin, or that is already cooked, such as croquettes or fritters, is fried at a higher temperature of 177°C (350°F). A high temperature fast-heat food that is cooked too long at a lower temperature becomes too dry and hard.

Also to be considered is the intermittent use of the low-heat input fryer. Although the high-heat input fryer may operate continuously at the proper speed to cook a food at 163–177°C (325–350°F), to cook it in the same period of time and give a comparable product, the low-heat fryer must start cooking at 191–196°C (375–385°F) and make full use of stored heat of the extra degrees. Then it must wait to recover its heat. Even so, sometimes the quality of the food is damaged, and the exterior of the food is too dark and crusty. Obviously, the only answer is to reduce the basket load and cook at the lower temperature.

Every make and size of fryer has slightly different time-temperature characteristics in cooking each food material. Thus it is a vain effort to try to set up recommended universal time-temperature figures for each food that is fried. Tables 11.1 and 11.2 are given to show relative figures. In conjunction with the recommended time-temperature

TABLE 11.1. ***Deep Fat Frying Chart (Open)***

	Fast-recovery Fryer		*Conventional Fryer*	
Food Material	*Temp*	*Time (min)*	*Temp*	*Time (min)*
Chicken, 1.1 kg (2.5 lb)				
Breasts	152–163°C (305–325°F)	12	177°C (350°F)	10–13
Halves	163°C (325°F)	12–15	177°C (350°F)	12–15
Legs and wings	152–163°C (305–325°F)	10	177°C (350°F)	7–12
Thighs	152–163°C (305–325°F)	13	177°C (350°F)	12–14
Whole	163°C (325°F)	13–15	177°C (350°F)	15
Precooked and breaded	177°C (350°F)	4	191°C (375°F)	4
Croquettes	185°C (365°F)	4	191°C (375°F)	3–5
Doughnuts, raised	191°C (375°F)	1–2	191°C (375°F)	1–3
Fish fillets	177°C (350°F)	3–4	182°C (360°F)	3–5
Fish steaks, breaded	177°C (350°F)	6	191°C (375°F)	6–7
Fritters, fruit	177°C (350°F)	3	185°C (365°F)	2–5
Fritters, vegetable	177°C (350°F)	4–5	185°C (365°F)	4–7

TABLE 11.1. (continued)

Food Material	Fast-recovery Fryer Temp	Fast-recovery Fryer Time (min)	Conventional Fryer Temp	Conventional Fryer Time (min)
Onion rings, breaded	177°C (350°F)	3	177°C (350°F)	3–4
Oysters, large, breaded	177°C (350°F)	3–5	177°C (350°F)	3–5
Potatoes				
Blanched to done, 1.2 cm (0.5 in.) cut	191°C (375°F)	2	191°C (375°F)	2–3
Frozen French fries, blanched	177°C (350°F)	2–4	191°C (375°F)	2–4
Raw to blanch, 1.2 cm (0.5 in.) cut	163°C (325°F)	6	177°C (350°F)	4–7
Raw to done, 1.2 cm (0.5 in.) cut	177°C (350°F)	7	191°C (375°F)	7–10
Raw to done, 1 cm (0.38 in.) cut	177°C (350°F)	6	191°C (375°F)	6
Raw to done, 0.6 cm (0.25 in.) cut	177°C (350°F)	5	191°C (375°F)	5
Scallops	177°C (350°F)	3–4	185°C (365°F)	3–6
Shrimp, breaded	177°C (350°F)	2–4	185°C (365°F)	3–6
Veal or pork cutlets	177°C (350°F)	3–7	191°C (375°F)	4–8

Source: Armed Forces Recipe Service, Washington, D.C.

data, these figures may be used and adjusted by research to the proper process times and temperatures for almost any food to be fried. The main things affecting time-temperature figures are fryer heat input, load amount, and food particle size.

There are now computer controls, some of which indicate doneness in the food product by monitoring temperature changes in the frying fat, and others controlled by a dial setting based on particular food types, cut, and size. They adjust for load size, but frozen and room temperatures cannot be mixed. The latter devices signal when the basket load is too large (drops temperature more than 20 percent). They have a low-heat melt cycle, shut off the fryer if it fails to preheat to 38°C (100°F) in ninety seconds, exceeds 224°C (435°F), or if a fire occurs. It will shut off the fryer if it is not used in a set period of time.

TABLE 11.2. Pressure Frying Chart (varies with make)

Food	Frying Time (min)
Cauliflower	3
Chicken	
Disjointed, 0.7 kg (1.5 lbs)	7
Disjointed, 0.9 kg (2 lbs)	8
Halves, 0.7 kg (1.5 lbs)	7
Halves, 0.9 kg (2 lbs)	9
Whole, 0.9 kg (2 lbs)	12
Corn on cob	4
Fish fillets, 113 g (4 oz)	3.5
Fish, whole, 0.7 kg (1.5 lbs)	5
Oysters	2
Pork chops, 113 g (4 oz)	5
Pork tenderloin	4
Scallops	1.5
Shrimp, jumbo	4

Source: Jule Wilkinson, *The Complete Book of Cooking Equipment,* Revised Edition, CBI Publishing Company, Inc., Boston, 1975, p. 104.

Procedure for Most Fryers

Weigh or measure basket load having similar size pieces of drained and dry food in the same load. The fryer should be at thermostat set temperature before adding the load. Plan to have the fryer operating at full capacity when it is in use. When used for individual orders, this is not possible. Be sure that potatoes are washed free of loose starch and that breaded products are free of loose breading.

Place the fry basket of food slowly down into the fat. If it starts to foam excessively, raise the basket half way out of the fat until the foaming partially subsides and then lower the basket gradually into the kettle. It is well to use safety glasses while frying as a spatter of hot fat may ruin an eye. In manually operated fryers, after the product has cooked about one-third of its cycle raise the basket from the fat and give it a brisk shake. This should be done again two-thirds of the way through the cooking cycle. This shaking breaks apart foods cooking together and helps even out color. If the product floats, turn it over halfway through the cooking cycle. Be sure that all food is below the fat for at least part of the cooking time. Do not depend on the foam since it cooks but slightly. Batter coated foods should be dropped into the empty fry basket after it has been placed in the fryer to avoid their sticking to the basket. Pastries should be kept submerged during frying for an even color.

At the end of the prescribed cooking time, the food should be examined. If it must be cooked through, a piece should be opened to see if it is cooked. Is the product of the proper color and crustiness? If the latter two are correct but the product is not cooked through, the food probably needs more cooking time at a lower temperature to avoid overcooking the outside while the heat is working its way to the product center. On the other hand, if the product was cooked through but the color was too light, the product probably must be cooked at a higher temperature for a shorter time. This high temperature reduces grease soakage to some extent.

If the batter comes off the chicken during raw-to-done frying, it is usually caused by the chicken's shrinking away from the coating allowing it to break up. To avoid this shrinkage, the chicken can be precooked in the steamer prior to coating and fried for a shorter period.

After frying, lift the fry basket of food from the fat, give it several gentle shakes, and allow the fat to drain from the product for a minute. It may be hooked over a bar on the back of the fryer for this period of time. The basket, then, can be inverted, gently dumping the fried product either into a pan carpeted with grease-absorbent material or on a rack that will allow the fat to drain off the food. It is desirable to have the food served immediately so that the moisture will not work out from the product interior and soften the crust. If the fried product must be held for some time, infrared lamps or heaters help to evaporate the moisture as it comes close to the surface of the fried food. Do not salt product until immediately before service, since salt draws moisture that softens the crust. Remove crumbs within the fryer by means of a crumb tray or hand sieve before frying, between batches, and after frying, particularly with breaded foods. Do not salt food in the basket over the fryer. Salt and crumbs hasten fat deterioration.

Cutlets or fish squares may be fried in a single layer in the bottom of a basket, or one can devise a tray that will fit down into the basket without touching the first layer of food, and a second layer of product may be placed on the tray. Some baskets are made with supports similar to letter holders so that fish squares or small fruit pies may be fried in a vertical position without touching. This makes maximum use of the fryer.

When the fryer is on standby, the thermostat should be set back to 93–107°C (200–225°F) and the fryer covered to reduce the rate of fat deterioration. The fry basket should be kept in the fryer during this period so that it does not get cold and add to the heat demand when food is fried.

Foods Not Commonly Fried

Brussels sprouts and whole snap beans may be fried for one and a half to two and a half minutes at 177°C (350°F). Carrot halves or slices, whole okra, and cauliflower flowerets may be fried for one to two minutes at 163°C (325°F). Onion halves may be fried for three minutes at 177°C (350°F). Two-inch slices of zucchini squash may be fried from four to six minutes at 163°C (325°F).

Other foods not commonly fried include whole and sliced mushrooms, pork and veal patties, and extruded shrimp and potatoes.

Special Applications

If the fryer is not in frequent use for frying, consideration should be given to using it for other purposes with and without the use of fat.

If one plans ahead when buying a fryer and gets one with a thermostat that will control down to 79°C (175°F), he may use the fryer for roasting meat, particularly beef. A roast approximately 3.6–5.4 kg (8–12 lb) in size, that will be covered by the fat, is placed in the fryer at 191°C (375°F) and the thermostat is lowered immediately to 79–85°C (175–185°F). A meat thermometer is placed in the coldest place in the meat to tell when the meat is done. Usually it roasts in about the same time as in a 163°C (325°F) oven and the product has a crust and looks and tastes like an oven roast but has a roasting loss of only 15 percent. There is little smoke or steam generated after the first few minutes as cooking takes place below 100°C (212°F). However, water is expressed from the meat and must be drawn off from the bottom before using the fryer again or boil-over will result.

Potatoes may be baked in twenty to twenty-five minutes by piercing each end of the potato with a fork and then immersing them in fat at 163–177°C (325–350°F).

Griddled or fried food can be kept hot by floating it in a pan set in fat at 177°C (350°F) or lower. Fat controlled below 93°C (200°F) makes a good double boiler when a pan of food is set in a rack or floated in it. Eggs may be broken out of the shell and scrambled or soft or hard cooked to be used for garnishes.

When the fry kettle is emptied of fat and filled with salted water, it is ideal for use as a rapid-heat kettle for cooking fragile vegetables such as asparagus or broccoli in the fry baskets. It may be used for other vegetables, as well as for water cooking ham and other meats to care for a serving line shortage or special order. It is very satisfactory for large- or small-batch cooking of pastas. Vegetables in #10 cans may be set in it for preheating prior to being put on the serving line. Boil-in-bag frozen foods may be set in the letter-file basket used for fish squares and pies for rapid timed-cooking or reheating.

Alternatives to the Fryer

Probably the easiest way to serve fried food without a fryer is to buy it prefried and reheat it on a sheet pan in the oven. Many schools use this technique. The old method was to fry in a range-top pan or kettle. This makes it difficult to maintain the fat at the proper temperature, and sometimes splashes or boil-overs result in fires. Of similar danger is the technique used by some institutions and restaurants, that of frying in a roast pan half full of fat in the oven. Some have used this technique for many years without accident or fire. It is dangerous and should be discontinued. Common frying problems and their causes are given in table 11.3.

Saving Energy

1. Fry kettles should be insulated with at least two inches of rock wool or fiberglass. This will reduce energy consumption 25 percent.
2. The deep fat fryer should always be covered, except when food is added to or removed from the basket, to reduce radiating energy losses. Care must be taken to lift the *back* of the cover first to prevent steam burns on arms of operator.
3. Fat should be melted in the steam jacketed kettle or steamer before it is added to the fryer. This

TABLE 11.3. ***Frying Problem Solving***

Causes	*Problems*							
	Fat Darkens Too Much	*Fat Smokes Too Much*	*Fat Foams Excessively*	*Improper Browning*	*Food Greasy*	*Objectionable Flavor*	*Too Much Fat Absorbed*	*Too Much Fat Used*
Inferior fat	X	X	X			X		
Overheating or hot spots	X	X	X					
Improperly prepared food	X	X		X	X	X	X	
Poor or too-infrequent filtering	X	X	X			X		
Inadequate cleaning or rinsing of kettle	X	X				X		
Poor ventilation		X						
Excessive foam formation				X	X		X	X
Overloading kettle				X	X		X	X
Slow kettle recovery				X	X		X	X
Too low frying temperature				X	X		X	X
Failure to clean out gum			X					
Too much frying fat			X					
Keeping food in fat after it is done					X	X	X	X
Improper draining after done					X	X	X	X
Poor quality of food prepared						X		
Contamination of shortening	X	X	X			X		
Breakdown of shortening	X	X	X			X		
Poor fat turnover	X	X	X	X		X		
Drip back of exhaust oil						X		

uses less energy than melting it in the fryer would.

4. The fryer should not be preheated any longer than necessary (7–15 minutes) to bring it up to use temperature.
5. A small fryer should be used for standby and small quantity frying.
6. Pieces of a uniform size should be used in a basket load and the frying time should be gauged according to piece size.
7. Blanching or precooking most foods in steam reduces the total energy consumed, lowers fat consumption by half, and reduces the size of fryer needed.
8. While most foods can be cooked from frozen to done in a fryer, energy conservation requires that they be thawed first in the refrigerator. Other foods should be brought as close to ambient temperature as is safe before cooking. Another possibility is keeping foods to be fried in the residual heat of an oven to get them hot and lower the amount of energy needed for frying.
9. A dry food requires much less energy to cook than does a wet one. Allow baskets of food to drip dry, or blot them before frying. Loose water can be shaken off. Loose crumbs, too, should be shaken off before frying, because they affect the life of the fat and use up energy.
10. In electric fryers, the fat should always be lo-

cated above the level of the heating elements for greatest efficiency. In gas fryers, the flames should be adjusted to blue and should just contact the bottom of the fry kettle or side, to avoid incomplete combustion and decrease heat transfer losses. The U.S. Navy took the top coil of the electric fryer and placed it in the fryer bottom.

11. If frying in quantity, as large a fryer as is available should be used; many small batches are less efficient than a few large ones. Each fryer should be used to capacity. Frying a 1.8 kg (4 lb) load will use 20 percent less energy than a .9 kg (2 lb) load.
12. Fryers should not be so overloaded that the fat falls below 149°C (300°F) during frying, since this increases cooking time and the fat absorption rate of the product. The fryer should be turned off when not in use. If it usually takes too long to raise the heat of the fryer fat to use temperature, the temperature of the fat should be lowered to 107°C (225°F) and the fry kettle covered with a heat-reflective lid.

Cleaning

Care of Fat during Cleaning of Fryer

While fat is in use, it should be strained from time to time with a skimmer to remove surface debris and the strainer on the bottom of the fryer should be emptied since the loose material aids in breaking down the fat.

When the used fat at 66–93°C (150–200°F) is removed from the fryer, it should be passed through a mechanical filter designed for filtering fat or, at the very least, be filtered through a paper or cloth filter that will remove most of the suspended material. Filter aids may be used. If one desires, once or twice a month he may place the fat in a steam jacketed kettle at no more than 93°C (200°F) and sprinkle a few gallons of water over the top of the fat. The water going down through the fat takes with it much of the suspended material left after filtering. The water and some of the fat are drained from the kettle bottom and placed in a kettle for refrigerating and separation of the hardened clean fat from the soiled water. The U.S. Navy calls this process washing the fat. Most operators consider the process too time consuming.

To clean the fryer (daily or twice a week), observe the following steps:

1. Shut off power on switch.
2. Drain the fat when it is below 93°C (200°F) from drain beneath the fryer. Pour fat from small removable kettles, or siphon it from those without a drain.
3. Rinse debris down kettle interior with dippers of hot fat.
4. When fat is removed, wipe out visible residue from the kettle. Hot water may be used to flush the kettle.
5. Portable kettles should be taken to the pot sink for washing. Fixed kettles should be filled with a mixture of hot water and fryer cleaner, usually about two ounces of cleaner to each gallon of water. Trisodium phosphate may be used, but lye or soap composition cleaners should not be used.
6. Boil mixture for twenty to thirty minutes. It may be left overnight. Lift heating elements to raised position out of water.
7. Brush all surfaces with a stiff brush. Take care to clean places where burned-on fat accumulates. Some heating elements may be cleaned by burning off accretions. Ash may be brushed off.
8. Drain water-detergent mixture and rinse kettle several times with a 1:20 vinegar and water mixture to remove and neutralize the detergent. Wipe off all brushed areas with the mixture.
9. Flush all surfaces with clean water to remove the vinegar taste.
10. In the meantime, take fry baskets to the pot washing sink and scrub and rinse all surfaces.
11. Refill fryer with well-filtered fat to about one inch above heating elements.

Maintenance (Weekly)

1. Inspect kettles for leaks.
2. Check thermostat against thermometer to ascertain that it shuts off power or gas to the heating elements at the set temperature and turns it back on at the proper temperature.
3. Check all control and display lights for proper operation.
4. Check placement of thermostat capillary tube to be sure it is in a position where the basket will not strike or dislodge it.
5. In gas fryers, inspect burners for proper flame adjustment and check pilot burner control.
6. Observe drain valves for leaking and smooth operation.
7. If a fryer has a basket lift-out device, check this for timing and smoothness of operation. Gears and slides should be lubricated properly.
8. Adjust burner for best gas-air mixture.
9. Inspect all removable parts for loose connections and proper functioning. Look especially for grease deposits that should be removed immediately.

QUESTIONS

1. Outline the procedure in the general use of the deep fat fryer.
2. Why do customers buy fried foods?
3. On what factors does success in frying depend?
4. Name ten specification requirements for purchase of a deep fat fryer.
5. What is the main advantage of a pressure fryer?
6. How does one increase the productive capacity of a fryer?
7. What are the steps in cleaning the fryer?
8. What percentage of fat load should be used each day?
9. Name five inspections made in a fryer maintenance program.
10. List five uses, other than frying, to which a fryer may be put.
11. List five energy-saving measures to use with deep fat fryers.

BIBLIOGRAPHY

ANON. 1959. A do it yourself frying research kit. Proctor and Gamble Distribution Co., Cincinnati.

ANON. 1966. Deep fat frying procedures. Proctor and Gamble Distribution Co., Cincinnati.

ANON. 1973. It's the care that counts. *Cooking for Profit* 40, No. 266, 57–60.

ANON. 1974. Hot ideas for deep frying. *Restaurant Executive,* March 1974, 10–33.

CHANG, S.S. 1967. Chemistry and technology of deep fat frying. *Food Technology* 21, No. 33, 33-36.

COYN, I.S. 1967. Fry kettle arithmetic. *Cooking for Profit* 34, No. 202, 32–41.

KEATING, R.T. 1969. Deep fat fryers in the school kitchen. *School Lunch Journal* XXIII, No. 9, 60–64.

MORGAN, W.J. 1971. Deep fat frying. *Cornell Hotel Restaurant Administration Quarterly* 11, No. 4, 82–89.

Tilting Fry Pans

The fry pan, also known as tilting skillet, braising pan, and sauté pan, is the most versatile piece of equipment in the kitchen. In form, it is somewhat of a griddle surface with four continuous vertical sides, which makes it, in effect, a flatbottomed kettle. It is bottom heated by gas burners or electric elements and, like the kettle, has a hinged cover that closes the open top.

In evaluating the fry pan, the U.S. Navy foodservice research found that of its 731 recipes, the fry pan was the best cooking device for 65 recipes and could be used for 542 others. It would braise, boil, simmer, griddle, deep and shallow fry, steam, thaw, poach eggs or fish, act as a bainmarie or heater for canned foods, or as a proof box or an oven, and would store hot bakery products. They found that it could be used as an extra kettle, griddle, or fryer when needed capacity exceeded what was available.

Many institutions and restaurants like the fry pan because it will save up to 50 percent in time and labor as well as saving some energy. Many times, all of the preparation steps can be carried out in the fry pan that otherwise might require the use of a number of pieces of equipment together with the requisite additional cleanup.

Description and Specification

Most fry pans are floor mounted in a sturdy tubular framework that may be painted or may be made of stainless steel. They should have feet that are adjustable through 2.5–5 cm (1–2 in.). There are trunnions on either side so that the kettle may be tilted down 90 degrees from the horizontal. Stops should be installed to keep it from going further. It is tilted by use of a self-locking worm and gear assembly that is operated by a hand wheel. This assembly should be tested for slipping by tilting the fry pan 45 degrees and observing any downward movement when resting the weight of an adult person on the pouring lip of the fry pan. If slippage occurs when the pan is fully loaded with hot food, it might be a human and financial disaster (figure 12.1).

Fry pans may be wall mounted on brackets similar to those used for steam jacketed kettles and ovens. A number of manufacturers build fry pans into counters with lifting devices to raise the rear of the pan so that the food will leave the pan over a front pouring lip (figure 12.2). Some of the smaller fry pans are mounted on a counter although, in many cases, this makes their tops rather high for easy use. Increasing use is made of fry pans in a framework on wheels so that the product can be prepared in the kitchen and then wheeled to the serving line or patio for service. Quick-disconnect gas hoses and electric connectors make this easy to accomplish.

The fry pan bottoms are made of steel 1 cm (0.38 in.) to 2.5 cm (1 in.) thick with the top surface being No. 302–304 stainless steel. The rest of the plate is ordinary sheet steel. Thickness of the stainless steel in the body and cover may be 12–18 gauge, and the finish is usually No. 4. At least one manufacturer coats the exterior of the pan with copper to promote better heat distribution.

The cover should fit tightly down into the fry pan and swing up on hinges mounted on the back.

FIGURE 12.1. Floor-mounted tilting fry pan. Courtesy Groen Division, Dover Corp.

FIGURE 12.2. Counter-mounted electric skillet. Courtesy Market Forge.

It should be counterbalanced by springs or other means. A heavy stainless steel cover that is not counterbalanced can slam down on a worker's hand, breaking or splitting fingers. The lifting handle should be fastened to the center of the front of the cover but project down to one end of the device, preferably to the right side. With this, the cover may be lifted without the worker's being in the path of the steam that might gush out as the cover is lifted. Some covers have a condensate drip shield under the cover, and at least one manufacturer has put a vent in the cover.

Heating may be by gas (figure 12.3) or electricity. Commonly this comes to the pan through one of the trunnions. The gas burners are placed across the bottom of the pan similar to those of the griddle to give maximum coverage. The electrical elements are commonly enclosed in tubes and clamped to the bottom of the pan as in a griddle. It is recommended that gas units provide at least 110–125 Btu per sq in. of fry pan bottom, and electric units have an input of 22–24 watts or more per sq in. However, most electric fry pans have considerably under this and range from 12.5–21 watts per sq in. Most American fry pans could use more energy input.

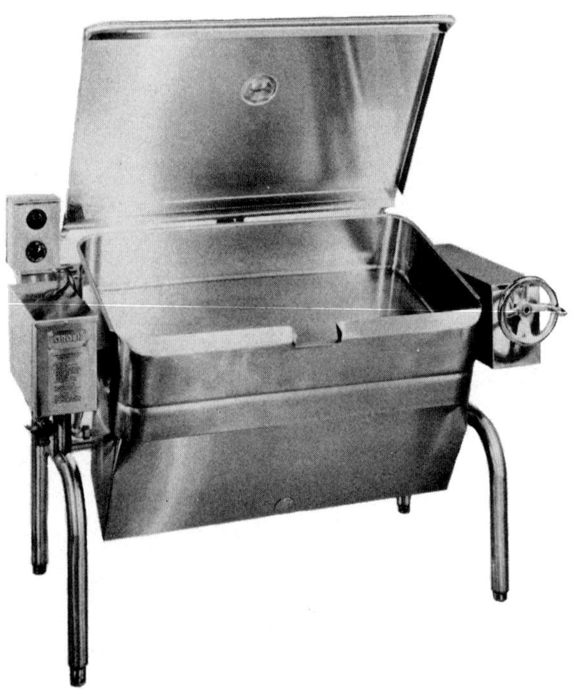

FIGURE 12.3. Gas tilting braising pan. Courtesy Groen Division, Dover Corp.

Gas unit controls are those usual for foodservice—gas flame regulation together with a pilot light or electronic igniter and air-gas mixture adjustment. The electric pans may have an on-off electric switch and a red indicator light to indicate when power is on, as well as a light to indicate when the elements are energized.

Both gas and electric fry pans have thermostats to control temperature. The range of temperatures provided varies with the manufacturer—38–204°C (100–400°F), 38–232°C (100–450°F), and 96–185°C (205–365°F). The thermostat should be accurate to ± 2.8°C (5°F) when the thermostat shuts off the energy at the set point and should cycle through a range of not more than 17–22°C (30–40°F). There should be a high-temperature limiting switch that will automatically shut off the energy input at about 27°C (50°F) above the thermostat's upper limit if the thermostat fails to function. This expedient may prevent a fire or ruined product. It should be capable of being reset easily. A few manufacturers have a sixty-minute timer.

Dimensions of the fry pan vary with the capacity desired and the design of the fry pan. Trunnion fry pans take more floor space than do those mounted in a cabinet and that lift the rear of the pan to pour the contents. A trunnion fry pan may have a 76-cm (30-in.) wide skillet, but overall the equipment is 140 cm (55 in.) wide. Some savings in area can be obtained by increasing the depth of the skillet from a usual 18 cm (7 in.) to a generally available 23 cm (9 in.) if volume increase is needed. If griddling area is needed, the cabinet fry pan is the only solution.

The fry pans commonly range in capacity from 87 liters (23 gal) to 151 liters (40 gal), with the skillet ranging in size from 41 cm (16 in.)

square to 61–107 cm (24–42 in.) wide, and 61–81 cm (24–32 in.) from front to rear with overall dimensions of 91–157 cm (36–62 in.) wide, 84–94 cm (33–37 in.) from front to rear, and 86–102 cm (34–40 in.) high.

The fry pans may be purchased with racks that may be inserted to provide support for pans of food being steamed. Pan holders are available that support the serving pan under the pouring spout as the fry pan is tilted. Usually they are purchased for a specific size of pan, and this must be noted in the specification.

In addition, the fry pan specification should state that the fry pan should conform to pertinent American Gas Association and Underwriters' Laboratories requirements and National Sanitation Foundation Standard No. 4.

Determination of Needed Capacity

With such a multipurpose piece of equipment, it is difficult to choose the product or products on which to base capacity calculations that will dictate size of equipment to be purchased. If the fry pan is to be used primarily for stewing, volume measurements like those used for steam jacketed kettles are used. These are based on commonly prepared products that require a maximum volume fry pan.

$$\frac{\text{number portions} \times \text{portion size} \times (\text{oz or ml vol}) \times 1.20\ (20\%\ \text{headspace})}{\text{128 oz per U.S. gal or 1000 ml per liter} \times \text{number of batches}}$$

= U.S. gal capacity, or liter capacity

Example:

$$\frac{200\ \text{portions} \times 4\ \text{oz} \times 1.20}{128\ \text{oz} \times 1\ \text{batch}} = 7.5\ \text{U.S. gal}$$

or

$$\frac{200\ \text{portions} \times 118\ \text{ml} \times 1.20}{1000\ \text{ml} \times 1\ \text{batch}} = 28.3\ \text{liters}$$

If the primary use is as a griddle surface, then the calculations will be the same as that used for griddles:

$$\frac{\text{number of portions per batch needed}}{\text{number of portions that can be cooked on 1 sq ft (930 sq cm) of fry pan}}$$

=sq ft or sq cm of fry pan surface needed

Example:

$$\frac{30\ \text{portions needed per batch}}{6\ \text{portions cooked per sq ft}} = 5\ \text{sq ft surface needed}$$

or

$$\frac{30\ \text{portions needed per batch}}{6\ \text{portions cooked per 930 sq cm}} = 4650\ \text{sq cm surface needed}$$

Actually, most purchases are based on the volume needed and the money and kitchen space available. Cooks then make adjustments for the variety of foods that can be prepared.

Basic Use and Operation

For the most part, the fry pan is operated in the same way as the equipment for which it would be substituting, whether it be fryer, kettle, griddle, 0 pounds pressure steamer, oven, or bainmarie. The major problem is that it cannot do all the functions at the same time and the cook must determine where it can be used most advantageously. Often this proves to be where the fry pan can perform successively required operations on a product without removing it from the fry pan—Swiss steak or pot roast (browning and moist heat cookery) or chicken cacciatore (cooking chicken, vegetables, and then the mixture).

Frying

Frying may be shallow or deep fat. Most cooks find the fry pan underpowered for deep fat frying. For shallow fat frying, they may use any fat depth from a fraction of 2.5 cm (1 in.) to 5 cm (2 in.) or more. Foods, such as chicken, may be turned several times during the process. Tongs are preferred to forks for the turning task as the product retains more juices. Frying is done at 177–204°C (350–400°F).

Kettle Cooking

The fry pan is ideal for cooking products such as vegetables that might be crushed in a steam jacketed kettle. It is excellent, also, for preparing stew meats and vegetables when it is desirable to brown or braise them in a small amount of fat at 177°C (350°F) first before adding the stocks and food materials that should be water cooked at a simmer or a boil. The cover is closed during kettle cooking. The fry pan can be substituted for an extra kettle for all kettle functions when a heavy kettle-cooked meal is scheduled. Cooking is done at thermostat settings of 93–107°C (200–225°F). Milk products should be kept below 93°C (200°F) so that they will not scorch.

Griddle Cooking

The fry pan, like the griddle, must be at the proper temperature and greased to prepare griddle cakes, fried eggs, scrambled eggs, French toast, hamburgers, and cottage fried potatoes. The cover is kept open. The high sides of the fry pan reduce spatter and restrain runny food products or those with small pieces. Residues from steaks, chops, or other meats that have stuck to the surface of the pan form the basis for gravy. Surplus fat is poured off, and a small amount of water is added. A sharp spatula is used to scrape the flavorful residue from the fry pan. This can be diluted, seasoned, and thickened to gravy consistency. Griddling is done at thermostat settings of 149–204°C (300–400°F) depending on the needs of the product. The fry pan is good for griddling fat-producing food because it can be tilted to drain away fat as it collects.

Sautéing

Sautéing is done at a little lower temperature than griddling. The temperature should be 107–143°C (225–290°F). The product is moved around as it cooks so that it is a lighter fry with no heavy browning. The cover is open.

Steaming

Steaming is commonly done with vegetables as they will not suffer the gross leaching out of nutrients or the losses of flavor and texture that they might in water cookery. Five centimeters (2 in.) of water are placed in the bottom of the fry pan to generate steam. A high thermostat setting should be used to provide heavy steam. The product is placed in perforated pans and set in a special rack that will hold it in the steam. Naturally, the cover is closed.

Holding

Products awaiting service may be placed in about 10 cm (4 in.) of water at 79°C (175°F) to be kept hot. In this way the fry pan becomes a bainmarie. Canned vegetables may be placed in water a little deeper and hotter to bring them up to service temperature. Without water, the fry pan becomes a hot storage for hot breads, pastries, and cakes. The cover is closed.

Poaching

This is usually done with 5 cm (2 in.) of water at a thermostat setting of 93–107°C (200–225°F). The water is acidified and salted for poaching eggs.

Proofing

A small amount of water is placed in the bottom of the pan to provide a humid atmosphere. The thermostat is set at about 38–60°C (100–140°F), and the product to be proofed is placed on a rack. The cover is closed.

Baking

Baking is not a preferred use for the fry pan, but in an emergency, it can be done. The product to be baked should be placed on a wire rack about 2.5 cm (1 in.) above the fry pan bottom. The cover should be closed tightly. The product will tend to brown on the bottom and not on the top. The thermostat should be set at about 204°C (400°F) to start. Experimentation may develop a better temperature. If a top crust is desirable, the vent on the cover should be left open.

Temperatures discussed in the preceding methods are estimates and actual practice may indicate that some other thermostat settings are better for the particular fry pan and cooking practices being used. Table 12.1 lists some suggested thermostat settings and cooking times for selected food products and the average fry pan.

Saving Energy

1. If the fry pan is used for steam or hot water cooking, hot water from the hot water heater should be used. Heated water is more energy efficient than cold water in bringing cooking water temperature up to the use point.
2. The cover should be closed during all cooking whenever possible, as this saves energy. The operator must remember to open the cover away from himself, to avoid burns.
3. The merits of insulating the fry pan are under little consideration in research at present. Placing heat reflectors and some insulation under the heating element and adding two inches of insulation along the outsides of the fry pan can reduce energy losses, however. Using covers made of two layers of metal with air sealed in between them is also helpful.
4. Pans used for cooking within the fry pan should be dark colored and made of thin, heat-conductive metal.

Special Applications

The fry pan may be filled with water and used for hot soaking of pans with cooked-on soils.

Slightly dried breads can be softened by placing them in the fry pan on a rack over small amounts of boiling water.

Where there are energy connections, the fry pan with the special pan-holding rack can be used on patios, in buffets, or in serving lines as a service cart or steam table. With a wire rack covering its bottom and the vent in its cover open, it serves as hot, dry storage for fried or griddled food.

At least one institution has used the 23-cm (9-in.) deep fry pan in an emergency to sterilize dishes. It was filled with water and kept at sterilizing temperature while racks of dishes were dipped into it.

A fry pan that has exposed infrared heating elements in the cover and the bottom can be used as a meat roaster or cooker. The bottom elements are covered with stainless steel drip protectors.

Alternatives to the Fryer

Since the fry pan is an alternate cooking device for a number of conventional pieces of equipment, these pieces of equipment can be used in its stead for the functions they do best. The steam jacketed kettle can be used for boiling, simmering, some steaming, and some pot roasting. The oven may be used for some pot cooking, holding, and its usual roasting and baking. The deep fat fryer can be filled with water for water cooking and with fat for frying. The griddle griddles, fries, sears, and browns. The range pot cooks, holds, and pan fries, although this is dangerous, and its ovens bake and roast.

Cleaning

The procedure for cleaning a fry pan is:

1. Turn off energy source and clean the fry pan as soon as possible after use.

TABLE 12.1. Cooking with the Fry Pan

Product	Thermostat Setting	Cooking Time (min)
Bacon	177°C (350°F)	2–5+
Beef, pot roast	brown meat 149°C (300°F); add sauce	10–15
	simmer 107°C (225°F) until done	120–180
Beef Stroganoff	brown 177°C (350°F)	10–15
	simmer 107°C (225°F)	60
Chicken cacciatore	braise chicken at 163–177°C (325–350°F);	25
	braise vegetables at 149°C (300°F);	15–20
	mix and cook at 107°C (225°F)	20–30
Chicken, fried (pieces)	149–177°C (300–350°F)	20–25
Chop suey	brown 204°C (400°F)	15
	simmer 107°C (225°F)	75
Eggs, hard cooked	107°C (225°F)	10–12
Eggs, poached	107°C (225°F)	2–3
Eggs, soft cooked	107°C (225°F)	5–7
Hamburger, 85 g (3 oz)	177°C (350°F)	4–5
Pancakes, 10 cm (4 in.)	204°C (400°F)	4–5
Potato pancakes	177°C (350°F)	12
Spaghetti and meat sauce	brown 177°C (350°F)	10–20
	simmer 107°C (225°F)	60–120
Swiss steaks	brown 149°C (300°F)	15
	add vegetables and cook at 121–135°C (250°–275°F)	60
Vegetables, fresh (steamed)	keep water at rolling boil	
Asparagus		15–20
Beans, green, cut		20
Beets		60–90
Broccoli		20
Cabbage		10–15
Carrots		25
Cauliflower		12–15
Corn on cob		10–15
Potatoes (medium)		25–30
Spinach		10
Vegetables, frozen (steamed)	keep water at rolling boil	
Beans, green, cut		15
Broccoli spears		12–15
Carrots, diced		10
Carrots, sliced		15
Corn on cob		10
Corn, whole kernel		10–12
Spinach, leaf		20–25

Source: Tilting Skillet Facts on Parade, Market Forge, Everett, Mass., April, 1974.

2. Flush all pan surfaces with warm water. Scrape surfaces on which food sticks with a stiff piece of metal such as a dough cutter. Use a special lime-removing cleaner for mineral deposits. Do not use steel wool or scouring powder as this scratches the surface and makes future cleaning more difficult.
3. For hard-cooked-on soil, use 28 g (1 oz) of a manufacturer-recommended cleaning solution per 7.6 liters (2 gal) of hot water and cover all of the affected areas. Soak for thirty minutes to one hour.
4. For less difficult-to-remove soil, use the cleaner at the rate of 28 g (1 oz) per 11 liters (3 gal) of hot water and brush all surfaces of the kettle including the exterior and both surfaces of the cover.
5. Rinse all surfaces with a flushing of clear warm water.
6. Flush all surfaces with a sanitizer. An additional rinse of fresh water may be used, but it is seldom necessary.

Maintenance

1. Check temperatures of the central bottom of the fry pan against an accurate griddle thermometer. At the point where the thermostat shuts back the gas or electricity, the thermostat and thermometer should be within 2.8°C (5°F). However, a difference of up to 5.6°C (10°F) is permissible.
2. Check gas flames to ensure that the air-gas mixture is correct and that the flames make proper contact with the fry pan bottom.
3. Check gas pipe connections for possible leaks and electric wires for frayed insulation or loose connections in the connectors.
4. Lubricate hinges, gear, and trunnions with lubricant suggested by manufacturer.
5. Be sure that baked-on soil and hard water accretions are removed.

QUESTIONS

1. What are the various functions that can be carried out by use of the fry pan?
2. For what functions is the cover kept open, and for what ones is it closed?
3. How is the fry pan used as a steamer?
4. What are the various systems used for mounting the fry pan?
5. How is the tilting mechanism tested for slippage?
6. What design feature is used to adjust for the heavy cover weight?
7. In what way is the design of the fry pan similar to that of the griddle?
8. What are the desirable energy inputs for the gas and electric fry pans?
9. In computing the volume needed in a fry pan, what head space is provided above the product?
10. What is the most important benefit of using the fry pan in cooking?

BIBLIOGRAPHY

ANON. 1966. The versatile tilting braising pan. *Cooking for Profit* 35, No. 205, 43–46, 118.

ANON. 1967. A new twist in fry pans. Reprint. *Food Service Magazine*.

ANON. 1971. Modern tilt toward a complete cooking center. *Food Service Magazine* 33, No. 6, 16–18.

ANON. 1973. Gas fired tilting braising pans. *Cooking for Profit* 40, No. 266, 38–40.

ANON. Braising pans, the first choice for versatile one step cooking. Manual 900b. Groen Division, Dover Corp., Elk Grove Village, Ill.

ANON. Production capacity of all Market Forge equipment. Bulletin No. 39C. Market Forge, Everett, Mass.

NATIONAL SANITATION FOUNDATION *Food Service Equipment Standards 1978*. Ann Arbor, Mi.

Griddles

A griddle is a food-cooking device that transfers heat from its source to the food by means of a metal plate coated, or not coated, with a film of fat. In most instances, it cooks one side of the food at a time. The expedients used to enable cooking both sides of the food at the same time include: (1) a fixed shelf with infrared elements which cover the back of the griddle; (2) a hinged cover with infrared elements that come down over the product; (3) a heated metal plate, similar to that under the food, that presses down on top of the food; and (4) a deep cover that goes over the product and makes contact with the griddle around the product. This traps the steam given off from the food so that it can be used to cook the top of the food while the griddle cooks the bottom.

The griddling process has the following sought after effects: (1) coagulation of protein (eggs, meat and fish); (2) development of flavor (browning meats and toasting buns); (3) development of crispness or crust (potatoes, bacon, or griddle cakes); (4) melting off fat (sausage, bacon, or hamburgers); (5) tenderizing of tissue (steaks); (6) drying (griddle cakes, buns, and bread).

The griddle has wide application for both quantity cooking and short-order preparation. It does have the disadvantage of being wasteful of energy. The bottom radiates almost half of the generated heat, the metal of the griddle absorbs and stores heat that may never be used, and the top loses heat whenever and wherever it is not covered with food.

Description and Specification

A griddle is usually flat although some are ribbed to give meats a parallel bar or grid effect and drain off grease. It may have shallow grease gutters on one to four sides or have deep troughs along the front and/or back or on either or both sides into which to drain and scrape food grease or debris. Instead of a trough, some manufacturers have smaller rectangular ports. Either troughs or ports drain down into removable grease receptacles that may be 1.9–7.6 liters (2–8 qt) in capacity.

Griddles may be made of iron, steel, or sheet or cast aluminum. While the aluminum probably has the best temperature distribution characteristics, steel is considered best overall. It is not as porous as the iron but has better heat distribution and is not as soft as the heated aluminum. Chrome-coated steel forms a transparent chromium oxide film that makes the steel even less porous. This speeds cooking, provides these griddles with good product-release qualities, and allows easy cleaning. It does not radiate as much heat as regular steel griddles.

Most griddles are 1.1 or 1.3 cm (0.45–0.5 in.) thick although some are as much as 2.5 cm (1 in.). The 1.3-cm thick griddle preheats quicker, absorbs less heat, responds to needed temperature increases, and is better for heavy loads than the thicker one. However, the thicker one is more even in temperature distribution and probably is better for light loads where even coloration is important.

The griddle is usually heated by gas or electricity. The flames of gas impinge on the bottom of the griddle and the waste products go up a flue. The burner may cover 15–30 cm (6–12 in.) of griddle width, and usually a single thermostat will govern one or two burners although they may control more. The thermostat should be in 13.9°C (25°F) increments through a usual range of 66–232°C (150–450°F). Ignition may be from a constantly running pilot light or one of the new electronic ignition systems. To provide the maximum production, it is desirable that the griddle have the maximum heat input that the food can properly conduct to its interior without overcooking the exterior. U.S. Navy research indicated that a gas griddle should have at least 110–125 Btus of gas per 6.45 sq cm (1 sq in.) of griddle surface.

With electrically heated griddles, the elements may be either imbedded in the metal or clamped onto the bottom of the griddle. Usually the elements are sealed in metal tubes to protect them. As with gas, the heat derived from electricity should be that necessary for maximum production, frequently 24 watts or more per 6.45 sq cm (1 sq in.) of griddle surface.

Since the corners and edges of the griddle lose their heat more rapidly than the center, the elements should be arranged to provide more heat in these areas. It was only a few years ago that griddles would vary 72°C (130°F) from their hot centers to their cooler corners. In quantity production of griddle cakes, some cooks found that they could prepare more per hour if they never placed cakes in the corners. Wiring, other than elements, should be grease resistant and placed where it is difficult for grease to contact it.

Griddles with gutters on four sides suffer from reduced capacity as cooks will drop griddle cakes and eggs well back from the edge to avoid the mess of cleaning them out of the gutter. The 7.6–15-cm (3–6-in.) fence was developed to surround the griddle surface tightly on two or three sides to permit griddling out to the ends and to keep scrambled eggs or hashed browned potatoes on the griddle surface while acting as a splatter guard, as well (figure 13.1).

In preparing a specification for a griddle, one considers, among other things, the following:

1. the foods to be griddled; this may dictate how the griddles will be split up as to size
2. the amount to be prepared and in what time as this will indicate needed size
3. what area and space is available for griddles
4. griddle preheat and cooling time
5. energy source most available and least expensive
6. availability of maintenance

FIGURE 13.1. Standard electric griddle with fence. Courtesy Vulcan Hart Corporation.

Foods to be Prepared

If foods are to be mainly short-order or heavy-demand foods such as hamburgers, it is probably best to specify a fast-heating aluminum or 1.3-cm (0.5-in.) steel griddle. If the load is to be light-demand foods such as griddle cakes, eggs, or French toast, the evenness of the 2.5-cm (1-in.) thick griddle might be a consideration. If a variety of foods using different cooking temperatures is to be prepared, griddles with multiple thermostats should be specified, or better yet, instead of dividing up the surface of a 1.8-m (6-ft) griddle among two or three products, provide smaller griddles, one to a product. Not as much energy is lost by using the small griddle instead of partially loading a large one.

If the foods are to be runny or composed of many small pieces, it is best to buy a griddle with a stainless steel fence around at least three sides and do any scraping to the trough in front of the griddle. If shallow frying is desired, the usual three-sided stainless steel splash guard plus a fourth across the front may be used to make a shallow fry pan. Griddles built in this way are not easy to empty, scrape, or clean.

Griddle Space Characteristics

A griddle may be of almost any width from 15 cm (6 in.) to many feet wide, and from 0.3–1.2 m (1–4 ft) deep (from front to rear). Most of those generally available are from 0.6–2.5 m (24–96 in.) wide, and 45–60 cm (18–24 in.) deep. While the width of the device is close to that of the griddle surface, the depth of the device can be 10–23 cm (4–9 in.) greater to allow for the gutter or grease trough, controls, and guard rail.

In height, counter top griddles may use legs (fixed or adjustable) in heights of 0–20 cm (0–8 in.) to present the griddle surface at about 0.9–0.96 m (36–38 in.) from the floor, depending on the height of the counter or stand. Some units are drop-ins that fit into an oblong hole in the counter and present the griddle surface 0.7–1.3 cm (0.25–0.5 in.) above the counter. Other griddles use an iron stand with legs of angle iron or tubular steel or legs alone to present the griddle surface at 76–107 cm (30–42 in.) from the floor. The griddle top should be about 5 cm (2 in.) below the worker's elbow if a straight spatula is used and 10 cm (4 in.) if an offset one is used. A number of griddles are installed as integral parts of range tops. They may use all or share part of the range top with open burners, solid hot-top pot-heating elements, or unheated table units of various widths. The splash guard fence, or mere raised edge, around the griddle surface must be added to the griddle surface height.

Heating Units

If using gas, the burners should have American Gas Association approval and should be inspected to ensure that a maximum of the griddle bottom surface is being impinged on by flame. Spaces between the flames will usually be cooler in temperature, making products such as griddle cakes irregular in color. Most burners used for griddle and hot tops are rectangular in shape with their long axis from front to rear or side to side. Btu input should be 100–125 per 6.45 sq cm (1 sq in.) of griddle area, with the higher level being more desirable.

Electric griddles using resistance wiring enclosed in metal tubing should be so arranged on, or in, the bottom of the griddle so that all of the top surface is close to the element beneath it. Particular care should be taken that a heating element extends along the edge and into the corners. At least 24 watts should be provided for each 6.5 sq cm (1 sq in.) of griddle surface.

Preheating Times

Preheating times for griddles vary according to the griddle material, the thickness of the griddle, the amount of applied heat, and the griddle surface area. To reach 177–204°C (350–400°F) should take no more than fifteen minutes and preferably no more than seven to twelve minutes.

In purchasing griddles, cooling times, although of some importance to cleaning them, may not be available.

Pretesting Griddles

Griddles should be pretested to determine whether they meet the cooking times indicated by the manufacturer. More important is the testing for evenness of heating over the griddle surface. This is done by the following procedure:

1. Turn on all elements at the same time with thermostats at the same temperature.
2. When the thermostats turn the heat down or off, load griddle with the griddle cakes in order of front to rear and left to right.
3. When left front cake is properly browned, turn all cakes in the same order that they were placed on the griddle originally.
4. When left front cake is done, remove all cakes and place them on a sheet pan or table in the order in which they were on the griddle.
5. Examine both sides for color differences, which indicate unevenness of griddle heating.

Determination of Needed Capacity

In calculating needed griddle capacity, one selects the commonly prepared product that makes the greatest demand on griddle capacity. Usually, this is the hamburger. Then one must determine how many are needed in what period of time. Assuming that the griddle will hold 20 portions in one batch load, the following formula may be used:

$$\frac{\text{serving line rate per min} \times \text{time (min)}}{\dfrac{\text{60 min}}{\text{batch cycle min}} \times \text{portions (batch) on 61-x-91-cm (24-x-36-in.) griddle}}$$

or

$$\frac{8 \times 60 \text{ min}}{\frac{60}{10} \times 20} = \frac{480}{120}$$

= four 61-x-91-cm (24-x-36-in.) griddles, or
= two 61-x-183-cm (24-x-72-in.) griddles

The batch cycle time is computed by adding the various components—10 seconds to place hamburgers on griddle, 3.5 minutes to cook on one side, 1 minute to turn, 3.5 minutes to cook on the other side, 1 minute to remove hamburgers from griddle and 50 seconds to scrape the griddle, or 10 minutes, total time.

Another way to determine needed capacity is on the square foot basis. If the hamburgers are 7.5 cm (3 in.) in diameter, 16 of them would cook on 0.1 sq m (1 sq ft) of griddle area every 10 minutes. Thus, if one needed 300 hamburgers per hour, the calculation would be:

60 min per hr ÷ 10 min per batch
= 6 batches per hr

300 hamburgers needed ÷ 6 batches per hr
= 50 hamburgers per batch

50 hamburgers per batch ÷ 16 hamburgers per 0.1 sq m (1 sq ft) griddle = 0.4 sq m (4 sq ft) (approx)

One griddle 61 x 61 cm (24 x 24 in.) would be needed.

Basic Use and Operation

In the past, the griddle has been placed in the center of the kitchen, crowded under the kitchen hood with the range, oven, and other cooking equipment. Fast food short-order cooking brought it out next to the kitchen partition, close to service and, in some cases, placed it on the service side of the partition or on the serving counter. The military placed griddles in the cafeteria service lines with enough capacity to serve steaks to ten to twelve men per minute.

The griddle, like the deep fat fryer, should be thought of as part of a short-production line (figure 13.2). There should be table space to the left of the griddle for raw material and for making food ready for griddling. To the right of the griddles should be receptacles with racks for the cooked food. Infrared lamps may be placed over these to keep the food hot and to vaporize the moisture that might make its way from the interior of the food and soften the exterior crust. If there is a shortage of table space, the cook has space on one side of the griddle only, or in the case of the griddle with a depth of 30–46

FIGURE 13.2. Griddles used in conjunction with other production equipment. Courtesy Vulcan Hart Corporation.

cm (12–18 in.), a cutting board of 25–30 cm (10–12 in.) deep in front of the griddle is used for the purpose. Using tables across an aisle from the griddle should be discouraged. The cook, under these conditions, faces away from the griddle and cooking food about 60 percent of the time. If a griddle is established in a battery of other equipment without tables, possibly wheeled tables can be brought up at right angles to the ends of the griddle.

To provide raw material, a refrigerator may be set close to the griddle. Ideally, one should have a drawer type refrigerator mounted under the griddle.

At times, griddles are placed in a frame mounted on wheels. With proper energy connections, these can be used wherever needed—in the kitchen, on the serving line, in a buffet, or out on a patio. They may be mounted on a table with adequate space on each side, have leaves that lift up and lock into place on each side of the griddle, or use other fixed or portable tables.

Making Griddle Ready for Use

When new, the griddle may be coated with a preservative. This should be removed with a grease-removing chemical. After installation by the distributor's or manufacturer's representative, the griddle should be tempered. This is the filling of the pores of the griddle surface with grease. It is usually accomplished by heating the griddle surface up to 204°C (400°F) and then coating it with cooking oil. After five minutes of baking, the residue of the oil is wiped off and the griddle is ready for use. Teflon and chromium-coated griddles do not have to be tempered.

Cooking on the Griddle

The thermostat is set at the proper temperature for the product to be cooked. When the power-on light goes off, the griddle is ready for loading. Most griddles are first coated with a cooking fat especially formulated for griddling. This has a good flavor and is resistant to breakdown and gumming. Fat foods such as bacon do not require a greased griddle. The food is placed on the griddle so as to use a maximum of the available area; unused space radiates and wastes heat.

Care should be taken to see that the food fits flat on the griddle surface. Steaks and chops will curl away from the griddle surface if the edge of the product is not cut vertically in a number of locations. Weights may be placed on curling foods if this does not damage their appearance. To speed hamburger griddling, they may be mashed flat on the griddle with a spatula. However, some people feel that this forces the liquid out of the hamburger and makes it less juicy.

After each load is removed, the griddle surface should be scraped with a sharp-edged spatula into the gutter or port and on into the grease container. After regreasing, the griddle is ready for reloading.

The time-temperature relationship (table 13.1) for each food depends on the type of food—eggs, griddle cakes, meats etc.—its consistency and thickness, any precooking, amount of contact with the griddle, and the degree of doneness or browning desired. In addition, it is influenced by the griddle's thickness, type of metal and surface, heat input, and cycling range of the thermostat. These will not be discussed in detail because of the variability of foods and equipment. However, if browning is the main reason for using a griddle, such as in preparation of breakfast, minute steaks, or precooked hashed browned potatoes, the cooking temperature should be high and the time short. If the product is thick and cooking or heating through is essential, the temperature must be lower and the cooking time longer. See table 13.2 for causes of imperfect products.

Special Adaptations

The griddle is not a versatile piece of equipment. A few of the modifications of design or use of the griddle follow.

Two of the more efficient griddles provide heat on both sides of the cooking food. Starting with the

TABLE 13.1. Suggested Griddle Times and Temperatures

Food	*Size*	*Temperature*	*Time (min.)*
Bacon		177°C (350°F)	3
Canadian bacon		177°C (350°F)	3
Cheese sandwich		191°C (375°F)	3–4
Eggs, fried		149°C (300°F)	2–4
Eggs, scrambled		149°C (300°F)	2–4
Frankfurters		163°C (325°F)	4
French toast		177°C (350°F)	3–4
Hamburger	71 g (2.5 oz)	177°C (350°F)	4
Hamburger	92 g (3.25 oz)	177°C (350°F)	5–7
Pancakes	10 cm (4 in.)	191°C (375°F)	3–5
Potatoes, American fried		191°C (375°F)	4–6
Potato patties		191°C (375°F)	3–6
Steak, breakfast	227 g (8 oz)	218°C (425°F)	5
Steak, minute	170 g (6 oz)	204°C (400°F)	3–5
Sausage links		177°C (350°F)	4
Sausage patties		177°C (350°F)	4–5

Source: Jule Wilkinson, *The Complete Book of Cooking Equipment,* Revised Edition, CBI Publishing Company, Inc., Boston, 1975, p. 94.

TABLE 13.2. Causes of Imperfect Products

Imperfection	*Cause*
Eggs are tough	too high cooking temperature
Food cooks too slowly	griddle overloaded griddle underheated food put on griddle at bottom of heating cycle
Food is grease soaked	drainage from griddle surface is impeded
Food sticks to griddle	griddle not tempered pots used on griddle surface foods too cold not enough fat on griddle improper temperature setting
Griddle cakes are soggy	cakes stacked when removed from griddle
Hashed browned potatoes do not brown	too low cooking temperature
Lacks brown outside when cooked through	too low cooking temperature
Meat is tough after cooking	needs cooking longer at lower temperature
Overcooked outside and underdone inside	too high temperature

basic griddle, one uses infrared units in and over the griddle back shelf or in a hinged housing that comes down over the food to provide top-side cooking. The other uses solid plates or grids in a hinged housing so that the grids make contact with the top and bottom of the food, thus providing conduction cooking on both sides of the food. In addition, steam is trapped to add to the cooking speed.

The chromium-surface griddle is quite fast and requires a minimum of effort to clean it.

Another variation of the griddle is made of heated rows of rotating tubes on which frankfurters spin as they cook. With its movement and evenness of cooking, it makes for good exhibition cooking.

New griddle designs use heating elements immersed in gasifiable liquids or heat pipes to generate a vapor that impinges and condenses on the bottom side of the griddle. If the generator is well insulated, this equipment should be energy efficient and heat evenly. In Europe, a griddle is used that is heated by liquid which is centrally heated and circulated about the kitchen to heat various pieces of equipment.

To overcome the slowness of cooking on the

conventional griddle, the griddle iron can be used to press the product against the griddle surface. In some instances, operators strive to make an acceptable product by cooking only one side of the product. The easiest way of doing this is to use the deep cover that envelops the food and entraps the cooking steam and heat around the product because its rim is in contact with the griddle surface. Another method of cooking uses the pressure of the spatula to make good contact of the hamburger with the griddle. In this case, the product is not turned.

One fast food chain places a rehydrated dried onion and water mixture on the griddle and places a square hamburger with five holes over this but not touching the griddle. After the mixture is seasoned, the bun is placed on top. The hamburger is never turned.

If griddles have a fence around three or four sides of the griddle, it is possible to cover the entire surface with Western sandwich mix or hamburger and then score the mass into sandwich squares.

If the griddle has a grease tight fence completely around the griddle surface, 2.5 cm (1 in.) or more of fat may be placed on the griddle for shallow frying of various foods.

Some cooks use the griddle as they would a solid-top range to heat pots or keep pans of food warm. This is inefficient in its use of energy, and the surface must be tempered again before being used for griddling.

Occasionally, the griddle is used for baking rolls or biscuits. A rack holds the bakery product about 2.5 cm (1 in.) above the griddle surface. A vented deep cover is placed over it. The products brown well on the bottom but poorly on top.

Several makes of griddles use the heating elements of the griddle to provide heat for a broiler beneath it. Used primarily for top browning and cheese melting, it comes equipped with a shelf. There are several shelf levels or distances from the elements.

Alternatives to the Griddle

Probably the alternative most used is the frying pan or skillet used in conjunction with a range. This is particularly good for cooking individual portions and when demand is intermittent. Another device, growing in use, is the high-sided fry or sauté pan. This device can be used for frying, kettle cooking, and griddling, among other things. It is probably superior to the griddle for products such as scrambled eggs or hashed browned potatoes as it surrounds them on four sides. Steam jacketed kettles are often used for scrambling eggs.

Products made on the griddle may be made in ovens at times. The product may be given a griddle-like crust in a deep fat fryer and the finish cooking is carried out in the oven.

Saving Energy

1. To avoid wasting energy, use the entire surface of the griddle whenever possible. Covering the surface with a Western sandwich mix or omelets and then cutting the product in squares will conserve heat. Overlapping griddle cakes and whole eggs will also utilize more of the heated surface.
2. Individual servings will use less energy on a griddle if cooked on one side only and topped with a bell cover. Two-sided griddles should be considered.
3. Griddle surfaces should be covered with an insulated and reflective cover when on standby. A thin griddle surface and a low standby temperature help reduce needed energy. A thin griddle speeds preheat time and does not store energy wastefully.
4. Griddled food is an expensive use of energy unless it has been precooked by a less expensive means, such as steam. Examples of foods that can be steamed and then browned are hashed-browned potatoes, various meats, and vegetables. Eggs and fish are damaged by a double cooking.

5. Foods to be griddled should be at room temperature or above unless this temperature endangers health. Eggs in shell and bacon may be at room temperature while fish cannot.
6. A small amount of cream added to cottage-fried potatoes will give a good brown color and shorten cooking time for precooked potatoes.
7. A mechanical griddlecake dropper and an egg dropper that covers the entire surface at once shortens the length of time that the griddle surface is unproductively bare. A unit that will turn over an entire batch of food at one time is also helpful.
8. Black steel griddle tops radiate and lose much heat while chromium and shiny steel save most of the heat until it is conducted into the food by contact. Foods that must be cooked at a low temperature, such as eggs, should be cooked at the lowest possible temperature to take advantage of the energy used in preheating. Use no more sections of the griddle than necessary. The griddle should be shut off when not in use, and scraped after every batch is cooked, since griddle residue acts as a barrier to heat transfer and wastes energy.
9. The air-gas ratio of gas griddles should be adjusted to a good blue flame that makes contact with the griddle bottom but does not spread to the griddle sides or up the flue. Placing a reflective surface and insulation under the burners improves energy efficiency.

Cleaning

While there are some differences in the ways in which individuals clean griddles, in general, the procedure is as follows:

1. Allow the griddle to cool down to between 65–93°C (150–200°F).
2. In the meantime, empty the fat container.
3. Scrape the griddle surface with a sharp spatula.
4. Make a slurry of good griddle cleaner and water and spread it over the griddle surface with a cloth. Let stand for the established time, if indicated, otherwise about ten minutes.
5. Wipe or scrape residue into drain trough. Wipe trough contents into fat container. Wipe off other surfaces which have been struck with grease or residue.
6. Rinse off residue from griddle and other surfaces with warm water and wipe with a dry cloth.
7. Empty fat container and wash in pot sink. Drain dry and replace in griddle.
8. Temper griddle surface before using griddle again.

Maintenance

1. At least once a week inspect the griddle for hard grease deposits or loose parts.
2. Check fuses, thermostats, lights and other controls.
3. Periodically check the thermostat against a good griddle thermometer. Be sure that the thermostat cycles according to the manufacturer's maintenance manual. Check griddle surface for cold spots which might indicate defective heating elements.
4. Check for levelness. Some operators like to have the griddle tilt slightly toward the grease container or trough. This is the only variation from absolute level that should be tolerated.
5. In gas griddles, check for proper flame adjustment in the burner and pilot light. Adjust burner for best gas-air mixture.

QUESTIONS

1. List the effects that griddling has on food.
2. Of what metals are the griddle plates made?
3. Of what capacity are the grease receptacles?
4. Is a thin or a thick griddle best for fast cooking?
5. What should be the least input in gas and electricity per square inch, or square centimeter, of griddle surface?
6. What is the advantage of the stainless steel fence around the sides of the griddle?
7. How does one pretest a griddle for evenness of heat?
8. What should be the relationship of the griddle with supporting work tables?
9. How is the griddle tempered and used?
10. What is the procedure for cleaning a griddle?
11. List five ways of reducing energy consumption in griddle use.

BIBLIOGRAPHY

ANON. 1975. A griddle station designed for high productivity. *Cooking for Profit* 42, No. 284, 52.

AVERY, A.C. 1969. The griddle. *Cooking for Profit* 35, No. 197, 42, 44 and 46.

BREY, H.S., MAYER, M.L., and PARDO, J. 1962. *The Evaluation of Naval Shipboard Griddles.* U.S. Naval Supply Research and Development Facility, Bayonne, N.J.

LONGREE, K., and BLAKER, G.G. 1971. *Sanitary Techniques in Food Service.* John Wiley and Sons, New York.

KOTSCHEVAR, L., and TERRELL, M.E., 1961. *Food Service Planning: Layout and Equipment.* John Wiley and Sons, New York.

SCHOMAN, C.M. 1960. *Influence of Electrical and Temperature Characteristics of Griddle on Griddling Operation.* U.S. Naval Supply Research and Development Facility, Bayonne, N.J.

TERRELL, M.E. 1971. *Professional Food Preparation.* John Wiley and Sons, New York.

WILKINSON, J. 1975. *The Complete Book of Cooking Equipment.* CBI Publishing Company, Inc., Boston.

Broilers

A broiler is a device for dry heat cooking. It cooks mainly with radiant and infrared heat waves that are emitted from charcoal, coke, ceramic, gas flame, or electric coil in a metal tube. Usually it cooks only one side of the food at a time, although there are a few, including some conveyor broilers, that cook the food on both sides at the same time. There are several that cook the bottom of the food on a griddle or solid grid and use a hinged swing down broiler to cook the top.

Generally, either gas or electricity is used to provide the heat, although charcoal, coke, or wood are used in a few commercial broiling devices as well as in many home backyard broilers. Broilers are available in many designs, but most are cavities with a heat source in the top and the food is lifted up to it on grids. The next most common design is that of a waist-high grid supported over the heat source of ceramic or metallic radiants.

The charred flavor of many meats and some seafood derived from broiling is relished by some people. It is not a new way of cooking, although the backyard broiler is a modern phenomenon. Cavedwellers, and later the Indians and pioneers, did much of their cooking by placing meat on rocks facing the fire or suspending meat, poultry, and ears of corn over the campfire coals, broiling style. Of all the equipment used in the institutional kitchen today, the broiler has been improved the least from an ancient method of cooking. Martha

Washington had spring- and weight-driven spits to facilitate even broiling of meats and poultry over wood coals. The only real differences are that today the spit is driven by an electric motor and the heat comes from gas or electricity (figure 14.1).

FIGURE 14.1. Continuous broiler used to cook barbecued chicken. Courtesy Crown-X Inc.

The broiler is not a very versatile method of cooking; it is primarily a surface activity limited to certain fat meats, poultry, and fish. True, other meats and fish can be cooked after application of a marinade or fat coatings, but they tend to suffer from too much drying action. Broiling is used, also, to brown and give a crisp exterior to foods cooked through by other means such as meats, poultry and casseroles, to broil certain vegetables including tomato and potato slices, and to melt cheese in sandwiches and on pie. The broiler may be used to reheat entrées, particularly individual plates of foods cooked by other means.

The charbroil or hearth type of broiler is sometimes used as an exhibition-cooking device. It may be set up in a restaurant window, in an island near the center of the restaurant, or in a partially enclosed area at the rear of the dining room. A frequent showy leap of flame, the odor of charring meat, and a chef with a flair sell much broiled food. The charbroiler is not a comfortable device over which to work because of the heat radiated up and into the face of the cook. (figure 14.2).

Description and Specification

Broilers take many forms but the following are the most common:

FIGURE 14.2. Hearth type gas broiler. Courtesy U.S. Range Co.

1. upright heavy-duty or hotel broiler
2. back-shelf broiler or salamander
3. hearth type or charbroiler
4. combination griddle broiler (see Chapter 13)
5. rotisserie broiler
6. infrared broiler (see Chapter 8)
7. conveyor broiler

Upright Heavy-duty or Hotel Broiler

This is a top-heated gas or electric unit with a lever and a spring counterbalanced grid that slides out against safety stops for loading. Distances from the heating elements are adjustable in increments of 3.8–20 cm (1.5–8 in.). The exterior is usually covered with at least 16-gauge stainless, black-japanned, or other heat-resistant finish steel. The frame is best if made of all welded steel or angle iron although a few are heavily bolted.

In most cases, the heat is derived from gas or electrically heated ceramic or metal alloy elements or direct gas flame that provide radiant heat. Some of these come up to the temperature for using in three to five minutes while others take up to fifteen minutes. Infrared broilers take a maximum of one and a half minutes. Reflective broiler interiors help to direct more of the radiant heat back toward the grid and the broiling food. At least one broiler has heat from beneath as well as from above, thus obviating the need to turn the product and thereby speeding the broiling process.

Beneath the grid is a sloping grease trough that leads into a grease receptacle. All parts should be removable or easily accessible for cleaning. Gas broilers must have a flue to remove the gas combustion products and smoke, and most others have flues with dampers to remove the smoke and fumes. These should be carefully regulated so that they do not adversely affect the gas flames or remove more of the heat than is necessary during removal of undesirable waste products. The overhead ceramic units tend to burn up the smoke and grease in the air.

The grids on which the broiling takes place are usually made of warp-resistant cast iron or steel. In the upright heavy-duty broiler, the grids have areas ranging from 0.30–0.55 sq m (475–850 sq in.). Most of these grids pull out within slides against safety stops that can be released to remove the grids for cleaning. Wide spaces between the grids through which food might fall are undesirable. A lever permits the raising and lowering of the grid in a number of fixed positions. Some broilers have drop-down doors, but most are open fronts.

It is desirable that the broiler cavities be insulated with a high-temperature-resistant material as this will reduce heat loss and make the broiler more comfortable around which to work. These large units, when heated by gas, use up to 100,000 Btu per hour at temperatures of 816–1093°C (1500–2000°F) for radiant units and 538–816°C (1000–1500°F) for infrared. The infrared uses less gas and cooks faster. The electric broilers commonly have an input of 12–14 kw with at least one having an input of 16 kw. Usually the broiler is controlled in one to three temperature settings using three heat controls similar to those on ovens.

The broilers may be mounted on a conventional or convection oven or on a table or stand in one to three tiers (figure 14.3). Except in space-short situations, one broiler is preferable because it can be installed so that it is easy to see into and operate, whereas two or three together are inconvenient from a height standpoint. Exterior dimensions vary from 81–91 cm (32–36 in.) in width, 77–102 cm (30.5–40 in.) in depth, and 31–61 cm (12–24 in.) in height. The broiling grids range in size from 57–66 cm (22.5–26 in.) in width, and 33–75 cm (13–29.5 in.) in depth. One model has two 64-×-57-cm (25-×-22.5-in.) grids side by side.

The Back Shelf Broiler or Salamander

This is very similar to the heavy-duty broiler except that it is smaller. Usually it sits over the back of a range to which it is attached. It is used primarily for browning the tops of casseroles and similar dishes, melting cheese, broiling short orders of a single or few orders of meats, removing the rareness

FIGURE 14.3. Broiler used in conjunction with microwave oven and conventional oven.

from cuts of roast beef, and similar jobs demanding overhead heat. Where a heavy-duty broiler may have 4839 sq cm (750 sq in.) of grid area, a salamander is usually about 2128 sq cm (330 sq in.) in area and has a production rate of about one-third that of the larger broiler.

The exterior of a salamander is usually the same as the range on which it is mounted, and the interior is much the same as the heavy-duty broiler but with smaller dimensions and heat input. The salamander is about 81–91 cm (32–36 in.) wide, 42–57 cm (16.5–22.5 in.) deep, and 76–103 cm (30–40.5 in.) to its top above the range top. The actual height of the broiler ranges between 37 and 45 cm (14.5 and 17.7 in.). The grids range from 1483–3419 sq cm (230–530 sq in.) in area. Heat input ranges from 30,000–44,000 Btu per hour for gas and approximately 5 kw for electricity.

Counter Top Broilers

These take many forms but usually are small versions of the heavy-duty broiler, charbroiler, or the infrared oven and will not be discussed in detail. These and the cheese melter have their place in the fast food restaurant but are used very little in hotels, cafeterias, institutions, or table service restaurants. In most cases, they do not have doors and are not readily adjustable in distance from the heat source, although they may have two or three slide shelf settings. A common size is 81 cm (32 in.) wide, 48 cm (19 in.) deep, and 48 cm (19 in.) high with grids 60 x 37 cm (23.6 x 14.5 in.).

Char-Hearth or Underfired Broiler

This is a late model charcoal broiler that uses gas or electricity to get the charcoal effect with less effort and faster time. It uses a heavy grate to support ceramic or refractory materials that are heated from beneath to form a radiant bed of coals under the cast iron grids which hold the food. Some have electric heating elements in the grids to provide self cleaning and bottom heating broiling elements. In the ceramic type, juices drip on the radiants to generate flames and smoke that impart the typical charcoal appearance and flavor while the grids burn typical marks into the meat. The system is dangerous from the standpoint of flash flames rising up into the exhaust filters and exhaust system. It is recommended that the nearest filter or unit be no less than 122 cm (48 in.) from the broiling meats.

The charbroil is commonly limited to the cooking of meats, preferably those that cook fast. Often it is demonstrated in restaurant windows to attract customers and in restaurant dining rooms to spark the ordering of high-priced steaks and chops. The units may be mounted on floor stands or on counters (figure 14.4). A few are set on top of ovens or storage shelves.

The floor mounted gas charbroiler may use various ceramics or flare plates to generate radiant or infrared heat beneath the grids that hold the food. The frame is usually welded steel angle iron and is only rarely bolted. The sheathing can be stainless steel or sheet steel with a heat- and rust-resistant finish. Under the heating elements are sloping plates directing fat that escapes into a drawer or other container. In gas units, one to three burners are operated by each control, which may have both a high heat for preheating and a low setting for cooking operations. With the electric units, in most cases the electric elements are imbedded in metal rods that alternate with the grid bars. They are emplaced in the grid itself or placed below the ceramics. The enclosed broiler assembly is supported on pipe legs made rigid on two sides by gussets. It is desirable that the feet be adjustable so that the broiler can be leveled easily.

Widths of the hearth broiler vary from 53–130 cm (21–51 in.), depths vary from 60–97 cm (23.5–38.3 in.), and heights from floor to grid top may vary from 86–99 cm (34–39 in.). The grids may vary in width from 53–122 cm (21–48 in.) and in depth from 37–61 cm (14.5–24 in.).

The counter top broiler is similar in all aspects to the floor-mounted broiler. Some of them are interchangeable. They may have short plastic or stainless steel legs up to 10 cm (4 in.) high or rest flush on the counter. At least one unit uses the same heating element for broiling beneath and above (figure 14.5).

Another variation is a griddle placed over the heating elements with the broiler beneath the elements. The various counter units range in width from 30–231 cm (12–91 in.), in depth from 53–91 cm (21–36 in.), and in height from 30–43 cm (12–17 in.). The grids vary from 30–81 cm (12–32 in.) in width and 41–76 cm (16–30 in.) in depth.

FIGURE 14.4. Counter type hearth broiler. Courtesy Lincoln-Wearever.

FIGURE 14.5. Unit with broiling done from below and above. Courtesy Magikitch'n Equipment Corp.

Gas units may use as much as 150,000 Btu input and electric units up to 16.5 kw.

Rotisserie Broiler

This utilizes from one to three refractory type gas burners, each with about 30,000 Btu, in the rear or center of a vertical unit. Two to seven spits rotate food mechanically in front of the elements as it slowly broils. Some use a carousel type of unit and others a continuous type of conveyor. These units are used mainly in poultry stores, markets, and delicatessens selling barbecued meats.

An infrared barbecue 74 x 46 x 99 cm (29 x 18 x 39 in.) may do twelve chickens weighing 0.9 kg (2 lb) per hour while one which is 102 x 66 x 112 cm (40 x 26 x 44 in.) may do forty chickens per hour.

Checkpoints in Selecting a Broiler

The following checkpoints should be observed when selecting a broiler:

1. Buy from a reputable dealer who will maintain the unit.
2. Be sure that the heat is properly concentrated on the food and reflected away from unproductive surfaces to reduce energy costs.
3. Specify grids and heating elements of non-warping materials, very rigid in design. Grids should be easy to slide out and placed against a safety stop. They should raise and lower in definite increments, and it should be easy to load, turn, and remove the product.
4. Require variable heat controls with at least two settings: preheat and cooking. More are desirable.
5. Request that the unit should preheat in ten to fifteen minutes for radiant units and thirty to ninety seconds for infrared.
6. Have separate controls for increments of the broiler width if the grid is over 46 cm (18 in.) wide in case all the broiler surface is not needed at once.
7. Be sure that flues are adequate to remove combustion products, smoke, and fumes but will not interfere with gas flames and the broiling process.
8. Ask for broilers of 16-gauge or heavier steel which are insulated, if possible, and have reflective linings.
9. Check to see that the unit is easy to disassemble for serving and cleaning and that it is easy to reassemble.
10. Be sure there are adequate means for removing grease and that the danger of grease igniting and burning in the storage container is obviated.

Determination of Needed Capacity

Capacity determination in a broiler is difficult to calculate because of the variables that must be considered:

1. Number of portions that can be placed on a given size grid.
2. Where food is located on the grid. In overhead broilers the food at the back of the grid heats much faster than that in front; in hearth types, the food around the periphery of the grid might not cook as fast as that in the center.
3. Distance of food loaded on the grid from the heat source.
4. The type of food and its thickness. Dense beef and thick cuts of meat cook slower and have to be placed farther from the heat than fish and thin cuts of meat.
5. The amount of heat given off from the heat source toward the food.
6. Required degrees of doneness along with any precooking or postcooking that may be done.
7. The variety of products to be broiled. It may

be necessary to reserve certain broilers for high sales items that demand special broiler conditions.

8. The degree of charring, the amount of basting, and the amount of turning.
9. The probable volume of foods to be broiled.
10. Availability of alternate methods and equipment that can be used in place of the broiler at peak time.

In the last consideration, steaks may be browned in the broiler during slack periods and refrigerated or frozen until the needed periods when they may be heated in the conventional or microwave oven for service. The former is often used for banquet service and the latter for short-order cooking.

If a broiler is to be a capacity-cooking device, one can determine the amounts of food that one needs to cook in what time period and determine the area of grid in a broiler necessary for the job. Thus, if a given broiler at a certain setting will cook the steaks in ten minutes plus two minutes for loading and unloading, then five batches per hour are possible. If it is expected that 100 steaks per hour will be sold, then one needs 100 divided by 5, or 20 steaks per batch, and sufficient grid area must be available. If only 10 of the test steaks can be broiled per batch in the test broiler, then two broilers of that size are necessary. It is well not to accept advertising literature as authoritative on capacity as often it errs on the side of overoptimism. It is best to run tests with the equipment on the products to be prepared to determine the numbers that can be cooked and in what time period, including cooking, loading, unloading, and cleaning times, if any.

There are a few rules of thumb promulgated by various manufacturers, but they should be verified:

1. A 3065–4644-sq-cm (3.3–5-sq-ft) broiling surface will handle 34–45 kg (75–100 lbs) of meat or fish per hour. The fish should not require as long a time to broil as the meat.
2. A broiler holding 48 hamburgers per batch will do 960 per hour.
3. A broiler holding 24 New York strip steaks will do 200 per hour.
4. A broiler with 3225 sq cm (500 sq in.) of grid area will cook 280–198-g (7-oz) tenderloins per hour.
5. A broiler with 4839 sq cm (750 sq in.) of grid area will cook 370–198-g (7-oz) tenderloins per hour.
6. A backshelf broiler with a grid area of 2127 sq cm (330 sq in.) will cook 120–198-g (7-oz) tenderloins per hour.

Basic Use and Operation

The same factors considered in broiler capacity determination must be considered in utilizing the broiler (figure 14.6).

Depending on the thickness, density, and fat coating of the material to be cooked and the degree of charring and doneness desired, the cook must decide on a heat setting, distance from the heat source, position on the grid, and times before turning and removal from the broiler. If the food is thin and it is important that the product be charred, the grid should be set near the heat source, the food placed to the rear of the grid, and the heating source turned to high. Sometimes, the thin food is cooked from the frozen state. If the food is thick or dense in structure, the food must cook slower. Thus it is set further from the heat and more toward the front of the grid, or the heat may be reduced.

In general, the broiling procedure is as follows:

1. Foods are selected and cut for broiling. The best foods are those that are tender and have a fair fat content such as steaks, lamb chops, chickens, sausage, hamburgers, calves' liver,

and bacon. To a lesser extent, fat fish fillets and fat- or marinade-coated foods may be broiled. Most cooks avoid broiling fresh veal and pork although some pork chops are broiled. It tends to toughen them. Where a number of pieces are to be broiled at the same time, they should be similar in size and thickness. Fat around the edges should be slashed to avoid curling.

2. After the grid is preheated, food is placed on it so that the food covers most of the surface that is at the same temperature. Grids may be greased before cooking to prevent sticking.
3. Temperature is set at high or preferably medium but seldom, if ever, at low except to keep food hot.
4. Grid level is set so that thin meats are 2.5–5.1 cm (1–2 in.) from the heat source and thick meats 7.6–12.7 cm (3–5 in.) from the heat source.
5. Food is cooked until at the proper color or degree of doneness. Total cooking time should be divided for the two sides of the product. When turning meats, it is better to use tongs rather than a fork to avoid losing juices. Doneness in a meat may be checked by feel of resilience in the meat. In general, frozen foods should be thawed before broiling. An exception to this would be some very thin steaks. Poultry is usually salted before broiling but steaks are not as the salt draws out the juices. Generally, fatty foods are cooked at a lower, slower temperature than lean foods; this reduces excessive fat crystallization. It is well to baste lean fish with fat as this prevents excessive drying out and increases temperature around the product. Room temperature foods cook faster than refrigerated ones.
6. Broiled foods should be held under an infrared heat lamp, in the oven, in a food warmer, or in the broiler under low heat and some distance from the heating elements. Forming a crust is usually a function of the amount of fat in a meat.

Some quoted, but not tested, broiling times at medium heat setting are (sources: Lincoln-Wearever, McGraw Edison Instructional Manuals, and Wilkinson, *Complete Book of Cooking Equipment*):

Product	*Time and Special Instructions*
Lobster	16–19 min, put weight on tail
Liver	4 min
Spring chicken (1/2)	24–35 min, broil underside and then top
Hamburger (thin)	2–5 min, sometimes not turned
Hamburger, 2.5 cm (1 in.) thick	12 min
Steak, 2.5 cm (1 in.) thick	rare, 6–8 min medium, 10–14 min
Pork chops, 2 cm (0.75 in.) thick	8–12 min, usually a bit dry if well done
Strip steak, 5.1 cm (2 in.) thick	17–20 min
Tomato half	15 min
Lamb chop, 2.5 cm (1 in.) thick	14–20 min
Ham slices, 2.5 cm (1 in.) thick	16–20 min
Bacon	4–5 min

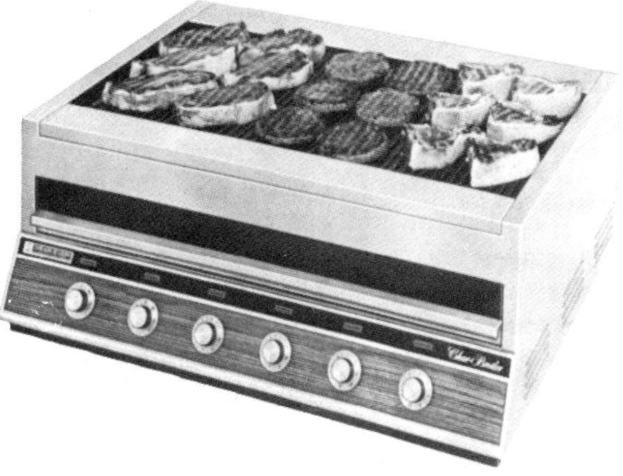

FIGURE 14.6. Utilizing hearth broiler to cook meats. Courtesy Lincoln-Wearever.

Fish fillet, 1.2 cm (0.5 in.) thick	4–5 min, do not turn
Fish steak, 2.5 cm (1 in.) thick	7 min, turn

Special Applications

The broiler may be used for melting the cheese on open-faced sandwiches, on pie slices, French onion soup, and casseroles. Often it is used for browning the tops of foods cooked by other means—chicken, baked potatoes, acorn and other squashes, and shrimp scampi.

The broiler can be used to brown meringues and baked Alaskas. It is used frequently to reheat slices of meats, vegetables, and other foods. Sometimes it is used as a conventional oven if the setting is low and the food is some distance from the heat source.

Alternatives to the Broiler

A broiler is not necessary in a kitchen except where the restaurant advertises broiled food. Foods may be cooked in an oven, griddled, pan fried, or deep fried to provide products much like the broiled foods. While these may not be as showy in preparation, they can be made to be as good tasting and, in most cases, the process used is not as dangerous. The U.S. Navy, famed among the services for its fine food, uses few, if any, broilers.

A substitute for a broiler can be made in conventional electric and infrared ovens by providing a rack that will hold a food up close to the oven's top heating elements. In both of these ovens, it is well to broil the food, particularly fat foods, in a pan with sides slightly higher than the product so that, in the event of a fire, a sheet pan can be inverted over it to smother the fire.

Saving Energy

1. Broilers waste heat both when in use and on standby. Their greatest asset is the coloration and charred flavor they provide for a few foods.
2. Infrared broilers should be used wherever possible, since they preheat faster and penetrate deeper, providing broiled characteristics faster than radiant-heat methods.
3. Broilers need to be fully loaded if they are to be energy efficient. When on standby, the broiler should be turned down to its lowest point and, if it is sectionalized, only a single section should be on standby. All exhaust fans should be turned down or off during standby. The broiler should be preheated no more than absolutely necessary—broiling can be started before the broiler is up to use temperature.
4. If there is a considerable demand for broiled food, a small broiler may suffice if the most commonly broiled foods can be precooked in steam. Typical broiled color and flavor may be achieved with accelerated temperature. Fish and other fragile foods, however, should not be precooked before broiling.

Cleaning

The overhead broiler must be allowed to cool before cleaning. Then:

1. Remove the grids. This is usually accomplished by pulling them out against the safety stops and then raising the end of the grids to a 45-degree angle to disengage them. The grid is then removed to the pot sink where it is allowed to soak. After soaking, it is scrubbed with a soft wire brush and a mild detergent, rinsed in fresh water and allowed to dry.
2. Scrape the inside panels of the broiler with a long-handled scraper and then wipe hard with a cloth dampened with a mixture of detergent

and water. Use no abrasives or caustics. Loose water and brushes and water should not be used in the broiler compartment. Rinse by cloth dampened in fresh water.

3. Remove baffles, fat container, trays, drip trays; pour out grease and wash in the pot sink with a gong brush and hot water and detergent. Rinse in fresh hot water, drain and replace after wiping dry. When replaced, water may be placed in the drip trays to facilitate later cleaning.
4. Clean gas burners with scraper and brush, and ream gas ports with a wire of proper size. Electric elements should be self-cleaning.
5. Wipe exterior of the broiler with a cloth dampened in detergent and water, and then rinse with a cloth dampened with fresh water. Use no abrasive or caustic. Exterior may be buffed dry with a soft cloth.

Maintenance

There is not much maintenance to a broiler except for checking the heating elements for proper flame, if gas, and adjusting to a strong blue flame. The electric elements should require little maintenance unless they burn out, and then the absence of heat should make replacement obvious.

There may be some buildup of carbon deposits that will interfere with the operation of burners or sliding of grids. These should be scraped off as should the buildups between elements of the grids.

QUESTIONS

1. What are the two main types of broilers from the standpoint of heat source placement?
2. How does lean fish have to be treated before broiling?
3. What is the secondary value of the hearth broiler?
4. What are the various types of broilers?
5. What type of heating provides the shortest preheat time?
6. What happens to the grease that is forced out of the meat in a hearth-type broiler?
7. How does one determine needed capacity in a broiler?
8. What is the greatest danger from a broiler? Why?
9. What are the factors that influence the speed of cooking a food in a broiler?
10. What decisions does a cook have to make as to settings in an overhead broiler? What influences these decisions?
11. What is the reason veal is not broiled?
12. How can an electric oven be modified to be a broiler?
13. What are the kitchen substitutes for a broiler?
14. How does one clean an overhead broiler?
15. How does one clean electric heating elements?
16. List two of the most effective energy-saving measures in broiler use.

BIBLIOGRAPHY

ANON. Undated. *Dietitians' Manual.* American Gas Association, New York.

ANON. Undated. Broil (Bulletin No. 736). Anetsberger Brothers, Northbrook, Ill.

ANON. 1977. Charbroilers, a product roundup. *Cooking for Profit* No. 324, 11–13.

KOTSCHEVAR, L., and TERRELL, M. 1977. *Food Service Planning: Layout and Equipment.* 2d ed. John Wiley and Sons, New York.

JERNIGAN, A.K., and ROSS, L.N. 1974. *Food Service Equipment: Selection, Arrangement and Use.* Iowa State University Press, Ames.

LONGREE, K., and BLAKER, G. 1971. *Sanitary Techniques in Food Service.* John Wiley and Sons, New York.

WEST, B.B., WOOD, L., and HARGER, V. 1967. *Food Service in Institutions.* 4th ed. John Wiley and Sons, New York.

Steam Jacketed Kettles

The workhorse of the foodservice establishment must be the steam jacketed kettle. It can prepare complete meals within itself or finish-cook many of the foods which are precooked in other equipment (figure 15.1).

Our forefathers cooked in large kettles suspended over the fire, and these were later fitted into

FIGURE 15.1. Steam jacketed kettles form the basis of kitchen cooking.

openings in brick furnaces. For some foods this was too hot or uneven in temperature, so pans were suspended over, or put into, pots of boiling water. To save the steam, the upper pot fitted down against the rim of the lower pot, and the double boiler evolved. With information derived from the infant canning industry, development of the steam jacketed kettle was sparked. Many of the older ones were made of copper, thus the origin of the U.S. Navy cooks' term *coppers* for steam jacketed kettles.

During World War II, most of the coppers began to be made of painted steel with stainless steel liners. Many institutions still have these kettles bought from war surplus. There were also many shipboard kettles made of aluminum. Some of these made shipboard conditions so hot that they insulated their kettles in U.S. Navy shipyards. U.S. Navy research evaluated one from the battleship, *New Jersey,* and found it to be quite energy efficient. Since it adds about 75 percent to the cost of the stainless steel kettle, most operators prefer to use uninsulated kettles although manufacturers can provide insulated kettles. After hours of use, the exterior of an insulated kettle remains cool to the touch.

Description and Specification

A steam jacketed kettle is a moist-heat cooking device manufactured from hemispherical metal shells of different sizes. The smaller one is inserted into the larger one and fastened to it in a way that provides a 5-cm (2-in.) space around its bottom and up its sides to form a pressure vessel with one-half, two-thirds, or full jacketing. Capacities in the interior hemisphere range from 946 ml (1 qt) up to 757 liters (200 gal.) or more.

In the operation of the kettle, the steam inlet valve is opened allowing steam under pressure to enter the jacket. The boiler steam at about 45-kg (100-lb) pressure, comes in through a steam-reducing valve set at the rated pressure of the kettle. If the pressure is too great, a safety valve in the side of the kettle opens at 2.3–4.5 kg (5–10 lb) above the rated pressure to prevent rupturing of the vessel. This is checked by the American Society of Mechanical Engineers.

As the steam condenses on the outside of the inner shell, it gives up its heat to the metal and falls to the bottom of the outer vessel as water. This water is removed by a steam trap. The heat in the metal of the inner vessel is conducted through, and transfers to, a media, usually liquid, inside the kettle. The liquid carries the heat to the food by convection. The amount of heat that is imparted is controlled by the amount the steam intake valve is opened.

If the steam system is shut off and cold water introduced near the condensate valve, the steam trap is made inoperative by closing a valve next to it. Water is removed by a valve opened by the safety valve. Then heat moves in reverse, first to the liquid media, to and through the metal shell, and thence to the circulated water where it is picked up and goes down the drain or is used for another purpose. A direct gas expansion refrigerated coil system inside or outside of the inner shell can perform the same cooling function.

The greatest use for large kettles is the cooking of potatoes, rice, pasta, stews, soups, poultry, pot roasts, Swiss steaks, pie fillings, and similar products. The smaller ones are used for small amounts of the above plus progressive cooking of vegetables, gravies, sauces, eggs, bakery fillings, desserts, and other items cooked in small quantities.

A specification for a steam jacketed kettle should include:

1. Size needed. This should be determined by the usual quantity of food to be prepared in it plus head space for foam which boils up as well as increases in volume. The capacity can be the needed volume plus 10–25 percent. In U.S. Navy ships, the latter was the rule because of the ship's motion. Overall dimensions should be included. These may be obtained from manufacturers' specifications.

2. Type of jacketing. Small kettles use one-half

jacketing which means that the lower hemisphere comes halfway up the side of the inner hemisphere (figure 15.2). The partial, or two-thirds, jacketed kettle is usually tall and uses a minimum of floor space. The full jacketed kettle, as a rule, is shallow and low and uses much floor space, but it does not allow food to be crushed at the bottom of the kettle. The specifications should state whether the kettle is to be shallow or deep.

3. Tilting (trunnion). Most of the smaller kettles tilt either forward or to one side. In some cases, the pivot is on each side of the kettle, and in others, it is in front of the kettle. In the smaller kettles, the motive power is a hand-powered lever that tilts the kettle forward (figure 15.3). Usually, the kettle is bottom heavy and will swing back to the upright if the handle is released. Some do not. Larger kettles are tilted by a wheel operated by hand that drives a screw enmeshed in a gear on the kettle pivot. The friction of this is frequently great enough so that if the wheel is released, the kettle movement stops. Care must be taken to see that slipping does not occur between screw and gear as serious accidents can happen. This linkage may be tested by tilting the kettle and then striking the lip edge of the kettle with a heavy weight or by sitting on the edge.

4. Type of stand. Available are pedestals that are a single column extending either from the bottom of the kettle to the floor or, in the case of tilting kettles, starting where a bow joins the two pivots beneath the kettle. The pedestal may be mounted flush to the floor or on a small raised platform. In either case, the mounting should be water-tight to prevent organic material accumulating under or inside the pedestal. Spoiling of the material will cause foul odors. Also, there is the tripod mount which is three tubular legs extending from the sides of the kettle to fixtures by which it can be fastened to the floor. Four-legged stands, as well as tubular assemblies, may be obtained for tilting kettles. Most expensive, but easiest to maintain, are the wall-mounted brackets for either fixed or tilting kettles (figures 15.4). While these can be supported by a heavy wall or counterbalanced by a

FIGURE 15.2. Half jacketing in steam jacketed kettles.

FIGURE 15.3. Trunnion kettle mounted on table top.

FIGURE 15.4. Wall-mounted steam jacketed kettle with mixer. Courtesy Groen Division, Dover Corporation.

kettle on the other side, most are mounted on L-shaped metal supports within the wall and supported by the brace under the floor. Small kettles should be mounted on tables of various heights that will bring the working height down to where the worker can use it easily. Preferred are small table-mounted tilting kettles that are mounted in pairs and tilt toward each other over a common drain and pan base. This means that it should be specified that both handles should be on the side of the kettle where the worker will be. Kettles pouring toward each other reduce possibilities of having the cook burned by spills.

5. Materials, gauges, and finishes. Although a few aluminum and copper kettles are still made, most are manufactured of No. 304 stainless steel (chromium 18–20 percent, nickel 8–12 percent, and the remainder steel) and 14-gauge which is 0.2 cm (0.078 in.) thick. The finish may be No. 6 or 7 (semi-mirror or 200-grit bright luster) or some other sturdy easy-to-clean combination.

6. Height of front lip of kettle from the floor. This may vary from 91–130 cm (36–51 in.). The draw-off of the kettle must be high enough from the floor to allow placing all utensils to be used under it, and to facilitate cleaning beneath it. The top edge of the kettle should be beneath the worker's elbow height to make it easy to use and clean. This should be balanced against the space that can be made available for the kettle. A shallow kettle may be desirable from a human engineering standpoint, but if there is not sufficient room for it or if such area is expensive, then a taller kettle must be used.

7. Type of draw-off. This must be specified

along with the type of valve. At one time the draw-off used was a dairy type where the pipe dropped straight down to a tee connected to a pipe that led out from under the kettle to a valve. The tee provided a place for food to collect since it did not drain. Now most kettles have a tangential draw-off that is almost a continuation of the bottom curve of the kettle and runs parallel to the floor. Today, most are the sanitary compression disk type with a few of the close-coupled drain valves being used. The sanitary compression disk type is the simpler but is more susceptible to leaks.

8. Covers. Most covers are one piece, fastened to the rear of the kettle by a hinge and counterbalanced by a cover-activator spring or weight. This partially overcomes the heavy and dangerous weight of the cover. The design should prevent drip from the cover of the kettle from running back into the kettle. It is preferable to have the hinge 45 degrees to the left of the rear so that, as the cover is opened, the cloud of imprisoned steam will not be released into the face of the worker. Table top kettles have one-piece completely detachable covers that are lifted off by hand. Covers are made of the same metal as the kettle but sometimes may be of a lighter gauge. Covers should conform to local health codes (figure 15.5).

9. Mixer. While food manufacturers have had mixers installed in their kettles for many years, they have been a comparatively recent development for foodservice. In most cases, they take the form of an exteriorly mounted motor with two drive shafts. One drives a scraper-mixer where hard metal or plastic shovel-type fingers move material from the kettle surface to the interior where beaters of various types can be installed to operate from the second shaft. These may be paddle, whip, beater, bar, or turbine types. A thermometer may be part of the assembly. A scraper-mixer assembly does away with a hot cook's flailing away at a mass of

FIGURE 15.5. Single piece cover for steam jacketed kettle. Better mounting would be 45 degrees to the right.

seething food material, increases the efficiency of the heat transfer process, and evens out and speeds the cooking process in addition to the effects of the beater attachments. The mixer may be purchased as a separate piece of equipment on wheels and moved to, and plugged in for, any kettle of proper size and dimensions, or it may be placed between two kettles and used in each (figure 15.6).

FIGURE 15.6. Steam jacketed kettle with scraper mixer. Courtesy Groen Division, Dover Corp.

10. Type of heating. This is probably most important. The cheapest, of course, is the use of an existing steam source if it is adequate for its regular duties in addition to the steam-jacketed kettles. It takes approximately 0.08 boiler horsepower per 3.8 liters (1 gal) of kettle capacity, or expressed in another way, one boiler horsepower produces about 15.6 kg (34.4 lb) steam per hour.

If the steam supply is not adequate, one has two choices. One is the use of self-contained units integral with the unit which heat pure water with gas or electricity to produce their own steam. The other is to have a small separate boiler to provide steam for the various pieces of steam-operated equipment. A smaller edition of the boiler may be used in the base supporting two or more table top kettles or the supports of larger kettles. A warning, in all cases, is to be sure that there is adequate steam for the equipment to be heated.

11. Electrical requirements. These should include voltages, phase, cycle, and wattage desired and the need for all assemblies to have the Underwriters' Laboratories approval.

12. Displays, meters, and controls and temperature indicators. Included here might be the hand steam control (this should be placed where it can be reached without the operator's being burned), the safety valve, pressure gauge, thermometer, water level indicator, low water cutoff, pilot light, thermostats, pressure limit switches, water breaker, or anti-siphon, and others.

13. Approvals. In addition to Underwriters' Laboratories approval for equipment using some electricity, one should have American Gas Association approval for gas-heated equipment, American Society of Mechanical Engineers approval to verify that the pressure vessels are safe, and the National Sanitation Foundation approval for the sanitary aspects of the equipment.

14. Accessories. Practically all manufacturers have a number of pieces of equipment that make steam-jacketed equipment easier to use or broaden its applications. Included are cold water and faucet, water meter (accurate, at least, to 3.8 liters (1 gal), pour lips for table top kettles, whip, brushes, paddle, operating handles for small tilting kettles, food pumps, troughs and dump trays (sliding or fixed), cover actuator, drain strainer, basket inserts, supporting frame or bracket, pan holder, heating/cooling valve system, and boiling control (figure 15.7 and figure 15.8).

15. Installation details. These vary according to the type, size, and location of the kettle to be installed. They may include: steam, electricity, gas, water inlet and water drain connections, leveling and bolting down, the ensuring of adequate space for opening the cover and tilting the kettle as well as the various checks that must be made. See table 15.1 for a list of available steam jacketed kettles.

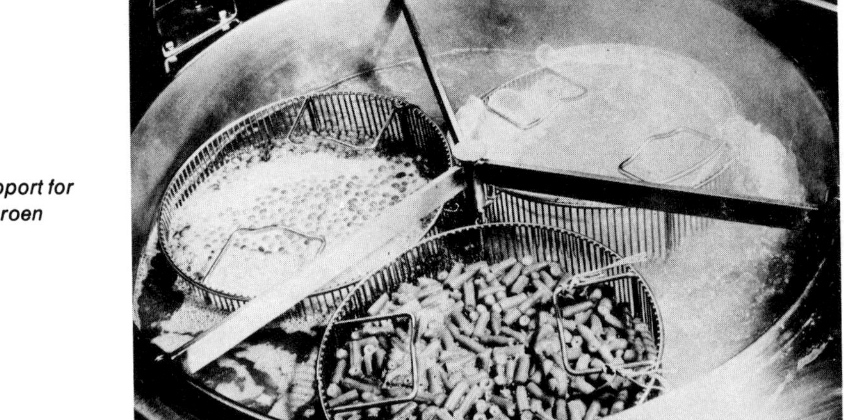

FIGURE 15.7. Multiple basket support for steam jacketed kettle. Courtesy Groen Division, Dover Corporation.

FIGURE 15.8. Steam jacketed kettle with internal stirring device is versatile. Courtesy Crown-X Inc.

TABLE 15.1. Steam Jacketed Kettles Available

Capacity	Jacketing	Mounting
0.9 l (1 qt)	1/2	TT
3.8 l (4 qt)	1/2	TT
4.7 l (5 qt)	1/2	TT
5.7 l (6 qt)	1/2	TT
7.6 l (8 qt)	1/2	TT
9.5 l (10 qt)	1/2	TT
18.9 l (20 qt)	1/2	TT
37.9 l (10 U.S. gal)	2/3	F, T
76 l (20 U.S. gal)	2/3 or full	F, W, T, TW
95 l (25 U.S. gal)	full	F
114 l (30 U.S. gal)	2/3 or full	F, T
151 l (40 U.S. gal)	2/3 or full	F, W, T, TW
189 l (50 U.S. gal)	full	F, T,
227 l (60 U.S. gal)	2/3 or full	F, W, T, TW
303 l (80 U.S. gal)	2/3 or full	F, W, T, TW
379 l (100 U.S. gal)	2/3 or full	F, W, TW
473 l (125 U.S. gal)	2/3 or full	F
568 l (150 U.S. gal)	2/3 or full	F
757 l (200 U.S. gal)	2/3	F

F = floor mounted; T = tilting; W = wall mounted; TW = tilting, wall mounted; TT = tilting, table mounted.
Source: Wilkinson, *Complete Book of Cooking Equipment*, CBI Publishing Company, Inc., p. 34.

Determination of Needed Capacity

In calculation of the steam jacketed kettle capacity, one must know the volumes and number of food portions to be prepared and the desired headspace (distance between the top of the cooking product and the top edge of the kettle). As the average person has a somewhat difficult time in calculating this, most operators calculate it as a percentage of the food volume and add it. Thus the following formula evolved:

$$\frac{\text{Number to be fed} \times \text{portion size (ml or oz)} \times \text{\% acceptance} \times \text{\% headspace + product}}{\text{1000 ml or 128 oz (1 U.S. gal)} \times \text{number of batches}} = \text{volume in liters or U.S. gallons}$$

Example:

$$\frac{\text{200 portions} \times \text{118 ml portion size} \times \text{50\% acceptance} \times \text{1.15 (15\% headspace)}}{\text{1000 ml} \times \text{2 batches}} = \text{6.8 liters (1.8 U.S. gal)}$$

or

$$\frac{\text{200 portions} \times \text{4 oz portion size} \times \text{50\% acceptance} \times \text{1.15 (15\% headspace)}}{\text{128 oz (1 U.S. gallon)} \times \text{2 batches}} = \text{1.8 U.S. gal (6.8 liters)}$$

The requirement would be a 7.6-liter (8-qt) kettle.

The food chosen for the calculation should be one that is prepared frequently and makes heavy demand on the capacity of the kettle. It should not be the product that is seldom prepared and makes the heaviest demand on kettle capacity. Buying a kettle for this capacity means that, most of the time, one would be preparing food in too large a kettle and wasting energy.

Basic Use and Operation

As every food recipe has its own procedure for developing the desired food product, each type of kettle has its special directions for using it at maximum efficiency. In general, the procedure is as follows:

1. Rinse the kettle with draw-off open. If cover has been closed, this may not be necessary. This ensures that nothing has dropped into the kettle since washing.
2. Close outlet and check to see if desired strainer or disk is over the opening of the kettle drain.
3. Fill kettle with proper volume of liquids or weight of solids. Use no more liquid than is necessary as this water must be heated and

excess water leaches too many water soluble nutrients from food, particularly vegetables. If adding thick products, fill the drain with water first. Use hot water.

4. Close cover and turn on steam. Proper use of the cover is important since 0.46 sq m (5 sq ft) of water loses 17,000 Btu per hour.
5. If a simmer of 85°C (185°F) is desired, check the temperature of the kettle contents frequently with a thermometer.
6. Turn down steam to maintain desired temperature.
7. Stir to maintain even temperature of temperature-sensitive foods.
8. When cooking is complete, shut off steam and remove food immediately to avoid overcooking. Be sure that cooking is coordinated with service so that food does not have to be held for long periods of time. Before removing foods, one may draw off the water through the drain before dipping or pouring out solids. Largely liquid foods may be drawn out by gravity through the draw-off or assisted by a food pump. Drain liquid from pipe several times during cooking and add it back.
9. Fill empty kettle with warm water above the high mark made by the previously cooked food. Let stand until kettle can be cleaned.

The shallow kettle may be used for braising. The procedure used is:

1. Preheat with cover closed.
2. Prepare meat in uniform pieces of 2.3–4.5 kg (5–10 lb) by seasoning with salt and pepper and coating with flour. Uniformity of piece size is necessary to ensure that when one piece is done, all of them are done.
3. Oil the surface of the kettle where the meat will make contact and leave a small amount on the kettle bottom.
4. Turn up heat to highest input and place meat around kettle bottom so that each piece is in contact with hot metal if possible. Do not cover. Brown for fifteen to twenty-five minutes, then turn at least once for an equal browning.
5. Add small amount of liquid—meat or vegetable stock, tomato juice or some form of milk.
6. Close cover and reduce heat. Renew liquid if necessary. Turn product several times during cooking. Cut pieces require thirty-five to forty-five minutes per 0.45 kg (1 lb); rolled roasts require ten to fifteen minutes more per 0.45 kg (1 lb).
7. When tender (fork passes through freely), remove meat for slicing.
8. Use remaining liquid for gravy.

See tables 15.2–15.5 for typical cooking times and uses of different types of steam jacketed kettles. Figures 15.9 to 15.11 show different types of kettles.

TABLE 15.2. Frequent Cooking Uses for Deep Steam Jacketed Kettles

Casserole combinations
Eggs, scrambled or in shell
Frankfurters
Gelatin
Gravy
Ice cream mixes
Pasta: macaroni, noodles, spaghetti
Pie fillings
Poultry
Puddings
Vegetables, dried: beans, lentils, peas
Vegetables: fresh and frozen

TABLE 15.3. Frequent Cooking Uses for Shallow Steam Jacketed Kettles

Braised meats: beef, veal, and pork roasts
Corned beef
Gravies
Hearts, liver, kidney, tongue
Preparation of Swiss steaks and pot roasts
Roast lamb and ham
Roast pork and pork chops
Stocks

TABLE 15.4. Cooking Uses of Tilting Table Top Kettles

Eggs, scrambled and soft cooked
Fish stews, clams and oysters
Gravy
Lobster and shrimp
Preparing jellied salads
Puddings, pie fillings
Reheating foods
Sauces
Soup in small amounts
Stewing fruits
Vegetables, fresh and frozen

TABLE 15.5. Representative Steam Jacketed Kettle Cooking Times

Food	*Approximate cooking time (min)*
Applesauce	20
Asparagus, fresh	20
Beans, green, fresh	20
Beans, lima, dried	30–45
Beans, lima, frozen	12–14
Beans, wax, frozen	10–12
Beef stew	210–270
Broccoli, fresh	15–20
Brunswick stew, simmer	180
Brussel sprouts, frozen	6–8
Cabbage, shredded	10–25
Carrots, fresh, sliced lengthwise	25
Cauliflower, fresh, sectioned	12
Celery soup, diced celery	35
Chicken for stock	180
Chili con carne	150
Clam chowder	20
Corn, frozen, whole kernel	6–8
Corn meal	10–15
Creole sauce, simmer	30
Curry, using cooked lamb	30
Eggs, soft cooked	3–5
Eggs, hard cooked, simmer	30
Farina	5–10
Fowl, 1.4–2.3 kg (3–5 lb)	150
Greens: mustard, collard, and turnip	30–40
Hominy, grits	25–30
Kale	10–12
Macaroni, noodles, spaghetti	15
Okra	10–12
Onion, dehydrated (soak 30 min), simmer	20
Onions, boiled	15–20
Parsnips, quartered	20
Peas, frozen	15–20
Pork chop suey	10–15
Pork roast, barbecued (1.8–2.3 kg) (4–5 lb)	110
Potatoes, boiled	25–30
Potatoes, dehydrated, sliced	15–25
Potatoes, dehydrated, diced	20
Rice	13–16
Shrimp, boiled	5
Spinach, fresh	8–10
Squash, summer, sliced	20
Turnip, sliced	40
Vegetables, canned, simmer	10
Vegetables, mixed, frozen	12–14

Source: Cooking the Modern Way, Groen Division, Dover Corporation, Elk Grove Village, IL

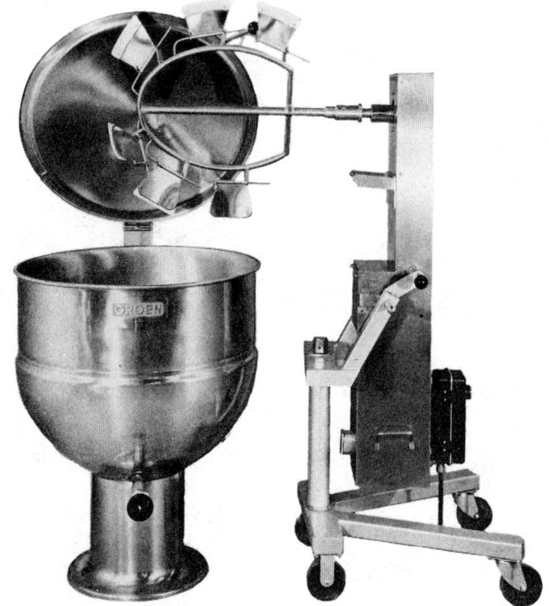

FIGURE 15.9. Pedestal-mounted steam jacketed kettle with wheeled mixer. Courtesy Groen Division, Dover Corp.

FIGURE 15.10. Table top self-contained steam jacketed kettle. Courtesy Groen Division, Dover Corporation.

FIGURE 15.11. Mixer kettle used in preparation of vanilla custard. Courtesy Groen Division, Dover Corporation.

Follow these hints on successful use of steam jacketed kettles:

1. Have the kettle installed so that a portable table may be wheeled up beside it, or a rack hung on its side for holding ingredients and serving pans for loading.
2. To have cabbage wedges hold their shape, cook 68 kg (150 lb) in 7.6 liters (2 gal) of water with kettle cover closed.
3. Reheat canned or precooked meats in serving pans placed crisscross fashion in the bottom of the kettle with a small amount of water and the cover closed.
4. Cook barbecued chicken and other meats with their sauces in the steam jacketed kettle. Finish by cooking chicken in a single layer in serving pans in an oven set at 218°C (425°F) for fifteen minutes.
5. Whole shell eggs are less likely to get heat-cracked shells if they are at room temperature before cooking.
6. Having the cover closed while bringing a liquid to a boil in a steam jacketed kettle reduces energy consumption 5–10 percent. When the product has reached boiling, it takes one-quarter to one-third the power to maintain this temperature if the cover is closed.
7. Vegetables cooked in soft water are more tender than those cooked in hard water. Tea made from soft water is clearer. Coffee made from hard water is better.
8. Red, yellow, and green vegetables maintain better color if cooked uncovered. Red vegetables keep color better if cooked in a slightly acid medium.
9. Vegetables should be carefully timed inasmuch as many vegetables will change from natural color and become flat and tasteless if overcooked.
10. While most vegetables may be cooked from the frozen condition, energy economy is attained by thawing them in the refrigerator first except under short-order conditions. Corn on the cob should always be thawed before cooking.

Frozen blocks of vegetables should be broken or cut into small squares to promote evenness of cooking. Frozen vegetables usually require about one-half the time of fresh ones to cook.

11. In cooking of meats, the higher the cooking temperature, the greater the loss of water, fat, and water-soluble nutrients.

Special Applications

If an institution does not have deep fat frying equipment, a thermostatically controlled electric insert can be custom made to turn the kettle into a fryer. After frying, the insert may be removed, wiped clean, and hung on the wall until needed. If steam is shut off, the electric insert provides emergency water heating.

If one is troubled by excessive heat in the kitchen, steam jacketed kettles can be purchased with insulated jackets that radiate little or no heat. An uninsulated 227-liter (60-gal) steam jacketed kettle can radiate 8200 Btus per hour.

A quickly prepared baked potato can be made by boiling the whole fork-pricked potato in a brine of 591 ml (2.5 cups) salt per 3.7 liters (1 gal) of water for twenty to twenty-five minutes and then broiling it for five minutes.

Using a 48 percent glycerin solution in a steam jacketed kettle will save 1.5 minutes in hard cooking eggs and a 60 percent solution will save 3.5–5 minutes. Prunes and poached eggs will cook in one-half their regular time.

Steam jacketed kettles may be used to make coffee. The old method of soaking a porous cloth sack of coffee grounds for a tested period of time or until the brew reaches a certain strength to taste is rather uncertain. A more reliable arrangement is to have a leacher that fits into the top of the kettle and holds the coffee grounds while a pump on the drawoff forces water as a spray over the grounds for a tested period of time to get a certain strength brew. The amount of water sprayed evenly over the grounds, the temperature of the water, the thickness of the layer of the coffee grounds, and the time the water is in contact with them must be carefully coordinated.

Refrigerated jacketed kettles can be used for cooling drinks, solidifying gelatin, or making puddings.

The U.S Navy uses the steam jacketed kettle to wash frying fat. The liquid fat from the fryer is poured into the kettle and heated to 96°C (205°F). Approximately 7.6–15 liters (2–4 gal) of water are sprinkled over the top of the fat. As it sinks down through the fat, the water picks up the suspended solids and carries them to the bottom. There, a small amount of fat and water are drawn off and refrigerated to solidify the clean fat. This can be lifted off the water and reused. The remaining clean fat can be returned to the cleaned fryer.

Water meters on which a desired volume can be set are a boon. Metering is done automatically and the cook can set the meter, turn on the kettle heat, and go and collect the rest of his ingredients. When he returns, the kettle has the desired amount of water at the desired temperature and can start cooking without waiting.

The steam jacketed kettle may be used to reheat canned foods for service and cans of frying fat for placement in the fryer. It may be used to heat any quantity of hot water.

Alternatives to the Steam Jacketed Kettle

While the steam jacketed kettle is the basis of institutional cooking, other equipment can perform most of its functions, although perhaps less efficiently. For instance, most foods may be cooked in pots set on a range, in a bainmarie, steam table, or oven. It is possible to fill the deep fat fryer with salted water and use it together with fryer baskets to cook fragile (asparagus, broccoli) and other vegetables, ham, sausages, and similar foods to maintain a serving line or for short-order cooking.

Some foods can use standby, or residual heat, of the oven for cooking. Rice and pasta cook well at about 107°C (225°F). Sauces being reduced in volume may be cooked without stirring in an oven. Infrared ovens may be used to heat frozen foods, cook eggs or meats, and with careful attention may do the other kettle jobs, as well.

Saving Energy

1. When bacteriologically and chemically safe, foods should be at, or above, room temperature before they are cooked in the steam jacketed kettle. Cooking time may be reduced if the pieces of food are small; this reduces energy consumption.
2. A minimum amount of water should be used to cook each food. Energy consumption is low if the cover of the kettle is kept closed, and food nutrient losses are reduced as well. The liquid left after the food is removed is usually suitable for gravies, and will not require expensive volume reduction.
3. Kettles that are capable of simmering should be bought. Fast boils should never be used unless food volume is being reduced. Slow boils should be used if the simmer is too difficult to maintain, because a slow boil requires only one-third to one-quarter of the energy of the fast boil. Using mechanical or electric timers is helpful.
4. Insulating the kettle exterior adds about 75 percent to the kettle cost but it makes the kettle more comfortable to work around, reduces the load on the ventilation or air conditioning systems, and lowers energy costs greatly.
5. Using mechanical scraper/mixers reduces the energy wasted when the cook mixes the contents by hand, improves efficiency of heat transfer, decreases cooking times, and, in some cases, lessens the need to raise the cover, which wastes heat.
6. Insulating all steam pipes, preheating steamer boilers no more than 15–20 minutes, using softened water in steam systems, and checking steam pipes and traps for leaks all reduce energy usage.

Cleaning

The procedure for cleaning a steam jacketed kettle is as follows:

1. Shut off steam before draining kettle.
2. Open cover, remove food, and drain. Allow kettle to cool. Remove drain screen or disk. Flush kettle with warm water.
3. Close drain and fill kettle with hot water and detergent. Fill above soil level. Draw some water from draw-off and add back to kettle.
4. According to amount of soil, soak thirty to sixty minutes.
5. Scrub kettle inside and out with a stiff bristle brush. Do not use steel wool. Scrub cover and kettle exterior including frame and legs.
6. Drain kettle and remove valve parts. Brush parts. Clean drain by brushing from valve to base of kettle.
7. Rinse kettle and all washed parts.
8. Reassemble and close draw-off. Add chemical sanitizer to draw-off and let stand five minutes. Drain.
9. Close valve and replace drain screen or disk.
10. Wipe cover, outside of kettle, and frame. Close cover.

Maintenance

A steam jacketed kettle is not a kitchen device that demands a great amount of maintenance, but there are a few points that should be checked periodically. They include:

1. The safety valve should be "popped" (actuated) at least once weekly. Move the lever on the safety valve while it is under pressure so that a puff of steam is ejected. This ensures that the valve is not stuck. Some operators do it daily.
2. The draw-off valve should be checked for leakage. If it leaks, it should be ground into the seating until it does not leak, or it should be replaced.
3. The pressure indicating valve, safety valve, and other displays and controls should be checked against a standard at least once annually.
4. The kettle steam inlet valve and all pipes into the kettle should be checked weekly for leaks.
5. The steam trap should be checked at least weekly to ensure that it is not passing excessive amounts of steam.

QUESTIONS

1. What is the pressure range at which steam jacketed kettles usually operate?
2. What is the purpose of the safety valve and what is the weekly procedure for ensuring that it is operating properly?
3. What specific metal and finish are commonly used to make steam jacketed kettles?
4. What makes a steam jacketed kettle heated by steam better than one heated by water at 100°C (212°F)?
5. What are the types of stands available for kettles?
6. When opening the kettle, how does one avoid clouds of steam coming out into the face of the operator?
7. What are the sources of steam for steam jacketed kettles?
8. What organizations provide approvals on parts of the kettle?
9. What is the temperature for a simmer?
10. What should be done before removing food from a kettle?
11. List five ways to increase energy efficiency when using the steam jacketed kettle.

BIBLIOGRAPHY

ANON. 1950. Groen Manufacturing Company Operating Manuals. Numbers 110–114. Groen Manufacturing Company, Elk Grove Village, Ill.

ANON. 1971. *Cooking the Modern Way with Stainless Steel Steam Jacketed Kettles*. Groen Division/Dover Corporation, Elk Grove Village, Ill.

ANON. Market Forge Operating Instructions S 108–109. Market Forge, Everett, Mass.

DUNN, T.C. 1962. *Quality Quantity Steam Cookery*. 1962 Commercial Gas Sales School. New Haven, Conn.

KOTSCHEVAR, L., and TERRELL, M.E. 1963. *Food Service Layout and Equipment Planning*. John Wiley and Sons, New York.

NAVY-MARINE CORPS RECIPE SERVICE. 1963. Bureau of Supplies and Accounts, Navy Department, Washington, D.C. NAVSANDA Publication 7.

SKINSTAD, J. 1966. *All Steamed Up Over Steam Kettles*. James Skinstad, Santa Ana, Calif.

TERRELL, M.E. 1971. *Professional Food Preparation*. John Wiley and Sons, New York.

WILKINSON, J. 1975. The *Complete Book of Cooking Equipment*. CBI Publishing Company, Inc. Boston.

Steamers and Pressure Cookers

While the top of the range is still the center of activity for the old-time chef, the steamer and pressure cooker bear the bulk of the modern cook's food preparation (figure 16.1). The reasons behind this are legion:

1. The speed of the device enables preparation to be "as needed" as contrasted to the old preparation long before the service period.
2. Maximum preservation of color, texture, moisture, and yields.
3. High level retention of nutrients as compared to pot cooking—gives about 40–50 percent more soluble solids and vitamin C.
4. Constant temperature and exact cooking time (scientific).
5. Reduced amount of attention needed from employees as equipment is automatic, mechanized, or electronic in many ways.

FIGURE 16.1. Small batch pressure cooker. Courtesy Lincoln-Wearever.

6. Equipment occupies minimum amount of floor space (one-half that of other equipment), has minimum of heat radiation surfaces, and uses energy efficiently.
7. Equipment may be used to cook almost everything except those foods requiring browning, charring, or a crust. As a general rule, 0.45 kg (1 lb) of steam cooks 1.8 to 2.7 kg (4–6 lb) of food.
8. Steam softens baked-on crusts and soils.
9. Steam saves about one-half on fuel as compared to range cooking.

As far as disadvantages are concerned, there are few:

1. The equipment is faster in speed than older cooks can use readily so they are prone to overcook with it.
2. It does not provide a crust or a charred flavor.
3. The cook cannot observe the food being cooked, since most pressure cookers cannot be opened while in use. Although the new zero-pressure steamer can be opened at any time, it vents steam constantly in order to move it across the food, thus wasting much steam.

The steamer and pressure cooker might be described as devices which cook food by the application of moist-heat steam at 0–6.8 kg (0–15 lb) pressure directed onto the food. This cooks not only by transfer of the heat of the steam and condensate water but, more importantly, from the latent heat of fusion given up by the steam's condensing on the food.

Saturated steam is steam that is the same as that which comes off a pot of water boiling on the range at room pressure.

Dry saturated steam is formed only when enough heat has been used to evaporate the water. If this steam is heated, or if heat results from releasing steam that has been under pressure, it becomes superheated steam. Foods cooked in it are subjected to temperatures above 100°C (212°F). The addition of 4.7 Btu per 0.45 kg (1 lb) of saturated steam will produce a temperature of 105.6°C (222°F) or 5.6°C (10°F) of superheat.

Latent heat of vaporization is the heat necessary to change water to steam. As the pressure in the heated vessel increases, temperature of vaporization increases and latent heat decreases. Although latent heat decreases with added pressure, total heat increases. Wet steam contains droplets of water. This means vaporization is not complete.

For effective use, the steamer or pressure cooker must be well designed and controlled, with a capacity that will support the production rate required. An adequate amount of clean steam must be available. Know the tested loads and processing times for the product to be prepared and keep the device clean and well maintained.

Description and Specification

The choice of a steamer or pressure cooker depends on the quantities of food to be prepared, the speed of preparation needed, degree of automatic control needed, and the probable source of steam (figure 16.2). For hospitals, schools, and industrial

FIGURE 16.2. Two-compartment low pressure steamer. Courtesy Vulcan-Hart Corporation.

cafeterias, the large compartmented steamer is best. For small restaurants, the forced convection oven and the pressure cooker do the job.

The units may vary in size from 58 cm (23 in.) wide, 41 cm (16 in.) high, and 53 cm (21 in.) deep using one-third size pans 7.6 cm (3 in.) deep up to those 99 cm (39 in.) wide, 183 cm (72 in.) high (or higher), and 84 cm (33 in.) deep preparing 247–317 liters (7–9 U.S. bushels) of food. The units may be circular like the Wearever or Hobart units or may be in oblong cabinets as are the Market Forge or Vulcan Hart units (figure 16.3). The smaller units require special pans, and the large units utilize the 30-x-51-cm (12-x-20-in.) solid or perforated steam table pans in depths of 6.4, 10, and 15 cm (2.5, 4, and 6 in.) and, in a few cases, 20 cm (8 in.) deep. Others use the steam table pan in one-half or one-third sizes. There is some use of 46-x-66-cm (18-x-26-in.) and 51-x-61-cm (20-x-24-in.) sheet and roast pans. It is well to remember that as one uses the larger and deeper pans, there is more likelihood of uneven heating. Some operators prescribe that a 46-x-66-cm (18-x-26-in.) pan should be used in no greater depth than 2.5 cm (1 in.)

FIGURE 16.3. High pressure units using small special pans. Courtesy Hobart Corporation.

In efforts to get more production into the same space, some steamers are stacked to where the upper decks are too high and the cook cannot see into the upper compartments or handle the pans from them safely. Cabinets or various other bases may be used to hold the cooker at the proper height. Adjustable feet may be used for small adjustments such as those for an uneven floor.

For materials, the fronts are usually stainless steel. One manufacturer uses No. 300 (18–8) series stainless steel. The sides, top, and framework may be made of heavy-gauge welded stainless steel or steel with baked-on enamel. The backs may be of any of these plus aluminized steel. The pressure chamber may be made of stainless steel or seamless aluminum. In the smaller units, doors may be made of flexible stainless steel, cast aluminum alloy, or cast aluminum with stainless steel facing. The doors of the larger steamers are usually in two major parts, one of which is hinged, has a latch and a hand wheel that drives a screw through it to force the floating, gasketed inner section tightly against the body of the steamer. Most of the high-pressure cookers have one piece doors and use the steam pressure in part to hold the door and its gasket firmly against the frame. The door cannot be opened until the steam is released.

Each compartment has stainless or other steel liftout shelves and universal pan supports that may be used for various depths and sizes of pans. The control and display system varies considerably but may include dials to show steam inlet and pressure chamber pressures, fifteen and sixty minute timers, on-off switch and lights that indicate that power is on, the unit is exhausting air, the proper pressure is reached, the timer is on, and lastly, the process is complete. This last is accompanied by a buzzer to attract attention. Frequently, there is a strainer on the incoming steam line and a steam trap at the steam exit to keep water from building up in the device and at the same time, save steam. The floor of the steamer slopes to the drain and trap.

Steam for the cooker may come from a number of sources. If the steam is clean without harmful chemicals such as boiler cleaning compounds, almost any reliable steam from an adequate steam source may be used. Where steam is not clean but is of adequate pressure, it may be run through a heat exchanger. This will convert drinking grade water to steam which, in turn, can be used in the cooker. A third alternative is to use a compact boiler heated by gas or electricity (figure 16.4). The electrically heated unit has an electrically heated element immersed in the boiler water. It is close to 100 percent efficient. The gas unit can

FIGURE 16.4. To provide steam cooking in restaurants without steam, special boilers or electrical or gas heated units such as this one are used. Courtesy Market Forge.

transfer heat from gas flames to the interior of the boiler by means of highly conductive heat fins or heat tubes that carry the burned gas and air mixture through the boiler to turn the water to steam. The heat fins are probably about 50 percent efficient in their use of the available heat while the heat tubes are 60–65 percent efficient. In computing steam needed, one-half to two-thirds of the total requirements calculated from the number of compartments are used.

The steam that enters the cooking compartment can be at 0 kg (0 lbs) pressure where it is at 100°C (212°F). It may be at higher temperatures if superheated by a heater or if released from a greater pressure. It can be at about 2.3 kg (5 lb) pressure, the most common pressure for the large compartmented steamers. This is 108°C (227°F) at sea level. At 4.5 kg (10 lb) pressure, this will give 116°C (240°F), and the commonly used "pressure cooker" operates at 121°C (250°F), although few actually reach this temperature (one cooks at 6.1 kg (13.5 lb) pressure and another at 5.4–6.4 kg (12–14 lb) pressure).

If the cooker has a great amount of air mixed with the steam, it will not provide 108°C (227°F) at 2.3 kg (5 lb) pressure or 121°C (250°F) at 6.8 kg (15 lb) pressure. Consequently, in common with the home pressure cookers, most commercial cookers vent off this air before building up to pressure. One 0-kg (0-lb) pressure cooker vents continuously during the cooking period thus obviating the possibility of air pockets, but adding to steam consumption.

In the older and slower cookers, the steam entered the bottom of the cooker and slowly found its way to the food over the sides of the pan (figure 16.5). Most of the new fast or jet cookers direct the steam onto the food from many directions; thus cooking starts immediately and is completed quickly.

In specifying a steam cooking device, one can cover a multitude of details if he indicates that it must conform to the requirements of the National Sanitation Foundation, the American Society of Mechanical Engineers, the American Gas Association, and the Underwriters' Laboratories.

FIGURE 16.5. The oldest of the steamers is the 5-pound large compartment unit. It is slow.

Voltages from 108 to 440 volts and one to three phase can be provided for in the equipment, if properly covered in the specification. Information to include in specifications is as follows:

1. make and model number, if decided, and steam source
2. outside and inside dimensions
3. steam pressure to be used, temperature control, pressure reducing valve
4. electrical characteristics—voltage, phases, amperage, wattage
5. pressure gauges, safety valve, times and other displays or controls desired
6. internal racks and supports (should be removable for cleaning)
7. heavy-duty one-piece door gasket, steam strainer, and steam trap
8. pans expected including perforated ones and sizes that make maximum use of the interior space
9. materials, preferably stainless steel, stand, and locking system if there is a choice
10. a request for instruction, cleaning, and maintenance manuals
11. NSF, ASME, UL and AGA approval

Timers are sometimes accessories and must be ordered (figure 16.6). Of greater sophistication is the automated timer.

FIGURE 16.6. Both pressure cookers and steamers require timers since the cook cannot view cooking food.

Multiple slide racks and usually racks for pans other than the standard 30 × 51 × 6.4, 10, or 15 cm (12 × 20 × 2.5, 4, or 6 in.) deep, or 46-×-66-cm (18-×-26-in.) pans must be additional purchases. Some have slide adapters (figure 16.7).

A very desirable accessory is a faucet with a flexible stainless steel hose. It can be used for hot or cold water or both.

Table top pressure cookers can be mounted on a heavy-duty stand that may, or may not, be an additional expense.

FIGURE 16.7. Racks must be in increments that will handle the pans desired.

Determination of Needed Capacity

Each manufacturer has a number of rules of thumb that he provides customers to determine sizes of equipment they need for various purposes. For instance, a Hobart Model 25 pressure cooker may be recommended for 250 servings per hour, the Hobart Model 75 for 750 servings per hour, the Model 85 for 2000 servings per hour, and various combinations of these sizes for other requirements. Market Forge recommends one compartment of a 2.3-kg (5-lb) steamer for 300 meals or less and one of their Steam-It models for 100 meals or less.

One general capacity chart for low-pressure and high-pressure cookers is given in table 16.1.

If one needs 800 85-g (3-oz) portions of regular cut potatoes per hour and you select a fast 6.8-kg (15 lb) pressure cooker accommodating three pans 30 × 51 × 6.4 cm (12 × 20 × 2.5 in.) which will prepare 450 85-g (3-oz) portions per hour, dividing 800 by the 450 portions that can be provided by one cooker indicates that two cookers are needed. The only real difficulty with this method of calculating needed capacity is that sometimes over-zealous salespeople give erroneous information as to the number of batches that can be cooked per hour. The safest procedure is to run actual tests on the product that will be used most frequently and will place heavy demands on the equipment. After testing, the needed capacity can be determined.

TABLE 16.1. General Capacity Chart for Pressure Cookers

Meals per Hour	*Low Pressure 2.3 kg (5 lb) or less*	*High Pressure 6.8 kg (15 lb)*
Under 200	1 1-compartment	1 compartment
200–500	1 2-compartment	2–3 compartments
500–750	1 3-compartment	3–4 compartments
750–1000	1 3-compartment or 2 2-compartment	4–6 compartments
Above 1000	1 2-compartment per 500 meals	1 compartment per 200–300 meals

Source: Wilkinson, *Complete Book of Cooking Equipment,* and Market Forge Instructions.

Basic Use and Operation

Installation

The steam or pressure cooker should be placed as close to the serving area as possible so as to encourage the cooking of vegetables as they are needed for service (figure 16.8). Pressure cookers may be placed in, or directly behind, the serving line. The larger low pressure cookers do not lend themselves to this location because the wide-swinging doors use too much space. The heavy-duty steamers may be pedestal, wall, builtup base, or leg mounted. Clearance of about 15 cm (6 in.) between equipment and floor should be allowed for ease of cleaning. A drip pan or depressed floor drain is desirable.

As with other front-opening equipment, it is advisable to place the smaller cookers toward the back of the cooking table so that table space for making products ready and for efficient loading and unloading may be made available. The large units should have tables across the aisle in front of them so that loading and unloading may be done with one motion. Shelved carts may be utilized in front of the cookers. Less desirable are tables at the sides of the cookers since this requires two-motion loading and spillage of liquids may result. Where tables are used, they should be the same height as the table or cabinet on which the cooker rests. Steam cookers should be neither too high nor too low. It should be easy to see and reach into them. Thus, they should be placed between waist and chest height.

It is desirable to have a water source on a flexible hose nearby. This makes addition of water to pans and cleaning easier. The tables should have raised edges to keep things from sliding off. Where a small pressure cooker is used to maintain a serving line with vegetables, a drawer-type freezer should be placed under it or, less desirable, a vertical freezer beside it. All exposed pipes should be insulated so that they will not present a burn hazard or waste expensive energy. While most waste steam goes down the drain, many operators see the necessity of placing the cooker under a hood to capture and remove surplus steam and radiated heat. In the average kitchen, it is probably not absolutely necessary to place the steam cookers under canopy hoods.

Steamers should be level and bolted to the floor or table.

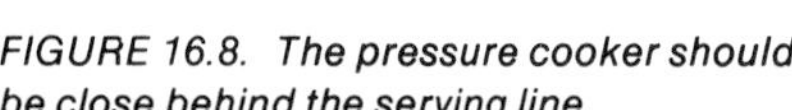

FIGURE 16.8. The pressure cooker should be close behind the serving line.

Steam Cooking Basics

With a source of steam available instantly, steam cooking is an extremely fast cooking medium. When heated, water requires 1 Btu to raise 1 lb of water 1°F. Thus to raise 0.45 kg (1 lb) of water from 16.7°C to 100°C (62°F to 212°F), 150 Btus are needed, but to change that 0.45 kg (1 lb) of water to 0.45 kg (1 lb) of steam (latent heat of vaporization) at the same temperature, 970 Btus are required. When the steam enters the cooker, it impinges on the food and gives up its heat (latent heat of fusion) while condensing to water. The hot water of the condensate then gives up Btus as it cools down to the temperature of the food.

Using water at 0°C (32°F) as a base, 1150 Btu would be required to provide 0.45 kg (1 lb) of 0-kg pressure steam; 1156 Btu, 2.3-kg (5-lb) pressure steam; 1160 Btu, 4.6-kg (10-lb) pressure steam; and 1164 Btu, 6.8-kg (15-lb) pressure steam.

Each make, and sometimes model, of steam or pressure cooker has its own procedure for operation included in the instruction book received with the device.

The step-by-step procedure for one 2.3-kg (5-lb) pressure cooker is:

1. Preheat to 1.8-kg (4-lb) pressure before loading to promote uniform steam flow and fastest result when food is added.
2. Place pans of food in cooker compartment.
3. Close compartment and latch.
4. Seal door by turning handle until door seal is tight.
5. Turn on steam and cook. Set timer if manual or automatic.
6. When food has cooked for recommended time by clock or timer, shut off, exhaust steam, and remove food. There are some units which shut off and reduce steam pressure automatically.

In a small pressure cooker, the procedure is much the same:

1. Open door by unlatching and pulling door out.
2. Load cooker.
3. Swing door into opening and engage locking bars, tighten door.
4. Set time by turning past the two-minute setting and then to recommended time. The pilot comes on then, the generator valve closes, and water enters the generator. Steam is generated and flows into the cooking chamber.
5. Defrost food until the temperature reaches 103°C (218°F) when the steam drain closes and timer starts. When pressure of 6.1-kg (13.5 lb) is reached, the generator reduces steam production to maintain pressure. This continues until the time reaches zero.
6. When the buzzer and flashing light indicate the process is completed, open the door and unload the cooker.

If the unit has a broiler, the food being browned should be steam cooked, and the browning action should not be continued more than thirty minutes. Care must be taken not to have the browning unit on when the door is raised or it will damage the gasket. The broiler has its own timer.

Timing is critical in the use of the steamer. It is faster than the range pot or steam jacketed kettle. Because of this, cooks have a tendency to judge cooking times by those used for the slower devices and thus overcook in the steamers. To assist with the timing process, most manufacturers provide food cooking time guides. The accuracy of these guides is dependent on adherence to a specific set of operating conditions and, even then, they can be faulty. The military tested 6.8-kg (15-lb) pressure cookers, and in one they found that foods for which 1 minute cooking time was recommended actually took 2–2.25 minutes for a total cooking cycle of 5.65 minutes. Use of recommended cooking times for other cookers was no help as they cooked the same product in 3.8, 7.1, 16.5, and 4.7 minutes, respectively.

It is necessary for each operator to establish his own cooking times for the conditions under which he operates and the equipment that he has purchased. Some of the variables include:

1. Altitude which affects the temperature of the steam. Steam at high altitude at 0-kg (0-lb)

pressure is lower in temperature than at sea level. Cooking times are greater.

2. Capacity of steam sources and size of pipes conducting it.
3. Type and size of pan. The deeper the pan, the greater the cooking time.
4. Amount of food in the pans. The greater the amount, the greater the cooking time.
5. The food material—type, form, piece size, temperature (frozen, chilled, or at ambient), air space around pieces of food, degree of doneness desired, and media surrounding the food.
6. Design of steamer, placement of steam inlet, steam pressure, steam circulation, degree of superheating of steam, and amounts of air mixed with the steam.

Every operator of a steamer should work out by actual test the process times for the products he plans to cook. He should standardize the amounts he will cook, the form and piece size, the depth of product in the pan, and other variables under his control. If he prepares a product in a variety of ways, he should develop the process time for each. After they are established, the procedural details and times should be posted in a waterproof cover beside the steam cooker.

The best way to conduct a test for correct time is to prepare the food using the directions which the operator uses now and plans to use in the future. Then cook the food according to the manufacturer's times. If the product comes out grossly overcooked, reduce the cooking time 25 percent, or if mildly overcooked, reduce it 10 percent and try again. Keep narrowing the time change. If the product is underdone, reverse the procedure and add to the cooking time. It is important to be precise in the ways that the food is prepared for cooking and in the cooking times used in the steam cooker with each repetition. There may be some variation in the quality of the food prepared in a steam cooker because of the variations in the food material, but these can be held to a minimum. Some of the cooking times recommended by the manufacturers of various steamers and pressure cookers are found in table 16.2.

Additional Information

1. Most frozen vegetables can be steamer cooked directly from the frozen state if complete thawing is not feasible. Large solid blocks should be cut or broken into small blocks to promote even cooking. Corn on the cob should always be thawed in the refrigerator before cooking. This will save energy, both in the refrigerator and the steamer. Cooks have found that prethawing contributes to better and more even cooking in the slower 6.8-kg (15-lb) cookers. If the juices are not to be saved, vegetables should be cooked in perforated pans. If the juices are to be used, the products should be raised out of the liquid to obviate leaching out of flavor and soluble nutrients.
2. To avoid water-taste meats, cook them in perforated pans or, better yet, cook them on a rack resting in the solid pan so that juices may be saved for soups and gravy.
3. Steam roast beef, pot roast, and poultry in the steamer and then brown the meats in a 218°C (425°F) oven. Save liquids for sauces.
4. Precook chicken halves at 6.8-kg (15-lb) pressure for five minutes or more, freeze them, and then prepare them for service in a fryer at 185°C (365°F) for five minutes.
5. Cook cornbread in sheet pans in the 2.3-kg (5-lb) steamer for twenty minutes. Sheet pans may also be used for cooking dumplings prior to placing them on the steamer-prepared stew. One can undercook stew and then place uncooked dumplings on top of the stew and steam until the dumplings are done.
6. Foods to be fried may be partially, or fully, cooked in the steamer and then fried for a short time in hot fat to give the desired crust and color. Batter fried foods are not as apt to shrink away from the batter crust if precooked in the steamer. Foods that take a long time to fry normally may be fried quickly with less fat absorption if blanched. Many foods that need

TABLE 16.2. *Manufacturer's Recommended Timer Setting*

Food	*2.3-kg (5-lb) Cooker (min)*	*6.8-kg (15-lb) Cooker (min)*
Asparagus, frozen	10–15	1.5
Beans, green, fresh	15–25	1
Beans, green, frozen	10–15	1
Beans, lima, frozen	10–15	1.5
Broccoli, fresh	10–20	1
Broccoli, frozen	8–12	1
Cabbage, cored and cut	14–20	1.5
Carrots, fresh, sliced	18–25	2
Carrots, frozen, diced	9–13	1
Cauliflower, fresh	10–20	0.5
Cauliflower, frozen	11–15	0.5
Chicken pieces, blanched	18–30	6
Corn on cob, fresh	10–15	4
Corn, whole kernel, frozen	9–13	0.5
Eggs, poached (greased pan)	6–8	0.5
Eggs, scrambled	6–8	4 + 2–3
Fish fillets	8–15	1
Onions, fresh	15–20	5
Peas, fresh, shelled	3–5	1
Peas, frozen, loose	6–9	1
Potatoes, French fry cut, fresh	15–20	5
Potatoes, 3 in. regular cut, fresh	20–30	5–6
Rice	22–27	7
Spaghetti	20–26	7
Squash, summer, 1 in. slice, fresh	3–6	3
Turnips, fresh, diced	25–35	1.5

Where a spread of minutes is given, the small number is for a few pans and the larger one for capacity.
Source: Market Forge, Everett, Mass.

an oven browning or crust can be cooked more quickly if steamed first.

7. Old onions should be steam cooked in water to give them a fresh onion flavor.
8. Custards may be steamed in serving pans if the cups are surrounded by water and covered with foil.
9. An advantage of steam cooking is that foods can be cooked in the same pans in which they are served, as a general rule.
10. Porcupine meat balls may be prepared by combining 237 ml (1 cup) of uncooked rice with 0.9 kg (2 lb) of hamburger. Steam until the rice is done and serve with a spicy tomato sauce.
11. Steaming of meat will usually give 5–6 percent greater yield than roasting.
12. When cooking rice, use about 1.4 liters (1.5 qt) of water to 0.45 kg (1 lb) of rice. For spaghetti, use 1.9 to 2.8 liters (2-3 qt) of water to 0.45 kg (1 lb) of spaghetti. Cook both about twenty to twenty-two minutes in a 2.3-kg (5-lb) steamer or seven minutes in a 6.8-kg (15-lb) steamer. Pressure should be released slowly to avoid overflow of pans.
13. Foaming in rice and spaghetti can be reduced

by pouring 15 ml (1 tbsp) of oil on each pan of the product.

14. When greasy foods have been prepared in the steamer, close the compartment and go through the preheat part of the process to rid the compartment of grease.
15. When using multiple compartments, fill and bring one up to pressure before starting a second one.
16. To avoid pressing a new gasket out of shape, close the door loosely and turn on steam. Tighten the door only enough to stop steam flow around the gasket.
17. Lobsters, shrimp, scallops, and other fish are highly acceptable, if steamed.
18. Steam cooking lends itself well to the cooking of fragile vegetables such as asparagus and broccoli inasmuch as they do not break up in cooking because they are not stirred.
19. Cook green vegetables only until barely tender. One extra minute might mean loss of the bright green color.

See table 16.3 for some problems and their causes associated with the steamer and pressure cooker.

TABLE 16.3. Steamer and Pressure Cooker Problem Solving

Causes	*Problems*									
	Food cooked unevenly	*Food overcooked*	*Food undercooked*	*Door gasket leak*	*Pressure does not release*	*Low chamber pressure*	*Loose door*	*Safety valve goes off*	*Buzzer or light does not work*	*Cooker does not operate*
Too much food in pan	X									
Too large pieces	X									
Too much mashing of food	X									
Timer is inaccurate		X	X		X				X	
Pressure control working improperly		X	X			X		X		X
Thermostat working improperly		X	X					X		X
Thermostat set wrong		X	X					X		X
Dirty gasket				X			X			X
Defective gasket				X			X			X
Twisted gasket				X			X			X
Material under gasket				X			X			X
Clogged drain line					X					X
Trap malfunction					X	X				X
Clogged strainer						X				X
Jammed door screw							X			X
Hanger bolts maladjusted							X			X
Defective safety valves								X		X
Defective buzzer and/or light									X	

Special Applications

Use the steamer to:

1. Freshen stale breads, day-old pastries, leftover entrees and vegetables, gravies, and sauces.
2. Loosen foods which have baked on pans.
3. Soften peppers or cabbage leaves for stuffing and whole apples for baking.
4. Quickly prepare whole fish, chickens, or turkeys for boning.
5. Cook brown bread, puddings, and other ordinarily baked products that do not need high dry heat to form crusts as cakes, pastries, and pizzas do.
6. Steam country sausage. Cook for one hour on a rack in a steam table pan and pour off the fat before oven cooking it for fifteen minutes at 177°C (350°F).
7. Reheat canned foods. Do not remove the top of the can until service. If can is not needed, it may be returned to the storeroom.
8. Steam corned beef without water for twenty to twenty-five minutes per 0.45 kg (1 lb).
9. Partially cook baked potatoes and acorn squash. Finish-cook in an oven with a higher-than-usual temperature or in a low-heat broiler.
10. Hard-cook eggs. Eggs for garnish or egg salad may be broken out into a greased steam table pan, hard cooked in the steamer, and sliced or chopped as necessary for use. A steam table pan will hold four dozen eggs and should be cooked from six to eight minutes in a 2.3-kg (5-lb) steamer. Scrambled eggs may be prepared by beating them with milk and steaming.
11. Steam blanch fruits to assist in the removal of their skins. It takes two to three minutes from the time the steam is turned on to loosen orange skin in either 2.3-kg (5-lb) or 6.8-kg (15-lb) steamers. For grapefruit it takes about four minutes.
12. Precook baked apples. Then cover with glaze and finish in a hot oven or broiler.

Alternatives to Steamers and Pressure Cookers

Most frequently used as a substitute for steam cooking is pot cooking on the range. However, pot cooking uses more labor, operational steps, and energy than steam cooking. It may take 62,000 Btu for 13.6 kg (30 lbs) of fresh potatoes on a range top but only 17,000 Btu in the faster steamer. A comparison is given below.

Range Top	*Steamer*
1. Place potatoes in large pot.	1. Place potatoes in small steam table pans.
2. Fill pot with water.	2. Spread potatoes in pan and place in steamer.
3. Carry and place pot on range (heavy job).	3. Close and turn on steam, set timer.
4. Turn on heat and bring to boil.	4. Remove potatoes when time is up (one-half time and one-quarter of the fuel used in range top cooking).
5. Cook potatoes (hot work).	5. Place potatoes in steam table.
6. Test potatoes for doneness.	6. Wash pan.
7. Carry potatoes to sink when done for draining (dangerous).	
8. Pour off water and lose water-soluble nutrients.	
9. Transfer potatoes to service pan.	
10. Wash pot and service pan.	

The steam jacketed kettle has many of the advantages of steamers but does require the heating of water in addition to the product. It requires stirring, emits clouds of steam, radiates much heat, and is inconvenient to unload as food must be dipped out or run into floor level containers.

More vitamin C is retained in broccoli and Brussels sprouts if they are cooked in steam rather than in water or a range pot.

Ovens may be used for cooking foods such as rice and spaghetti since they do not require so much attention as range top cooking demands. Despite considerable insulation, ovens radiate much heat which is lost. They are also a slow means of cooking.

Little used is the deep fat fryer which may be filled with water and used for a rapid heating pot or cover and used as a rather dangerous steamer.

Improved Steamer Design

An indication of a modern design modification is the new Groen steam cooker, which spurts steam on all sides of a single portion of food, cooking it in seconds. This development will promote cooking foods to order, thus minimizing the problems of leftovers and holding food at elevated temperatures, which hastens food deterioration.

Saving Energy

1. Steam equipment should be used as close to capacity as possible for efficient energy use. This may mean that several sizes of steamers will be needed for the various quantities to be cooked.
2. The package boiler that produces the steam should be insulated with 12.7 cm (5 in.) of insulation and the piping that carries the steam from the boiler to the steamer with 5.1 cm (2 in.) of insulation. Placing the boiler and steamer close together helps to reduce steam losses. While it is not usually done, insulating the steamer would reduce energy losses and decrease the load on the ventilating system. Most manufacturers consider that the temperature difference between steam and ambient air is not great enough to pay for insulation.
3. The higher the steam pressure of the cooker, the less the number of Btu required to cook a given amount of food. For example, six pounds of rice require 42,000 Btu to cook in a zero-pressure steamer, but 12,000 Btu are needed under 15 pounds of pressure. Also, the more the incoming steam impinges directly onto the food, the greater the speed of the cooking and the less the energy use. Similarly, the smaller the piece size, the faster it cooks. Smaller pieces also facilitate even cooking, since larger pieces tend to overcook on the outside.
4. Small pressure cookers are good for cooking to order, which decreases leftovers. They are also easier to fill to capacity, which provides more efficient energy use.
5. Consider precooking many foods in the pressure cooker or, to a lesser extent, the steamer, and finish-cooking them in the oven, deep fat fryer, broiler, or griddle. Some foods that can be cooked this way are full-size turkeys and beef roasts, corn bread, chickens, chops, and baked potatoes. Turkeys cooked this way use less energy and give 5–6 percent greater yield.
6. The steamer or pressure cooker can substitute for most range-top cooking operations except for pan frying. Steamers will cook 30 pounds of potatoes using 17,000 Btu, while the range requires 68,000 Btu.

Cleaning

For the most part, steamers and pressure cookers are somewhat self-cleaning, but a procedure for cleaning should be set up. It should be posted adjacent to the steamer. The following is a suggested guide that might vary according to the model and manufacturer of the steam cooker used:

1. On completion of use, open door and allow unit to cool.
2. Press safety latch and lift out shelves. Wash these with brush in pot sink or in mechanical potwasher or dishwasher. Rinse well.

3. Scrub chamber with stiff bristle gong brush using hot water and detergent mixture. Check compartment drain for adequate functioning.
4. Clean outside of unit by same method.
5. Rinse well inside and out with clean hot water.
6. Close door, turn on steam for several minutes, and then open door and allow to dry.
7. Reinstall shelves and latch into place.
8. Wipe outside with dry, lint-free cloth and set door ajar.

When spills occur during operations, they should be cleaned up immediately.

Maintenance

Each manufacturer has recommended procedures for providing daily and less frequent maintenance for various pieces of equipment. These usually come as instructions with the equipment. Obviously, it is impossible to record maintenance procedures for all of the various pieces of steam equipment.

A step-by-step procedure to follow on one piece of equipment might be:

1. Lift lever of safety valve when unit is under pressure to ensure freedom of operation.
2. Check adjustment of hanger to bolts to provide tight fitting of inside door against the steamer front.
3. Check gaskets for cuts, breaks, depressions, looseness, and steam leakage.
4. Check indicator lights for proper functioning.
5. Check all gas and steam controls. Where a gas heater is used, check the pilot light and the burner for a good blue flame.
6. Watch for water leaks.
7. Look for any aberrations in boiler performance.

Other factors that may be checked weekly or monthly are:

1. Accuracy of timers against a stop watch.
2. Accuracy of pressure gauges.
3. Lubricate screw for tightening door (some use graphite and some use grease). Include in lubrication hinges and other locations where metal moves around a pin as well as the toggle swivel on handle.
4. Blow out steam line for each deck.
5. Check steam trap for proper removal of water without too much loss of steam. Disassemble and clean elements. If the steam trap does not close within two minutes after starting, replace it.
6. Remove and clean steam inlet strainer.
7. Flush out and clean boiler periodically. Replace anode when corroded.

QUESTIONS

1. What are the advantages of steamer and pressure cooking over range top pot cooking? Over steam jacketed kettle cooking?
2. What is the secret behind the fast cooking of steam?
3. What is the latent heat of vaporization? Latent heat of fusion?
4. At what three steam pressures are most steamers and pressure cookers operated?
5. What is the standard size of pan used in most steam cookers? In what depths does it come?
6. What is the predominant material used in steam equipment?
7. What controls and displays do most steamers have?
8. What is the design feature responsible for the effectiveness of the most efficient gas steam boilers?
9. What are the agencies usually responsible for approval of steamers?

10. What is the safest way to determine needed cooking capacity of steamers?
11. What are work table placement considerations in the use of steamers?
12. Before an operator places a new steamer into use, what should he do relative to steam cooking times?
13. What is the effect of altitude on steamer operations?
14. How does one determine accurate cooking times for a steamer?
15. How does one get the characteristics of roast beef on meat cooked in a steamer?
16. How does one avoid the sticking together of steam cooked rice and spaghetti?
17. What is the benefit of using the steamer to heat canned foods?
18. What foods cannot be cooked properly in a steamer?
19. How is the steamer cleaned?
20. What are the major points checked in the maintenance of a steamer?
21. List five methods for conserving energy in steamers or pressure cookers.

BIBLIOGRAPHY

ANON. 1971. Steamer Specification Sheets. Vulcan Hart Corp., Louisville, Ky.

ANON. 1974. Service Manual for Wearever Hi-Speed Steam Cookers. Wearever Food Service Equipment Co., Fort Wayne, Ind.

ANON. 1975. The Cleveland Convection Steamer. Cleveland Range Co., Cleveland, Ohio.

ANON. 1975. Pressureless convection steam could revitalize your operation. *Chef Magazine*, June-July.

ANON. n.d. *Market Forge Newsletter*. Market Forge, Everett, Mass.

ANON. n.d. *Market Forge Test Kitchen Bulletin*. Market Forge, Everett, Mass.

BREY, H.T., MAYER, M.L., and PYOUS, J.E. 1964. *Evaluation of Pressure Cookers*. U.S. Naval Supply Research and Development Facility, Bayonne, N.J.

HOLMAN, H. 1975. Steam: Combating the energy food crunch. *School Food Service Journal* XXIX, No. 1, 33–46.

SANSTADT, H. 1972. Around the menu with steam cooking. *Cooking for Profit Fortieth Year* No. 4, 41–50.

WILKINSON, J. 1975. *Complete Book of Cooking Equipment*. CBI Publishing Company, Inc., Boston.

Refrigerators and Freezers

Most people in quantity foodservice consider the refrigerator to be indispensable, yet two centuries ago the only refrigeration that was known was a cool cellar, cave, or a cold winter. A large proportion of the world's people today have little contact with refrigeration on a day-to-day basis. Meals are planned to use fresh unrefrigerated ingredients, and all food is eaten or thrown away.

If a food cannot be salted, pickled, smoked, or dried, the only alternative that many people have is to cook it and continue to cook it whenever it starts to spoil. I have had fish in the Philippine Islands that was cooked four times before it was eaten.

During wars, most of the front-line troops see little refrigeration. In World War II, troops under fire ate canned foods and packaged dried foods or "C" and "D" rations. Directly in back of the lines were "field kitchens" or the U.S. Armed Force "mess trucks" that prepared canned or dried foods ("B" rations) and either carried it up to the troops or had them come in small groups to eat it. What was not eaten was thrown away or shared with hungry civilians. Refrigeration did not enter into the military scheme of feeding except to a limited extent in rear areas. In military operations of the future, it is planned to move refrigeration farther to the front.

Although the Chinese, Greeks, and Romans stored ice and snow in underground pits and insulated them with straw, hay, and sawdust before the birth of Christ, controlled refrigeration did not enter into our scheme of feeding until approximately 1775. Then ice was cut in winter and packed in sawdust or shavings before it was put in sawdust-insulated boxes or storerooms as refrigeration. With the advent of railroads into the Pocono Mountain section of Pennsylvania and the Catskill area of New York, ice was brought to the big cities.

By 1890, natural ice could not keep pace with the demand, so mechanical ice machines were developed. They were so successful that the demand for natural ice declined rapidly. However, it was not until 1918 that the ice machine was miniaturized so that cold could be produced in an insulated box without the messy handling of ice. Mechanical refrigeration developed rapidly between 1918 and 1941.

What is Refrigeration?

Refrigeration is the removal of heat from a body or material. The process is carried out by placing the warm material next to the cold one. The heat from the warm material migrates to the cold one until the two materials are the same temperature. In most refrigerators, this is not possible because of the quantity of food to be chilled. Cold air which is cooled by proximity to the refrigerator's evaporator coils is circulated around the warm food and chills it. The warmed air goes back to the coils to give up the heat it has gained and be chilled again. The foods thus chilled are, for the most part, above 0°C (32°F) and are "refrigerated."

If the food being chilled is to be frozen or lowered to temperatures below 0°C (32°F), much more heat must be removed than if it were to be refrigerated. It takes only 1 Btu to reduce 0.45 kg (1 lb) of water 0.56°C (1°F). However, to convert that amount of water at 0°C (32°F) to ice requires the removal of 144 Btu. Then, when this ice is thawed, it removes 144 Btu from the air. It was this cooling ability that our forefathers used in their ice boxes.

Most of what the foodservice industry calls "freezers" are not freezers but frozen food-holding equipment. While they may freeze food in time, they do the job slowly and the ice crystals that are formed rupture the food cell structure because the crystals are too large.

What Does Refrigeration Do in Foodservice?

1. It slows bacterial action by lowering the food temperature to the point where bacteria grow poorly. Freezing temperature is low enough to stop bacterial action.
2. It decreases chemical activity so that foods do not develop rancidity and other off flavors readily. It reduces the rate of beef aging. Freezing is even more effective in slowing chemical activity.
3. Life processes are slowed so that fresh fruits and vegetables do not mature as fast as at ambient temperature. This allows them to be stored for longer periods of time.
4. It changes the forms of some foods. Gelatin goes from a fluid to a semisolid under refrigeration; ice cream, from fluid to a solid when certain amounts of heat are removed in freezing.
5. It changes textures of some foods. Greens become crisp, bacon is brittle, and butter gets hard.
6. It removes moisture from uncovered foods. Lettuce and other greens lose their crispness, gelatin develops a skin, meat shrinks, and root vegetables and fruits shrivel.
7. It develops coldness typical of some foods—puddings, custard, salads, and fruits.
8. It concentrates by evaporating or freezing water out of a liquid in the form of ice.

Refrigeration Systems

There are many ways of cooling, for example, use of ice, evaporative cooling, steam jet, air cycle, solid carbon dioxide, liquid air, nitrogen, thermoelectric, absorption, and vapor compression. A number of them are actually variations of vapor compression. This is the one that most concerns us here as it is the basis of most foodservice refrigeration.

Vapor compression refrigeration uses the principle of a heat pump. A refrigerator cavity and the food placed in it are full of heat that must be removed. A compressed gas is expanded inside a pipe in the cavity. This becomes heat thirsty and soaks up the heat in the refrigerator like a sponge and carries it outside where the heat is wrung out of it. Then it returns to the refrigerator for another load.

The pipe in which the gas is expanded is the evaporator. The expanded gas with its load of heat is pumped out of the refrigerator by a motor- or engine-driven compressor that then compresses the gas, which becomes very hot. The hot gas is passed through a condenser or heat exchanger where the heat is removed by air or water and may liquefy. This cooled gas is stored in a tank or receiver until needed inside the refrigerator to soak up heat again. At that time, an expansion valve actuated by the thermostat opens and lets some of the compressed and cooled gas expand into the evaporator coil where it soaks up the excess heat in the refrigerator cavity.

In foodservice, refrigeration finds its way into quite a number of pieces of equipment. Included are:

1. Reach-in refrigerators or freezers. These are cabinets where a door swings open or a drawer may be pulled out to reach cold food (figure 17.1). They may be under the counter or take vertical space from the floor almost to the ceiling.
2. Walk-in refrigerators or freezers. These rooms are large enough for a person to enter. They may occupy part of the foodservice building or be placed outside. The walk-in may be compartmentalized (figure 17.2).
3. Roll-in refrigerators. Like the roll-in oven, the refrigerator will handle a complete wheeled rack of food as a unit. They are much in demand in school lunch operations to handle large numbers of prepared lunches awaiting heating and service.
4. Pass-through refrigerators. These may be like

FIGURE 17.1. Reach-in refrigerators may be placed throughout the kitchen area.

the reach-in refrigerators except that they have doors on both sides so that they may be loaded from the kitchen side and unloaded as needed on the serving line side. Some are built into the wall and others use part of a space left in the wall.

5. Counter refrigeration. These units once were pans filled with fine ice or snow for chilling and presenting salads, juices, chilled desserts, and similar foods. Ice may be used today, but often it is kept from melting by mechanical refrigeration in the plates or coils beneath the ice. The food may be placed directly on the refrigerated plates (figure 17.3).
6. Display refrigeration. These may be display counters like those in a delicatessen, glass-doored refrigerators, or open frozen food display cases such as those in a supermarket.
7. Mobile or portable refrigerators (figure 17.4). While almost any small refrigerator on wheels

FIGURE 17.2. The walk-in refrigerator must be placed where it can support a major preparation area. Courtesy Vulcan-Hart Corporation.

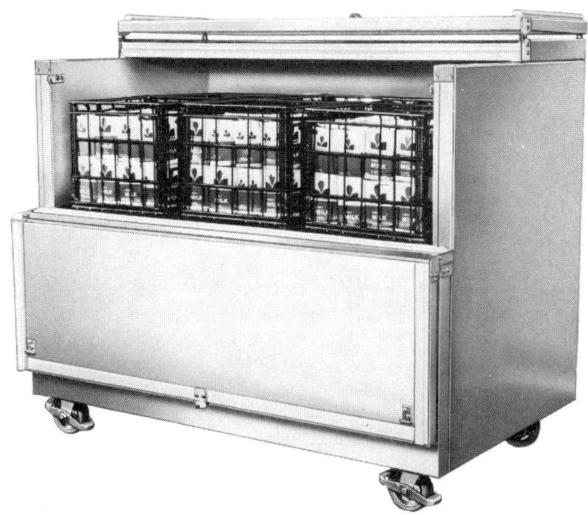

FIGURE 17.4. Mobile refrigerated carrier-dispensers can be effective. Courtesy Glenco Refrigeration Corporation.

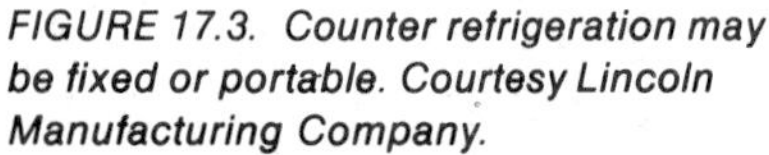

FIGURE 17.3. Counter refrigeration may be fixed or portable. Courtesy Lincoln Manufacturing Company.

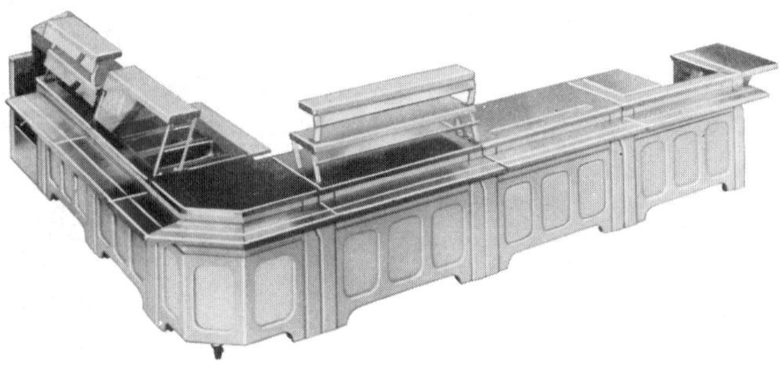

may fit this category, there are special refrigerators on wheels which are lightweight enough to be handled in a loaded condition by a single individual. The insulation is thinner and less effective than that in a conventional refrigerator, and the refrigerating unit does not operate when the refrigerator is in transit.

8. Other refrigerated devices. These include beverage dispensers including milk, soft ice cream, or milk shake machines, chest-type ice cream or milk carton dispensers or storage cabinets, ice machines and dispensers, butter and lettuce dispensers, and many more.

Description and Specification

In general, whatever form it may take, the refrigerator or freezer should be rugged in construction, have a durable finish and heavy-duty hardware, be easy to sanitize and maintain, and have a trouble-free quiet mechanism that rather precisely maintains a set temperature.

Exterior

Formerly most refrigerators were covered on the outside with wood, but today most are covered with corrosion-resistant steel, usually 18–24 gauge, either No. 302 which is 18–8 (18 percent chromium and 8 percent nickel), or Type 430 with No. 4 finish, although some have a No. 7 finish. Other refrigerators are steel coated with white porcelain glass baked at 816°C (1500°F), or with synthetic enamel baked at 149°C (300°F), or plastic laminates. Seamless fiberglass is also used for refrigerator exteriors, as is aluminum, type 3003H, which is about 0.76–1.0 mm (0.3–0.4 in.) thick with anodized or aluminited finish. Walk-ins are available in stainless steel, galvanized iron, and various combinations.

All exteriors should be of seamless construction either through welding or pressing, except for the walk-ins which usually have panel construction.

The refrigerator base may be of 14-gauge corrosion-resistant steel or other heavy metal.

Insulation

Refrigerator and freezer insulation or heat barrier was formerly sawdust, then mineral rock wool, foil laminates, shredded redwood bark, and corkboard were used. None of these is used much today. Glass fiber and foamed glass came into use during World War II followed by styrofoam and finally Freon-blown polyurethane foam that is usually foamed in place. The insulating value or the ability of a material to slow down heat penetration is usually given in "k" values. This value is the number of British thermal units of heat that are transmitted through a 30-cm (1-ft) square of the material 2.5-cm (1-in.) thick in one hour. Conductivity of insulators is as follows:

Material	*Conductivity as k factor*
corkboard	0.28
cellular glass	0.40
concrete	6.0–10.0
fiberglass	0.26
hardwood (maple)	1.25
masonite	0.33
pinewood (white)	0.79
polyurethane	0.14
sawdust	0.45

Source: Bureau of Standards

From these figures, it can be seen that fiberglass is almost twice as good an insulator as is sawdust, and polyurethane is twice as good as fiberglass. Thus, refrigerators that formerly required 20 cm (8 in.) of sawdust could get by with 10 cm (4 in.) of fiberglass or 5.2 cm (2 in.) of polyurethane. It is important that insulation be vapor sealed on the outside against entrance of moisture. When cork was first used, the seal consisted of tar and felt. This was superseded by polyethylene, well lapped and sealed. I feel the latter should still be used, for although foam glass, styrofoam, and polyurethane are impervious to water vapor, the fabricating process leaves some routes of access to water vapor and helps pass heat.

It is felt that the minimum of insulation for reach-in refrigerators should be 5.1 cm (2 in.) of polyurethane and for freezers 7.6 cm (3 in.). For walk-ins, insulation may be advantageously increased up to double these amounts. Examine a refrigerator that has been working at 32–38°C (90–100°F) and above 80 percent RH (relative humidity). Where small patches of condensed moisture drops show on the outside surface, it indicates faults in construction that allow free flow of cold to the outside. Where there is a thin moisture film over considerable surfaces, the insulation is too thin.

The panels of the walk-ins are locked together and are sealed by felt, vinyl bulb gaskets, insulation on insulation, or polyvinyl chloride.

Interiors

The interiors, too, should be of seamless construction. The materials may be white porcelain, fiberglass, stainless steel, anodized aluminum, galvanized iron, and baked enamel. Most of the walk-in refrigerators of the first four types. Galvanized iron is little used for reach-ins.

The reach-ins have switches that turn lights on when the door is opened and off when it is closed.

Most reach-in refrigerators have evaporators in the top of the refrigerator cavity. They may be of finned copper or aluminum tube construction that may or may not be coated to protect against airborne corrosive acids. Older units allowed the air distribution to rely on the fact that cold air is heavy and drops down in the refrigerator. Today, most refrigerators have a fan and a diffuser to draw air over the coils and then blow the cold air around the cavity. To even out distribution, the cold air may flow down hollow walls on the sides and then out ports along the way from top to bottom. Some use hollow mullions that carry cold air down between sections or in back of each section of the refrigerator.

Walk-in refrigerators usually have the evaporator on the back wall or on the back side of the top. A fan and diffuser blow air along the top of the refrigerator, and as it loses force, it drops down over the stacked or shelved foods.

The food in reach-ins is usually stored on heavily tinned, chromed, galvanized, or stainless steel wire or expanded metal racks. These are adjustable in 2.5–5.1 cm (1–2-in.) increments by keys that fit into slots in the cavity corners. These slots may be used to hold pan slides, as well. The shelves in one-half or a full section may be built as an assembly that will slide out onto a dolly, or the section may be mounted at floor level so that a wheeled rack may be rolled into the refrigerator (figure 17.5).

FIGURE 17.5. Many shelf combinations are possible in reach-in refrigerators in addition to regular shelves and wheeled racks. Note some of the possibilities. Courtesy Hobart Corporation.

In walk-ins, the floor may be the floor of the room, a sheet of steel without insulation, or it may be insulated like the rest of the refrigerator (figure 17.6). It may or may not have support elements under the floor. There may also be a metal floor of heavier gauge than the sidewalls. If the floor is insulated, the room floor may be depressed to allow carts to run into the refrigerator, or a ramp may be built up to the door level. There may be slatted

FIGURE 17.6. The most desirable walk-in refrigerator is one where carts may be moved in easily at floor level. Courtesy Vulcan-Hart Corporation.

floor boards to distribute air and weight. A few have floor drains.

Racks may be hung from the walls, be on stationary supports or be on wheels. These latter are preferable as the racks may be loaded on the receiving platform and then wheeled as a unit into the refrigerator without rehandling the food. Supermarket carts may be used for this purpose. To get more food into walk-ins, shelving may be put on wheels and arranged so that food may be stored without aisles. When a particular rack is needed, the racks are moved as little as possible until the desired rack is released. However, most kitchens use fixed location shelving.

Refrigerating System

Refrigerators may have the compressor and condenser in the bottom or the top of the cabinet or in some remote location that is cool and which will not add heat to the kitchen. The top location is better than the bottom as one can get about 1.4 cu m (49 cu ft) in a top-mounted unit and only 1.1 cu m (39 cu ft) in a bottom-mounted unit.

Most foodservice refrigerators use mechanical compressors to concentrate the refrigerant. Of these, the most common type is the "reciprocating piston" that compresses gas by moving up and down in a cylinder like that in a car. The "rotary" system is an off-center rotor that squeezes the gas against the side of a circular compression chamber. The "centrifugal" unit compresses the gas into a restricting cylinder by use of a fan.

In each case, the gas or refrigerant (ammonia, sulfur dioxide, carbon dioxide, methyl chloride, or most usually one of the Freons) is heated by the compression and must be cooled. Cooling may be accomplished by evaporating a liquid off the coils in which the compressed gas is carried, running water over the coils, or blowing cool air over them. As the gas is cooled and liquefied, it is stored in the receiver until released to expand and take up heat through a thermostatically controlled expansion valve into the evaporator as it is needed to maintain a cool temperature within the refrigerator.

The evaporators may be manually defrosted by shutting off the refrigerator and opening the door, or it may be possible to reverse the refrigeration cycle by making the evaporator the condenser until the ice is melted off. The water is caught in a pan or run to a drain. Then there are automatic defrosters that accomplish the process automatically, at timed intervals. Usually the water runs into a pan outside the refrigerator where it is evaporated by the heat of the condenser. Water from large units is usually directed into a floor drain.

Doors

The reach-in may have one to three or more vertical sections. Each section may have one full length door or two half doors on one or two opposing sides (figure 17.7). A three section refrigerator may have up to twelve half doors. The doors may be self-closing by torsion action or gravity action cam lift. At an angle of about 100° the door will stay open, and at 120° it will come up against a self-stop. Door gaskets may be heavy, soft, easily cleaned vinyl with or without magnetic properties. In some refrigerators these gaskets snap out easily. There are usually heated cables around the door that evaporate condensed moisture. The chrome-plated hinges should be heavy duty. Latches may be magnetic and be coupled with a key lock. Some use positive interlock latches.

Refrigerators in serving areas often have double sliding glass doors that are self-closing. These are not usually feasible for kitchen use. In pass-throughs where they are used, the door on the kitchen side should be hinged to prevent cold loss.

The doors may be of the same material as the body of the refrigerator inside and out and have at least 5.1 cm (2 in.) of polyurethane insulation. The doors may have double-pane glass windows or be solid. Walk-ins may have full length doors with the same amount of insulation as the walls. They may be hinged on either left or right and be any size to handle mechanized materials handling equipment. The large central commissaries may have sliding doors that may be operated manually, by pressure plate, or photoelectrically.

To obviate frequent opening of walk-in refrigeration, some institutions and restaurants use up to 2.5-cm (1-in.) plexiglass in chrome-plated frame doors so that workers can see who or what is in the refrigerator. Some commercial users claim that the door pays for itself in one year of use.

As reach-in storage below waist height is hard to use, some kitchens have this storage as self-closing drawers with supports to hold full or half size steam table pans. This may be under counter or along the entire front of a reach-in refrigerator.

Controls and Displays

As most refrigerators are automatic in their functioning, there are not many controls or displays

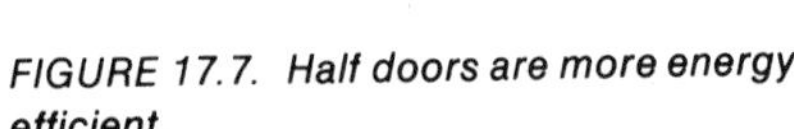

FIGURE 17.7. Half doors are more energy efficient.

needed. Most refrigerators have an internal temperature adjustment, an indicating thermometer, and a warning light that may flash when temperature is higher than that set. Some have an audio alarm and a few have a dew-point compensator control.

Dimensions and Compressor Horsepower

The average one section reach-in refrigerator is 71 cm wide x 83 cm deep x 208 cm high (28 x 33 x 82 in.), contains 0.67 cu m (24 cu ft) of storage space, and requires a 1/4 horsepower compressor. A two-section unit is 137 cm wide x 83 cm deep x 208 cm high (54 x 33 x 82 in.), has 1.46 cu m (52 cu ft) of storage space and uses a 1/3 horsepower compressor. A three-section unit may be 213 cm wide x 83 cm deep x 208 cm high (84 x 33 x 82 in.) with 2.0–2.2 cu m (70–80 cu ft) of storage space and use a 1/2 horsepower compressor. Freezers have compressors two to three times the horsepower of refrigerators.

The walk-ins are built over a wide range of sizes. For instance, one manufacturer makes refrigerators 1.5 x 1.2 x 2.4 m (5 x 4 x 8 ft) up to 3.7 x 9.4 x 2.4 m (12 x 31 x 8 ft) with compressor sizes from 1/3 horsepower to 3 horsepower for refrigerators and 3/4 horsepower to 5 horsepower for freezers.

Determination of Needed Capacity

There are a number of rules of thumb for estimating the space needed in refrigeration. Some are given here:

1. 0.028–0.04 cu m (1–1.5 cu ft) usable space per person per day
2. 0.07–0.14 cu m (2.5–5 cu ft) per seat in a fine restaurant
3. 4.45 cu m (159 cu ft) inside for 250 school meals
4. 7–11 sq m (75–120 sq ft) inside for 400 employee meals
5. 30–37 sq m (320–400 sq ft) inside for 400-bed hospital with centralized tray service

Some consultants calculate freezer space as one half that for refrigeration. A commonly used set of figures for space per meal is:

Meat and poultry	283–850 cu cm (0.010–0.030 cu ft)
Dairy	198–425 cu cm (0.007–0.015 cu ft)
Vegetables and fruit	566–1133 cu cm (0.020–0.040 cu ft)
Total	1047–2408 cu cm (0.037–0.085 cu ft)

The lower figure is for schools and the higher figure for fine table service. One might take an average figure for hospitals and employee feeding.

The U.S. Department of Agriculture calculates needs for a school lunch kitchen by multiplying the number of meals to be served by the 0.95 kg (2.1 lb) of food needed per meal and multiplying this by 0.45 (percent of food requiring 2.2–4.4°C (36–40°F) and multiplying this number by the number of days for which meals must be stored. The total amount of food is divided by 6.8 kg (15 lb) to get the cubic feet of storage required in a walk-in refrigerator assuming that only one-half of the total space could be used for storage. In the reach-in refrigerator calculation, the total amount of food to be stored is divided by 10 kg (22 lb) to get the amount of cubic feet required. Then one needs only look for a refrigerator that has the needed capacity in cubic measurement. Some consultants add a factor of 15–25 percent for future needs and to cover possible errors.

If one has no previous experience on which to base refrigeration requirements, the method used by the U.S. Navy is the most accurate. If the delivery period is one week, then a number of one-week menus with the assistance of the pertinent recipes and the number of portions needed per week are used to calculate the amounts of each refrigerated food in kilograms (pounds) needed per week. This number is multiplied by the cubic meters per kilogram (pound). An example would be 0.0009 cu m (0.033 cu ft) per pound for frozen peas. In the U.S. Navy every food used was calculated in this way. The total number of cubic meters (cubic feet) is added and multiplied by a factor of 2 to compensate for aisles and unusable space in a walk-in refrigerator. For reach-ins the factor would be far less than 2 as there is less unused space. Probably 1.25 would be as good as any. On submarines, the U.S. Navy used no factor as the refrigerators were loaded solid in reverse order of projected use, and the submariners literally ate their way into the refrigerators.

Freezers

When computing the capacity needed for a food freezer, the calculation is somewhat different than that for refrigerators or holding freezers. Food must be brought from the temperature as received to the final frozen temperature, and enough tons of refrigeration must be provided. The calculation in American figures alone is given in table 17.1, although the answer could be calculated equally well in

TABLE 17.1. Calculating Food Freezer Capacity

Refrigerator needs

2 sides		*2 sides*		*Top*		*Fiberglass insulation factor*		*Temperature differential*		*Hours*	
2(10′ x 7′)	+	2(8′ x 7′)	+	(10′ x 8′)	x	.26	x	(90°–0°F)	x	24	
8 in. insulation (divisor)											= 23,306 Btu

Floor (10′ x 8″) x 6.0 concrete insulating factor x (90°–0°F) x 24 / 12 in. thick	= 86,400 Btu
	109,706 Btu
*Factor for other losses	1.25
	137,133 Btu

	Weight		*Specific heat thawed*		*Temperature change*		
Beef need	1000 lbs	x	.77 Btu	x	(50°–32°F)	=	13,860 Btu
			Latent heat of fusion				
To freeze	1000 lbs	x	100 Btu			=	100,000 Btu
			Specific heat frozen		*Temperature change*		
	1000 lbs	x	.40 Btu	x	(32°–0°F)	=	12,800 Btu

	126,660 Btu
Total	263,793 Btu

Required to be removed	263,793 Btu	= 1 ton compressor required
One ton of refrigeration	288,000 Btu	

*There are calculations that may be used to determine the "other losses" but it is simpler to use 25% to compensate for lights, door openings, people in the refrigerator, and unknown losses.

TABLE 17.2. Specific and Latent heats of Commonly Frozen Foods

Food (1 lb.)	*Specific Heat Before Freezing (Btu)*	*Specific Heat After Freezing (Btu)*	*Latent Heat of Fusion (Btu)*
Beef (fat)	.60	.35	79
Beef (lean)	.78	.41	102
Fish	.76	.41	101
Pork	.60	.38	66
Eggs	.76	.40	98
Milk	.90	.46	124
Apples	.71	.39	92
Berries	.89	.46	125
String beans	.92	.47	128
Peas	.80	.42	108
Poultry	.80	.41	99

metrics. The operator wants a blast freezer that will freeze 1000 pounds of beef from 50°F to 0°F. He wants the walk-in to operate in a 90°F ambient and to have 8-in. walls of fiberglass and a 12-in. floor of concrete. The dimensions of the walk-in are 10 by 8 by 7 ft.

Basic Use and Operation

When a refrigerator is contemplated, what type it should be, its capacity, and its placement are prime considerations. For bulk storage and considerable volume, the walk-in, particularly those that permit entrance of carts and wheeled racks, is desirable as the food can be handled in large units and without multiple handling. Some of the reach-ins have been modified to be roll-ins but they are usually limited to one type of product per cart or shelf assembly.

For cook support, the reach-in is usually best as its door can be opened, the food removed, and the door closed faster than with a walk-in. The most used items may also be placed at the most efficient height. Some kitchens have pass-throughs between the meat or vegetable preparation areas and the cooking areas which obviates taking the ready-to-cook foods back to the walk-ins and makes them available when needed. Sometimes a walk-in will be placed centrally with bulk storage, providing reach-in facilities for either the cook or service personnel. Then the cook can go into the refrigerator and place all the needs for a meal in front of the reach-in doors, so he will not have to reenter the walk-in until the next meal.

Reach-ins are often used to thaw frozen meats as it is unsafe to thaw them at ambient. This is a slow process in the average refrigerator, often taking two days, as its temperature will drop close to −18°C (0°F) before it starts its slow rise. To speed the thawing process, special refrigerators are designed with heaters to hold a safe temperature above freezing. They can be operated as conventional refrigerators when thawing is not being done.

Pass-throughs are used between the production area and the serving area so that the salad and dessert personnel can prepare items ahead or watch the rate of consumption and produce only enough to maintain a certain reserve level. Some institutional operations prepare individual salads or desserts and place them in a portable refrigerator. This can be wheeled into a space in the wall behind a cafeteria serving line and be plugged in to maintain a refrigerated temperature. Cleaning is made easy by the fact that they can be rolled to the cart or potwashing area for cleaning.

Bulk food storage capacity for refrigerators has been discussed. Capacity needed in cooks' refrigerators is usually regulated by the practices of each cook. In a small facility, a single section will usually do, but in most facilities a cook will need two sections.

Reach-ins used for salads or desserts usually must have the capacity to hold a certain number of sheet pans or racks of individual salads or desserts or they must have space for a number of serving pans. Capacity requirements can be calculated easily.

Placement of refrigerators is often an afterthought and, in many cases, is wasteful of manpower or causes unsafe food-handling practices. It once was customary, particularly in institutions or the military, to place refrigerators along a corridor leading into the kitchen. In some cases, walk-ins were free-standing outside the foodservice building. Supposedly, the reasoning behind this design was to keep the mess and movement of receiving and storage out of the production area and to store the large amounts of food close to where they were received. This is wrong! Food should be stored as close to the point of first use as possible to reduce the costly travel of cooks and other preparation personnel and to provide storage of perishable foods close to the point of use. The meat storage should be in or close to the meat preparation area. The fruit and vegetable refrigerator should be close to the vegetable and salad preparation area.

Reach-in refrigerators should have tables in front of their doors to speed loading and unloading and to reduce labor by making one-motion loading and unloading possible. Using tables beside the refrigerator means that each insertion or withdrawal necessitates not only both a backward and a forward movement but doing this around an open door as well.

Speed of Refrigeration

Among others, the following factors affect the speed at which foods refrigerate:

1. The Btu that can be removed per hour per unit of cubic space and the effectiveness of air circulation.
2. The specific heats of the foods being refrigerated. Specific heat is the number of Btu that must be removed to lower 0.045 kg (1 lb) of product 1°F.
3. The amount of food to be refrigerated.
4. The temperature at which the food enters the refrigerator and the temperature to which it will be refrigerated. In the interest of energy conservation, if a heated food is not a food poisoning hazard, such as foods containing protein, it is recommended that it be brought to room temperature before it is placed in the refrigerator.
5. The container in which cooling takes place. It is most effective if the food can be placed on a wire rack without packaging. Aluminum is good packaging, but various foams, heavy cardboard, and the other insulators are poor. The less space between the top of the product and the top of the pan, the better.
6. The thickness of depth of product. While thick gravy in a stockpot might take several days to cool, if it is poured to a depth of 5.1 cm (2 in.) in an aluminum pan, it may cool in two to four hours. The U.S. Navy recommends that leftovers not be over 7.6 cm (3 in.) in depth when refrigerated.
7. The amount of surface exposed per kilogram or pound of food is important as the more the surface, the faster the cooling.
8. The amount of stirring given the cooling food.

TABLE 17.3. Recommended Cold-Storage Conditions

Foods	*Temperature [°C (°F)]*	*Relative Humidity (%)*
Butter and cheese	1.6–4.4 (35–40)	85
Eggs	0–7.2 (32–45)	95
Fish	−1.1–4.4 (30–40)	85
Meats	0–2.2 (32–36)	85
Vegetables and fruits	0–2.2 (32–36)	95

If all factors were optimum, one could calculate the time to refrigerate an amount of food by the following formula: Amount of food times (food temperature before refrigerating minus food temperature after refrigerating) times specific heat of the particular food divided by the Btu removed by the refrigerator per hour.
Example:

100 lbs fish × (70–35°F) × 0.76 Btu ÷ 2550 Btu (46 cu ft refrigeration per hour) = 1 hour

or

45 kg fish × (21–1.6°C) × 3.01 Btu ÷ 2550 Btu = 1 hour

3.01 Btu is an adjustment to the .76 Btu for above metrics.

Recommended cold-storage conditions are given in table 17.2. Although greens keep best close to 0°C (32°F), green beans, cantaloupe, okra, pumpkins, sweet peppers, winter squashes, and sweet potatoes do better around 10°C (50°F). However, they can be kept for several days at 0°C (32°F). Mature green-ripe tomatoes should be held at 13–21°C (55–70°F) and ripe ones at 10°C (50°F); however, the U.S. Navy found they could keep firm, red-ripe tomatoes for well over a month at 2°C (35°F).

As most refrigerators act as a water pump removing moisture from uncovered food to the evaporator coils, salad greens tend to wilt and meats lose weight rapidly. The solution used to date for the problem has been to wrap foods in vapor barrier materials. A more acceptable solution would be the use of larger diameter evaporator coils so that the temperature differential between the refrigerant and the refrigerator air would be no more than 6°C (10°F) and moisture pumping would be slowed, or stopped, allowing the relative humidity to rise from 20–30 percent to 85–95 percent. Care would have to be taken to have enough air circulation to remove water droplets that might condense on the food because of the raised humidity level but not enough to cause food surface drying. These refrigerators can be specified.

Hints on Refrigeration Use

1. Remove all waste leaves and unnecessary packaging before placing food in the refrigerator. They slow cooling of food.
2. Mark all foods so they can be recognized quickly. Where important, mark with the date that it was placed in the refrigerator.
3. Place new foods to the rear and move old stock to the front. If possible, continue to use the same shelves for each product as this assists in quick identification and removal.
4. Place material on the shelves loosely. Leave space between packages and between packages and walls for good air circulation. Cover prepared food with thin vapor barrier material to protect against bacterial and odor contamination and prevent drying.
5. Use sheet pans and other solid pans no more than necessary as they block the flow of cold. Where utensils are used, they should be good temperature conductors like aluminum.
6. Limit solid masses or liquid foods to a thickness of 5.1–10 cm (2–4 in.). Frequently stir liquids to get them through the 60–4°C (140–40°F) danger zone quickly.
7. Never store raw foods above cooked foods as they may contaminate the sterile items.
8. Never refrigerate potentially dangerous leftovers such as meat, poultry, eggs, fish, gravies, and creamed foods more than 36–48 hours. If longer storage is contemplated, freeze them immediately after removal from service. If the food is hot, cool it quickly by spreading it in thin layers in the pans and placing them in moving cold water or air.
9. Where only small amounts of a perishable food will be required per batch, remove the product from the refrigerator in small quantities as needed.

10. With the walk-in, if possible, it is desirable to handle a food as a unit from Receiving to Service areas. Some facilities have trimming facilities at Receiving so that the waste can be removed and the product placed in a wire cart or wheeled rack and taken as a unit without further handling to the refrigerator. Then, when needed in preparation, it goes as a unit.
11. In walk-ins, food needs to be placed on shelving off the floor. Preferably, the shelving should be of wire or metal straps well separated for good air circulation and on wheels to permit quick movement to the point of use and ease cleaning of the refrigerator.
12. As in dry storage, the most used foods in walk-ins should be stored close to the door between waist and chest height. Most used food combinations should be placed close together so that the refrigerator need be open no more than necessary and the worker need not spend excessive time searching in the refrigerator.
13. Workers should be encouraged to plan their openings of the walk-in or reach-in refrigerators. They should remove a maximum of needed items at one time so that the refrigerator need not be opened frequently. Similarly, when the refrigerator is loaded, it should be preplanned so that the food to be stored is positioned close to the door and the area where it will be stored is known when the door is opened.
14. To reduce cold air loss when the door is opened, some walk-ins have hanging sheets or strips of plastic or air curtains where a sheet or air is blown from top or bottom and drawn in from the opposite side.

Special Applications

The freezer can be used to reduce the amount of water in a liquid material by freezing out the water as ice. This is the way our forefathers made applejack from hard cider.

The freezer can be used to dry similar to the way frozen clothes dry during the winter. Air blowing over thin frozen pieces of foods will dry them by sublimation (going from ice to the vapor phase without going through the liquid phase).

Alternatives to Refrigerators and Freezers

During the winter the outside air can, and is, used to refrigerate and freeze. Fishermen catching fish through the ice have frozen their catch for ages.

In the summer, the job of refrigerating becomes more difficult. Cellars, caves, wells, and cold springs were used by our ancestors. Evaporative cooling has been used in some areas. A coarse cloth may be loosely wrapped around the food to be cooled and then placed where a breeze will blow on it while the cloth is kept wet. In many parts of the world, this technique is used to cool both food and rooms.

For preservation purposes, there are many alternatives—cooking, canning, dehydrating, salting, concentration, chemical preservatives, smoking, and others.

Saving Energy

1. Manual defrosting saves more energy than automatic systems.
2. Lights should be turned off inside the walk-in refrigerator when no one is inside. An outside light should indicate when the interior lights are on.
3. Trips to the refrigerator should be planned to minimize opening the refrigerator door. All foods should be well marked, grouped in most-used combinations and located in the same place as much as is possible. Rubber curtains should be placed on the inside of the doorways to re-

duce cold losses when the doors are open. Walk-in refrigerators with reach-in doors should be purchased so that the cook can plan a day's menu and place the necessary food in front of the reach-in door.

4. Doors of walk-in refrigerators should be wide enough that carts can be pushed through them for loading and unloading food. A better plan is to place foods, as received, in arranged lots on wheeled racks or carts so that they can be wheeled into the refrigerator as a unit until needed and then pushed to the food preparation area. Gross trimming and washing of vegetables can be done on the receiving platform along with the removal of superfluous packaging. These all decrease energy use.
5. The condenser should be kept free of soil and the evaporator coils free of ice.
6. If food safety will not be threatened, freshly cooked foods should be brought down to room temperature before they are refrigerated. This does not apply to protein foods, which should be refrigerated as soon as possible. When thawing foods, plan ahead so that thawing can take place in the refrigerator. This will help keep the refrigerator cool, free of charge.
7. Half doors should be used instead of full-length doors, unless they are specifically needed. This reduces cold air spill-out. Pullout drawers with various pan holders, set below waist height, should be used wherever possible. Polyurethane insulation 7.6 cm (3 in.) thick should be used for refrigerators and 10.2 cm (4 in.) of insulation should be used for freezers. Use self-closing doors and drawers.
8. To avoid wasteful air leaks, make sure the refrigerator is level and the doors are air-tight.
9. Consider selecting Plexiglas doors, which let light into the refrigerator and permit the contents to be seen, possibly lowering the number of times the door is opened.
10. Refrigerators should be checked frequently for short cycling and loss of temperature control.

Cleaning

1. Spills should be cleaned up as they occur.
2. Fingerprints around the door should be wiped off daily.
3. At least once weekly, transfer the refrigerator contents to another refrigerator so that the refrigerator can be shut off for defrosting.
4. Remove the racks and wash them top and bottom, rinse and dry them at the pot sink. Shelf supports, removable air ducts, and food files can be cleaned in the same way.
5. Wash the refrigerator interior with a mild detergent and a germicide that does not leave a residual odor. As cleaners, one may use soda ash, baking soda, borax or other recommended commercial detergents. If soils are resistant, one can use mild abrasive cleaners such as magnesium oxide, fine pumice, French chalk and similar products. Do not use strong soaps or harsh abrasive scouring powders.
6. Rinse all surfaces and wipe them dry with a soft dry cloth.
7. Clean glass with a good glass cleaner.
8. Clean the condenser once a month with a whisk broom and a tank type vacuum cleaner. If it is greasy, spray with a strong detergent and rinse with clean hot water spray. Wipe up all water.
9. Wipe loose water off evaporator coils and water collector if they are easily accessible. Replace all removed equipment and start refrigerator.
10. Wipe off exterior of refrigerator with a mild detergent and water, rinse and wipe dry with a soft cloth at least once a month. Doors and front will have to be cleaned weekly. Wipe off door gaskets at the same time.

Maintenance

1. Clean condenser coils as indicated above. A condenser 25 percent clogged can increase operating costs 200 percent.

2. At least twice a year clean the fans inside and out with a good grease remover, and wash this off with detergent and water.
3. Lightly oil hinges and latches.
4. Check door fit by closing it on a slip of paper at least once on each side of the door. If the paper slides out easily, check the refrigerator for levelness from side to side and front to back. Then examine the condition of the door gasket. If worn or abraded, replace it.
5. Check the defrost cycle to determine whether it occurs when it should and if it removes all of the ice on the evaporator. Ice should never be over 0.3 cm (0.125 in.) thick. If ice is not removed, bring in the maintenance worker. At the same time, check the evaporator coil temperature against manufacturer's specifications.
6. Daily check the refrigerator interior for proper distribution of the contents for good cooling action. Be sure food is not too close to evaporator, fans, and duct openings.
7. Check condenser for adequate air circulation in front of coils.
8. Check the indicating thermometer with a thermometer placed in the center of the empty cavity.
9. Be sure that moisture condenses only on the evaporator coils of walk-in refrigerators. Look for it in the following locations:

   a. Around the perimeter of the door. This usually means a burned out heater wire that should be replaced if drips occur here.

   b. Just inside the door or behind the door gasket. If ice condensate is evident, it is probable that the cause is poor door sealing and levelness of the refrigerator. The condition of the gasket should be checked.

   c. The ceiling. When ice condensate gathers here, the usual cause is the door is being open too much and the evaporator fan is drawing in the moist kitchen air which condenses on the cold ceiling.

   d. The floor. Ice here in a walk-in freezer may be caused by the evaporator drain pan's heater burning out, the drain line being clogged, the evaporator fan starting before the defrosted water drains out of the evaporation which blows water on the floor, or water which was used to clean the floor not being completely removed.

   e. On electric contacts or controls. Ice here is usually caused by the control's being in line with the moist air being drawn in by the evaporator. The control should be moved to where the incoming air does not hit it.

   f. In cracks and crevices. Ice forming here is usually caused by lack of a vent that will prevent a vacuum's forming when air is chilled. As there is no way for air to come in easily, it is drawn through weak spots in the insulation causing these to deteriorate and ice to form in the cracks. The vent must be heated to prevent ice from forming there.

   g. In cracks between the panels making up the walls. Condensate and ice here are usually caused by faulty assembly. Often it can be corrected by relocking the panels or applying caulking along the locking seams.

QUESTIONS

1. When was the first mechanical refrigerator developed?
2. What is refrigeration?
3. What does refrigeration do for foods?
4. What are the major components of the vapor compressor?
5. Name ten mechanically refrigerated pieces of equipment.
6. What are the main coverings for reach-in refrigerators?

7. What is the k value of an insulation?
8. What important treatment is made to corkboard?
9. What are the most common refrigerants?
10. What is done to prevent condensation of moisture around a door opening?
11. What is the best placement of walk-in refrigerators?
12. Where should tables be placed in relation to reach-in refrigerators?
13. What factors affect the speed with which a food will refrigerate?
14. What products are best stored at 10°C (50°F)?
15. What is the procedure for storing food in a reach-in refrigerator?
16. What is the optimum way of handling food in a walk-in?
17. What is the procedure for cleaning a reach-in refrigerator?
18. How does one check door fit?
19. What is the maximum thickness of ice that should be permitted on refrigerator evaporator coils?
20. What causes ice on a walk-in refrigerator floor?
21. Describe five ways that refrigeration can be made more energy efficient.

BIBLIOGRAPHY

ANON. 1966. Schmidt walk-in handbook. C. Schmidt Co., Cincinnati, Ohio.

ANON. 1974. Equipment guide for on-site school kitchens. Program Aid No. 1091. U.S. Department of Agriculture, Washington, D.C.

ANON. How to get maximum performance from your electric refrigeration equipment. Publication No. 75 TEC 974. The Electrification Council, New York.

CHASE, R. 1964. Walk-in refrigerator design analysis. *Kitchen Planning* 1, No. 3, 15–18, 106.

FARRALL, A. 1963. *Engineering for Dairy and Food Products*. John Wiley and Sons, New York.

KOTSCHEVAR, L., and TERRELL, M. 1977. *Food Service Planning Layout and Equipment,* 2d Ed. John Wiley and Sons, New York.

LEY, S.J. 1980. *Foodservice Refrigeration*. CBI Publishing Company, Inc., Boston.

LITMAN, C. 1957. Making refrigeration work for you. *Institutions* 40, No. 5, 188–192.

LONGREE, K., and BLAKER, G. 1971. *Sanitary Techniques in Food Service*. John Wiley and Sons, New York.

PHELAN, J., PRINCE, G., KALIN, M., and FROHLICH, L. 1971. Cooling it. *School Lunch Journal* XXV, No. 1, 25–44.

SMITH, L.L. and MINOR, L.J. 1977 *Food Service Science*. The Avi Publishing Co., Inc. Westport, Ct.

STOWIK, W. 1974. Discussion on humidity, the culprit (leaflet). Vollrath Refrigeration, River Falls, Wis.

Dishwashers

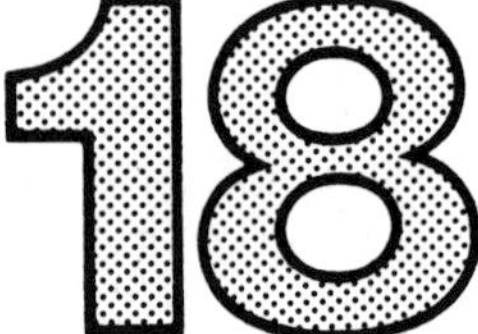

One of the most costly, but least considered, operations in foodservice is dishwashing. Using 8–12 percent of the sales dollar, dishwashing involves the operation of the most expensive piece of equipment in the kitchen by what are often the lowest paid workers. In addition to the interest on what might be an $8,000–$10,000 investment, everything about dishwashing is expensive—space, water, dish losses, detergents, rinse-aids, electricity or gas, overhead, indirect costs, and labor.

In 1952, 70 percent of the dishwashing dollar was spent on labor, but fifteen years later this had shrunk to 49 percent. Why? The mechanical dishwasher was the answer. As the cost of labor skyrocketed, the use of mechanical dishwashers increased greatly. However, it was a mixed blessing. The total cost per dish has increased only a quarter of a cent from one cent. In terms of the dishwashing dollar, the indirect costs have increased greatly—interest on investment, detergents, and cleaning supplies have doubled, hot water has almost quadrupled in cost, and dish breakage and loss have increased from 10 percent to 14 percent.

Dishwashing has come a long way from the days when it was wholly a hand operation using only two sinks and drainboards for soiled and clean dishes, lye soap, lukewarm water, and largely transient labor.

Strong soaps were used "to get dishes clean." Often the bars of soap would be cut up in a can with a perforated bottom and hung on the hot water faucet to dissolve as the hot water ran into the sink. Sometimes the wash solution would be too strong and the worker would suffer skin loss or dermatitis. The advent of milder-on-the-skin detergent helped.

Another problem was low water temperature. The worker would start the water at a temperature at which he was comfortable, about 43°C (110°F), and soon it would be down to ambient in both wash and rinse tanks. The dishes often had films of fat on them, did not dry well, and certainly were not sterile. Some chlorine was used for a sanitizer, but dish drying was still a problem as they would have to use a towel to dry them. Some dishwashers started to use long-handled racks so that, as the dishes were washed, they would be stacked in the rack immersed in water hot enough to sanitize. When filled, the rack would be lifted out onto the drain board to dry partially. A slotted drain rack into which the dishes would be inserted could be added. This separated every plate, and they would air dry quite well.

Keeping the wash and rinse water hot was a problem. In some cases, the hot water was allowed to run into the two sinks at a slow rate throughout the entire washing period. However, this diluted the soap in the sink. Then steam was injected directly into the sink water, but often temperature was hard to control and steam burns occurred. Today some of those who still wash dishes by hand use thermostatically controlled steam injection or electric tubular heaters as required by law. Also, as required by federal regulation on interstate carriers and many state regulations for intrastate applications, three sinks are used for washing, rinsing, and sanitizing.

While many churches, schools, small institutions, summer hotels, and small restaurants still use hand dishwashing, most dishes are now washed by mechanical dishwashing machines. By definition, a dishwasher might be described as a device for bringing a mixture of detergent and hot water in contact with the soil on dishes forcefully, flushing away the soil which it loosens with copious quantities of water, rinsing off the soil and detergent with clean water, heat sanitizing the dishes, and assisting in the drying of them.

There are many types of dishwashing machines. A few of the more common are described here:

1. Immersion dishwashers. A rack of dishes is immersed in a tank of detergent and hot water while a large pump in the tank wall swirls the liquid violently and abrades the soil away. The rack of dishes is lifted out and placed in another tank for rinsing. This device is used in some kitchens for potwashing as well. It is a minor dishwasher.

2. Single tank, stationary rack (also called door type). Dishes in a rack are washed by jets of water and detergent pumped from below and generally from above also. Nozzle assemblies may be stationary or whirling, and the base holding the rack may be stationary or move back and forth. Rinsing and sanitizing takes place without removing the rack as fresh, hot water at adequate temperature from the hot water line sprays over the dishes after the wash cycle (figure 18.1).

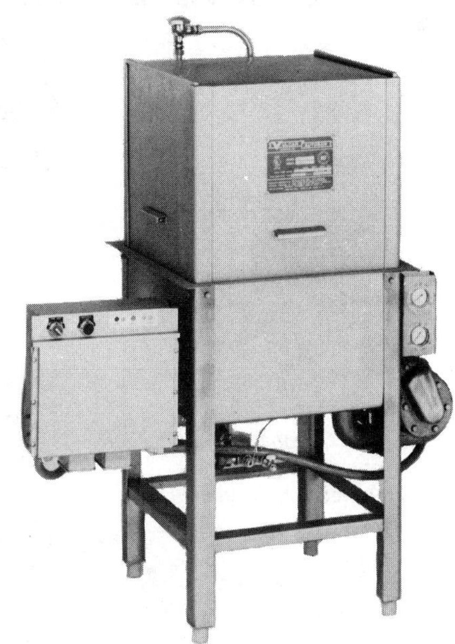

FIGURE 18.1. Single tank, stationary rack mechanical dishwasher. Courtesy Vulcan-Hart Corporation.

3. Conveyor-rack type. These may use a single tank as in the single tank machine or use two tanks and a prerinse (figure 18.2). A pair of motor-driven chains engage the rack of dishes and draw it through the machine where the prerinse, wash, power rinse, and final rinse operations are performed on the dishes. After ejection, the hot dishes are allowed to stand on the dish table until dry. Then, usually, the dishes are removed from the racks and stacked on dish carts. The racks are reused and hand or conveyor carried to the soiled end of the dishwasher. To reduce breakage and handling labor, it is recommended that glasses, cups, and often bowls be transported in the racks in which they are washed. This increases the number of racks that must be stocked but seems to be worth the expense and the extra space required.

4. Flight type dishwasher. These are similar to the conveyor type except that instead of using individual racks, the conveyor is one continuous rack and the dishes must be placed against pegs or bars, as in a rack, at the soiled dish end of the machine and removed at the discharge end (figure 18.3). To permit the dishes to dry, the conveyor extends away from the exit end of the machine a suitable distance. Racks of glasses, cups, bowls, or silverware may be placed on top of the conveyor pegs to permit washing and handling as a unit. If the dishes or racks are not removed, they come against a strike bar that turns off the conveyor motor.

5. Carousel type. This provides a closed circuit conveyor where the dishes will continue to go

FIGURE 18.2. Conveyor-rack type machine designed for operating around the corner of a narrow room. Courtesy Vulcan-Hart Corporation.

FIGURE 18.3. Flight type machine with prewash, wash, power rinse tanks. Courtesy Insinger Machine Company.

through the machine if not removed. It may consist of a chain with lugs that will engage a rack set on it, or it may be made up of a continuum of racks or pegs attached to a conveyor chain. In either case, they slide around to the entrance of the dishwasher, through it, and back to the loading point on tables (figure 18.4).

6. Low-temperature type. This dishwasher can be the single-tank or multitank type, and run with or without conveyors. Its attraction is based on the fact that it uses 49°-60°C (120°-140°F) water—preferably the latter—rather than the 82°-90°C (180°-195°F) temperature range of conventional dishwashers. This reduces energy costs, but increases chemical costs, since the dishes must be sterilized chemically. Also, if relative humidity in the dishroom becomes high, it is difficult to air dry dishes, even with the use of a rinse aid.

For low-temperature dishwashing, water at no more than 6 grains hardness (102.6 parts per million of lime and magnesia) is desirable. Hardness may be tested with special kits, but you may ask the local water company to furnish the information or have a detergent salesman perform the test. Desirable water pressure is usually 18–20 pounds psi, and desired water volume is 257 liters (68 gal.) per minute. When setting the temperature gauge, keep in mind that water below 54°C (130°F) will not remove tallow fat. To sanitize dishes, use about 50 parts per million chlorine, as chlorine levels about 85 ppm will leave buildup on ware. Silver plate, however, should not be washed with this method because the chlorine will react with the silver. Last, the wash-rinse cycle of most low-temperature dishwashers runs for about 90 seconds, permitting the washing of approximately 37 racks of dishes per hour.

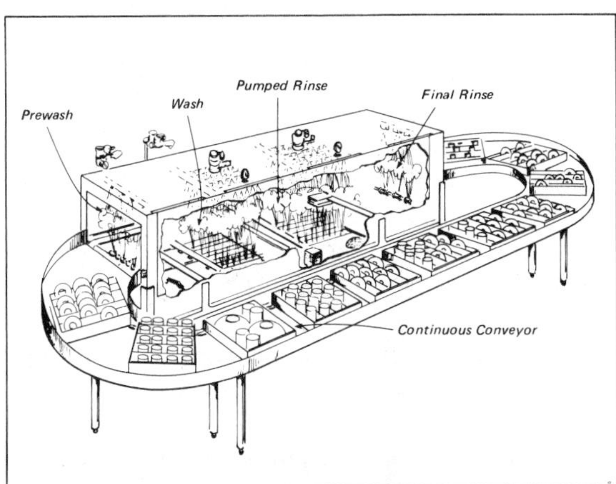

FIGURE 18.4. Carousel type dishwashing system. Courtesy National Sanitation Foundation.

There are other types of dishwashers that will not be covered here—undercounter, ultrasonic, pulse-type, glass washers, silverware washers, and others.

Description and Specification

When one talks about a dishwasher, he is usually thinking about a mechanical device that takes soiled dishes and treats them so that they become acceptable judged by sight, touch, and bacterial safety.

Alone, or in conjunction with support equipment, the dishwasher carries out the following functions that should be discussed:

- scraping
- washing
- rinsing
- sanitizing
- drying

Scraping

As dishes arrive from the dining room in the waiter's hand, on a tray, in a bus box or cart, or on a conveyor, they are usually covered with a gross soil that would, in aggregate, place an undesirable load on the dishwasher (figure 18.5). This soil, made up of crusts, meat residues, uneaten vegetables, gravy, and other edible and inedible material, must be removed.

The basic means of removal consists of a bare hand or hand in a rubber glove brushing the plate

FIGURE 18.5. Scraping area using a trough with water running through it. Over this are racks for cups, glasses, and bowls.

residue into a garbage can or garbage grinder. Repelled by this proximity to garbage, some workers use a plastic or rubber scraper. Others bang the soiled dish on a rubber collar around an opening leading to the garbage grinder or garbage can to loosen and remove the plate waste. Another means of soil removal is performed by passing the plate under a heavy plume of water directed over the mouth of the garbage grinder. Somewhat similar is the use of a flume of water in a trough. The dishes are dipped in the fast moving stream of water, and the garbage is washed into the garbage grinder. Some units are designed to reuse the water.

Scraping may take place after the dishes are placed in the dishwashing rack. The rack of dishes is slid over a drain assembly that either collects the gross garbage in a tray or diverts it into a garbage grinder as a hand-directed spray on a flexible hose washes it from the dishes. The scraping may take place as prewashing in the dishwashing machine, as the dishes in a rack, or, on a conveyor, pass under jets of water and collect the solid garbage in trays. This is the first section of some dishwashers but is omitted on others.

Dishes and silverware with soil that is too dried on to be removed in the dishwasher are often allowed to stand for a period of time in a soak sink of warm water and detergent.

Washing

The heart of the dishwasher is the washing section where a mixture of 60–71°C (140–160°F) water and detergent is drawn into a powerful pump and then forced under pressure into pipes and either fixed or whirling arms above and below the dishes in racks or on conveyors (figure 18.6). This mixture is forced out of orifices in a heavy spray that has a flushing action that first loosens the soil and then washes it down over perforated trays that remove the gross soil. The water-detergent mixture returns to the wash tank. As it comes in contact with the dishes, the water should be in a solid sheet of water since drops of water in a spray do a poor job of soil removal. Water from the rinse tank constantly flows into the wash tank providing a surplus that leaves through an overflow to a sewer taking with it some of the floating scum from the water surface. The detergent thus lost must be replaced by an automatic detergent dispenser or added periodically by hand. The detergent concentration should be maintained somewhere between 0.15 and 0.30 percent for most detergents, although in the past, the Public Health Service has recommended 0.45 kg (1 lb) of detergent per 189 liters (50 gal) water, or approximately 0.24 percent. Actually, it varies according to detergent and should be checked.

Rinsing

The residual soil and detergent are removed from dishes over a rinse tank similar to the wash tank using the same type of pump and spray assemblies and a flush of water at a minimum of 71°C (160°F) (figure 18.7). Prior to leaving this area, the dishes are subjected to a final rinse of water direct from the water heater and usually a booster heater that brings the water to at least 82°C (180°F) and no higher than 91°C (195°F). The curtains between tanks should be in place so that the spray from the rinse tank does not raise the temperature or dilute the wash water too much.

The single tank machine, of course, does not have a rinse tank, so the final rinse does the whole rinse. Single temperature machines use 74°C

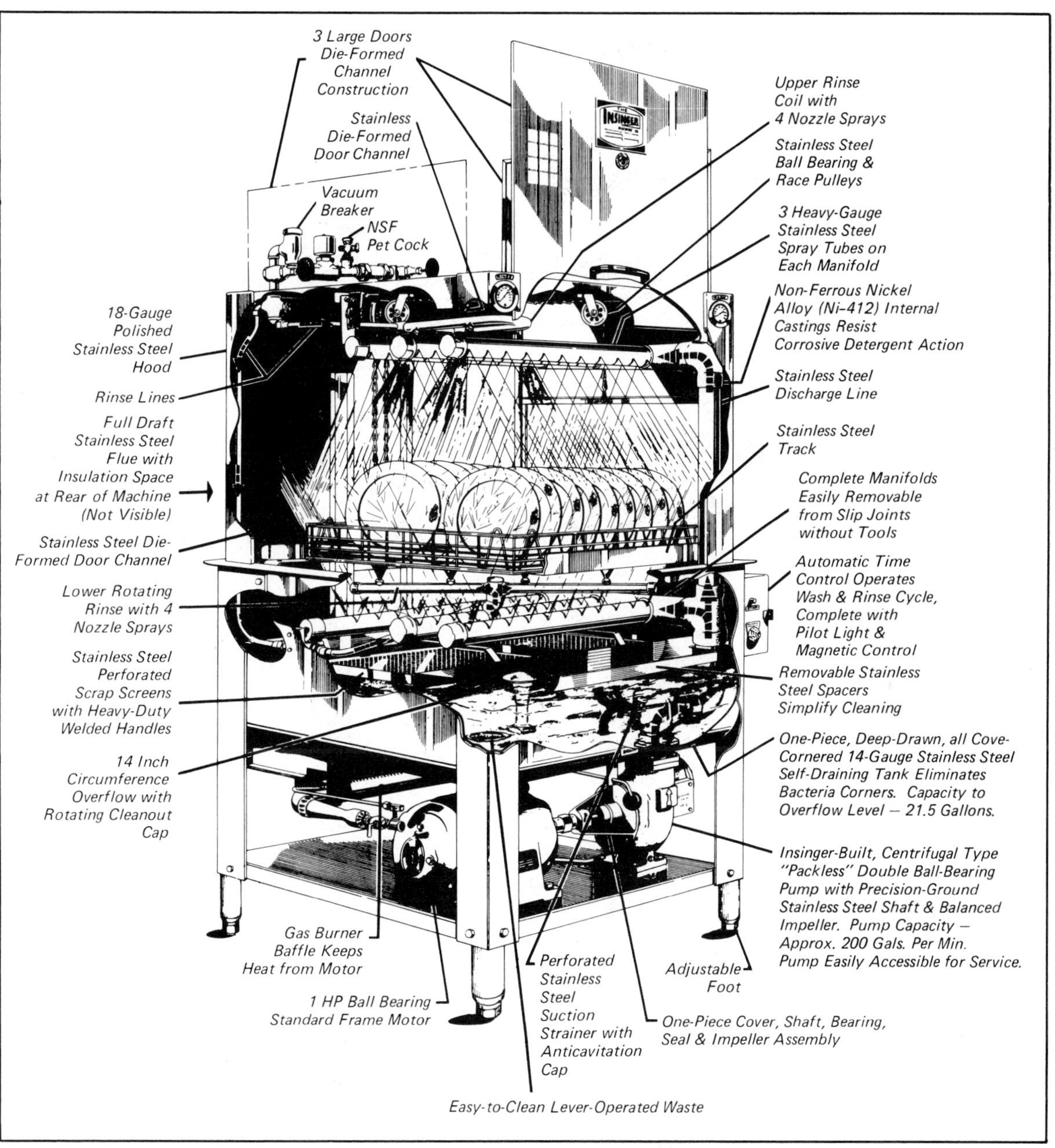

FIGURE 18.6. Single-tank dishwasher and washing spray. Courtesy Insinger Machine Company.

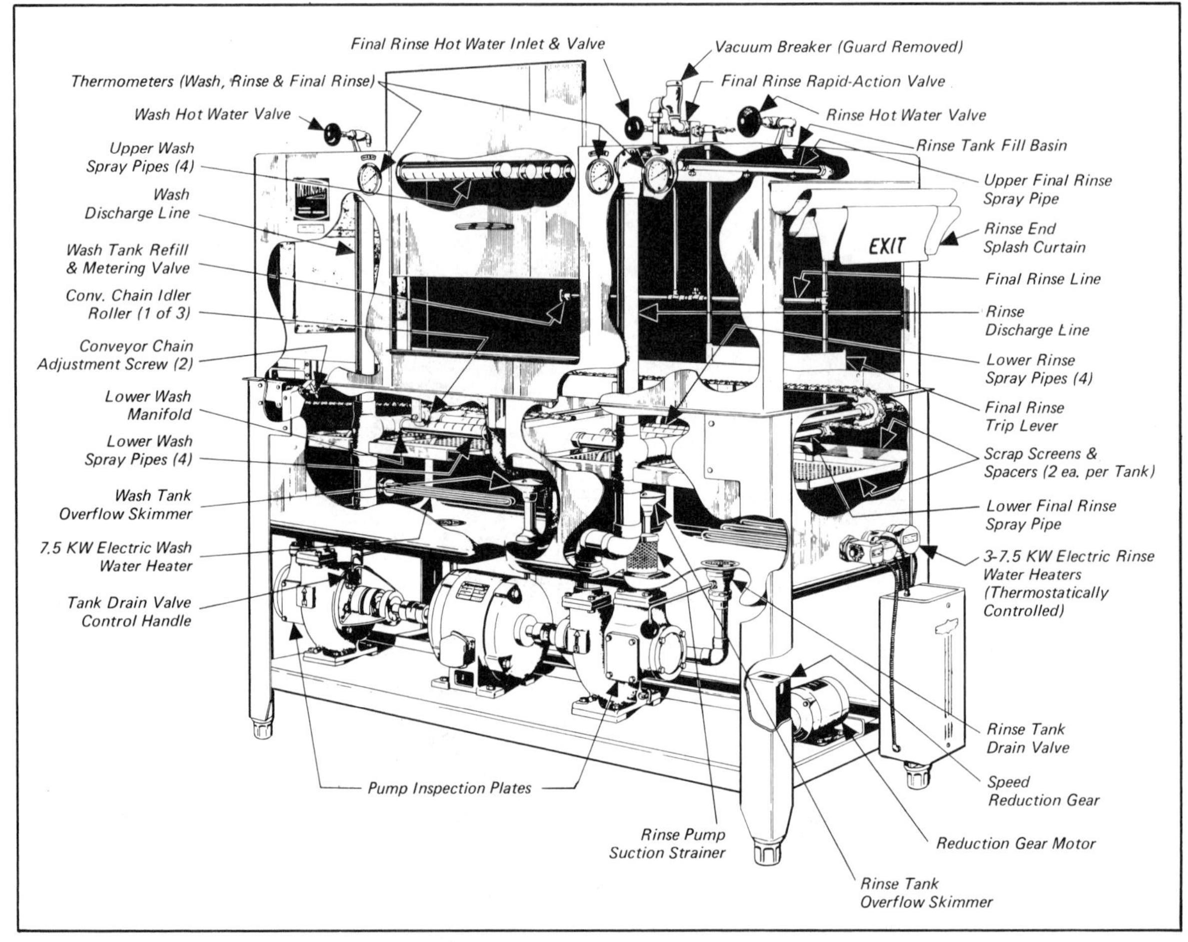

FIGURE 18.7. Double-tank dishwasher showing power rinse and final rinse on right side of machine. Courtesy Insinger Machine Company.

(165°F) water in both wash and rinse cycles while chemical sanitizing machines may use 49°C (120°F) water for both wash and rinse.

Sanitizing

Sanitizing of dishes is important as they are used by a number of people who might transmit pathogenic microorganisms to both dishes and flatware. Potentially dangerous bacteria grow rapidly in food residues on the utensils and must be destroyed.

In most dishwashers, the sanitizing takes place by heating the surface of the utensil to a temperature where microorganisms cannot survive. The dish surface may be up to a temperature of 64°C (147°F) when it leaves the wash tank, 68°C (155°F) when the power rinse stops, and 72°C (161°F) after passing the final rinse. Paper thermometers that change color at the desired temperature or small maximum recording thermometers may be used to check maximum temperature. Thermocouples drilled through to the dish surface and cemented into place may also be used. As it leaves the dishwasher, the dish temperature drops rapidly and is back to 41°C (105°F) within 40 seconds. If the combination of heated waters does not get the dish surface up to 71°C (160°F), probably the combination of time and temperature is not sufficient to completely sterilize the dish.

In chemical sterilization, the rinse water at a temperature of 49°C (120°F) should bring the equivalent of at least 50 parts per million of chlorine or 12.5 parts per million of iodophore to the surface of the dish.

Drying

The wet dish is not acceptable to the customer or the health authorities. The toweling of wet dishes is not acceptable to the sanitarian as it is a prime way of carrying contamination from one dish to another. Thus, the dishwasher or its auxiliary equipment must provide a dry dish.

Most dishwashers dry dishes by heating them to the point where moisture evaporates from them quickly. The success of this drying action depends on many factors. Included among these are the following:

1. The temperature to which the dish is heated. This depends on the material from which the dish is made, the temperature of the water in the dishwasher and the time which it is in contact with the dish.
2. The time the dish retains its heat after leaving the dishwasher. This depends on the material from which it is made.
3. The use of a rinse-aid in final rinse. A rinse-aid reduces the surface tension of water drops and causes them to flatten out. This exposes more water surface area, resulting in faster evaporation.
4. The time the dish is allowed to stand to evaporate its moisture load. This usually depends on the length of the dish table or conveyor beyond the exit of the dishwasher and the celerity with which the dishes are removed from the racks or conveyor. The thoughtful designer allows space for four racks outside the dishwasher and comparable length of space in the flight-type machines. Dishwashing personnel must be trained to allow maximum drying time before removing and stacking the dishes.
5. The relative humidity of the dishroom which is an important factor seldom recognized. If it is high, dishes will not dry. To prevent high humidity in the dishroom and the subsequent wet dishes, it is important to have the dishroom well ventilated. The most effective ventilation will remove the moisture that is emitted from the entrance and exit ends of the dishwasher by means of hoods and then evacuate the gathered steam to the building exterior.

If previously mentioned measures are not sufficient and further high humidity air removal is impractical, sometimes it is necessary to blow heated or unheated air across the dishes as they leave the dishwasher to promote drying. In an era when high energy consumption is frowned on, forced air drying, particularly with heated air, may be used less.

Design

Dishwashers are designed so that there is a machine to fit into almost any space, load from any side, discharge in any direction, handle any number of dishes, utilize various numbers of workers, and cost from $2,000 to $10,000 or more. All of these are not available in any one machine, but in the vast number of machines available, there is something for every need. There are single and multiple tank machines that can stand in a corner, sit along a wall, or be placed under a counter.

Door-type Rack Machines

A door-type rack machine is usually single tank and built for a 41-x-41-cm (16-x-16-in.), 46-x-46-cm (18-x-18-in.), or 51-x-51-cm (20-x-20-in.) rack. The operator opens the door in front, or on either side, and places, or slides, the rack in from a table. The next rack may push the washed rack out the other side onto a table to dry. For dimensions, the machine may be 51 x 51 cm (20 x 20 in.) or 66 x 66 cm (26 x 26 in.) deep and 150–168 cm (59–66 in.) high with the door closed or 196 cm (77 in.) with the door open. The panel material is 16-gauge No. 302 type with No. 4 mill finish (12-gauge galvanized iron is an option) while the frame is welded steel. There may be one or two counterbalanced doors that slide up. Sometimes the doors are 18-gauge to make them lighter. The other panels may slide up, and the top comes off for ease of cleaning. The wash tank capacity is not too important but may be approximately 76 liters (20 gal).

The pump that drives the wash water for the sprays is operated by a 1/2 HP motor for the smaller machines and a preferred 1 HP motor for the larger ones. In the first case, 454 lpm (liters per minute) (120 gpm, gallons per minute) are pumped and the larger unit pumps 681 lpm (180 gpm). The pump impeller is made of stainless steel or Ni-Resist. Inside the wash compartment, stainless steel arms revolve above and below the rack of dishes. Each arm has twelve nonclogging stainless steel nozzles. In addition, there are two revolving rinse arms to provide 5.7 liters (1.5 gal) of 82°C (180°F) rinse water as required by most sanitation codes. For this temperature of water, a gas, electric or steam-heated booster is usually required. The wash tank has gas, electric, or steam injection heaters to maintain the wash water at 66–71°C (150–160°F). The wash cycle must be at least 40 seconds long (can be 43–45 seconds), and the rinse cycle at least 10 seconds (can be 12–15 seconds), which means that a 51-x-51-cm (20-x-20-in.) rack of dishes must receive at least 348 liters (92 gal) of wash water and 6.5 liters (1.73 gal) of rinse water. The single tank, stationary rack machine with a single temperature of 74°C (165°F) washes for 40 seconds and rinses for 30 seconds. This is controlled by an electric timer. There are perforated stainless steel trays to gather the gross soil washed from the dishes.

For a chemical sanitizing machine, the wash water must be at least 49°C (120°F). After the wash cycle, it may be dumped and a rinse with sanitizer drawn after the cycle is dumped. The final rinse is saved to be the wash water for the next rack. The total of wash and rinse water must be 303 liters (80 gal). The addition of both detergent and sanitizer is automatic.

There are round machines that operate the same way as the square machines but use 44 or 53 cm (17.5 or 21 in.) diameter round racks.

Conveyor-type Machines

Conveyor-type dishwashers use a conveyor to move the racks of dishes from a table on one side of the machine through the machine to a table on the other side. In the process, the dishes can be prewashed, washed, rinsed, sanitized, and heated to speed drying. While human hands must slide the rack from a table to where the lugs on the dishwasher conveyor can engage it, the remainder of the process is automatic, including removal from the machine. The conveyor dishwashers may be single-tank, two-tank, or three-tank (figure 18.8).

In the single-tank machine, the one tank has the hot wash water at 68°C (155°F) and detergent. The rinse water at 82°C (180°F) partially, or wholly, goes into the wash water. The rinse is usually at line pressure. In a two-tank machine, one is the wash tank and the other a power or pumped rinse followed by a final rinse immediately before the rack leaves the machine. A three-tank machine is similar to the two-tank machine but is preceded by a prewash tank that removes the gross soil and catches it in perforated trays. This prewash may be placed in front of the single tank machine, as well. There are also blowers and blower heat-dryers 183 cm (72 in.) long, 76 cm (30 in.) wide, and 201 cm (79 in.) high that may be placed at the discharge end of the dishwasher to dry the dishes.

These tanks may vary in length. One manufacturer has single tank machines 91 cm (36 in.), 102 cm (40 in.), and 127 cm (50 in.) long. Add a 61-cm (24-in.) prewash to each of these and there

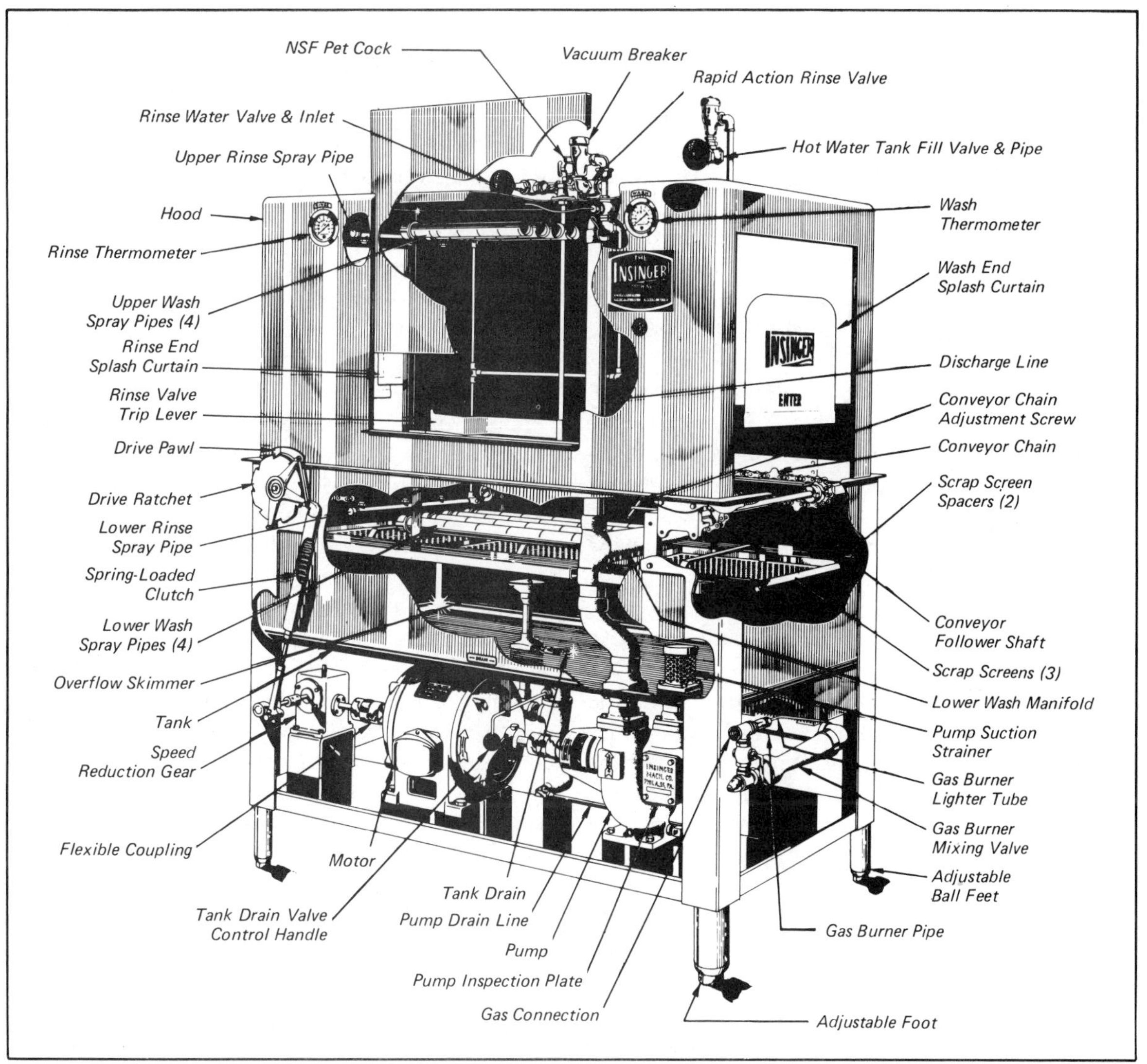

FIGURE 18.8. Single-tank conveyor type machine. Courtesy Insinger Machine Company.

are three more dishwashers. The two-tank machines use the above single-tank modules to get 183-cm (72-in.), 203-cm (80 in.), and 254-cm (100-in.) machines. Again the 61-cm (24-in.) prewash tank may be added to each. The width is 61 cm (24 in.) and height 146 cm (57.5 in.) in all cases. To keep steam and splash within each compartment, curtains separate them. There are curtains at the entrance and discharge ends of the dishwasher also. Failure to use a curtain between the wash and rinse tank can cause the wash tank to overheat. In all machines that use it, the prerinse tank holds 58 liters (15.3 gal). The 91-cm (36-in.) tanks hold 82 liters (21.7 gal), the 102-cm (40-in.) tanks hold 89 liters (23.6 gal), and the 127-cm (50-in.) ones hold 108 liters (28.5 gal). The pumps are driven by motors as follows: prewash pump by 1/2 HP motor, 91-cm (36-in.) tank pump by 1 HP, and 102-cm (40-in.) and 127-cm (50-in.) tanks by 1 1/2 HP motors. The conveyors require 1/4 HP motors. They vary in speed from 152 cm (5 ft) per minute to 259 cm (8.5 ft) per minute depending on the length. The conveyor tracks, pawls, and pawl bars are usually made of stainless steel.

Where the door-type machines use whirling spray arms, the conveyor machines use fixed arms, spray boxes, and slotted pipes with various types of nozzles. Some have more water coming from the top while others have more coming from the bottom units. The wall panels, top, and tanks, are 16-gauge, No. 302 stainless steel with a No. 4 finish. The frame is welded iron or steel and may be stainless, if desired.

Flight-type Machines

The monsters of the dishroom are the flight-type machines (figure 18.9). While conveyor machines can start washing as the rack enters the machine and allows for dish drying on tables outside the machine exit, the flight type machine must have conveyor space for loading prior to entering the wash or prerinse chamber and space for dish drying on the conveyor outside the rinse chamber. Made of 14- or 16-gauge, No. 302 or No. 304 stainless steel panels with No. 3 or No. 4 finish and a welded steel frame, most flight-type machines are similar to the rack conveyor-types except for the design and placement of the conveyor.

A flight-type machine may range in length from 2.9 m (9.5 ft) to over 6.1 m (20 ft) and in width from 0.61–0.91 m (2–3 ft). In the small machine, the loading section might be 0.76 m (2.5 ft), the wash-rinse hooded section 0.91 m (3 ft), and the unloading section 1.2 m (4 ft). In a large machine, the loading area might be 0.91 m (3 ft), the prewash 1.2 m (4 ft), the wash-rinse 2.4 m (8 ft) and the dry-unload section 1.5 m (5 ft).

The conveyor may be 51–76 cm (20–30 in.) wide and be made up of pegs, fingers, or bars of plastic such as nylon or polypropylene reinforced with stainless cross rods. These provide slots into which plates may be inserted to present the best possible angle for flushing away the soil. The narrow conveyors will take the 42-x-57-cm (16.5-x-22.5-in.) trays while the wide one will take the 46-x-66-cm (18-x-26 in.) sheet pan or the large oval tray. The tops of these dish supports supply an

FIGURE 18.9. Flight type Hobart dishwasher with prewash, wash, rinse, and long drying area outside of machine. Dishes are being loaded into dish dollies. Courtesy Crescent Metal Products, Inc.

even surface on which racks of glasses, bowls, cups, or silverware may be placed for washing. The conveyor may be driven by a 1/2 HP motor at speeds of 1.5–2.6 m (5–8.5 ft) per minute. There is a switch operating off a pressure plate to stop the conveyor if a dish fails to be removed.

The narrow machines commonly have 1 HP motors to drive the pumps and the wide machines have 2 HP motors.

Special Dishwashers

Using functional sections and dish or rack conveying systems developed for the dishwashers previously discussed, dishwashers can be devised to fit into almost any space. A narrow alcove arrangement can be devised so that a rack can be fed into the machine along one wall of a corner and come out at right angles to this along the other wall. This can be done in either direction and with any number of sections.

The carousel dishwasher is usually a conventional device with a conveyor that joins the discharge end of the dishwasher with the loading end on the same plane. It is a closed circuit dishwasher where the washer can be loaded and unloaded from the same location. It can be of a rack construction where racks of various types are towed around an oval, square, rectangular, or triangular course on tables or it can be of a flight-type. The dishwasher sections can be placed together as in a conventional dishwasher, or they can be separated by hooded sections.

The carousel dishwasher has the advantage of being easily operable by one worker at times when the machine is operated at less than capacity. Operating a dishwasher at less than capacity is frowned on from a utility conservation standpoint. Another advantage is that its shape permits it to operate around a pillar or other occupied space.

Accessory Equipment

The accessory equipment items for dishwashers are legion. Only a few will be mentioned here. Pre-

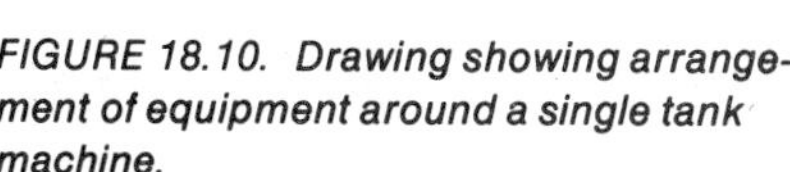
FIGURE 18.10. Drawing showing arrangement of equipment around a single tank machine.

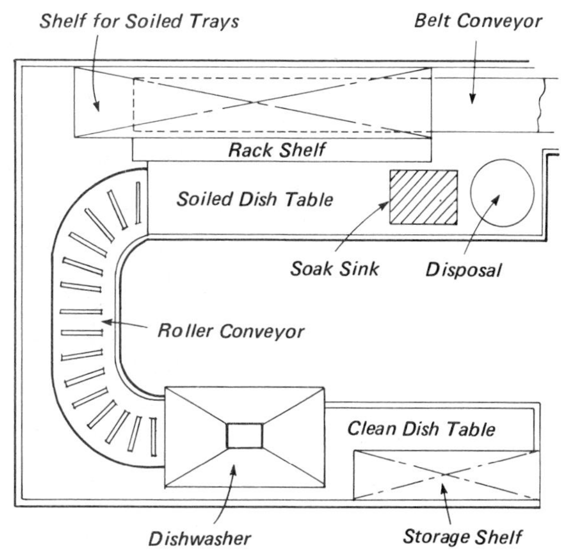

Layout of Remote Dishwashing Department

FIGURE 18.11. Dish scraping area with incoming tray conveyor, shelf to hold rack. In background is spray to prewash racks of dishes.

viously mentioned were the hand spray and prewash rack support over a garbage grinder, the trough type of scraper, the blower and blower-heater assembly for dish drying, the scraping table with jet or plume of running water, and the collar around an opening leading down into a garbage can.

In addition, one can get soak sinks for silverware and hard-to-remove soils on dishes. Sometimes a silverware rack is placed in the sink and when filled to the proper level is removed and passed through the dishwasher. There are tables leading into and out of the dishwasher. Over the entrance table where the dishes are sorted, scraped, and racked, it is usual to have one or two canted rack-holding shelves to provide easy loading of cups, bowls, and glasses and sometimes to store racks that will later be placed on the table and loaded with plates or trays (figure 18.11).

Large operations with flight-type machines have separate scraping facilities for handling, scraping, and stacking of dishes and racks of cups, bowls, glasses, and silverware. These are then slid on connector tables to the loading end of the dishwasher.

As humidity becomes too high in the average dishroom due to escaping steam from both ends of the dishwasher, hoods should be used to capture the moist air and vent it to the outside.

Whether they be round or square, dishwasher racks are made of wire, strap metal, molded plastics, or fiberglass (figure 18.12). Construction is such that dishes or silverware are presented to the top and bottom dishwasher sprays in such a way that little or no shielding occurs and the flushing action of the water strikes the dishes at the best angle for maximum soil removal. As metals mark dishes, metal racks are usually coated with plastic such as Plastisol.

FIGURE 18.12. Plastisol-coated dishrack outside a single-tank dishwasher.

The flat racks for washing several layers of flatware are in some disrepute; there is much masking action in washing, and after going through the dishwasher, the ware must be toweled to get it dry. A more effective means uses a number of removable round open-work plastic cups or cylinders set in a carrier with an overall handle similar to the milk bottle carrier. In these, the flatware can be inverted with the handles down and the soiled ends exposed to the washing action of the dishwasher. After washing, the individual cylinders can be inverted over empty cylinders so that only the handles of the ware are exposed. Then the cylinders can be placed in a suitable holder in the serving line for sanitary dispensing.

Determination of Needed Capacity

Determining needed dishwasher capacity usually is a matter of finding a machine whose advertising literature or salesperson indicates it will care for the dishes of the number of customers anticipated. This commonly means that a much too large or small machine is purchased. The dish count should be ascertained and a machine found that will handle that number in the time required or desired.

The dish count might average twenty per customer in a fine table service restaurant, fifteen in a family restaurant, ten to twelve plus a tray in a cafeteria, and six to eight in a counter operation. One should multiply the number of customers per hour by the pertinent dish count per customer. Then calculate the number of racks required by dividing the total number of dishes by the number one can get into the large rack (twenty to twenty-five) or into the small rack (sixteen). The glass, cup, bowl, and flatware racks should be added. If trays are involved, eight of them make up a rack load. Some estimators add 20–25 percent to care for human inability to keep the dishwasher fully loaded. If the total number of racks is determined, then it is a simple affair to find a machine that will handle that number per hour.

This method, too, is somewhat misleading as it is based on the supposition that dishwasher capacity should be based on the number of dishes produced during the heaviest serving periods. To do this requires an oversized dishwashing machine and too much labor. If an adequate number of dishes is available and there is enough table space, it is better to use a smaller machine and either stack the dishes and wash them over a longer period after the meal or wash them throughout the meal and stack the overage for washing when the rush subsides. If either of these methods is used, then the capacity of the machine in racks per hour is calculated from the total number of racks of dishes, flatware, and trays to be washed divided by the number of hours the dishwashing operation is to last.

It is more difficult to determine adequate capacity of the flight-type machine because conveyor width, distance between the bars or rows of pegs, and belt speed enter into the calculation along with a percentage allowance for probable failure to keep the conveyor fully loaded. A flight-type dishwasher's capacity per hour can be determined from the following formula:

$$\text{Capacity} = \frac{120\ (W \times V)}{D} \times 0.70$$

where: W is width of the conveyor in inches

V is speed of the conveyor in feet per minute

D is the distance between the rows of pegs or bars in inches

0.70 is a practical average percentage of a full load for the conveyor to use in planning

Example:

$$\text{Capacity} = \frac{120\ [28.5\text{ in. (width)} \times 5\text{ ft. (speed)}]}{2\text{ in. (distance between pegs)}} \times 0.70 = 5{,}985\text{ pieces}$$

In metrics, the 120 factor would be 4.0.

With a conveyor belt width of 57 cm (22.5 in.):

Belt Speed	*Dish Capacity Per Hour*
152 cm (5 ft) per min	4,725
244 cm (8 ft) per min	7,560
366 cm (12 ft) per min	11,340

With a conveyor belt width of 72.4 cm (28.5 in):

Belt Speed	*Dish Capacity Per Hour*
152 cm (5 ft) per min	5,985
244 cm (8 ft) per min	9,576
366 cm (12 ft) per min	14,364

Subtracted from these capacities would be the number of linear feet of conveyor taken up by cup, bowl, glass, and flatware racks. Thus, 20 racks × 51 cm (20 in.) per rack = 10 m (33 ft) of conveyor. A conveyor moving at 1.5 m (5 ft) per minute × 60 minutes = 90 m (300 ft) per hour. This means that the 10 m (33 ft) taken up by racks would reduce its capacity by one-ninth, so that for a dishwasher with a capacity of 4,725 dishes per hour, the racks would reduce its dishwashing capacity to 4,200 dishes.

Basic Use and Operation

Success of the mechanical dishwasher is dependent on a properly scraped dish being adequately wetted with a combination of a well-formulated detergent and water at an adequate temperature and their flushing away the soil with copious quantities of water. This is followed with a hot water power rinse and final rinse to remove soil and detergent and raise the dish temperature to where it is sanitized and the surface moisture will evaporate quickly after the dish leaves the machine. To help with this evaporation, a rinse-aid is sometimes added to cause the drops of water to spread out into fast-drying sheets.

To operate the dishwasher:

1. Check tanks for any garbage, flatware, or other foreign materials.
2. Replace or check to see if the rinse and spray arms, the pump inlet strainer, scrap trays, and curtains (on conveyor machine) are properly in place.
3. Turn on, or check on, heating system to booster heater.
4. Close tank drain valve and open fill valves. Leave out one scrap tray until tank or tanks are filled to overflow drain and then shut off fill valve, replace scrap tray, and close access door.
5. Either add proper amount of detergent to the wash tank or fill the detergent dispenser. If rinse-aid is used, check its level.
6. Turn on heat to tanks and check nozzles for clog. If clogged, ream them out with a probe (usually a piece of wire).
7. Check rinse and final rinse to ensure that they are up to temperature.
8. Turn on pump and conveyor switches and observe spray patterns and pressures.
9. When detergent dispenser indicates the wash tank has the proper detergent level and all tank temperatures are correct, dishwashing may start.
10. Remove paper and gross quantities of food from dishes by scraping with hand, rubber glove, or spatula. Do not use another dish as this may remove the dish glaze.
11. Dishes may be flushed or prewashed under a spout of water over a garbage grinder drain, placed in racks, and flushed with a hose spray unit or run through a prewash section of the dishwasher. This makes the wash cycle of the dishwasher more effective. Dishes that have obvious caked-on soil should be placed in a sink or pan of detergent and water to soak prior to washing.
12. Flatware should be removed and placed in a soak tank. If the ware is to be washed in a flat

rack, it may be placed in the soak tank and when filled to the proper level (one should be able to see the bottom of the rack), lifted out and run through the dishwasher. Cups, glasses, and sometimes bowls should be placed in racks designed to protect and present them to best advantage to the wash and rinse sprays. They should be placed with open end down.

13. Where the silverware is to be washed vertically in round or square containers, the ware should be placed very loosely in the containers with tines, bowls, and blades up.
14. Place plates in the racks or on the flight-type conveyor so that they are displayed without crowding or overlapping. All surfaces must be exposed to the sprays so that there are no pockets that will not drain quickly.
15. Start the racks or dishes through the machine.

    a. In the door-type machine, open the door and slide in the rack and either push the wash lever on the manual machine or start the operating switch on the automatic machine. At the end of forty seconds or more, switch the lever from wash to rinse for ten to fifteen seconds, no more or less. Then the racks from both the manual and automatic machine may be removed.

    b. With the tray conveyor machine, the rack is pushed to where the lugs of the conveyor engage the rack. The dishes face up and toward the machine. Facing the dishes down with the backs toward the machine once a week improves cleaning. The dishes in the rack as it emerges from the dishwasher should never be touched until completely dry. Preferably they should have been out of the washer at least thirty seconds if treated with rinse-aid, two minutes if not. This permits the dishes to dry before they are removed from the racks and stacked. Rather than relying on timing, it is recommended that four racks be out of the washer before dishes in the first rack are removed.

    c. When using the flight-type conveyor, a rinse-aid should be used and dishes should be allowed to be as far from the machine as possible before removal. With trays, it may be necessary to wipe the lower edge dry when removing them from the conveyor as plastic or fiberglass trays do not store up enough heat to allow complete drying.

    In all three of the machines, it is good energy and manpower utilization to keep the machines fully loaded when they are operating. As the dishes are removed, they should be stacked and placed in proper dispensers. Dishes which are soiled should be returned to the soak sink.
16. When washing is complete for each serving period, the pump, conveyor, and heat switches should be turned to off. The side panels should be opened, the tanks of wash and rinse water dumped, the scrap trays and pump inlet screen cleaned, and the tanks flushed out. Clogs in the nozzles may be cleaned with a stiff wire.

Hints on Dishwasher Use

1. Wash dishes as soon as possible after use to obviate drying on of soil.
2. Wash dishes as soon as possible after they arrive at the dish table. This prevents dishes from being stacked too high and broken.
3. Soft water washes dishes cleaner and helps preserve the machine.
4. Do not presoak dishes unless absolutely necessary. It uses excessive labor and causes dish breakage.
5. Dishroom workers should be encouraged to place dishes of a kind together when they stack them and lift them when removing them from the stack. Sliding dishes together or apart removes the glaze.
6. If possible, avoid stacking wet dishes as moisture causes friction that may result in dishes sticking together or being broken.

7. Avoid use of abrasives on dishes as they tend to remove the protective glaze.
8. As replacement of china and glassware amounts to 0.5–1.5 percent of the sales dollar, definite steps should be taken to prevent dish breakage:
   a. Put up a display of china and glassware on the wall of the dishroom showing the replacement cost of each.
   b. Train busing personnel to place heavy items in the center of the tray and keep flatware separate from the dishes in the bus boxes.
   c. Give dishroom workers pay incentives for reducing dish breakage losses.
   d. Do not permit workers to dump dishes from bus boxes or trays onto dish tables or stack them in tall stacks.
   e. Use protective rubber or plastic on dish handling tables when racks do not have to be slid.
   f. Set up definite traffic patterns for movement of soiled and clean dishes out of the dining room and in the dishroom.
   g. Use busing carts wherever possible as more tables can be bused per trip to the dishroom, fewer dishes are dropped and broken, and worker loads are far less. In handling clean dishes after washing, use of wheeled self-leveling dish dispensers and other types of dish carts to return the dishes to the service area can reduce handling, labor, frequency of trips, and dish breakage.
   h. Place a guard on the flight-type dishwasher conveyor to prevent overshoot as it is being loaded and reduce consequent dish breakage.
   i. Use one weight of china. Heavy china plates tend to break lighter weight plates when they are stacked together.
   j. When possible, transport dishes, particularly cups and glasses, in the dishwashing racks as it helps to protect them.
   k. Consider the use of rubber-backed carpets in the dishroom wherever approved by the Department of Health. They reduce dish breakage greatly.
   l. Train and supervise the dishroom worker. Look in on him and let him know when he is doing a good job. This should be done at least once a day.

Dishwashing Deficiencies and Their Causes

1. Films caused by insufficiently softened water, baked-on protein films, or carryover of detergent from wash tank because of poor rinsing.
2. Foaming caused by too high sudsing detergent or dissolved solids in wash water.
3. Grease films caused by insufficient alkalinity level, water temperature or volume too low to melt fats, or misfunctioning equipment (nozzles clogged or worn).
4. Spotting caused by high rinse water hardness, low water temperatures, inadequate time between rinsing and removal from racks, use of a type of dish that gets insufficiently hot, not using rinse-aids, and high dishroom humidity.
5. Staining of coffee cups caused by the coffee or tea compounds. Removal requires a chlorine or oxidizing stain remover. With plastics, do not use abrasives and use only an oxidizing stain remover. Chlorine will remove the glaze as well as the stain.
6. Streaking caused by high alkalinity of water, high dissolved solids level, poor power rinsing, or final rinse not functioning.
7. Unclean dishes caused by insufficient detergent, too low (or too high) wash water temperatures, insufficient or poorly distributed spray water, masking by poor racking, insufficient washing or rinsing times, poor scraping or prerinse, or dried or baked-on soils.

Special Applications

Probably the most frequent use of the mechanical dishwasher, other than for washing dishes and flatware, is for cleaning lightly soiled pots, pans, and kitchen hand utensils or for rinsing them after they have been handwashed.

They may be used for cleaning the ventilation hood filters as washing, rinsing, and sanitizing takes place.

In some institutions, they have sectionized the duckboards in the kitchen and dishroom areas so that they can be washed in the dishwasher. Refrigerator racks, cutting boards, coffee urn leachers, the detachable parts of molders, mixers, and similar equipment are often cleaned in the dishwasher.

The dishwasher may be used to heat canned or pouch-pack foods prior to service. It avoids the overcooking that comes from reheating on the range, in the steamer, or in a steam jacketed kettle. It may be used to wash fruits and vegetables that are served or cooked with their skins on.

Alternatives to the Dishwasher

The most apparent substitute for the mechanical dishwasher is hand dishwashing as many harried managers, who have had to make the substitution, can testify. The usual procedures in hand dishwashing are:

1. Scraping and prerinsing is similar to that used for machine dishwashing. Scrape with hand, rubber glove, or spatula and prerinse in a water plume or spray rinse.
2. Water is drawn to a desired level in wash, rinse, and sanitize sinks. Usually, the wash water must be cooled to the 49–52°C (120–125°F) temperature that the dishwasher can tolerate. The proper amount of detergent based on a measured amount of water is added. Washing is done with a stiff bristle brush.
3. From the wash sink the dishes are rinsed in the rinse sink of hot water. It is well to place them in a basket with the basket handles sticking out of the water, so that the dishes will drain well when removed from the sinks. Some rinses are set up so that the hot water constantly runs into the sink and runs out through an overflow. This keeps the water clean.
4. The basket of dishes is immersed in the third sink of water at 77°C (170°F) or above, for at least thirty seconds and preferably two minutes.
5. Finally, the basket of dishes is removed to the drainboard to drain and dry.

Another alternative to the mechanical dishwasher is the use of paper, plastic, or aluminum disposable utensils. These are used in many fast food restaurants and in hospitals where contagion may be a factor.

Saving Energy

1. Select a dishwasher with a power prewash that uses the overflow water from the wash cycle without heating the water further.
2. All dishwasher gaskets, particularly pump gaskets, should be checked frequently for leakage.
3. Reduce the buildup of water scales by using softened water, since water scales can hinder the process of heat transfer.
4. Place boosters and other hot water heaters as close to the dishwasher as possible, to save energy losses in pipes. Hot-water tanks and hot-water piping for the dishwasher should be insulated. For hot water tanks, insulation should be at least 12.7 cm (5 in.) of polyurethane. Check the water pressure of the final rinse, since pressure of about 25 pounds psi wastes hot water and energy, and may cause spray nozzle to atomize inefficiently. Check the final rinse temperature too; it should be above 83°C (180°F) but below 93°C (208°F).
5. The dishwasher should be fully loaded when in use and completely shut off (including boosters) when not in use. Periods of use should be at least 30 minutes long.

6. Humidity in the dishroom should be kept low, so that dishes can air-dry properly, and so forced air dryers and heaters, which have high energy consumption, need not be used. Placing ventilators at each end of the dishwasher helps prevent dishroom humidity buildup. Wetting agents should be used to spread out water clumps and facilitate drying.
7. Hot water heaters for the kitchen should be turned down to 22.8°C (75°F) at night.

Cleaning

1. At the close of the use day, the detergents and rinse-aids dispensers should be shut off, along with gas, steam or electricity that is used to heat water in the tanks or booster heater.
2. Open the drains to all the tanks to remove the water while it is yet hot, and thus scum on the tank walls will be less.
3. Open side doors and remove and clean as well as rinse scrap trays and wash rinse arms. Remove the caps from the ends of the arms and brush them and the slots with brushes furnished by the manufacturer. Check rinse jets and clean them with a stiff wire. Scrap trays and curtains may be put through the machine before cleaning it.
4. Remove all debris from the tanks and scrub them with a stiff brush, detergent, and water to remove adhering soils. Rinse all surfaces with a hose. Thoroughly clean overflows, strainers, pump inlets, and filters. Clean detergent dispenser electrodes.
5. Remove all curtains, scrub them with a stiff brush, and thoroughly rinse them with a hose if they have not been washed in the machine. Hang them up to dry. The National Sanitation Foundation has recommended that two sets be used so that one set can dry while the other set is being used.
6. Clean the dish tables and the dishwasher exterior and wipe dry. Clean detergent and rinse-aid dispensers.
7. Dishwasher may be left disassembled until the next day to air dry.
8. Wash arms and jet nozzles should be cleaned at least once a week. Assemble them after cleaning and run a tank of detergent and water through them for a few minutes before scrubbing and rinsing the tanks.

Maintenance

Maintenance varies with the design of the machine, and the operator will be well advised to follow the procedure recommended by the manufacturer of his particular machine. Check the following items:

1. All water valves, drains, and pumps for leakage. Particularly check as to whether the final rinse shuts off when the rack is not over it. Check that rinse and final rinse are flowing at proper rates.
2. Nozzles and pipes for reduction in size due to lime scale. Use manufacturer recommended acid delimers to remove the deposits. This operation should be supervised closely.
3. Nozzles for excessive wear. If they become too large, they will not clean dishes properly and should be replaced. All nozzles should be operating and proper dish coverage should be ascertained and corrected, if need be.
4. Accuracy of the thermostat by immersing each in a wide-mouthed thermos container of hot water while sensing the same water with a good mercury thermometer. Thermostat display and thermometers should agree. Temperature at dish position will be 5.6–11.1°C (10–20°F) lower than the thermostat-sensed temperature.
5. Amount of heat. If a heated dish dryer is used, check that no more heat is used than is required.
6. The detergent level in the wash tank. Adjust the dispenser if necessary.

7. Flames for proper flame color if gas heaters are used. Electric immersion heaters should not be coated with lime.
8. Belts and conveyors for unusual wear and adjust where necessary. Lubricate all conveyor bearings and speed reducer as indicated by the manufacturer.
9. Draft at the steam and heat collectors at each end of the dishwasher. Excessive drafts would cool the wash and the rinse waters.

QUESTIONS

1. What is the present cost of mechanical washing of a dish?
2. What are the problems of hand-washing dishes?
3. What provides the cleaning action in the immersion type dishwasher?
4. What are the five functions carried out by dishwashing?
5. In what ways can scraping be accomplished?
6. What are desired temperatures of prewash, wash, power rinse, and final rinse in a conveyor machine?
7. What two means are used to sanitize dishes in a mechanical dishwasher?
8. How does one ensure dry dishes without the unsanitary threat of towels?
9. What is a carousel-type dishwasher?
10. What is the capacity formula for flight-type dishwashers?
11. What is the step-by-step procedure for operating a mechanical dishwasher of the rack-conveyor type?
12. List ten steps to be taken to reduce dish breakage.
13. List, in order, the steps in hand dishwashing.
14. How does one clean a mechanical dishwasher?
15. List five of the maintenance steps that should be taken with a mechanical dishwasher.
16. List five ways to save energy when operating dishwashers.

BIBLIOGRAPHY

ANON. 1966. Important facts about commercial dishwashers. *Commercial Current Events* 18, No. 5, 2.

ANON. 1974. How to get maximum performance from your electric warewashing equipment. The Electrification Council, New York.

ANON. 1976. Food service equipment standards. National Sanitation Foundation, Nov., 96–123.

KOTSCHEVAR, L., and TERRELL, M. 1977. *Food Service Planning: Layout and Equipment.* John Wiley and Sons, New York.

LONGREE, K. 1972. *Quantity Food Sanitation.* Wiley-Interscience, New York.

LONGREE, K., and BLAKER, G. 1971. *Sanitary Techniques in Food Service.* John Wiley and Sons, New York.

MILLER, S. 1963. Sanitation and dishes: Aspects old and new, part I. *Journal of the American Dietetic Association* 43, No. 1, 23–33.

RICHARDSON, T. 1968. Training guide to dishmachine maintenance and cleaning. *Institutions Magazine* 62, No. 3, 115–118, 136.

SCHNEIDER, N., and JAHN, E. 1968. *Commercial Kitchens.* American Gas Association, New York.

Coffee Makers

While coffee is not native to the New World, more of it is now raised in Brazil than anywhere else, and Americans consume more of it than anyone. At one time it was estimated that Americans drank 440 million cups each day. Since being smuggled into Martinique in 1723, coffee has become big business, not only from the sale of the beans but also from sales of coffee-making equipment, coffee shops, and the beverage itself.

This is all rather surprising as coffee has little nutritive value or appetizing appearance to attract customers but must depend on a unique taste and a mild stimulating effect to wield its magic. However, there are few other foods that can do as much to make or break a foodservice business as the quality of its brewed coffee. Thus it is important that foodservices sell a brew made from a coffee blend and roast that conforms to the expectations of its customers and that the strength, quality, and temperature of the brew are consistently good. Normally this is produced by properly designed and operated clean equipment using the proper amount of good water, the accepted blend, roast, and grind, and the proper time and temperature of extraction.

Coffee drinkers from the West prefer a light roast while those from the South like a heavier, darker roast that is sometimes supported by chicory in locations such as Louisiana. Most of the rest of the United States likes a medium roast.

There can be blends of about 100 varieties of coffees, but the one selected is a purely local decision although some of the national coffee distributing companies have developed some national tastes. The U.S. Navy used a blend of 70 percent Brazilian and 30 percent Colombian coffee.

Strength, too, may vary, although the amounts of soluble solids in the beans is considered to be much the same; actually, it is not. A blend of Latin American coffees may be 32 percent or 145 g (5.1 oz) of solubles per 454 g (1 lb) while an Angolan coffee is 36 percent or 164 g (5.8 oz) of solubles and a Colombian coffee 30 percent or 136 g (4.8 oz) of solubles. Most users consider a coffee to have 34 percent or 156 g (5.5 oz) solubles. What varies most is the percentage of these solubles that goes into the brew and the degree to which the brew is diluted. Coffee experts indicate that properly extracted coffee grind loses 18–22 percent of its solids to provide a brew with 1.15–1.35 percent solids in the brew. Thus the ratio of coffee grind to water recommended is 454 g (1 lb) grind to 7.6–9.5 liters (2.0–2.5 gal) of water with the better coffee using the least water. For institutional use some operators extract at the ratio of 454 g (1 lb) of coffee to 11.4 liters (3 gal) of water and they remove 24 percent of the solids from the grind which means that some of the undesirable bitter elements are included. U.S. Navy men preferred this to the less extracted brews. If more dilute brews are desired, more water may be added to a properly extracted brew.

What is a properly extracted brew? It is one where 18–22 percent of the weight of the grind has been extracted. This includes the desirable aromatic flavorful solids but not the undesirable bitter elements, of the 156 g (5.5 oz) solubles present per pound, extraction of only 82–99 g (2.9–3.5 oz) is desirable. Experience has shown that according to the fineness of the grind, water of medium hardness at 88–96°C (190–205°F) must be in contact with the total grind for a certain period of time.

Each type of coffee maker uses a specific grind. The most common of these are given in table 19.1.

TABLE 19.1. ***Screen Size and Type of Grind***

	Amount Held Back (%)		
Screen size	*Regular Grind*	*Drip Grind*	*Fine Grind*
14 mesh	33	7	none
28 mesh	55	73	70
Pan (dust)	12	20	30

Source: Facts about Coffee, The Coffee Brewing Center, New York, p. 3.

If regular grind is placed in a drip grind coffee maker, the 14-mesh retained grind will be underextracted while fine grind would be overextracted. As a general rule, the following extraction times are suggested: for regular grind, six to eight minutes; for drip grind, four to six minutes; and for a fine grind, one to three minutes. To get the proper extraction in these periods, all the grounds must be equally wetted, that is, have equal access to the 96°C (205°F) water. Thus the area and thickness of the grind bed and the equal distribution of the available water over the bed are important.

The time of extraction, that is, the minutes that the water is in contact with the grind, is influenced by the depth of the grind, the porosity of the filter cloth, paper, screen, or plate, and the quantity and hardness of the water.

As most of the solids are extracted early in the process and settle to the bottom of the urn, it is necessary to agitate the urn contents to equalize solids throughout the brew. This is done by aeration, repouring some of the urn contents, or mechanically agitating the brew.

A large part of the acceptability of coffee is its temperature. To ensure hot coffee after it has been poured into a cold cup it must be held in the urn at 85–88°C (185–190°F); most coffee makers are designed to store coffee at this temperature. Temperatures above this range cause breakdown of the brew and temperatures that are lower lead to cold, less acceptable coffee. Coffee brew held much over thirty minutes suffers from loss of aroma and flavor and develops bitterness. One hour is the limit suggested by many for holding coffee. When making coffee, perform the following steps:

1. Select a coffee blend desired by the potential customer.
2. Select a coffee maker that provides the needed cups of brew per hour and that can be easily operated and cleaned by available personnel. It should be able to hold coffee at desired temperature and quality for an adequate period of time. Select leacher proper for grind and amount of coffee.
3. Use a grind of coffee suitable for the coffee maker.
4. Place grind in leacher to a depth of not less than 2.54 cm (1 in.) or more than 5.1 cm (2 in.). Thickness of grind should be consistent.
5. Pour the proper amount of water at 96°C (205°F) or above over the grind so it wets all the grounds evenly and will pass through in the prescribed time. Urn should be kept covered as much as possible to hold in aroma. The leacher should not sag into the brew.
6. Remove leacher and spent grind.
7. Draw off and pour over about 3.8 liters (1 gal) of water per 454 g (1 lb) grind to mix and even the solids throughout the brew. Do not pour over grind.
8. Hold the brew at 85–88°C (185–190°F) less than one hour. U.S. Navy men preferred coffee held no more than one-half hour.

Good coffee should be pleasing, fragrant, clear, and sparkling. There should be no floating grounds. The aroma should not be acrid, rancid, or oily. There should be enough dissolved solids to be evident in the mouth.

Description and Specification

Whether a foodservice operation wants to prepare a few cups of coffee or many gallons, there is dependable equipment available. It may be completely manual in operation or entirely automatic or some combination of these. It may be mounted on a counter, side table, cart, or on the floor. There are many ways of bringing the water into contact with the coffee grind for extraction purposes. These include, among others:

1. Kettle brewing. Add the free grind to the boiling water or in a cloth bag.
2. Percolation. Grind is held in a metal basket while steam formed in the bottom of the pot forces water up a tube to a deflector that distributes the water over the grind.
3. Vacuum. Two bowls are used; one holds the water and is heated and the other holds the brew and a filter. The top bowl fits tightly into the lower bowl where steam forms to force the water up a glass tube into the top bowl to contact and extract the solubles from the grind. When the unit is removed from the heat, the brew is strained through the filter down into the lower bowl from which it is served.
4. Half-gallon automatic. A small amount of brew is prepared in glass carafes. Operator must measure the weight of the grind carefully, but thereafter the machine takes over to regulate the amount of water to be poured over the grind, the temperature, and timing.
5. Automatic urns. These are usually in capacities of 11.4–75.6 liters (3–20 gal) and are pushbutton operated. Temperatures of water, pour-over, automatic timing, and mixing are done by the urn (figure 19.1).
6. Twin-urns. These are usually a three-piece battery with a water boiler and two urns. The

FIGURE 19.1. Double-tank coffee urn. Courtesy Bleckman Equipment Corporation.

pour-over method is used, but this may be done manually, by siphon system or by pump. It ranges in size from 11.4–75.6 liters (3–20 gal).

7. Combination urn. This utilizes a boiler that surrounds the urn liner and ranges in size from 11.4–189 liters (3–50 gal). The brews are all made by the pour-over method whether it be manual, pump, or siphon.
8. Batteries. These are similar to the twin urns in that they use a separate water boiler with total capacity of 11.4–379 liters (3–100 gal). They are commonly used with the siphon and a water meter to indicate water withdrawal.
9. Steam jacketed urns. These are the monsters of the coffee making world and run from 76–568 liters (20–150 gal). They use pumps to pour-over the leaching water and may, like steam jacketed kettles, use partial or full jackets. The U.S. Navy carried this a step further by having the kettle refrigerated so that iced coffee or other cold beverages could also be prepared in it.

It is not possible to describe all the available coffee makers, so only a few will be described here.

One-Half Gallon Automatic

This uses a minimum of space and may be 25 cm wide x 46 cm deep x 56 cm high (10 x 18 x 22 in.) for a two-decanter unit and 66 cm wide x 46 cm deep x 64 cm high (26 x 18 x 25 in.) for a five-decanter unit. The tank and cabinet are of 18–8 stainless steel. Pour-over is by gravity flow. A nonclog spray head is used along with a ceramic-coated warmer plate. Supposedly, water volume accuracy is good, and water is aerated to prevent its becoming flat. The carafes may be of glass or stainless steel (figure 19.2).

Twin Urn

This urn made of 18–8 Type 302 stainless steel is highly polished (No. 7) for serving line use. It is insulated with glass wool. The water chamber is of heavy-gauge copper while the coffee chamber is ribbed to add strength. It is available with electric immersion heaters that may provide 6 or 10 kw. Another manufacturer boasts of heat inputs of 12 and 15 kw in similar urns. Usually the greater the heat input, the faster it recovers in temperature to make the next batch. This company offers an 11.4–31.3-liter (3–8-gal) urn in dimensions of 89

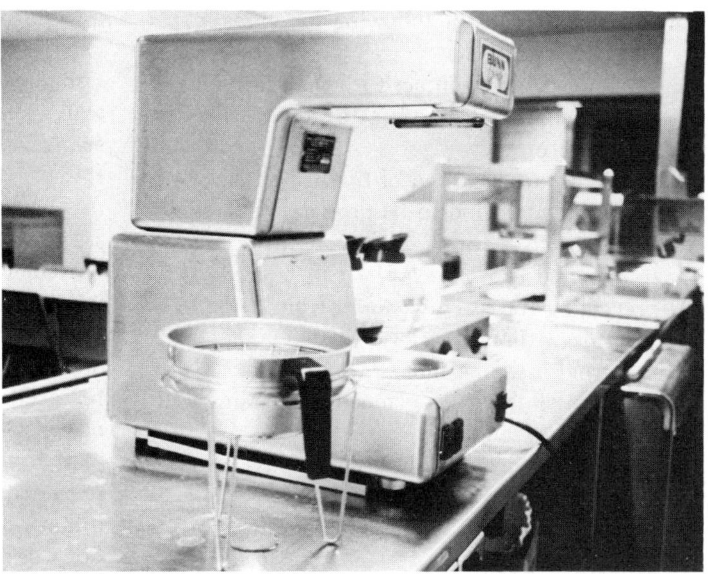

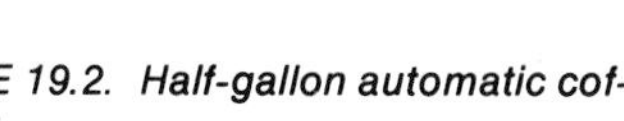

FIGURE 19.2. Half-gallon automatic coffee maker.

cm wide x 51 cm deep x 74 cm high (35 x 20 x 29 in.) and 38–57-liter (10–15-gal) urns with dimensions of 89 cm wide x 61 cm deep x 102 cm high (35 x 24 x 40 in.) A push button actuates the automatic pour-over of the proper amount of water. A switch is also available for one-half batches. A manual button is also available. Dial thermometers are available for reservoir or brew temperature measurement. Faucets may be of metal dairy-type or spring-loaded plastic (figure 19.3).

The reservoir, whether it is separate or surrounds the brew tanks, may vary according to manufacturer from the amount to make two-urn loads of brew up to three to four times this amount. Desirable is the feature where the reservoir quickly refills itself and comes up to brewing temperature.

FIGURE 19.3. Twin coffee urn. Courtesy S. Blickman Inc.

Heating

Heating of the reservoir water may be done by immersion type electric or steam coils, usually of copper, or by gas flames impinging on the bottom of the water reservoir. Insulation of the urn, particularly the reservoir and brew chamber, is desirable. Some means should be used to insulate the prepared brew from the cooled water of the reservoir.

Leachers

Coffee leachers have the following functions:

1. keeping water in contact with the grind for the prescribed period of time to get the desired extraction
2. providing an even bed of the proper size and depth for the grind to be properly extracted
3. draining off the brew quickly after the extraction period
4. preventing the leaching water from going over the side without making proper contact with the grind or being filtered
5. keeping all the solid grind from passing into the coffee reservoir
6. allowing a maximum of brew to pass into the coffee reservoir
7. keeping the grind from sagging into the finished brew

Leachers may be a cloth urn bag, paper filter, metal strainer, or perforated metal plates. Descriptions of these follow:

The cloth urn bag is usually made of cotton with thread size and weave that will restrain the flow of water sufficiently long for the desired leaching of the grind's soluble solids to take place but not long enough for the undesirable bitter elements to be extracted. It has a flat bottom which will set squarely in the gridded basket and has sides high enough to restrain the grind from overflowing into the brew. Before the cloth leacher is used, it should be rinsed in hot water to remove the sizing. Some operators recommend that this rinse water should be about 60°C (140°F) so that the sizing will not swell and fill the space between the threads. Others do not see this as a problem and use water as hot as possible. The cloth leacher soaks up coffee oil and darkens, and this will become rancid if left out in the open air. When not in use, the bag should be stored under cold water. When overly clogged with "fines" or too rancid in odor to give a good cup of coffee, it must be replaced. The U.S. Navy found that leachers made of Dacron lasted three months or many times that of the cotton ones. The bag should be well supported in the leacher basket so that the grind is uniform in depth and the bag does not dangle down into the brew.

The paper filter is similar to the cloth filter except that it is used only once and the problem of "fines" carryover into the brew is least in this filter. It is fragile when wet so must be well supported by the leacher basket and interior support. The paper filter is sometimes used flat over a perforated metal base with a perforated plate holding it in place.

The metal strainer is made of wire mesh woven to provide the filtering action proper for the type of grind, thickness of bed, and amount of pour-over water. When new, it works very well, but the spaces between the wires tend to fill up with "fines," and if not reverse-flushed and carefully cleaned, they will clog and allow the water to overextract the grind. Many times the users give up trying to keep the strainer clean and poke holes in it and use a paper filter to regulate the extraction.

The perforated metal plates use the principle of two perforated metal plates fitting together closely so that the holes in one are offset from the holes in the other. The filtering action takes place as the brew going through the holes in the top plate is stripped of solids as it moves horizontally between the plates to the holes in the bottom plate. The placement and sizes of the two sets of holes must be carefully designed or the strength of the brew may vary. The two plates must be handled carefully as warping of either will affect the extraction rate and filtering efficiency. I have used this type of leacher in the top of a steam jacketed kettle coupled with a pump connected to the draw-off and a good spray nozzle to convert the kettle into a coffee maker. Accurate timing and water temperature provided a constant strength brew.

Other things one may look for in coffee makers, particularly urns are:

1. Coffee and water level glasses to coffee reservoir and water boiler to show amounts of coffee or water present.
2. Either air-stirrers or pump to stir the brew after extraction.
3. Thermostats to control temperature of water or brew or both. These are adjustable if the pour-over water temperature is too cold or boiling, or the brew is too cold or too hot.
4. Bypass is available in some units to allow water other than that poured over the grind to go into the coffee brew reservoir. This may obviate overextraction of the grind or may provide necessary dilution of the brew.
5. Timers to time water pour-over to leacher. In some units this is a push button control.
6. Two sets of faucets so that patrons may draw from both sides of the urn or so that workers may draw from the back of the urn as the customer draws from the front in the serving line.
7. A low water cutoff to shut off heat to the urn if the level in the water reservoir falls below a certain point. This prevents burn-out of the elements.
8. Automatic refill of the water reservoir to the desired level after a batch has been made. This is usually a desirable feature.
9. Leacher adapters that decrease the area of the leacher bed so that one-half and one-quarter batches may be made during slack periods of demand.

Materials

Most coffee urns are made of 18-gauge No. 302 or 304 stainless steel. While the water reservoirs are usually of any noncorrosive metal, much controversy takes place over the materials of the coffee brew container. Although most metals except soft solder are little affected by coffee, some do give the brew a metallic taste. In increasing order of concern are: silver, nickel, copper, aluminum, chromium, and tin plate. Monel and stainless steel impart little flavor except in long holding. Almost completely inert to coffee are glass, porcelain, and similar ceramics; however, these may be damaged easily by contact with heavy metallic instruments. While glass is commonly used for decanters, stainless steel is the main material used in large coffee receptacles. Several urns have Teflon liners for the steel urns.

No. 7 polished stainless steel or chrome is commonly used for coffee maker exteriors in cafeteria serving lines, but some atmosphere may be added by using some of the many vinyl and other exteriors simulating wood and fabrics.

Where handles get hot, wood or some of the plastics are used to keep them at temperatures under 51.6°C (125°F), at which they may be handled.

Determination of Needed Capacity

Because of coffee's short use life, determining the proper capacity of coffee-making equipment to purchase is fraught with many considerations. Certainly, an operator wants to have quality coffee brew ready to serve when the customer requests it, but coffee brew is expensive and deteriorates rapidly. Its production must be carefully regulated and scheduled.

If a cafeteria serves six people per minute, and four of these six people take 0.18 liters (6 oz) of coffee, calculating the size of the urn it should be using is not too difficult if one has one item of information, the length of time to make a batch. Thus, if the total time to make a batch is ten minutes, it may be calculated this way:

$$\frac{10 \text{ minutes} \times 4 \text{ portions per minute} \times 0.18 \text{ liters (6 oz) per portion}}{1 \text{ liter or } 1 \text{ gallon (128 oz)}}$$

$$= 7.6 \text{ liters (1.9 or 2 gal)}$$

As one batch of coffee would need to be made while the other is being served, this would have to be a twin 7.6-liter (2-gal) unit.

Also to be considered is the fact that the grind absorbs about 0.9 liters (1 qt) of water for each 454 g (1 lb) of grind used and this amount is not available for service.

Basic Use and Operation

As previously indicated, a specific coffee brew is the result of many factors:

- blend of coffee beans and the way they were handled
- roasting (mild, medium, or dark)
- grind (amount, packaging, storage, degree of fineness, and use of)
- coffee-making device (percolator, urn, drip, or vacuum, etc.)
- leacher and the way it is used
- cleanliness of urn and leacher
- water (solubles, temperature, distribution, timing, and amount)
- postextraction mixing and service (temperature, container, age of brew, additives, and other factors)

All in all, coffee making is a complex process that has had to be simplified to make it workable in quantity foodservice.

Coffee and blend. Most foodservice establishments are urged to use a blend of varieties and origins with which their customers are familiar and which the customers like. In most cases, the coffee salesperson is the best one to consult initially as he delivers to others in the area. After that, the restaurant's customers will keep the operator informed as to the desirability of the coffee blend and the coffee quality. If the coffee is to be held on the premises for a week or more, it is well to keep roasted beans unground as they are three to five times more stable than ground coffee. If ground coffee is bought, it should be canned under vacuum pack, nitrogen, or carbon dioxide. Ground coffee loses 20 percent of its freshness in two to four days; in twenty days it has lost 50 percent of its flavor. It is stale in five to eight days. Refrigerating the grind slows its deterioration, and freezing it virtually stops breakdown. Care must be taken to keep the stored grind away from odorous materials as it quickly picks up the off odors.

Roasting. This has been discussed in some detail with the recommendations that one use the degree of roast common to the area. Exceptions to this may be ethnic restaurants of countries where strong roasts are common such as Turkey, Greece, and others. Also, if one serves a demitasse, he may want to use a strong roast or strong brew or both.

Grind. The size of particles of coffee left after the bean has been ground or mashed may be expressed in a variety of ways. The most common of these are: steelcut, cornmeal, regular, coarse, percolator, medium fine, drip, Silex, vacuum, and pulverized. Most of these are mixtures of various sizes of particles with a predominant percentage being of one size in a particular grind. These percentages are usually determined by use of screens where the amount of grind that goes through or is restrained is regulated by the number of certain size wires per inch. For instance, a 14-mesh screen, or 14 wires to the inch, will retain 33 percent of a regular grind, 7 percent of a drip grind, and none of a fine grind. The grind should be used promptly, kept refrigerated or frozen, where possible, and kept free of mold, insects, off odors, and old age. While the grind may be purchased in bulk or ground in-house, a preferred method is to secure the grind in bags where the amount in each provides one coffee-maker loading. It simplifies in-house measuring, makes brews more consistent in strength, and avoids open grind containers. Some popular amounts per bag are 85, 397, 454, and 907 g (3, 14, 16, and 32 oz).

Coffee-making devices. These have been discussed previously, but it should be emphasized that one should select a coffee maker that can make the quantities of brew needed in the time frame required, that the available workers must be able to turn out quality brew, the cleaning procedure must be uncomplicated and the coffee maker or makers must fit into available space, use available utilities and drains, and be economical to purchase, install, use, and maintain. It must be said that there is a coffee maker for almost every quantity foodservice need.

Leacher. This has been discussed. Its importance cannot be overemphasized. The time that water of proper temperature is in contact with the grind is all important and this is regulated by the pour-over rate and the leacher. A properly designed leacher governs the thickness of the filter bed. It also controls the amounts of filterable solids that find their way into the brew to some degree. Improperly designed filter baskets allow the filter bag to dangle into the brew which causes undesirable overextraction of some of the grind.

Water. Some hardness in the water is desirable to provide the best brew but hard water is apt to form lime in the coffee maker interior and it passes through the grounds more quickly than soft water. Softened water where sodium ions are substituted for calcium does not turn out a satisfactory brew, nor does distilled water. Medium hardness water is preferable, and if some softening of available water is desirable, it should be done by use of polyphosphate filters as this does not damage coffee quality. Most operators accept the premise that, "If the water tastes good, use it!" One should avoid waters with high ammonia, chlorine, iron, or other abnormal flavor contents as they affect the coffee adversely.

Postextraction mixing. This is necessary to even out the soluble solids and color of the brew. Most of the color and solubles come over early in the extraction process, and, being heavier, they settle to the bottom while the late colorless liquid drops on top and does not mix in. Thus it is necessary to draw off and pour over 3.8 liters (1 gal) of brew per 454 g (1 lb) of grind extracted. Some urns use air or pumps to agitate and even out the solids and color in the brew.

Coffee service. Coffee brew does not maintain its good qualities of taste and aroma beyond sixty minutes. The U.S. Navy limited holding to thirty minutes in their Standards of Production as sailors preferred coffee held no more than thirty minutes. However, some operations permit a holding time of ninety minutes. Holding temperatures prove to be important as the customer seems to prefer coffee at 71–74°C (160–165°F) in his cup which means it must be at 85–88°C (185–190°F) in the urn. Because holding temperatures above 88°C (190°F) cause the brew to break down quickly, they should be avoided. Certain additives must be provided with the coffee as it is served. While 27 percent of the customers may like their brew black without cream or sugar, 26 percent like it with these additives. Cream, alone, is preferred by 15 percent and 9 percent like sugar alone with their brew. Eight percent never drink coffee, and the remainder use cream or sugar substitute.

Procedures Used for Various Coffee Makers

Half-Gallon Automatic

1. After rinsing a new cloth filter in hot water, place it, or a paper or metal filter, in the brew chamber.
2. Add 113 g (4 oz) but not less than 91 g (3.3 oz) of dry coffee grind so that it rests evenly in the filter.
3. After checking water temperature (it should be 96°C (205°F), start flow over the grind. It should take not less than three minutes twenty seconds or more than four minutes twenty seconds to extract the coffee brew from the grind.
4. As the filter finishes dripping, remove it and rinse out the filter in hot water. If cloth, store it in cold water.
5. Some operators wait ten minutes for the brew to stabilize and then stir it several times with a spoon to ensure even distribution of solids (figure 19.4).

Vacuum Coffee Making

1. Start water heating to a boil in lower bowl. Heating may be by gas or electricity.
2. Place cloth or metal filter in bottom of top bowl. If cloth, rinse the filter in hot water before use. Add 28 g (1 oz) of fine grind coffee to the bowl for each 0.47–0.59 liter (16–20 oz) of water in the lower bowl.

FIGURE 19.4. Half-gallon coffee maker with half of coffee served.

3. When the water boils in the lower bowl, insert the upper bowl into it with a screwing motion.
4. Reduce the heat so that the water will not be forced too vigorously into the upper bowl. This movement of water should take about one minute. The grind-water mixture should be stirred the first twenty seconds.
5. When the water has finished moving into the upper bowl and steam has started bubbling in the brew, the two bowls should be removed from the heat.
6. In about three minutes, the air should cool in the lower bowl, and the resultant vacuum should draw the brew through the filter down into the lower bowl.
7. When empty, the upper bowl should be removed, the cloth filter rinsed and stored in cold water, and the bowl rinsed thoroughly.
8. The bowl or decanter of brew is then placed on a heating unit and maintained at 85–88°C (185–190°F).

Urn Coffee Making

1. Rinse out urn with hot water.
2. Be sure water reservoir is filled with fresh water and brought up to at least 96°C (205°F).
3. If new, the cloth filter should be rinsed out in hot water and placed in the leacher basket and coffee grind added in depth of 2.5–5.1 cm (1–2 in.). It should be drip grind in the amount of 454 g (1 lb) to each 7.6–11.4 liters (2–3 gal) of water depending on the strength of brew desired.
4. Pour the requisite amount of water over the grind. Be sure all the grind is evenly wetted and receiving an equal contact with water. Total contact between water and grind should be for four to six minutes. If more time is needed, the water should be reduced and the necessary water added directly to the brew. Replace cover between pourings if done by hand.
5. Immediately after brewing, the leacher should be removed, and if cloth, the leacher should be rinsed out thoroughly in hot water and stored in cold water.
6. The brew should be thoroughly mixed by means of air, pump, or hand pour-over at a rate of 3.8 liters (1 gal) per pound of grind. No pour-over water should be poured through the extracted grind as undesirable bitter elements will be extracted.
7. Rinse urn with boiling water after each use.

Brewed coffee should not be reheated for use the next day. U.S. Navy research found that:

1. Those who use both milk and sugar in their coffee have the greatest sensory tolerance in their brew.
2. Those who drank it black preferred a medium brew.
3. Those using only milk preferred a strong brew.
4. Those who used only sugar wanted a fairly weak brew.
5. Most of the people desired a brew made with one pound of grind and three gallons of water. They liked the slight extra bitterness.

Coffee Treats

Iced coffee, much desired in summer, is made from a brew extracted at a rate of 454 g (1 lb) of grind to 5.7–7.6 liters (1.5–2 gal) of water. Do not refrigerate overnight. After cooling to room temperature, pour about 0.18 liters (6 oz) into a 0.35-liter (12-oz) glass and fill glass with ice. Add cream and sugar to taste.

Café au lait is half a cup strong coffee and half a cup of hot milk poured together with much flourish.

Mocha Java is half hot, normal strength coffee and half hot cocoa with several small marshmallows floating on top.

Viennese coffee is simply very strong coffee, sweetened and served with a dollop of whipped cream.

Spiced Viennese coffee is a spicy treat made for six servings by pouring three cups of extra strong, very hot coffee over four whole cloves, two cinnamon sticks, and four allspice berries and letting it stand ten to fifteen minutes. The resultant brew is strained into cups, topped with whipped cream, and sprinkled with nutmeg. It is served with sugar.

Demitasse is a strong coffee made from a dark roast but not as dark as some Turkish coffees. Its strength is obtained by using 5.7–6.1 liters (1.5–1.6 gal) of water per 454 g (1 lb) grind. It is served in small cups. To complement it, serve it with sugar, lemon peel, liqueurs, or a spice mixture of cardamom seed, whole cloves, and broken cinnamon stick.

Espresso or Italian coffee is made in a macchinetta or espresso maker. The macchinetta is a drip pot made up of two containers, the upper of which has a spout, and the lower unit which has two sieves and holds the coffee and the water. The water is heated to a boil, and the two containers that are fitted together are inverted and water makes contact with the grind and drips into the container with the spout without further heating.

The espresso unit uses steam to force hot water up into the very fine, dark grind as in a vacuum coffee maker except that there is twice as much grind per given volume of hot water. It is served in 0.12 liter (4 oz) cups with lemon peel and possibly sugar and liqueurs. Do not offer cream!

Cappuccino is similar to café au lait except that the mixture is sometimes two-thirds very strong or espresso coffee and one-third steaming milk sprinkled with cinnamon or nutmeg and topped with whipped cream.

Coffee diablo is a popular New Orleans specialty made by placing pieces of lump sugar, eight cloves, one short cinnamon stick, one cut-up orange or lemon peel, and four jiggers of cognac in a chafing dish. The brandy is lighted and the mixture stirred. After a minute or so, four cups of demitasse coffee are added while continuing to stir. It is strained into four brûlot cups and served.

Irish coffee is an Irish drink popular in San Francisco. It is made by placing two teaspoons of fine granulated sugar into a wine glass of hot coffee. After it is mixed, two tablespoons of Irish whiskey are added and topped off with whipped cream. Do not stir in the cream!

For coffee royale start with strong demitasse coffee and fill a demitasse cup two-thirds full. Strictly speaking, coffee royale is made when a dash of cognac is added but white creme de menthe, curaçoa, kummel, Cointreau, bourbon, or rum are also good.

Cinnamon coffee is somewhat similar to spiced Viennese coffee but uses one stick of cinnamon in contact with two cups of hot strong coffee for one hour. When cool, serve in glasses with sugar and heavy cream using cinnamon sticks as stirrers.

Special Applications

Coffee makers have a few uses other than the making of coffee. Most of these are limited to the use of the hot water for instant coffee, tea, bouillon, instant soups, and hot cocoa or chocolate. Hot water may be used to rinse out the cup or coffee server before filling it with brew, and hot water may be provided for those people who wish to dilute their coffee.

Alternatives to Coffee Makers

If the coffee maker breaks down, instant coffee plus some source of hot water is the best solution as it offers a choice of both regular and decaffeinated coffee. If needed in quantity, one may use a range pot or steam jacketed kettle to make it by the old institutional method:

The correct amount of water for the amount of grind to be used must be measured. It will usually be 454 g (1 lb) to 9.5–11.4 liters (2.5–3 gal) of water. Bring water to boil and immediately reduce heat to slow boil.

Rinse out a clean cloth bag in warm water and squeeze it half dry. Half fill it with the requisite amount of regular grind and tie the bag shut. Submerge the bag in the 93°C (200°F) plus hot water. Push it up and down and move it around for eight to ten minutes. Do not boil it!

At the completion of brewing, remove the bag, gently press it to remove excess brew and prepare to serve coffee immediately. Hold at the usual coffee holding temperature. The bag may be emptied, turned inside out, and rinsed well in hot water and then submerged in cold water until next use. By that time the modern coffee maker should be fixed.

Another technique involves heating the proper amount of fresh water to be used in the old coffee pot until it comes to a rolling boil. Lower heat until water is just below boiling and add the proper amount of regular grind. Stir in well and then steep for eight minutes. If grounds have not settled, add one cup of cold water per pound of grind. Pour brew through a strainer into serving container and discard grounds.

Cleaning

Part of the secret of good coffee is clean equipment. Every surface coming in contact with coffee grind or brew can accumulate accretions that will produce undesirable odor or flavor that carries over into the brew. To avoid this problem, follow the basic procedures for cleaning large coffee makers.

Before each use, which includes each batch, rinse the urn to remove any sediment, old coffee brew, or at the start of the day, any cleaning residuals. This should involve placing one or more gallons of water in the device and brushing all coffee contact surfaces. Draw off soiled water and rinse all interior surfaces with clean fresh water. The urn is then ready for the next batch.

Repeat the process just described several times at the end of the use day. Take the faucet apart and clean it, being careful to rinse thoroughly. Brush the drain pipe leading into the urn and urn glasses. Rinse all surfaces with fresh water. Place a gallon or more of fresh water in the urn until next use. At that time, drain out standing water and rinse urn with fresh water before first use.

Do a more thorough cleaning at least twice a week. With jacketed reservoir at least three-quarters full of water, fill the urn at least three-quarters full of water, fill the urn at least three-quarters full and heat contents while adding urn cleaner recommended by the manufacturer. Let stand thirty minutes. Scrub the inside of the urn and clean the lug nut in the urn base. Drain the urn but save some of the detergent water to wash the urn glasses, faucets, and pipes thoroughly. Rinse all interior surfaces with fresh water three or four times, brushing surfaces each time. Check spray heads to be sure all holes are open, and if not, ream out with a wire. Wipe all outside surfaces with cloth and detergent and fresh water, then wipe dry with soft cloth. Leave some water in the urn. Scrub risers and urn baskets with detergent mixture and rinse thoroughly. Air dry. Never use soaps, scouring powders, or other abrasives.

The urn bags or filter clothes should be rinsed in hot water before being used the first time and after each batch of coffee. They should be stored in cold water. They should not be washed in detergent or soap, and, when worn or have strong odors, they should be discarded and replaced.

Maintenance

Each type and make of coffee maker has its recommended maintenance procedure or at least checking measures and corrections to be applied to those deficiencies that may be treated in-house.

The most common of these are thermostat defects that cause pour-over water or brew temperature to be too low or too high, usually too low. In most cases, a screw driver operating on the thermostat will correct this. If not or the thermostat does not cycle, usually it means that the thermostat must be replaced. A hand-held thermometer should be used frequently to check the temperature of the pour-over water and the stored brew, and needed corrections should be made.

Sometimes the heat input is insufficient for other reasons. If the unit is gas heated, the gas-air mixture may be incorrect, giving a yellow flame, or the quantity of gas may be insufficient. Steam units commonly suffer from clogged pipes, poor removal of condensed steam water, or similar problems. Electric coils do burn out, wires break, or the units become coated with lime, making them inefficient. Lime can be removed by deliming, but burned out heaters must be replaced.

If faucets leak, those of metal may have to be reground or replaced, while those with soft plastic interior parts usually must have the plunger replaced. It is a minor job.

Other maintenance problems specific to each coffee maker can be ascertained similarly and corrected. Pipes are examined for leaks, electric wires are checked for loose connections, urn glasses are examined for cracks, breaks, and leaks, leachers for bent or broken supports, and brew is checked for excessive sediment indicating defects in the leachers, the bed of grind is observed for evenness of extraction and tunneling, the spray nozzle is examined for clogging, and the area around the urns is checked for leaks in reservoirs. The brew should be tested with a coffee hydrometer to ascertain whether the proper extraction is occurring.

QUESTIONS

1. What are the desirable qualities of coffee brew?
2. What percentage of the grind should be extracted as soluble solids?
3. What are the main parts of a coffee urn?
4. What is the least affected material commonly in contact with coffee brew? What material is most used?
5. What should the temperature of pour-over water be? What should the temperature of the brew in the urn be?
6. What are the types of leachers? Describe each.
7. If one does not have a coffee maker, how can coffee be made?
8. What coffee blend and coffee roast does one select?
9. How does one determine needed coffee maker capacity?
10. How is the coffee urn cleaned?
11. What is the procedure for making urn coffee?
12. How can one tell if an urn is making proper strength brew other than by taste?
13. What are the most commonly used grind to water ratios?
14. What are the most commonly used coffee making devices?

BIBLIOGRAPHY

ANON. 1960. Best in beverages. *Institutions* 46, No. 1, 140.

ANON. *Facts about Coffee*. The Coffee Brewing Center, New York.

KATZENSTEIN, A.W., and BENARDE, M.E. 1955. *Coffee Brewing*. U.S. Naval Supply Research and Development Facility, Bayonne, N.J.

KOTSCHEVAR, L.H. 1974. *Standards, Principles, and Techniques in Quantity Food Production*. CBI Publishing Company, Inc., Boston.

KOTSCHEVAR, L.H. and TERRELL, M.E. 1977. *Food Service Planning: Layout and Equipment*. John Wiley and Sons, New York.

STEIN, H., and RICHTER, H.W. 1959. Study of *Automatic Coffee Makers*. U.S. Naval Supply Research and Development Facility, Bayonne, N.J.

Food Mixers

The food mixer is a device for integrating solids into solids, liquids and solids, and liquids into liquids to make homogeneous mixtures. In addition, it incorporates air, diffuses, disperses, develops gluten, or develops a specific crystalline structure in a food mixture. It can have attachments that heat, cool, mix, beat, knead, whip, emulsify, slice, sieve, strain, chop, grind, and perform other functions as well. It is the most versatile piece of mechanical equipment in the kitchen.

The food mixer can take many forms—a motor-driven propeller in a vat of liquid or semiliquid material, the scraper-beater of an ice cream machine, the mixer steam jacketed kettle and mixer pressure cookers, the horizontal bread mixer, the homogenizer, the overhead motor vertical mixer, the high-speed blender with the motor at the bottom of the device, and its close relative the vertical cutter-mixer, formerly known as the schnellkutter when it was brought from Germany. There are other mixing devices used mainly in the baking and food manufacturing industries. The one that will be discussed here is the vertical mixer with overhead motor that is most popular in America.

Description and Specification

The vertical mixer is generally available in sizes of 4.7–132 liters (5–140 qt), but the commonly bought capacities are 19, 28, 38, 57 and 76 liters (20, 30, 40, 60, and 80 qt). Up to 19 liters (20 qt), the mixer is table or wall mounted, and mixers larger than this are set on the floor (figure 20.1). While form and mechanism vary somewhat between manufacturers, in general, a housing parallel to the floor holds the motor, gearing, shaft, and mixer rotating mechanism. This housing is supported by a vertical shaft that, in turn, is supported by two feet under the housing which rest on a table or the floor. The mixing bowl is held over the feet by a sliding yoke attached to the rear shaft. As the yoke is raised by action of a lever, wheel, or motor, the mixing bowl is moved up around the mixing beater. When the action is reversed, the bowl is lowered away from the mixing device. If the mixer bowl is large and heavy, this lowering places it down on a special three-or four-wheel dolly or cart whereby the bowl can be rolled to wherever its contents will be used.

The supporting elements can be of cast iron or steel and the housing can be made of welded steel around the vertical support and motor-gear housing that makes up the head of the mixer. The exterior of the mixer may be painted with high-quality acrylic baked enamel or tough epoxy finish or it may be sheathed in polished aluminum or stainless steel. The agitators may be made of cast aluminum, tinned, or chrome-plated or stainless steel and the bowls of tinned steel or stainless steel. While they cost three times more, it is recommended that stainless steel bowls be used because the tinned bowls must be retinned after a period of use and, at times, they can darken the color of the food.

In the housing or head is the motor gearing which may be all metal, a combination of nylon and metal, or a combination of metal gears, pulleys, and a drive belt. The combinations are used to take up the shock of starting the mixer, particularly in heavy mixtures. Some mixers have a system of springs to relieve the strain of sudden starts. The motors vary in horsepower from 1/6 to 5 HP. Where heavy doughs are to be mixed, it is well to get a motor 1/2 HP larger than is usual for that size mixer. Some people feel that hand wound motors are best.

The gears or belt drive the planetary agitator which moves in a horizontal plane around the inside of the bowl in one direction while driving the

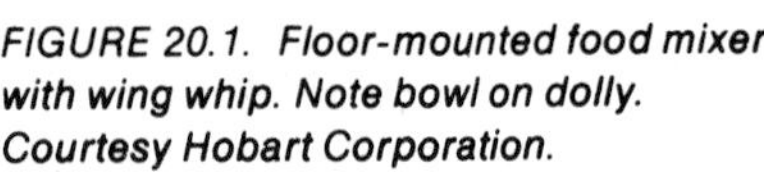

FIGURE 20.1. Floor-mounted food mixer with wing whip. Note bowl on dolly. Courtesy Hobart Corporation.

shaft on which the beater is fixed in the opposite direction. This is so that the beater stirs all of the bowl contents and will reach a different area of the bowl on each revolution. The bottom of the revolving shaft usually has a pin that juts out on each side so that, as the beater slides up on the shaft, the pins go into slots in the beater housing, first vertically and then at right angles so that, operating against the drive of the motor, it is effectively locked in place. To remove the beater, it is twisted and slid in a reverse path.

The bowl sits on the yoke that, in turn, is connected to the vertical shaft on a slide. On the end of the yoke arms are vertical pins that fit into holes in two metal projections or a rim that stick out from opposite sides of the mixing bowl. The back of the bowl is held by a slit into which the bowl edge fits, a hole into which a pin from the bowl fits, or a hand clamp or latch that is turned down against the bowl edge. Some mixers have other clamps beside the supporting pins on the ends of the yoke or against the rim of the bowl further back along the yoke arms.

If smaller mixer loads than those requiring a full mixer are desired at times and one does not want to buy another mixer, it is possible to get adapter rings that will support a smaller bowl. Smaller attachments to fit the smaller bowl will have to be purchased. A 76-liter (80-qt) mixer may have 57-, 38-, and 28-liter, (60-, 40-, and 30-qt) adapters, a 28-liter (30-qt) mixer may have a 19-liter (20-qt) adapter, and a 19-liter (20-qt) mixer may have an 11-liter (12-qt) adapter. A 4.7-liter (5-qt) mixer occupies little more area than a home counter mixer that is 24 x 39 cm (9.5 x 15.5 in.), but a 132-liter (140-qt) floor mixer may occupy a floor area of 74 x 115 cm (29.25 x 45.38 in.).

A part of the housing is a speed control that usually has three or four levels of speed, although a few may have as many as nine speeds. There is an on-off switch. A timer is a good investment, particularly if mixing times are made a part of the recipes used.

The mixer speeds of beaters and power take-off on various makes and sizes are different at the various speed settings. As an example, a 76-liter (80-qt) mixer may have:

Speed	*Agitator (RPM)*	*Attachment Power Take-off (RPM)*
first	55	102
second	96	179
third	181	336
fourth	318	591

Usually there is a power take-off that drives a variety of food preparation equipment. It often consists of steel housing into which is slid part of the housing of the device that will derive the power from the mixer. A thumb screw or clamp holds it in place. In the center of this housing is a shaft that connects with the drive shaft of the mixer. Attachments that may be purchased especially to use this power take-off include, but are not limited to, a dicer, coffee mill, food chopper, juice extractor, tool sharpener, vegetable slicer, and a shredder. While all of these sound useful, be sure they can, and will, be used at the location of the food mixer. Often it is better to have separate devices located at the point of most efficient use. For years the U.S. Navy bought most of these attachments for every mixer and found that most of them gathered dust in warehouses and were sold finally as scrap and salvage.

As part of the vertical supporting shaft is some means for raising and lowering the mixer bowl. For the smaller mixers, this is merely a lever that ratchets into gear teeth in the back of the bowl support yoke to do the movement. In larger mixers, a hand-wheel and gearing drive the yoke movement, while in others, a motor provides the power to move the yoke and bowl.

There are a considerable number of agitation accessories made of cast aluminum or tinned or chromed steel that fasten on the single vertical shaft (home mixers have two shafts usually) to do the particular type of mixing desired. The most common of these are:

1. The flat beater of interconnected bar construction is normally used with medium consistency foods for mixing, creaming, rubbing, and mashing (figure 20.2). Among other uses are making cakes and icings and mashing cooked vegetables. It uses medium speeds.

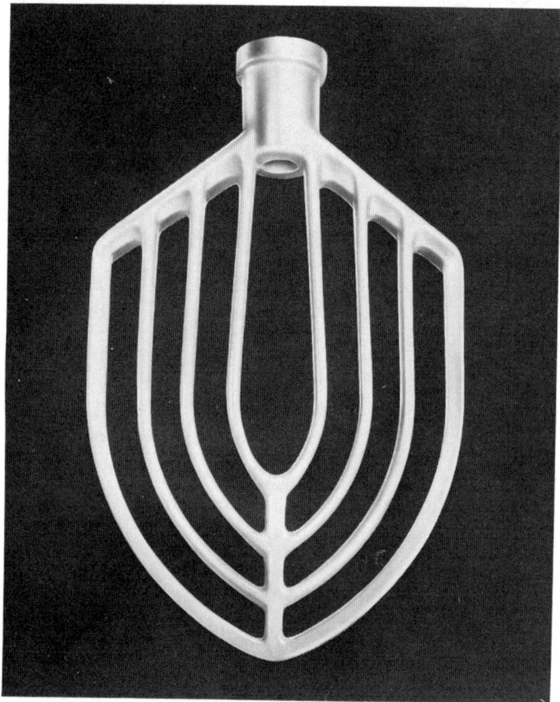

FIGURE 20.2. Flat beater. Courtesy Hobart Corporation.

2. The wire loop or whip of coarse wire-rib construction comes in a number of forms (figure 20.3). This is used with light ingredients most often to incorporate air. Whole eggs, egg whites, and frostings are often prepared with the whip. It uses high speeds.
3. The dough arm or hook is a heavy metal bar in a single loop used to mix heavy ingredients such as bread doughs that require extensive folding, stretching, and kneading (figure 20.4). It uses low speed.
4. The pastry knife, a blade in a single loop, provides a cutting action to incorporate short-

FIGURE 20.3. Wire whip. Courtesy Hobart Corporation.

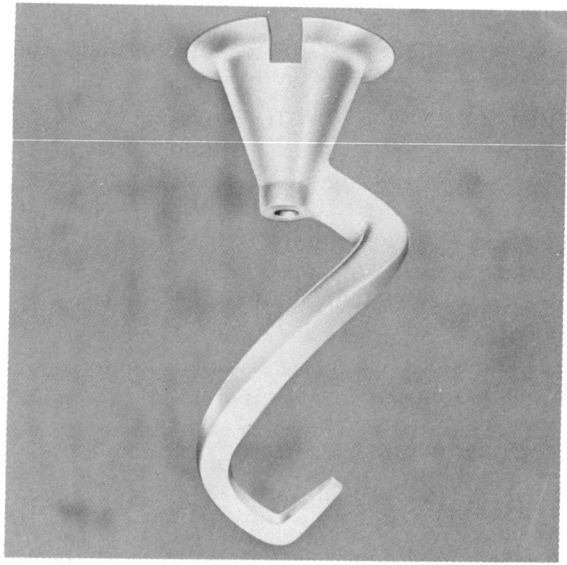

FIGURE 20.4. Dough arm. Courtesy Hobart Corporation.

ening into flour without overdeveloping the gluten (figure 20.5). It is used for pie crusts, pastry shells, and similar mixes. It does not incorporate air and uses low speeds.

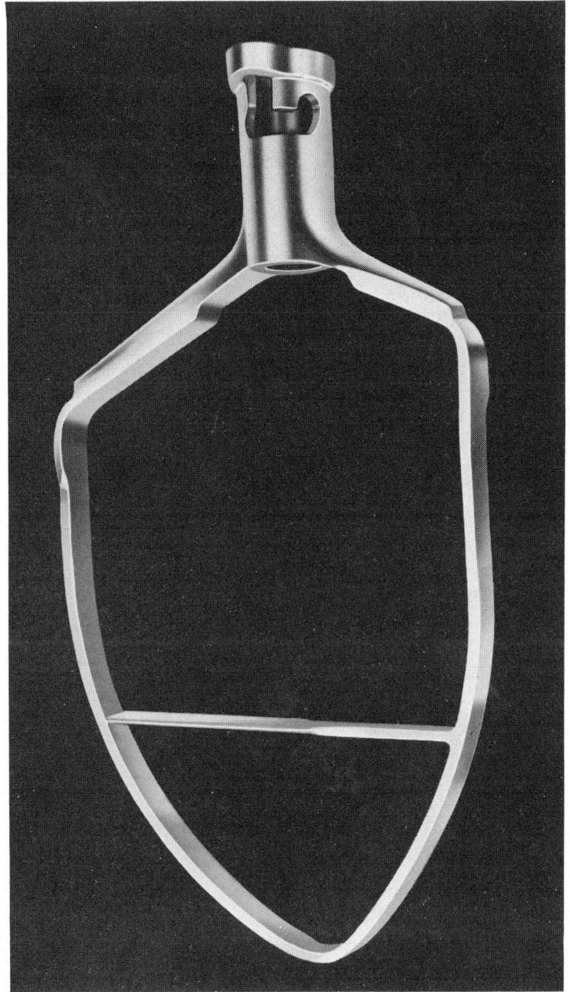

FIGURE 20.5. Pastry knife. Courtesy Hobart Corporation.

5. The wing whip, heavy metal loops joined by wires in two to six wings, is used to whip materials too heavy for the wire whip (figure 20.6). It is used for creaming, making mayonnaise, or whipping potatoes and vegetables. It uses medium to high speeds.

FIGURE 20.6. Wing whip. Courtesy Hobart Corporation.

6. The sweet dough hook, which is halfway between a dough hook and a flat beater, provides creaming, rubbing, folding, and stretching but not to the degree of the dough hook and flat beater. It is used with mixtures not too high in gluten and uses medium speeds.

The most frequently used mixing attachments are the flat beater, pastry knife, wire whip, and dough hook. In most cases, the others are unnecessary.

There are other attachments or features that might be of use to some operators. They include:

1. hot-cold water jacket for mixer bowl
2. colander sieve, a roller for making purees, soup, removing skins, and seeds.

3. splash cover for mixer bowl
4. oil dropper for making mayonnaise and salad dressings
5. shelf for holding pans below power take-off attachments
6. extension to sides of bowl for splashing mixtures
7. dolly or truck for carrying mixer bowl
8. wall mounting (eliminates base and the problems of cleaning beneath the device) (figure 20.7)
9. high-rise feature (brings the mixer bowl up to height where materials can be easily seen without bending over); strongly recommended

In general, the following questions should be asked in specifying a mixer:

1. Does the chosen machine have adequate capacity and performance to meet production needs?
2. Does its capacity mesh with the equipment that it is to support? Does it provide for an oven deck or total oven load?
3. Is space available for the selected mixer and its attachments next to it?
4. Is the mixer designed for convenient use? Are the attachments easy to connect and disconnect? Is the bowl easy to install and remove and is the human engineering good?
5. Does it have adequate speeds, timer, and raising and lowering mechanism?
6. Does mixer have the requisite attachments and stainless steel bowls?
7. Is machine easy to clean and maintain? Is local maintenance available for the particular make of machine?
8. Does the mixer use available electrical current?
9. Is mixer safe to use?

FIGURE 20.8. Mixer combined with pressure cooker, steam jacketed kettle, refrigerated kettle, and potato peeler.

FIGURE 20.7. Wall-mounted mixer that can be folded out of the way.

Determination of Needed Capacity

Capacity in food mixers demands consideration of more space than the volume of materials that will be placed in the mixer bowl. Of great importance is the increase in volume that will occur in mixing given volumes of the materials that will be prepared in the device. For example, as an average, a 19-liter (20-qt) mixer will mash only 6.8 kg (15 lb) of potatoes, whip only 3.8 liters (4 qts) of cream, 0.9 liters (1 qt) of egg whites, mix 7.6 liters (8 qts) of pancake batter, 9.5 liters (10 qts.) of mayonnaise, 7.3–7.7 kg (16–17 lb) of pie dough, 9.1 kg (20 lb) of layer cake, 5.4 kg (12 lb) of fondant icing, 10–11.3 kg (22–25 lb) of heavy bread dough, and 4.1 kg (9 lb) raised doughnut dough. The extra space is needed to take care of the increases in volume of the foods.

To a lesser extent, degree of splashing controls needed capacity, but this is included in the aforementioned capacity. Splashing may be thwarted by use of bowl side extensions or splash covers. Time of processing may be of some importance as it controls, to some degree, the batches that can be prepared but since few mixers are used full time, it will not be considered here. Needed amount per batch is the usual capacity-controlling factor.

If one has a three-deck oven, each deck of which will hold two 46-x-66-cm (18-x-26-in.) sheet pans and one wants to use it to bake plain cake, one makes a simple calculation:

3 decks × 2 pans per deck = 6 pans

6 pans × 3.2 kg (7 lb) cake batter per pan
= 19 kg (42 lb)

Thus, if a 19-liter (20-qt) mixer will handle 9.1 kg (20 lb) of cake batter, then a 38-liter (40-qt) mixer would be needed for 19 kg (42 lb). Other calculations can be conducted similarly.

Basic Use and Operation

The basic procedure for using the mixer is as follows:

1. Place bowl in position and fasten catches or clamps.
2. Slide proper agitator up on shaft and lock it in place over the shaft pin.
3. Raise bowl to mix position and check clearance between beater and inside of mixer bowl. It should be between 0.15 and 0.32 cm (0.08 and 0.12) in.). It should not touch as it will abrade away metal and discolor food.
4. Select speed, 1 for low speed and 3 or 4 for high. If speed is changed, power should be off during the shifting. It is important that the machine be at slow or stop for smooth engagement of the clutch. The machine should be stopped to scrape down the sides of the bowl. To ease the shock on the gear chain when the mixer is restarted, the bowl can be lowered before starting the mixer and gradually eased up around the moving beater.
5. On completion of adding of ingredients and the mixing cycle, shut off the mixer and lower the bowl onto the dolly. Be sure the beater has stopped before doing any scraping of bowl or beater. Remove beater. Unlatch bowl and wheel to point of further use.

The procedure for using the mixer varies for each type of product and often for each cook or baker. The following are a few of the procedures that were standardized by one of the military services:

Straight dough bread mixing. Place water, salt, sugar, and nonfat milk in mixing bowl. Add flour, yeast suspension, and shortening and mix at medium speed until smooth and elastic at medium speed (fifteen minutes). Allow dough to ferment to almost full capacity (is double in volume and starts to sag). Punch down and let stand thirty to forty-five minutes. Scale loaves and make up.

Sponge dough bread mixing. This procedure differs from the straight dough in that about 80 percent of the flour, part of the water, the yeast, and yeast food are mixed and allowed to ferment until a piece of the sponge will break cleanly with little stretch. Then the resultant sponge is returned to the mixer where the remainder of the flour, water, salt, sugar, milk, and shortening and other ingredients are added. The mixture is then mixed in the same manner as the straight dough and handled like it thereafter.

In the early mixing stage the dough is rough, lumpy, wet, and sticky with no dough development. At the next stage, the dough becomes smooth, semielastic, pliable, and starts to dry. The dough is developed when it becomes dry, elastic, and does not cling to the back and sides of the bowl. If it is overdeveloped, it softens, becomes wet, sticky, and stringy and breaks short.

Sweet dough mixing. Place sugar, salt, and shortening in bowl and mix one minute at second speed. Dissolve yeast in water and add eggs and milk, and blend with first mixture. Add sifted flour and flavoring and mix about four minutes or until a smooth dough is formed. If the dough is to be made into a roll, it need not be developed in the mixer but if dough is to be made up after a short rest, then it should be developed in the mixer.

Muffin mixing. This procedure is used for griddle cakes, brown bread, corn bread, dumplings, and fritters, as well as for muffins. Sift dry ingredients (flour, sugar, baking powder, salt, and spices) into mixer bowl. Add mixed liquids (beaten eggs, water or milk, vanilla, and melted shortening if directed by recipe) and blend them into dry ingredients until just mixed. If shortening has not been added before, it should be added and mixed in. Muffin, cornbread, and dumpling batter should be mixed only to the point that all dry ingredients are moistened.

Biscuit mixing. Sift dry ingredients together several times, blend in shortening until it is an homogeneous dough, roll out, and cut.

Batter-type cake mixing (creaming method). All ingredients should be between 24–27°C (75–80°F), and the flat beater is used. First, sugar and shortening are creamed at low speed until waxy and workable. Mixing continues at medium speed until the mixture is light in color and fluffy in texture. Scrape down sides frequently. By now sugar and shortening have a good attachment for each other. Add eggs and mix at medium speed. The eggs help to emulsify the shortening, and air is incorporated. When the mixture is creamy, the dry ingredients and liquids are added alternately while mixer proceeds at low speed to develop the gluten (four to seven minutes).

Quick mix cake. All ingredients are mixed with a whip for five minutes at speed 1 to wet ingredients, two minutes at speed 3, two minutes at speed 2, and one minute at speed 1.

Multiple-blend cake. Fat and flour are blended at low speed for three to five minutes, and the bowl is scraped down frequently. Salt, sugar, soda, or baking powder, and one-half to three-quarters of the liquid are added and mixed at the same speed for three to five minutes. Then the remaining ingredients and liquid are added for a further mixing for three to five minutes.

Uncooked icings. With all ingredients at 22°C (72°F), cream butter or shortening and flavoring until light and creamy. Gradually add sugar, salt, and liquid. Finally whip at high speed for five minutes.

Pie crust mixing (mealy crust). Using pastry knife, mix all the fat with all the flour until it resembles coarse cornmeal. Then add the salt to the water and add to the mixture and mix lightly. Excessive mixing will give a tough crust. A modification of this is called the paste-mix method and involves reserving part of the flour to make a paste and adding that to the flour shortening mixture.

Mixing mayonnaise. First, the egg yolks are beaten at high speed for five minutes or until light and thick. A mixture of salt, cayenne pepper, mustard, and sugar is added to the beaten egg yolks and beaten at high speed for an added three minutes. The oil and vinegar are added alternately in very small amounts (a dropper attachment may be used) while being blended at high speed for approximately seven minutes.

Other mixer basics. In general, most foods prepared in vertical mixers are better when prepared in a small batch as compared to a large one.

In mashing potatoes, start at medium speed and finish at high speed.

If flaky pie crusts are desired, limit the mixing action after adding water (about forty seconds) and the fat will stay in large pieces. Also, it helps to keep the mixing action at 15.6°C (60°F) and add the water at 4.4°C (40°F). If fat is too cold, the crust will be too cold to roll properly and if too warm, the crust will not be flaky. Allowing the dough to rest about fifteen minutes after mixing allows the gluten to hydrate, decreases shrinkage, and makes crust easier to roll. Some bakers ripen a crust twelve to twenty-four hours.

Never add sugar to bowl first as the sugar crystals scratch the bowl.

Mashed potatoes should never be held in a tinned bowl as the tinned surface darkens the potatoes. Tinned bowls will be attacked by certain starches, fruit juices, and other foods.

When a small mixer is used in several locations, it should be mounted on a cart with locking wheels.

Make sure no grease or oil are on the whip or mixer bowl when whipping egg whites or eggs as volume will be lowered.

Alternatives to the Vertical Food Mixer

Hand mixing was used before the advent of the mechanical mixer, and it can be used today for quantity mixing as well as the small batches for which it is still used. The greatest problem would be with mixing thick or viscous materials or high-speed whipping. Human strength, consistency, speed, and mixing thoroughness cannot compete with the vertical mixer.

The horizontal mixer in various barrel increments does a good job of mixing bread but is limited to the bakery and is not as good for batters and pie crusts.

The vertical cutter mixer, which is a bottom-actuated high-speed mixer, can be fitted with various attachments, beaters, and cutters that make it as versatile as the vertical mixer.

There is a great variety of specialized mixers that are used in food manufacturing and which can be used in foodservice but the vertical mixer and the vertical cutter mixers are so versatile that there is no particular need to clutter up kitchens with overspecialized mixers.

Cleaning

1. As soon as possible after the machine has been turned off, remove the bowl and beaters and take them to the potwashing sink for washing with a gong brush, hot water, and potwashing detergent. Be particularly careful to clean out

where the beater fits over the shaft. Rinse well in hot water and air dry. Pieces may be scalded to remove any vestige of oil that might hinder beating of eggs. The bowl and beaters may be rinsed with a mild vinegar rinse before the final rinse and drying.

2. Scrub machine with hot detergent and water and a gong brush taking particular care with the beater shaft, bowl saddle, shell and base.
3. Rinse all surfaces with a clean cloth from which hot fresh water has been wrung.
4. Wipe all exposed surfaces with a clean dry cloth.
5. Hang beaters on a rack beside the mixer and place the mixer bowl bottom side up on a wire shelf after its interior is thoroughly dry.

Maintenance

Each make of mixer has its own prescribed maintenance procedure and these should be ascertained and followed to the letter. These are general instructions:

1. The bowl yoke slide and attachment hub to the power take-off must be oiled periodically with several drops of tasteless mineral oil.
2. Motor and transmission should be lubricated only according to the manufacturer's directions.
3. If work is needed on any of the parts inside the housing, use only a factory-qualified repair service as all parts are precision machined and exact alignment is mandatory.
4. Be sure all surfaces except those that are oiled are wiped clean after every use and that any paint removed is replaced with a touch-up kit.

QUESTIONS

1. What are the two main mounting locations for vertical mixers?
2. What are the main capacities of mixers used in foodservice?
3. What is the function of the planetary movement?
4. Name four of the most used agitators. For what is each used?
5. How many speeds do most mixers have?
6. Of what metals are mixers made?
7. With what are the mixer bowls coated? Which is the best? Why?
8. How does one mix smaller than capacity loads in a mixer?
9. What functions are provided by use of the power take-off?
10. What are some of the most important accessories other than those in question 9?
11. List five questions that should be answered before buying a vertical mixer.
12. How does one calculate needed mixer capacity?
13. What are the steps in making sponge dough bread?
14. What mixing caution is necessary to get a flaky pie crust?
15. What is the caution on the use of sugar in a mixer?

BIBLIOGRAPHY

ANON. *Food Operations Reference Manual.* Bureau of Supplies and Accounts, U.S. Navy.

KNIGHT, R.F. 1969. The mixer: a most versatile and useful machine. *School Lunch Journal* XXII, No. 4, 16–20.

KOTSCHEVAR, L.H., and TERRELL, M.E. 1977. *Food Service Planning: Layout and Equipment.* 2d Ed. John Wiley and Sons, New York.

McCARTHY, F. 1949. Modern food mixing. *Food Industries* 21, 1577–1586.

TERRELL, M.E. 1977. *Professional Food Preparation.* John Wiley and Sons, New York.

WEST, B.B., WOOD, L., and HARGER, V.F. 1965. *Food Service in Institutions.* 2d Ed. John Wiley and Sons, New York.

Vertical Cutter/Mixers

The vertical cutter/mixer or the schnellkutter, as it was known when first brought to this country from Germany after World War II, is a highly versatile and speedy food mixing and cutting machine. It will mix, cut, chop, blend, emulsify, grate, grind, mash, stir, homogenize, cream, whip to some extent, develop gluten, crush ice, crystallize, and make crumbs. Based on the principles that made the Waring blender a household word, the vertical cutter/mixer has its motor attached to the bottom of the mixer bowl and has integral cutting-mixing blades rather than a separate housing with detachable bowl.

The vertical cutter/mixer performs most of the functions of the vertical mixer with much greater speed (figure 21.1). In fact, the speed is beyond the comprehension of the average cook. The older cook often has trouble making the mental adjustment to the processing times which may be one-quarter to one-tenth of those of conventional mixers and cutters. Consequently, many products are overmixed or cut too fine. All too often large sums of money are expended to buy the vertical cutter/mixer and then, because of a few poor quality products due to overprocessing, the device falls into disuse.

In common with the steamer and pressure cooker, the vertical cutter/mixer is rarely used for the great variety of functions that can be performed in it. Some of this is due to ignorance of the capabilities of the cutter/mixer, some is due to

FIGURE 21.1. Vertical cutter mixer with water support above and drain.

overselling the functions without clearly demonstrating them, some is due to lack of experimentation, and some comes from fear of the device. Many times only one of a staff is trained to use the vertical cutter/mixer with the idea that he will train the rest of the staff. Often this training is not carried out, and if the trained operator leaves, the device is not used.

The vertical cutter/mixer, like other labor-saving devices, should not be purchased unless it saves enough money in labor and material over its life to pay for itself or it performs some necessary function that no less costly device will perform. When installed, everyone on the kitchen staff who might have occasion to use it should be trained to use it efficiently and safely and to care for it properly.

Description and Specification

The VCM (vertical cutter/mixer) mixes or cuts food up to ten times faster than commonly used equipment. The driving force is a heavy-duty motor that turns a shaft directly up through the bottom of the mixing bowl at high speed. The usual two speeds of 1750 RPM and 3500 RPM use a motor with 4½ HP at the low speed and 5½ HP at the high speed in the 23.7-liter (25-qt) VCM. In the 56.8-liter (60-qt) VCM, the slower speed provides 20 HP and the high speed 25 HP. There are also 37.9-liter (40-qt), 75.7-liter (80-qt), and 123-liter (130-qt) models of the VCM with comparable horsepowers. The bowls are made of stainless steel for the smaller models and 75.7-liter (80-qt) VCM and aluminum in the 56.8-liter (60-qt) and 123-liter (130-qt) ones. The motor speeds are regulated by three speed controls: off, low, and high. These are a lever type that has a flange that interlocks with the cover so that the power must be shut off before the lid can be raised (figure 21.2).

The hinged cover is made of polished cast aluminum, and it has a horizontally sliding viewing port in it. This may be opened to view the contents of the bowl or closed to prevent splash (figure 21.3). A hand cannot enter the port. The cover is locked in place against a gasket between the cover and bowl by a hinged bracket latch mounted on the bowl. This pulls up over a metal bar projecting from the cover. The flange on the speed control will not allow the cover to swing open with the power on even if the latch is unfastened.

The bowl is mounted in a tubular steel frame with two wheels for the small units or in a cast iron stationary base painted with gray enamel for the larger VCMs. The larger ones have a tilting pivot that is attached below the bowl in the top of the motor housing. There is a position lever attached to the pivot to hold the bowl in any desired position. A locking pin can be used to fasten the bowl in either the vertical or horizontal position. The exterior dimensions for the vertical cutter/mixer range from 51 cm (22.5 in.) wide, 74 cm (29.25 in.) deep, and 119 cm (46.75 in.) high for the 23.7-liter (25-qt) one, to 80 cm (31.5 in.) wide, 110 cm (43.3 in.) deep, and 176 cm (69.13 in.) high for the 123-liter (130-qt) size (figure 21.4).

There is a cast aluminum mixing baffle that throws material from the periphery of the bowl toward the center where it is drawn down into the

FIGURE 21.2. Vertical cutter mixer open and thus inoperative. Note heavy motor beneath and viewing port in cover.

FIGURE 21.3. New lower powered mixer with plastic see-through cover. Courtesy Hobart Corporation.

FIGURE 21.4. New table top vertical cutter mixer. Courtesy Berkel, Inc.

knives or mixing assembly. The mixing baffle is operated by hand from the top with a handle in the smaller mixers and by ½ HP to 1 HP motors in the larger models.

There is a variety of modifications and attachments that may be purchased. The basic cutting action is accomplished with beveled cutlery grade stainless steel knives attached to a removable sleeve that fits over the central cast aluminum drive shaft. There are narrow knives for cutting vegetables and broader, thicker blades for chopping up blocks of frozen meats. There are also narrow and wide wave cut knives. A hone comes with the VCM to sharpen the blades. There are slant ring adjustments on the bottom of the shaft to place the blades low for small batches and high for large batches. The sleeve is held on the shaft by a knurled nut or preferably a wing nut. The knurled nut requires an easily misplaced wrench to remove it at times, while the wing nut can be loosened with a tap by the heel of one's hand. A special sleeve has blades on pivots that rest close to the shaft when the motor starts giving little torque in a viscous dough, and then they wing out as speed increases to get full cutting-mixing action.

A mixing sleeve or shaft made of cast aluminum has dull canted blades that act as a motor boat propeller does to draw products down from the surface in a vortex to the bottom of the bowl and then up along the sides of the bowl to the top again. A stir-mix shaft is used for small quantities. A similar sleeve provides a grating action for cheeses and products of that nature by means of small rough serrations on the surfaces of the blades.

With the original schnellkutter came a speed-reducing assembly that fastened to the top of the drive shaft. To this were fastened wire whip assemblies, a slicing and shredding attachment exterior to the bowl, and a sieving attachment. In addition, it had an homogenizing baffle that, when used in conjunction with the narrow blades, could be used to process salad dressings and ice cream mixes and to reconstitute dry milk solids. Also available was an ice-crushing baffle for continuous ice-crushing operations, and, where necessary, a water jacket for the bowl, and a vacuum lid.

The present VCM has a perforated basket liner for the mixer bowl. It is held in place by the cutter assembly. On removal of the cutter assembly, all of the product in the bowl can be lifted out and drained at one time. It is used for chopped greens.

Determination of Needed Capacity

As with the vertical mixer, the capacity of the vertical cutter/mixer is rated by how much finished product it can hold. In addition, the vertical cutter/mixer must have sufficient space to operate on all contents in an even fashion for there may be an added media such as water in salad green cutting. The determination of these capacities along with processing time is a trial-and-error process that varies with the amount and piece sizes of the foods processed. As with the vertical mixer, one wants a VCM that produces enough product at a time for a cooking batch. To get the capacity required, the operator should consult table 21.1. The VCM that prepares the batch sizes needed should be the one selected. The data given is from manufacturers and is not research tested by an outside agency; however, the times in parentheses represent my research.

Basic Use and Operation

As occurs with most high-speed foodservice equipment, the personnel who operate the VCM have difficulty adjusting their thinking to the much shorter processing times over conventional processing equipment or hand processing. Other deterrents to its use are fear of the whirling knife and lack of knowledge of techniques to achieve maximum benefits from the device.

Before using the VCM in any way, the worker should be briefed on a few safety precautions:

1. Never raise the cover until the motor has stopped.
2. Never place the hands in the bowl for any purpose while the knives are in the bowl. Remove the knurled or winged nut from the shaft and lift out the knife assembly on its sleeve and place it in a safe location. Replace the nut on the drive shaft.
3. Never store anything in the VCM bowl except the knife assembly, and that should not be stored on the drive shaft.
4. Never poke any solid object into the bowl through the viewing or inspection port for any reason.
5. Have a wall mounted switch as well as that on the VCM and be sure that both are off before placing hands inside bowl.

TABLE 21.1. VCM Product Usage and Capacity Details

Product	Speed	Time* (sec)	Method	VCM 25 [kg (lb)]	VCM 40 [kg (lb)]	VCM 60 [kg (lb)]	VCM 80 [kg (lb)]
Bread crumbs	high or low	120 (90)	continuous	2.7 (6)	3.6(8)	7.7 (17)	10 (22)
Bread dough, medium	low	60–90 (120 heavy)	continuous	10.9 (24)	16.3 (36)	22.7 (50)	38.6 (85)
Cake batter	low	60–90 (240)	continuous	18.1 (40)	29.5 (65)	40.8 (90)	54.4 (120)
Cheese, chopped	low	10–15	continuous	6.8 (15)	9.1 (20)	18.1 (40)	22.7 (50)
Cookie dough	low	20–40	continuous or jogging	9.1 (20)	14.5 (32)	21.8 (48)	31.8 (70)
Dough, sweet Danish	low	50–60	continuous	10.9 (24)	16.3 (36)	22.7 (50)	32.7 (72)
Frostings	high	120	continuous	13.6 (30)	22.7 (50)	27.2 (60)	45.4 (100)
Hamburger	low	25 (35)	continuous or jogging	9.1 (20)	18.1 (40)	27.2 (60)	36.3 (80)
Liver paste	high	180	continuous	14.5 (32)	18.1 (40)	27.2 (60)	54.4 (120)
Meat loaf	low	50–60	continuous or jogging	11.3 (25)	13.6 (30)	22.7 (50)	31.8 (70)
Pie dough	low	12–20	jogging	9.1 (20)	13.6 (30)	18.1 (40)	27.2 (60)
Pizza dough	low	60	continuous	10.9 (24)	16.3 (36)	22.7 (50)	38.6 (85)
Potato, mashed, chopped	low	10	jogging	10 (22)	15.9 (35)	18.1 (40)	31.8 (70)
Potato salad	low	50–60	jogging	13.6 (30)	18.1 (40)	27.2 (60)	36.3 (80)
Salad dressing	low	120–180	jogging	5.7 l (6 qt)	8.5 l (10 qt)	47.3 l (50 qt)	79.5 l (84 qt)
Tossed salad lettuce heads	low	2 (3)	jogging	5–6 heads	8–10 heads	14 heads	24 heads

*In parentheses under time are times which I found to be different from those advocated by the manufacturer.
Source: Adapted from Hobart Corp. information.

A typical procedure might be that used for preparing lettuce for tossed salad in a VCM 40:

1. Check that both wall and machine switches are off.
2. Raise cover and remove turning handle and mixing baffle by unscrewing the retaining screw at the outside top of cover.
3. Place perforated basket down over drive shaft and be sure it is well seated before placing knife sleeve down over drive shaft. Fasten it in place with the knurled or wing nut.
4. Fill bowl one-half to two-thirds full of cold water. Ice cubes may be added to keep the lettuce crisp.
5. Remove cores and wrapper leaves and add eight to twelve heads of lettuce to water so that they float. Add other previously presliced and precut vegetables.
6. Close lid and pull locking bracket over bar projecting from lid.
7. Turn wall switch on. Turn machine switch on and then off several times (jogging method). Check degree of cut through viewing port or inspection cover after each jogging maneuver.
8. Turn off wall switch, unlatch cover, and raise it.
9. Remove locking nut and knife assembly.
10. Lift out basket of greens. Hold out of water for several minutes to drain, and then store greens for use. Water may be used for next batch.

There are two techniques for operating the vertical cutter/mixer. In the continuous method, the mixer is turned to low or high speed and operated until the prescribed time has elapsed. In the jogging method, the power is turned on and off while turning the scraping baffle and examining the product for proper particle size after each jog. This last method protects against the possibility of overcutting, one of the problems in using the machine.

Hints for Operation

1. When using the VCM for chopping large blocks of frozen food such as meat or eggs, use the wide knife assembly because the narrow knives may be broken and scar the bowl interior.
2. To get more product into the bowl and promote more even cutting, cut large pieces into smaller ones before placing them in the bowl.
3. When adding solid vegetables to salad green mixtures, preslice them.
4. Chill cheese to –2.2––1.1°C (28–30°F) before chopping it to avoid lumping.
5. When placing products of varying consistencies into the bowl, put liquids in first (do not exceed 80 percent of bowl capacity). Solid ingredients with shortenings should always be added last.
6. If mixing hot ingredients, the process may be facilitated by leaving the viewing port open to permit exit of steam. A towel may be used to prevent splash out of the port.
7. Lower blades when chopping small quantities.
8. When in doubt as to which assembly to use, try the narrow knife assembly.
9. When chopping meat, try to remove all gristle and bone before processing.
10. When cutting small amounts, distribute them evenly around the bottom of the bowl.
11. Keep cutting knives sharp by honing them with the stone that comes with the machine.
12. When using the VCM for a number of products, plan a sequence that will obviate the need for cleaning the bowl thoroughly between products. Thus, if salad greens are chopped first, the bowl may be wiped clean with a cloth to remove green particles, and then salad dressing could be made. This could be followed with cole slaw, sandwich filling, meat loaf and sausage.
13. Whipped potatoes may be made from instant potato mix by placing the proper amount of water at 82.2°C (180°F) in the bowl. Follow this with milk, seasonings, and margarine. Funnel potato mix into the viewing port. Operate at low speed for sixty seconds, shut off power, open cover, remove knife assembly, and empty bowl after scraping it down.

Special Applications

As all but the mixing action may be designated as special applications and these have been delineated, they will not be discussed here.

Alternatives to the Vertical Cutter Mixer

For the mixing action, one may use the regular mechanical vertical or horizontal mixers and air whippers, or do the job by hand using bowls or pots for containers and spoons, paddles, or whips for the stirring action. For small quantities, it may be possible to use small table top electric blenders or portable propeller mixers using electric motor power.

For cutting action, one may do the job by hand using a knife, hand grinder or cutter, or hand choppers. Mechanical and electrical equipment includes a multitude of vegetable cutters, choppers, grinders, and even meat tenderizers. While these are more precise than the VCM, they are much slower. In work done by the U.S. Navy, it was found that the VCM time as compared to conventional mechanical equipment in preparation was:

1. 9.1 kg (20 lb) sliced onions, one-quarter the time
2. 9.1 kg (20 lb) chopped celery, one-tenth the time
3. chopped lettuce heads, one-tenth the time
4. grated cheese, one one-hundredth the time
5. mixing cake, one-third the time
6. mixing mayonnaise, one-eighth the time
7. mixing bread, one-tenth the time.

Cleaning

Suggestions for cleaning the VCM are:

1. Clean the cover, gasket and bowl rim with warm water and mild detergent mixture using a soft cloth, rinsed in clean water, and then replace gasket.
2. Install the knife assembly and mixing baffle.
3. Fill the bowl two-thirds full with warm water plus a small amount of sudsing detergent.
4. After closing the lid and leaving the viewing port open, run the VCM at low speed and briefly at high speed while turning the mixing baffle counterclockwise. Turn off switch on machine and the one on the wall.
5. After being sure that the blades have stopped moving, raise the cover, remove the locking nut from the pivot, release locking handle and tilt bowl to pour the water into a drain or portable container. The bowl interior may be rinsed with a hose while in a tilted position.
6. Return bowl to vertical position, and if not previously rinsed, either rinse with added fresh water or remove cutting assembly, inspection cover, and mixing baffle and rinse bowl with a cloth wet with fresh clean water. Wash, rinse, and dry removed parts separately. Wash the exterior of the VCM with fresh hot water and wipe dry with a soft cloth.
7. One may replace knives and use their air movement to finish drying the bowl exterior. Remove knife assembly and leave in bowl but not on drive shaft. Always leave nut on the shaft. Replace the mixing baffle and inspection cover. Lower cover but leave inspection cover (viewing port) open to aid in continuing drying of bowl.

Maintenance

There is little to the maintenance of the VCM except to keep the various blades sharp and to provide the maintenance prescribed by the manufacturer. Some operators place several drops of vegetable oil around the mixing baffle pivot after each use. The machine is designed to require a minimum of maintenance.

QUESTIONS

1. Name five uses for the vertical cutter/mixer.
2. Why do older cooks have difficulty with the VCM?
3. What should be the economic consideration in the purchase of the VCM?
4. In what sizes does the VCM come?
5. What is the main safety caution one should exercise in the use of the VCM?

6. What is the basic functional assembly most used in the VCM?
7. What expedient is used to speed passage of lettuce heads through the cutter blades?
8. What is the main advantage of the VCM over other kitchen equipment?
9. What is the cleaning procedure for the VCM? What caution should be exercised in cleaning cover gasket?
10. What cutting assembly should be used to cut 2.27 kg- (5-lb) blocks of beef into hamburger?

BIBLIOGRAPHY

ANON. Undated. How to cut and mix with Hobart VCM. Hobart Corp., Troy, Oh.

LANEY, M.G. 1976. Vertical cutter/mixer (unpublished). Purdue University, West Lafayette, Ind.

LONGREE, K., and BLAKER, G.G. 1971. *Sanitary Techniques in Food Service.* John Wiley and Sons, New York.

SPEAR, A. 1966. *Laboratory Study of Cutter-Mixer Combination.* U.S. Naval Supply Research and Development Facility, Bayonne, N.J.

Food Waste Disposals and Trash Compactors

Food Waste Disposals

While food waste may be placed in cans, dumpsters, and bags and be carried off to a land fill, most kitchen operators would prefer to grind it and mix it with water until the sewer will carry it away—no mess, no fuss, and no smelly cans. However, it is not that simple. Some cities feel that they do not have the proper sewer lines or perhaps sewage disposal plants to handle food waste effluent. In some areas water is in short supply and not available in the quantities needed as a food waste vehicle. Thus, it is important to check with local authorities before considering a food waste disposal.

Most food waste disposals operate on the principle of the hammer mill in that the food waste is held on separated bars while whirling bars or a serrated disk strike at it. Feeding may be by gravity (dropping down upon the whirling hammer), a screw conveyor, or a flume of water. Water helps position the food waste disintegration, cleans out the grinder, and makes up a part of the effluent that carries away the ground food waste.

There are two main types of food waste disposals. One is the horizontal, down-swing hammer-mill type and the other is a vertical waste disposal with fixed tooth impeller, swinging hammer, and rotor shredder. The vertical unit is gaining most favor as it occupies the least floor space and can be mounted beneath a dish-scraping or vegetable-trimming table easily. It is less noisy, weighs and costs less, and requires less maintenance than the horizontal unit.

In the purchase of a food waste disposal, one must find one that will:

1. Handle the type of food waste produced—bones, vegetable trimmings, etc.
2. Grind it fine enough for the water and sewer to carry it.
3. Take the volume of food waste produced.
4. Not require excessive water, probably not more than 11 liters (3 gal) per minute.
5. Resist tendency to jam and, when it does, have a reduction procedure which is easy to carry out (usually the simplest expedient is to be able to reverse the rotor by changing the motor direction).
6. Not provide aerosols or spatter that may contaminate nearby foods or equipment.
7. Protect against the accidental introduction of flatware and if it does get into the grinder, handle it without damage to the grinder.
8. Safeguard the operator against getting his hands in the grinder or being hit by objects thrown out by the grinder.
9. Be easy to clean and simple to maintain.
10. Operate at low noise, vibration, and power levels.

Description and Specification

While it is impossible to describe in detail all of the food waste disposals, some of the desirable features and general design characteristics will be described.

Most of the disposals have vertical housings of iron alloys or steel covered with tough enamel over rust-resistant base coating. At least one has a stainless steel lining or facing in the grinding chamber. These housings are reinforced at the top, the area where the grinding action takes place, and at the base where the motor housing and three or four feet are attached. The interior of the housing, particularly where the rotor travels, has various combinations of bars, chopping lugs and cutter screens that act in concert with the swing hammers, bars, burrs, knives, and cutters on the rotors. These grind bones, chop, cut, and pulverize foods to the point that they will wash down between the outside edge of the rotor and the housing. From there they are whirled around the periphery of the housing and out the drain. Some have an eductor connection at the exit point which causes a drawing of air from the grinder interior, thus reducing the possibility of bacterially contaminated aerosols coming out into the room to contaminate clean dishes.

There are a variety of feed assemblies. The simplest one is a 14-gauge Type 302 stainless steel cone that guides the food directly down onto the rotor. It may have a rubber or neoprene scraping block leading into it, or a bowl-sink assembly may be used. Others have an oblong feed pan that slopes down into the grinder from the side. It is usually covered on top. In dishrooms where silverware may inadvertently be dropped into the feed pan or trough, the pan will slope down to a reservoir a short distance from the disposal and then slope up into the disposer. The low point is supposed to trap the flatware. Others use small traps of various design for the same purpose. To reduce spatter, some designs have strip curtains at the entrance to the disposal.

More complex scraping facilities use a trough leading into the grinder. Pump-driven water carries the food waste. In some cases, the water is recovered in large measure and recirculated. The water serves both to flush the dishes and carry the soil to the grinder. Another system uses a plume of water over the disposer cone to flush gross soil from dishes held under it and provide water for the grinder. A slide holds a rack of dishes over the disposal, where a hand-held spray faucet is used to remove the soil from the dishes.

Often the motor is set vertically on the base and has a waterproof housing. It drives the rotor through a direct connecting shaft. In accordance with the size of the disposal, the motors usually range in power from 1/3 to 10 horsepower. There are larger units for special purposes. The bearings may be roller or ball type.

The primary differences in food waste disposals involve design of the grinding rotors and the housing in the vicinity of the rotor. A few different designs will be discussed here.

One design uses four removable tool steel bars set into slotted grooves 90 degrees apart at right angles to the drive shaft. They whirl at a close tolerance distance from vertical cuts in the sizing (comminuting) ring on the housing. On the top surface of the rotor are deflectors that force the food waste to the outer edge of the rotor where it is ground between the whirling bars and the serrations in the sizing ring.

A second design uses two breaker lugs on the periphery of the rotor to crush large objects so that they may be ground between the rotor and serrated outer ring. It has curved vanes to direct the food waste into the grinding surface.

A third uses the principle of the burr mill and has two round conical disk plates, one of which is fixed. The opposing surfaces are fluted so that the food waste is ground as it travels down the disks while the space between them gradually decreases. As the food waste reaches the periphery, added teeth grind it between the rotor and housing ring. Lugs bolted to the top of the rotor execute the initial breakup of the food waste and distribution on the rotor.

A fourth uses two opposing replaceable steel knives on top as radii from the shaft to the edge of the rotor. In addition there are 64 3-mm (0.12-in.) cutting notches in the periphery of the rotor. The stator chamber has three adjustable knives set 120 degrees apart.

Finally, a fifth design uses a stainless steel grind table or rotor that has two integral rind ripper lugs to reduce large particle size and two swivel-mounted impellers that swing outward forcing the waste against the outer teethed ring (figure 22.1). A knifelike cutting disk at the periphery contributes to the grinding process. The stainless steel grind ring also has teeth with cutting edges.

Determination of Needed Capacity

It is difficult for the inexperienced person to calculate disposal size needed. He must use the tables furnished by the various manufacturers and the experiences of those who have had a well-known make of food waste disposal. The makeup and quantity of the food waste dictate the size of disposal that should be used. All other things being equal, it is better to err on the side of ordering one that is too large rather than getting one that is too small since the smaller units are more prone to jam. Table 22.1 gives one manufacturer's specifications for disposals with the indicated horsepower for the specified number of customers and uses.

The U.S. Navy tested disposals with a standard food waste made of 20 percent beef bones 1.2 x 3.8 x 3.8 cm (0.5 x 1.5 x 1.5 in.), 54 percent vegetables (spinach, carrots, beets, green beans, turnips, lettuce, celery, cabbage, and potatoes), 25 percent fruits (grapefruit and banana skins), and 1 percent paper napkins. Because the disposals were forced to take as much food waste as they could handle as times were taken, pounds per hour were obtained. Inability to grind bones was disqualifying. If an operation generated 408 kg (900 lb) of food waste per hour, it required a 3-HP unit from one of two manufacturers. It was found that, from the standpoint of capacity, freedom from jams, handling of bones and similar factors, the 3-HP unit was the minimum size that could be used. Units under this size could not handle the bones and jammed. The U.S. Navy also tested reactions to introductions of silverware and the production of aerosols. The models approved produced no aerosols and did not jam on flatware.

Basic Use and Operation

There is little advice to offer on the operation of a food waste disposal except to avoid using one for materials and capacities it cannot handle. No disposal with a motor under 3 HP seems to grind big bones consistently or compensate for introduced flatware. The operator must watch any

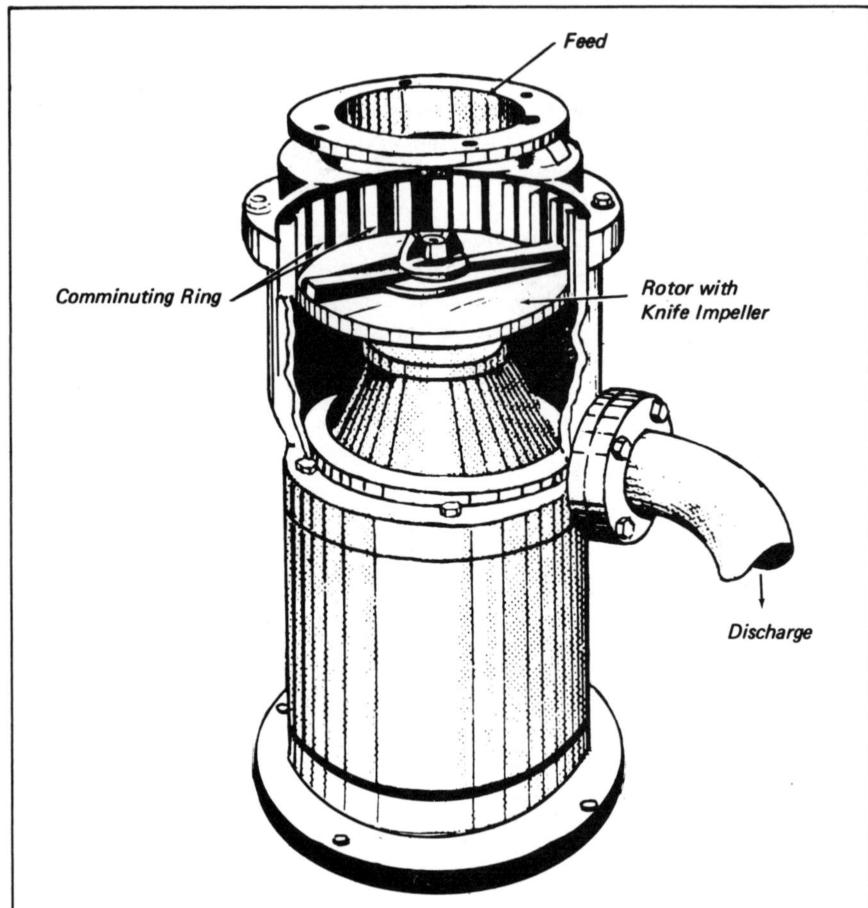

FIGURE 22.1. Impeller type garbage grinder that grinds garbage between impeller and serrated edge.

TABLE 22.1. One Manufacturer's Specifications for Disposals

	Persons per Meal		
Use	100–150	200–300	750–1500
Soiled dish table	1 HP	2 HP	5 HP
Vegetable preparation	3/4 HP	1-1/2 HP	3 HP
Salad preparation area	1/2 HP	3/4 HP	1-1/2 HP
Pot sink	1/2 HP	3/4 HP	1-1/2 HP
Meat preparation area	—	3 HP	5 HP

Source: Insinkerator Commercial Disposers, Insinkerator Division, Emerson Electric, Racine, Wisconsin.

disposal, and if he observes that the food waste bounces around without being consumed, the unit is being forced beyond its capacity. Sometimes it will slow down, jam, and stop if overloaded.

The amount of water is regulated to keep the rotor and grinder surfaces clean and transport the ground waste down the drain system. The U.S. Navy prescribed that this be no more than 3 gal per minute but some trough operations used outside the military use up to 60–70 gal of water movement per minute. As water becomes short in supply or more expensive, the reuse of trough operation water may become more important and should be considered in this type of operation.

One should avoid allowing materials that might not grind properly such as some papers, plastic films, foils, metals, string, cloth, rubber, and other similar materials. Also to be avoided are hard-shelled crabs, lobsters, oysters, and clams as well as greases that may solidify in pipes or disposal. Foams that ride on water surface may not grind.

Food materials and kitchen wastes that can be ground include: fruit rinds, skins, peels, pits and seeds, vegetable tops, peels, whole vegetables, spoiled foods, husks and similar parts, some paper napkins, sugar packets, straws, paper cups, milk cartons, small paper plates, soft-shelled crabs, shrimp, and other soft shells, chicken, pork, steak, fish, and other bones if not too large.

Alternatives to Food Waste Disposals

Most of the alternatives to food waste disposals are simply the methods and equipment used before they came into use. The basic substitute is the garbage can that may, or may not, provide fuel for a pig farm. This is dependent on state health regulations. If it is permitted and does go to a pig farm, such food waste must be completely edible. If it does not, it may be mixed with inedible food waste because it will wind up as landfill somewhere. It may be cut into small pieces so that it will use only one-quarter to one-fifth as much garbage can space as conventional garbage does in the can or it may be compacted so that it makes a dense package for reduction of storage and trucking space.

Cleaning

1. Before attempting to clean the disposal, the main electric switch to the disposal should be turned off to avoid inadvertent turning on of the device while the hands may be inside the housing.
2. The steel cone, tray, or flume into the disposal should be removed, if necessary, to get into the chamber on top of the rotary disk. Any string, paper, film, or other unground residue should be removed by hand. Avoid scraping hands on sharp bars.
3. Using a hose, wash down disposal interior with water as hot as can be obtained. If food residues remain on the rotor or disposal inner wall, they should be scrubbed with a stiff bristle gong brush at the same time as the surfaces are flushed with hot water.
4. All removal parts such as pans, guides, and cones should be taken to the potwashing sink, scrubbed in detergent and hot water, and rinsed and air dried. Then they may be reassembled back on the disposal.
5. The fixed surfaces that might have come in contact with food waste or liquids should be scrubbed down with a stiff bristled brush, hot water, and dishwasher detergent. The surfaces may then be rinsed with fresh hot water and wiped dry with a soft dry cloth. The surfaces that come in contact with food waste may, or may not, be treated with a bactericide and water before the rinse.

Maintenance

Most of the maintenance of the disposal is that recommended by the manufacturer of the particular make of disposal. Some manufacturers allow the adjustment of the bars on the rotor, others recommend that only a skilled repairworker do this as the disposal interior can be destroyed by improper adjustments to elements on the rotor. Some units provide for pulling (lifting out) the rotor in cases of stoppage; others do not.

Most units have some means of reducing jams. One of the simplest means is where the rotor can be removed. Others have a wrench that attaches to the top or bottom of the rotor shaft or a reversible motor so that it can be reversed, thus relieving most jams. If they cannot be released easily, the operator should use a professional repair service.

Some units have bearings that are permanently lubricated; in other cases they must be oiled or greased. The manual that comes with the disposal should tell what needs to be done along the maintenance line.

Trash Compactors

The trash and garbage cans have long been a cross to bear for the foodservice industry. The flock of garbage cans behind the average restaurant requires the care of at least one part-time worker in most cases. Simple incinerators solved most of the problem by burning that trash and garbage that could be coaxed into flame, but they added to air pollution and are outlawed in most communities today.

The garbage grinder came forth to handle most garbage, but city growth, outmoded sewers and overworked sewage treatment plants caused many cities to forbid their use. Shredders, pulpers, and crushers decreased the space occupied by plastic, paper, cans, and bottles in trash cans but each was but a partial solution to the problem of too much trash. The obvious solution was compaction.

The open trash truck gave way to the compactor truck that crushed several loads of trash into the space formerly occupied by one. Then restaurants began to have both garbage and trash chewed up and compacted into easily handled bags and boxes one-fourth to one-twentieth the volume formerly occupied by garbage and trash in cans. Most of these monsters at the restaurant back door are simple hydraulic machines that drive pistons sideways or down into loosely packed garbage or trash. The sides and bottom are restrained, and in the case of the side compressed units, the top is as well.

While the average restaurant generates about two cans of refuse each day, it is estimated that a compactor will reduce this volume of trash to one-half with a similar reduction in costs for handling. The compactor does reduce odors, pests, vermin, and fire hazards. Also, it reduces the need for trash sorting, trash storage space, and pilferage protection. It provides a degree of environmental control, time saving, improved economics, 24-hour operation and long life. Most compactors will reduce one week's trash collection to that usual for one day or a weekly $60 cost to $10. When one considers that the United States discards about two billion pounds of waste per day, this can amount to quite an amount of money saved. Whether one uses the garbage can or other means is merely a matter of economics and what is available. Usually a compactor is 59 percent cheaper than incinerating, 47 percent less than pulping, 26 percent less than shredding, and 100 percent less than cans of trash.

One must choose a trash compactor with considerable care as one that is too small will jam or function poorly, while one that is too large is costly and occupies too much space for the job that it performs.

Description and Specification

Compactors come in two general forms—the horizontal moves parallel to the earth's surface and the vertical unit moves a piston down to press garbage and trash into a smaller than usual space. Customarily, the first has the greatest capacity, uses the most floor area, and is least used in commercial or institutional foodservice. The latter uses a minimum of floor space and is usually automatic. They may be bought or leased. A compactor that will handle 26.8–68.8 cu m (35–90 cu yd) of trash per hour may cost $1500–$4000, while one that compacts 95.6–191 cu m (125–250 cu yd) of trash per hour may cost in excess of

$12,000 and weigh from 113–4536 kg (250–10,700 lb).

The vertical compactors range in height from 107 to 231 cm (42 to 91 in.), 51 to 5690 cm (20 to 224 in.) in width, and 48 to 351 cm (19 to 138 in.) in depth. Typically they use an hydraulic system where a trash bin may hold about 0.17 cu m (6 cu ft). The machine weighs about 374 kg (825 lb) and uses a 115 volt, 1 HP motor operating at 15–20 amperes. The ram with a piston diameter of 5.1 cm (2 in.) and a 15-cm (6-in.) plate or pusher operates through a distance of 68.6 cm (27 in.) at a pressure of 114 kg per sq cm (1650 psi) to provide a compaction ratio of 5 to 1 up to 20 to 1. Some have two pistons to handle an increased volume of waste. They may have sanitizer-deodorizers that spray about 0.5 liters (1 pt) a day.

The compactor may be made of 10-gauge steel panels in the compression changer and stainless steel or a decorator vinyl-coated steel on the exterior. Most operate through a compaction cycle of approximately thirty seconds and have safety interlocks that prevent the door being opened while the machine is being operated or the bag is not in place. This takes motors that in the usual machines range between 1/3 and 5 HP. Generally, they will compact down into bags or boxes .042–0.224 cu m (1.5–8 cu ft).

Determination of Needed Capacity

A typical restaurant generates two pounds of waste per person per meal. If all waste compacted equally, computations on compactor capacity would be easy. However, this is not the case as waste may range all the way from that which is largely paper, cardboard, and wooden boxes weighing perhaps 3.6–4.5 kg (8–10 lb) per 0.028 cu m (1 cu ft) to a Type 3 garbage, largely animal and vegetable waste where the same volume of waste may weigh 13.6–15.9 kg (30–35 lb).

Most sales personnel use rule of thumb to designate a size of unit for a given operation. This is usually based on past experience. For instance, a school cafeteria with 400 or fewer students may use a one-bag unit while one feeding 400–1400 students will use a two-bag unit, and one feeding 1400–4000 students requires two of these larger units. A medium-sized industrial cafeteria may use one two-bag unit.

Compactors are sometimes purchased on the basis of the space that is available for them. As an example, a single unit may occupy 0.56 sq m (6 sq ft) of floor space which means that if a restaurant requires two of these to handle its trash, it must have at least 1.12 sq m (12 sq ft) of floor space plus adequate aisle frontage before it can consider using them.

Another basis for purchase of compactors is the number of pounds of trash generated calculated against the rated waste capacity of the compactor in weight. This is rather risky as a given compactor will not handle equal weights of garbage of different densities and moisture contents. Waste that is largely paper will have but 10 percent moisture and will give a 10 to 1 and up to 15 to 1 compaction ratio. Waste that is made up of animal and vegetable material and has 70 percent moisture is lucky to get a 3 to 1 or 4 to 1 compaction ratio.

The surest way to determine the capacity of a compactor one needs in a particular operation is to test the machine of one's choice with the typical waste for which it will be used. Determine the time the unit takes to compact 100 pounds of this typical trash, taking into account the cycle of time to make the machine ready, process the trash, and remove it from the machine. From this data, compute the pounds of trash that can be handled per hour. Then the buyer has only to decide if this trash handling capacity is sufficient, too little, or too much. If compactor is under capacity, too much of a worker's time may be required, or some of the trash may have to be disposed of uncompacted. If the compactor is over capacity, the machine stands unproductively idle part of the time.

Use

As each manufacturer's compactor has its specific operating instructions, these will not be discussed here. It is well, though, to emphasize the need for safety. Most of the compactors do have door interlocks that shut off power to the unit when the door is open similar to the operation of microwave and forced convection ovens. Where these interlocks are not present, either the machine should be avoided or the users should be carefully selected and trained. Serious accidents can occur.

Alternatives to Compactors

Reduction of space occupied by waste is not a new phenomenon. For many years many operators have been taking steps to reduce the space occupied by their trash. Both ends have been taken out of tin cans and the walls flattened. Can cartons and other cartons have been unfolded, flattened, and baled. In many cases, the cartons have been reassembled and used.

Then there are other mechanical monsters that pulp paper and other organic wastes, press out the water, and place it in cans at just a fraction of its original volume.

The easiest way to treat the waste situation is not to have any at best or have much at worst. Some of the solutions include:

1. Buy prefabricated meats without bone or excess fat.
2. Use ready-cut salad greens.
3. Use no food items that the customer is not expected to eat.
4. Reduce portion size so nothing is left to become garbage.
5. Provide nothing other than what is on the menu unless the customer asks for it.
6. Plan uses for leftovers.
7. Buy vegetables in frozen, canned, or ready-to-cook state.
8. Feed garbage to pigs if health authorities allow and burn combustibles if permitted.
9. Reduce size of napkin and replace boxes with bags.
10. Shorten sipping straws.
11. Eliminate disposables.

QUESTIONS

1. What is the garbage grinder or disposal?
2. Where is the food waste disposal located?
3. What moves the food waste through the disposal? Where does the ground residue go?
4. In general, how is the garbage grinding done?
5. What horsepower range is obtainable in disposals?
6. How is the food waste disposal cleaned?
7. What materials may not be ground?
8. What are the ten requirements that a food waste disposal should fill?
9. What are the alternatives to using a food waste disposal?
10. How does one tell when the disposal is overloaded?
11. Why are trash compactors desirable in foodservice?
12. How much refuse does the average restaurant generate?
13. What feature prevents injury while compactor is operating?
14. Why is it difficult to compute needed compactor capacity?
15. Name five measures that can be taken to reduce compactor requirements.

BIBLIOGRAPHY

ANON. 1975. Food waste disposal systems by Gruendler. Gruendler Crusher and Pulverizer Co., St. Louis, Mo.

ANON. 1971. Now the Trend is to Waste Compactors. *Food Service Magazine 33,* No. 4, 57–61. April, 1976.

COMBS, W.H. and CRAIG, S.N. 1965. Waste Disposal Methods. *Modern Sanitation and Building Maintenance* 17, No. 9.

DEBAUN, W.H. 1969. The food waste disposer is not a trash machine. The Salvajor Co., Kansas City, Mo.

GIAMPIETRO, F. and GARR, J. 1976. Compactors Cut the Waste out of Garbage and Refuse Handling. *Restaurant Business* 75, No. 2, 76–78, February, 1976.

MAYER, M.L. RYBERG, M.E., and SEIDENBERG, I. 1960. *A Comparison of the Functional Characteristics of Vertical-type Garbage Grinders for Navy Use.* U.S. Naval Supply Research and Development Facility, Bayonne, N.J.

Miscellaneous Small Mechanical Equipment

From the days when Martha Washington used a clock mechanism to turn the roasting spit in the fireplace, cooks have sought to find mechanized equipment that would lighten the work load of food preparation and cooking. With the growing shortage of skilled foodservice personnel, machines that can do many of the tasks that only experienced cooks could do become increasingly important. Some of those pieces of mechanical equipment that will be discussed here, but to a lesser degree than those to which complete chapters were devoted, include: meat tenderizer, food slicer, vegetable cutter, food grinder, food shaper, vegetable peeler, and meat saw.

Mechanical Meat Tenderizer

The mechanical meat tenderizer is an underused and undersold piece of equipment (figure 23.1). Most salespeople sell it solely on the basis of its ability to cut and tenderize the tough fibers in a flat piece of meat which would not be used as a dry heat steak meat normally. They do indicate that it has a knitting action which pulls the chopped fibers together so that the piece of meat will not fall apart if picked up by one corner.

It would seem that the foodservice operators who use them would be pressured by the seemingly limited application of the tenderizer to do some

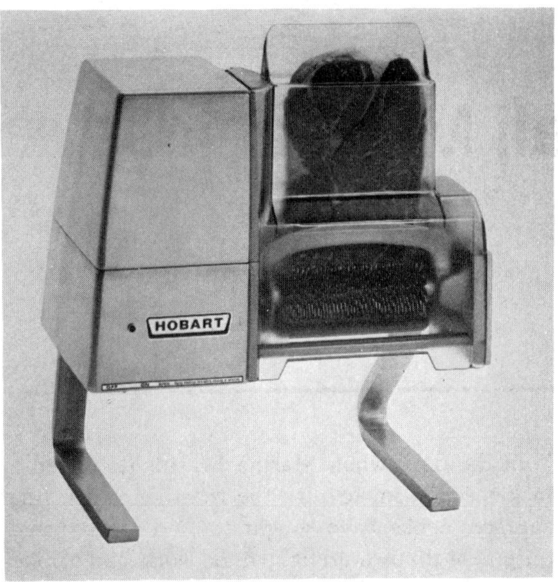

FIGURE 23.1. Mechanical meat tenderizer showing meat going through serrated knives. Courtesy Hobart Corporation.

research for other applications. However, this does not appear to be the case. If the potential buyer is perturbed by the probable limited use of the equipment, he does not buy it. This means that the rather inexpensive piece of equipment does not get an opportunity to do the many things that it does well—tenderize and knit together tough meat, make steak-size pieces of meat from stew beef, blend various types of meat (pork and veal) into new meats, incorporate cheese, onions, garlic, and other agents into the steak, produce poultry steaks from small pieces of turkey and chicken meat which increases the number of portions per bird, chop coarse and fine slaws, and cut hashed-brown and French fried potatoes.

Design

There are many designs for the tenderizer, but in the main, the device is composed of two motor-driven intermeshing rows of round disk knives (figure 23.2). Usually they are set up in combinations of solid disks and serrated disks. The outer edges of the serrated blades cut the tough fibers, and the indentations between the short blades pull the chopped fibers and knit them together. The heavy stainless steel blades separated by stainless steel spacers on a stainless steel shaft may be cutting, cutter-knitter, or knitter blades. The blades vary some in size. Tenderizing and knitting blades may be 5.9 cm (2.3 in.) while scoring blades are 5.2 cm (2.06 in.) and frozen meat scoring blades 4.8 cm (1.9 in.). Each shaft is set in a cast aluminum lift-out frame where the shaft can turn in bronze bearings. A lift-out handle goes over each set of blades, and a set of stainless steel cleaning combs directs the meat into the blades and keeps residue from accumulating between the knives. The two shafts fit together and can be lifted out as a unit.

The knife assembly fits into a cast aluminum housing where it is locked in place. The housing includes a 1/2-HP motor totally enclosed and powered by 115 volts, 60 cycle, and single phase. The units may be purchased for other voltages. The unit is geared down to a workable speed. Over the cutting assembly is a plastic guard, sometimes made of Lexan, that provides a chute to guide the meat between two sets of blades and then out of the machine. The chute is shaped and raised high enough so that fingers cannot get down or up into the blades. If the shield or guard is moved, the motor shuts off. Some machines have a pilot light which indicates when the power is turned on to the device, although raising the guard has made it

FIGURE 23.2. Knife assemblies for various meat tenderizers.

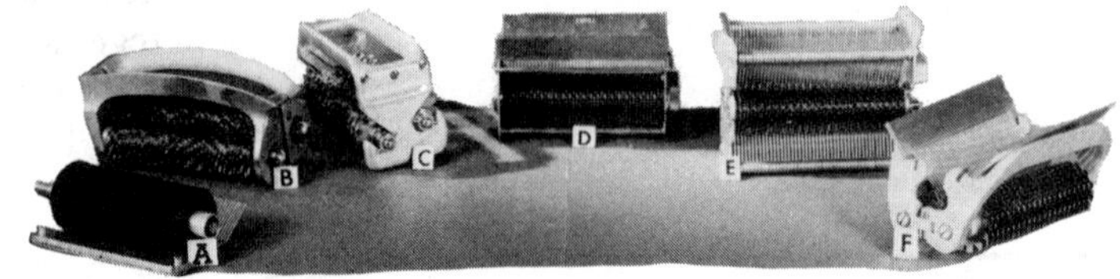

inoperable. Stainless steel bars or feet provide the base.

Dimensions of the tenderizers vary considerably. The one described is approximately 50 cm wide x 27 cm deep x 48 cm high (19.5 x 10.5 x 19 in.) and weighs 26 kg (57 lb).

Usually the tenderizer will handle pieces of meat as large as the size of the feeding opening or throat which in the described unit is 3.5 x 21 cm (1.38 x 8.25 in.). Capacity varies according to the size and complexity of the product being tenderized or fabricated and the dexterity of the operator.

FIGURE 23.3. Tenderized steaks that can be made from various odd-sized pieces of meat.

Use

In general, a piece of meat of the weight that will constitute a portion and of dimensions that will slide down the feeding chute easily is loaded into the feeding opening (figure 23.3). The machine makes cuts on both sides of the meat, and the meat is flattened and extended in area. Turning the resultant piece of meat 90 degrees and running it through the tenderizer again further tenderizes it. Steaks thus tenderized should griddle cook in about half the time of regular steaks of comparable weight and thickness.

If steaks are to be made of small pieces of meat, they are run through the machine individually, stacked together to make the proper weight of steak, turned 90 degrees and passed through the tenderizer to knit the pieces together, flatten them into steak shape, and tenderize the meat (figure 23.4).

To blend two or more kinds of meat, a relatively thin slice of each is passed through the tenderizer. Then they are stacked together, turned 90 degrees and passed through the unit again.

To add other ingredients, two or more relatively thin slices of meat are passed through the tenderizer individually. The onions, cheese, garlic, parsley, fat pieces, bacon, sausage meat, or other ingredients are placed between the two tenderized meat strips which are then turned 90 degrees and passed through the tenderizer again. These are prone to falling apart and must be handled with care until cooked, particularly if too much of ingredients other than meat are used.

Cabbage or lettuce heads to be chopped coarse or fine and potatoes must be sliced to a size that will fit into the loading chute. Usually one tries to place the leaves of the greens so that they will come into contact with the knives at right angles to the lines of the leaves.

When making the poultry into steaks, the larger pieces of white meat are best cut into steak-size pieces of meat by hand. The white meat scraps and the dark meat can be treated the same as stew beef. I monitored a research project where the operator was able to bone out a 5.6 kg (12.25-lb)

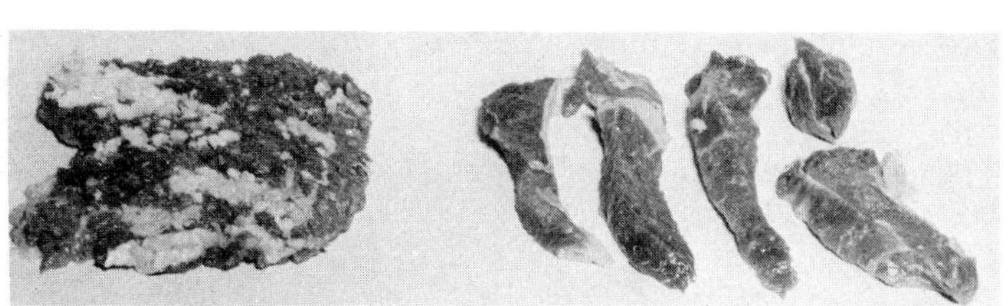

FIGURE 23.4. Tenderized steak that can be knit from a number of small pieces of meat.

turkey to 2.9 kg (6.4 lb) of boneless, skinless meat from which he knitted 24 113-gm (4-oz) turkey cutlets. These were all cooked in fifteen minutes as compared to hours for a whole turkey.

Alternatives to Tenderizing Equipment

Most professional cooks tenderize meat by pounding it with a serrated-surfaced mallet, the back of a cleaver, or the cutting edge of a knife. While in the Philippines, I observed the natives tenderizing carabao (water buffalo) by pounding it with a rock or the edge of a heavy native knife. Sometimes they would pound papaya leaves into the meat to tenderize it. In California, the abalone slices were observed being tenderized by hoisting a rock with block and tackle and then letting it drop on the abalone slice, thus mashing the tough fibers.

Many of the cut-rate roast beef and steak houses are using a soaking or sprinkling of chemical meat tenderizers, many of which are papaya based, to digest partially and thus tenderize their low grade (often standard grade) meats. At least one packer injects a tenderizing agent into the blood stream of an animal immediately before slaughter so that it is well distributed into all tissues. Some packers inject tenderizer into the meat they sell.

There are other types of tenderizers. One is a strictly cube steak machine cross-cutting squares into one side of the steak about 0.6–1.3 cm (0.25–0.5 in.) apart and the same depth into the meat. The steak is turned 90 degrees and cut again, giving the meat a cubed appearance on one side. Another device used in processing plants forces sharp blades down into steaks and roasts, thus cutting fibers and tenderizing it.

Cleaning

While meat tenderizers made by different manufacturers might have minor differences, the cleaning procedure, in general, is:

1. Be sure to turn machine switch to off and disconnect the outlet plug.
2. Raise and remove cover. In some makes a knob or latch needs to be unfastened. Wash it inside and out in warm water and detergent and sterilize in hot water.
3. Remove knife assembly and frame by sliding or lifting it out of the housing.
4. Unlatch locking plate and remove blade assembly and then the two stripper plates. All should be washed in a pan of hot water and detergent using a gong brush. Clean each part separately. Do not allow them to be together or to bump together in the pan. Rinse thoroughly in hot water.
5. Wash the housing and supports with a cloth dampened in the warm water and detergent mixture and rinse with cloth dampened in clean hot water.
6. Assemble tenderizer in reverse order to disassembly. Be sure all locking pins and latches are securely fastened.

Food Slicer

Almost all meat eaten as steaks, roasts, or chops has been sliced across its long muscle fibers to shorten them as is done in the meat tenderizer. This makes the meat more tender. Even with the use of the chemical tenderizers, the fast food roast beef sandwich houses would be out of business if they could not serve a relatively tender product made that way by slicing it thin crosswise to its grain.

The primary purpose of the slicing machine is the cutting of slices of consistent thickness whether it be of roast beef or tomatoes. This happens as the product to be cut is pressed against the knife-sharp edge of a whirling disk. The thickness of the slice is regulated by the distance that the food projects beyond the disk when presented at a right angle to its edge. This distance can be adjusted usually from paper thickness up to 1.9 cm (0.75 in.) (figure 23.5).

FIGURE 23.5. Mechanical meat slicer showing knob that adjusts gauge plate to proper slice thickness. Courtesy Berkel, Inc.

Design

Slicers come in a wide variety of sizes and additional equipment. Although slicers may be hand-powered or electric motor-driven, only the latter is important to large scale feeding. A typical unit will be described along with some of the variations.

The cutting element is a round carbon steel or cast stainless steel blade about 25 cm (10 in.) to 45 cm (17.75 in.) in diameter that may be hollow ground or bevel ground, or the whole disk may be concave. The diameter of the blade regulates the crosscut of the product. Power is transmitted from a ¼- to 5-HP motor of various possible voltages to the blade by a special gear that meshes with an aluminum-bronze worm wheel so that the knife moves at 285–360 RPM. All bearings should be permanently lubricated. Most of the slicers have attached knife sharpeners that make it easy for the unskilled worker to keep the blade in sharp condition. There is usually an additional motor to move the carrier back and forth when the feed is mechanical. Small models are moved by hand.

The thickness of the slice is controlled by a regulator or gauge plate that can be adjusted to give slices from paper thinness up to 3.2–3.8 cm (1.25–1.5 in.) thick, although 1.9 cm (0.75 in.) is usually maximum. The carriage holding the food can be mounted to present the food to the tilted blade at an angle of 45 degrees to the table top so that gravity can assist the feeding process and the slices will fall flat, or the feeding can be parallel to the table top where the machine does all the moving of the product and a mechanism picks up and stacks the slice as it falls. In most cases, the feeding trough has a right-angle top surface. The trough should be able to handle meat 19 cm (7.5 in.) in diameter and 30 cm (12 in.) wide (figure 23.6). To protect fingers while the product is pushed toward the blade, most machines have a pusher or feed grip with a spike, barred, or corrugated face to hold the product while the hand operates safely behind the pusher plate. The feeding trough operating on a slide may be hand or machine operated to move the food toward the

FIGURE 23.6. Meat slicer showing pusher or feed grip on top.

blade and, after the slice is complete, back to start another slice.

In most cases, manufacturers try to have food contact surfaces of stainless steel and all other surfaces of anodized aluminum or some type of easy-to-clean thermoplastic or enamel. They want to comply with the National Sanitation Foundation standards.

As accessories, there are square and round vegetable hoppers that hold small and large food pieces as they are sliced (figure 23.7). Similar are the multiple feeding slides that offer several lines of food to be fed at one time. Some units have a spike-type holding device that clamps and holds even the small piece of food rigidly as slices are cut from it. There are some machines that recover the slice as it leaves the blade and stack it with or without sheets of paper. Some include a heavy plunger to push those foods that rebound from the blade. One has an infrared lamp for keeping meat hot during slicing. Most units have some type of blade cleaner.

For controls, most machines have on-off switches and slide- or knob-actuated product thickness controls. Several have two or more speeds, and at least one has a light showing when the power is on to the machine. Several have variable speed controls for the sliding food table that can be regulated to give from one slice per minute to at least fifty-five per minute.

Use

The slicer is primarily considered as a device for cutting meat slices of consistent thickness. As an entrée, these may run from 0.3 cm (0.125 in.) to 2.5 cm (1 in.) or more in thickness, but for beef houses that serve roast beef sandwiches made from low-grade meat, the meat is sliced paper-thin. Where used for these two purposes, the slicer is usually table-top-mounted close to where the entrée or sandwich plates are assembled. If used for other purposes, the foods must be brought to where the slicer is located. This reduces utilization (figure 23.8).

Where maximum use of equipment is the rule, the slicer is recognized for the many tasks it can perform. Rather than move food about, the slicer is mounted on a cart with locking wheels so that it can be moved easily to wherever it can be used—salad preparation, cheese and cold cuts slicing, vegetable preparation, and similar tasks. The cart should be of a height where the loading area is at, or slightly below, elbow height. The various attachments should be placed on a shelf below the slicer. An electrical receptacle of proper voltage and wattage should be planned for each point of projected use.

The food moves down in the chute or trough and slides along the gauge plate table as it is slid back and forth by hand or motor. It is sliced by the

FIGURE 23.7. Two electric meat slicers with right-angle feeding troughs. Note round vegetable hopper beside machine on right.

FIGURE 23.8. Meat slicer in use for slicing ham. Note many other products that can be sliced. Courtesy Hobart Corporation.

spinning knife blade to which it is presented at right angle. The closer the gauge plate surface is to the same plane as the knife, the thinner the slice; the farther it is from the plane of the knife, the thicker the slice, although it is still parallel to it. This is regulated by an adjustment knob. Meat is always presented to the blade so that it will cut at right angle to the meat grain, thus crosscutting the meat fibers and tenderizing the meat. To prepare for the next slice, the carriage carrying the chute is pulled back until the food clears the knife edge and slides down against the table or gauge plate, thus measuring the next slice. Then the carriage moves forward again to make the next slice.

On the smaller slicers, a hand pusher applies pressure against the top of the product to hold it firmly during slicing and move the unsliced food down against the gauge plate to prepare for the next slice. Never should the worker's hand push directly on the small food pieces as he may miscalculate and get too close to the knife or his hand may slip off the product into the path of the knife.

When cutting some type of a constant size product such as a ham or chicken roll, the slice should be weighed as soon as the size of slice is evenly regulated to make sure that the desired portion weight and yield per pound is being achieved.

When vegetables are being sliced, they should be placed in the chutes or holders so that the proper shape and crosscut of slice will be attained. This is important particularly with such products as tomatoes, cucumbers, squash, or eggplant. Sometimes sticks of carrots are desired, and putting them through the slicer twice in a lengthwise position may be desirable. Cubes for stews and vegetable dishes may require three cutting operations. While the slicer may be used for many products, the relative efficiency of doing the task with the slicer as compared to hand cutting or using another type of cutter must be determined by actual tests.

Slicing of roasts of meat is a well-known application for the slicer, and its use for tomatoes, carrots, cucumbers, squash, and eggplant have been mentioned. Less well known is the use of the slicer for cabbage and lettuce cuts, slicing lobster tails, slicing vegetables for cream style dishes, cutting French or Italian breads, slicing onions, cutting corn from the cob, slicing parsnips, turnips, and rutabagas, cutting cooked poultry for various a la king and casserole dishes, cutting cooked and raw potatoes for numerous purposes, slicing oranges and lemons, and many others. The slicer cannot be used for all cutting operations, but with some ingenuity, it can be used for many more than it is today.

Cleaning and Maintenance

The cleaning procedure for the slicer varies somewhat according to the product that has been sliced. A beef tallow is much harder to remove than lettuce juice. However, in the main, the following procedure will suffice:

1. Be sure the electric plug is removed from the receptacle.
2. Remove those parts that are easily detached to the pot sink. They are usually the trough or chute, pusher and receiving pan, but may include drip pan, slice deflector, and knife guards. These should be washed in hot water and detergent and rinsed in hot water. They should be air dried.
3. The knife should be washed with a cloth dipped in hot water and detergent. Be careful to rub toward the edge rather than from the edge to avoid cuts. The blade may be rinsed with a cloth and clean hot water and allowed to air dry. Some manufacturers advocate that the blade be cleaned while in motion but I do not approve of this.
4. The remaining part of the motor, gear housing, and stand should be washed and rinsed in the same manner as the blade. Some slicers have a prop or stand so that one side of the slicer may be supported in a raised position to ease cleaning beneath it.
5. After the basic slicer is dry, the parts which were washed in the pot sink may be retrieved and reassembled so that the slicer is ready when needed.

It is desirable that the slicer be capable of being disassembled without use of tools since tools tend to be misplaced.

For the most part, maintenance is not a problem with the slicer. With sealed oil bearings, little must be oiled except possibly the chute slicer and the pusher slide. After every washing, two or three drops of light oil on the slides will suffice. Some operators oil the surfaces of the blade with vegetable oil.

The major maintenance problem is keeping the knife sharp. Most slicers have a permanently mounted knife-sharpening assembly that, when used according to instructions, keeps the knife in razor-sharp condition. In some cases, this is a one-step procedure and in others, two. Most machines require that a shop sharpen the blade at infrequent intervals.

Food Molding Machines

A food molding machine is a device for forming a semisolid food material into a standard, constant sized portion that is easy to handle and cook. In most cases, the device substitutes for hand forming. The food material, whether it be a meat mixture such as hamburger or a vegetable-fish mixture such as a fishcake, is usually placed in a hopper where it is forced down into a mold. The mold is then extricated from the hopper usually by sliding from beneath it. The molded product is then punched from the mold onto a belt, into a pan, or onto the surface of a sheet of paper. Then the mold retreats to the base of the hopper for reloading. In any case, it must be decided whether the device will save enough labor to pay for itself or if consistency in portion size or weight is important enough to warrant use of a food molding machine. The low degree of compression from food molding machines is desired by some foodservice operators, since it gives a lighter product and more portions.

Design

Each food molding or shaping machine has different design characteristics, and describing all of them would be of little educational value. Only one will be discussed in any detail with occasional mention of others.

In most cases, the food-holding hopper is made of stainless steel in capacities from 11.3 kg (25 lb) to 90.7 kg (200 lb). Propellers of similar metal force the food mixture toward the base and into a depression in a circular 4–15-hole aluminum plate or turntable that moves under the hopper. As the circular plate moves from under the hopper, a nickel-silver piston pushes the patty up out of the depression, and it is scraped off onto a paper or some receptacle. Another type of unit forces the patty down into a slide. All food contact surfaces should be of stainless steel if not otherwise indicated.

The weight of the patty is regulated by the depth of the piston in the circular plate, 0.5–1.9 cm (0.2–0.75 in.), and the diameter of the patty as established in the top of the turntable. The latter can produce patties in diameters of 6.4–12.7 cm (2.5–5 in.) and, in conjunction with the patty depth, allows patties in weights from 28–354 gm (1–12.5 oz). Meatballs can be made in diameters of 1.9–5.1 cm (0.75–2 in.) and weights of 7–57 gm (0.25–2 oz). Capacity may be as high as 3600 patties per hour in one machine and 10,000 patties or 43,200 meatballs per hour in another. Some units use a diverter to remove the patties; others, a revolving spatula.

Several models use neoprene plastic belts to remove the patties from the machine; others, a wire bar belt. Some place paper between the patties, and in other cases this must be done by hand, if at all. Release of sticky products is eased by use of a crumb box that coats the inside of the mold with crumbs before the mold fills. The most common motor sizes run from ¼ HP to 1 ¼ HP. Most machines have patty counters.

Some units score the patties with cross depressions or knife cuts, and one pierces the patty with needles. Several manufacturers have interchangeable mold plates that allow any desired shape of patties to be fabricated—chopettes, ovals, fish cakes, chicken legs, squares, and sausages. Another manufacturer has one that fastens onto the meat grinder head, and as the meat is extruded, a roll of paper comes out under the meat and the squares or oblong meat patty and paper are cut off together.

Use

Most often the method of using the food molding or shaping device is specific to each manufacturer's equipment. In general, the food hopper is filled with food before the equipment is turned on, and care is taken to keep the food level at least half full in the hopper so that the patties will be well formed and consistent in density. The patty thickness indicator is checked. If the unit is multi-speed, the indicator is set to a speed where the worker can keep the hopper loaded, check and take away the finished patties, and keep the paper roll or patty-divider sheets loaded into the machine. Usually the worker will throw the first few patties back into the hopper, as they may be malformed. Before starting production, he should also weigh several patties to ensure that they meet specifications. If they do not, he should make the necessary adjustments to the piston of the machine.

If malformed patties start to come out of the shaper, the operator should turn it off until he finds the source of the trouble. Often the trouble will be found to be a low level in the hopper, but it may be that the food has changed in consistency or that some part of the machine has worked loose or become blocked. Another cause may be that the food may have bridged; that is, the paddles have not been able to force it into the mold.

Alternative to the Food Molder

The food shaper-molder is an expensive piece of labor-saving equipment, and one should calculate whether the advantages of having it outweigh its cost of procurement and operation. If the molder is not a good buy, then one must buy prefabricated items, use one of a variety of hand molding devices or do it entirely by hand. The three techniques most frequently used are:

1. Form patty in a ball and then compress it to patty thickness between the hands or on the table.
2. Portion meat with an ice cream scoop (#20), and place it between two layers of waxed paper. Press to flatness with the bottom of a can or glass.
3. Roll meat out on a sheet pan or table until it is the desired thickness. Wax paper may be used between the rolling pin and the meat. The meat may be cut into squares using a knife or cut in circles as biscuits are by using a #2 or #2 ½ can or a cookie cutter.

Cleaning and Maintenance

Depending on the particular manufacturer and model of machine, the usual procedure in cleaning the food molder is:

1. Be sure the machine is disconnected from the electrical outlet.
2. Remove all food material from the hopper. This may be done by running the machine until it is empty or removing the propeller and paddles and scraping out the residue.
3. Remove all detachable parts and take them to the pot sink for washing in hot water and detergent. Then rinse them in hot water and air dry. Some hoppers may be detached, but others may have to be tilted to clean on the machine.
4. Using a pan of hot water with detergent and a gong brush or cloth, thoroughly clean all food contact surfaces. Rinse with clean hot water. With protein mixtures where sanitation and bacterial populations are a problem, a chemical sanitizer may be necessary. Allow to air dry.
5. Wipe off all other external surfaces with a moist cloth and rinse and wipe dry with a cloth.
6. Reassemble machine and cover until next use.

Maintenance procedures are specific to the particular machine, and generalizations cannot be made. This information should be obtained from the manufacturer, placed in a waterproof cover, and placed by the machine for quick reference by the operator. Things that should be included are daily, weekly, and monthly maintenance, necessary adjustments and checks, lubrication, and trouble-shooting procedures.

Food Cutters or Choppers

To make tough food materials edible and make the preparation of food mixtures feasible, cooks have slaved for long hours over wooden cutting surfaces with knives cutting and chopping food into small pieces. Thus, one of the earlier items of kitchen labor-saving equipment that was developed was the food grinder. It consisted of a small hopper into which food was dropped or forced until picked up by a turning screw in a confined space and forced through a grid of sharp-edged holes and extruded looking like a bundle of spaghetti. Most early models were hand operated.

Today there is a wide variety of cutting and chopping devices. Some were developed for the food manufacturing industry and adapted, mainly in size, to foodservice. The units are usually variations of the old food grinder. A popular variation utilizes the power take-off of the upright food mixer. When the device is needed away from the vicinity of the mixer, a table top power unit similar to the head of the mixer is used. It can be used to power other equipment as well.

Another device commonly known as the bowl chopper uses a slow turning bowl designed in a round trough shape to carry relatively small pieces of food through fast-spinning knives that chop it ever smaller into a paste (figure 23.9).

There are a number of devices that use back and forth slides or whirling disks on the surface of

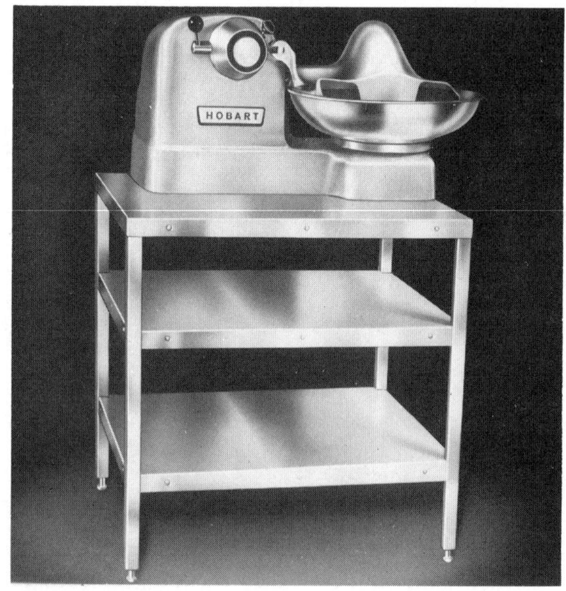

FIGURE 23.9. Bowl type food chopper. Courtesy Hobart Corporation.

which are various configurations of knives (figure 23.10). When food is pressed against these from hoppers or chutes, it is sliced, chopped, cubed, or waffled. They come in sizes that range from small hand-driven table models that might also be used in the home to large floor-based units that are commonly used in central commissaries or manufacturing plants.

Construction

The electrically driven grinders or choppers can use either gears or chains to drive the tinned steel worm operating in a tinned steel housing. The motor and drive housing may be plastic, anodized aluminum, or stainless steel. The tray that holds the food to be ground may be of tinned or stainless steel. The tinned steel adjusting ring holds the perforated plate that usually has 0.3 cm (0.125 in.) holes through it, although 0.48 cm (0.19 in.) and 0.6 cm (0.25 in.) holes are available in some machines. Between the driving screw (worm) and the plate is a four-bladed knife that is driven by the worm. It scrapes against the inner surface of the plate, cutting tissue and fibrous material forced into the plate holes so that they can be ejected to the outside. At least one manufacturer has an additional knife in front of the plate-scraping knife, which chops the meat before it is forced into the plate.

A wooden, plastic, or aluminum stomper is used to force food from the holding tray down into the grinder to where the screw, or worm, can seize and force it against the plate. Generally, the horsepower of a unit to chop a given amount of product is:

Motor Horsepower	*Food Chopped per Minute*	
	kg	*(lb)*
1/4	1.8–2.3	(4–5)
1/2	5.4–6.4	(12–14)
3/4	6.4–9.1	(14–20)
1 1/2	10.9–11.3	(24–25)
3	16.8	(37)
5	27.2	(60)

The bowl chopper is driven by a 1 HP motor and may have a 46–cm (18-in.) diameter stainless steel bowl. Within the bowl is a two- or three-knife assembly. This assembly is covered by an anodized cover interlocked with the electric switch so that it cannot be opened while the knives are in motion (figure 23.11). Some of these choppers have power-drive hubs similar to those on the upright mixer so

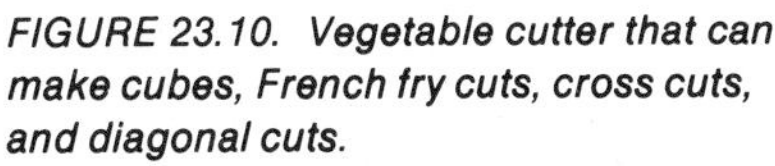

FIGURE 23.10. Vegetable cutter that can make cubes, French fry cuts, cross cuts, and diagonal cuts.

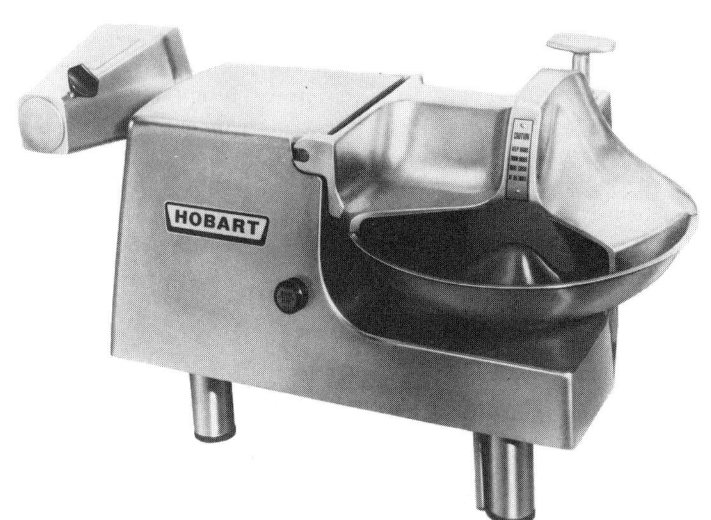

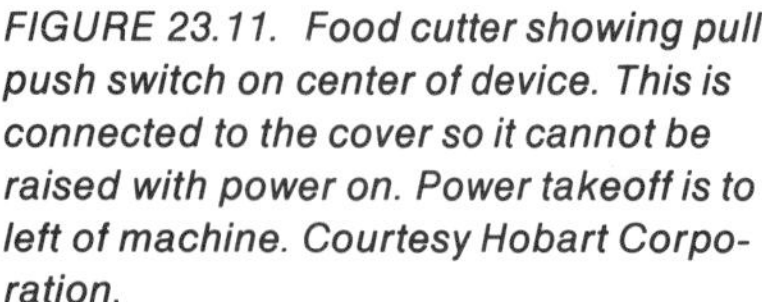

FIGURE 23.11. Food cutter showing pull-push switch on center of device. This is connected to the cover so it cannot be raised with power on. Power takeoff is to left of machine. Courtesy Hobart Corporation.

that various power-driven attachments may be used as well.

Another device used primarily for cutting vegetables and fruits uses two vertical feed chutes while the knives move horizontally back and forth at right angles to the direction of the feed. One of the chutes may cut strips 1.1 cm (0.44 in.) square while the other cuts strips 0.48 cm (0.19 in.) square. Metal plungers may be used to force the food down into the blades. I recommend a tray to hold the food to be cut. The same unit has a circular blade-holding disk powered by the same motor with two chutes, one of which presents the food at right angles to the vertically spinning knife and the other unit presents the food at approximately 45 degrees or on the bias to the knife disk. Both have metal or plastic plungers to force the food against the blades. Thickness of slices may be varied between 0.038 cm (0.015 in.) and 1.0 cm (0.38 in.). Also available are grater plates, shredder plates of various thicknesses, chunk lettuce cutters, onion and celery chop-dicers, potato dicers, and trimmer knives for sizing vegetables. The unit is powered by a 1/3 HP motor and has a cast aluminum housing and stainless steel blades. If the cover is raised exposing the blades, a safety switch cuts off the power.

Use

As each device has its own directions for use and none are complex, they will not be discussed here. Most of the units require some coarse precutting of the product so they may be placed into the device for precise cutting. Some foods must be presented to the blades in a certain way to get the desired typical cut, but in most cases the instruction is simple and the worker can learn it in a few minutes.

Cleaning and Maintenance

Most of the food cutters and choppers are simple to clean. Most of them require only a simple rinsing between the various batches of foods processed in them. Exceptions to this are the grinders and choppers used with meats and dairy products or for making pastes. They should be cleaned between batches. The other equipment should be cleaned at the end of the day in this manner:

1. Before cleaning the meat grinder, I recommend passing bread crusts (heels) through the machine. It helps in the later cleaning process. The chopped bread should be discarded.
2. Be sure that the switch is at off and the cord plug removed from the receptacle.

3. Remove all parts that are easily detached such as the grinder ring, grinder plate, knives, feed screw, plungers, holding pans, housings and such to the potwashing area. Do not place knives, knife holding disks, or grinder plates in the sink but place on the drain board and wash while held in the hand in detergent and hot water. Rinse while held in the hand in hot water and place on drain board out of harm's way to dry. The plates may need use of an ice pick or small brush to clean the holes.
4. Other removable parts may be placed in the pot sink, scrubbed in detergent and hot water, and placed in a wire basket as washed. The basket of parts may then be dipped into hot water for a few minutes and placed on the drain board to air dry.
5. The fixed in-place part of each device should be wiped clean of gross soil and then washed with hot water and detergent by use of a gong brush or cloth and then rinsed with water as hot as possible. The device should be left open for a few minutes to air dry and then the exterior parts should be wiped dry with a soft cloth.
6. It may be desirable to lubricate the interior of the grinder screw housing and screw lightly with vegetable oil before placing it back together with the knives, cutting plate, and retaining ring. The unit may be left disassembled until use as the selection of cutting plate may change, but I prefer to assemble the unit to protect the loose parts from loss, damage, and contamination.

Vegetable Peelers

One of the undesirable features of foodservice that lingers in many people's minds is that of removing the skin from vegetables so that they may be cut and cooked in some way. Many former military men can remember only the long hours spent on KP (kitchen police) peeling potatoes. The job is not as onerous as it once was because of the mechanical peeler. Prepeeled and precut and, in some cases, preblanched and prefried potatoes may be purchased in the major cities, and canned, dehydrated, and frozen vegetables are available.

While potatoes may be peeled by heat treating them to melt the pectic layer beneath the skin so that the skin may be sloughed away, most potatoes are abrasion peeled. In abrasion peeling, the raw potatoes are dumped into a cylinder that is coated on the inside with sharp-edged grit. In the bottom of the peeler is a wavy, abrasive covered disk that is motor driven to whirl the vegetables and strike them against the peel-removing grit. To clean the grit and remove the peel, water flows over the peeler interior and the vegetables. Usually some hand trimming is necessary to remove peel from potato indentations and cut out eyes and blemishes.

Design

Most vegetable peelers used in foodservice are of the vertical cylinder type (figure 23.12). A few central commissaries, university systems, and foodservice chains use lye peeling or horizontal abrasion peelers. The potatoes move down over inclined, rotating, fine-grit coated rollers as the peel is worn away. The degree of peel removal is regulated by the degree of incline. Both methods require some hand trimming after the peeling operation.

The vertical peelers vary some in design between manufacturers and designed load. These peelers are sized according to the pounds of potatoes they can handle per batch. A given manufacturer may have a line of peelers 6.8-kg (15-lb), 13.6-kg (30-lb) and 22.7-kg (50-lb) capacity driven by motors of 1/3, 1/2, and 3/4 HP, respectively. One 22.7-kg (50-lb) model, for example, has a stainless steel cylinder with vertical rubber ribs to bump the vegetables toward the center. Rather than the usual power-driven iron disk imbedded with carborundum to abrade away the peel, this manufacturer uses a carborundum-imbedded lightweight plastic.

FIGURE 23.12. Mechanical potato peeler. Note timer on side, vegetable discharge on top left side, and peel trap beneath. Courtesy Hobart Corporation.

A few peelers still use carborundum imbedded not only in the rotating disk but also in the walls of the peeler. In research performed under my direction, it was evident that a medium-coarse grit to remove a minimum of potato and an undulating disk to agitate the potatoes are the essential design requirements for a good potato peeler. Too coarse a grit removes too much potato at a strike, and too little agitation of the potatoes increases the likelihood of those potatoes on the bottom of the peeler being overly abraded on their bottom sides while the remainder of the potatoes remain unpeeled.

Most peelers have a cover of plastic, aluminum, or stainless steel. To catch the peel residue before it finds its way to the sewer, most peelers have a peel trap that slides under the peeler drain. The peel, washed from the potatoes by a spray of water injected over the potatoes as they abrade, is caught in the trap and removed by hand. A trap door may be raised to discharge the peeled potatoes into a tub or onto a trimming table. While most potatoes are peeled by guessed times or observation of the potato condition, one can get a synchronous timer that can be set in fifteen-second increments for up to four minutes. This is recommended, since the skilled cook can determine the proper peeler load and peeling time for a particular truck load of potatoes and then turn the job over to an unskilled worker, who will weigh or measure the peeler loads and use the times established by the cook.

Operation

The principles involved in abrasion peeling of potatoes are as follows:

1. The potatoes must move with considerable velocity so that when they strike the imbedded carborundum, a thin chip of peel and potato are gouged from the potato. With the newer machines, the velocity obtained in the potato is not as important as the velocity with which the potato is struck by carborundum imbedded in the whirling disk.
2. Excessive abrasion on one side of the potato must be avoided. This is done by good agitation of the potatoes in the peeling chamber. Part of this is accomplished by the undulation of the abrasive disk and part by the rubber baffles around the chamber interior.
3. The interior of the peeler must be flushed with water to remove the loosened peel from the potatoes and clean the small pieces of potato from the carborundum.

4. The shape of the potato, the age of the potato, and depth of eyes are important, along with consistency in size. The best peeling potatoes are fresh, of a consistent size and shape (almost round), and have shallow eyes.
5. Peeling time, as affected by peel thickness and peel eye depth, is a matter of judgment. The tendency is to over-machine peel, to reduce hand trimming.

I advocate removal of 85 percent of the peel by machine and the remainder by hand trim. With new potatoes, this may mean a peel time of one minute, but old thick-skinned potatoes may require up to three minutes of machine peeling. Any time over this should be viewed with suspicion because it usually means that excessive peel and potato are being removed to reduce trimming action.

Cleaning and Maintenance

The steps in cleaning any mechanical potato peeler are:

1. Flush peeler thoroughly with cold water immediately after use. Usually this is done with a forceful jet of cold water from a hose in order to clean the potato from behind the chips of carborundum. It is considered easier to remove with cold water rather than hot, which cooks the material behind the carborundum.
2. Stop the machine and remove the top along with the abrasive disk. Every interior part is reflushed and scrubbed with a gong brush and warm water. The disk is scrubbed in the sink. It should not come in contact with metal as the carborundum may be broken or worn off.
3. Remove the peel trap and flush and scrub it before replacing it.
4. Take all removable parts to the pot sink, wash in hot water and detergent, rinse in fresh water, and replace.
5. Wash the exterior of the machine in water and detergent, rinse in fresh water, and wipe dry with a soft cloth.

As for maintenance, use that prescribed for the particular machine. Mainly, it involves lubrication of the main bearing and replacing the carborundum at the factory when it is worn.

Meat Saw

While known as a meat saw, this machine has many more uses than sawing meat. Primarily, these are in the frozen food area. Blocks of frozen food lend themselves to portioning and dividing on the saw. Steaks may be crosscut from a frozen fish, chops cut from a pork loin, ham steaks from a ham roll, and portions cut from a block of frozen vegetables.

Many foodservice operations have no meat saw because of the general availability and reasonable cost of prefabricated meats. In studies done when with the U.S. Navy, I found that prefabricated meats and poultry were cheaper than those that we could fabricate. Add to this the high cost and shortage of commercial butchers, space, and equipping costs of butcher shops and utilities and the case is overwhelmingly on the side of the prefabricated items.

Design

If one can see enough benefit from a meat saw to pay for the many costs of owning it, there are a number of good machines available to fill the need (figure 23.13). Historically, a fixed floor-mounted device had a cutting platform at table height for ease of sliding heavy pieces of meat from scales or support tables. Today, table top portable saws are available that can be stored beneath the table when not in use.

Typically, a power driven meat saw has an enclosed base approximately 56 cm (22 in.) wide and 46 cm (18 in.) deep, and with 15 cm (6 in.) adjustable legs, total height is 178 cm (70 in.) and table height is 89 cm (35 in.) from the floor. Including the overhangs and carriage travel a floor

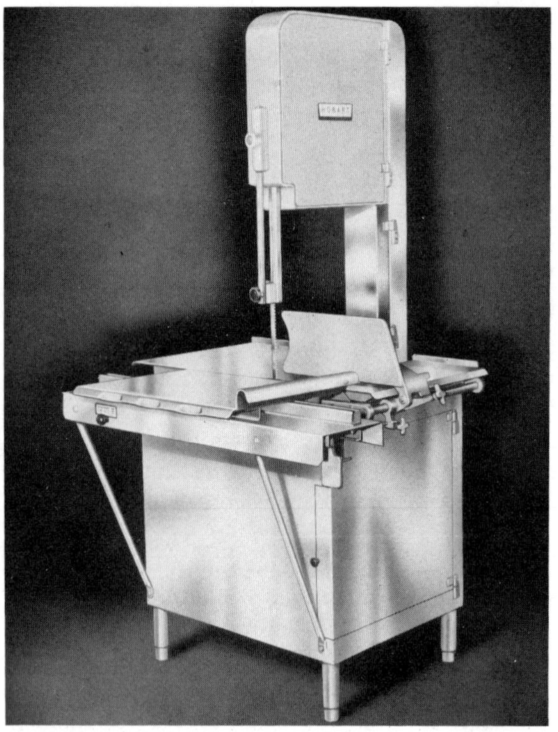

FIGURE 23.13. Electric meat saw with overhead unit that houses one pulley. Note the gauge plate beneath it and the food carrying table to the left. Courtesy Hobart Corporation.

area at least 109 cm (43 in.) wide and 86 cm (34 in.) deep must be allowed. The continuous steel belt saw blade 1.6 cm (0.63 in.) wide and 284 cm (112 in.) long rides on two large cast iron pulleys, one above the cutting table and one beneath. A saw of the size being described may have a standard drive from a 2 HP motor, or if desired to operate at twice the speed, it may be powered by a 3-HP motor. The push-pull control is on the front of the machine. The motor is beneath the table top.

The blade tension is sensed accurately and the results made available to the operator on an eye-level indicator. A nearby handwheel operates under positive tension so that the operator can adjust the saw tension according to need. Both the upper and lower pulleys have easy-to-remove cleaners and blade guides. It is important that they can be removed without tools because of the ease of losing tools.

The cutting table itself is heavily reinforced stainless steel and should be large enough to permit some stacking of meat slices, steaks, and chops. In the typical saw being described, this surface is 46 x 91 cm (18 x 36 in.), and overhead and side clearance permits the cutting of a piece of food 43 cm (17 in.) high and 33 cm (13 in.) or more wide. Behind the blade is a gauge plate 17 x 38 cm (6.75 x 15 in.) of epoxy–sealed cast aluminum that can be adjusted by a vernier to a precise product thickness. The food to be cut is loaded on a 41-x-53-cm (16-x-21-in.) ball-bearing-carried table at a right angle to the blade edge. It moves precisely in a track. All moving parts should be enclosed to prevent accidents. A pusher plate should be provided to move the food up against the track for the next slice and to avoid having the fingers in the proximity of the blade. While food-contact surfaces should be of stainless steel or anodized aluminum, the other surfaces of housings may be of baked-on epoxy enamel or similar protective coating.

Use

The major use of the meat saw is for cutting steaks or chops from large or primal bony or frozen cuts of meat. With fish, this is quite simple. The dressed, scaled, and trimmed fish is placed crosswise on the moving table against the raised forward support so that it is at right angles to the guide surface and so that, as it moves against the saw blade teeth, a crosscut slice is formed. The guide is adjusted according to the slice thickness desired. After a slice is cut, the sliding table is returned to a position so that the fish is clear of the blade. Then the fish is pushed up against the guide again, thus measuring another steak. The table, in sliding the fish against the saw blade, cuts another slice and pushes the first slice away from the blade. Not until then should the first steak be touched. It can be removed and stacked or be allowed to fall off the edge of the table into a pan. As the end of the fish approaches the saw blade, a pusher should be used to move it forward against the guide. A clamp should be used to hold it tightly during the sawing.

Meats may be cut in similar fashion, but remember that the saw is cutting the muscle fibers short and across muscle grain, thus making the meat as tender as possible. It takes a skilled operator to know how the muscles are running in a shoulder to cut it to best advantage. Poultry is somewhat dangerous and difficult to cut due to its odd shape and the difficulty in using the various guides, clamps, and pushers. Many operators cut poultry without the use of the guides. This is where accidents happen.

Cleaning and Maintenance

Both cleaning and maintenance of meat saws are dependent on the design of the particular saw, but for cleaning, in general, the steps are:

1. Be sure power to the machine is shut off.
2. Remove sliding table, gauge, and pan. Wash, rinse, and dry them at the pot sinks.
3. Loosen the blade tension, remove the blade guard and coil the blade. Remove the scrapers, blade wheels, rollers and guides to the pot sink for scrubbing in hot water and detergent with a stiff brush. Rinse in hot water until they are hot and remove them to a wire rack to air dry. Be careful in cleaning the blade to avoid striking the teeth on metal as this dulls the saw. Care must be taken to avoid scratching the worker.
4. Clean the rest of the machine that might be subject to juices and solids of food using hot water and detergent. Use brush and cloths. Rinse in hot water and wipe dry.
5. Reassemble in reverse order to disassembly.

QUESTIONS

1. What is the operating principle of the mechanical meat tenderizer?
2. What are the various functions that can be performed by the mechanical meat tenderizer?
3. Of what material are the blades and holding assembly made?
4. What safety feature is important in the design of the chute leading into the knives?
5. How does one make steak-size pieces of meat out of bits and pieces?
6. How is the meat tenderizer cleaned?
7. How is the thickness of the meat slice regulated in the food slicer? What variations may be obtained in slice thickness?
8. Of what material is the slicer disk made?
9. How does one get the food in front of the knife edge without endangering the fingers?
10. How does the meat slicer provide tenderized meat?
11. On what is the food slicer usually located? Why?
12. What attachment is used to slice tomatoes?
13. What is the operating principle for most food molding machines?
14. What regulates the thickness of the patty? the size of the patty?
15. How are the patties removed from the food molder?
16. How does one make patties without a mechanical maker?
17. What is the device one uses for making an avocado paste? How does it operate?
18. How is the meat grinder cleaned?
19. What is the principle on which the mechanical potato peeler operates?
20. What keeps the abrasion peeler grit effective in removing peel?
21. What are the design characteristics of a peeler that avoids overremoval of potato peel and potato?
22. How is the mechanical vegetable peeler used to provide consistent effective peel removal?
23. What is the design of the meat saw? How is slice thickness regulated?

24. What is the alternative to the meat saw in a steak house?

25. How is the meat saw used? How is it cleaned?

BIBLIOGRAPHY

ANON. 1951. *A Comparative Evaluation of Various Mechanical Meat Tenderizers.* U.S. Naval Supply Research and Development Facility, Bayonne, N.J.

ANON. 1964. *Federal Specification, Meat Slicer, Hand Operated and Meat Slicing Machines, Electric.* U.S. Government Printing Office, Washington, D.C.

ANON. 1965. Auxiliary kitchen corps. *Institutions Magazine* 56, No. 9, 105–114.

ANON. *Masterpiece Tenderizers,* Service Manual Model 704 and 704A. Berkel, Inc., La Porte, Ind.

GIAMPIETRO, F.N. *Is Your Kitchen Obsolete?* Berkel, Inc., La Porte, Ind.

KOTSCHEVAR, L.H. and TERRELL, M.E. 1977, *Food Service Planning: Layout and Equipment.* 2d ed. John Wiley and Sons, New York.

LONGREE, K., and BLAKER, G.G. 1971. *Sanitary Techniques in Food Service.* John Wiley and Sons, New York.

PROCTOR, B.E., and NICKERSON, J.T.R. 1956. *Investigation of Optimum Methods and Equipment for Efficient Potato Peeling for Shipboard Use.* Department of Food Technology, Massachusetts Institute of Technology, Cambridge, Mass.

TERRELL, M.E. 1971. *Professional Food Preparation.* John Wiley and Sons, New York.

Materials Handling in Foodservice

In most industrial development, one of the prime considerations is the assembly of a materials handling system. This system involves the movement of materials and products from the time they are received as raw materials until they are packed and shipped as finished products. In foodservice, materials handling has seldom been considered as an integral part of the design of the overall system as the weight of the material moved is far less per worker than in most other manufacturing operations.

In foodservice, the emphasis should be on a system that will make the worker travel less as materials move through the foodservice establishment. At present the foodservice worker turns out only $12,000 to $15,000 of salable product per year while one in food manufacturing turns out $40,000 worth. Some increased productivity can result by study of the worker's planning and movement. More can be done by mechanizing and automating production and service equipment, and most can result from decreasing the worker's wasteful movement of materials (figure 24.1). Materials handling uses more labor than any other aspect of most manufacturing, and foodservice is not different in its use of labor for this purpose.

In foodservice, materials handling does not add value to the food products, but it does provide time and place utility to them. It seeks to eliminate the need for itself but, failing this, it aims to make every human involvement as minimal and as pro-

FIGURE 24.1. Sheet pans of desserts being moved on multislide transport. Courtesy Crescent Metal Products.

ductive as possible between Receiving, Service, and Sanitation areas. This chapter will discuss those elements of the highly developed industrial materials handling philosophy as it has been modified to emphasize the human rather than the materials movement. Much of the equipment is similar and is used for the same purpose as in other industrial manufacturing, but its application is to save labor, particularly as pertains to worker travel.

Principles

All material movements and storages should be minimized. In foodservice the following examples, among others, may be used to demonstrate this action:

Use a multishelved cart in one well-planned trip through the kitchen to gather and hold all ingredients and utensils needed for a recipe in the work center (figure 24.2). Use enclosed hot and cold carts or open racks that will wheel into hot or cold cabinets to carry large quantities of ready-to-serve foods from Preparation, Cooking, or Storage areas to the Service area. Use busing carts instead of hands or trays for clearing tables and taking

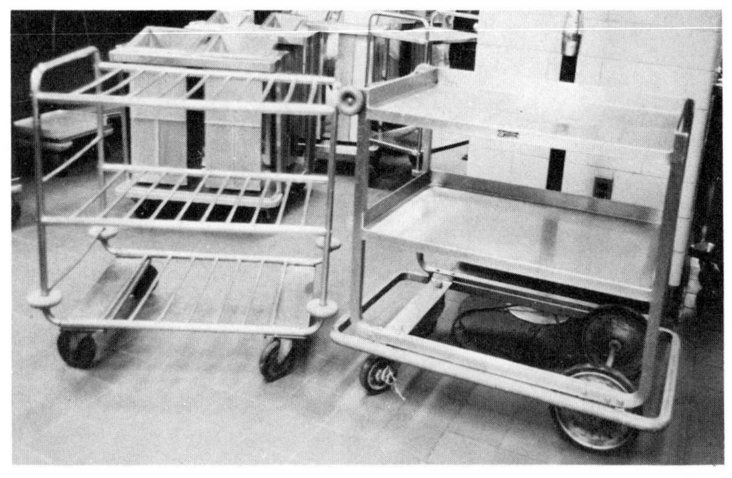

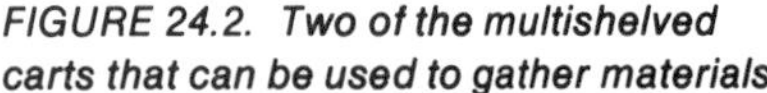

FIGURE 24.2. Two of the multishelved carts that can be used to gather materials.

soiled ware to the dishroom. Carry clean ware from dishroom in quantity by use of wheeled self-leveling dispensers and other types of dish carts. Have potwasher collect soiled pans and utensils at the various work centers periodically and return the clean ware during the next collection by use of a wheeled rack. This will greatly reduce the walking that higher-paid cooks need to do.

Plan the kitchen layout so that the work centers and pieces of equipment that operate successively on most foods most frequently are adjacent, or in the same vertical plane, and are arranged in the order of their most frequent interuse while progressing toward service. This includes placement of tables beside deep fat fryers, griddles, ranges, steam jacketed kettles, fry pans, and mechanical equipment. Have tables close in front of ovens, broilers, reach-in refrigerators, steamers, and other front-opening equipment. Where this is not possible, bring up portable tables close to the height of the equipment; this will minimize steps. Plan assembly of salad, entrée, sandwich, and dessert plates so that everything to be done on the plate is completed before moving on to the next one.

Materials should not be moved more than several steps by hand by the worker unless absolutely necessary. (See figure 24.3.) If adequate preplanning is not done, many kitchen and service workers will "make work" by moving foods and dishes in small quantities and by hand when the work load is light. Thus, when the kitchen worker is rushed or the waitress cannot keep up with service demand, the habit of doing things by hand and in small quantities dominates the actions. Busing and serving carts help alleviate this situation. Food pumps, perforated liners, or suspended baskets quickly empty steam jacketed kettles, and bulk battering and breading of fried products will speed this process. Conveyors, carts, and pallets to move supplies from Receiving to Storage, use of carts to move clean dishes to the service area, and use of carts to move foods from Storage to Preparation to Storage to Cooking and to Service are examples of ways to eliminate moving materials by hand.

FIGURE 24.3. Heated banquet cart being used to move entrées and cart on left loaded with dessert items. Courtesy Crescent Metal Products Inc.

Materials that must be put down should be prepositioned to eliminate the need for rehandling. Positioning food for its next movement or operation is often forgotten, or at least not planned. Mechanically peeled potatoes being trimmed should be dropped into the steamer pan in which they will be cooked or into a stockpot on wheels so that they can be wheeled into storage without individual rehandling. Some cooks drop them into fry baskets placed on scales.

Materials and utensils should be stored close to the point of first use. (See figure 24.4.) Food materials which do not deteriorate rapidly and which will be used in a short time should come from Receiving to the point of first use. This requires some planning to build storage facilities at the first use point but, where feasible, it usually obviates the need for a round trip into the storeroom. Some thoughtful managers have the product weighed or measured into batch lots at Receiving and transport it on a rack or supermarket-type basket cart to the point of use. Root vegetables, squashes, melons, apples, pears, pineapple, avocados, plums, and other similar foods lend themselves to this handling. Canned and other dry packaged foods can be brought from Receiving to point of first use in a similar manner.

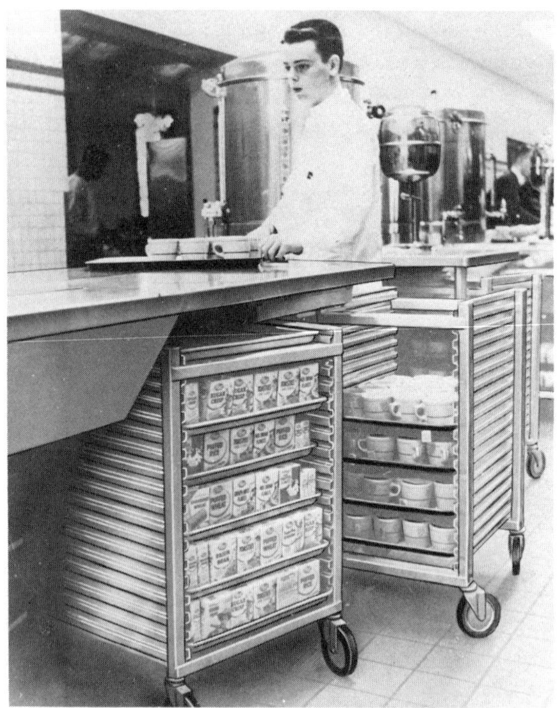

FIGURE 24.4. Cereals and cups stored close to point of first use. Courtesy Crescent Metal Products Inc.

Foodservice often neglects to plan work centers so that pots, pans, and hand utensils are no more than a step away from the point of their first use. Centralizing storage of these items in Potwashing or an area close by to save the potwasher steps is fuzzy thinking. Costs go up when the higher-salaried chefs and cooks must take steps to get their tools and, similarly, to take them to the potwasher when they are soiled. The potwasher should be equipped to collect soiled ware and return it to the point of first use when it is clean.

Movement of materials should be over the shortest and straightest routes. Facility planning has the greatest effect on this factor. Fast food and some chain restaurants have gone to great lengths to make food movement distances between Storage and Service as short as possible. This expedient has helped to reduce overall as-served food costs by lowered labor costs. All refrigerator, preparation, cooking, and service equipment is grouped around the one or two cook-servers. Grouping equipment and tasks around the workers would help larger facilities as well. Short lines of preparation and cooking equipment at right angles to service and frequent walk-throughs are necessary for longer lines of equipment because they help reduce having to walk around long lines of equipment.

Mechanical aids should be used when men must lift more than 22.7 kg (50 lb) and women 11.3 kg (25 lb). (See figure 24.5.) Two- and four-wheeled trucks, pallets, and pallet trucks, conveyors, and

FIGURE 24.5. Heavy-duty pallet trucks for carrying multicase pallet loads.

hand and electrically operated lifts help with this. Where large drums are used, special hand trucks and cradles for tilting are available. Placing heavy loads on table tops adjacent to equipment where they will be used permits sliding or rolling loads heavier than those noted above and provides a base for dumping them into something such as a fry pan or kettle.

Use gravity to aid the flow of materials. Institutions, central commissaries, and a few other large kitchens use gravity to move materials on slides and wheeled, roller, or braked belt conveyors and similar equipment from a truck body to the receiving platform and at times from ground level to basement storage. Of greater importance is the use of drop deliveries.

It is standard in foodservice, while working at a table, to reach up over the rim and down into a pan or pot to grasp a piece of food on which to work and then reverse the procedure to remove the food to the table top or cutting board. After operating on the food, it is raised up again and dropped over the edge of a nearby pan. It is much better to tilt the pan holding the food material on its side so it is spilled adjacent and close to the cutting board. This obviates having to reach up and over into the supply pan. After the food has been worked on, it should be slid over the edge of the table to drop into a pot just below the table's edge (drop delivery). Gravity has been used twice: first, to supply the material; second, to deliver it.

The optimum use of gravity was observed in a state institution where potatoes flowed by gravity from a dump truck at ground level into a bin near the basement ceiling. A trap door in the base of the bin allowed a calculated amount of potatoes to flow into a mechanical potato peeler. The peeled potatoes spilled onto a counter where they were hand trimmed and dropped into a tray leading into a mechanical slicer that cut them into French fries. They fell from the slicer into a pot partially full of water that was placed on a wheeled pot dolly. This eased moving it to the cooking area. At the cooking area, a wire basket insert lifted the entire load of potatoes to a drainboard for draining.

Use conveyors when food or materials must be moved over a fixed path repeatedly. (See figure 24.6.) Conveyors of various types have been used to good advantage in large feeding operations to remove trays of soiled dishes from dining rooms to dishrooms (figure 24.7). In most cases, the customers have done the busing, so no employees are used until the dishes have reached the dishroom. Some restaurants use the top of a conveyor belt to move prepared food from the kitchen to the service area and the top of the returning part of the belt to take soiled dishes to the kitchen area. Hospitals and some central commissaries that prepare individual school lunches use the conveyor to provide an assembly line where the workers stand still and the conveyor brings the tray or compartmented dish past them for addition of the food items. One system uses a flume of water to bring a prepared food item to the serving station on a raft or high-sided container. Another system uses a conveyor to take soiled dishes from various busing stations in racks to the dishroom, through the dishwasher, and then back to the busing station where a magnetic code on the rack actuates the system to

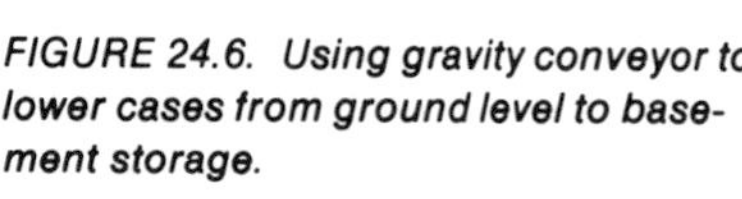

FIGURE 24.6. *Using gravity conveyor to lower cases from ground level to basement storage.*

FIGURE 24.7. *Using conveyor to move soiled dishes over fixed route to basement dishroom.*

kick the rack off the conveyor. Several systems have round counters moving horizontally or continuous conveyors to move food items past the customer until he fills his tray. At one point, the conveyor goes through the kitchen, where it is restocked.

Movement of the food material through the foodservice facility should be in one direction. Where food moves back and forth and from side to side, usually workers must move it, and multidirectional movement adds to the distance food must move. It also adds to the labor cost, to say nothing about the probability of food quality deterioration and possibilities of accidents. This is why kitchen designers strive to arrange work centers along a hypothetical food flow line in the order in which the food is operated on as it proceeds from Receiving to Service, thus eliminating back and forth movement within well-planned work centers. The designer arranges equipment in the order that it is most often used in each particular work center to reduce back and forth movement of food and skipping of equipment.

One of the problems has been that the refrigerator, which is used to hold foods until the next operation can be performed on it, is often used for initial storage. Thus, if used, it is a considerable step backward along the food flow line. To avert this, some kitchens have pass-through refrigerators and landing or short-term storage tables that are

FIGURE 24.8. *Tote boxes that stack easily when full and nest when empty.*

placed between work centers along the food flow line. This prevents the need for backtracking.

Design pots, pans, and storage containers for ease of movement by workers or materials handling equipment. The various food handling containers should be designed to make them easy and safe to handle by the workers and should permit trouble-free stacking in storage or during movement (figure 24.8). The containers should be of a size and shape that allow the worker to apply maximum strength with minimum danger to himself. Handles are placed above the center of gravity and should be of a proper diameter and no wider than the space between the elbows. They are set away from the container so that they will not shut off blood circulation to the fingers or press them painfully against the side. They should be far enough from the floor so that a straight back and leg muscles can do the lifting. Flanged or inset covers, brackets, or bases are designed to permit stacking of the containers so they will not slide from one another and fall when moved.

Equipment, frequently moved, should be furnished with wheels to reduce human effort in its use. (See figure 24.9.) Moving equipment to clean beside or behind it is often a strenuous task and, although desirable, is sometimes neglected because of the difficulties involved. Purchasing the equipment with large wheels eases the movement problem and encourages better sanitation. Movement of stack ovens and heavy ranges is not a task

FIGURE 24.9. *Heavy broiler on wheels which make it easily transportable to place of use by one person. Courtesy Magikitch'n Equipment Corp.*

for the weak worker, so at times wheels are placed on light equipment only. Certainly, equipment used in several locations in the kitchen should be on carts, wheeled stands, or tables. Where work space in a work center is in short supply, some kitchens place all seldom-used equipment on wheels and store it remotely. Care should be taken so that it will fit into the locations where it will be used. The working level should be close to elbow height and the wheels of the stand should lock if the equipment tends to vibrate or cause the unit to move when it is in use. Equipment of multilocation use most often placed on wheels includes food slicers, food shaping machines, vegetable cutters, food grinders, and small mixers.

Much service equipment is placed on wheels to make multiuse rooms into dining rooms, reorganize a serving line for certain meals, increase the number of serving lines when necessary, and provide for patio brunches, barbecues, and buffets or smorgasbords. Almost all service equipment except that requiring steam or gas is readily converted to wheels, and with a bit more difficulty, gas equipment can be moved about with the use of bottled gases or quick-disconnect gas lines.

Buy foods and other foodservice materials in package shapes and sizes that make them readily usable. Buying materials in 113-kg (250-lb) barrels or 45-kg (100-lb) bags may appear to reduce purchasing costs, but this can be an illusion. If the workers cannot move the container of material to the point of use and must go to the material constantly rather than having it at the point where it is used most often, labor costs increase. Flour, sugar, detergents, potatoes, cooking and frying oils, and salt are materials most often packaged in containers too heavy or awkward for the workers to handle. In some cases pots and pans, too, are ill designed in shape and capacity.

Collect and store garbage at the points where it is generated, and have a low-paid worker collect it and remove it to the garbage room rather than having cooks carry their own.

Commonly Used Equipment

Gravity Conveyors

While little used except in large restaurants, institutions, central commissaries, industrial cafeterias, and food factories, the gravity conveyor costs little except for the initial purchase. Gravity does the work. The most common type is the metal chute, either in a straight or spiral shape, with or without sides (preferably with sides). It moves a product horizontally while gradually lowering it vertically. The initial force applied to the package, the angle of incline of the chute, and the weight of the package operating against the friction of the package, slide, and side material regulates the speed of movement on the chute. To stop the package at the bottom of the chute, a buffer of some kind can absorb the shock. The package may drop off the chute on a resilient surface, the angle of fall can decrease, or the end of the chute may turn up so that loss of gravity plus the friction of the surface of the package on the chute stops the package. Abrupt stops sometimes damage packaged materials, particularly those in glass containers when a phenomenon known as "water-hammer" operates against the vacuum to shatter the jars.

The gravity chute can be used for cases of canned foods and bags of potatoes, onions, flour, sugar, and similar materials. In foodservice, they are used primarily to unload trucks and freight cars onto the receiving platform or from Receiving to basement storage.

Gravity conveyors may be made of sheet metal for the bottom and side-guides. This chute needs little maintenance, but is usually thought to be awkward and difficult to move about for use in a number of locations. The most commonly used conveyors are the roller and skate wheel types where two pieces similar to those on an aluminum ladder support rollers or small wheels above the level of the side pieces (figure 24.10). Friction is far

FIGURE 24.10. **Roller conveyors in a dishroom move trays and pans quickly from belt to scraping area.**

less than for the metal chute because the rollers or wheels turn on friction roller or ball bearings. Packages moved on conveyors must be more rigid and free of surfaces that give under pressure than those used on slides. Gravity will carry the packages much further horizontally with less vertical drop on wheels or rollers. While the slide must be wider than the package to be used, the roller wheel conveyors are usually about three-quarters of the width of the package being carried unless the roller supports or other side elements are used as guides. The package must fit between the supports. Where changes of direction are necessary, accessory guides are used.

Gravity conveyors may be used for distances from 0.6 to 61 m (2 to 200 ft) but when the package has reached floor level, it must be hand, or otherwise, lifted to the top of another conveyor for another gravity drop. In some places a power-driven belt conveyor does the lifting. Turns are usually no less than a radius of 0.8–0.9 m (2.5–3 ft), and an outside turning guide is necessary. Usually turns are 30–60 degrees. For a considerable drop in a small area, commonly a spiral conveyor or chute is used. Softer packages require greater incline. The incline grade in distance per 0.3-m (1-ft) depth of drop of conveyor for various packages is as follows:

Package	*Incline Grade*
apples, bushel basket	1.6 cm (0.62 in.)
canned foods case, full	1.3 cm (0.5 in.)
soft drink cases, empty	1.3 cm (0.5 in.)
soft drink cases, full	1.6 cm (0.62 in.)
sugar in paper bags	2.5 cm (1 in.)
tote pans	0.6–1.3 cm (0.25–0.5 in.)
wire milk case	1.6 cm (0.62 in.)
wooden box case	1 cm (0.38 in.)

The following information might be needed to develop a specification for a gravity conveyor or chute:

1. Nature of material being handled. A conveyor for bagged flour would have to be wider and steeper than one for cases of canned goods.
2. Dimensions of the material to be handled. The packages must fit between the side guides if a chute is used and not unbalance it if a conveyor. It must not be too long to go around necessary curves.
3. Weight of material or its weight density. While a 7-cm (2.75-in.) channel frame can handle 13.6-kg (30-lb) packages of a certain width with supports 3 m (10 ft) apart, if the supports are placed 1.5 m (5 ft) apart, the conveyor will support 73 kg (160 lb). If the frame is increased to a 12.7 cm (5 in.) channel and the supports remain 1.5 m (5 ft) apart, the conveyor will carry 839 kg (1850 lb).
4. Distance that the product must be carried. If distance is too great, lifts must be integrated to permit continued use of gravity.
5. Frequency of use. A heavy traffic conveyor must be more rugged than one used occasionally.
6. Special requirements or accessories needed. Converging conveyors, spurs, switches, turntables, wall, floor or ceiling supports, special stops, and other special requirements must be noted.

Powered Belt Conveyors

Conveyors that derive product movement by use of continuous belts driven by motor-driven pulleys are known as belt conveyors (figure 24.11). The belt may cover the entire carrying surface or it may be a strip-type belt rising slightly above slide rollers or skate wheels on each side to assist with the carrying. Belt conveyors in foodservice are used, primarily, for carrying soiled dishes from Dining Room to Dishroom; prepared food from Kitchen to Service; hospital trays, airline trays, and school lunch dishes during meal assembly, and supplies from Receiving to Storerooms.

In foodservice, most of the continuous belts are made of two-ply polyester, polycarbonate, butyl Teflon, or neoprene. On the top or commonly used surface, the belt usually slides in a slider pan made of 14-gauge stainless steel with a 5.1–7.6-cm (2–3-in.) margin on each side of the belt. Total width of the slide is commonly 5.1–7.6 cm (2–3 in.) wider than the trays that will be used on it. One manufacturer recommends 25-cm (10-in.) belts in 43-cm (17-in.) slides for trays or bus boxes, 28-cm (11-in.) belts in 29-cm (11.5-in.) slides for loose dishes and glasses, 33-cm (13-in.) belts in 34-cm (13.5-in.) slides where belts must make 90 degree turns with loose dishes and racks, and 46 cm (18 in.) in same width slides for loose dishes, racks, or areas where there may be spillage. The edge of the belt is higher than the center. Side walls should be 5.1–7.6 cm (2–3 in.) on the open side of the conveyor and 15–20 cm (6–8 in.) high on the wall with a slope toward the conveyor.

The drive unit is at the end of the conveyor toward which the belt is moving. This pulls the belt rather than pushes it. The size of the motor depends on the head-shaft pull of belt friction. This, in turn, is a function of belt length, width, material, slide pan, and the loading on the belt. A conveyor of 3m (10 ft) length might require a ¼ HP conveyor motor and a ¾ HP motor for one 12-18m (40-60 ft) long. A 90-degree turn may require an added 25 percent. On the end opposite the head-shaft pull or driving drum is an idler drum. Some long belts have two or more drive motors.

The underside of the belt is supported by idler

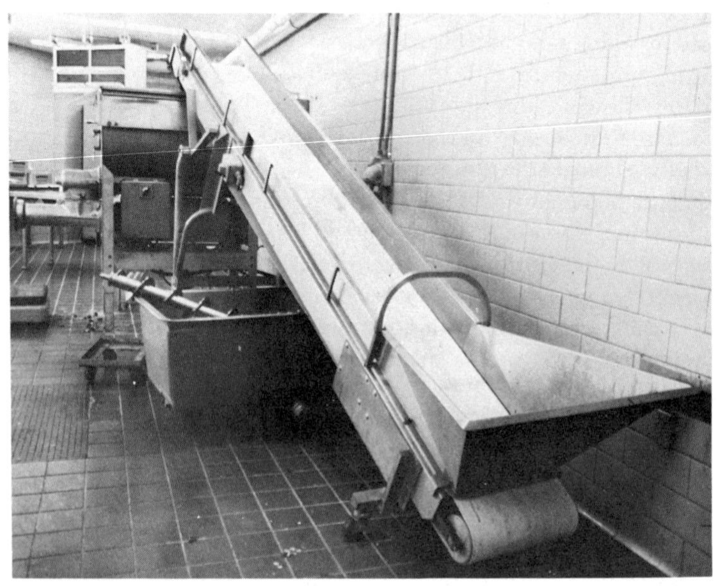

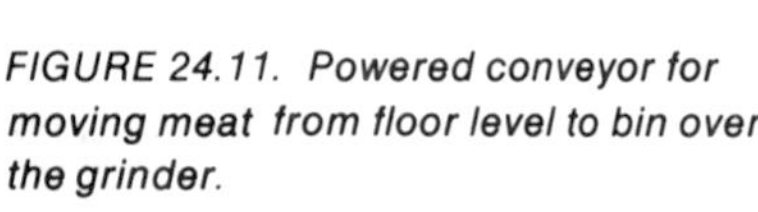

FIGURE 24.11. Powered conveyor for moving meat from floor level to bin over the grinder.

rollers. The belt can be tightened or loosened. Switches may be on the side or close to the floor for foot operation, particularly for tray assembly belts. The conveyors may be varied as to speed. Because the belt may move from 6.1–15 m (20–50 ft) per minute with an average of 9.1 m (30 ft), most conveyors have a brake to prevent coasting. Most have an arm or pressure type plate at the drive end of the conveyor to shut off the conveyor if the workers fail to unload it.

Some conveyor belts are washed continuously. This can involve a chute at the drive end to carry away flatware left on the belt to a basket. Sprays are applied to both sides of the belt, and a nylon brush operates on the dish contact side, both scraping food residue into the chute and scrubbing it. Squeegees on both sides of the belt remove all remaining liquid. As the belt leaves the idler wheel, the underside is sprayed to lubricate its path over the slide pan.

The conveyors may be fixed in place or portable. The portable units are generally used for tray or plate assembly. They are usually not over 9.1 m (30 ft) long, and most are not over 3–6.1 m (10–20 ft) long and 30–61 cm (12–24 in.) wide.

Chain Conveyors

These are often used in place of belt conveyors in dishrooms, although generally, they are about 30 percent more expensive. In their usual form, they use Delrin or Lexan thermoplastic slats or plates mounted on a link or slider chain that runs in a channel or slot in the bottom of the slider pan. To reduce the wear of metal to metal, contact takes place on easy-to-replace wear strips. Sometimes the plates are hinged vertically as well as horizontally so that they can make 90–180 degree turns easily. A relatively new type of chain conveyor is one where magnets on the chain beneath the steel-imbedded slider pan pull trays, which slide on top. The most common type of chain conveyor is that used in carousel dishwashers. Racks are attached to the chain or engaged by metal projections on the chain. These chains move horizontally.

Mechanical Lifts and Dumbwaiters

These use a hoist, chain, or cable as a conveyor mechanism to support arms, trays, buckets, or platforms. In foodservice these carry trays, serving pans, clean or soiled dish carts, or food transports that must be moved vertically between floors of a school, hotel, hospital, factory, or nursing home. Whereas the conveyor uses a slider pan to keep the conveyor belt confined, the lift or dumbwaiter uses guide rails or tracks to keep the carrying platform steady. Most are powered by electric motors in the top or basement of the operating shaft, and the carrying platform is connected to the motor by wire cables. Safety locks to the guide rails stop the platform if the motor fails or a cable breaks. Operation of the control mechanism is similar to that of an elevator except that it is exterior to the lift.

Dumbwaiters are commonly 61 cm wide × 61 cm long × 91 cm high (24 × 24 × 36 in.) for foodservice use and they can usually carry three trays 51 × 39 cm (20 × 15.5 in.). The worker can select the floor, or the device may be oriented to one floor. If the door of the dumbwaiter shaft is opened, the dumbwaiter stops to avoid injuring an unwary worker who might stick his head or hand into the opening. Some units will not allow the door to open unless the lift or dumbwaiter is stopped inside. The ultimate is a cart lift for hospitals where the cart automatically goes to the proper floor and then electronically follows a wire imbedded in the floor to the proper service station.

I observed one industrial setup where soiled dishes on trays from several widely separated dining rooms on various floors went by chain conveyor to vertical conveyor (not discussed because of infrequent use) where they were lowered to a subbasement and then consolidated by horizontal conveyors into one vertical conveyor which raised them to the dishroom at basement level. Here they were scraped, washed, and assembled in carts for transport by elevator back to the various floors and service areas. Carts were transported manually.

Two-wheel Hand Trucks

This is a one-man cart designed to transfer the bulk of a dead weight load to two wheels (figure 24.12). A flat bar frame is slid under the load. The worker uses the axle joining the two wheels as a fulcrum and two side rails attached to each side of the bar frame as levers to lift the load off the floor. Then, balancing the load with its center of gravity over the axle and resting against the side rails, he wheels the load to the point of use. By pushing the side rails forward, the load is lowered to the floor. Cross brackets make the two side rails rigid, and grips on the top end of the rails provide easy hand grasp.

The hand truck is available in two general models. The Eastern model has a tapered frame, most of which is inside the wheels. The Western model has parallel arms and frame, and the wheels are located inside the frame.

Four-wheel Hand Trucks

As used in foodservice, customarily these consist of a rigid wood, steel, or aluminum platform supported by four wheels attached to the platform by stout brackets (figure 24.13). The wheels may be distributed with a wheel to each corner (2–2) or one at the center of each end and two on opposite sides of the middle (1–2–1). The wheels may be made of iron, steel, soft rubber, hard rubber, nylon, polyurethane, and other materials. The metal wheels are noisy, bouncy, and hard on concrete floors. The soft rubber wheels are easy riding and quiet when new but tend to develop flat spots when they stand in a loaded condition for a long time. Then they become bouncy. Hard rubber wheels roll well and last a long time but are bouncy and noisy. Polyurethane wheels are probably best for foodservice as they have good load-carrying characteristics, roll well, and are quiet and easy on kitchen floors. Wheels should be water, chemical, and fat resistant, durable, and strong enough to support the desired weight. Good quality roller or ball bearings should be selected. It is well to remember that as the wheel gets larger, the force to push it decreases, and as the width of the wheel increases, the force necessary to push it increases. Casters with large swivels wear carpets less than those with small swivels. Wheels with slightly rounded edges also wear carpets less than those that are square edged.

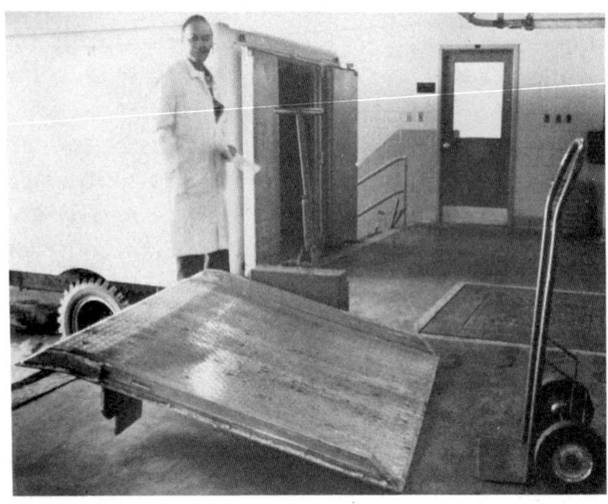

FIGURE 24.12. Two-wheel hand truck (right) with a portable ramp (left) to bridge space between platform and transport.

The size or diameter of the wheel should be specified; the tendency is to select the cheaper small wheels, which will catch on small obstructions. For most kitchen uses where equipment is rolled only a few feet on relatively smooth floors, one can get by with casters on wheels 7.6–10.1 cm (3–4 in.) in diameter. For longer distances where heavy loads must be pushed by a single person, wheels should be 12.7–15.2 cm (5–6 in.) in diameter, preferably the latter. Conveyor-towed trucks should have 20.3-cm (8-in.) casters, and tractor-towed should have 25.4-cm (10-in.) wheels. The sturdiness of the caster specified depends on the load to be carried and the frequency of use. If considerable maneuverability is desired, then swivels that move the wheel around a vertical pivot may be used on all four wheels. For most purposes, two rigid wheels at one end of the cart and two on swivels at the other end are desirable and cheaper. Where hand or machine work must be performed

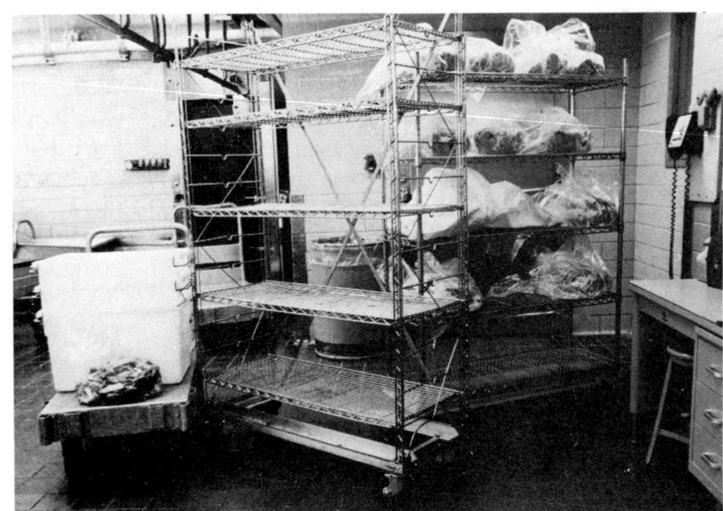

FIGURE 24.13. Four-wheel hand truck (left) generally used in kitchens for moving foods, pans, and other materials. Wheeled racks for refrigerator use (right).

on a cart, wheel locks operated by the worker's toe are often desirable to stabilize the work surface.

Carts are seldom differentiated from hand trucks (figure 24.14). A truck is often thought of as a heavy-duty carrier with the essential load-carrying platform close to the floor. In contrast, a cart has load-carrying shelves, bins, or flat surfaces up to about chest height and racks, wheeled shelving, or cabinets extending up to 1.8 m (6 ft) or more. However, there does not appear to be any hard and fast definition; here they will be treated together. Factors to be considered in this variety of wheeled vehicle are:

1. It should be easy to pull, push, and turn yet not threaten to fall over. The base should be broad but not protrude.
2. It should be sturdy enough in construction to serve the purposes for which it is being purchased. It should not be excessively heavy as this adds to costs and generally to handling weight.
3. Casters should be of a size and construction suitable for the terrain, load and use for which the equipment is designed.
4. Design of the kitchen should be checked to determine if it lends itself to the use of wheels

FIGURE 24.14. Insulated tray or cart. Courtesy Lincoln Manufacturing Co. Inc.

(I could not use wheels on most U.S. Navy ships because of the ship's motion, inadequate widths of aisles, unsatisfactory flooring, and obstructional items.) Some small kitchens would get little benefit from use of carts as food and dish distances are too close together.

5. Construction should be checked. Is it sturdily welded or riveted so that it will not come apart? Is floor clearance adequate to clear all floor obstructions and ease cleaning under it? Is equipment put together so that it is easy to keep clean? Does it meet NSF requirements?
6. Are carts designed with human operation in mind? Are latches easy to manipulate, handles or bars easy to grasp, all spaces available to sight and reach, controls and displays easy to see and use?
7. Are carts equipped with rubber or neoprene bumpers to protect walls against inadvertent striking?
8. Are carts on which electric equipment is operated provided with adequate grounding?
9. What have been the experiences of other operators nearby with the equipment under consideration?

Carts

Materials Handling Carts

These usually have one level of platform 5.1–10.1 cm (2–4 in.) above the wheels, but they may be multishelved. The platform may be made of wood, soft sheet steel, galvanized steel, stainless steel, or aluminum with a frame of steel or aluminum. There is usually a waist high cargo support at one or both ends. To the top of at least one support may be attached a push-rail, although the top of the cargo support is often used for this purpose. They are open on both sides. Multishelved carts may be limited to waist height or may be above head height. Usually the shelving is fixed to the height of the product for which it will be used, but in a few it is adjustable. Some merely have slides or supports into which sheet or steam table pans may be slid. Some have slides that handle several sizes of pans. A few have a support column on one side of the dolly base, and the shelves or slides are cantilevered over the base so that they can be loaded or removed from three sides. Materials carts may be used for tote or bus boxes, bakers' pans, pie plates, roast pans, steam table pans, trays, dish racks, and garbage cans.

Mobile Base Carts

Where a table top piece of equipment needs wheels, it may be placed on a cart that will allow it to be used at a most efficient height (elbow height). This may be between 41–91 cm (16–36 in.). It is well to have sufficient space on each side for holding both unprocessed and processed food. The wheels should be capable of being locked when the equipment is in use.

Portable Work Tables

These should be available to support equipment that does not have adequate work area nearby. They should be close to the working height of the equipment that they support and have locking wheels. Equipment that needs this support most are deep fat fryers, steam jacketed kettles, ranges, griddles, broilers, ovens, and floor mixers. Cutting boards on work tables are often useful.

Cabinets

Where the product must be protected or a special atmosphere provided, the cart has sides and doors (figure 24.15). With these one may provide equipment to heat, cool, and humidify the contents according to need. Some are insulated to make them more energy efficient, but in most cases this adds to the effort to move them. Materials are usually aluminum or stainless steel, although some that are going to be used for serving line support may be covered with various plastic and fiberglass paneling. While most heating, refrigerating, and humidity equipment is electric, other means may be used. Alcohol lamps may be used to heat, and

FIGURE 24.15. *Mobile heated cabinet with insulated walls and door.*

ice or reusable disks or sheets of a frozen chemical may be used to refrigerate for short time use.

Other Carts

The number of other special purpose carts used in foodservice is staggering. They include, among others, silverware, tray, rack, and dish carts in a great variety, condiment carts, coffee and sandwich carts, roast beef slicing carts, salad bars, serving carts, dessert wagons, portable bars, trash and garbage carts, janitor carts, portable cashier stations, and bowl carriers (figures 24.16 to 24.20). Most of the carts use angle steel tubes or aluminum channel members for support, and 16-gauge, Type 302, No. 4 finish stainless steel or comparative aluminum for platforms or decks.

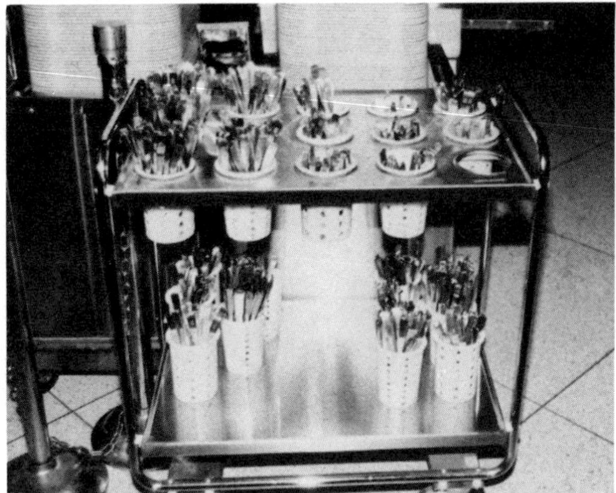

FIGURE 24.16. *Silverware cart for serving line.*

FIGURE 24.17. *Dish carts with self-leveling dispensers.*

Work Center Considerations

Receiving

Chutes, conveyors, truck lifts, ramps from platform, pallet trucks, materials carts, wheeled shelf racks, dollies, rollers, pallet-lifting trucks, blowers (used by large central commissaries and food factories to move flour and sugar), and overhead trolleys that carry meats are used to move food and other materials from various transports to the

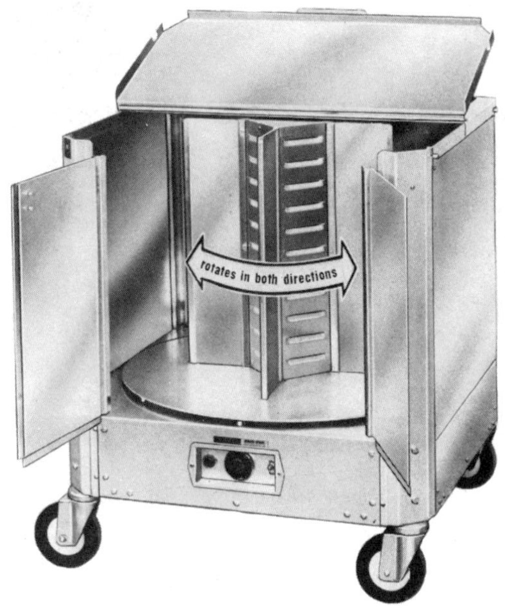

FIGURE 24.18. Dish cart on which platform for holding dishes revolves. Courtesy Crescent Metal Products Inc.

receiving platform (figure 24.21). After checking the delivered product against purchase order and invoice, they are used to move the materials into storage. Leaving as much waste as possible at Receiving reduces the labor of removing it from the kitchen.

Storage

In large operations, the cased and bagged materials remain on pallets and carts until it is time to move them to the point of use. Waste may be removed, food cleaned and weighed or measured into processing batch lots at Receiving, and then one- or two-basket carts similar to those used in supermarkets may be used to transport them into storage and later to point of use. Wheeled racks similarly are loaded at Receiving and then handled as a unit until processed. It must be emphasized that wheeled vehicles need either floor-level or low-ramp access and adequate width and height of egress to the storerooms to be effective. Otherwise, the transports must be left outside the door and materials hand carried in and out of the storeroom. To aid access to storerooms without using physical effort, electric eyes or pressure plates that are activated when the vehicle approaches the door may be used. Some cold storerooms may be left opened during working hours and air curtains or

FIGURE 24.19. Variety of dish-holding and rack-carrying carts.

FIGURE 24.20. Self-leveling dispenser cart at clean end of dishwasher. Courtesy G.S. Blakeslee and Co.

FIGURE 24.21. Lift for two-wheel skid (left) and dolly for pans and hand truck (right).

ribbon curtains used to keep the cold in and warm air out. To avoid constant opening of walk-in refrigerators, several manufacturers add reach-in doors to walk-ins so that the frequently used items may be placed in front of the reach-in doors. This reduces retrieval time and energy losses.

Bake Shop

Pallets, materials handling carts, shelved carts, and possibly hoses and water meters bring in supplies and three- or four-wheeled dollies carry the mixer bowl about the bake shop. The dough trough carries the mixed dough into the proofing room. Wheeled racks bring empty pans to the panning area and full pans from there to the ovens. Cooling racks hold the baked product. If the oven is a conveyor or reel type, the mechanism takes the product through the hot cavity and thence back to the point of origin. In essence, it is a piece of materials handling equipment. In commercial bakeries, practically everything moves by conveyor or wheeled racks. Some large institutions use push-through ovens where entire racks of baked product are pushed in on one side and, as others are added, forced out the other side with the product baked.

Meat and Vegetable Preparation

Most meats come from storage in tote pans set into wheeled racks and, after processing, the same carts are used to move it back to storage prior to cooking. To reduce this travel, pass-through refrigerators between Meat Preparation and Cooking may be used, and there may be some between Vegetable Preparation and Cooking. To ease materials handling, tables in both Meat Preparation and Vegetable Preparation are of stainless steel at the same height so that products may be slid instead of carried. Wherever possible, drop deliveries of finished products into pots or pans on wheels are used to reduce handling and facilitate movement of product after preparation. Salad greens, as they are cut, are usually placed in a round-bottomed bowl (bird bath) set in a wheeled rack so that after the mixing of the greens they may be taken to a table for making individual salad or moved to the salad service area. Salad and dessert dishes are brought to the area in wheeled carriers. Desserts, as they are portioned, are usually placed on sheet pans and carried to the serving line on shelved racks.

Cooking

Carts and wheeled racks or pass-through refrigerators bring most of the food material to the Cooking area while wheeled racks from the Potwashing area bring the necessary pots, pans, hand utensils, and cooking equipment parts.

Holding

Food may be placed in steam table pans before or after cooking, if prepared in bulk. These pans are transported to the serving line in heated cabinets for insertion in gaps behind the portion of the serving line that they support or in carts or open racks for insertion into fixed heated pass-throughs behind the serving line. Food pumps are sometimes used with steam jacketed kettles in large central commissaries to fill serving utensils that are moved by conveyors to cart loading.

Service Area

Self-leveling dish dispensers and other types of dish carts bring dishes to the serving line. Trays, silverware, and napkins are brought to the serving line by special carts. Griddles may be wheeled into the serving line for griddling to order. Self-leveling glass rack dispensers or rack caddies make glasses available at the water dispenser. In some cases, the condiments are dispensed from wheeled tables at selected locations in the dining room or serving line. Glass rack units are located beside milk and soft drink dispensers, cup and saucer dispensers by coffee and tea urns, and paper or ceramic dish dispensers by the soft ice cream machine.

The tray makeup area for most hospitals is made up largely of materials handling equipment —tray, dish, plate, silverware, and menu card stand dispensers, hot and cold foodservice units, possibly portable griddle and beverage dispensers, and finally, plate or tray covers, depending on the type of carrier which carries trays to the patients.

Dishwashing

While soiled dishes may be brought to the dishroom by busing cart or dish conveyor, clean dishes and flatware are removed to the service area in a multitude of specialized dish, rack, tray, and flatware carriers that can double as dispensers (figure 24.22). Some are self-leveling in that they bring the dishes up to using height; others require a certain amount of bending by the customer to reach the ware stored close to the floor.

QUESTIONS

1. What is materials handling?
2. What is the emphasis of industrial materials handling as contrasted with foodservice materials handling?
3. What are the principles of foodservice materials handling?
4. What regulates the speed of travel on a gravity conveyor? How is product movement stopped on a gravity conveyor?
5. As packages become softer, is the incline needed greater or less than for hard packages?
6. What information is needed to develop a specification for a gravity conveyor?

FIGURE 24.22. ***Self-leveling glass rack holder (left) and dish dollies (right).***

7. What is the most used material for belt conveyors?
8. Is the driving of a belt conveyor done on the end of the conveyor toward which the belt moves or the end from which the belt comes?
9. What is the least expensive conveyor?
10. Of what metal is the slide in which the belt moves made?
11. What is the usual length of a portable belt conveyor?
12. What is the safety mechanism of the dumbwaiter?
13. What is the difference between the Eastern and the Western type of two-wheeled hand truck?
14. What is the desired wheel diameter on carts that will be used frequently?
15. What is the difference between a cart and a cabinet?
16. What is the materials handling equipment at Receiving? in the Dishroom?

BIBLIOGRAPHY

ANON. 1964. Conveyors. *Volume Feeding Magazine* 22, No. 5, 83–85.

ANON. 1969. *New Automated Food Cart Gets Off at the Right Floor by Itself.* Servo-Lift Facts, Boston.

ANON. 1974. Conveyor systems. *Kitchen Planning* 11, No. 1, 32–41.

APPLE, J.N. 1963. *Plant Layout and Materials Handling.* 2d ed. Ronald Press, New York.

GIAMPIETRO, F.N. 1977. How mobile equipment can enhance your facility. *Restaurant Business* 76, No. 2, 132–138.

KOTSCHEVAR, L.H. and TERRELL, M.E. *Food Service Planning: Layout and Equipment.* John Wiley and Sons, New York.

Service Equipment

After food has been prepared and/or cooked, it must be assembled on a plate or tray and made available to the consumer. The equipment involved in doing this varies according to the size and type of foodservice establishment, the money available, and the desires of management and the customer.

The simplest setup is to serve from the cooking equipment that cooks the food, and in the case of camps and other small feeding operations, this is often the only serving equipment used. This means that the range is the service equipment in most of these places. In many types of fast food operations the cooking equipment is, or is closely associated with, the serving equipment. Included in this category are many of the hamburger, pizza, chicken, seafood, and similar restaurants. It is not until one gets into the large serving line and shopping center or carousel types of cafeterias and the table service restaurant that serving equipment becomes complex (figure 25.1). As the carousel or moving circular unit is not yet used to any considerable extent and table service restaurants vary too greatly, the line cafeteria will be the only one discussed here. Most of the equipment used for service in table service operations in the kitchen or in waitress stations is similar to service line equipment.

Tray Dispensers

Most people have been familiar with cafeteria serving lines since they were in grade school, but

FIGURE 25.1. Carousel type serving unit where the counter does the moving. Courtesy B/W Metals Company Incorporated.

they may not know the reasons behind some of the serving line equipment design and arrangement. First in line must be the trays (figure 25.2). The customer needs to have a flat surface on which to assemble the dishes of foods that he selects. In some cases, as in the military, the tray is compartmented and the food is placed directly on the tray by the server. Presentation of the tray to the customer before he enters the serving line may be from a self-leveling dispenser where a spring-loaded or otherwise counterbalanced frame constantly lifts the stack or stacks of trays to approximately 91 cm (36 in.) from the floor for ease of removal. Shelf-type dispensers without the self-leveling feature are available but are rated less desirable as the customer must bend over as the stack of trays is depleted. Tray dispensers may be built into, or adjacent to, the serving line but most are placed on wheels as enclosed cabinets or open pipe-type frame assemblies. Usually all exterior material is stainless steel, although some enameled or Formica side panels with stainless or chromed steel for the cap and other wearing surfaces may be used. While a bit small, most of these cabinets use 10.1-cm (4-in.) diameter rubber or polyurethane swivel casters. Some have rubber bumpers on the corners or around the base. Wheels permit loading of the trays at the dishwasher and wheeling the unit to the service line, and they require no further handling until it is empty.

Many of the tray dispensers come in combination with flatware dispenser and napkin dispensers, but I prefer that these be placed at the end of the serving line or on an island in the dining room so that the customer may choose exactly what he needs after he has made his food selection.

FIGURE 25.2. Combination tray and silverware dispenser.

Tray Rail or Slide

Wherever the customer puts his tray down in the service area to make selections or pick up condiments or flatware, he needs a table top or, as is most often the case, tray rail or slide for his tray (figure 25.3). In a conventional cafeteria, the tray rail extends along one side of the line of serving equipment while the serving personnel are stationed along the other side, which is usually closest to the kitchen. The tray rail permits the customer to slide his tray while he makes his selections. In the shopping center type of cafeteria, the service is broken up into islands or, in some cases, a sawtooth arrangement of short serving line sectors to encourage the customer to move about to the various serving islands that have the foods he desires. The idea is to avoid having people standing in lines at locations where they will not be selecting a food and are being delayed by someone who is making a selection. A shopping center service will handle many more customers per hour than a conventional service line, and because much of the service is by the customer, the number of service personnel is reduced.

Wherever the customer does stop to make a selection, he should have a tray rail or other surface to support his tray while he uses his hands to service himself or handle dishes. Tray rails commonly provide a surface approximately 30 cm (12 in.) wide (figure 25.4). The surface may take a number of forms, but the most frequently used is three or four 2.5-cm (1-in.) stainless steel rails supported in stainless steel channels and by brackets of similar metal bolted into the serving

FIGURE 25.3. Tray slide around a portable serving line. Courtesy Lincoln Manufacturing Co. Inc.

equipment. Another type is a flat solid 14-gauge stainless steel tablelike top with bull-nose edges. A variation is to reduce sliding friction on the tray by effecting several lengthwise V-shaped or rounded ridges along the solid tray slide. On portable service equipment, the bracket holding the tray rail can be folded so that the rail hinged on the equipment side will fold against the equipment while it is being moved.

Hot Tables

The order of arrangement of equipment is not fixed along the route that the customer follows from entering the serving area until he reaches the checker or cashier to pay for the food he has accumulated on his tray. Some designers place the cold foods and their supporting equipment first and the hot food, including soup and beverage, closest to the cashier so that the customer has a reasonable chance of eating hot foods when he reaches his table. However, this is by no means standard. While institutional facilities may place low cost and bulky foods early in the serving line to fill the customer's tray before he reaches the more expensive items, a restaurant or hotel may reverse the arrangement so that customers choose the more expensive or best profit items before they realize that there are cheaper things available to satisfy their hunger. No attempt will be made here to prescribe a standard arrangement because there are various preferences for arrangement to fit different service situations. In some situations the service equipment is sectionalized and placed on wheels so that it may be moved to where it is needed and arranged in the most efficient order and shape of line for a given meal (figure 25.5).

The basic element of most serving lines is the hot food table, which essentially is a support for the approximately 30-x-51-x-6.4-, 10-, 15-, or 20-cm (12-x-20-x-2.5-, 4-, 6-, or 8-in.) steam table pans in various multiples over a reservoir of water (figure 25.6). This may be heated by thermostatically controlled gas, electric, or steam heating elements. While the basic opening is 30 x 51 cm (12 x 20 in.) for that size of pan, the long dimension may be divided for one-half, one-third, two-thirds, and one-fourth size pans. With or without the use of an adapter bar, the short dimension may be halved to allow the space to be filled with two long pans, one-

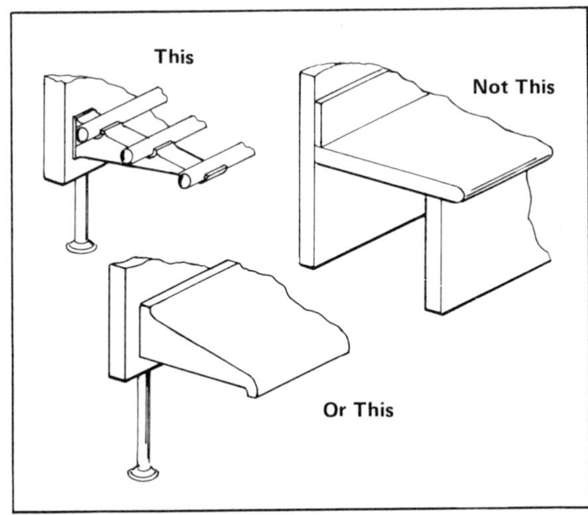

FIGURE 25.4. Sanitary consideration in tray slides. Courtesy National Sanitation Foundation.

FIGURE 25.5. Hot food service (left) and cold food service (right). Courtesy Lincoln Manufacturing Co. Inc.

FIGURE 25.6. Hot food serving counter with meat server on left, then oblong steam table pans with round units to the right. A cutting board and plate storage are on front of unit and serving shelf over it. Courtesy Star Metal Corporation.

sixth size and even one-ninth size pans. With other adapter units, round serving pans of various sizes may be used. Although not used to any considerable extent, hot tables with openings for pans up to 46 cm (18 in.) wide may be obtained.

The hot food table may be obtained in standard sizes that will hold one, two, three, four, six, or eight steam table pans 30 x 51 cm (12 x 20 in.) and custom-made units are limited only by available floor space in capacity. The most common unit will hold four pans. It might be 1.8 m (6 ft) long, 0.9 m (3 ft) wide, and 0.9 m (3 ft) high with adjustable 20-cm (8-in.) tubular steel legs giving some 4.4 cm (1.75 in.) latitude on this. A 1.9-cm (0.75-in.) or thicker cutting board of Richlite, maple, or stainless steel about 23–30 cm (9–12 in.) wide may extend over the top of the rear of the table. The top of the unit may be of 14-gauge satin finish stainless steel with the front and ends of 20-gauge or various types of woodlike and other veneers, fiberglass, or formed plastics. An 18-gauge stainless steel shelf beneath the cutting board will hold plates. A full width stainless or galvanized steel shelf may extend across the bottom above the legs. The base may be enclosed with either sliding or hinged doors. The water or steam pan may be 12.7–20 cm (5–8 in.) deep and extend beneath all the openings, or each opening may be an enclosed unit with individually controlled electricity. Thus it may provide a dry or wet heat to the pan above it, and each unit may be thermostatically controlled.

These hot tables may have a glass or clear plastic enclosure that allows service while protecting the food against contamination from the customer and provides a serving shelf above them (figure 25.7 and figure 25.8). Stainless steel covers are available to cover the individual serving pans in the hot table. Some have plastic or glass shields that act as protection for the food from customer sneezes while allowing him to reach beneath them to obtain a preportioned food.

At least one manufacturer provides hot tables together with the other basic serving line equipment in decorator colors. They insert and lock into portable units so as to make a rigid, yet attractive, serving line that can be assembled according to need (figure 25.9).

Cold Tables

As many salads, desserts, appetizers, and other foods are served in the cold condition by design, no serving line would be complete without one or more units to display and preserve the cold freshness of these foods. In the past most of the cold display tables were constructed of galvanized steel and filled with crushed or flaked ice to provide the refrigeration. Then a venturesome manufacturer borrowed a page from the supermarkets and refrigerated walls and sometimes the bottom of the oblong depressed serving tables. In most cases it was found that to maintain the even, cool atmosphere of a supermarket showcase required a table that was too deep. The manufacturers then removed the side coils and raised the bottom refrigerated plates so that the dishes of food placed in it were more visible (figure 25.11). Some difficulties were encountered in providing satisfactory cooling for a large salad, salad bowl, or deep dish

FIGURE 25.7. Food serving unit with plastic food protection shield over food. Courtesy Crescent Metals Products, Inc.

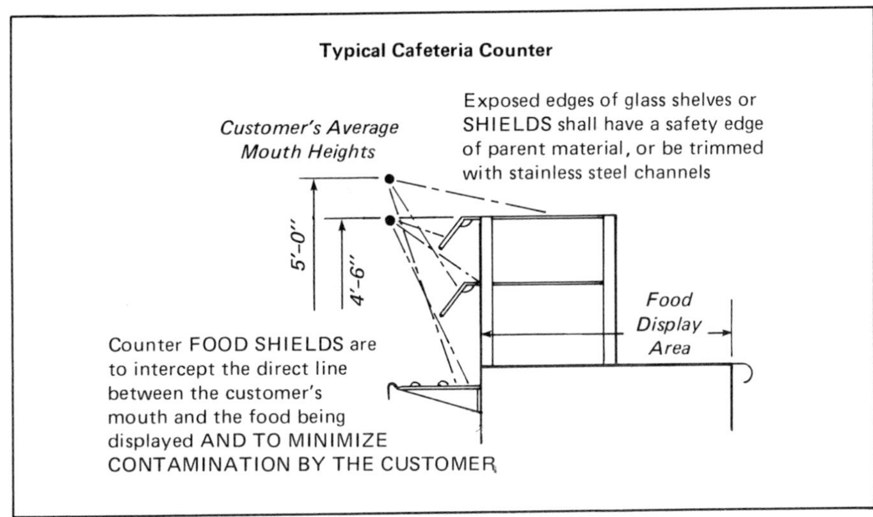

FIGURE 25.8. Proper placement of protection shields at two shelf levels. Courtesy National Sanitation Foundation.

of pudding. Many cafeterias and buffeterias are now placing the ice back in the cold pans as it can be brought up around the side of the dish to provide a cooler atmosphere in addition to a striking background for the food. The refrigeration system is used to slow the melting of the ice.

There is little standardization of the cold pan. One manufacturer makes pans 1.2, 1.8, and 2.4 m (4, 6, and 8 ft) long, 86 cm (34 in.) wide, and 0.9 m (3 ft) high with adjustable legs 4.4 cm (1.75 in.). The pan may be obtained with a 2.5 cm (1 in.) or 8.9-cm (3.5-in.) deep solid bottom and 8.9-cm (3.5-in.) deep perforated bottom. It can be drained. The top surfaces and pan interior are 14-gauge Type 304 stainless steel with a 12.7-cm (5-in.) apron front and rear. The sides and front are made of 18-

FIGURE 25.9. A quickly assembled serving counter available in decorator colors. Courtesy Lincoln Manufacturing Co. Inc.

FIGURE 25.10. Hot pass-through food cabinets supporting hot section of serving line.

gauge bonderized and zinc-coated steel coated with synthetic enamel. Some use 18- or 20-gauge stainless steel, others Formica, and some use simulated woods and other coatings to have all of the serving line present a similar appearance. The insulation of the pan and cabinet beneath it is 5.1-cm (2-in.) polystyrene. The refrigerated cabinet has 20-gauge stainless steel interior. The compressor runs from 1/4–3/4 HP, depending on the length of the pan; the condenser is air cooled. The unit may be put in a remote location if the compressor or condenser heat is a problem. The cold air is blown around five enclosed sides of the pan and throughout the insulated space below the pan. This space is used for storage of foods to replenish those removed by the customers. As an option one can get the cold pan without the refrigerator beneath it. Stainless steel shelves are put into the space. I feel that refrigerated pass-throughs above waist height behind the line are preferable storage for cold pan refill items as it is difficult to see into undercounter refrigerators unless they are made up of pull-out

FIGURE 25.11. Cold pans. Courtesy Lincoln Manufacturing Co. Inc.

FIGURE 25.12. Cold pass-throughs behind cold serving section of serving line.

drawers or swing-out or slide-out shelving attached to the doors (figure 25.12).

Of a similar nature is the refrigerated display case that is merely an upright refrigerator with single- or double-pane sliding glass doors so that the customer may view refrigerated salads, canned soft drinks, juices, or desserts, slide the door left or right, and remove his choice; the spring weight loaded door will close itself in most cases. This should be a requirement. The refrigeration unit is in the base, which may or may not be insulated and used as an added refrigerator.

Another much-used device of comparable design is the sandwich bar and refrigerator. In the place of the single refrigerated pan top one has one or more 30-x-51-cm (12-x-20-in.) die-stamped pan openings into which may be placed one to nine sandwich spread and garnish pans with or without the use of adapter bars. Across the back of the unit a 17.8–30 cm (7–12 in.) wide cutting board provides a surface for fabricating and cutting the sandwiches. Some units use part of the unit's top surface as stainless steel table top on which to place plates of prepared sandwiches. Some have glass-enclosed housing with glass sliding doors on the rear to protect the foods. Space beneath may be used for a door or drawer refrigerator (which I prefer) or it may be used as shelving for sandwich plates, loaves of bread, or utensils. In this unit, too, the refrigeration unit may be included or located remotely. Covers may be put on the pans when the sandwich unit is not in use.

Ice Cream Cabinets

When most ice cream desserts were dipped to order from 9.5–38-liter (2.5–10-gal) containers, it was easiest to do this from a container that was below the counter top. As a result, most ice cream cabinets were designed with this concept in mind—units that would hold one to innumerable of these containers. Most of these were self-contained refrigeration units with up to 7.6 cm (3 in.) of polyurethane or comparable amounts of polystyrene, glass wool, cork, or other insulators. The exteriors were of stainless or enameled steel, aluminum, and various plastics. The interior of the ice cream cabinets was usually galvanized steel, although some had stainless steel, anodized aluminum, or plastic linings. Most had insulated tops with the outsides of the same stainless steel or enameled steel as the cabinet exterior and the interior of stainless steel, plastic, or zinc-coated steel. Insulation was similar to that of the cabinet and had a sealing breaker strip between the overlapping flange of the cover and cabinet top. Most tops were hinged in the middle so that each half would cover one or two cans of ice cream. Usually the split-hinged top could be lifted completely from the cabinet when placing the cans in the freezer, but only one half would be folded back when the ice cream was being dipped.

The ice cream cabinet is little changed today. Some cafeterias have found hand dipping of ice cream is not economical because of the labor cost, but the cabinets continue to be used for prepackaged ice cream. They are ill-designed for this function as the customer cannot see into the reach-down cabinets without difficulty. To correct this, some cafeterias use cold pans with direct expansion plates in their pan bottoms to merchandise preportioned flat-bottomed dishes of ice cream or prepackaged ice creams of various types. A few use spring-loaded self-leveling shelves to bring the ice cream up to where it is visible.

More and more cafeterias are using soft ice cream, frozen custard, frozen yogurt, slush, and milk shake machines somewhat similar to those used in the fast food dairy bars. The only difference is that in many cases the customer operates the machine, so the machine's drawing mechanism is turned toward the customer in a serving line or in an island in a shopping center cafeteria.

While there are many makes and designs of machines for continuous freezing of soft desserts, most of them operate on a similar principle. A mixture of milk products, sugar, gelatin, or similar thickeners, and flavors, coloring, nuts, fruits, and syrups and sometimes eggs for both flavor and whipping ability is fed into a steel cylinder around which a compressed gas, usually one of the Freons, is expanded, making the metal surface very cold. Ice crystals freeze to the surface and while yet quite small, they are scraped off by sharp blades revolving around the interior of the cylinder. Part of the scraping assembly is a beating arrangement that whips in air, thus increasing the volume of the mixture. The assembly moves the frozen dessert to the discharge mechanism as well.

The incorporated air is known as "overrun." While a regular ice cream may have 100 percent overrun, which means 50 percent of air by volume, a soft ice cream usually has 40–80 percent overrun, which means 20–40 percent of air by volume. Overrun is commonly measured by the reduction in the weight of the original mix. An ice cream that weighs 2.08 kg (4.6 lb) per gallon when the mix weighed 4.17 kg (9.2 lb) per gallon has 100 percent overrun. To provide prompt freezing when needed, the mix should be stored at close to freezing temperature and kept adequately refrigerated in the freezer storage tank. While the ice cream can be frozen in the soft ice cream machine until it reaches –8.4°C (19°F), more can be produced in a given period of time if it is drawn at –5.6°C (22°F).

In choosing a machine for continuous freezing of desserts, the following factors should be considered:

1. The unit selected should blend well with the other service equipment. In most cases, this means that it should be largely stainless steel.
2. The freezer should be easy to assemble, disassemble, clean, and sanitize so that all echelons of foodservice personnel can perform this function. Equipment should require a minimum of tools because tools get lost.
3. Care should be exercised in assuring that the equipment complies with all health regulations so that the mix in the hopper is protected against bacterial and other contamination as well as temperature rises.
4. Operating noise level should be ascertained before purchasing the freezer as loud machine noise tires workers and repels customers.
5. Be sure that there is a local repair service of

good repute for the selected equipment, and be sure they carry an adequate supply of spare parts. The equipment should be covered by an adequate warranty.

6. Check to see that the compressor and beater drive motors are of sufficient capacity. Reasonable motor horsepowers might be:

Unit	*HP Compressor*	*HP Beater*
3.78-liter (4-qt) shake freezer	3/4	1/2
6.62-liter (7-qt) shake freezer	1	3/4
3.78-liter (4-qt) soft ice cream	1	1
6.62-liter (7-qt) soft ice cream	1 ½	1 ½

One manufacturer has soft-serve machines that vary in width between 41 and 66 cm (16 and 26 in.), in depth between 74 and 84 cm (29 and 33 in.), and overall height between 85 and 165 cm (33.5 and 65 in.) including the adjustable legs or swivel wheels. The lesser heights are table mounted; the greater heights, floor mounted. The widest freezers have dual freezing shells; the narrow ones, a single shell. The mix hopper for most of these units had a capacity of 18.9 liters (20 qt) per freezing shell except for the smallest ones that held 9.46 liters (10 qt).

Dish Dispensers

While some of the hot and cold serving tables have shelves beneath the server sides of the units for the storage of dishes, many others do not and must depend on self-leveling dispensers (figure 25.14). These may be located in the counters beside the serving tables, or better yet from an efficiency standpoint, wheeled self-leveling dispensers may be used. They may be loaded in the dishwashing room and then wheeled up beside, or into, that part of the serving complex that they support.

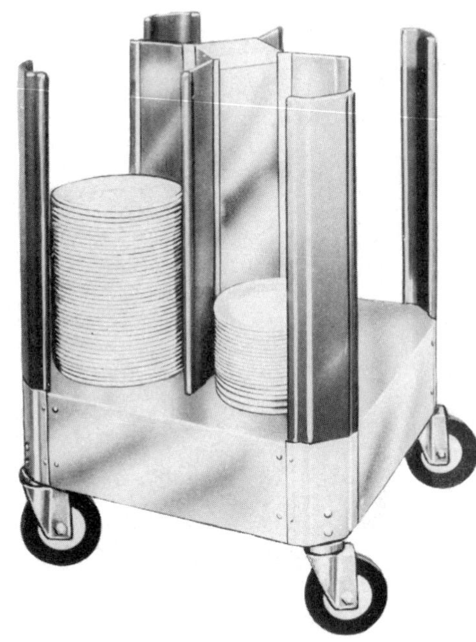

FIGURE 25.13. Plate dispenser. Courtesy Crescent Metals Products, Inc.

Based on principles similar to the self-leveling dispenser of trays, there are similar dispensers for plates, bowls, and vegetable or dessert dishes adjacent to the cold tables. Self-leveling dispensers are used adjacent to the coffee-brewing equipment for coffee cups, saucers, and sometimes disposable cups and covers as well. The cups are usually in cup racks, but the self-leveling dispenser is commonly used to hold the racks. By having these dispensers on wheels, much multiple handling of dishes can be obviated. As they come out of the dishwasher, the plates may be loaded into the self-leveling tube dispensers while the racks of cups and glasses are loaded into dispensers that hold the complete racks. They are handled only once before the customer or server removes them from the dispenser.

FIGURE 25.14. Heated plate dispensers.

Most self-leveling dispensers are spring actuated and adjustable to the weight of the plate or rack used. Usually they are loaded to capacity but not to a height where they will fall off. For saucers, dishes, plates, or bowls, the stainless steel tubes have a stainless steel spring that supports the head of similar material. The interior diameter of the tube may vary from 11.9 cm (4.7 in.) to 32.2 cm (12.7 in.) with 8.9-cm (3.5-in.) posts on top to steady the dishes placed in the tube. The tube may be set into a fixed counter, a wheeled stainless steel enclosed cabinet, or a tubular frame of 2.5-cm (1-in.) stainless steel also on wheels. In both of the latter two cases, the wheels are of 10.1 cm (4 in.) diameter and of a nonmarking material. The corners are protected by rubber or composition bumpers.

Heated cabinets commonly have 2.5 cm (1 in.) of fiberglass or other insulation inside the enclosed frame. Heating is accomplished by thermostatically controlled resistance heater strips of a wattage suitable for the size of cabinet. As an example, a four-tube plate unit might be provided with a 1000 watt unit.

Coffee urns and griddles have been discussed. Some of the other available service equipment that will not be described includes stainless steel tables, glass shelves with sneeze guards, butter patty dispensers, bread dispensers, tea dispensers, infrared lamps and roast-slicing stations, silverware and condiment dispensers, water dispensers, menu boards, and others. Successful service equipment merchandises the products, provides an attractive well-integrated atmosphere, keeps the customer from feeling self-conscious, and safeguards the food and customer while he makes his food selection.

QUESTIONS

1. What is the first piece of equipment in a serving line?
2. What types of tray rails are used?
3. What is the special advantage of the shopping center cafeteria?
4. Why would a particular type of food be placed first in a serving line?
5. What is the basic size of opening in the hot table? What are the various sizes of containers placed in it?
6. How does one protect food from customer contamination in a hot table?
7. How are hot tables heated?
8. What is the main function of the mechanical refrigeration in a cold table? What are the main depths in cold tables?
9. What is the reason for not having doors on refrigerators beneath the cold pans?
10. What are the components of a sandwich bar?
11. What are the operating principles of the ice cream freezer?

12. What are the advantages of using a soft ice cream machine in a serving line instead of conventional hard ice cream cabinets?
13. What are the particular advantages of using mobile dish dispensers over fixed shelving or dish dispensers?
14. What in a self-leveling dish dispenser raises the dish up to customer level?
15. In what way is the self-leveling dish dispenser utilized with glasses?

BIBLIOGRAPHY

ANON. 1973. *Knight Cafeteria Equipment*. Stanley Knight Corp., Des Plaines, Ill.

ANON. 1976. Take in service, Texas style. *Cooking for Profit* 44, No. 306, 29–32.

KOTSCHEVAR, L.E., and TERRELL, M.E. 1977. *Food Service Planning: Layout and Equipment*. John Wiley and Sons, New York.

TERRELL, M.E. 1971. *Professional Food Preparation*. John Wiley and Sons, New York.

Saving Energy in Foodservice

The two percent of the nation's energy used by the foodservice industry may seem too small to be of any importance in an energy reduction program. When joined with hundreds of similar programs in other industries, the total effect can be considerable on energy use in United States. The effect is not entirely in British thermal units but in dollars as well. The National Restaurant Association estimates the average foodservice establishment can save 20 percent on its energy consumption. This means that a small company can save \$800 on its annual \$4,000 energy bill, and a large company can save \$4,000 on its \$20,000 bill.

Savings like these are not impossible. I found in some U.S. Navy installations that only 40 percent of the energy entering the kitchen was used productively. The remainder was being lost by radiation from equipment and pipes, leaks from steam and water pipes, through ventilation systems, and in excess lighting, equipment use, and heating.

Energy conservation is not solely the responsibility of the manager and some designated energy conservation officer but should receive constant attention from every worker in the establishment. The employees should be given lectures and training sessions on how to recognize energy losses and take proper corrective action. Incentive programs should be set up to spur employees to look for ways to reduce energy usage, and outstanding achievements in this should be recognized.

Most of the energy losses that do occur in foodservice happen because we have always had cheap energy and it cost less to waste it than it did to design and manage to save it. Today, this is not the case. It is possible with energy conservation in existing facilities to reduce burgeoning utilities bills 20–30 percent and in new buildings designed for saving energy, the reduction can be 40 percent or more.

Buildings

As far as energy is concerned, buildings cannot be thought of as solid impervious structures, but should be looked upon as sieves in which the holes leaking out energy must be covered with insulation, draperies, and other thermal-resistant construction. Keeping the heat in during the winter and keeping it out during the summer is the aim. Walls, ceilings, and sometimes floors, must be insulated to provide barriers to heat movement. Doors and windows need to be weather stripped, double windows used, and shading provided by means of eave overhang, exterior shading, or screens, awnings, reflecting films, and proper use of blinds, shades, and draperies. A single pane of glass passes 20 times as much heat as a well-insulated solid wall of the same size.

In cold climates, the roof should be black in color to absorb the heat of the sun. In hotter zones, the reverse is true. The roof and walls should be colored in reflective silvers and whites or other light colors to repel the heat intrusion that requires so much air-conditioning and ventilation to remove. Dual-pane storm windows or plastic coverings save on heat lost in winter and gained in summer. If heat-absorbing glass is used in a window, a fan should blow over it to move the heat into the room. Double and triple windows with drying glass between them can cut costs 20–50 percent. Storm windows without shade can reduce solar heating 15 percent in summer. Wood framing transmits 24 percent of outside heat, but wood is twice as expensive as aluminum. Large windows on a building's south side can reduce winter bills by 30 percent but need reflective screening in summer. Small north windows can reduce winter heating bills 20–40 percent and can be opened in summer. The heat or cold of the outside air should be used (i.e., windows opened) wherever feasible to make interior spaces more livable. Some estimates indicate that 18 percent of the nation's energy is used to regulate indoor temperatures.

Because heating, cooling, and ventilating use so much energy (almost a third of foodservice energy), it must be monitored closely. One way to reduce this energy consumption is to watch the room thermostat closely and lower it from 24°C (74°F) to 20°C (68°F) in winter which will reduce energy requirements for heating 18 percent and total kilowatt consumption 3 percent. Conversely, raising the thermostat from 23°C (72°F) to 26°C (78°F) in summer reduces air-conditioning requirements 30 percent and kilowatts 5 percent. Keeping relative humidity high in winter makes the lower temperatures more pleasant. Filters in the furnace in winter and air conditioner in summer must be kept clean or energy consumption may increase 50 percent.

Some operators dehumidify rather than air condition their kitchens during the summer, to make their workers more comfortable. A lower humidity causes perspiration to evaporate more readily, thus cooling the worker.

Staggering start-up times of kitchen heating and air-conditioning equipment over several hours can be used to lower the demand or the charge made for having a needed high volume of electricity. Roasting and baking at other than peak hours may help, too.

It has been found that nightly lowering of the thermostat 6°C (10°F) in cold weather and raising it the same amount in hot weather will save 8–10 percent on energy used for heating and air-conditioning purposes, respectively. Another suggestion is the use of heat exchangers that will take their heat from the hot exhaust duct to heat the kitchen intake air. Despite some previously engineered ventilation figures, it has been found that air removed in ventilation can be reduced up to 50 percent. Some of the new high-velocity air baffle ventilators can reduce cubic feet per minute two-thirds and cost of heating the air an equal amount.

Certainly those kitchens that are air conditioned can reduce ventilation 50 percent if smoke and steam removal is adequate. Shutting off the ventilation during slack production periods will reduce energy consumption.

Selection of air conditioners with high energy-use efficiency is mandatory. The most efficient air conditioners are those that have high EERs (energy efficient ratios). This is obtained by dividing the rated Btu removed by the wattage used (available on attached plate on machinery). The higher the EER, the more efficient the air conditioner. Some air conditioners are 50 percent more efficient than others. In determining whether to use window-type or central air conditioning, remember that the latter is usually 10–15 percent more efficient. To avoid having to heat cold air that is drawn in from outside to replace smoky indoor air in winter, simply recycle the stuffy indoor air. Condense the excess moisture, filter the solid materials through conventional filters, and use activated charcoal to absorb the odors.

Rooms in which nothing will freeze or deteriorate from the heat need not be cooled or heated. Doors to these rooms should be kept closed. Heating or cooling ducts going through these rooms should be insulated. In some cases it has been found that infrared lamps directed on the receiving area at the time of receiving is more efficient than trying to heat the area. Steam and hot water pipes should be insulated, wherever they are. Hot water heaters and refrigeration condensers should be placed in rooms that can be closed off from the rest of the inhabited facility and well ventilated, particularly in summer.

Hot water heaters should be heavily insulated. One with 12.7 cm (5 in.) of insulation is 8 percent more heat efficient than one with 5 cm (2 in.). Similarly, a steam pipe losing 73,000 Btu can reduce this loss to 3,919 Btu with 5 cm (2 in.) of insulation and 2,600 Btu with 7.6 cm (3 in.). Water used in washrooms can be reduced to 49°C (120°F), and other water can be maintained at 60°C (140°F) unless higher temperature is needed for sanitizing. Then, heating at the point of use should be considered. The lower the temperature of the water in the hot water tank, the less the energy used in heating or maintaining its temperature and keeping the water hot in the pipes.

Hot water heater and heating boiler burners should be checked frequently to ascertain whether energy-efficient blue flames are the rule and to provide proper maintenance where they are not. Fuel–air ratios are important, as too much air means that too much heated or cooled air is going up the stack and too little air means that wasteful incomplete combustion occurs. Consider lowering the hot water tank thermostat to room temperature at night.

General airing out of the facility, if desirable, should be done by opening the doors early in the morning in summer and right after lunch in winter.

Lighting

Lighting is about 10 percent of the foodservice operator's energy bill. It is probable that this item can be reduced about 30 percent with application of some care. To do this, one must start with the building. Rooms painted with light colors, carpeted with light-reflecting carpets and having light-colored draperies and furniture demand less light. One can reduce light demands by using fixtures that bring the light down closer to, or direct it onto, the diner's table in the dining room and the work surface in the kitchen. Light levels should be only as high as that needed to perform the task. One can tell doneness of foods and read penciled directions with 30–50 FC (foot candles, the amount of light from one candle measured one foot from the source), although some illuminating engineers and state regulatory agencies prescribe 70 FC. Corridors can be lighted satisfactorily with 10 FC of light while some storerooms can be lighted with 30 FC. Where fine figures must be read (office) or at the exit end of the dishwasher where cleanliness must be ascertained, 70–100 FC are needed.

While the incandescent lamp presents the customer's complexion and the as-served food in the best light, some of the new fluorescents are almost as good in color definition and produce four times the light of the incandescents for the same amount of electricity.

There are other sources of light that provide more lumens (units of luminous flux from a point source having an intensity of one candle) per watt of electricity that can be used for exterior lighting. Compared to incandescent lamps they are:

Incandescent	17–22 lumens per watt of electricity
Mercury	56–63 lumens per watt of electricity
Fluorescent	67–83 lumens per watt of electricity
Multi-vapor	85–100 lumens per watt of electricity
Sodium	105–130 lumens per watt of electricity

In many older facilities, replacing older fluorescents with new can be up to 14 percent more efficient. Some get the color effect of incandescent lamps by substituting a pink fluorescent for one of the white ones. PAR floodlights give the same light as reflector floodlights but at half the wattage. Where people remain briefly in a room, twist-time switches will shut off the light automatically at the end of a set time. (Some restaurants have restroom hot water faucets that shut off automatically, as well).

Lighting, in general, is inefficient in its use of electricity as only about 25 percent of the current becomes light. The rest becomes heat that helps warm the room in winter and must be removed in summer. Lights can generate 25–60 percent of the air-conditioning load. Where tests show that there is too much light, one may remove some of the lamps or use bulbs of lower wattage. On the other hand, sometimes it is possible to replace two bulbs with one having the same lumen output but using less wattage.

Training, too, enters into lighting conservation. Workers should be trained to shut off lights that are not needed. Switches can be color coded to be turned on or off when certain tasks are being done—food preparation, cooking, service, cleanup, or no activity. In most instances, "lights out" after working hours should be the policy both inside the building and for signs outside. Outdoor lights can use up to 10,000 watts of electricity nightly. If outdoor lights are needed, however, using automatic timers that turn lights on and off is recommended.

Existing lights will put out more lumens if the lamps and fixtures are clean. Aging bulbs and dirty fixtures can reduce original light output up to 50 percent.

Equipment

Energy losses related to foodservice equipment are rather all encompassing, including improper specification, design utilization, cleaning, and maintenance. The most common energy waster is that of using too large equipment so that it is not used to capacity. Partial loads are baked and roasted in large ovens, dishwashers are kept operating at half capacity or less, steam jacketed kettles and range pots are operated with partial loads, griddle and range tops are heated over all of their surfaces although only partially covered with food or pots, and the fryer is used for partial loads or stands idle between loads with power on.

Other gross deficiencies include insufficient or no insulation, preheating too far in advance of use, leaks of various types of energy, poor transmission of heat from source to food, poor scheduling, faulty techniques, not using more efficient cooking temperatures, poor heat transfer due to improperly cleaned surfaces, poorly adjusted heating units, among others. Consult the *Saving Energy* sections in the various chapters on foodservice equipment, to improve energy use in individual types of equipment.

Heating, Ventilation, Air Conditioning, and Refrigeration

The first thing to consider is making the establishment airtight. All cracks, doors, and window frames should be caulked. A 1/16–1/8-inch crack can leak cold air, adding at least $180 per year to the heating bill.

Both reflective and insulative draperies should be used. The former should be drawn when the sun hits the windows in summer; the latter should be drawn when the sun leaves the window in winter. Vestibules should be built around doors to provide a trap for outside air when the door is opened.

Ample insulation should be installed in the walls and attic. It may help to install it in floors, as well, to keep out unwanted heat or cold. Reflective material should be placed under the attic skylight, if any, in summer. Attics should be ventilated in summer and made airtight in winter.

Overhanging eaves and awnings keep sun off windows in the summer. Placing special reflective screens on windows also helps to keep the building cool.

Heating and air conditioning needs must be properly gauged to avoid purchasing overly large, energy-wasting units. If possible, select a central air conditioning system, as it is 10–15 percent more energy efficient than individual window air conditioners.

Condensing coils, fans, and pipes of air conditioners must be kept clean. The National Bureau of Standards states that this will reduce cooling costs 10 percent. Dirty filters and evaporator coils, too, can add 40 percent to air conditioning costs. In addition, curtains and equipment that might block air conditioning and heating vents must be moved to allow free air movement.

All pipes and equipment carrying hot or cold air or hot water should be insulated. A bare pipe radiating 73,000 Btu can be reduced to 4,000 Btu with the addition of 5.1 cm (2 in.) of insulation.

Relative room humidity should be maintained at 40–45 percent, the level studies have shown to be most comfortable. To compensate for the drying effect of heat, room humidity must be raised in winter. When air from outdoors is heated, its humidity must also be augmented. Rooms must be dehumidified in summer, since humidity can reach an uncomfortable 90–95 percent, left unchecked. Low humidity allows perspiration to evaporate on the skin, providing a cooling effect.

Refrigerator condensers and hot water heaters should be placed in little used, well-ventilated rooms, to avoid having to compensate for the heat that they generate. Rooms that are not needed may be closed off from heat or air conditioning if they contain nothing that will be damaged by an unregulated temperature.

Where fresh air is brought in through wall ventilators, adjustable baffles should be used to avoid having an oversupply of wind.

Ventilation hoods over equipment should be checked. Place a smoking candle or a small smoke pot on the front of the equipment to determine whether ventilation hoods are functioning. Often, air volume can be reduced 50 percent without impairing smoke and fume removal. If the equipment is gas fueled, it is advisable to run equipment vents close to, or into the hood.

Energy could be saved if the following equipment were shut down at night:

- Cooling and condenser fans on air conditioners
- Chilled water and condensing pumps
- Air supply and exhaust fans
- Boilers that supply absorption units

Outside air may be used to cool air conditioner, refrigerator condensers, and unoccupied rooms, and to ventilate rooms filled with cigarette smoke, at night and early in the afternoon.

Keep in mind that heating or cooling even a few degrees more than necessary uses energy needlessly. In winter, maintain a 20°C (68°F) temperature; in summer, keep temperature between 23°–26°C (75°–78°F).

Making Restaurant Grounds Energy Efficient

One of the best exterior energy reducers is the planting of large deciduous (leaf-bearing) trees where they will shade the building, windows, and grounds. The shade provided by the trees lowers the air temperature around the building in summer. In winter, the trees shed their leaves so that the sun can heat the building. A fully shaded house will require only half the air conditioning that an unshaded house will use.

Many restaurants have asphalt or concrete close to the building. Asphalt may reach 41°C (106°F) in summer and concrete 46°C (111°F). Substituting grass, which reaches only 26°C (80°F), is a considerably better idea.

Dense shrubs, in addition to being attractive, provide a dead space and block off cold winds when placed close to a building. They may save 20–30 percent on fuel. Arborvitae, hemlock, spruce, and yew are all effective windbreakers. Planting groves of trees on the windward side of the building is helpful since they cool the air by the evaporation of their leaf moisture. An unshielded house may be 8–10 degrees warmer in summer. Windbreaks in general, whether they be dense lines of trees, solid high fences, or other wind screens, reduce air penetration of the building. If one windbreak is used, 25–30 percent may be saved in energy; if two are used, up to 60 percent may be saved. Windbreaks prevent heavy snow drifts from accumulating on the side of the building.

QUESTIONS

1. How can one design a new restaurant to be energy efficient? What percentage of energy reduction should be achieved?
2. What color should a roof be in a warm climate? In a cold climate?
3. What is EER? How is it calculated?
4. What is the average set room temperature in summer? In winter?
5. What causes lumen output reduction in light fixtures?
6. What foot candle production does Avery recommend for light fixtures?
7. When should a restaurant be aired out in summer? In winter?
8. Name two ways in which restaurant grounds can be altered to reduce energy use inside the building.
9. At what humidity level should a room be kept in summer? In winter?
10. Where should a hot water heater be placed?
11. Name five ways of keeping sun from windows.
12. How is a ventilation hood checked for possible air velocity reduction?
13. How can an attic be made more energy efficient?

BIBLIOGRAPHY

ANON. 1973. Checklist: commercial cooking energy conservation. *Hoosier Chef* XIII, No. 12, 8, 9, and 13.

ANON. 1975. *Guide to Energy Conservation for Food Service.* Federal Energy Administration, Washington, D.C.

ANON. 1975. *Energy Management and Energy Conservation Practices for the Restaurant Industry.* Canadian Restaurant Assoc., Toronto.

AVERY, A.C. 1974. You can save energy. *Institutions Volume Feeding* 74, No. 6, 41–45.

AVERY, A.C. 1975. Changing Foodservice for Energy Savings. Lecture given to Canadian Restaurant Assoc., Toronto.

AVERY, A.C. *Your Restaurant and the Energy Crisis.* Cooperative Extension Service, Purdue University, West Lafayette, Ind.

Arranging Equipment in a Foodservice Facility

One can give every consideration to the selection of the proper type, design, and capacity of equipment for a foodservice facility, but if that equipment is poorly placed in relation to the raw material that will be used in it, the other supporting pieces of equipment, overall food flow, and proximity to point of service, much of the value of the equipment is lost. The manager is responsible for making his wants and needs, as well as those of the operation, known to the foodservice consultant who will prepare plans from which the architect and contractor will build a food facility.

In kitchen design one should:

1. Provide a kitchen in which a minimal number of skilled and unskilled workers will be able to prepare and serve the necessary amounts of optimum quality foods in accordance with the advertised menu and established standards of preparation and service.
2. Select proper equipment in proper size and place it so that it will allow service of the food at its maximum quality with the speed expected of the particular type of operation (instantaneous for fast food and cafeteria and to-order for a table service restaurant).
3. Minimize food losses and costs.
4. Utilize a minimum of building space and construction funds.
5. Require a minimum of utilities with low maintenance costs.

6. Provide a safe comfortable working environment that will attract workers and utilize them at maximum efficiency.

To accomplish this alone or with the assistance of a foodservice consultant or architect requires that the manager collect much information or make pertinent assumptions that can be used for planning purposes. This is a partial list of what must be known before purposeful planning can be started:

1. Type of sponsor. Sole owner, partnership, corporation, franchise, government, or other.
2. Type of operation. Fast food (hamburger, hot dog, fish, steak, roast beef, pizza, taco, chicken and other), self-service or other service cafeteria, lunchroom, specialty house (see fast food list and add gourmet, ethnic, classical cuisine, seafood, and many others) in addition to smorgasbord, barbecue, shore dinners, school, college, hospital, nursing home, prisons, and other institutional feeding. This decision affects overall type of building, decor, location, and equipment.
3. Type of service. Walk-up, drive-up, self-service cafeterias, shopping center cafeterias and carousels, counters with stools or stand-up, serving carts and trucks, and table service. This decision affects cooking, serving, and dishwashing equipment.
4. The proposed menu. This, along with the prospective number of customers, expected volumes of each menu item to be sold, and the degree of raw material prefabrication to be purchased, regulates the amounts and types of storage and other equipment that will have to be provided. A labor-abundant institution may need tables and other equipment to prepare everything from the raw untouched state, while a city hospital may need nothing but storage, reheat, and assembly equipment to serve food that is purchased completely prepared and preportioned.
5. Raw material. Foods without any preparation, foods with partial preparation or some cooking, and fully prepared foods or ingredients. These decisions affect storage needs, preparation equipment needs, cooking requirements, manpower needs and in some cases, service equipment.
6. Frequency of deliveries from food and paper goods purveyors. This affects storage capacities required.
7. Service and eating times available. These usually regulate the types and numbers of service facilities and cooking equipment to be provided, the number of seats and tables, and, to some extent, the warewashing facilities required.
8. Health and business ordinances. These will be factors in the various decisions that will have to be made. As an example, can food waste disposals be used? Does canned garbage have to be enclosed or refrigerated? Can bulk milk dispensers be used? What facilities must be provided for workers? Can carpet be used in the kitchen?
9. What utilities can or must be used? Many new restaurants cannot use gas due to a short supply in the area. How much hot water will be needed and at what temperature?
10. Will the workers wear uniforms? If so, will they or the company be responsible for their purchase and care? If the company is to be responsible, is it more economical for the company to hire laundry service or operate its own for the uniforms and other linens? Is paper feasible for table service?
11. What staff facilities should be provided? What customer rest room facilities?
12. How much office space is needed?
13. How much of the old kitchen equipment will be used in the new kitchen? Will it be compatible with the new?
14. What numbers, types (skilled and unskilled), sexes, and degree of training are available in workers? How good is the management?
15. What money is available for carrying out the project?

16. Others include: Will butchering be done? Will baking be done? Will ice cream be bought or made? What types of flatware and dishes will be used? How will tables be served or bused—hand, tray or cart?
17. Standards of production. These might include all grilled, broiled, and fried items prepared when ordered, coffee prepared every half hour, vegetables prepared in three batches, soups, rice, pasta, and potatoes kettle cooked in one batch, no carry-over of coffee from meal to meal, and others.

Using this information, plus experience with similar facilities, the consultant or architect commonly modifies standard designs that he has in mind or on file or has tried before without considerable complaints from those who have used his services. Few consultants have worked in kitchens that they have designed and many have not seen them completed. He usually assays the adjustments required by those who hire him, the design situation, and the aforementioned collected information, but a food facility is rarely designed with the scientific exactness that a factory planner uses to maximize operating efficiency and minimize materials handling and labor costs.

In general, a factory designer analyzes the operations, amounts, and movements in the manufacture of each product and then develops a consolidation for all the products. From the data, he arranges work centers along a line or lines from Receiving to Shipping in the general order that they operate on the raw material. At the same time he minimizes the energy needed for moving them. Those work centers between which the greatest weight of material is moved will be closest together along the material flow lines. Within work centers the same applies after the types, numbers, and sizes of needed equipment are determined. Those pieces of equipment between which the greatest amount of materials move are placed close together and arranged in the order of their use. A possible factory layout design process is shown in figure 27.1.

Conventional Foodservice Layout

If the type of operation, menu, and desired feeding capacity of a proposed foodservice facility are similar to one the foodservice consultant has designed in the past, the new facility will often look much like the old. Plans of many designers are easy to identify as some of their design features never change.

The conventional foodservice layout procedure for a completely new concept will not be described in detail as it varies between consultants, particularly in the amount of analysis and science used. Some use tables developed by others to make their equipment selection and then move it around in the space available, varying table shapes and sizes and aisle widths until all the space seems to be well filled. If the customer does not complain, the designer feels he has done a good job.

The good foodservice consultants do their background work first, collecting all the previously noted information. They use the menu, together with expected average amounts of each food that will be needed for each period, to prepare production bar charts for each day of a typical week. The chart is arranged vertically, listing each meal and the menu items that must be prepared for it. Across are vertical lines equidistant from the hour of first equipment use to the time of the last equipment use. A horizontal equipment use bar is drawn across the hour bars and the equipment identified on the bar for the length of time equipment is used for each menu item and the capacities needed each time. From this chart the designer determines his equipment needs and capacities. Also, he can see when the same piece of equipment is needed at the same time or overlapping time, thus requiring two of the same piece of equipment. With a good knowledge of equipment, often he can use equipment for multiple purposes and decrease the types and numbers of necessary pieces and the space they occupy. In some cases, he can suggest prefabricated food items that negate the use of expensive or little-used equipment, or he might suggest labor-saving equipment that might provide

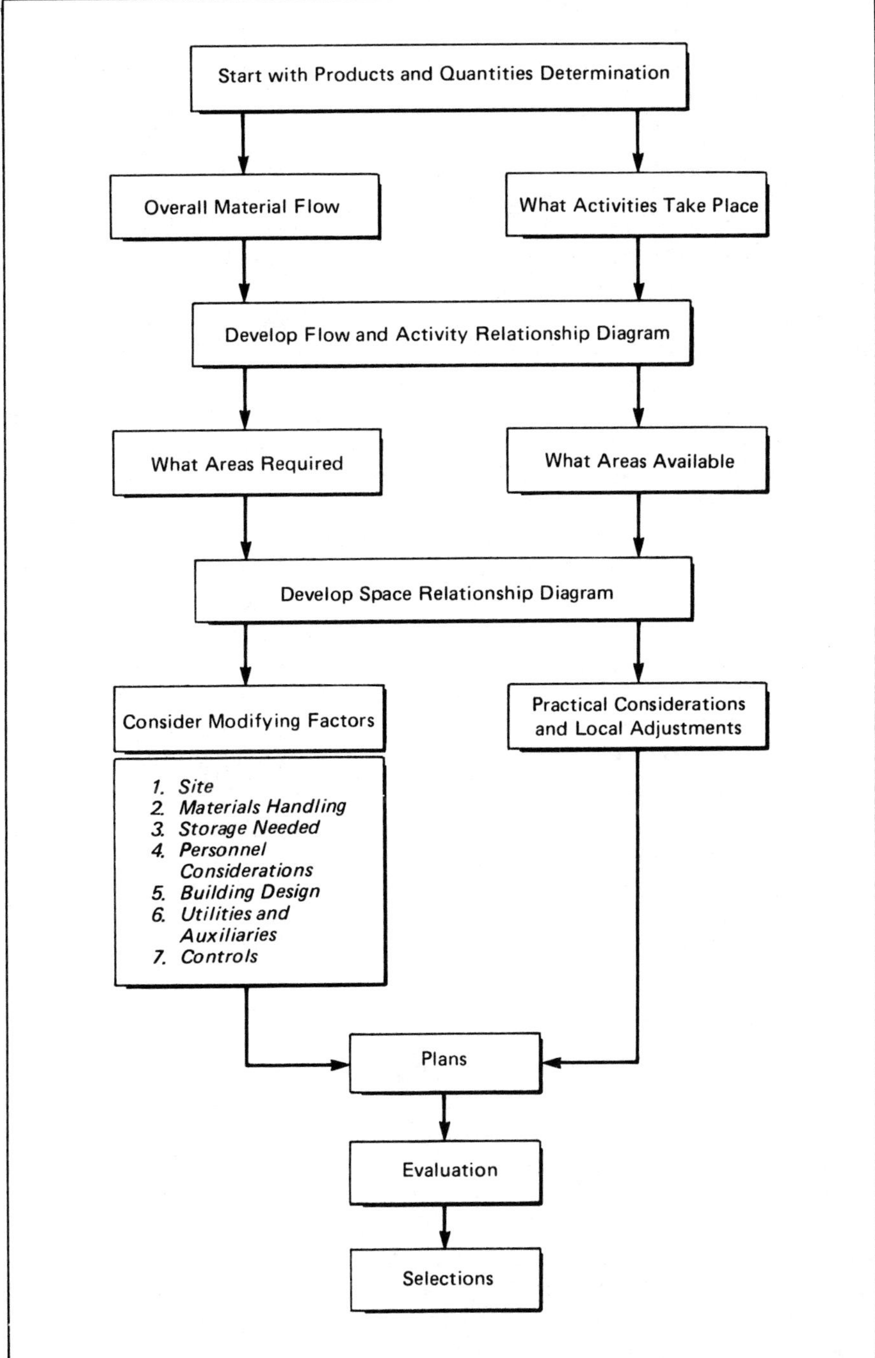

FIGURE 27.1. Factory layout design procedure.

an expensive skill or be a cost-saving substitute for a worker.

The designer allocates the equipment to the various work centers, which may be defined as the locations where one or more similar types of work are done often by one worker. The work centers usually, but not always, include:

1. Receiving. The place where food is received, weighed, or counted, checked against the order and invoice. It is then routed to the proper frozen, chilled, or nonrefrigerated storage or directly to the point of first use if space is available and the food will not deteriorate before it is used. Counter and platform scales and a table are usually available here along with a stand-up or sit-down desk. Conveyors or skids, and sometimes adjustable ramps or elevators, to bridge between truck and unloading platform are made available. I recommend that a one- or two-compartment sink be present, together with one- or two-compartment supermarket-type carts, so that greens and vegetables may be washed and broken into lots and meats may be divided into batch lots, then handled into cold storage units or points of first use as a batch unit without further handling. Most waste is left at Receiving. Goods received in truck or railroad car may be unloaded as pallet loads, thus necessitating a pallet truck of some kind, transferred to a four-wheel cart (preferably on the truck), and rolled off by ramp or moved by slide, gravity, or powered conveyor.

2. Storerooms. Must be sufficient in capacity to hold food and other supplies between replenishments and, if not too costly, should be large enough to allow purchases of least expensive truck and carload lots and also to allow buying of much-used foods when they are at lowest cost to hold for later use. Colleges, large chains, government groups, and institutions are usually best able to allocate the funds and space for this purpose.

Storeroom space of a minimal nature is commonly calculated on the basis of historical data that determines how many cases of No. 10 cans of whole tomatoes, 30 pound cartons of frozen peas, pounds of fresh or frozen hamburger patties, and other items will be needed between replenishments plus emergencies. The total number of cases of tomatoes would be multiplied by 0.029 cu m (1.02 cu ft), the space occupied by one case. The number of cases of frozen peas would be multiplied by 0.029 cu m (1.02 cu ft), and so on until the total space needed for freezer, refrigerator, and dry storage rooms are known. Use of shelving alters space needs very little. If the storerooms are walk-ins, necessary space must be added for passageways for personnel and carts. This might increase needed space by 100–150 percent. If foods are handled in pallet lots, more space needs to be added.

While many designers use fixed in-place permanent shelving, I prefer wheeled shelving that can be in the form of the supermarket-type carts with wall- or ceiling-mounted shelving above this height. Often used is the wheeled shelving that can be loaded with a preparation-load of food on the receiving dock, wheeled to the storeroom, and then to the point of use as needed. To make full use of the storeroom space, it is desirable to have the shelving adjustable to the height of the product to be stored on it. A desk, chair, vertical file for requisitions, and stock card file are desirable.

Where the storeroom is to be used as a central ingredient room, additions needed are a table on which to do measuring, table top scales, floor or medium-height platform scales, various volume measures, wheeled flour and sugar bins, and a variety of table top cannisters for various spices and other ingredients. Carts or wheeled racks will be needed to take the measured recipe components to the work center where they will be used.

3. Vegetable Preparation area. This may be vestigial if most fruits and vegetables are procured in ready-to-cook or precooked form, but if they are prepared from the raw state, a mechanical peeler, sinks, trimming benches or tables, vegetable slicers, choppers, cubers, and scales are necessary. If individual salads are prepared ahead of time, assembly tables, wheeled racks for transport and refrigerators, preferably those into which a whole rack of prepared salads can be wheeled, are used. Pass-through refrigerators between Vegetable Preparation and Meat Preparation areas and the Cooking area may be used so that the ready-to-cook products may be placed in them on one side and be removed by the chef in the Cooking area on the other side when he needs them.

4. Meat Preparation area. This is fast disappearing as more and more meats are portion-cut or cut into roasts ready to cook. Where butchering is done in-house, the usual equipment includes scales, meat saw, chopping block or cutting table or both, possibly a meat tenderizer or cuber, meat grinder, patty maker, and a sink.

5. Baking area. A full bakery is rarely planned except in large facilities. In most cases, it consists of scales, a mixer, ingredient bins, a makeup table, sink, sometimes a proofer, hot plate, and/or steam jacketed kettle, deck or forced convection bake oven, and cooling racks. At times the mixer does double duty in other work centers, particularly the Cooking area.

6. Cooking area. This is heart of the foodservice facility, and in some small operations the kitchen and the other supporting areas are a part of it, doubling as preparation and cooking equipment. In most cases, the cooking area is a judicious blending of storage, tables, cooking, and holding equipment whose makeup will depend on the type of operation and menu combination. While the cooking area for a pizza restaurant is a circle of mixer, refrigerator, topping material containers, dough, pizza preparation table, and pizza oven, that of a Chinese restaurant may be ranges, woks, steamers, cutting table, and refrigerator.

However, most table service, cafeteria, and institutional kitchens of any size have some combination of steam jacketed kettles, steamers or pressure cookers, griddles, deep fat fryers, broilers, and ranges interspersed with work tables, refrigerators, sinks, and access to a mixer. The cooking equipment is usually covered with a canopy hood to remove smoke, steam, fumes, and surplus heat. In conjunction with these, many, particularly table service restaurants, have a service area where ready-prepared foods are kept hot until plates or serving dishes are served. Commonly, moist foods are stored in steam tables and dry crusty foods under infrared lamps.

7. Holding area. Once this was the bainmarie, but this is largely in disrepute as it encourages food preparation too far in advance of service. The table service serving center has been mentioned as one type of holding area. Cafeterias normally use heated and refrigerated pass-through cabinets in the wall between the kitchen and the service area where the pans of ready-to-serve food are put in on the kitchen side and removed on the other side for placement in the serving counter as needed. It saves labor, particularly with refrigerated items, to place them into a wheeled refrigerator cabinet as they are prepared in the salad-dessert area and then wheel the whole unit into a space in the wall behind that part of the serving line that it supports. This may be done with hot items using heated cabinets.

8. Service area. The make-up of this varies according to the type of operation and service requirements, speed of service, variety of items to be served, as well as other factors. Many fast food restaurants concentrate both final preparation and service equipment around a walk-up or drive-in counter as indicated for the pizza restaurant. Table service restaurants of moderate size operate their final cooking functions of broiling, griddling, and frying on the back-bar across an aisle from a steam table and possibly a cold pan for salad plates and garnishes. Many have the pick-up area in the kitchen area in the form of an inverted horseshoe. As the waitress enters the area on the right, she places soiled dishes on a table in the dishroom to her right. At the next station she would pick up breads, desserts, salads, etc., as she proceeds around the horseshoe. Just prior to leaving the kitchen at that station she would pick up the hot entrée plate, vegetables, and hot breads and possibly the hot soup and beverage. More and more restaurants are serving breads, soup and beverages, flatware, and dishes from behind a barrier immediately within the dining room nearest the kitchen, from a service island or from a table along the wall. Where this can be done without offense to the customers, the expedients reduce steps and speed service.

Cafeterias have all of the service facilities in view of the customer. The steam tables, cold pans, bread and beverage service equipment, dessert displays, ice dispensers, and other equipment may be arranged in almost any order in straight lines or loops, using both sides of the equipment, saw tooth, in islands and various types of shopping centers. Some have a regular service line but place flatware, condiments, and water on an island in the dining room past the first cashier. This speeds the serving line, encourages the customer to take only that flatware he needs for what food he has on his tray, and reduces consumption of condiments as compared to having them at each table. Observant managers light the displayed food brightly and the tray slide area dimly. They place items that they want customers to take early in the line, where there is a bend in the line, or where the customer must wait.

I look on the serving line area as a good location to save food and also labor and eliminate leftovers, so I place as much final cooking equipment as possible in, or adjacent to, the serving line. This brings the cook into the service area, which reduces the needed number of serving personnel and enables the cook to listen to customer comments and learn where food improvement is needed. However, the major benefits derived are in being able to enhance food quality by preparing it fresh according to need, and looking ahead to the number of customers coming through the line. This reduces leftovers. A portable griddle can be placed in the serving line and, like the hearth broiler in an atmosphere restaurant, it can sell much high-priced food. The fryer and pressure cooker, in some cases, are placed on the back-bar. In one class of ships, a steam jacketed kettle was placed in the serving line for soup and hot cereals. It greatly increased consumption of these low-cost items.

9. Dishroom. This has the function of making soiled flatware and dishes table ready. The soiled dish table, prescraping facilities, garbage disposal, silverware washers and burnishers, dish prewashing, washing and drying equipment, as well as tables, dish transports, and carts for getting dishes back into service quickly must be carefully considered. In the order of desirability, dish removal from table service restaurants is best done by use of busing carts, then large trays, and, least desirable, by hand. Many school lunch, institutional, and industrial operations use self-busing where the customer takes his tray of soiled dishes to a window close by the dining room exit. Many fast food restaurants utilize single-service dishes to avoid the need for dishrooms. While this may increase cost to the customer, it does reduce labor, material, equipment, and space needs. It leaves the problem of increased waste disposal and its cost. In some cases, this can be reduced by incineration or compaction equipment.

10. Potwashing. This is often overlooked or relegated to a distant corner of the kitchen as it is not usually considered part of preparation, cooking, or service. However, it is vital to all three, is of considerable interest to health authorities, and can waste much labor. In its simplest form, potwashing is composed of two to four compartment sinks, soiled and clean utensil drainboards, garbage facilities, and clean utensil racks. As the size of the operation increases, greater use is made of mechanized potwashers and wheeled utensil racks to collect, return, and store utensils.

11. Office. In it are the desks and chairs for the managerial personnel, file cabinets for important records, typewriters, and calculating machines as required.

In most conventional layout design, little analysis goes into the arrangement of either work centers or equipment within work centers. The more thoughtful planners do think in terms of food flow through the kitchen and place the work centers operating on the food along the food flow line from Receiving to Service. Work centers may be arranged as shown in figure 27.2. Dotted lines show frequent personnel movement but not food movement.

While not related to food, most of the soiled utensils are generated in Cooking, Bakery, and Service, so Potwashing should be located close to all three. Dishwashing is related only to Service and Dining Room so it is placed close to them. As the manager is primarily interested in whether the food is being prepared expediently and serving lines are moving smoothly, he should be in a position to observe both from his office instead of being placed close to Receiving, as was the case formerly.

The food flow line is not always a straight line. It may be S- or L-shaped and in large commissaries, it is U-shaped as the food comes in for processing and leaves for the schools or other operations from the same platform. Some large institutions such as the U.S. Naval Academy have parallel lines for each major type of food production method—broiling, frying, griddling, water cooking, and roasting.

In conventional types of arrangement of equipment in work centers, usually a major piece of equipment is placed centrally and the other pieces of equipment are arranged around it without too much thought of flow. Thus, in a bake shop, the baker's table is the hub and the mixers, bins, sink,

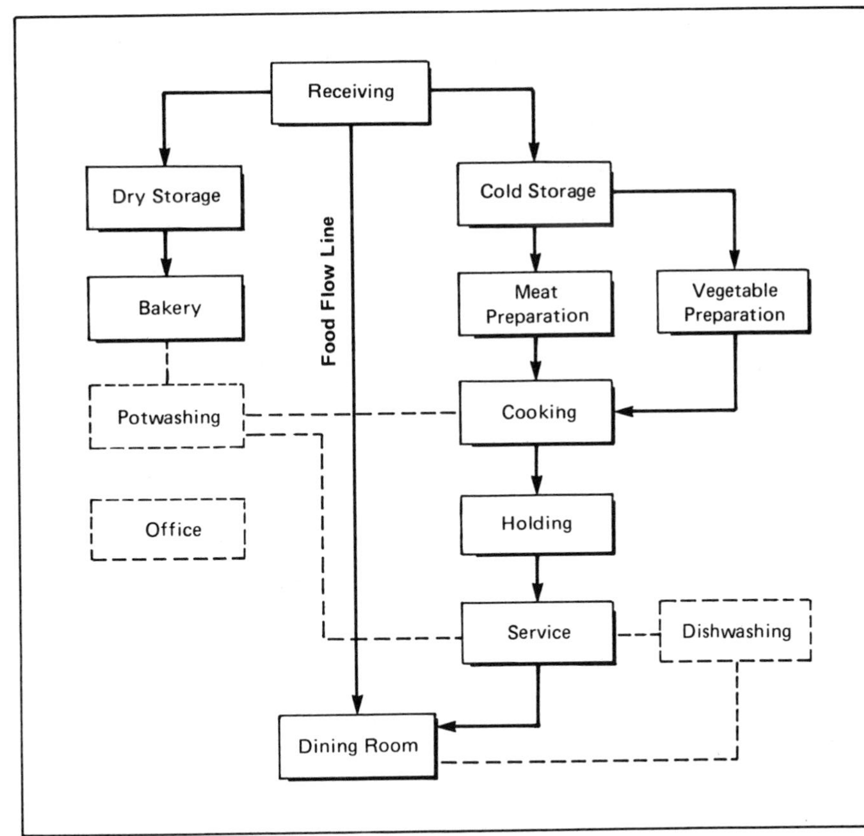

FIGURE 27.2. Food flow diagram.

racks, and ovens are arranged around it. The same applies in a pizza kitchen. In a butcher shop, supporting equipment surrounds the cutting table.

The Cooking area has long been the most poorly arranged of the work centers. The range has been the center of the work center and solid banks of similar types of cooking equipment extend in both directions from it. Often, in large kitchens, another solid bank of cooking equipment backs up to it to minimize the size of the canopy hood. Despite the fact that most of the cook's movements are between the equipment under the hood and tables, he has no tables under the hood. In most cases, he must cross a 1.2–1.5-m (4–5-ft) aisle. The cook averages about 60 percent of his time at tables. So for 60 percent of his working day he has his back toward the cooking food. In addition, he travels an interminable number of times back and forth across the aisle, each step of which is a possibility of slip, trip, or fall and the spilling or dripping of grease or other slippery material.

Avery Design System for Foodservice

The Avery Design System is a scientific approach based on Orpha Mae Thomas's *A Scientific Basis for the Design of Institution Kitchens* (1947) as modified by the U.S. Navy for developing the atomic submarine and destroyer galleys and by me to overcome deficiencies I observed in the navy studies (figure 27.3).

It is based on the premise that a kitchen should be arranged so that those work centers and pieces of equipment between which there is the

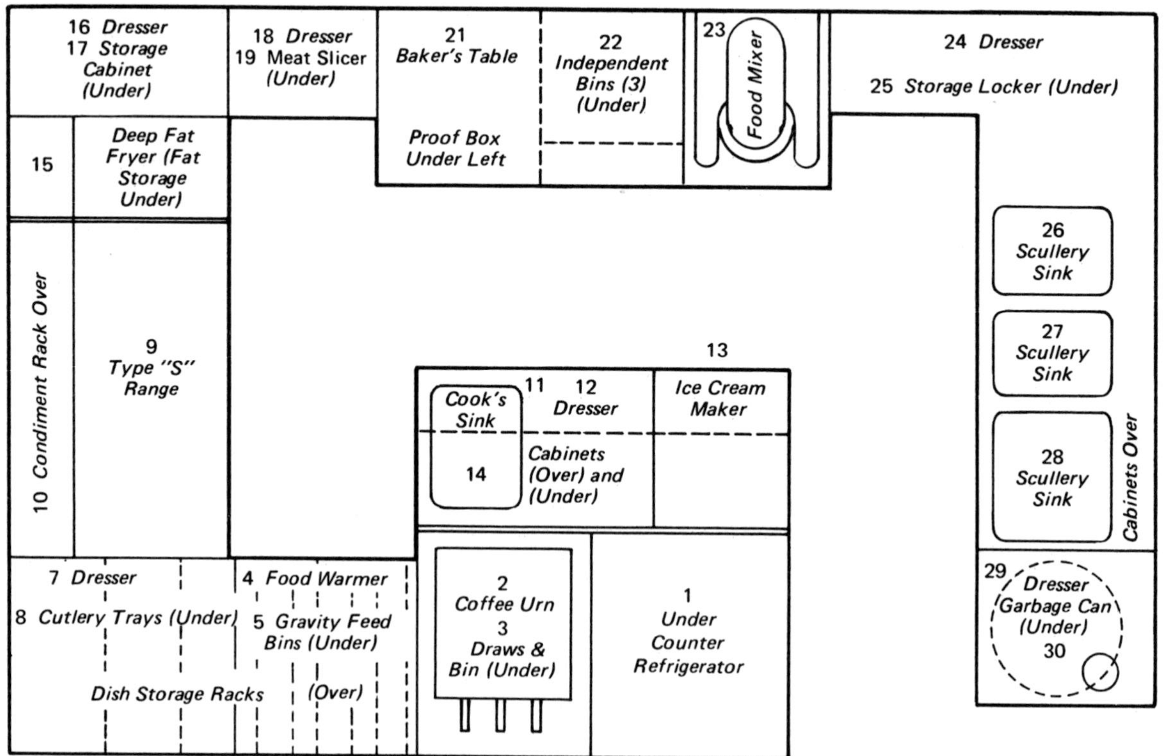

FIGURE 27.3. Layout of atomic submarine galley as planned by use of man-machine interaction study.

greatest human movement (as contrasted with the industrial engineer's weight of material) should be close together and arranged in the order that the food flows from Receiving to Service. This was determined to give scientific design to submarine and destroyer galleys by noting every movement of every kitchen worker between the various pieces of kitchen equipment. Thus, in the redesign those pieces of equipment between which there was the greatest movement were placed adjacent to each other or in the same vertical plane. Tables appeared beside ranges, griddles, fryers, mechanical equipment, kettles, and sinks. They were found to be best located immediately in front of broilers and small steamers and across the aisle from ovens, large steamers, and refrigerators. These changes modified the equipment under canopy hoods by adding tables and, in some cases, sinks.

The Avery Design System modifies the man-machine interaction data according to the level of wages of the particular worker making the movements. Thus, the movements of a cook, which are twice as costly as those of the lowest paid worker, are multiplied by two. While the industrial engineer would have one optimize the kitchen operations by work improvement study before doing the man-machine interaction study, I found that older foodservice workers resist change while working and being studied in familiar surroundings, so instead I optimized the design based on the collected data after collecting the man-machine interaction data (figure 27.4). This optimization was done with the aid of a tool that the U.S. Navy uses to develop tomorrow's ships. In my modification, it is known as the Ideal Design Development Chart (figure 27.5) and, as a working chart, the example

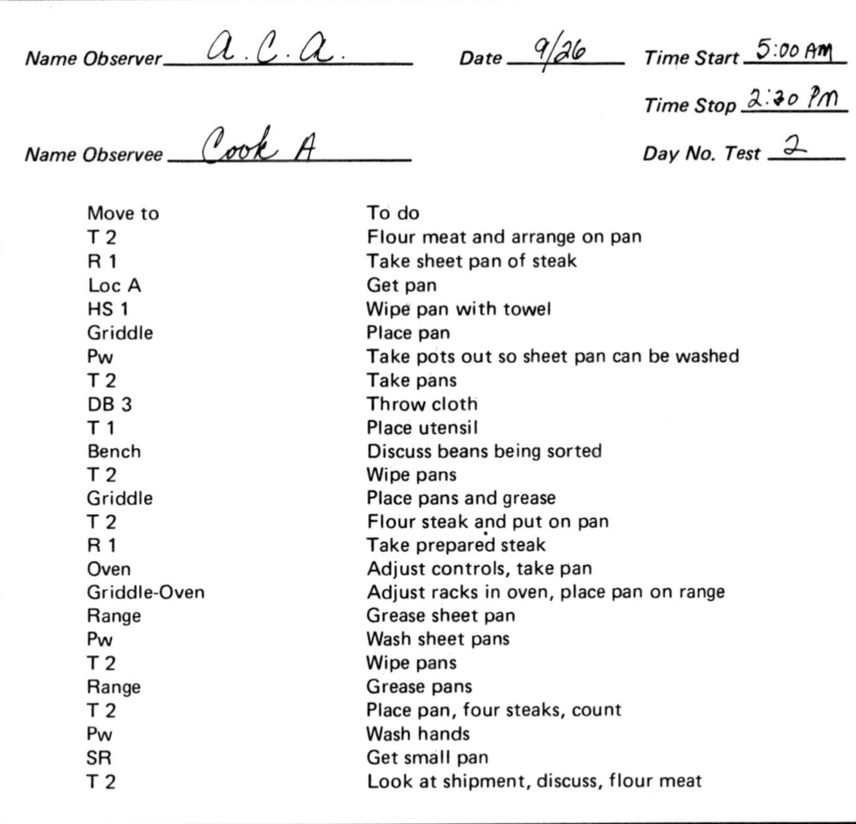
Name Observer a. C. a. Date 9/26 Time Start 5:00 AM

Time Stop 2:30 PM

Name Observee Cook A Day No. Test 2

Move to	To do
T 2	Flour meat and arrange on pan
R 1	Take sheet pan of steak
Loc A	Get pan
HS 1	Wipe pan with towel
Griddle	Place pan
Pw	Take pots out so sheet pan can be washed
T 2	Take pans
DB 3	Throw cloth
T 1	Place utensil
Bench	Discuss beans being sorted
T 2	Wipe pans
Griddle	Place pans and grease
T 2	Flour steak and put on pan
R 1	Take prepared steak
Oven	Adjust controls, take pan
Griddle-Oven	Adjust racks in oven, place pan on range
Range	Grease sheet pan
Pw	Wash sheet pans
T 2	Wipe pans
Range	Grease pans
T 2	Place pan, four steaks, count
Pw	Wash hands
SR	Get small pan
T 2	Look at shipment, discuss, flour meat

FIGURE 27.4. Form used to record the cook's movement from equipment to equipment, in order to place equipment between which there is greatest movement close together.

is expanded over a sheet about 61 cm (2 ft) wide. Every aspect of the prospective kitchen design that appears to need improvement is run through a chart individually. It can be done by an individual or a team of three or four innovative people. The chart can be used for solving of methods problems as well. Using the Avery Design System to redesign a state hospital kitchen which was planned by an architect, I was able to reduce worker travel 50 percent, use less area, and reduce feeding costs per patient.

One may use a shortened version of the Avery Design System with fairly good results. Gathering of the man-machine interaction can be simulated by drawing up a process flow chart showing each step and piece of equipment involved in the preparation of each major recipe. This type of study can be done in two or three days as contrasted with six months each for the U.S. Navy studies and six weeks for my hospital study.

Layout Design by Consensus

No matter how scientific a design may be, if an important worker in the kitchen has not had input, generally he will find fault with the ultimate design. An acceptable kitchen design can be achieved by consulting all of the important people on the staff who are involved with the kitchen as to what work centers and equipment should be close together. At least, they can give the designer the requirements as each of them see it. But, in most cases, each will be only repeating his past experience. I did not have my research done in time for the first atomic submarine, so old submarine commissary personnel were consulted as to needed design characteristics. The *U.S. Nautilus* looks much as did World War II submarines because these men could do little but repeat their experience in the old submarines.

What is Done?	*Why is it Done?*	*How Else Could it Be Done?*	*Ideal Action Selected*
What is action?	Why do it?	What actions could be used? Could any be combined with other actions? Can they be eliminated? List alternatives. Evaluate and select one best	Describe: Can it be improved in future? How?
When is it done?	Why is it done at this time?	When could it be done?	What is best time for action? Why?
What action precedes? What action follows?	Why does this action precede? Why does this action follow?	Select best What actions should precede? Select best What actions could follow?	What action should precede? Why? What action could follow? Why?
Where is action done?	Why should it be done there? Advantages Disadvantages	Where could action be done? Evaluate and select best	Where should action take place? Why?
Who does action? Who does what?	Why them? Advantages Disadvantages	Who else could do it relative to: degree of skill required? Availability at time of ideal action selected? Number required?	Who should do job in light of the ideal action selected?

FIGURE 27.5. Ideal Design Development Chart. In use it is spread out to be two to three feet wide to have more room.

To average out the requirements for placement of work centers and equipment in a new kitchen as seen by each of the staff who will operate it, I have devised a system from Richard Muther's *Simplified Layout Planning* known as Design by Consensus (actually averaging). Each person being consulted fills out forms on which he first evaluates the relative need for each pair of work centers to be close to each other on the basis of a scale of 4 (very important) to 0 (no importance) (figure 27.6).

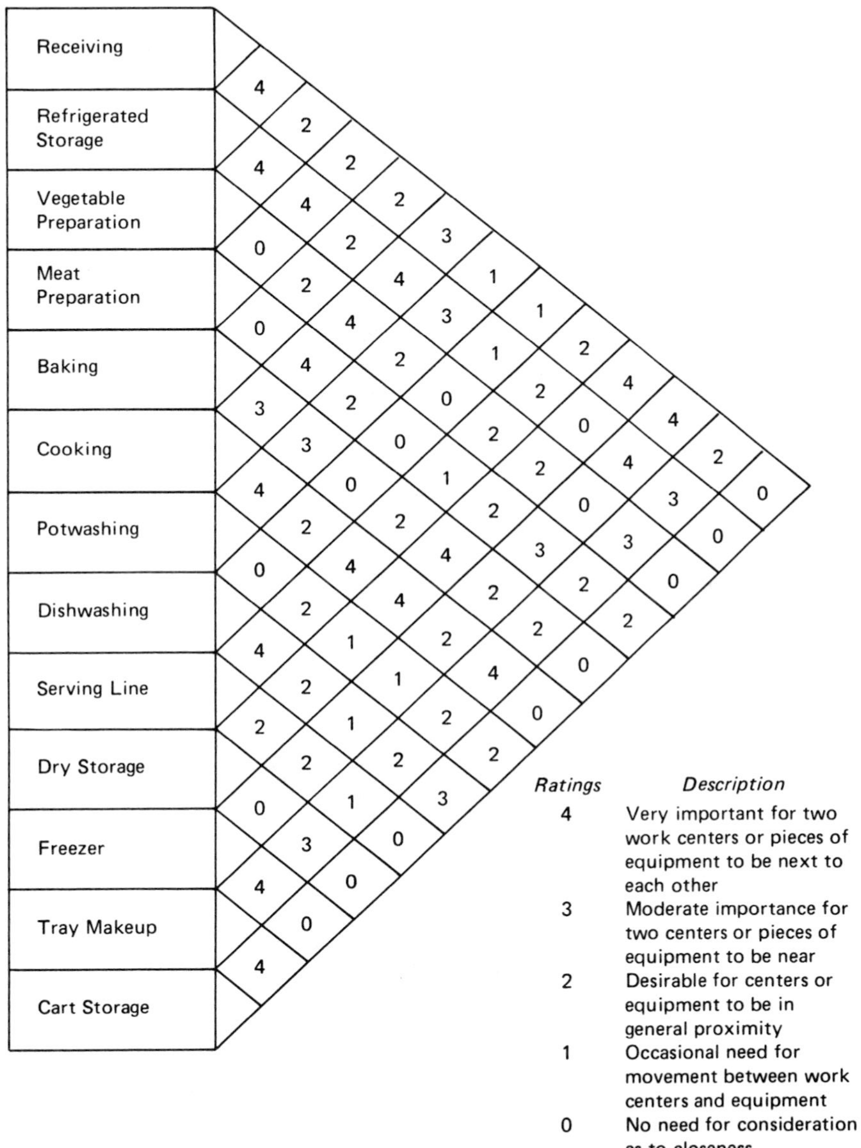

FIGURE 27.6. Workers' relationship chart that is first filled out for work center placement and then used with the equipment in each work center to arrange it.

Then he does the same for the equipment within each work center. Then the person conducting the study consolidates these ratings for all those individuals being consulted and strikes an average for each work center or equipment pair and learns which work centers and pieces of equipment should be close to each other (figure 27.7). If the designer feels that the opinions of one person are more important than the ratings of others, he may double or triple the values this person records.

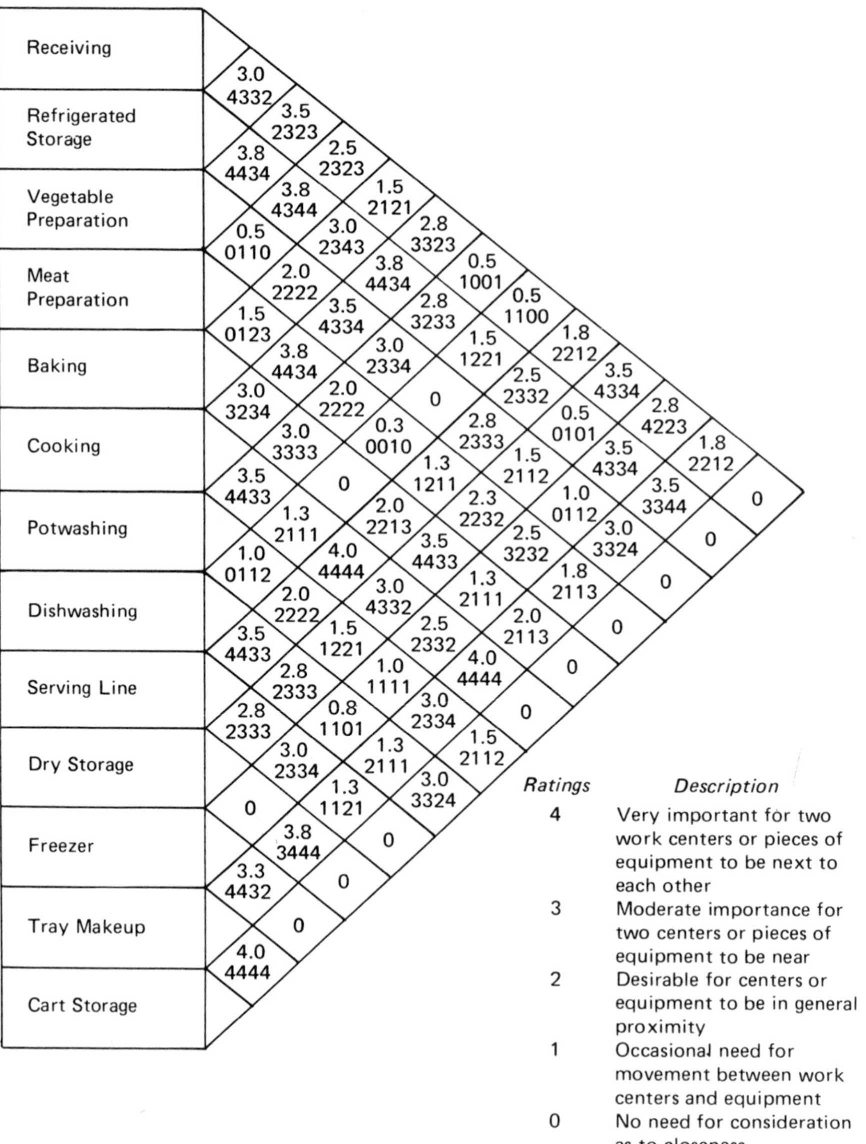

FIGURE 27.7. Consolidating or averaging all the thoughts of those being consulted.

Assembling the Layout

Whether he uses the conventional, Avery Design System, or Design by Consensus, the designer must prepare a layout indicating that the equipment will fit into the spaces available, with proper passages or aisles. Usually the food must come into the designated space at a specific point designated by the architect or owner and exit from the kitchen at designated points—elevators, doors, windows, pass-throughs, or dumbwaiters.

The designer uses two-dimensional templates of paper or three-dimensional models of the same scale as the outline of the space he wants to evaluate. I use a scale of 1 to 12; 1 cm on the drawing will equal 12 cm of equipment in the kitchen. Templates or models of all equipment are arranged in the kitchen space available, taking care to allow adequate aisles and work space around all equipment. If it all fits in like a jigsaw puzzle, the designer needs to make no adjustment. But, if there is space left over or unused, then he must decide to use it in wider aisles, bigger tables, more storage space, or give it back to the architect.

More often, since foodservice spaces are an afterthought in most industrial and institutional design, the planner must find more room. This can be done in consultation with the owner or manager by planning to buy some of the items that he has planned to do in-house in ready-to-cook or fully cooked form instead. Most common substitutions are prefabricated meats, ready-baked breads, rolls, and cakes, ready-to-cook or frozen vegetables, and precooked frozen entrées. Some fast food people eliminate dishrooms by adopting single use ware.

If the additional space need is small, narrower aisles and smaller tables may suffice. More use of vertical space may do the trick—double-deck ovens, using undercounter refrigerators, shelving over equipment, double-deck broilers, or single large rather than double small fryers. Sometimes substitution of higher capacity faster equipment can help—using forced convection ovens instead of a two- or three-deck conventional oven, using pressure cookers in place of steamers, using high capacity fryers and griddles, and similar substitutions that may be unfamiliar to the cooks but are necessitated by space limitations.

The first step in the layout process after making sure that the equipment fits is to arrange the work centers along the food flow line. Most will be as indicated in the conventional system, but make use of better information, if available. In the Avery Design System and Design by Consensus, those four to six work center pairs receiving the highest ratings as needing to be close together are given ratings of "A," the next six to eight "B," and the next eight to ten "C" (See table 27.1.) In a diagram of the space to be laid out and the food flow line, the A category relationships are placed in the space first and joined with four lines, then the B relationships are put in and joined with three lines indicating that there is much movement between these work centers and cross-traffic should be avoided (figures 27.8 and 27.9). Then C relationships are added, and here they are not allowed to interfere with the A or B relationships. They, too, should avoid traffic, but it is not as important as with the A's and B's. Any other relationships are arranged in places where they occur traditionally (figure 27.10).

Next, utilizing the space needs of each work center scale, squares are substituted for each of the work centers in its relative position. These, in turn, are drawn into the space available in a scale drawing. Finally, the equipment in each work center is arranged according to the man-machine interaction relationships or the opinions of those consulted in Design by Consensus (figure 27.11). However, these must be modified to some extent to put together the proper aisles and overall movement. I strive to keep the main traffic aisle through the kitchen away from that concerned with food production by giving the food flow line aisle the semblance of a dead-end aisle. This means that the main traffic aisle must be the obvious route for those not concerned with the kitchen.

In general, one seeks to arrange each work center so that it starts at the food flow line, loops to one side or the other, returns to the food flow line after working on the food. If the work center aisle is at right angles to the flow line, the food would start

TABLE 27.1. Importance Category Breakdown

Work Center Pairs	Consensus Rating	Category
Cooking and Serving Line	4	A
Cooking and Tray Makeup	4	A
Tray Makeup and Cart Storage	4	A
Refrigerator Storage and Vegetable Preparation	3.8	B
Refrigerator Storage and Meat Preparation	3.8	B
Refrigerator Storage and Cooking	3.8	B
Meat Preparation and Cooking	3.8	B
Dry Storage and Makeup	3.8	B
Dry Storage and Receiving	3.5	B
Refrigerated Storage and Freezer	3.5	B
Refrigerated Storage and Tray Makeup	3.5	B
Vegetable Preparation and Cooking	3.5	B
Dry Storage and Baking	3.5	B
Cooking and Potwashing	3.5	B
Serving Line and Dishwashing	3.5	B
Freezer and Tray Makeup	3.3	C
Refrigerated Storage and Receiving	3.0	C
Refrigerated Storage and Baking	3.0	C
Tray Makeup and Vegetable Preparation	3.0	C
Cooking and Baking	3.0	C
Baking and Potwashing	3.0	C
Dry Storage and Cooking	3.0	C

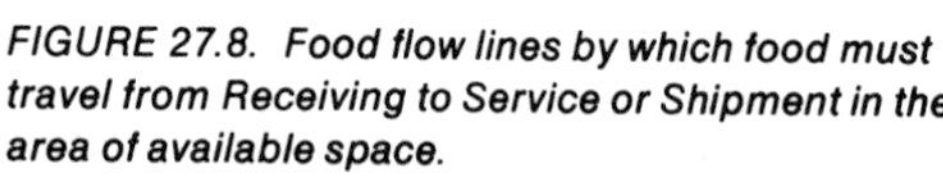

FIGURE 27.8. Food flow lines by which food must travel from Receiving to Service or Shipment in the area of available space.

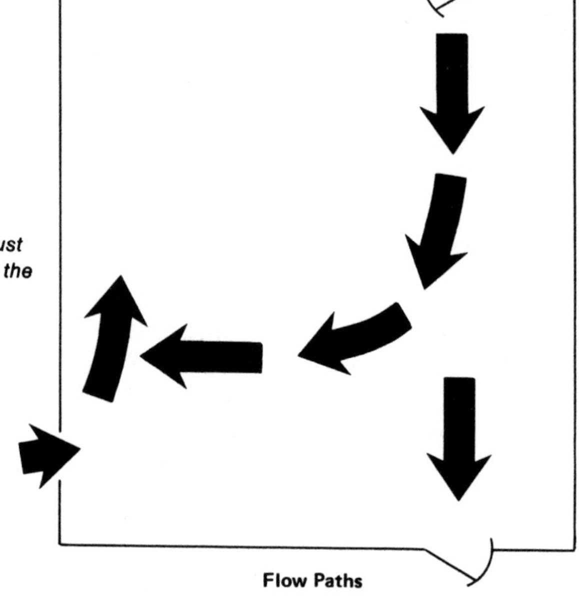

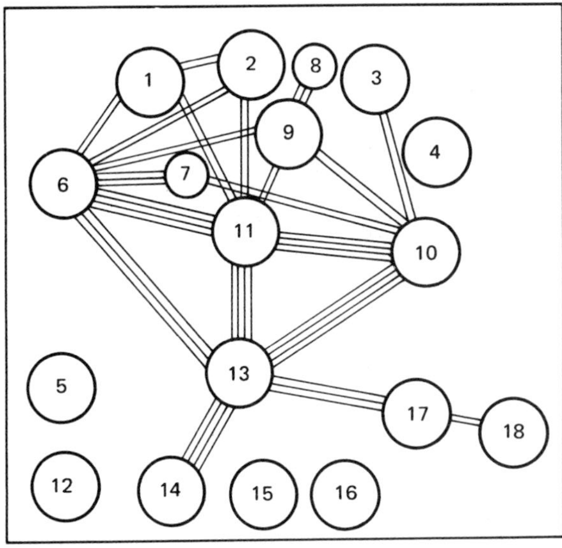

1. Storeroom	10. Refrigeration
2. Bakery	11. Production (Cooling)
3. Receiving	12. Dietitian's Office
4. Freezer	13. Tray Service
5. Serving	14. Tray Cart Storage
6. Potwasher	15. Diet Kitchen Office
7. Meat Preparation	16. Storeroom (Branch)
8. Tray Service (Branch)	17. Dishwashing
9. Vegetable Preparation	18. Dumbwaiter-Elevator

FIGURE 27.9. Work Center Activity-Relationship Diagram placing work centers along food flow lines.

at the flow line, move along the nearest side of the aisle and back the other side to the flow line. Thus, the equipment is arranged around the resultant loop in the order it might work on the food as indicated by the man-machine interaction study or the consensus opinion. A meat preparation work center might have the loop of equipment arranged with table, scales, meat saw, cutting table, meat tenderizer, table, meat grinder, meat molder, and pass-through refrigerator. The first and last are at the food flow line.

Where the work centers run parallel to the flow line, the work center equipment may be arranged along one side of the aisle in the order of its most frequent interuse while proceeding toward service, while another work center traverses the other side of the aisle. If the aisle is short and both sides of the aisle must be used for one work center, it is best to have the most frequently interused pairs of equipment on the same side of the aisle, but overall, the food will move from one side of the aisle to the other after two or three pieces of equipment have worked on it. Generally it flows in one direction.

Contrary to some consultants, I prefer to have the food flow line and major aisles at right angles to the service line or area. All long lines of equipment should be cut through with frequent pass-through aisles to reduce walking.

Further Kitchen Design Considerations

1. Provide water sources beside range, mixer, and kettles and close to the oven. Have a sink beside the range to drain pots.
2. Duplicate condiments, hand utensils, and pots and pans at each place of frequent use and provide facilities for making them readily visible and available.
3. Consult chapter 3 for recommended aisle widths and other design considerations pertaining to worker use of the kitchen.
4. Keep in mind the need for tables beside deep fat fryers, griddles, ranges, steam jacketed kettles (may use hang-on shelves), and mechanical equipment. Also important are tables in front of front opening equipment, directly in front of broilers and small steamers and across the aisle from ovens, large steamers, and reach-in refrigerators.
5. Consider handling as many loads as possible with carts. Using carts speeds service, busing, collecting ingredients and utensils in kitchen, and loading pass-throughs. For this last, consider using multiple rack units that can be loaded in the preparation area and then handled as a unit for storage and then for service.

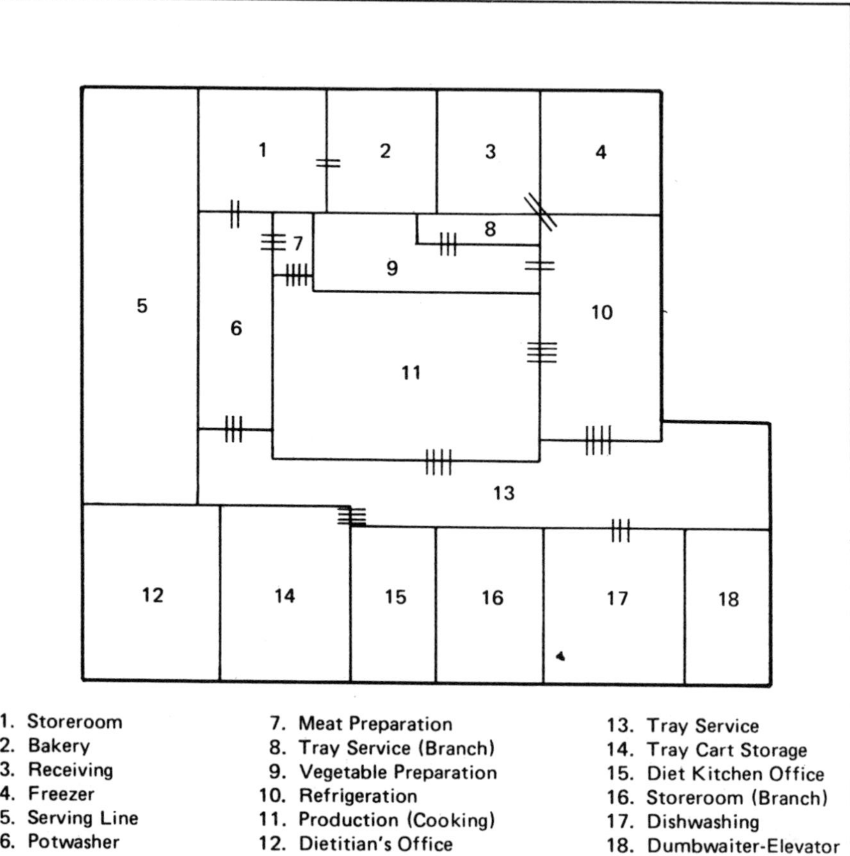

FIGURE 27.10. Using the Work Center Activity-Relationship Diagram of work centers (fig. 27.9), work centers are located in available space.

6. For hospital and school tray makeup belts, plan to have the hot food on one side located close to final preparation in the kitchen, and have cold items on the other side close to where they are prepared or next to wheeled, holding refrigerators that brought them from their preparation areas.
7. Consider the use of pass-through refrigerators between the Meat and Vegetable Preparation work center and Cooking to obviate having to carry ready-to-cook food back from the preparation areas to the walk-in cold storage and then back to the cooking area.
8. Place equipment used in several locations on wheels—food slicers, scales, food molding machines, small mixers, cutting boards, griddles, and similar pieces of equipment.
9. Place equipment that develops smoke, fumes, grease vapors, steam, and much heat under hoods.

QUESTIONS

1. Name the aims of kitchen design.
2. What information is necessary before kitchen designing can begin?
3. What is the difference between factory design and kitchen design?

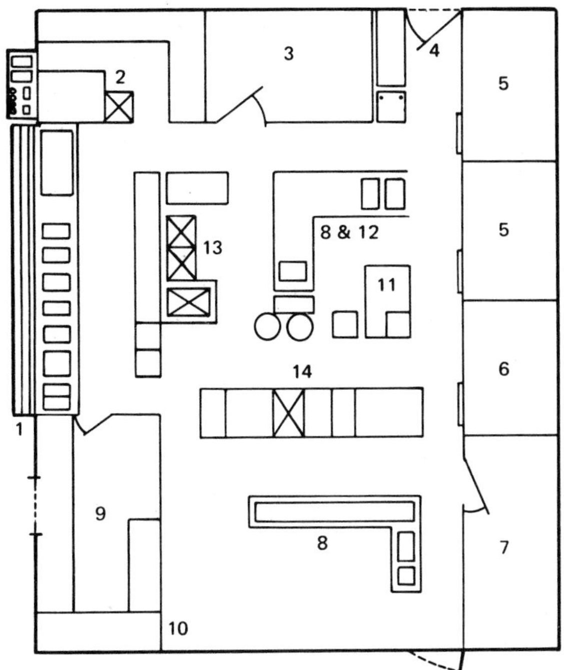

Sketch of Kitchen Layout

1. Serving Line
2. Bakery
3. Dry Storage #1
4. Receiving
5. Refrigerated Storage
6. Freezer
7. Dry Storage #2
8. Tray Service
9. Dishwashing
10. Cart Storage
11. Meat Preparation
12. Vegetable Preparation and Tray Service (Advance Preparation)
13. Pot Washing
14. Cooking

FIGURE 27.11. Equipment as arranged by group opinion consensus is placed into work center and improved with proper aisles and customary placement.

4. What is the basis or starting point of kitchen planning?
5. What are the most important work centers that are most often arranged in the kitchen?
6. What equipment is added to a dry storeroom to convert it to a central ingredient room?
7. What production equipment is usually a part of the average kitchen?
8. Where is the dishroom placed in the usual table service restaurant?
9. How can the design of the cafeteria line be used to reduce food losses?
10. With what work centers is Potwashing most closely related?
11. What can be done with the lighting to increase food selection in a cafeteria?
12. What is the general arrangement of work centers along the food flow line?
13. What are the usual patterns of food flow lines?
14. In conventional design, how is the equipment commonly arranged in the average work center?
15. On what information is the Avery Design System based?
16. How is the data collected in the Avery Design System used to arrange work centers and equipment?
17. How is the kitchen design optimized in the Avery Design System?
18. What is the basis of Layout Design by Consensus? What is the value of the system?
19. How are templates used in food facility design?
20. What is the preferred basis of arrangement of a work center?

BIBLIOGRAPHY

AVERY, A.C. 1958. Automation in the kitchen. *Journal of the American Dietetic Association* 34, No. 4, 369.

AVERY, A.C. 1961. Traffic flow—good layout cuts costs. *Cornell Hotel and Restaurant Quarterly* 2, No. 1, 51.

AVERY, A.C. 1967. Work design and food service systems. *Journal of the American Dietetic Association* 51, No. 2, 51.

AVERY, A.C. 1968. Simplifed food service layout. *Cornell Hotel and Restaurant Administration Quarterly* 9, No. 1, 114.

AVERY, A.C. 1969. *A Study of the Development and Evaluation of a New Kitchen Design System.* University of Missouri, Columbia.

FLACK, K.E. 1962. Arrangment and equipment of the physical plant. *Journal of the American Dietetic Association* 41, No. 1, 35.

KOTSCHEVAR, L.E., and TERRELL, M.E. 1977. *Food Service Planning: Layout and Equipment.* John Wiley and Sons, New York.

MOSKOWITZ, W., DYLLA, H., and SCHOMAN, C. 1958. *Submarine Galley Improvement Based upon Industrial Engineering Studies and Techniques.* U.S. Naval Supply Research and Development Facility, Bayonne, N.J.

MUTHER, R. 1973. *Systematic Layout Planning.* CBI Publishing Company, Inc., Boston, Mass.

NADLER, G. 1963. *Work Design.* Richard D. Irwin, Homewood, Ill.

PEDDERSEN, R.B., AVERY, A.C., RICHARD, R.D., OSENTON, J.R., and POPE, H.H. 1973. Increasing Productivity in Foodservice. CBI Publishing Company, Inc., Boston, Mass.

REED, R. 1961. *Plant Layout Factors: Principles and Techniques.* Richard D. Irwin, Homewood, Ill.

THOMAS, O.M.H. 1947. *A Scientific Basis for the Design of Institutional Kitchens.* Ph. D. dissertation, New York.

Glossary

AC An alternating current of electricity, which flows in two directions in a wire.

Accessories Additions to a standard piece of equipment that enable it to perform more functions. Care should be taken to choose only those accessories that will pay for themselves by frequency of use and quality of performance.

Acoustic Relative or pertaining to sound, hearing, or the science of sound, which involves the production, control, and effects of sound.

Aerosols Air-carried liquids that may contain deleterious bacteria or solids. In foodservice, aerosols emitted from garbage grinders and dishwashers are a source of concern, since they are possible contaminants of clean dishware.

AGA American Gas Association

Aluminized steel The aluminum-coated steel used in oven interiors to reflect unabsorbed heat back toward the food, to prevent loss of heat through the oven exterior.

Ambient Uncontrolled air temperature in a room or the outside atmosphere.

ASME American Society of Mechanical Engineers

Bainmarie A device for holding or heating prepared, cooked food between the cooking and service areas. It is powered by hot water, gas, electricity, or steam.

Bake shop The work center where breads, pastries, cakes, pies, and similar foods to be baked are prepared.

Baking Cooking by dry heat, usually in an oven but also over hot stones, heated metal, or similar heat source. Moist heat would put a hard crust or surface on the food.

Baking sheet A flat aluminum or steel baking tray, which sometimes has three shallow sides and one open end.

Basket, fry Basket made of woven wire, strap metal, or perforated sheets of metal, used to immerse food in fat during frying.

Basket inserts Open-wire baskets, usually three in number, affixed to the top of a steam jacketed kettle to permit cooking of three separate foods, usually vegetables, at the same time.

Battery of urns A two-urned coffeemaker that uses a separate boiler to make coffee and hot water for tea.

Beater, flat A flat bar framework of connected metal strips in a vertical mixer used to mix, cream, rub, and mash.

Blanching A quick scalding of fruits and vegetables in boiling water to soften the pectin layer under the skin so that the peel can be removed. In foods to be frozen, blanching sets color and, in some cases, texture.

Blender A tall, upright jar or metal container with propellers or knives in the base driven by an external electric motor. Blenders are especially useful in preparing mixed drinks or mixing raw eggs.

Board, cutting A laminated or solid piece of hardwood (usually maple or pecan), rubber-composition, or thermoplastic material on which food is placed to be cut. Wood or plastic is used to prevent damage to the knife edge, as would be the case on a steel or stone table.

Bowl, mixing The receptacle on the vertical mixer that holds solids or liquids to be mixed. It rests on a yoke that slides up and down on a vertical shaft.

Box, tote A portable receptacle for moving large quantities of foods or dishes. Usually has high sides for added volume.

Brackets (supports) Bracket-shaped supports on either side of a steam jacketed kettle or frypan that keep the equipment off the floor and allow it to be tilted for emptying and cleaning. Also called a *trunnion mount*.

Braising pan *See* Fry Pan

Breader (breading machine) A horizontal perforated cylinder in which food is tumbled in a breading mixture to give an even coating.

Breaker strips Soft, flexible strips of material placed between flat surfaces, such as table tops, to prevent water, food, debris, or liquid from seeping down between the fixtures.

British Thermal Unit (BTU) The amount of heat required to raise one pound of water one degree Fahrenheit.

Broiler A device for dry-heating foods by gas- or electric-powered radiant or infrared heat that is located either above the food, below it, or both. The food rests on an open metal grid. Product must usually be turned at least once.

Broiler, backshelf A broiler that is placed over the back of a range. Toasts sandwiches or browns products cooked on the range.

Broiler, char, hearth, or underfired A broiler whose source of heat is located underneath the food.

Broiler, continuous A broiler that uses a continuous conveyor to carry the product under the heat source, over it, or both. Can be the rotisserie type.

Broiler-griddle A combination broiling-griddling device that is usually used in small short-order restaurants. Can do both cooking jobs at the same time or independently.

Broiler, overhead A broiler that has its heating elements placed above the grid of food to be cooked.

Browning dish Dish that absorbs heat and browns food in a microwave oven.

Browning units Calrod heating elements in microwave ovens or steamers, which provides radiant heat that browns surfaces of food.

Burner, gas The part of a gas range or oven that produces the gas flame.

Busing Removing dishes and flatware from a customer's table after a course has been eaten.

Cabinet A cupboard or storage space, usually with doors, which may have wheels to make it portable. It may be insulated and temperature controlled to hold or transport hot or cold foods.

Calrod heating elements Tubular metal elements in which electric resistance wires are encased to protect them from being hit or broken. They may be round, as used in ovens or fryers, or flattened, as in range tops.

Canopy or hood A top cover placed over heat-producing equipment to catch steam and gaseous fumes before they dissipate into the room. The fumes are funneled outside the building through ventilators or ducts.

Capacity of equipment The maximum amount of food or material that a piece of equipment can hold, store effectively, or process in a given time period.

Charring Burning or searing food slightly to carbonize the food surface and give food a typical broiled flavor. Called charbroiling if done in a broiler.

Cheese melter A small countertop broiler used to melt cheese.

Chilled food Refrigerated food maintained at a temperature of 0°–13°C (32°–55°F).

Chromium A shiny hard metal added to steel to make it hard, non-corrosive, and shiny in appearance.

Chute A smooth slide that transports materials from a high to low elevation by gravity.

Clambake, New England A pit lined with hot rocks and a layer of wet seaweed, used to steam seafoods that are placed on its surface and covered with canvas.

Coffee, drip grind Coffee beans ground to the following ratio: 7 percent, 14-mesh; 73 percent, 28-mesh; and 28 percent pan or dust grind.

Coffee, fine grind Coffee beans ground to the following ratio: 70 percent, 28-mesh; 30 percent pan or dust grind.

Coffee grind The degree to which roasted coffee beans are ground. Mesh screens of varying sizes, or degrees of fineness, are used to produce regular, drip, and fine grinds.

Coffee maker, vacuum A coffee-making device that places boiling water in contact with the coffee grind and then draws the coffee solubles through a filter, by means of a vacuum, into a separate holding container.

Coffee, regular grind Coffee beans ground to the following ratio: 33 percent, 14-mesh; 55 percent, 28-mesh; and 12 percent pan or dust grind.

Coffee roast The degree to which coffee beans are roasted, prior to grinding, to develop the desired solubles and volatile elements.

Coffee urn A standard coffee-making device. A measured amount of water is poured or sprinkled over the grind for a proper brewing time. The desired brew is then filtered into a tank, where it is stored hot until service.

Compactors, trash Compressing devices that reduce the volume of garbage, paper, and other foodservice waste.

Compression disk A type of valve used in a steam jacketed kettle draw-off, which presses against a seat to shut off the liquid flow from the kettle.

Compressor, refrigerator Component that reduces the volume of heat-saturated gas and increases its temperature before it is moved to the condenser for air or liquid cooling.

Condensate Moisture that forms on cool surfaces. Water in the air near the cool surfaces condenses as droplets of water.

Condenser, refrigerator Unit that takes pressurized gas from the compressor and cools it by means of water or forced air so that the gas can be expanded in the evaporator and used to reduce heat in the refrigerator compartment.

Consultant, foodservice A person hired to design foodservice facilities and plan their management.

Convection steaming Zero-pressure cooking with steam. The convection unit moves steam through the cooking cavity to the exhaust.
Conveyor A fixed or portable device that transport material by using gravity, rollers, skate wheels, power-driven belts, inter-connected metal or plastic plates, or chain drives.
Copper U.S. Navy term for steam jacketed kettles, coined because most steam jacketed kettles were originally made of copper.
Counterbalance Additional weight placed on the outside of a kettle or fry pan hinge to make raising or lowering the lid effortless and safe.
Coupling device Means of transferring microwaves from the wave guide to the cooking cavity of the microwave oven.
Coving Rounding of the angle where two or three plane surfaces are joined. In foodservice, edges are coved to make them easy to clean.
Crusher, garbage Machine used to reduce the volume of glass, jars, metal cans, or cartons by applied pressure.
Cycle The frequency of the alternations or reversals of an electrical current. A cycle is two changes of direction. Sixty cycles is standard, but a current may have 25–50 cycles.
DC A direct current of electricity, which flows in one direction only in a wire.
Decibel A system for measuring sound levels on a scale, with zero representing a barely audible sound.
Deck A complete oven cavity with necessary heating element, controls, door, shelf, and possibly a timer and vent. One or more decks may make up an oven.
Deep fat fryer *See* Kettle, fry.
Design by consensus Developing a design for the layout of a kitchen by using an average of the written opinions of the kitchen staff as to how work centers should be arranged.
Design, kitchen The planned arrangement of equipment and work space in the kitchen to make the available space most efficient.
Dielectric A test given to determine the amount of electrical leakage through a given insulator, used to rate the effectiveness of the insulation.
Dishroom Area relatively close to both dining room and service area designed for cleaning and sanitizing dishes and flatware. It may have two or three compartment sinks for hand dishwashing or have a mechanical single-tank, a conveyor, flight, or other type of dishwasher.
Dishwasher, carousel A closed-circuit, conveyor-type automatic dishwasher that returns the cleaned dishes to the loading point, enabling the same worker to load and remove them.
Dishwasher, conveyor rack A conveyor-type automatic dishwasher that uses mechanically driven chains to take racks of dishes through the wash cycle.
Dishwasher, flight type A conveyor-type dishwasher that has rows of pegs or bars to hold dishes at the proper angle on the conveyor for optimum cleaning.
Dishwasher, mechanical A power-operated machine that cleans, rinses, dries, and sanitizes permanent ware dishes. Some dishwashers perform the prewashing operation also.
Dishwasher, single tank A mechanical dishwasher designed to clean a single, stationary rack of dishes.
Dishwasher, ultrasonic A mechanical dishwasher that uses sound waves to generate vibrations in the dishwashing liquids to clean the dishes.
Dispenser, dish A portable cart designed to hold, dispense, and transport stacked dishes. Some are self-leveling by means of a spring-loaded mechanism. May or may not be heated.
Dispenser, ice A unit that provides small quantities of ice in the serving line, bar, or service kitchen.
Disposal, food waste *See* Grinder, garbage
Doors, French Twin glass-paneled doors hinged at the sides that swing open at the same time. Usually found on convection ovens.
Dough arm A twisted metal bar attachment for the vertical mixer, which folds, kneads, and stretches heavy doughs.
Dough proofer A cabinet with controlled temperature and humidity to hold yeast-raised bakery products under optimum yeast-growing temperature and humidity conditions. May be electric, gas, or steam heated, and may be either portable or stationary.
Draw off A pipe drain with a valve that drains the liquid contents of steam jacketed kettles, fryers, and other types of equipment. Most valves are compression disks or the dairy type of valve.
Dumbwaiter A vertical hoist similar to an elevator but reduced in size, which transports a cart, rack, or tray between floors.
Economic Equipment Purchase Formula A simple calculation of estimates of expenses and savings used to determine whether a piece of equipment will be cost-efficient.
Enamel, acrylic A coating of synthetic resins placed on base metals such as iron or steel to protect against heat,

stains, water-detergent mixtures, and other food chemicals. It abrades readily.

Enamel, baked An alkyd paint, baked at high heat on a base steel or other metal, that provides an easily cleaned finish.

Enamel, porcelain Glass fused to a metal base at high heat to make a finish that is nonporous and resists scratching, rusting, and staining.

Equipment-purchasing specifications An accurate description of the technical details and capabilities of a piece of equipment that a purchaser wants to buy. The specifications include, among other things, the equipment classification (size, type, kind of energy used by appliance), scope (what the equipment will be required to do), drawings of the desired piece (if different from standard available equipment), and administrative details, such as how payment, bidding, and contract details will be handled.

Ergonomics The adaptation of tasks, equipment, and work environment to maximize the use of sensory, perceptional, mental, and physical attributes of the human worker. Also called "human engineering."

Evaporator The tube within the refrigerator that absorbs heat introduced by food, or air from an open door or insulation. A compressed gas in the tube expands to absorb the heat of the cavity.

Expansion valve Valve in the refrigerator that opens when the thermostat announces that cooling action is necessary, which releases compressed gas into the evaporator to provide the necessary heat removal.

FEDA Food Equipment Distributors Association

Flux A substance that aids or induces flowing of a solder in a foodservice equipment connection or seal.

Food choppers or cutters Machines with knives that provide tender or pulverized food products by cross-cutting tough tissues of meat or other foods.

Food molder A labor-saving machine used to make uniformly shaped items, such as fish cakes, hamburgers, and vegetable-fish mixtures.

Foodservice layout, conventional A hired designer's standard arrangement of equipment and workspace in a kitchen. System differs from design by consensus.

Foot candle The amount of light shed by one candle at a distance of one foot.

Free fatty acids Fats that have been broken down to more basic components. The presence of free fatty acids in frying fat is usually indicated by the fat's lowered smoke point.

Freeze-drying The removal of moisture from a frozen material to change it from the solid to the gaseous state without going through the liquid state.

Freezer A refrigeration unit that maintains food in a frozen state. Also, a device that will change food from the fresh to the frozen state by application of the latent heat of fusion.

Freon A liquid hydrocarbon used in a refrigeration unit to transfer heat from the interior of a closed space to the exterior.

Fryer, deep fat *See* Kettle, fry

Fryer, pressure A device that combines the techniques of frying and pressure cooking, which fries food in less time than a conventional fryer.

Frying pan A low-sided, usually flat-bottomed pan used for frying, which gives the same high-temperature fat-to-air treatment associated with griddles.

Fry pan A high-sided, covered, oblong or square flat-bottomed cooking pan heated by gas or electricity, which can be used for kettle cooking, frying, griddling, steaming, and other tasks. Also called a tilting skillet, saute pan, or braising pan.

Fusible link An element in the electric circuitry of a deep fat fryer, set up to melt if the fat temperature gets dangerously high because of a defective thermostat. The melting of the link breaks the electric circuit.

Gasket A rubber or plastic seal set between two metal or other hard surfaces to prevent the escape of heat, air, or liquids.

Gong brush A short-handled, fiber-bristled brush used in cleaning kitchen equipment.

Grid A flat network of cast-metal bars or a steel wire rack that food or pans are placed on in the oven, broiler, or other cooking appliance. The interconnected bars permit grease drainage and circulation of heat. Also called a *grate*.

Griddle A flat metal surface, heated by means of dry heat under its surface, that is used to cook food. The pores of the metal are filled with fat to keep the food from sticking to the griddle.

Grinder, garbage A device that pulverizes food waste so that it can be disposed of in a sewer.

Gutter An open trough found on a kitchen floor, roof, or on a cooking device such as a griddle, for carrying away surplus fat or water.

Head space Space between the food or liquid contents and the lid of a steam jacketed kettle, pot, fry pan, or deep fat fryers, provided to allow for foaming of contents. Also, the space between the top of a canned product and the bottom of the lid.

Holding cabinet Hot or cold storage unit for ready-to-serve foods.
Hone An abrasive stonelike material used for sharpening cutter blade edges.
Human engineering *See* Ergonomics
Ice cream freezer A mechanically driven device that incorporates air into the dessert mixture and freezes it very quickly into small crystals.
Ice cream hardening cabinet A low-temperature chest, well-insulated and refrigerated, used for freezing soft frozen desserts.
Ice cream holding cabinet A storage unit that holds ice cream and other frozen desserts at a desired temperature.
Infrared units Devices that generate infrared heat waves, which are absorbed by food. Infrared waves are shorter than light waves, longer than microwaves, and travel in straight lines.
Integral heating system A covered ceramic or plastic plate that acts as a small oven when it is heated from underneath by electricity. The underside of the plate is coated with heat-resistant material.
IPS The diameter, in inches or metric measures, of iron pipe size.
Iron, griddle A weight with a handle, resembling an iron somewhat, that presses food against the hot surface of the griddle, thus flattening the product and making cooking and browning faster and more uniform.
Kettle, fry The apparatus for deep-fat frying. Liquid fat is stored in a well and heated either from beneath (as with some gas units), or by gas-heated tubes or electric rods (calrod units) immersed in the fat.
Kettle, steam jacketed A pressure-cooking kettle manufactured from hemispherical shells welded together to provide a chamber between the two in which steam can be introduced. Heat is conducted through the metal to the contents of the inner hemisphere. Some have a tangential pipe draw-off or valve to release water and steam.
Kilowatt A measure of electricity equal to 1,000 watts.
Klystron unit A generator of microwaves from high-voltage electricity, used in the microwave oven.
Landing A table in front of an oven used to hold pans removed from the oven.
Latent heat of fusion Heat that must be removed from a substance to change it from the liquid to the frozen state, as in making ice, or from the gaseous to the liquid state, as in condensing steam.
Latent heat of vaporization The amount of heat needed to change water to steam.
Leacher A cloth bag, paper filter, metal strainer, or perforated metal container that holds coffee grinds in the process of coffee brewing.
Lighting, diffuse the use of translucent shields over a light source to spread or disperse the rays to eliminate glare.
Lighting, indirect Bouncing light off a reflective shield, wall, or ceiling to decrease glare.
Lime A compound, usually considered to be calcium, that forms a solid coating on water-contact surfaces, such as pipes, tanks, valves, and dishes.
Magnetron A unit that generates electrons from a heated cathode which, when moved under a radial electric and magnetic field, provides the microwaves used in radar and in microwave cooking.
Meter, water A device that measures the amount of water being used in a given apparatus. Some may be set to shut off the flow after a measured amount of water has been reached.
MHz (megahertz) A unit of measurement for an electronic wave frequency that is equal to one million hertz.
Mixer, dough A device for mixing bakery products, usually yeast doughs, to develop the gluten. It may be either vertical or horizontal.
Mixer housing Enclosure at the top of a vertical mixer shaft in which the drive motor, power take-off, and mixer gears are encased.
Mixer-kettle A regular steam jacketed kettle with a scraper-type mixer that improves heat transfer and food mixing. The mixer may be used for one kettle only, placed on a pivot between two kettles, or wheeled so that it can service a number of kettles.
Mixing baffle An accessory, usually of a vertical cutter/mixer, that scrapes mixed food off the sides of a bowl and returns it to the central mixing area.
NAFEM National Association of Food Equipment Manufacturers
Nosing The exposed edges of horizontal table tops, which project over the vertical panels or supports of the table.
NRA National Restaurant Association
NSF National Sanitation Foundation
Nut, knurled A serrated nut that is often used to hold the knife and mixer assemblies together on the drive shaft of the vertical cutter/mixer. A special wrench may be needed to loosen or tighten it.
Nut, wing A fastener with vertical bladelike elements that may be loosened and tightened without a wrench.
Oven, baking A heated cavity with shelves 7–8 inches apart normally used to bake breads, cakes, and pastries.

Oven, electric An electrically heated cavity with calrod units in the top and bottom, as well as around the sides, in some. It heats the foods in the oven by radiation, a small amount of conduction, and largely by natural convection.
Oven, forced convection A cavity, heated by gas or electricity, used to bake or roast foods by the forceful circulation of heated air around the food.
Oven, gas A gas-heated cavity in which the heat and waste products from gas combustion may be circulated through the cavity or impinge on the food's exterior.
Oven, general purpose A heated cavity that is intermediate to the roast and bake ovens and may be used for either.
Oven, mechanical An oven that uses revolving trays, reels, a Ferris wheel, or conveyor to move pans of food through a large heated cavity.
Oven, microwave A fast-cooking compartment heated by very short electromagnetic waves.
Oven, muffle An oven with an externally heated chamber, the walls of which radiantly heat the contents of the chamber.
Oven, pizza A high-heat oven with low height and several shallow floors, usually made of ceramic tile or transite, used primarily for baking pizzas.
Oven, pulse type An oven that cooks by alternating gusts of very hot and then cold air—to heat the food and then keep the product's surface from overcooking.
Oven, quartz An oven with a thick ceramic glass or quartz top and bottom, which produce infrared waves when heat is applied to them.
Oven, roasting A conventional oven with sufficient height to hold standing roasts of beef—approximately 12.5–14.5 inches in height.
Pan holder A bracket that holds a steam table pan under the pouring lip of a tilting steam jacketed kettle or fry pan.
Pan, holding An insulated holding or service unit cooled by ice, cold water, mechanical refrigeration, or some combination of these, which is used for holding cold food.
Pastry knife An accessory that is attached to the motor-driven mixer/agitator to cut shortening into the flour.
Peel A flat, spadelike surface with a long handle, used for moving products such as pies and pizzas into and out of the backs of deep ovens.
Peeler, vegetable A device for removing exterior coatings of vegetables, which uses abrasive grit to chip away the peel or steam to melt away the pectic layer under the skin.
Phase of electricity Arrangement of circuits or electric routing in an AC (alternating current) system—a single phase has two wires, a two-phase system has 3–4 wires, and a three-phase system has three wires, the latter two used for heavy loads.
Pilot light A constantly burning gas flame used to ignite the gas-air mixture emitted from gas burner units.
Pin lock A type of fastener used to clamp a lid against a chest or bowl, with a gasket placed between the two to form a seal.
Poaching Cooking in shallow acidified water that is kept just below the boiling point. The food, often eggs, is placed in a mold on the water.
Polar molecules Molecules which have a permanent electric dipolar movement.
Postextraction mixing The agitation of brewed coffee to even out the coffee solids.
Pouring lip A short spout on the top edge of a steam jacketed kettle or other apparatus that directs liquids poured out of the kettle to the center of the pouring edge.
Power factor The ratio of true power to apparent power, expressed by the following formula:

$$\frac{\text{Watts (true power)}}{\text{Volts} \times \text{amperes (apparent power)}}$$

Preheating Heating the cooking device before food is inserted to bring it up to operating temperature.
Pressure cooker An airtight appliance that cooks by means of steam under 5–15 pounds of pressure. Five-pound units are sometimes referred to as steamers.
Proofing Holding bakery items at a temperature and humidity that will provide optimum growth of yeast leavening.
PSI Per square inch.
Pulper A unit that chops and pulverizes kitchen waste in water. The pulper then extracts the reusable water so that the waste is greatly reduced in volume for disposal.
Purchase description A brief description of a specific piece of equipment that the buyer wishes to purchase, which includes the details of the desired purchase agreement.
Purchase order An authorization for a supplier to provide a piece of equipment with the characteristics indicated in the specifications, in exchange for an agreed-upon price.
Range A multipurpose waist-height cooking stove with an oven, usually heated by gas or electricity, and a flat top with several open burners.
Receiver, refrigeration A holding unit for the cooled, compressed refrigerant gas.
Receiving The kitchen station or work center where incoming deliveries of foods, materials, or equipment are

checked and weighed, if necessary.

Refrigerator A heat-insulated chest or box that permits foods to be held at a low temperature, which extends the storage life of many foods. It acts as a pump to remove heat from the interior.

Refrigerator, pass-through A refrigerator that allows food placed in one side to be removed through a door on the opposite side.

Refrigerator, reach-in A refrigerator with small doors, designed to lose a minimum of heat when opened frequently.

Refrigerator, roll-in A specially built refrigerator that will hold wheeled-in racks of food.

Refrigerator, thaw A low-temperature refrigerator for thawing frozen foods that warms food enough to change the ice in its cells to liquid but not enough to increase deterioration.

Refrigerator, walk-in A large refrigerator that can be walked into, which has a floor and an open central space.

Resistance wiring Wiring that slows the passage of electricity, thus generating heat.

Rotisserie A broiler, which may be a chain conveyor or carousel type, that moves food past a radiant or infrared heat source while rotating the product on a spit for even cooking.

SAFSR Society for the Advancement of Food Service Research

Salamander A small broiler, mounted on the back of a range, that browns the food surface.

Sauteing Cooking in a frying pan with a small amount of fat.

Saute pan *See* Fry pan

Saw, meat A power saw with offset teeth and a continuous band-saw blade, used for slicing and cutting frozen foods and meats.

Scale, platform A scale for weighing large quantities, affixed to a small flat platform which may be table- or floor-mounted or built into the floor.

Schnellkutter The original term for the vertical cutter/mixer.

Scraping block A round collar of rubber or other resilient material that fits on a metal sleeve in a dish table, under which is placed a garbage can or grinder. Soiled dishes can be rapped on the scraping block to remove loose garbage without damaging the dishes.

Shake maker A blending device with propellers driven from beneath or on shafts from above the upright tank, used to incorporate air, milk, ice cream, and flavorings, to make milkshakes.

Short-order cooking Cooking foods, to order, that require little time.

Silicone A coating that is applied to griddles and other cooking surfaces to prevent food from sticking.

Simmer Cooking in liquid at a temperature below the boiling point, (approximately 85°C or 185°F) to conserve food quality, vitamins, and minerals.

Skillet *See* Fry pan

Slicer, food A power-driven slicer that produces tender meats or other foods of uniform thickness. Tender meats are produced by cutting long tough tissues of food against the grain.

Smoke point A variable temperature at which fat starts to emit smoke, signaling that the fat is about to burst into flame.

Solder Any one of a number of fusible compounds that, when melted and pliable, are used to join metallic parts.

Spatula A square or rectangular utensil, long-handled and made of thin, flat metal or plastic, that is used to lift and turn flat foods in pans or on a griddle.

Specific heat The number of Btu (British thermal units) necessary to raise the temperature of a product one degree Fahrenheit.

Splash guard A fence, usually of stainless steel, set at right angles to the edges of a griddle to hold liquids or food in the cooking area.

Steamer A cooking appliance that subjects food to steam at 0–5 lbs pressure. The cooking action is caused by the steam condensing on the food.

Steam jacketed kettle *See* Kettle, steam jacketed

Steam, saturated When enough heat has been used to evaporate water, to the point at which the air holds all the moisture it can hold, saturated steam results.

Steel finish The degree to which a steel surface is polished or smooth, ranging from No. 1 (rough) to No. 7 (high gloss).

Steel gauge The measurement of steel thickness, which ranges from 8 to 24.

Steel, stainless (CRS) A corrosion-resistant steel used in foodservice with a composition of 18 percent chromium, 8 percent nickel, 0.15 percent carbon, and the remainder steel.

Stir-frying Cooking meat and/or vegetables in a shallow layer of fat, usually in a wok, while stirring frequently to obtain even coloration and doneness.

Stirrer, microwave A device for distributing microwaves throughout an oven compartment as the waves leave the coupling device, to promote evenness of heating.

Storage Space where foods and other materials are held until needed. Three types of storage are dry storage (room temperature), cold storage (0°-13°C, or 32°-55°F) and frozen (below 0°C or 32°F).

Table, cold *See* Pan, Holding

Table, hot A holding device, heated by hot water, steam, or electricity, that maintains hot foods at a desired high temperature.

Teflon A fluorocarbon resin that, when sprayed on cooking surfaces, prevents food from sticking and makes the appliance easy to clean.

Tempering The metal pores of the griddle are filled with grease and then heated to about 204°C (400°F) for five minutes to prevent foods from sinking into the pores and sticking. The griddle is tempered before it is first used and after each cleaning.

Tenderizer, meat A special appliance that tenderizes meats by shredding the long tough meat tissues with knives and then knitting them back into easily prepared individual portions, such as cube steaks. Chemical tenderizers are sprinkled on meat to dissolve tough tissue.

Thermocouple A kind of thermometer, made of two dissimilar metals fused together and connected to a meter, that measures electricity (resulting from heat applied to this junction) as degrees of temperature.

Thermostat A mechanical or electronic control for regulating temperature automatically.

Tilting skillet *See* Fry pan

Transite An oven-deck material made of compressed asbestos and Portland cement, which has a high level of heat conduction.

Tray dispensers Static or self-leveling storage carts for trays, located at the beginning of service lines. These may be built-in or portable.

Tray rail A pipelike rail support or metal projecting fence with raised edges, which the customer slides trays upon while moving through the service area.

Trunnion mount Supports located on two sides of the steam jacketed kettle or fry pan which, together with pivots and a self-locking worm gear, make it possible to tilt the kettle or frypan and pour the contents by turning a handle on the worm gear.

UL Underwriters Laboratories. The agency that inspects and approves electrical apparatus on equipment.

Vertical cutter/mixer A mixing and cutting device, driven by a motor under the bottom of the mixing bowl, similar to the Waring blender in concept.

Warranty A promise given by the manufacturer of equipment (through a distributor or sales agency) to stand behind and repair or replace designated breakdowns or defects within an established time period. A minimal fee may or may not be charged.

Washer, glass A unit for cleaning glasses which may be similar to a dishwasher in design or may use rotating brushes.

Wave guide A transmitter that moves microwaves from the generator to the cooking cavity of a microwave oven.

Whip, wire An attachment to the vertical mixer/cutter made of coarse wire, which incorporates air into egg mixtures and frostings.

Wok A shallow metal bowl, placed on a ring above a gas burner and used for stir-frying and cooking.

Index